ROBERT OWEN'S

MILLENNIAL GAZETTE

EXPLANATORY

OF THE PRINCIPLES AND PRACTICES BY WHICH, IN
PEACE, WITH TRUTH, HONESTY, AND SIM-
PLICITY, THE NEW EXISTENCE OF MAN
UPON THE EARTH MAY BE EASILY
AND SPEEDILY COMMENCED.

NUMBERS 1 - 16

" The Character of man is formed *for* him, and *not by* him."

AMS PRESS
NEW YORK

DUE TO POOR ORIGINAL COPY THIS REPRINT EDITION
DOES NOT MEET THE STANDARDS NORMALLY SET BY
AMS PRESS.

Reprinted from the edition of 1856-58, London
First AMS edition published in 1972
Manufactured in the United States of America

International Standard Book Number: 0-404-08454-0

Library of Congress Catalog Card Number: 74-134408

AMS PRESS   INC.
NEW YORK,   N.Y. 10003

ROBERT OWEN'S
MILLENNIAL GAZETTE;

EXPLANATORY OF THE PRINCIPLES AND PRAC-
TICES BY WHICH, IN PEACE, WITH TRUTH,
HONESTY, AND SIMPLICITY, THE NEW
EXISTENCE OF MAN UPON THE
EARTH MAY BE EASILY AND
SPEEDILY COMMENCED.

" The character of Man is formed *for* him, and *not by* him !"

No. 1.]   MARCH 22, 1856.   [PRICE 6D.

TO THE GOVERNMENTS ABOUT TO ENGAGE IN NEGO-
TIATIONS TO ADJUST THE PERMANENT PEACE OF
EUROPE.

THE time is propitious for great good to be effected, by laying a
solid foundation for the permanent peace, not only of Europe,
but of the world.

Why should the population of the world be longer governed
and educated on the principle of disunion, repulsion, irrationality,
and selfish ignorance, when it will be for the everlasting progress,
prosperity, and happiness of the population of the world, that it
should be governed, trained, and educated, on the principle
of union, attraction, rationality, and disinterestedness, or of
the true permanent interest of every individual of the human
race, whatever may be their present rank, condition, and position
in society.

In consequence of the past and present character of all having
been based solely on the principle of disunion, repulsion, and
irrationality, and of society being based and constructed of
necessity on the same erroneous principle, all have been by that
false education, and society has been by its false construction on
the same principle of error, made to become utterly incapable of
acting upon the pure and just principles taught by Jesus Christ,
the only principles which, when applied to practice, can make
man individually and society generally good, wise, united, and
happy, and these principles, fully understood and consistently
applied, are amply competent to produce and permanently maintain these four results. And what can man require more while
he remains upon the earth ?

The question is,—Will you, the governments about to negotiate for the permanent peace of Europe, give instructions to base
this peace on rational and Christian principles of union, attrac-

tion, and justice to all, or will you still found your new arrangements for the intended adjustment of the peace of Europe, on the old un-christian principle of disunion, repulsion, and ignorant self-interest, and thus make it impossible that Europe can become Christian in practice, or remain long at peace?

It is now a glaring hypocricy for Europe to call itself Christian. The essential and the only essential principles of Christianity are universal love and charity in every day practice, and to be consistent in these divine virtues from the commencement of each year to its termination. To make Europe Christian, rational, prosperous, and to secure its permanent peace, there is but one mode, and that is to base its government and the education of its population on the principle of union and attraction, the unchanging principle of nature from the beginning, and which all past generations have so ignorantly neglected and rejected.

I gravely put the question to you, the individual members of the leading governments of Europe, now about to transact most important public affairs,—Did any one of you make the smallest atom of your physical, intellectual, moral, or spiritual nature,— or decide upon the country and surroundings in which you were born? You must answer—No. Why, then, in the name of the most common common-sense, do you continue to govern and to educate the people as though you and all of human kind formed your own qualities of body and mind and decided upon your own surroundings?

You must know, if you know anything by observation and accurate reflection, that you can never establish Christian feelings, principles, or conduct, while you thus so irrationally act; and that by this unwise system of governing you create and maintain all the evils and sufferings which afflict the human race Can you not arouse yourselves from this lethargy of ignorance, and act like men possessing sound reason and judgment, and openly acknowledge the error of your education, and your determination to be no longer hypocrites and call yourselves Christians, when you oppose all that can lead to Christian practice? You have been hitherto, in mind and practice, pagans. Will you continue to remain so? Or will you now become Christian,—that is, consistent and rational, to have charity and love for our race, and educate and govern on this principle?

You have been taught to think this to be impracticable. You have been taught most erroneously. It is true that while you uphold the principle and practice of individualism, the practice of Christianity will continue an impossibility; for it is practicable only under the united system,—not as ignorant writers describe it, but in its full purity, when made to be consistent with the laws of nature, undefiled by the irrational and crime-creating laws of men.

The laws of men disunite the interests of the human race; while the laws of God and nature, if adopted and consistently acted upon, would strongly unite the interests of all, and make the entire of humanity as one, continuing without intermission through each succeeding generation to the end of earthly time.

The united system, which will arise from superseding human laws by God's laws, would gradually place all of our race permanently in a far more desirable position than any one has ever been, or can be placed in, under the government and false direction of the laws of men.

The difficulty, in the present falsely educated state of the mind and habits of the population of the world, is vividly known and strongly felt, by a long life practically and ardently engaged in preparing society for this change. But these difficulties, like so many other supposed impossibilities, are to be overcome by patience, perseverance, foresight, and wisdom, directed by the divine principles of charity and love for our race.

The path by which this great and glorious change is to be attained is obvious. To quietly and peaceably enter that path is now the only real difficulty to be surmounted.

The easiest and shortest mode by which this path can be entered is, perhaps, to form first a commonwealth of nations, and somewhat on the principles given to the world by the signers of the United States declaration of independance on founding the North American Republic of united nations. But some alterations and additions will be required to prepare for the change from the individual ignorant selfish system, opposing man to man and nation to nation, to the united system in which the interests of all will be provided for and permanently secured.

The next step will be to make each nation into a commonwealth, to be governed by its own population in accordance with the laws, rules, and regulations of the Great General Commonwealth of the World.

The third general step should be to divide such national commonwealths into the true and real commonwealths, in number according to the present population of each nation composing the world's commonwealth.

These true and real commonwealths will consist of populations not exceeding three thousand as a maximum.

By this outline arrangement, full justice will be done to every one from birth,—each one will be well cared for by society,—each one will have all his or her physical, intellectual, moral, spiritual, and practical qualities, faculties, and powers, cultivated to their highest point of utility for the individual and for society,—and each one will be so placed through life that he or she will possess and enjoy their full just equal rights, and be secured in life advantages never yet enjoyed by one of the human race.

By this simple outline arrangement, the population of the world may be gradually, peaceably, and naturally changed from their present irrational state of repulsion, conflict, competion, falsehood, poverty, ignorance, crime, and misery, to a new condition of existence, in which all will be made from birth to become good, wise, united, wealthy, sound in body and mind, and happy, with no other distinctions throughout society than those of age, divided according to the natural periods of life.

By this outline, honestly and fairly carried out and made to be consistent in all its parts, there could be no disease, no ignorance, no poverty, no disunion, no bad passions, no crimes, no vices, no bad habits,—but union, harmony, ever increasing prosperity, and unfailing happiness over the earth.

ROBERT OWEN.

Sevenoaks Park, Sevenoaks,
February 10th, 1856.

WHY DO THE NATIONS OF THE EARTH CONTINUE TO TROUBLE THEMSELVES IN VAIN?

IF nations now opposed in language and apparent interest could be induced to unite upon a fundamental principle in accordance with all facts past and present having reference to it, and agree to construct society upon that foundation, the only true one, and make all parts of this new society consistent with itself, they would form an entire system, new in all its extent, calculated to make man rational and consistent, good and wise, and to give perpetual peace, prosperity, and happiness to the race.

This principle is the knowledge, derived from all facts, that man is a being created with all his physical, mental, moral, and spiritual qualities unknown to himself and without his consent,—and that consequently, like all created existences, he cannot rationally be made responsible for any of these qualities or powers of body or mind, or spirit or soul.

As men from birth may be forced by particular training and education to believe any absurdity to be divine truth, and the most valuable divine truths to be the most injurious falsehoods—men have to this day been forced to believe that they are responsible for their physical, intellectual, moral, and spiritual qualities,—not one of which could they of themselves form.

They have also from birth been forced to believe that society based on unerring facts, and made in all its parts to be consistent with itself, could not exist, but must destroy itself. While this is the only system which by its purity and consistency will admit of the language of truth, and of a conduct ·void of offence to God and man—the only system that can unite the human race as one family into a cordial un·ending brotherhood, in which the interest of one would be the well-understood interest of all—nor would there ever be a jarring of feeling or interest from one end of the earth to the other.

The system which makes man responsible to God and his

fellow man necessarily creates a system of repulsion and all evil. While the irresponsible system will make man a new being in all his associations of ideas, in feeling, mind, and conduct,—will make him good and wise, and will well prepare him for the spirit spheres, when he shall have passed through his earthly life and commenced his new spiritual existence.

How uselessly and worthlessly edited are the leading journals of Europe and America, now the leading instructors of the peoples of both hemispheres. Look at their senseless leading articles about trivial evils or events which must continually recur while they support present ignorance in the formation of character and in the construction of every department of society. •

Why do these journals not go at once to the root of all evil, and explain how easily, by placing society on its only true foundation, surroundings may be now devised and executed which shall with the certainty of a law of nature enforce from birth through life a good valuable and superior moral character upon all,—and ensure annually, with pleasure to all, the creation of more wealth than the population of the world can consume, and a cordial unity among all of human kind?

To effect these results will be practical positive philosophy, and nothing short of this will deserve the name of true philosophy.

Found society on truth respecting human nature, make the surroundings consistent with that foundation, thus making the human character good and society permanently prosperous, and all will be in accordance and ever consistent with the eternal laws of humanity and of nature generally.

Here is the direct, plain, and simple road to a terrestrial paradise and permanent Millennium. Why then should nations continue to trouble themselves in vain, when the path to high happiness is straight before them, and so easily attainable?

Do the population of the world want more than a good character and wealth for all which all may at all times enjoy?

These can never be attained without the requsite surroundings to produce them. All the means to produce and maintain them now exist in superfluity throughout the world, and the science is known by which they may be now combined to produce these ever to be desired results. Why then do nations trouble themselves in vain?

PRACTICAL POSITIVE PHILOSOPHY.

PRACTICAL Positive Philosophy consists :—

1.—In a knowledge of the cause of ignorance, and how to overcome it.

2.—In a knowledge of the causes of poverty and the fear of it, and how to prevent both.

3 —In a knowledge of the cause of the disunion of the population of the world, and of the means to unite them

4.—In a knowledge of the causes which give a false and most injurious character 'o the whole of the human race, and of the means by which a truthful, good, and most beneficial one may with the certainty of a law of nature be given to the population of all nations.

5.—In a knowledge of the cause of crime, of the causes to pre-vent it, and how the latter may be made to supersede the former.

In short, *practical* positive philosophy consists in a know-ledge of the causes which produce and continually reproduce evil to the human race, and of the causes which will terminate those evils and produce good only to the future population of the world,—with the knowledge *how* the causes of good are to be made gradually, peacefully, and most beneficially for all to supersede the causes creating evil.

Evil is allowed most unnecessarily to continue; for it can be advantageously for all removed for ever from human society. While evil thus remains time becomes most precious,—life, espe-cially in advanced age, is very uncertain; therefore to effect this change from all evil to all good, in the shortest time and in the best manner, I suggest that the great powers — namely, Austria, France, Great Britain, Prussia, Russia, Turkey, and the United States of North America, should at the earliest period call a Congress of all civilized governments, to be represented in it by the heads of all the governments, assisted by their most talented ministers, in order to calmly deliberate on the shortest and best mode of quietly and peaceably changing the *existing irrational system of evil to all*, for the *rational system of society*, which, with the certainty of an unchanging law of nature, will *insure permanent good to all*.

This Congress should be held in London, the present metro-polis of the world, at the commencement of summer, say in May next, and if such Congress should be so called and held, I will undertake to make this rational and superior system of society so plain, that in principle and practice it shall be understood by all who have been taught to observe facts and to reflect upon them, and to make it easy for the present scientific and practical men of the world to introduce it gradually into practice in all coun-tries at the same time.

It should now be known that there is no possibility of uniting these two systems. The world must have the one or the other. It must have the evil and irrational system, with its necessary language of falsehood, or the rational system of good, with its necessary language of truth.

If governments are not yet prepared in all earnestness and good faith now to commence this change from all evil to all good, then I will call a Congress of the reformers of the world to meet in London on the 14th of May next, to consider how best to introduce this great and glorious change for all humanity and for ever.

EDUCATION.

THIS word, through all past ages, has been as little understood and as much misapplied as the word religion, and both have been the cause of immense long continued evil to our race. Had these words been rightly comprehended from the beginning, evil would have been unknown, and man would have commenced and progressed in numbers as one family, and the cordial brotherhood of the human race would have been to this day unbroken, and would as centuries advanced have increased in cordiality, friendship, and affection.

Education, then, means the formation of the character of each human being from birth to death. Each one *is* educated by the surroundings in which he is placed by society. And as his natural instincts, which are created for him, must receive all their *impressions* and *ideas* from these surroundings, he becomes to all intents and purposes the being of these instincts of his natural organization and of the kind and quality of the surroundings in which he is placed.

On this knowledge, irrespective of the difference in natural instincts, when the science of creating surroundings shall be explained and made known to the population of the world, each child as he comes into existence may with the certainty of a law of nature be forced by society to become an earthly *demon* or an *angel*, without any demerit in the one case, or merit in the other, on the part of the so formed demon or angel. The surroundings give the country, language, habits, manners, conscience, religion, occupation, ideas, and conduct, to every one. How important, then, is it now become, that the population of the world should now be taught the science of these surroundings, that without loss of time the human race may be formed into earthly angels. There are no human rational surroundings in any country for any class,—they have all originated from a false principle respecting human nature, and thus have these false surroundings produced only a false and very inferior character for the past race of man. Nor can a superior character ever be formed within any of the existing surroundings in which the population of the world is now placed. While if these surroundings were made rational, that is, in accordance with the laws of our nature, every one would at all times speak the language of truth only, in look, word, and action, become highly intelligent, and be good and superior compared with any now living in any country of which we have knowledge.

The surroundings which are found in all schools, colleges, and universities, in all nations, are not calculated to form a good, wise, superior, and happy character for any one; but on the contrary must form an inferior character in wisdom, goodness, and happiness.

A new era is about to arise over the earth, when man shall be made wise to his salvation from evil,—when the pure spirit of charity and love shall be made to pervade all from birth,—and when the world shall be governed in righteousness and peace, without human punishments—for the cause of crime will not exist.

Read, mark, learn, and inwardly digest what is here written, and soon the population of the world will be prepared to enter upon the millennial state of human existence.

The advanced spirits in the higher spheres of the spirit world are now most actively engaged in preparing men's minds for this great and all-glorious change, when old things shall pass away and all become new.

RELIGION.

The term " Religion " is applied by the human race to sanction every kind of absurdity and cruelty,—to cover all abuses in the conduct of men,—to keep the population of the world in ignorance and poverty, disunited, and in constant agitations of hatred of one insane sect for others, both at home and abroad. And all these evils are produced with the declared, and often sincere, desire to glorify and magnify the Great Creating Power of the Universe; while common sense, upon slight reflection, makes it evident that man can do no more good to universal wisdom and power than worms can do to man. Consider for a moment those harmless creatures using all their efforts to glorify and magnify the name of man. What an absurdity! And yet the distance between man and his Creator is infinitely more removed than is the worm from man.

Man's destiny is to attain goodness, wisdom, and happiness; and these can be taught him, not by religion as hitherto misunderstood, but by an education of surroundings which shall make his happiness to arise from his constant active endeavours to promote the happiness of his race, without diminishing the happiness of any one. To possess the pure spirit of charity and love for all,—and to be actively engaged in endeavouring to promote the happiness of all around us,—and to be merciful to the animal creation, is the essence of true religion—a religion which has no reference to words, forms, or ceremonies. And thus alone will the will of God be done on the earth as it is in heaven.

When human nature shall be understood, and its wonderful and superior natural qualities at birth shall be appreciated, and men shall abandon their insane and cruel laws, striving to oppose Nature's wise, good, and all merciful laws,—then will the population of the world be taught how to create around them surroundings consistent with Nature's laws—surroundings which will make it impossible for man to deviate from the straight path to goodness, knowledge, excellence, and happiness. Such is true religion.

CHEMISTRY AND MECHANICS.

THE importance of these two sciences, in their capability for promoting the happiness of the human race, is yet little comprehended by any parties engaged in governing the nations of the world. But the time approaches when their value will be known and appreciated.

They are capable of being made, and are destined, to destroy human slavery and servitude, and to make it practicable to form the human race into one family of equality according to age, and of cordial brotherhood, having one and the same universal interest. Extended knowledge will discover to our race that the right application of these two sciences in the direct business of life will not only render living slavery and servitude unnecessary, but will make a high aristocracy of the human race, and the life of man, when governed solely by the laws of his nature from birth, a life of happiness and of healthy rational enjoyment. By the aid of these two sciences, wisely applied, all the drudgery and unhealthy occupations of life, when society shall be rationally constituted, will be performed, and the life of man, when placed, trained, educated, and employed, according to the laws of his nature, will be a life of delightful physical and mental activity.

When society shall be properly constituted, and all shall be placed from birth within arrangements or surroundings in accordance with the laws of nature, how many faithful active slaves and servants will each of humankind require to create wealth, and to serve him or her in every capacity in which their aid can be required? Will it be ten, twenty, or fifty? The latter number, in the arrangements or surroundings proposed to be made for all in accordance with the laws of nature, would be equal to a host of living servants as employed under the present individual system.

But when the powers to be derived from chemistry and mechanism shall be understood, it will become obvious that each one of the human race may with ease and pleasure to all be aided and served through life, not only by fifty or a hundred of these untiring, unresisting, ever faithful servants, but by an unlimited number, far beyond the possible wants or wishes of any being made to be rational in mind and practice.

The public appears to be quite ignorant of the the progress which has been made within the last hundred years in the manufacture of these most valuable servants and slaves in Europe and America. The mass of the population of Europe and America little suspect the progress which has been made in this respect within that period, or they would not remain the stupid insane beasts-of-burden to their equally insane and almost as ignorant and unreflecting task-masters—to men so insane as in a few years to destroy and demoralise unnumbered millions of their equal fellow men,—consume most injuriously wealth beyond calculation,—and expend, in addition, hundreds, nay thousands of millions sterling, for no rational object, but to keep the masses ignorant of their rights and powers.

These two sciences, properly comprehended and rightly applied, are capable of very rapidly making our earth into a terrestrial paradise, to be inhabited by an order of aristocracy far superior to any now living in any quarter of the world.

Will it be credited by future generations that for centuries their ancestors had been far more anxious to expend a million to slaughter life and to destroy property, than to expend a hundred to prevent ignorance, poverty, disease, disunion, crime, and misery?

But, my friends of the human race, it is too horrible to the feelings of humanity to dwell upon the insane errors of the past and present. For some wise purpose, beyond existing progress in knowledge, they have occurred; and no parties can now be blamed for these evils, frightful as they are to us now that our eyes are opened to their magnitude. Evidently however our eyes are now opened to the causes which have led step by step to this acma of insanity, that those causes may now be superseded by others, which shall make man wise to his salvation from sin and misery.

Men! study this pamphlet, and all which I have previously written and published.

MONEY.

WHAT is money?—Something made by society to represent real wealth. What is real wealth?—That which is of use to man— and the more useful, the more valuable. Anything may be made to represent this wealth in exchange; but some things more advantageously than others. At an early period, iron, intrinsically the most valuable of all metals, was used in some countries for this purpose. Latterly by the most advanced nations, gold, silver, and copper, have been retained for this purpose. These now are not only valueless for this purpose, but are daily inflicting the greatest injustice and cruelty on the real producers of the most valuable wealth, and serious injury on those who are taught to believe that they are benefitted by this ruinous representative of wealth, and that they could not exist without it.

This specious circulating medium is the medium of idleness, injustice, and ignorance. Suppose gold, silver, and copper, to be at once annihilated, and that not an ounce of either could be found on the earth,—Would the real wealth of the world be destroyed? Would the population of the world stand still and starve?—Neither of these events would take place ; but the real wealth of the world would be speedily mightily increased, and soon it would be discovered that by simple rational proceedings wealth would be created annually to far exceed the necessities or even the desires of all, when their surroundings shall be made rational. The loss of these metals, less intrinsically valuable than iron and steel, would at once disclose to all nations—now blinded by gold, silver, and copper—that the true source of all wealth was not in these metals, but in the physical and mental powers of their respective populations; and that these populations, rightly surrounded, and properly aided by the sciences, could, with ease and pleasure to every one, create wealth—real valuable useable wealth—to an illimitable extent, and human labour of slavery and servitude would be soon rendered null, and of less than no value. For in a rational state of society, formed by rational surroundings, made to promote the happiness of humanity, slavery or servitude, both being bad surroundings, will never be seen. The child, to be rational, good, wise, and happy, must from its birth never see a slave or servant. He must be surrounded by rational superior men and women only, and by the most superior at the earliest period of its life.

What, then, is to create the representative of wealth ? Wealth itself,—which, while the change from the irrational to the rational system of society shall be in progress, will be by Notes representing the wealth created. These notes to be exchanged for a similar amount of wealth in any other article required. But very speedily wealth will be created so easily, pleasantly, and abundantly, that it will cease, like air and water, to require any exchangeable representative. Air and water are our most valuable wealth, and need no representative. The earth also, ere long, according to the irresistable law of progress, must become, like air and water, the common property of the human race. The earth is now most injuriously and unjustly held as private property, to the great loss and disadvantage of its present possessors and of the population of the world.

The evils necessarily arising from metal money must cease as soon as an unavoidable preparation has been made for the introduction of the Millennium, or the rational state of human existence upon earth. Metal money is the cause of immense crime, injustice, and misery throughout society, and is one of the surroundings which tend most materially to mis-form the character, and to make the earth a pandemonium. It has been so, is so, and will continue to be so, as long as metal money shall be used to create wealth, instead of wealth being made to create its own natural representative—the Labour Note, as circumstances prematurely forced me to introduce it in the Gray's Inn Road a quarter of a century ago, which would be, if men had been trained to be honest, a good and true representation of wealth.

SLAVERY.

SLAVERY is a grave offence against the slave, his owner, society, and the pure and undefiled religion of love and charity, taught by Christ, but not yet in practice by his professed disciples. The infant slave at birth possesses all the divine qualities of humanity fresh from his Creator, and, of every shade of colour, is capable of being made a good and valuable citizen of the world. These infants are capable of being so placed, trained, educated, and employed, by a new combination of rational surroundings, that they may be made to become at maturity far more valuable and much better members of society than any citizen now living in any country. Better and of more value, because all of every country have been to this day mis-placed, mis-trained, mis-educated, mis-employed, and mis-governed, and in consequence have been forced to become far more inferior, and of much less value to society, than all of humankind may be made to become, when they shall be from birth rationally placed, trained, educated, employed, and governed, through a new and rational combination of surroundings, formed in accordance with the laws of God and nature—thus creating consistency and unceasing harmony between man, nature, and God.

Slavery is a grave offence against the owner of slaves. The slave is an essentially bad surrounding to the master and family by whom he is kept as a slave. The master and his family must in consequence be deteriorated in all their faculties, physical and mental; and it is utterly impossible for them while retaining slaves in their service to become Christians,—except in name. They must of necessity be cruel hypocrites or grossly irrational; for as Christians they profess charity and love for the human race,—even to love their enemies; while in practice they are doing the greatest injury to their near neighbour—their slave; and not to benefit the master or his family, but to make both continually to profess one thing and act another.

Slavery is a grave and heinous offence against society. For while it is continued and sanctioned by human laws, and countenanced by custom, most injurious and irrational surroundings must be created and maintained, against the best interests of society; and while these inferior and deteriorating surroundings, which are absolutely necessary for the continuance of slavery, are in existence, they obstruct and prevent the possibility of introducing good and rational surroundings. And let it never be forgotten that, according to all past and present experience,—As are men's natural qualities, made by God, and their surroundings, made by society, so must men become. Bad and inferior surroundings must make bad and inferior men :—Good and superior surroundings must make good and superior men.

Will the *savans* of to-day, the scientific and wise men of the most advanced nations, have the kindness to make something like an approximate estimate of the difference in the amount and degree of happiness to be experienced, between a society made by its surrounding to become bad and inferior, and a society made by its surroundings to become good and superior ? And also of the difference in the difficulty of governing the society made to become irrational, and the society made to become rational? When they shall have solved these two problems, the advanced and prominent statesmen and the deeply learned political economists may be then requested to prepare a budget of the finances, or production and expenditure of these opposing societies.

These difficulties once fairly made known to the public, would, it is believed, settle the question for ever between bad and inferior, and good and superior surroundings of all nations and peoples.

Will the writers in the leading journals, daily and weekly, with the monthly periodicals, take up these subjects of deep and lasting interest to the human race ? And will they now abandon their waste of time, and the waste of the time of the population of the world, in giving to the public the endless local nothings, necessarily arising, and continually recurring, from the irrational surroundings which ignorance of human nature and its laws has induced all nations to create and maintain, in direct opposition to universal facts and self-evident deductions from them ? How much might they write upon these subjects to enlighten themselves and the public ! How evident is it to those who know the inward feelings of the best minds in society, that they are now yearning strongly for real knowlenge ! Not for cunning—how to attain money and position in society, but how to acquire and maintain happiness, or, in other words, how to attain the knowledge and the means by which they can be placed within rational and common-sense surroundings—such surroundings as will not only permit, but strongly assist them to acquire and practice the divine principles of universal love and charity, and to apply themselves with all sincerity, earnestness, and energy, to promote the happiness of all around them.

Who can so feel and act under the presesent irrational, opposing, repulsive, and false system of society ? Not one,—however he may be inclined to do so in all sincerity of purpose.

Such, however, is the state of society, arising from the error on which alone it is based, and such the involved entanglement produced by the contending and opposing interests arising of necessity from this false fundamental error, that slavery cannot now be suddenly abolished without producing great present evils, and even dangerous results to the peace of any nation which may attempt in ignorance to effect thus prematurely one of the most virtuous actions. While I was in the United States, and when my son Robert Dale Owen was an active member in their Congress, I was with him anxious to see this vexed question permanently adjusted, with the least ill-will and least injury to all parties. We saw the error of the violence of the two parties which divided the north from the south. I was intimate with John C. Calhoun, from 1824, to 1847 when I last returned from the United States. I was well acquainted through him with the strong educated prejudices of the south in favour of slavery, and how very sensitive he was himself upon this subject. I was also well acquainted with several leading Abolitionists, with their strong right feelings on the subject, and their many educated prejudices against the true spirit and right measures by which the evil of slavery was to be overcome. Both parties then exhibited and now exhibit a great want of a correct knowledge of human nature and of the new acquired productive powers from the sciences of chemistry and mechanics, when they shall be wisely applied. A knowledge of human nature would have given the slave-owner a knowledge of the high value which correct conduct would give to every infant of every shade and colour. A knowledge of the immense productive powers acquired within the last century would have enabled both parties to have discovered that these new powers, whenever understood and rightly applied, would render slavery not only unnecessary in any part of the world, but less profitable than free servitude, as long as society should find free servitude necessary and profitable. Thus knowing and to a considerable extent having the confidence of the leading advocates for and against slavery, I wrote a letter intended for the Washington journals of both parties—those journals being always open to my communications. The letter contained the substance of the plan stated, and I took it to Mr. Calhoun to ask his opinion of the practical measures I proposed, by which to gradually abolish slavery in the United States. He read it with strong sensitive feeling, and then earnestly intreated me not to publish it; for he said it would create an excitement that might be dangerous to both parties, north and south.

My friendship for him and my estimate of his many virtues and amiable private character induced me to accede to his wishes, and I withheld the publication of the letter. My experience from that period, (1845 or 1846,) has confirmed me in the views I then held upon the subject, and upon this gradual abolition of American slavery—a slavery so utterly unworthy of the nation assuming to be the leading nation in personal and national liberty and progress in civilisation. A nation which possesses such an extraordinary amount of advantages for entire independence of the rest of the world, ought to set an example to all other nations and peoples over the globe, of right, justice, and freedom from physical and mental slavery.

The conditions proposed for the gradual abolition of slavery in the United States were as follows :—

1st.—That from and after a day to be named, (say 1st of January in the following year,) all children of slaves shall be born free,—but the owner of the parent or parents of the new free born, shall well train or educate him or her, as the case may be, to become a good and valuable citizen of the United States.

2nd.—The owner shall keep a just account of the cost of keep and of education against the free born citizen, and against this account place the value of the services of the free-born, either male or female, and as soon as these accounts balance each other, then the free born to be at liberty to choose his or her own service or employment, and to receive their own earned wages or remuneration, making their own bargain.

3rd.—A commission of five to be appointed in each state— two from the south to see justice done to the owner,—two from the north, to see justice done to the slave,—and these four to appoint a mutual person to keep harmony by his aid and vote between all parties interested.

This is a short outline for the consideration of the parties now unwisely in conflict.

How long is the human race yet to be influenced and governed by violence, force, and hostile feelings, instead of the far more effective feelings of charity and love, of calm patience and wise consideration, all parties making due allowance for the educated prejudices and injurious surroundings of their opponents ! Surely the time is near at hand when all will see and feel the necessity of ceasing to obstruct its coming, as society is evidently preparing for this change.

REFORMATION OF THE WORLD.

As the world required to be reformed respecting its old notions of the flatness and fixedness of the earth, and of the movements of the heavenly bodies, so it now requires to be reformed on the subject of the human mind, to make it consistent and sane.

The preceding articles have been written to prepare the populations of all nations for this the greatest of all reforms that humanity can experience.

The errors arising from the infant and undeveloped state of man through the past early ages of his existence even to the present have filled his mind with the most contradictory, incongruous, and absurd notions and ideas respecting himself and society, and in consequence he is now the most inconsistent, immoral, and miserable being on the earth, having a language of deception in his looks, words, and actions. The best living have no real pretensions to be considered moral beings. They have yet to advance, in their upward and onward progress towards rationality or plain common sense, from the phase of animals inconsistent in their feelings, thoughts, words, and actions.

When they can be elevated to the rank of rational beings, they will be made to become from birth consistent in all their feelings, thoughts, words, and actions.

Truth, pure and undefiled with error, is always consistent; there can be no contradiction, incongruity, or opposition, between one idea and all the other ideas in the same mind, or in any two minds throughout the world, when men shall be made sane and rational.

The great reform now required is to adopt measures to change this inconsistent and immoral animal into a consistent and moral being.

To effect this change, the mind from birth must be filled with new ideas and new associations of ideas, each consistent with all the others, in order that there may not be two jarring ideas or two jarring associations of ideas in any mind throughout the population of the earth. Impossible as this result must appear to the inconsistent and of course irrational mind formed under the existing system of falsehood and deception, yet as soon as measures can be introduced to place, train, educate, employ, and govern men within rational surroundings, this change will become an easy every day practice, familiar in principle and execution to every one so placed, trained, educated, employed, and governed.

Hitherto the minds of men have been so undeveloped, that they have looked for consistency or truth in the opposing, contending, and absurd *Religions* of the world,—in the contending, opposing, and absurd arrangements arising from the ignorant selfish notions which have created the arrangements to uphold and perpetuate the demoralising practice of *Private Property*,—and in the varied absurd modes made over the world for priestly or secular *Marriages*, based as all have been upon the glaring falsehood " that man has been created with faculties to love or hate at his pleasure"—when every one knows by experience that this is an error fatal to truth and happiness.

These glaring fallacies and gross inconsistencies, forced from birth into the minds of all, must be destroyed root and branch, before it will be possible to make man a rational and moral being, and to enable him to express the truth in his honest look, word, and action.

But it will be now asked—Can these old established gross inconsistencies be now rooted out, and the prejudices and habits of unnumbered ages be now overcome ?

Yes. Truth is omnipotent, and will prevail over all error.

The Religions, Private Property, and human-made legal Marriages, with their endless evil consequences, all emanate from the glaringly absurd notion " that man makes his own physical, intellectual, moral, practical, and spiritual qualities ;"—while the experience of the human race, reverberating its knowledge through all ages to this hour, declares in unceasing sounds that man of himself is yet incompetent even to know how these divine qualities are forced upon him. And of the wondrous power by which they are devised, separately formed, and more wondrously combined, he is at this day profoundly ignorant.

How grossly insane must it then be to form the human character, base and construct society, and govern the population of the world, upon this glaring falsehood ?

But the time is at hand when truth will overcome all error,—when man shall be made wise to his salvation from all evil,—and when the population of the world will rapidly progress in peace and prosperity, until they attain a state of high excellence, active enjoyment, and permanent happiness,—or the Millennial State of human Existence upon the Earth, previous to their translation into the superior spirit spheres.

This is the change to be effected by the aid of the Spirits of our departed relatives and friends, who in the world of spirits are also assisted by the sages and prophets of olden times, and of all that is superior among them. Those who wish for scientific and valuable knowledge upon this new and wondrous phase in man's progress towards a superior life upon earth, will do well to consult the writings of Professor Hare, Judge Edmonds, Governor Tallmadge, Andrew Jackson Davis, the Rev. Mr. Ferguson, with many other works of deserved celebrity. Also the weekly and monthly journals devoted to the same subject, and to the experience of the Fox family, the Mettlers, Mrs. French of Pittsburg, Mr. J. C. Atwood of Lockport, and innumerable healing and superior mediums spread over the United States, and especially the Koons, Tippies, Davenports, for daily extraordinary material manifestations. The superior spirits communicating through these parties, and to myself, all agree that these new and truly wondrous and almost incredible manifestations are now made to prepare the public mind for the *reformation of the population of the world*, and to convince men that they will live in a superior state when they depart from the earth, and that their life is immortal.

To assist to hasten this good time that is coming, as no one is perhaps in a position in society to do it with so little inconvenience as myself, I have called a congress of the reformers of the world, to be held in St. Martin's Hall, Long Acre, in London, the present metropolis of the world, on Wednesday the 14th of May, at eleven o'clock, to commence business *precisely* at noon, and to continue day by day until the subject matter for the consideration of the congress shall be discussed to its completion, and practical measures shall be decided upon.

At this congress for the reformation of the world it will be proposed :—

That society shall be new based in principle, and the individual responsibility of man changed for the responsibility of the directing and governing powers of each division or aggregate of the population governed.

That individual interests shall gradually give place to a well devised united interest.

That Europe, including the whole of Russia and Turkey, be formed into a federative comonwealth, composed of the present kingdoms and states. Each kingdom or state to remain sovereign within its present limits, until the whole can be peaceably and advantageously combined into one harmonious whole, under such new surroundings that each one shall possess the greatest amount of rational liberty and permanent prosperity.

That the circulating medium at first shall be the notes of each state, guaranteed by the state,—afterwards by the united federative commonwealth ;—and as soon as the practical arrangements can be formed to produce by the aid of chemistry and mechanics wealth in perpetual continuance beyond the possible wants of the population, the necessity for any circulating medium will altogether cease ; for wealth will be made so abundant with pleasure to all parties, that, like air and water, it will be obtained without money and without price.

That when society shall be based and constructed on the laws of nature, the arrangements respecting the sexes will be also in accordance with the pure and unerring laws of nature. When the rational faculties of man shall be opened, and he shall be placed in a state of perfect mental freedom, which has not yet been attained by any portion of the human race, he will clearly perceive the gross ignorance and absurdity of the present sexual arrangements over the world ;—that they are directly opposed to the laws of human nature and of God ;—that they are well calculated to produce falsehood, deception, sexual disease, dissatisfaction, and misery ;—that through this error these evils are now produced throughout society to a frightful extent ;—and that were the sexual relations made to be in consistent accordance with the laws of human nature and of God, there would be no sexual disease, dissatisfaction, or unhappiness between the sexes.

That effective arrangements be made to do justice to every one from birth, by placing all within arrangements by which the physical, intellectual, moral, and spiritual, as well as the practical qualities, given to each by the Great Creating Power of the

Universe, shall be well trained, educated, employed, and governed through life.

That as society has given to the present population of the world its present grossly false ideas and habits, all who desire to be undisturbed in these insane ideas and habits, not of their choosing, may be allowed quietly to retain them if they can, and to be unmolested, like other lunatics, while they do not injure those around them who may have entered upon the rational life upon earth. These will of course pity the weakness of their poor deluded fellow mortals, for whom, in consequence of the maladies forced from birth upon them, they will have patience, forbearance, charity, and kindness, without ceasing.

That the new surroundings in which to place the human race shall all be made so as to enable man to live his life according to the divine laws of his nature :—those surroundings made under the existing insane system being as it were purposely devised to prevent his living according to those laws—the only laws which can make him good, wise, rational, united to his fellows, and happy.

That, seeing that parents are the least competent to train and educate their own children, all children will be equally and justly trained and educated within proper arrangements devised for the purpose, by the commonwealth, which will be the common Father upon earth, representing the Divine Common Father of Existences pervading the Universe.

These are the vital interests to all humanity, which will be fully discussed until their truth, unity, and everlasting benefits to our race shall be comprehended by the congress, so as to enable it to give the same knowledge to the public, in order that it may be understood as a whole, consistent in all its parts,—as must be all things made in accordance with nature's laws, as seen as far as human faculties can extend within the universe.

Before the time appointed for the meeting of this congress, the business proposed to come under discussion and to be decided upon will be systematically arranged and published, in order that the members attending may have time to reflect upon it, and come prepared to express their sentiments in short decisive speeches, adapted for practical results ; because it is intended that from this congress practical measures shall proceed, beneficial to the permanent interests and happiness of the human race.

THE OUTLINE OF THE BUSINESS AND THE ORDER OF DISCUSSING IT, TO BE PROPOSED TO BE TRANSACTED AT THE CONGRESS FOR THE REFORMATION OF THE WORLD.

THE proposed outline of the business and order of discussing it at the congress for reforming the world and introducing the Millennium into every day practice is the following :—

1st.—Two officers to be elected by the Congress, to be the President and Vice President of the Congress :—the latter to aid and assist the former when required, and to preside during any unavoidable absence of the former. The election to take place at noon on the first day of meeting. Immediately afterwards seven secretaries to be elected,—an English, an American, a French, a German, a Russian, a Turkish or Ottoman, and an Italian,—to report to their respective nations.

After these officers shall have been elected, four officers of order to be elected, who shall be conveniently placed in different parts of the assembly, to assist the President under his direction to preserve the requsite order while the congress is conducting business of such high importance to every class throughout the world.

2nd.—When these elections shall have been completed, and the secretaries and orderly officers have taken their stations, the President shall read or cause one of the secretaries to read the following :—

Preamble.

This congress is held with the pure intention of benefiting permanently the human race as one family, and ultimately, by gradual practical means, to proceed in peace with foresight and wisdom to adopt measures, uninjurious to any, to prepare the population of the world to form themselves, nation after nation, into one brotherhood, on the principle of a true and just equality according to age,—this being the only principle which can insure permanent peace and harmony throughout humanity. There will however always be the never ending varieties of character created by the natural combinations of the faculties, propensities, and powers, given at-birth to each individual.

That these ever-to-be-desired ultimate results can never be attained except through the knowledge of truth respecting the laws of human nature, and how to form all the arrangements of society to be ever consistent with those unchanging and unerring divine laws of humanity. These laws, when fully understood and rightly appreciated, may be now applied to practice in such manner, that with the certainty of a law of nature these results may be universally and permanently attained and secured for humanity through all future ages.

That these all glorious results cannot be given isolated to any individual, any one nation, or to any partial division of the human race.

That to attain these results, substantial arrangements must be devised and adopted, which in their progress in practice will proceed from individuals to nations, and from nation to nation, until the surroundings of the human race shall be complete to force, by the irresistible influence of those surroundings, one and all to become rational in feeling, thought, and action, and therefore, good, wise, healthy, united, wealthy, ever consistent, and happy. It is one of the all-wise laws of nature and of God, that one human being cannot be relieved and raised from the present state of irrationality and insanity, except by measures that will equally relieve and raise all to the same elevation of goodness, wisdom, rationality, and happiness. Hence the necessity for now adopting universal principles and practices.

That it is now evident to all who have powers given them to observe, reflect, and reason accurately, that, from the earliest period of human existence or infant state of humanity, to this day, man has been without a correct and comprehensive knowledge of his own nature, and that in consequence society over the world has been based on error, and constructed in all its parts in accordance with that error.

That this fatal mistake has given a false character and a language of falsehood to man, and made society over the earth a heterogeneous confused mass of the most gross follies and absurdities. Hence the repulsive feelings, the quarrels, fightings, and general disunion of the human race ; when it is now evidently the interest of all not to quarrel, not to fight, nor to be disunited, but to live within such surroundings as will make all attractive to each other, so as to form one family or brotherhood of united interests, and so to remain through futurity. The unreflecting have believed, and until they shall see a new state of things commence in successful practice will continue to believe, the attainment of these Millennial results to be impossible ; but those who by favourable circumstances have been enabled to expand their mind beyond the petty circles of class, creed, country, and colour, and to be competent to grasp at one view the entire of humanity, through the past to the present and through the future, know that until the incubus can be overcome and removed which deranges the faculties of the human race and afflicts them with insanity, the true base on which society should be founded and constructed cannot be adopted ; but that when this base shall have been adopted, it will be a straightforward practical proceeding to advance society into the long promised Millennial state.

This incubus, it must be evident to all who have acquired a knowledge of God's laws of humanity, is the insane notion that each one forms his own physical, mental, and spiritual natural qualities, and makes his own local and general surroundings. While the first indications of a sound mind acquainted with the facts of history, past and present, make it evident how impossible it is that the individual could know how he received these natural divine qualities, or how he came to be so surrounded. Yet with these facts, exposed to man generation after generation, society has been from the beginning until now based and constructed on the opposing supposition that each one decides upon and creates his own natural qualities and his own surroundings, making him responsible for the influences which he is obliged to receive from the combined powers of these two forces.

Reflection, unbiassed by the local insanities of class, creed, party, country, and colour, must now make it evident that this incubus has caused the past and present insanity of the human race, and produced all the evils which have affected mankind from the beginning even to the present hour. Remove this incubus— new base society on its true foundation — and construct it throughout to be consistent with that base, and the world will soon be reformed, and the true Millennial State enjoyed by all.

From that which has been now stated it must be evident that the first subject for discussion for a congress called to consider the means by which the world is to be reformed, must be to deliberate and decide upon the base on which the human character should be formed from birth to death, and on which society should be constructed to be consistent with that foundation through all its departments, so as to become permanently prosperous, and the entire population continuous in progress towards higher and higher physical, mental, and spiritual excellence and happiness.

This all-important point once decided,—that society shall continue to be based on individual responsibility to society, as heretofore, or on the responsibility of society to individuals,—will at once decide the future proceedings of this congress.

From men who meet for the purpose of reforming society over the world it will be naturally anticipated that they will decide in accordance with facts, and that these are universally known to give *all* power to society over the individual, and no power to the individual, except, perhaps, a small modicum to one in a million. The congress will therefore decide, that a reformation of the population of the world can be based only on the principle that God or nature and society form the individual, and that society should be responsible to the individual for that portion of his character which society forms. And as this portion includes the language, religion, habits, manners, conduct, the truth or falsehood of his language, the honesty or deception of his transactions with his fellow men, and in fact the truth or falsehood, wisdom or folly of all his sayings and doings through life, society must be so recreated as to make it responsible for the character in these respects of every individual committed to its charge.

And under wise foreseen arrangements or surroundings every individual may be placed from birth to death under the immediate and direct charge of society.

The principle of non-individual responsibility and the responsibility of society to the individual, with the practice of gradually creating new, good, and superior surroundings around all of the human race, being decided upon and agreed to as the foundation on which the business of congress should proceed, the investigation and discussion of the questions and business as stated in the programme will follow, and will call forth the highest qualities and powers of the most advanced members of the congress. But as the true criterion of truth is now known and can be always and in every case of difference referred to, there can be little chance of congress, after a full debate, coming to a false and injurious conclusion—for all false conclusions cannot fail to be ultimately injurious.

Some of the members of this congress may not perhaps be familiar with the universal criterion of truth, and therefore it is here re-stated from many of the published works of the writer. It is,—" that truth, in every case, on all subjects, must be throughout consistent with itself and in perfect accordance with every known fact." Truth must be one eternally throughout the universe, and admits of no inconsistency or contradiction to itself. All differences of opinion which may arise in this congress being referred to this criterion or touchstone of truth, may be always truthfully decided.

These principles being decided, the great questions then to be investigated will be—

1stly.—What are the surroundings which will best form the character of the human race ?

2ndly.—What surroundings will enable the population of the world to create the greatest amount of the most valuable wealth in the shortest time with health and pleasure to its producers ?

3rdly.—What surroundings will be the best for the circulating of this wealth justly and beneficially to all.

4thly.—What will be the best surroundings by which each social division and the aggregate of society over the world can be the best governed, beneficially for the governed and govenors ?

5thly.—What will be the best social surroundings by which to combine into one, for each division of society, the four preceding subjects, to be the most effective for the attainment of the objects stated ?

6thly.—What will be the best mode of inducing governments and people to carry into execution the resolves of this congress ?

7thly.—What practical measures will the congress recommend governments and people to adopt, to gradually attain the permanent peace of the world ?

The writer from long consideration of this subject has come to the conclusion that the object proposed in the preceding paragraphs may be immediately the most easily commenced and attained, by Great Britain and the United States forming, upon perfect terms of equality, a federative treaty to unite the two nations as one, to constitute the two empires in their extended dominions over the globe as one, undivided in all their interests and great objects for promoting the true civilisation of the world. Thus will each give to the other a splendid empire, without a particle of loss to itself; but as one light will give its light to another light without diminishing its own, so may the United States and Great Britain give each their full power to the other without any loss of power on the part of either. But soon both would discover that by this union the power of each would be far more than quadrupled. But even this will be but a small part of the ultimate benefit of this first divine transaction between rival nations. It will be an example that will be of necessity adopted by other nations. Such unions will possess so many important permanent advantages, that the example will be soon followed by other nations in their own defence. And Great Britain and the United States should hold out the hand of fellowship and friendship to the other states and nations, to federatively unite with them, until gradually, as other nations prepare themselves for such divine unions, the peace and union of the population of the world and its Millennial state shall be complete.

This outline of the proposed business of the congress for the reformation of the world and to prepare it for the long-promised Millennium, will suffice for the present. A more sytematic programme shall be arranged previous to the Congress, and published, in order that the members when assembled may be prepared for the business to be transacted, and to consider the practical measures which the Congress should recommend the people and governments most advanced in civilisation to adopt.

The time for mere words and much speaking is past ; and that for essential action in the right direction is near at hand. Let all civilised nations send their best men to this congress.

PROGRAMME OF THE PROPOSED PROCEEDINGS OF THE CONGRESS FOR THE REFORMATION OF THE WORLD AND INTRODUCTION INTO PRACTICE OF THE MILLENNIUM.

IN consideration of this being the first Congress ever held for the reformation of the world, and the subject being so new to the mass of the population of the civilized and most advanced nations, to prevent confusion and give order to its proceedings the following programme has been prepared, and will be offered for acceptance after the officers have been elected and the preamble read to Congress.

It is necessary to premise that the term God, as used in this programme, signifies that Power which eternally creates, preserves, and governs all things within the universe; or composes, decomposes, and recomposes the elements of the universe. And this statement is made, without pretending, from lack of knowledge derived from facts, to say in what form that Power exists, or the mode by which its wondrous results are attained and maintained in eternal action.

As the universe must be one ever consistent truth, the criterion of every other truth must be its consistency with the laws of nature, with itself, and with all facts; and that which is inconsistent with the laws of nature, with itself, and in opposition to facts, must be false, and when adopted in general practice must lead to endless errors and evils, and to a language and conduct of deception.

Every subject discussed at this Congress must stand the test of this criterion before it can be affirmed as one of the resolves of the Congress.

These self-evident truths being stated and agreed to, the following is the proposed Programme, or order of business.

After the first day, the business of Congress to commence each morning at ten o'clock, and to terminate at four; having a rest or suspension of business from one o'clock to half-past one.

The following questions to be discussed and decided upon in the order in which they are here stated.

1st. Question.—Will it be for the happiness of the population of the world that it should be in future governed by the just, merciful, beneficial, unchanging, and eternal laws of God,—or as hitherto, by the ever changing, conflicting, unjust, and cruel laws of men?

2nd Question.—What are the unchanging and eternal laws of God respecting humanity?

3rd Question.—Shall these laws of God be now recommended to be gradually introduced for the government of the human race?

4th Question.—What are the ever changing laws of men by which the nations of the earth are now attempting to govern themselves in opposition to God's laws, and thereby of necessity producing endless ever recurring evil?

5th Question.—Shall it be recommended by this Congress to the population of the world to gradually abandon these ignorant and demoralising laws of men in opposition to God's laws, and to supersede the former by the latter?

6th Question.—Will the language of truth or the language of falsehood be the most beneficial for the human race?

7th Question.—Will the laws of God admit of the language of Falsehood?

8th Question.—Will the laws of man admit of the language of Truth ?

9th Question.—Can the human race ever become good, wise, united, and happy, while compelled by men's ever-changing, unjust, and cruel laws, to speak the language of Falsehood ?

10th Question.—Can the human race avoid becoming good, wise, united, and happy, while governed by God's all-wise, just, and merciful laws, which admit of the language of Truth only in look, word, and action?

11th Question.—As all of the human race are born with the same natural faculties—although, most advantageously for all, combined in different proportions—is it not just, if practicable, to place all from birth within such surroundings, that each one, according to age and natural capacity, shall be equal in education and position ?

12th Question.—Is it not just that each one of our race should have his or her fair share of the duties and enjoyments of life ?

13th Question.—Is it just, or can it be beneficial to the population of the world, that individuals or any aggregate of individuals should oppress or injure other individuals or aggregates of individuals ?

14th Question.—As real useful valuable wealth can be easily and pleasantly produced by the physical and mental qualities of men, women, and children, according to their age, when aided by inventions in mechanism and other sciences, is it rational that any parties willing to be employed in creating wealth should be kept in idleness by the foolish laws and practices of society ?

15th Question.—Is it just, reasonable, or rational, that while any part of the population of the world is in want of wealth, any other part should be kept in useless idleness and luxury ?

16th Question.—Will it be for the happiness of the population of the world that all from birth should be trained and educated on the principle of repulsion for our race, or on the principle of attraction ?

17th Question.—Will it be for the happiness of the human race that each one from birth should be trained and educated, physically, intellectually, morally, and practically, to the extent of their natural faculties, in the best manner known or that may be discovered ?

18th Question.—Will it be for the happiness of the population of the world that each according to his or her natural capacities should be daily employed, physically and mentally, beneficially for themselves and society ?

19th Question.—Will it be for the happiness of the human race that all nations should now commence to create good and superior common-sense arrangements, in which gradually to place all of the human race ?

20th Question.—Will it be for the happiness of the population of the world that nations should continue to be divided in language, interest, and territory, or that they should be now federatively united, in order that nation after nation should by degrees become united in language, interest, and territory ?

21st Question.—Are the present divisions and classifications of society over the world rational, and calculated to create superior men and women ? Or are they grossly irrational, and calculated to degrade and keep the human race in a perpetual state of hostile degradation ?

22nd Question.—Will it be for the happiness of the human race that efficient substantial arrangements and surroundings should be now commenced to create, pleasantly for the creators, wealth in superfluity for all at all times, without competition or conflict of opposing feelings or interests,—or for the population of the world to continue its present most irrational and absurd, unjust, cruel, and ignorant mode of creating wealth ?

23rd Question.—Is it for the happiness of the human race that wealth should be distributed as it now is most unjustly and unwisely for all; or should such arrangements be now commenced as will create a surplus for all, and when such surplus shall have been created, should all be permitted freely to use what their nature requires without money and without price?

24th Question.—While the changes proposed, should they be adopted by the Congress and acceded to by governments and people, shall be in progress—will it be true wisdom to effect the circulation of the growing wealth by bank notes of the nations, guaranteed by each nation singly before its federation with others, and afterwards by the United federation ;—or to continue to limit the creation of wealth by the amount in circulation of metals intrinsically of less value than steel or iron ?

25th Question.—Will it be for the happiness of the human race that all should be placed in dwellings devised by the highest knowledge, skill, and talent, to be the most healthy and convenient for the enjoyment of existence through life, placed in the midst of well-devised superior surroundings, to-well-form character, usefully occupy time, and enable all to enjoy the substantial pleasures of a rational and wise existence, in peace, with order, and with a due foresight for the future ;—or that all should continue to live in the present random-built dwellings, without plan or system, in many cases amidst the most unhealthy demoralising surroundings, creating a large expenditure for little comparative comfort, and not one advantage for many which might be given at much less cost of labour and material?

26th Question.—Will it be for the happiness of the human race to live in large cities and towns, with all their many disadvantages ?—In isolated dwellings, with their different disadvantages ?—In colleges and universities, with their yet different disadvantages ?—Or to reside in dwellings so surrounded as to possess in high perfection all the real advantages of cities, towns, isolated positions, and universities, without one of their disadvantages ?

27th Question.—Will it be for the permanent high advantage of the human race that these surroundings should be so devised and combined as essentially to assist in forming a good and superior character for all placed from birth within them,—in enabling all to create wealth easily and pleasantly,—and in enabling all to govern and be governed, each one according to age, in such manner as to satisfy all, without any being oppressed, but each one to be well cared for from birth through life by the society around him ?

28th Question. — Will it be for the true and lasting happiness of the human race that these surroundings should be such as will tend to pervade the whole within them from birth with the pure spirit of universal charity, kindness, and love for the entire of humanity under all its differences, and create a feeling of merciful consideration for all that has life ?

29th Question.—Will it be for the happiness of the population of the world that each one from birth shall be so placed, trained, educated, and encouraged, as to express the truth on all occasions without the slightest deception in look, word, and action, so that falsehood and deception from birth should be unknown to the individual and to all of our race.

30th Question.—Will it be for the present and future happiness of the entire population of the world that these new proposed surroundings should be such as will enable society to gradually train, educate, and place all under such consistent and superior circumstances, that they will be prepared to constitute a part of one brotherhood of the human race, cordially united in feeling, interest, and langnage, equal in all respects in their position among their fellows, according to age and capacity, and thus introduce and commence the long promised Millennium upon earth ?

I am impressed to add the following, to assist to prepare the public yet more for the immediate introduction in practice of the Millennium.

All the powers, qualities, and faculties of man, — physical, intellectual, moral, spiritual, and practical—are directly formed by God's laws, and are therefore divine ; and these faculties, qualities, and powers are also combined in such manner in each individual and in the aggregate of individuals over the earth, as to form one humanity, complete when united in one feeling, interest, and language, each individual forming a necessary part of this magnificent humanity, which, thus united, will form of the human race one man containing all his varieties. These faculties, qualities, and powers, given to the individual, are admirably and wonderfully combined, mechanically, chemically, and spiritually, to secure the health, goodness, progress, and happiness of each and all, as soon as society shall have progressed so far as to comprehend these divine powers, and to learn how to place, train, educate, and employ each and all from birth through life according to the laws of man's nature.

The first lesson to learn the divine laws of humanity as given by God to each at his birth is :—

That man must eat to live, and must eat a sufficient quantity of wholesome food as a first preliminary to be healthy.

That he must daily duly exercise his physical, mental, and spiritual nature, in a salubrious atmosphere, as a second preliminary to be healthy.

That these faculties, qualities, and powers from birth, are of necessity under the direction of society, to be placed, trained, educated, and employed, rationally or irrationally.

That in the former case the individual will be so placed, trained, educated, and employed, that he will become consistent in mind and practice, good, wise, united in charity and love to all of human kind, and through life actively employed in endeavouring to increase the happiness of all around him ; and the earth will be gradually highly cultivated and beautifully laid out, peace will be permanent and universal, and the progress of humanity in all kinds of knowledge and in wisdom will be rapid and increasing, and the will of God will thus be done on earth as it is in heaven, and the promised Millennium will be attained, and man's earthly happiness will be great and progressive in each generation through futurity. For man to be virtuous, (that is to act in accordance with God's laws and to be happy,) is the highest worship and the only worship that an all-wise, all-good, and all-powerful eetrnal Creating Existence can desire from the beings created.

That in the latter case,—that is, while society so places, trains, educates, and employs all, as to make each irrational, to act in direct opposition to God's all-wise, just, good, and most merciful laws,—man must become, as he has become and is now over the earth, an unreasonable, or insane, opposing, quarrelling, fighting, contending, ignorant, and miserable animal, unsatisfied with his position in life from birth to death. And these are the natural or necessary effects now arising from society thus insanely placing, training, educating, and employing all in every nation over the earth. And while society shall continue to inflict upon the population of the world its insane laws in direct opposition to God's laws, the earth will be made as heretofore, and as it is now, the abode of irrational-made men, women, and children, gradually tending towards a pandemonium of absurd contradictions, inconsistencies, and most unnecessary misery for all classes, nations, and peoples.

The present mode of placing, training, educating, employing, and treating the human race over the earth, is erroneous, absurd, and irrational in the extreme ; this conduct being the true cause of all the ignorance, poverty, disunion, wars, contests, crimes, and misery prevalent throughout all nations and among all people.

The adoption of God's laws in all their purity and integrity is the only remedy. Any change short of this will be vain and useless.

Hence the necessity for the Congress to reform the world and to introduce into practice the long desired Millennial state of human existence upon earth.

Men and Women of all nations and colours !—Read, Mark, Learn, and Ponder well on that which has been now written. It is " consistent with itself and with all facts,"—and therefore it is true.

ROBERT OWEN.

Sevenoaks Park.

RESOLUTIONS TO BE PROPOSED FOR ADOPTION BY THE CONGRESS.

1st.—That there are two systems, a false one and a true one, by which to form the character and govern the human race. The first is based on the imaginary notion, opposed to all facts, " that man, individually, forms his physical, intellectual, moral, spiritual, and practical qualities of body and mind." The second is based on the knowledge, derived from all known facts, " that God creates these divine qualities at birth, and that society gives them a wise or foolish direction and character from birth to death." The first mode necessarily forms man into a repulsive, selfish, quarrelsome, fighting, inconsistent, irrational, and insane animal, ignorant of his own nature and of the eternal unchanging laws of humanity, and consequently so placed and trained that from birth to death, without intending or knowing it, he acts continually in opposition to his own and his fellows' permanent and highest happiness. The second mode, when introduced and consistently acted upon, will as necessarily form man into an attractive, generous, peaceable, consistent, rational, sane, and superior reasoning and reasonable being, who will be consequently so placed, trained, educated, and employed, that from birth to death he will become good, wise, healthy, united to all his fellows, wealthy, and happy, and will thus be well prepared for the change awaiting him after he shall have ceased to live upon the earth.

2nd.—That these two systems can never be united; because

the first requires for its support a language of falsehood and a conduct of deception, while the second could not exist with either falsehood or deception, but requires a language of truth and a conduct of straightforward, open honesty, without exception or deviation.

3rd.—That the past and present history of the human race proves that hitherto the first system has been alone known and acted upon by all nations, tribes, and peoples,—all having made the same mistake of principle on this subject; as our early ancestors erred respecting the principles of astronomy, and respecting our planatory movements ; and that the time has arrived in the due order of nature for this error, fatal to human rationality and happiness, to be peaceably abandoned, and the true system of society for forming the character and governing the human race to be now with the consent of all peoples and their governments adopted in principle and practice.

4th.—That the first system will lead, if continued, to universal confusion and a pandemonium upon earth ; while the second will lead to universal order and a terrestrial Millennial paradise.

5th.—That the change from the first to the second system for forming the character and governing the human race will be the soonest effected in peace, order, and with wise foresight, by the federative union of existing nations and peoples, brought about by their present respective governments.

6th.—That upon the adoption of the second system for governing and forming the character of the human race from birth through earthly life, (the time for which has now arrived,) the details of its practice for forming a superior character and governing wisely will be plain and simple, one step following another in due order, to make each part consistent with every other part, and all the parts forming a consistent, beautiful, harmonious, and perfect whole.

7th.—That, to expedite this change of system, from disunion, disorder, and misery, to union, order, and happiness,
delegates be chosen with care and foresight, after due deliberation, by a committee of   now to be appointed and nominated by this Congress :—such delegates so chosen to communicate with all civilised nations and governments simultaneously on this subject, to endeavour to induce them to adopt in good faith the second system, and immediately to take measures to carry it into execution without loss of time or of happiness to the people whom they now mis-govern.

8th.—That, to aid these delegates in their great and most important mission, a league of the people be formed in each civilised nation, to be called the League of Universal Union, to promote an accurate knowledge of the false and true system for forming the character and governing the human race, and to preserve peace and create good feelings in all these nations while the change shall be in progress.

9th.—That the Committee to be now appointed, and the Delegates whom they may choose, shall select a Central Board of Directors in London, to organise through the British Dominions at home and abroad the League of the People to produce Universal Union, and to aid in peaceably changing the false for the true system of society, and to promote the federative union of all nations, commenceing with a federative treaty upon terms of perfect equality between Great Britain and the United States of North America.

10th.—That the Board of Directors thus chosen shall also endeavour to induce the other civilised nations to form similar Central Boards of Directors to effect the same results within their respective national limits,—and thus prepare the way for a cordial union between all the governments and peoples of the civilised world, including Russia and Turkey.

11th.—That a Committee be now also appointed who can devote their time to call upon the wealthy members of society and others to subscribe to forward this great and glorious change for all humanity ; and that a subscription be now made to cover the expense of this Congress.

Then will follow the usual concluding resolutions.

ROBERT OWEN.

February 26th, 1856.

No. 2 will be published 1st of April, and No. 3 1st of May.

London :—Published by the Author at 16, Great Windmill Street, Haymarket : and sold by J. Clayton and Son, 223, Piccadilly ; Holyoake, 147, Fleet Street ; Truelove, 240, Strand; Goddard, 14, Great Portland Street, Cavendish Square ; Farrer, 21, John Street, Fitzroy Square; and all Booksellers.

ROBERT OWEN'S
MILLENNIAL GAZETTE;
EXPLANATORY OF THE PRINCIPLES AND PRACTICES BY WHICH, IN PEACE, WITH TRUTH, HONESTY, AND SIMPLICITY, THE NEW EXISTENCE OF MAN UPON THE EARTH MAY BE EASILY AND SPEEDILY COMMENCED.

"The character of Man is formed *for* him, and *not by* him!"

No. 2.]   APRIL 1st, 1856.

WHY SHOULD THE GOVERNMENTS OF THE WORLD LONGER ATTEMPT TO SUPPORT A SYSTEM OF SOCIETY BASED ON FALSEHOOD, WHICH CONTINUALLY CREATES EVIL TO ALL, AND OBSTRUCTS THE PROGRESS AND HAPPINESS OF THE HUMAN RACE?

WHY? indeed, when the straight path to goodness, unity, wisdom, and happiness, is now opened to the world, should its rulers persevere in maintaining a system which of necessity must inflict misery on every one of our race?

Surely the experience of the past has now developed so much of the reasoning faculties of humanity, that when facts innumerable and ever recurring are plainly placed before the most advanced and least prejudiced by error of the human race, so much common sense will arise in their mind, as to exhibit in vivid impressions the gross folly and irrationality of proceeding another year without adopting effective practical measures to prepare, in peace and with wise foresight, for an entire change from this system of *all error* to that of *all truth*,—from a system based in opposition to all facts, to a system in perfect harmony with all facts bearing on humanity and the constitution of society.

It is a good sign of the times when the Emperor of the French publicly states that the Prince Imperial. the child of France, shall have his character formed to advance the progress of the age. It is confirmatory of the great, glorious, and divine truth, that any character, from the worst to the best, may, by the adoption of proper means, be given to every one born with the natural faculties and qualities of humanity.

If the Emperor can thus announce to France and to the world that the Prince Imperial, the child of France, shall have a character given to him to advance the progress of the age,—Why not now adopt decisive measures to form the character of every child of France to advance the progress of the age?

And if Napoleon the Third can thus determine that his son *shall* have his character formed to advance the progress of the age,—Why shall not the sovereigns of all other nations also determine that their sons and daughters shall have their characters formed to advance the progress of the age?

But, far beyond all other considerations,—Why, now that the secret is made public, and the truth is thus published to all nations and peoples, that any character, good or bad, can be given to all children, whether born princes or peasants,—should not every child of man over the earth have a character formed for them to advance the progress of the age?

Rejoice, all ye true friends to humanity! whatever may be your colour, country, creed, or class, that the Emperor of the French —the extraordinary man, Napoleon the Third—has announced to the world that his first-born shall have a character formed *for* him to advance the progress of the age, and thus assents to the all-important truth, that society may now make arrangements to give *any* character to the human race— a truth which, if the mental faculties of men had been more developed, would have been long since demonstrated by the experience of the character given so decisively to all the varied nations, tribes, and peoples, over the earth.

After this divine disclosure to the human race,—surely universal measures will be speedily adopted to prevent any nation or people from forming any inferior characters,—much less thieves, robbers, murderers, or any that shall become malicious, revengeful, jealous, selfish, or uncharitable.

Will not all now discover that it has been a gross error, for want of a higher development of our mental faculties, that any of our predecessors had their characters formed to be so very inferior as history describes them to be?

And especially, after so much glaring experience attained in our age, that any one of the present generation should have had his character so formed as to be selfish, cruel, unjust, without charity or love for his race, to be poor, and ignorant, and to be despised for being poor and ignorant.

But as the light now shines, let us rejoice in it, and forget the demon darkness of the past!

These characters of misery will now soon cease to be formed by a society which was undeveloped and insane when it formed such characters. The light is now come into the world through the mediumship of Napoleon the Third, Emperor of the French, and he stands forth prominently as one of the most important and influential mediums of this extraordinary age, when so many mediums of note have been given to the world.

No! the governments of the more civilised nations can no

longer support a system, which is so false and injurious that it is opposed to the introduction of truth upon all subjects the most important for man to know and fully comprehend, and which inflicts continually upon the human race, of every colour, country, creed, and class, evils almost too much for humanity to sustain and live.

There are but two systems, the bad and the good, by which the world can be governed. While man remained undeveloped and in mental darkness, the bad was preferred and was universal. The sun of knowledge arisen—the darkness is exposed—the bad can no longer be maintained :—the good is opened before us—its advantages are so numerous that soon all will adopt it, and the bad will be for ever abandoned, and its evils will only be remembered as a foil to increase the happiness to be derived from the good, and will be estimated as the preliminary cause, perhaps, absolutely necessary to prepare for and to produce the good.

Why, then, should any of the governments of the world longer attempt to retain a system based on falsehood and repulsion, opposed to truth and attraction, and destructive of goodness and happiness over the world ?

SHAKERISM *V.* OWENISM.

A LETTER TO ROBERT OWEN, BY A SHAKER.

(Copied from the Spiritual Telegraph,—a weekly paper published at New York, U. S.)

NEW LEBANON, *January* 16th, 1856.

To ROBERT OWEN :

Respected Friend—As a member of the society of *Shakers* at New Lebanon, N. Y., I find myself in possession of several numbers of your " *New Existence of Man upon the Earth,*" and others of your pamphlets. Be pleased, in return, to receive the thanks and well wishes of our Brotherhood for the same, but still more for your persevering benevolent labours in the cause of poor perverted, distressed, and oppressed *Humanity.*

When some of the disciples of Jesus Christ informed him that they had found a man casting out devils in his name, and forbade him, because he followed not with them, they looked for a meed of praise for their zeal. But, instead thereof, they received a rebuke for their *sectarianism.* The noble and ever-to-be-remembered response of Jesus was, " Forbid him *not ;* for he that is *not* against us, is *for* us." Every doer of good to man stands in some relation to Jesus and his disciples. Our motto is :— " Peace to him that is *nigh,* and to him that is *far off.*"

Extremes meet. *Robert Owen* and the *Shakers* of America have for half a century been the antipodes of each other—the two opposite ends of the entire class of Reformers, who are agitating the minds of the human family " for better or for worse." Our mutual object has been to inaugurate the Millennium upon earth ; and we both think that object is accomplished.

You aim to create a *new earth*, wherein shall dwell righteousness. The *Shakers* aim to create a *new heaven*, as well as a *new earth*. *You* have been impelled by the motive power of *truth*, operating on the *natural plane*, exercising common sense, philosophy, science, and, (may I also add without any disparagement ?) " worldly wisdom." They (the *Shakers*) by the motive power of *Revelation* alone, which, quickening the conscience as the *primal* faculty of the spiritual senses when moved upon by the religious element, has resulted to them in wisdom—not their own, and for which they, as men and women, take no credit—*supernal*, and, as they believe, *Divine* wisdom.

Your initiatory or *first* purpose was to establish Communities in which the institution of *Private Property* would have no place ; where *War*, in all its phases, would be unknown, and violent antagonisms and burning competition would cease ; where Peace, Wealth, and Unity, would cause the tears on the cheeks of suffering mortals to stop midway, and turn to gentle dews of friendship and affection. To accomplish this laudable and philanthropic enterprise, (after making several costly but unsuccessful attempts in your native country,) you gathered together in the *new world* some of the best material the civilised portions of the earth could produce for the accomplishment of your undertaking ; yet, notwithstanding you were favoured with all the advantages of wealth, talents, and numbers *within*, and sympathising thousands *without*, it terminated in an entire failure. Some twenty different communities were attempted on the same principles ; still not one of them remains at the present time. This field of labour was abandoned on the plea that the present generation was not prepared, and that the only feasible plan was to commence with the proper education of children. *Spiritual* influences, of course, were not then, to you available.

As a *converse* :—The initiatory or *first* purpose of the *Shakers* was simply from the *religious* plane, as moved by the love of God, the fear of God, the dread of hell, and the desire of heaven, —with which they were inspired by *spiritual* intelligences with whom they daily (and often hourly) communed—individually to *cease from doing evil*; i. e., to refrain from all that their own consciences, when aroused to the highest state of activity by supernal influences operating upon them, decided to be contrary to that spiritual light by which they were illumined.

This light shone back upon their whole past history with an intensity not to be appreciated by any except those who have in some measure experienced its effects; recalling to the consciousness of the person influenced thereby so vivid a recollection of every particular transgression, error, and sin, against either themselves, their fellow-men, or God, during the entire of their former life, as brought the matter just as present with them as at the time of its actual commission or perpetration. From the guilt, horror, and condemnation which this spiritual retrospection of themselves produced, their Spirit friends distinctly informed them that they would never find releasement until they *circumstantially* narrated, in the presence of some supernaturally-appointed person or persons, and as a confession to the Divine Being, each and *every* identical sin, error, or transgression, *exactly as it occurred*, and also made restitution (as far as it was in their power) for every wrong committed against a fellow being.

After obeying these—*to them*—sacred and divine injunctions, the most extraordinary results often followed. Their whole soul would be filled with joy unutterable, finding expression in shaking or dancing with all their might; shouting or speaking in some language with which the person in his or her normal state was perfectly unacquainted; and other equally singular and marvellous operations, which secured to them from outsiders the appellations of witches and wizards—inspired by the devil, etc.

The *fact* that this inspiration led them to be good to each other, and to clothe the naked and feed the hungry, even when they were of their own persecutors, has tended gradually to soften the prejudices and to puzzle and perplex the orthodoxy of the religious world.

From this time, the young Shaker novitiate was *inwardly* laid under the most solemn obligations *never to repeat* any act which had been a subject of his or her confession; *forsaking sin* and righting wrongs being the only form of atonement or repentance toward God, that the ministering Spirits would accept. Again, they were not merely to "cease to do evil," but were also to "learn to do well,"—to practise every active virtue.

And now an unlooked-for and very unexpected consequence flowed from this novel manner of being "converted," and of "getting religion," which distinguished its subjects from all other so-called Christians in existence. It was a distinction so palpable that "all men" could easily perceive it, how natural or external soever they might be in their own state and condition. They loved one another so genuinely, so practically, that each one felt it a privilege and a duty to let every other brother and sister possess all that they possessed, and enjoy all that themselves enjoyed. "They had all things common," and laid claim to nothing as *private* property, whether in chattels, land, or houses. They thus learned by experience that the direct tendency of their new, *spiritual* religion, was not only to throw all who would embrace it into the form and relation of *community*, but that it was a legitimate, an inevitable effect.

Now let me ask, my friend Robert,—Is not the foregoing the solution of the great problem of your life—of the age—how to form a community having in itself the seeds of *perpetuity* ?

Jesus said,—"Take *no thought* for your life, what ye shall eat, or what ye shall drink, or wherewithal ye shall be clothed ; for your heavenly father knoweth that ye have need of all these things. But seek ye *first* the *kingdom of heaven* and its righteousness, and all *these things* shall be *added* unto you."

Look now and consider. Has it not been the desire, the constant wish, of your big, benevolent heart, to gather the people into communities, that, *as the prime object*, they might be fed and clothed ? Has not this been the mainspring of your life-long labours—to educate the ignorant, to feed the hungry and clothe the naked, to *lower* the *rich* and *elevate* the *poor* ? And have you not thus sought as an *end*, that which, though in itself intrinsically *good*, is but an *effect* of an end ? In fine, have not your people hungered more after the *fruits* of the kingdom of heaven, (or the Millennium,) than they have after " the kingdom of heaven" itself, " and its righteousness," with the faith that, once in possession of *that*, " all other good things would be added," as certainly as that water will run down hill, or as that vegetation will spring from the bosom of the earth, when conditions are at all favourable ?

In the spirit of humility, and with sincerity and a heartfelt respect for you and your friends in the cause you advocate, I submit these questions, and again inquire if *here* is not revealed the *true cause* of the universsl failure of the *mere earthly man* to form a community ?—And also the *true cause* of the *spiritual man*, as before described, without possessing a tithe of the external worldly wisdom advantages—without even thinking or caring about a Community or Socialism—having been instinctively drawn into it by laws to him as unseen and unknown as were those that organised and fashioned him in his mother's womb ?

Let me recapitulate the incipient stages in the process of forming all hitherto successful communities. A man or woman receives a heavenly, spiritual ministration, which convinces him that there is a God,—convicts him of sin,—and teaches him how, and constrains him, to confess and forsake it,—implants in his soul such a fear and love of God as for ever restrains him thereafter from wilfully committing any known sin,—and so deeply imbues him with a love to all who in like manner have found God, as to subdue his selfishness, pride, and lust, and induce him to become one with them, in heart and feeling—one in all things pertaining to *earth and heaven*. This is a perfect Community— GOD, the *primal cause ;* the *Spirits* whom he has sent, the *media ;* LOVE, the *agent ;* and " ALL THINGS COMMON," the *consummation.*

These are not idle words, or unproved fancies and theories. If so, I had even now held my peace. For full well do I know that facts—stubborn, actual facts—are what earnest men and women in this day are loudly calling for. They are heart-sick of words, *words*, WORDS ? " Give us now," they say, " something tangible, that our eyes can see, our ears hear, and that our hands can handle, of the *word of Life;* which for ages our so-called *Christian* priests have vainly preached to us about."

So strong and deep is this cry from the heart of hearts of the human race, that God himself has heard and answered it ; and He will continue to answer it, as fast as it arises from individuals, classes, or nations, until every man and woman upon the earth shall be as fully convinced of the following propositions as they now are of the existence of the sun :

That there is a God ;—an immortality ;—a spiritual no less than a natural world ;—and the possibility of a social, intelligent communication between their inhabitants respectively ;—a time and work of judgment, to which all will progress, in either this or the Spirit-world, and in which each individual will read, from the book of his own immortal memory, " an account of all the deeds done in the body," so that he may, *if he will*, put off the unfruitful works of darkness, and lay hold of eternal *truth*, and thus find an endless progression in faith, virtue, knowledge, brotherly kindness, and love to God and man ; or an equally endless progression into the bottomless pit of " the lusts of the flesh and of the mind," that will not only " war against the soul," but will continually separate it further and further from the fountain of all goodness.

(Frequent instances have been recorded in the public prints of the latent unlimited powers of the human memory, as exhibited in individuals who, *while falling* from a building or scaffold, or during the process of DROWNING, have had every transaction of their lives, to the minutest particular, pass in review before them.)

Friend Robert, it is a fact, which cannot be called in question, that *Eighteen Communities of Shakers* are now in existence in the United States, all of which have been founded upon the principles and in the manner above briefly set forth. It is also a fact that some of them are more than fifty years old. These all claim to be of *spiritual* origin ; to have spiritual direction ; to have received, and to receive, *spiritual* protection ; that in them is brought forth an entirely " *new code of morals, laws, and religion ;"* forming a system distinct from every other on the face of the earth ; being separate from all other governments, civil or religious ; and looking to God only as their great and good Father and Mother, who, by their ministering *Spirits*, ever have watched, and ever will continue to watch over them for good, so long as they continue to be their simple and obedient children in *millennial truths*.

Here, then, is a *new system, spiritually* originated in Old England herself, owing its existence to the agency of a *woman* or female Messiah, as the *first* Christian Church was founded by a man, or the Messiah in the *male* order; comprising a " new code of laws, of classification, of government, of social arrangements, of training, of education ;" the life of which is *love ;* and its fruits a social unity of all interests,—civil, religious, political, external and internal ; a *millennium*, and, for more than half a century, calling itself " *The Millennial Church !*"

What mark does this Church lack that should be upon the true second Christian Church of the millennial age ? Is this not the " kingdom" which " the God of heaven" was to " set up ;"? (See Daniel, seventh chapter.)

It appears that you, my friend, are now a Spiritualist. *Spiritualism* originated among the *Shakers* of America, after spiritual " darkness had covered the earth, and gross darkness the people " thereof, for more than twelve hundred years. And it was also to and among them, a few years ago, that the *avenues* to the spirit world were first opened, when for seven years in succession a revival continued in operation among that people, during which period hundreds of *spiritual mediums* were developed throughout the eighteen societies. In truth, all the members, in a greater or less degree, were mediums. So that physical manifestations, visions, revelations, prophecies, and gifts of various kinds, (of which voluminous records are kept,) and, indeed, " divers operations, but all by the same spirit," were as common as is gold in California.

These *spiritual* manifestations were constituted of *three* distinct degrees. The *first* had for its object, and was judiciously adapted to that end, the complete convincement of the junior portions of the associations—junior either in years or in privilege. The *second* had for its object a deep work of judgment—a purification of the whole people by Spirit agency. Every thought, word, and deed, was open to the inspection of the atttending Spirits ; even the motives, feelings, and desires, were all manifest to their inspection. " *Judgment began at the house of God.*"

The *third* had for its object a ministration of *truth—millennial* truths—to various nations, kindreds, tribes, and people in the *spirit world*, who were hungering and thirsting after righteousness. " These all died in faith, not having received the promises; God having provided some better thing for *us*, that *they* WITHOUT US should not be made *perfect ;*"—" which things the angels desire to look into."

Spiritualism, in its onward progress, will go through the same *three* degrees in the world at large. As yet it is only in the *beginning* of the *first* degree, even in the United States. By inquiry I presume you can put yourself *en rapport* with some of the spirits who have visited our people, and perhaps procure some further information upon this subject, which might be of interest and profit to you.

The *Shakers* are the only people on the earth who will not, in their turn, become the subjects of *Spiritualism* in its present and two succeeding degrees. Spiritualism is the angel that John saw " come down from heaven, having great power, and the *earth* was *lightened* with his glory." After the *earthly man* is lightened and enlightened by it, he will then need *salvation from sin*, and will *feel that need*.

If the *advocate of women's rights* wishes an exemplification of his views, he will find it in a *Shaker village*. Nor can the *tee-totaller* go to a better locality for *sobriety* and *comfort*. The *slave* and his *tyrant master* can here learn to call each other *brother*. The *peace man*, or *non-resistant*, may here lay down his weapons, and learn to *practice* what he finds much easier to preach—*his own precepts*.

On the 14th of May, 1855, you claim to have inaugurated the *Millennium* upon earth. If so, it must have been upon *Christian* principles. For " other foundation can no man lay than that which *is* laid, which is Jesus Christ."

You say, in Part VII. of the " *New Existence of Man upon the Earth*," that the " true Christian life was opened in part to the then Pagan world, which was the first coming of *Divine truth*—he (Jesus Christ) also promising that there should be a *second* coming of the same divine truth, in after ages, when men's minds would be able to bear it." This is *true; as it is* also when you say, " all the *governments* of Europe and America are mere Pagan governments, assuming the *name* of *Christian*, without a particle of Christianity. except in words, in their religion, laws, classifications, social arrangements, education, or language. All are opposed to Nature and to God."

Again, you ask " Where shall I go to find a religion, code of laws, government, etc., etc., where individuals love one another? Where is this love now seen? In the contending armies of Europe and Asia? In the diplomacy of modern nations? In the party spirit, so keen and violent among the advanced or said-to-be progressed Americans? In the keen competing spirit of trade and commerce? In the conspiring ambition of statesmen and politicians? Or in the hatred of the contending religious sectarianisms over the world?"

I answer: The love you seek is not in any of these; nor is it in any part of the wide world with which you are acquainted. In all this you and I agree; and I now respectfully invite such an investigation into the system of Shakerism, or the Second Christian Church, as will make you and other candid inquirers as perfectly acquainted with its principles, doctrines, precepts, and practices, as you now unquestionably are with all other systems and organizations in Christendom.

The pleasure derived from your visit to New Lebanon is still green in our memory, and I trust that nothing in this letter will be understood as in the least designed to underrate your past labours, or to discourage your future efforts to give a new construction to the social organizations of the world—those of England in particular. Nor have I intended to convey an impression that such a construction is *not necessary* or *practicable*, although such new organizations may probably not take the precise form now existing in the minds of yourself and coadjutors.

The alchymists did not find the philosopher's stone that should turn everything to gold ; but nevertheless we, through their labours, have found the science of chemistry, without which we should but very imperfectly understand how to produce or prepare the elements of our subsistence.

We regard you as one of the instruments in the hands of God to forward His divine purposes respecting the human race in the *natural* or earthly *order* of *generation*, etc.

In the mind of Deity the whole world is as a vast machine composed of multifarious wheels fitting into and moving each other ; all of which, as the prophet Ezekiel saw in vision, move straight forward to accomplish the unseen purposes of the great all-controlling *Builder*. And should you, as one of His *employées*, be honoured so much as to only be the means of *pulling down* the old "*worn-out*" and corrupted religious and political institutions of the present age, you will have performed a work which, while it will *immortalize your name*, will be of the utmost *advantage*, as preparing the way for that higher, or *Gospel*, order, which God has from the beginning purposed shall be established in every nation under heaven. And we, as a people, shall ever feel thankful at the recollection that you were engaged by, and have so far carried out the intentions of, Divine Providence, in so praiseworthy and beneficent a work.

And now, with sincerest respect, believe me to remain, as ever,

Yours, in the cause of truth,

F. W. EVANS.

Shaker Village, New Lebanon, N. Y.

[Robert Owen's reply to this letter,—for which there is not room in this number,—will be given in No. 3.]

INSANITY OF THE POPULATION OF THE WORLD ; ITS CAUSE AND REMEDY.

THAT the population of the world ever has been and now is insane, its past history of contests and fightings, and its present opposition to progress in knowledge and to attain and enjoy rational and superior happiness, are undeniable demonstrative proofs.

It will be found to be true wisdom to train the human race in a correct knowledge of its own nature and qualities, on the principle of attraction, in the language of truth only, in a knowledge through the senses of things and their qualities as they actually exist around us, and to be so educated from birth as to understand the all-importance of the material and mental surroundings in which the human race should be placed, and how to create those surroundings which shall make man a rational being,—consistent in mind and practice,—filled with the spirit of love and charity for his race,—devoid of all injurious passions,—and continually stimulated to endeavour to increase the permanent and substantial happiness of all around him. Such will be man, and such the state of society, as soon as the principle which has hitherto made the human race of necessity the opposite of all that has been stated can be withdrawn, and the only principle which can make it sane and rational can be introduced and made to become universal.

Will it be possible in distant future ages to make our descendants to comprehend how, for unknown centuries, their ancestors had been trained to believe the contradictory absurdities which are now from earliest life forced into the mind of all, and to pursue the insane practices thence necessarily ensuing ?

All are now taught that God, the Great Creating Power of the Universe, creates all things ;—and that without him nothing was made ;—that in him we live, move, and have our being ;—that man of himself can do no one good thing ;—but that for all his qualities and powers of body and mind he is altogether dependent upon his Creator. All this is consistent with facts, consistent with itself, and eternally true. It is rational, and in accordance with the highest human reason and wisdom. But, in opposition to these facts and eternal unchanging truths, the teaching of the world has been, and to a great extent now is, that man is bad by nature, that he made himself at some former time bad, and that in consequence his offspring without exception is born bad, and that therefore all are prone to evil as the sparks fly upwards ;—that man thus making his physical, intellectual, moral, spiritual, and practical qualities bad and inferior, he must be responsible, first to society, and then to his Creator, for those physical, intellectual, moral, spiritual, and practical qualities, which the Creator without man's knowledge forced him to possess at birth, and which society trained and educated and directed from birth.

Now with such human teaching, opposed to all facts and to common sense in its first degree, how could man ever become rational in mind or conduct ?

Such contradictory teaching must of necessity make man perfectly irrational in his thoughts, feelings, and language, a perpetual imbecile or hypocrite.

Unpleasant as this statement must be at first to the feelings of those thus made from their birth to become insane, it is nevertheless a truth necessary now to be told to the world, as the first step to prepare its population to become rational in mind and practice, to acquire wisdom, and attain and enjoy happiness. It is indeed truth alone which can set the nations free.

Who, now, mis-instruct and mis-lead the human mind in the more civilised parts of the world?

Religions and governments have hitherto, and do yet to a considerable extent. But who that has eyes to see, ears to hear, and a mind to comprehend, cannot perceive that these old powers are rapidly becoming less influential day by day, and that soon their reign of power over the human mind must give place to the teachings of the press. The teaching is by the daily and weekly journals of Europe and America and the European and American Colonies; but at present especially by the London *Times*, the *Illustrated London News*, and the *New York Daily and Weekly Tribune*. Others are endeavouring to follow in their wake and come in for their share of influence, and especially the *Daily Telegraph* in London, and *Chambers' Journal* in Edinburgh.

But those named dare not yet teach truth,— teach that which is by far the most important for man to know. Were they at once to speak the language of simple truth, so insane have the populations of all nations been made by the contradictory and absurd dogmas of all religions and the irrational laws of all governments, that if simple truths of the highest importance to the well-being, well-doing, and happiness of the human race were taught by these now leading journals, such teaching would for a time deprive them of a large majority of their present mistaught readers.

It cannot therefore be expected that the proprietors of these journals should so act as to drive away their readers. But when they become rational, they will desire to instruct their readers in real knowledge and true wisdom. The proprietors of these journals have however now made so much independent capital by the public, that they can afford to become gradual true teachers, and the greatest benefactors to their fellow men. They might gradually prepare the minds of their present readers to study facts, to reason consistently from those facts, and by degrees convince them that that only can be true which is always consistent with itself and in accordance with all facts known or that can be known by the latest discoveries. It would be an easy matter for these journalists, now that they possess the ear and to a certain extent the confidence of the wealthy and most influential members of society in the civilised districts of the world, to gradually convince them that they have hitherto most lamentably mistaken their own interests. That they have preferred the *cause* which *must* produce *repulsion*, to the *cause* which *must* produce *attraction,*—the *cause* which *must* produce *ignorance,* to the *cause* which *must* produce *knowledge,*—the *cause* which *must* produce *poverty,* to the *cause* which *must* produce *wealth* beyond the *wants* or *desires* of humanity,—the *cause* which *must* produce *folly* and *gross absurdities,* to the *cause* which *must* produce *wisdom* and *rational conduct,*—the cause which must produce falsehood, to the cause which must produce truth only in look, word, and action, or perfect sincerity,—and the *cause* which *continually creates evil,* to the *cause* that would *create unceasing good.*

This is the insanity which the proprietors and editors of these leading journals should apply their whole mind, power, and influence to overcome. They are called upon by their position in society, and by the wealth which they have gained from the public, to take the place now held by the best and most successful physicians or [other superintendents of the best conducted lunatic asylums. They should treat their reading patients who are out of asylums, with similar foresight, kindness, and consideration for their educated maladies, as these humane and talented persons daily and hourly exhibit towards *their* patients *within* asylums. The cases are the same, only varied in the kind and degree of the symptoms of lunacy ;—with this difference, that the patients *out* of the lunatic asylum, do infinitely more harm to their fellow lunatics than those confined *within* them.

But this universal lunacy can be cured only by a universal remedy. These *out patients* require to have entirely new surroundings made, in which to place them, and in which they would by degrees, in peace and quietness, lose their lunatic propensities one after another.

These surroundings, properly devised, arranged, and executed, would more effectually cure the patients now out of the asylums, than those well constructed buildings with their arrangements cure those within them. The arrangements for the former might be made much more complete than those that are now made for the latter. It is well said that the first step towards the cure of an evil is to discover its cause. The cause of all human evil has been discovered to be the insane notion forced into the minds of all from their birth, " that they make and direct their own " physical, intellectual, moral, and spiritual qualities, and are responsible for them." While it is evident from attention to universal facts, that the individual does not and could not make one of these divine qualities. The cure, then, of the present insanity of the human race, is to be effected by directing the natural faculties of all from birth to those unchanging facts and laws of human nature which will enable them to acquire a knowledge of themselves, the most important of all knowledge ;—to know that their creator gave them every one of their natural qualities, propensitics, and powers ;—that these are all good and absolutely necessary to the progress in knowledge and the happiness of the individual and of society,—and that the power has been given to society to make these natural qualities, propensities, and powers, the cause of good or evil to the human race ;—of good when directed to act in accordance with God's laws,—of evil when directed to oppose them.

It is now evident from the infant and undeveloped state of humanity, that until this period man has been so ignorant of his own nature, that, in direct oposition to all facts and to his own progress in knowledge, love, and wisdom, he has had the divine qualities of his nature so directed by public opinion, created by society, that they are made continually to produce evil instead of good. The *Great Change*—the *Revolution* of *Revolutions*, is now at hand, when the natural qualities, propensities, and powers of the human race shall be so directed, that progress and happiness to all must be the gradual result, and that, in peace and without competition, all of humankind shall become lords of the earth, freely roam over it, and enjoy its fertility and paradisaical beauties.

The means now abundantly exist to attain these results. Who shall—who can, prevent the attainment of this happiness for all ? None.—For the prospect of its certain practical attainment will prepare the world for this Millennium,—will destroy the present individual ignorant selfishness which is the only obstacle now to be overcome.

You leading and independent journalists of the civilised world should immediately begin to prepare the public for this change. But if you have not moral courage or knowledge for this glorious task, others will rise up to perform it ; for this *Great Work* is now to be done, and will be done.

QUESTIONS TO BE CALMLY CONSIDERED AND TRULY ANSWERED BY THE HEADS OF RELIGIONS AND THE RULERS OF NATIONS, IN ORDER TO SECURE THE PERMANENT PROGRESS IN WISDOM, PROSPERITY, AND HAPPINESS OF THE HMUAN RACE.

1st Question.—Are the natural faculties, propensities, and powers—physical and mental—of man, formed by himself at birth, or by the Great Creating Power of the Universe ?

2nd Question.—Are the country, climate, language, religion, government, laws, class, sect, party, habits, manners, ideas, associations of ideas, and conduct of each one of human-kind, produced by the will and decision of the individual,—or are they produced, from his birth through life, by the influences impressed on his natural physical and mental powers by the surroundings in which he is placed by nature and society ?

3rd Question.—Which is the most rational, just, and beneficial to the human race,—To make the individual responsible to God for the divine powers of humanity which God alone could give him ? Or that the Creator of these qualites should be responsible for them to the individual ?

4th Question.—Which is the most rational, just, and beneficial to the human race,—To make society responsible to the individual, for his language, religion, instruction, habits, manners, ideas, association of ideas, and conduct, (all given to him by the surroundings formed for him by society, assisted by the surroundings of nature,)—Or to make the individual responsible, for these and the qualities and powers given to him by the Power which created them, to the society which trained and taught him all the acquired knowledge, beyond his instincts which he possesses ?

5th Question.—Are the characters of men formed by the union of the divine qualities of nature, given to them at birth, and the surroundings—good, bad, or indifferent, inferior or superior—which society places around them through life ? Or do they decide upon their own natural qualities, and upon the good or bad, inferior or superior conditions in which they are placed from birth through life ?

6th Question.—Would a rational being, if he had the will, power, and choice, ever make himself inferior,—physically, mentally, morally, spiritually, or practically,—when he could make himself perfect in all these respects ?

7th Question.—When adult society possesses the means and ample power to make the surroundings in which to place all the infants of the human race, and to make them such as to compel all of them to grow up to maturity good, intelligent united in feeling and interest, wise, prosperous, and happy,—while society creates such surroundings as to force the great majority of mankind to be inferior, poor, ignorant, disunited in feeling and interest, irrational, anxious about wealth, and miserable ; and to force the remainder unjustly to oppress and degrade the many, and also to be irrational in their spirit, mind, and conduct, —Can society, while so acting, be considered otherwise than insane, and deserving the deepest sympathy for their mental malady ?

8th Question.—Are the unchanging, good, merciful, and wise laws of God and nature respecting humanity,—or the ever-changing, ignorant, unjust, and cruel laws of man, the best by which to form the character and govern the human race ?

9th Question.—Will the language of truth or of falsehood produce the best character and the most happiness to the human race ?

10th Question.—Will the conduct of undeviating open honesty, in look, word, and action,—or the conduct of deception, produce most happiness to the population of the world ?

11th Question.—Will the spirit of repulsion, disunion, quarreling, fighting, and national wars,—or the spirit of attraction, union, peace, progress, charity, and love, be the best to instil into the minds of all from birth to death ?

12th Question.—Do not the laws and teaching of men create the spirit of repulsion, disunion, quarrelling, fighting, and national wars, with the language of falsehood and conduct of deception?

13th Question.—Will not the laws of God and nature respecting humanity create in all the spirit of attraction, union, peace, progress, charity, and love for our race ?

14th Question.—Can the language of truth be universal with the laws of men ? Or the language of falsehood be admitted with the laws of God and nature ?

15th Question.—Can undeviating open honesty exist with the laws of men ? Or deception of any kind with the laws of God and nature ?

16th Question.—Should wealth create its own circulating medium, and be unlimited in its production, when there is power and material to produce it ? Or should the production of real wealth, while greatly wanted, be limited in its amount by a metal circulation ?

17th Question.—While society is in the transition state from irrationality to rationality, and before wealth shall be made superabundant for all,—Will not National Bank Notes, guaranteed by the entire wealth and power of the nation, be the best temporary circulating medium ?

18th Question.—Cannot the population of the world, when trained, educated, employed, and placed rationally from birth, easily and pleasantly, with the aid of the sciences of chemistry and mechanism, create more wealth than it will desire to consume ?

19th Question.—Will it not be for the interest and happiness of the human race to have such surroundings made as will destroy all motive to contest and competition about wealth, by making it perpetually superabundant beyond the wants of the human race ?

20th Question.—Is not the greatest mine of wealth over the earth to be obtained by rationally training and educating all the physical, mental, moral, spiritual, and practical qualities of the human race, and by rationally employing and placing all through life?

21st Question.—Is it not just, and will it not be permanently beneficial, that arrangements should be formed, if practicable, to place all of the human race under such surroundings as will give every one within them an equality of education, wealth, and condition, preserving in full purity the advantages to be derived from the beautiful and most beneficial varieties, arising from the endless combinations of the divine human faculties,—varieties so essential to the progress and highest happiness of our race ?

22nd Question.—Will it be for the permanent happiness of the population of the world that all the varied natural qualities of every one should be cultivated from birth, and be brought out into beneficial action? Or that the present most insane neglect or misdirection of these faculties should be continued?

23rd Question.—Is it a mark of wisdom, or of insanity, to create and maintain institutions which place the individuals belonging to them under such conditions that their interest and duty are always opposed to each other?

24th Question.—Is it not the duty of the priesthood of the world to endeavour to make all of the human race good, intelligent, united, wise, and happy? And is it not their apparent interest to keep them ignorant, divided, and subservient to the will of the priesthood?

25th Question.—Have not the priesthood kept the mass of the people of the world in ignorance, disunited, and subservient to their will?

26th Question.—Could not general arrangements be now made to give in one year more knowledge, goodness, unity, and happiness, to the human race, than the priesthoods of the world have given them through the past period of human existence?

27th Question.—Are not the members of the profession of the law over the world so trained, educated, and placed, as to have an apparent interest in keeping men disunited? And is it not the highest duty of all to endeavour to unite the human race as one family?

28th Question.—Cannot the laws of God and nature be now made most beneficially to entirely supersede the irrational laws of man, as they now exist in opposition to God's all-wise laws?

29th Question.—Are not the members of the medical profession so placed by society that their duty and interest are in opposite directions—it being their apparent interest that their patients should be afflicted with disease, while it is their duty to keep them in health?

30th Question.—Could not the population of the world be trained in one generation to understand and practice the laws of health better than they have been instructed on this subject through all past time?

31st Question.—Are not the members of the military profession trained and placed in a position in which their apparent interest and their duty are opposed? For are not their rank and pay more rapidly increased in a period of war than in peace,—and is it not the duty of all to create and preserve peace, so as to render all warlike proceedings as unnecessary as they are injurious?

32nd Question.—When society shall be based on its true principle, and the character of all formed from birth to be rational,—Will there be the slightest necessity for any one of these professions?

33rd Question.—Will not, under the circumstances just mentioned, the continuance of these professions be highly injurious to the members of each profession, and to the public?

34th Question.—Are not these professions now the sole means by which the ignorant but assuming hereditary few have so long kept the many in ignorance and poverty, and have so sorely afflicted and mis-governed the human race?

35th Question.—Are not these professions based and supported on the grossly absurd notions that man by his will can determine his belief and his feelings of love and hatred? And do not the all-wise laws of God eternally declare that man *shall* believe according to the strongest conviction made upon his mind, whether he desires it or not,—and that he *shall* love that which is made most agreeable and lovely to his individual constitution or organisation, and dislike and hate that which is made to be the most disagreeable and hateful to his organisation or natural feelings?

36th Question.—Are not these professions mainly instrumental in enforcing upon all these irrational notions respecting human belief and feelings?

37th Question.—Can society ever become rational while any one of these professions are maintained to coerce and corrupt society?

38th Question.—Have not all the varied artificial arrangements for the marriage of the sexes been based on the insane notion that both could love and hate according to their own will and pleasure? And does not the experience of every one prove the absurdity of these notions, and the endless demoralisation and consequent miseries which they inflict upon the human race?

39th Question.—Do the artificial arrangements for the union of the sexes in the eastern, or those in the western divisions of the world produce the most demoralisation, evil and misery?

40th Question.—Would not all these sins and sufferings be prevented by society in all its arrangements being based and consistently constructed on the good, wise, just, and merciful laws of God and nature—laws which, but for the four professions previously named, would become obvious to every one, as soon as they shall be rationally placed, trained, educated, employed, and governed?

41st Question.—Is it sane to attempt longer to continue a system which places, trains, educates, employs, and governs all, in such manner as of necessity to force all to think and act continually in opposition to their own interest and happiness, and that of all their fellows,—while it will be now so easy and pleasant, peacefully and gradually to supersede it over the world, by a system based on truth, derived from all known facts, and which will make it impossible that any one could be placed, trained, educated, employed, and governed otherwise than to become through life good, enlightened, wise, united cordially to his fellows, happy in this life, and well prepared for a future immortal existence?

These questions will be reasoned upon and answered in the next number, to be published on the 1st of May next, that it may be in possession of the public a sufficient time previous to the Congress of the reformers of the world, to be held on the 14th of May, to consider how best, in peace and beneficially for all, to change an insane for a sane system of society, and thus to secure through futurity, as soon as the change shall be made, the happiness of every child of man through his life. These questions, or as many of them as time will permit, shall be attempted to be truly answered, without mystery, mixture of error, or fear of man, in this 3rd number.

EQUALITY AND INEQUALITY OF THE HUMAN RACE.

I have received from a superior medium living at some distance from me, a letter of which the following is an extract :—

" I told the spirits I was writing to you, and they have sent a short message upon an old subject."

I may inform the reader that this medium has long been enabled to see and speak with superior spirits, in the most easy and natural manner, while she is in her normal state. The following is the message sent to me by the spirits.

" Private property is an accursed thing. It is the cause of " evils and miseries innumerable. It causes hatred and all man- " ner of sin. The love of it is selfishness,—and selfishness is " the evil power.

" Yet equality is for ever an impossible thing. Men are not " equal in any of the gifts of nature, and God himself makes " distinctions."

" Nobility of soul is the only true nobility,—and this may as " often be found in men of low origin as in men of birth and " education."

That which the spirits have so well expressed is the substance of all that can be said upon this important subject.

It is true that without a certain equality among the human race there can be no real goodness, justice, unity, peace, nor happiness. This is the practicable equality of education and condition. Without this there can be no cordial and permanent unity among the human race,—no chance of creating a brotherhood of the family of man, or of destroying the selfishness created by individuality of property and interests.

But this equality of education and condition can be attained only when the parties to be thus put upon an equality shall be trained in the spirit, principle, and practice of attraction, to fit them for such superior state of human life, and when their surroundings shall be all made in unison with this new life of attraction.

When the character shall be formed from birth on the principle of attraction, and all the surroundings of man's devising and construction shall be in perfect accordance with that principle, then will it be easy of practice to have for the human race an equality in training and educating, employing, and placing all, so that *all* shall become superior men and women, to any of the past or present generations of our race.

Yet will it be eternally true, that no two of human kind can ever be made to become the same.

Among our race there will ever be the same distinctive varieties, as is so perceptible in all the creations of the Great Creating Power of the Universe.

And this variety is that ingredient in our natural formation which can alone give zest to human existence, and which everlasting varieties, under the spirit of attraction, will bring out of the great storehouse of humanity a host of good and lovely qualities, such as have hitherto lain dormant under the principle of repulsion, and which in the aggregate in each generation will constitute humanity, or the full formed man and woman.

It is the combination only of these good and lovely qualities, that will constitute the real wealth of the world,—and this wealth should be at all times free for the use, improvement, and happiness of all under the action of the divine power of the electric telegraph, by which, under the new surroundings about to arise over the world, a daily communication may be made to and from the most divided distances upon the earth.

These arrangements will constitute that beautiful harmony throughout the population of the world, of universal unity with universal variety,—a state in which monotony or listlessness will be unknown, and in which a motive will ever exist to excite to the due physical and mental activity to create the best wealth and the highest rational enjoyment of life, day by day, through all the years of earthly existence.

It is now most evident that the Great Creating Power of the Universe has created man to attain, through a process and period for experience, a high state of knowledge, of goodness, of wisdom, and of permanent happiness, while upon earth; and to be thus prepared for a higher and far more beautiful immortal existence, when he shall enter into his second life.

This change from the principle of repulsion and disunion to that of attraction and cordial union will prepare the human race to understand, receive, and adopt in practice, the true religion, as taught by Jesus Christ.

And how simple and beautiful is this divine religion !

" Love to God and love to man ;"—only to be practised under a system of equality, and without private property or individual interest. And herein consists the essence of religion and of happiness,—of all that is necessary to insure the well-being, well-doing, and permanent welfare of every child of man. These principles, with the practices which will necessarily emanate from them, will be, when explained in the spirit of charity and love, readily received and adopted by the human race, and all dissentions henceforward will cease and die their natural death, and the human mind will attain such peace as will prepare it for rapid progress in the right direction,—such peace of mind and such happiness as the population of the world has never yet experienced.

But this practical equality must not be required from those who have been trained, educated, employed, placed, and governed, in surroundings which have emanated from the system based on repulsion, and with the practice of private property. The habits of individuality and selfishness are too deeply rooted in their educated constitution to admit of the enjoyment of happiness under such a revolution in their feelings, language, and conduct.

Yet a new generation, under the new surroundings created on the principle of attraction, will not only have no difficulty in this new action, but will derive the most exquisite pleasure from its adoption, and will never relinquish it.

And during the transition from one system to another—from the false to the true—the present generation will experience much happiness in seeing the progress of the change, and in the consciousness of the future well-being of their children.

PEACE ;—LAW ;—ORDER. THE PRACTICAL MODE OF FORMING CHARACTER.

How enormous are the evils which arise from punishing instead of preventing bad habits, vices, and crimes !

How utter is the blindness of mankind in not patiently and perseveringly tracing each evil to its true origin !

How gross the irreligion and infidelity of not acting in faithful accordance with God's laws, as declared to man by Nature's unchanging operations !

What folly and wickedness is it to apply human legislation and instruction solely to pluck the leaves of error and evil, while the branches, trunk, and root of these evils are not only untouched and uninjured, but the roots of this tree of evils are carefully watered and manured !

How absurd is the farce of religions and governments pretending to teach the people morals and wisdom, while their own practices and the greater part of their instruction teach them to be immoral, and keep them in ignorance !

What insanity is it to preach to tell the people to love their neighbours as themselves, when all their previous instruction and the entire formation of their character have been based on principles tending to create strong repulsive feelings and violent religious and other hatreds !

What greater insanity to give merit and reward, and to attribute and inflict punishment, for any belief whatever, now that it is made glaringly evident that all are compelled to believe as they do believe !

What irrationality is that of telling people to be good, by those who by their false instruction and conduct make them bad, and who could, by, to them, an unseen force, compel every one to be far better than these professed instructors have yet made any one in any country over the world !

What weakness of intellect is it for professed teachers to say that man is bad by nature,—when God has given only divine qualities to each at birth, and now gives to society the knowledge how to divinely cultivate these qualities from birth !

What absurdity to permit poverty to exist, when, by the most simple arrangements, unadulterated wealth of superior quality may be made at all times to superabound beyond the possible wants of the population of the world when they shall be placed within rational and common-sense surroundings !

What an error in governments and people not making proper arrangements to unite federatively with each other over the world, to secure their progress in knowledge, wisdom, wealth, and happiness, and thus to make peace permanent over the earth !

What irrationality, insanity, and madness, in society in all countries, will it be, if man continue longer to attempt to sustain a worn-out system which has fully performed its destined work, and which now can produce only falsehood, disunion, wars, and fightings, and maintain ignorance, superstition, bigotry, and religious hatred, with other endless evils—all of which, by a system of truth without mystery, mixture of error, or fear of man, can be prevented !

How erroneous will it be to endeavour to enforce the present worn-out system of falsehood, leading to all evil, when it will be now so easy for governments and people to introduce the system of truth, leading to all good for the human race !

Will the language of truth and conduct of honesty, or the language of falsehood and conduct of deception, best promote the peace, progress, and happiness of the population of the world ?

Will the scarcity, competition, and conflicts about wealth be the most advantageous for the human race,—or to have it annually produced so abundantly as to admit of its being freely used by all without money and without price?

Will it be true wisdom to continue arrangements which greatly limit the creation of wealth, and which stimulate motives to deteriorate its qualities,—or now to introduce new and superior arrangements to produce easily and pleasantly superior wealth illimitable in amount, sufficient at all times to saturate the population of the world with it, without competition or contest ?

NEW EXISTENCE OF MAN UPON THE EARTH.

IT will now be understood by all who attend to the subject, that I advocate a system in principle, practice, and spirit, the reverse in all respects of the system adopted by men from the beginning, and continued to this day. These two systems are so opposed to each other, that, like fire and water, they cannot exist together, —for the water will quench the fire, or the fire will dry up the water.

It is in vain, therefore, to think of ever uniting the two in principle, practice, or spirit.

The system, therefore, which I advocate, cannot be introduced into any existing Cities, Towns, Villages, or Isolated Residences.

It will not admit of any of the laws of men, opposed to the laws of God and nature,—and all human laws, although ever changing, have been made in opposition to the laws of God and nature.

It will not admit of one of human kind being neglected from birth, or not trained, educated, placed, and employed, in such manner,—physically, mentally, morally, spiritually, and practically,—in accordance with the laws of God and nature, that the character shall be made consistent, rational, and sane, in mind and practice, so as to become, with the certainty of a law of nature, good, wise, united to the race, ever prosperous, and happy.

It will not admit of any distinctions among the human race, except those of age, and of capacity for producing happiness to all.

It will not admit, therefore, of ignorance, poverty, disunion, evil passions, bad habits, inferior manners, vice, or crime, among any portion of the population of the world.

It will not admit of the practice of endeavouring to buy cheap and sell dear.

It will not admit of one individual, or any combination of individuals, to oppress any portion of the human race.

It will not admit of a variety of languages, opposing interests, feelings, or territories.

It will not admit of violence to humanity under any form, or, unnecessarily, to any living creature.

It will not admit of slavery or servitude among the human race.

It will not admit of the creation of wealth being dependant upon a metal circulation.

It will not admit of a language of falsehood, conduct of deception, or secrecy of any kind in the transactions of the human race.

It will not admit of any one being trained and educated in false principles, injurious practices, or to acquire an unkind spirit.

It will not admit of any surroundings in which to place a child of humanity, except those which shall be directly calculated to make it rational and sane, in mind and practice,—that is, to be through life consistent in goodness, wisdom, and happiness, and ever occupied in promoting the happiness of all around it, knowing no limits short of the entire race.

It will not admit of angry words or personal violence.—because human beings, trained, educated, employed, and governed, in accordance with the laws of God and nature, will never have a motive to induce such conduct. And all will know that anger and violence are irrational feelings, and lead to insanity and madness. The system by which men have governed the population of the world from the beginning to this day, is the first phase of humanity;—a phase apparently necessary to develope the rational faculties of our race, and to prepare the way, as it has done, for the second or rational system, in which all the divine qualities of humanity will be advanced to a much higher state of maturity, and, perhaps without a third phase, to their earthly state of perfection.

The reign and existence of the first system, with all its errors and miseries, are evidently coming to their termination over the earth,—all nations are in a commotion of great excitement, without knowing the cause. Their minds are confused;—they know some great change is approaching,—but they know not what this change is to be. The divine faculties of humanity are now too developed in all nations to admit of a change to a worse state in their condition,—but they will admit of one that will permanently produce wisdom, goodness, unity, prosperity, and happiness to all. And such is the change that will be introduced throughout the world by this second or rational system to supersede the first.

The first, although irrational in principle and practice, must be for some time longer retained and supported, to prevent too sudden a change, creating confusion, ill-will, or violence,—and to give the population of the world time to effect the change with order, foresight, and wisdom, in peace, and with the willing consent of all; because each might have his choice to live and die in the first system, or to become a member of the second; or to remain in the first, and place their children within the new surroundings of the second, so as to have them trained and educated to become truthful, rational, prosperous, and happy beings, among their fellows and equals in principles, practices, and spirit.

TWO SYSTEMS FOR THE GOVERNMENT OF THE WORLD.

It is now evident that in the order of terrestrial creation there are two systems, a first and a second, for forming the character and governing the human race.

The first, for man in his ignorant, inexperienced, and undeveloped state, to stimulate him by pain, or evil, so called, to develope all his faculties, and force him to necessary physical and mental exertions, to make discoveries in various arts and sciences, to prepare for the commencement of the second state or phase of progress, in which goodness, wisdom, and happiness will be universally attained. The first, with all its evils and consequent sufferings, being necessary in the order of nature, to force humanity onward to produce the second.

The first is based, in opposition to facts and God's laws of nature, on imaginary notions respecting humanity. The second is based on God's immutable laws of nature.

The first is the immediate origin of evil. The second will be the immediate origin of good to the human race.

The first, although necessary to develope human faculties, is false, and requires a language of falsehood and a conduct of deception for its continued support. The second will require a language of truth and a conduct of honesty over the world, without deviation in look, word, or action.

The first, of necessity, trains the human race to be repulsive in their general character. The second, from like necessity, will train and educate all to become attractive, and to acquire lovely qualities only.

The first tends to perpetual ignorance, poverty, disunion, disease, and crime. The second will dispel these evils, and will produce over the earth knowledge, wealth, union, health of body and mind, and goodness.

The first creates physical and mental weakness, disease of body and mind, confusion of intellect, inconsistencies, irrationalities, and folly. The second will create physical and mental strength, order, consistency, rationality, and wisdom.

The first encourages and enables the few to oppress and degrade the many, physically and mentally, by keeping them in ignorance and poverty. The second will equally elevate and physically and mentally strengthen all, by training, educating, employing, and placing all within such surroundings as will make them to become *wise* and *wealthy*.

The first creates superstition, bigotry, and ignorant religious hatred—the most injurious of all hatred. The second will create a spirit of universal never-ceasing charity, kindness, and love for the human race, irrespective of colour, country, creed, or class.

The first creates all manner of artificial distinctions between

man and man, and trained inequalities throughout society over
the world. The second will know no distinction but that of age,
and will give to each of the same age a similar education and
position in society, or, as near as practicable, an equal condition
through life.

The first, of necessity, disunites the human race in interest and
feeling. The second will unite them in both.

The first giving great merit and high reward for some particular belief or profession of belief, whether real or assumed, and
punishes and degrades for an opposition to that particular belief.
The second neither gives merit nor demerit, rewards nor punishes,
for any belief whatever,—knowing that belief is not an act of
the will of man, but the result of the strongest conviction, true
or false, which is made on the mind of the individual, and that
all are compelled to believe or disbelieve in accordance with this
strongest conviction.

The first gives and promises great merit and reward, present
and future, for loving and hating according to its artificial notions
and dictates. The second will give no merit or reward for loving
or hating anything or person,—knowing that humanity is so
created that it must like and love that which is agreeable to its
organisation, and dislike and hate that which is disagreeable to
its organisation;—and that loving and hating are not acts of the
will, but of the instinct of feeling, and therefore are natural and
necessary to happiness. Also, that the only practicable mode by
which man can be made to love his neighbour as himself, is by
training, educating, and placing all from birth in such surroundings as will form them to grow up with lovely qualities only, and
then all will be compelled by the laws of their nature to love all.

The first makes religion to consist in words, forms, and ceremonies,—the words and the actions being generally in direct
opposition to each other. The second makes religion to consist,
not in words, forms, or useless ceremonies, but in the heartfelt
constant desire and practice to make all around them happy,
making no distinction of colour, country, sect, sex, or class.

The first trains, educates, employs, places, and governs man,
in such manner as to compel him to become most ignorantly selfish. The second will train, educate, employ, place, and govern
all in such manner as will utterly root out and destroy in all this
individual selfish feeling, and instead thereof will create a new
spirit of universal charity and love, which, through life, will pervade the feelings, and will direct every action to be consistent
with that divine spirit.

The first is continually occupied in making and repealing
unjust, cruel, irrational, and often most impractical laws, keeping
the human race in a perpetual ferment of insane contests, and
puerile, but often violent conduct,—laws, too, which are always
opposed to Nature's or God's unchanging laws. The second will

study to comprehend and righteously apply God's just, merciful, all-wise, and most beneficent laws,—laws which alone can produce a rational, or sane and happy existence of man upon earth.

The first, owing to the error on which it has been based, creates around all, more or less, the most irrational, absurd, and injurious surroundings,—all said to be intended to promote goodness, prosperity, and happiness of the race, while they are, in reality, directly calculated to create wickedness, prevent prosperity, and destroy happiness. The second will create such a new combination of rational superior surroundings, as will compel all who shall be born, trained, and live within them, to become wise, good, prosperous, and happy.

The change from the first to the second system for forming the character and governing the human race, is the natural progress of God's creation of humanity, towards a more rational and perfect state of man's existence upon the earth, and to better prepare him while in the earthly form for a more pure and a higher state of existence in the life to come, when the terrestrial has performed its duties, and dies its natural death, or effects its destined change for immortality.

MEANS OF HAPPINESS.

With the means now placed at the disposal of the human race it will be easy to make all of the family of man, united, good, intelligent, wealthy, ever prosperous, wise, healthy, and happy. Shall these means be now so applied as to accomplish this great and good work ?

Why, in the name of common sense, should the population of the world longer remain in its present divided, opposing, degraded, and miserable condition ?

It is already in possession of the most ample means to insure perpetual goodness, prosperity, and happiness, to every one who shall be born through all future ages. And the means now possessed, although ample to effect the results stated, are capable of rapid illimitable increase, so that the progress of the human race may proceed from year to year, from age to age, and from century to century, without stay or retrogression, to an illimitable extent of excellence in all things, and in the enjoyment of a rational terrestrial existence.

Why, then, should any portion of the human race be allowed longer to remain ignorant poor, disunited, opposed to one another, oppressed, degraded, or miserable ?

The heads of existing religions and governments are the unconscious obstacles now in the way of this ever-to-be-desired progress.

They have been trained, educated, occupied, and placed from their birth under such degrading surroundings as have kept them ignorant of themselves, of human nature, and of the means of giving happiness to themselves or to others. They require as much sympathy for their educated errors as those whom they mis-instruct and mis-govern. The pure and genuine spirit of charity and love is now required to pervade the mind of all, to calm reproach, overcome anger, destroy the desire for vengeance or revenge, and to create the divine spirit of forgiveness—not for one or a few, but from all for all,—because " they know not what they do" against themselves and all others.

Happiness for all has now become a broad plain open path, in which all may proceed with ease, comfort, and high satisfaction, not only without interruption from others, but with the assistance and aid of all their travelling companions. Why, then, should the means which the Great Creating Power of the Universe has placed at the disposal of man for the happiness of his race remain unused or mis-applied ?

CREATION.

WHAT is Creation ? Whence its origin ? It must have a cause ; and that cause must itself be eternal and uncreated ; because from nothing something could never arise, or become an existence.

This Eternal Uncaused Existence is unknown to man, except as far as the faculties which have been given to him enable him to perceive and comprehend so much of the creation as is within the reach of the mental and spiritual power which he possesses.

The mental and spiritual faculties given to man enable him to perceive self-evident truths, or truths which demonstrate themselves. Such are those truths which have been now stated.

There are also self-evident deductions from self-evident truths, as demonstrable as the truths which are self-evident.

Therefore, although this Uncaused Eternal Existence is in its essence yet unknown to man, it is a self-evident deduction from the Facts of the Creation, that that Uncaused Cause possesses the wisdom and power existing throughout Creation.

The operations of Creation proceed by a regular process, which, to the extent of man's present experience, is uniform and unchangeable.

This process is called a law of nature, in all its variety of action.

This process of Creation appears to human capacity and experience to be an unceasing operation of composing, decomposing, and recomposing certain elements, which men suppose to be eternal self-existing elements, or emanations from the Unknown

Uncaused Cause, eternally existing in a manner and with attributes beyond the present capacity of humanity to comprehend. And no man has yet by searching found out God—the name given to the Unknown Uncaused Cause, whence all things proceed, with whatever qualities and powers they possess.

Man is an emanation from this Unknown Uncaused Cause, or God.

And when this power shall make known its mode of existence and of action to man, then will men know God, and not before.

The universal desire in man to know God is a strong presumptive proof that in the due order of time, in the continued process of Creation, man shall be enabled to know, and perhaps to see and comprehend this, at present, incomprehensible Eternal Power.

From the self-evident truths which have been herein stated, it is a self-evident deduction that man can do no good to God, nor be responsible to the power whence he derives all his powers, physical, mental, and spiritual ;—and therefore that it is vain and useless longer for men to differ in anger about what God is, or is not,—or about any worship of the Creating Power of the Universe.

Whatever may be the form, or ceremony, or phrase of words, intended for worship, it must be senseless, and, if possible, degrading to a Power which creates, directs, and governs the Universe.

It will then be true wisdom in man to cease all his differences about what God is, or what God desires ;—because no man knows either the one or the other, except as declared in the unchanging laws of nature, as these are continually developed in the never ceasing process of Creation ;—and Creation is the only true book of God,—a book which is ever open to all men, in all ages, over the world,—and from which alone all knowledge or certain truth can be discovered and attained.

From this book all wisdom that man has been created to know must be acquired ; and this is the only book in which truth without mystery, mixture of error, or fear of man, can be found,— and wherein truth is always consistent with itself, and in perfect accordance with all facts, known, or that can be known.

The power that creates, having progressed man to this point in his onward course towards higher knowledge and greater perfection, now opens to him another leaf of this divine book, and therein shows him the path which he must pursue to attain goodness, unity, health, wisdom, and happiness.

It shows him that these results can never be attained—

By society making man responsible for what he does not create :—

By society leaving him from birth in ignorance, and surrounded from birth with inferior conditions, when superior may be easily made for all :—

By society making laws directly opposed to the laws of the Creation :—

By the matured in age teaching and training the young in principles and practices of repulsion and opposition of feeling and interest :—

By society making arrangements for individual interests to be opposed to general or united interests :—

By society forming arrangements to artificially divide the population of the world into opposing classes and opposing nations, or into the ignorant and educated, or into poor and rich.

It is now, also, self-evident, from the entire experience of the human race, that a family divided against itself cannot be prosperous and happy. So it is with the family of man. It is trained, educated, employed, placed, and governed, on principles of disunion, calculated to create continual feelings of opposing interests, and to prevent all from perceiving the interminable road to ever increasing goodness and happiness, which will arise to the human family when it shall be trained, educated, employed, placed, and governed, on principles of union, instead of principles of disunion, division, and opposing interests.

The divine book of the Creation has written in every page of its progress the superiority of union for the production of happiness over separation and division. And yet man, disregarding this divine instruction, has made all his arrangements to divide human feelings and interests, — except in forming armies and navies to destroy property and life and to create ruin and misery.

Let there be similar arrangements made to create wealth, form the character, and to govern society,— and the progress and happiness of the human race would know no limitation.

The Creation of the Earth for Man's Existence upon it, it is now evident, has been produced to give him existence, knowledge, goodness, wisdom, and happiness, through the unity of his race.

For union is not only material strength, but it is also wisdom, perpetual prosperity, and happiness, necessarily flowing from the charity, love, and sympathy, which unity will produce.

The Creation of the earth and its heaven has been for the progress and high happiness of man, as soon as he shall be sufficiently developed to know himself and how to unite cordially with his fellows.

" By this,"—said Jesus Christ, the Great Reformer of *his* age of the world, " shall ye know that you are my diciples," (or the genuine followers in practice of the truths which I teach,) " that you love one another."

THE REFORM OF THE WORLD.

Who in this age can imagine anything so impossible?

What does it mean? What is it? How insane to talk of it, when all the powers of the world are opposed to it?

It is premature by some centuries!

These are the nutural sayings and exclamations of the misdirected puny intellects trained and formed under a false, ignorant, and most irrational system—a system opposed to facts, to common sense, and to reason.

These sayings and exclamations proceed from minds just awakened as from a dream, not knowing well whether they are yet awake or still dreaming.

Had they been trained, educated, and placed, under a system in accordance with all facts, consistent with itself, and in harmony with the laws of God and Nature,—a system based on truth, and constructed in accordance with common sense, and right reason,—they would have discovered that, with past experience and the gigantic means which the sciences have developed to aid man, the reform of the world, or the entire change of the principles and practices of society in all nations and among all peoples, is but a plain, simple, and direct process, as soon as the true base, on which society should be founded and constructed, and the characters of all shall be formed, can be made obvious to a generation which from birth have had their minds filled with erroneous and conflicting ideas—a generation wrongfully trained, educated, employed, placed, and governed.

As soon as the rulers of society can be made to discover their own best and highest interests, they will agree to re-base society, re construct it, and to form the character of the human race, on the principle of attraction,—and thus quietly and peaceably, with wise foresight, supersede over the world the old, now thoroughly worn-out system of repulsion, violence, contention, and fighting.

They will then perceive that to establish permanent peace over the world,—to commence progress in knowledge in a right direction,—to create a superfluity of superior wealth for all at all times,—to secure a rapid progressive prosperity for all,—to unite all cordially as one family,—and to gradually make the earth a terrestrial paradise, and men and women good, wise, and happy, would naturally follow, step by step, such change from the fundamental error on which society has been, to the fundamental truth on which it should be based.

And to accomplish this requires only the will of the people, whose well-being, well-doing, unity, and happiness, depend upon this change being now effected in harmony between the people and their present governments.

It is therefore concluded that there is now derived from all past experience in the history of our race, a sufficient development of humanity among the most advanced in all nations, to to create and direct the public will to desire, and unanimously desire, that this change should now commence and be cordially promoted by the people and their governments.

What are the practical steps necessary to prepare all nations for this " good time coming "—to commence the glorious era and new dispensation of humanity to inaugurate the Millennial state of Man upon Earth ?

Let the seven great powers now select each their best man for the purpose, to form a Congress of these seven nations, (a greater number would retard progress,) to consider, first, the best mode of federatively uniting all nations in one commonwealth ; second, for this great commonwealth to guarantee to each nation as now existing, peace and quietness from all foreign attacks, while its internal improvements, from the change of an erroneous for a true system for forming character and constructing society, is in progress ;—third, that a model commonwealth, based and constructed on this true principle, should be made in each nation, for an example, and from which similar commonwealths would be formed, in which gradually, as they were finished, all the population of the nation could be received.

By this simple process, the present population of the world would be prepared for, and gradually introduced into new and superior surroundings, scientifically devised and executed to compel every one born and trained within them to become good, wise, united, and happy,—and to become not merely children of France, of Great Britain, of Germany, of Russia, of Italy, of Hungary, of Poland, of Turkey, of Japan, of China,—but really and truly children of the Great Commonwealth of the world,—knowing in their new brotherhood no distinction of colour, country, creed, or class,—free and independent, yet universally united, citizens of of the world.

Space and time will not now admit of more upon this subject, but let this suffice for some preliminary to the preliminary congress for the reformation of the world, to commence at noon on the 14th of May next, in St. Martin's Hall, Long Acre, London.

ROBERT OWEN.

Sevenoaks Park, Sevenoaks,
   March 31st, 1856.

London :—Published by the Author at 16, Great Windmill Street, Haymarket : and sold by J. Clayton and Son, 223, Piccadilly ; Holyoake, 147, Fleet Street ; Truelove, 240, Strand; Goddard, 14, Great Portland Street, Cavendish Square ; Farrer, 21, John Street, Fitzroy Square ; and all Booksellers.

ROBERT OWEN'S
MILLENNIAL GAZETTE;
EXPLANATORY OF THE PRINCIPLES AND PRACTICES BY WHICH, IN PEACE, WITH TRUTH, HONESTY, AND SIMPLICITY, THE NEW EXISTENCE OF MAN UPON THE EARTH MAY BE EASILY AND SPEEDILY COMMENCED.

" The character of Man is formed *for* him, and *not by* him !"

No. 3.]   MAY 1st, 1856.   [PRICE 6D.

REPLY TO BROTHER EVAN'S LETTER TO ME, ON THE PART OF THE SHAKERS' COMMUNITIES IN THE UNITED STATES, AS PUBLISHED IN THE *NEW YORK TRIBUNE*, AND IN THE *SPIRITUAL TELEGRAPH*.

FRIEND EVANS,—

Your letter is at this moment of deep interest to society.

It is well-timed, and I thank you cordially for your kind words respecting myself, and your communities for their frequent disinterested hospitality when I visited any of them,—which I did as often as an opportunity offered.

I did so, because I was desirous of witnessing the effects on character of public property devoid of any private property, and also the effects from a system of celibacy on both sexes :—the first in accordance with my views of the laws of God and nature, —the second, according to my impressions, in direct opposition to the laws of God and nature.

My visits to your communities confirmed these impressions ;— but, constituted so erroneously and inconsistently as society has been and is, you could not have succeeded without the union of both.

Your communities have been a first preliminary step toward a rational and superior Millennium upon earth. The mission of your communities is to prove to the world that humanity possesses within itself, even when, as your first societies were, under great disadvantages, the inherent power of association to produc a superfluity of wealth for all ; and also to prove that men and women married by any of the artificial modes devised by the priesthoods or legalities of the world, can never unite in communities without soon experiencing the evil passions arising from the sexes being united by the ignorant laws of men, instead of by the all-wise, good, and merciful laws of God.

There never has been, there never will be, a cordially united community composed of the two sexes while artificially united by the ignorant and unjust and most cruel laws of men.

To live in permanent comparative harmony in a community, both sexes must live in celibacy ; but to live permanently in perfect harmony, they must be united by God's laws,—that is, according to their God-made affinities ;—God being a much better judge of these affinities than priests, lawyers, or legislators—all of whom have been trained, educated, employed, and governed, to form, for them, a most absurd, irrational, and incongruous character—a character so erroneous that not one of the members of these divisions of society has any sound knowledge of human nature, or how to unite men and women to constitute a rational state of society—a state in which the good and superior qualities of humanity will be alone and always called into action.

There needs no other demonstration of the past and present insane or undeveloped state of humanity over the world, than to consider the three most popular institutions which have been so sedulously cultivated by the priesthood, and in consequence madly maintained in all ages of the world and in all divisions of our race.

Even at this advanced period of human experience the thoughtless, unreflecting, and mistrained, as well as the educated, deem it impossible that society could be held together without it maintained, by fire and sword if necessary, these three murderers of the reason, common-sense, and happiness of the human race.

The First of these deep-rooted universal evils, is the ever-contending, hate-creating SECTS, all called RELIGION, with their insane CREEDS, which the supporters of each are taught to believe is *THE* TRUE RELIGION.

As man from birth may be taught to believe any absurdity to be divine truth, the mass educated within the circle of their creed are made from birth conscientiously to believe *that* creed alone to be divine truth.   Yet all so trained and educated to become sincere in their convictions believe, as they are taught to do, that all the innumerable creeds or sects opposed to their own are false and utter absurdities, and are suprised that men could believe such palpable contradictions to facts.

Now a moment's calm and unprejudiced reflection, when such can be obtained, will make it certain that peace, unity, progress in real knowledge, and happiness, can never co-exist with any one of these conflicting creeds, or with any isolated sect calling itself *the true religion.*

These creeds are directly calculated to force all trained to be sincere in them to become so insane, that their faculties of reasoning are destroyed, and on subjects connected with what *they* call *religion* their judgments are not only useless, but highly injurious to themselves and their opponents.

Creeds and sects of party religions are opposed to the happiness of the human race. They will therefore never enter into the true terrestrial Millennial state, or the "New Existence of Man upon the Earth."

The Second of these popular universal evils, is that of the prejudices insanely created in favour of PRIVATE PROPERTY and INDIVIDUAL INTERESTS opposed to UNIVERSAL INTEREST.

This is the education of man in the first principles of individual selfishness—the early destroyer of many of the best principles of humanity, and the implanter of avarice and of many of the worst passions forced by error into humanity.

As soon as the first glimpse of rationality can be introduced into society, and man can be taught the rudiments of common sense,—private property and individual interests will be superseded by new surroundings, which will establish the principle and practice of public property and public interest, to the entire exclusion for ever of private property and private interests.

None but those trained from birth to become insane will ever expect to see truth, justice, goodness, charity, and love, the practice of any society living under a system based on private property. The arrangements which are necessary to support private property and individual interests must divide man from man, and generate dishonesty, injustice, and cruelty.

Such arrangements must be in the nature of things opposed to progress in good feelings, charity, and love,—to knowledge, to unity, to the natural increase of wealth, and to good fellowship over the world.

It hardens the heart, blunts the best feelings of humanity, and makes all to hate their neighbours who may be opposed to their accumulation of private property, or who may be in the way of their individual interest.

It is, in connection with sectarian creeds, a most demoralising principle of the present system.

Volumes may be written to detail the endless evils which private property and individual interests have inflicted and continue to inflict on the human race. And this gross error is daily increasing the demoralisation and misery of all nations and people.

The evils arising from religious contending creeds, private property, and individual opposing interests, are now too numerous, too obvious, and too severe on humanity, not to be perceived, and in most cases felt by every class in society. Nor will time or space permit me to enter upon this most fruitful part of the subject.

Their demoralising influences are everywhere seen and felt, and speak trumpet-tongued to the suffering from them in all countries.

The Third popular cause of insanity over the world is the deeply cherished prejudices in favour of some one of the innumerable artificial arrangements called MARRIAGE, made by Priests, Lawyers, and would-be Legislators and Law-givers.

These wise men of the world, when they make laws, never think of referring for knowledge to the laws of God. But when their ignorant, unjust, and cruel laws are examined, and are compared with the laws of God and nature,—what a mass of absurd folly and puerilities do they present to a rational mind familiar with the obvious laws of that power which creates man with all his divine faculties, propensities, instincts, qualities, and powers!

Has God created men and women with the power to love and hate at their will and pleasure?

Has he not given to all humanity such a combination of these divine natural qualities, that each of human kind *must love* that which is the *most agreeable and pleasant* to the *God-given qualities* or *natural organisation* of *each?*

And is not every one *compelled* by his divine combination of the human faculties to *dislike* or *hate* that which is made to be the most disagreeable and unpleasant to him or her?

Wha an opposition, then, to the common sense of unprejudiced humanity is it, for men to make laws and institutions in direct hostility to God and nature's eternal and unchanging laws, —laws of affinity which pervade the entire creation!

How egregious must be the folly of men thus through so many centuries of human existence senselessly to fight against God and nature!

When is this insane conduct on the part of man to terminate?

Do men vainly imagine they can ever successfully contend against God and nature?

Are family dissentions not yet rife enough?

Are not the poisonings and other murders of your infatuated human laws of marriage yet numerous enough?

Are the sexual diseases created alone by your insane laws of marriage not yet sufficiently deplorable and dreadful?

Are the cloaked miseries and horrible sufferings of the poor most-cruelly-used prostitutes not yet sufficiently extended to terminate for ever the 'cause of them, and of so many unnameable married afflictions?

Will you, the so called good and pious men, and men of the world, ostrich like, hide your heads in the mysteries of senseless contending creeds, and not withdraw them to look these glaring abominations in the face, but continue to imagine that your large bodies of ignorance and selfishness are unseen, and that the evils are unfelt by the population of all nations?

Cease, ye Priests, and Law-givers, longer to contend against God's most wise, just, and merciful laws, every one of which is directly calculated, when understood and rationally applied, to give health, strength, goodness, unity, and happiness to the entire family of man!

Which of the laws of men has stood the test of time ?

Which of the laws of God has not stood the test of time ?

Are not God's laws more than ever required to-day to give peace and happiness to men and women ?

And also to make society rational on this subject—hitherto so grossly misunderstood ?

But, as the human race has been trained, educated, and placed, what would be the immediate confusion and direful events among all classes in all nations were the marriage laws of men to be at once abrogated ?

Would men and women act with the instinctive wisdom of the animal creation in their sexual relations, and like them produce good only ? No such thing. So insanely have all been trained and educated, that their immediate conduct would not bear comparison with any tribe of animals.

In consequence of men's educated ignorance of their own nature, while this old system is maintained by the authorities of the world the marriages of all countries must remain as they are now.

The only relief which laws or governments can give to the people so trained, is to form a common-sense bill of divorce, to be in force while the new arrangements for rationally forming the character and governing men, women, and children, shall be in progress.

The present system for forming character and governing could never train men and women so to understand their own natures as to act rationally in their sexual relations. This can be effected only when they shall be trained from birth under the true system of society, and within the external surroundings which that system will create.

I readily admit that the surroundings within your eighteen communities of Shakers are far more rational than any now in the outer world, as you call it, because they prevent poverty and its many evils. But, friend Evans,—your better surroundings in this and several respects will not do for the true and full Millennial state of man's new existence upon earth.

The new surroundings must be of a far different and superior character. They must include, among other differences, arrangements to well-form the character of naturally produced children, from their birth through every stage of life ; and for each sex to have, from fifteen or sixteen years of age, equal independant arrangements, so that our respective individualities shall be as well provided for as our universal social nature.

Until our individual and social qualities shall be effectually provided for in the new surroundings, they will be too defective to satisfy universal humanity.

Men and women have individual natures, differing from each other as their natural faculties at birth are made by God to differ in their combinations ; and the arrangements in the new Existence of Man upon the Earth must amply provide for this endless individual natural variety, or they will be too incomplete to become universal and permanent.

The principles and practices of your societies can never become universal ; and the phase to which knowledge has developed the human faculties now requires universal true principles, and practices always in accordance and ever consistent with these true principles.

To attain these results,—the only ones deserving the attention and consideration of those who desire to reform the world,—true first principles must be adopted, and from these, and in perfect accordance with them, the character of all must be formed and the entire of society constructed.

To form character and construct society to be consistent and rational is therefore a science as fixed and certain as any known science—as fixed and certain as the science of mathematics.

The laws which govern the universe govern the science of forming character and constructing society.

These laws are so fixed and certain, that if a bad character and an inferior society are desired, the laws by which both can be secured are at once obvious. And if, on the contrary, a superior character and a rational and happy society are wished for, the laws to effect both are now equally obvious, and can be far more economically attained and maintained than the false and inferior systems for governing mankind.

But the superior system can never be obtained by ignoring any part of human nature as given to man by the Great Creating Power of the Universe.

Humanity consists of animal instincts and propensities,—intellectual and moral qualities,—and a spiritual nature, wonderfully devised, combined, and enclosed in a physical body.

These are all necessary for the physical growth, health, and continuance of the species, for mental and moral progress, and for the happiness of the spirit within us.

Now when all these animal instincts and propensities, and all the intellectual and moral faculties, are exercised up to, and not beyond, the point of temperance for each, the body and mind will be always healthy ; every exercise, physical and mental, will give its due share of happiness to the spirit within, and the earthly life of each individual will be a long life of physical, mental, and spiritual enjoyment—the life evidently intended that man in the course of creation should attain, after the species had passed through certain necessary stages of development.

Your societies ignore the natural and necessary propensity and instinct for continuing our race, and the earth under your principles and practices would soon become a desert, and the object of the earth's creation would thus be frustrated.

But there is no probability—even with your many advantages from public property and freedom from the fear of poverty—that your societies can much increase; and they ought not to do so.

I must declare the truth without mystery, mixture of error, or fear of man, to all, and especially to your societies, in which there is I believe a greater practice of truth than in any other society, except, perhaps, among some of the North American tribes of Indians.

It, then, appears to me that you greatly err in opposing one of God's most evident laws of humanity—a law most necessary to the continuance, health, and happiness of the human race.

The founders of your sect desired to establish a community of public property, in order to terminate poverty and the fear of it, knowing how much crime and misery poverty and opposing interests created.

They appeared instinctively to feel that public property and the artificial marriages of the priesthood, or any law-made marriages by men, could never exist together.

The world yet wants the first successful community of artificially married men and women. It is an impossibility.

What, then, were they to do? Either to abandon their great, and as it appears overwhelming desire to establish a community of public property and mutual interests, and admit the sexes to unite according to their natural affinities, as God and nature intend they should;—or to bring the two sexes together on the Shakers' principle of celibacy.

When the first Shaker society was formed, public opinion, even in the United States, was so far undeveloped, that no society of persons of both sexes would have been permitted to live without they submitted to priestly or lay artificial and unnatural marriages.

The founders of your society therefore adopted the other extreme, and established the equally unnatural principle of celibacy.

They presumed that they knew better than the Creator of man how to direct this necessary propensity for the continuance, health, and happiness of our race.

The Priests and Legislators of the world, being equally ignorant of human nature and of God's laws of humanity, also presumed that they knew better than God how to direct this propensity; and experience proves through all past time how much disorder, disease, crime, and misery, they have by their gross impiety and ignorant presumption inflicted upon themselves and the entire family of man.

They were too ignorant to comprehend that God directed the sexual instincts of all animals virtuously and beneficially, and that if Priests and Legislators, all grossly ignorant of God's laws of humanity, had not opposed these laws by their puny efforts to supersede them, God would have virtuously and beneficially directed the sexual propensities of animal humanity, as well as those of all other animals.

And which do you suppose knows best how to direct these instincts of Man—The Power which has so wonderfully created and combined them in our nature ? Or the Priests and Legislators of the world, who have thus far demonstrated their total ignorance of humanity and of their own nature ?

But it must not be mistaken that artificial marriages are a necessary part of this false, evil, and now, fortunately for the human race, worn-out system ; and while men shall be so grossly undeveloped in their observing and reasoning powers and rational faculties as to maintain this system, these artificial and evil-producing marriages must also be maintained.

When artificial marriages go, the entire system must go ; for as each part—creeds, private interests, and artificial marriages—is necessary to support the others,—they must all be maintained intact, or quietly superseded by the rational system, true in principle and practice, and all the surroundings of men must be made to be consistent with those true principles.

Thus—friend Evans—your society is in a fatal error when it advocates celibacy ; and the sooner you can now make arrange ments to abandon it, without breaking up or injuring your otherwise highly valuable mode of life, the better it will be for your communities and for society.

Your mission has been to exhibit to the world the practicability of men and women in a state of celibacy, under many great disadvantages, creating more wealth than the real wants of such populations require.

Your societies are now called upon to show the world the ease with which—aided by the advanced discoveries in the sciences, and the many new inventions—any well ordered community can create a superfluity of wealth of good and superior quality beyond their requirements, when these communities are living naturally in accordance with the laws of God, — while they increase as nature requires to replenish the earth, and assist to make it a terrestrial paradise, and the abode of men and women made angelic in mind and conduct.

Celibacy is not a law of God.

Universal propagation throughout the vegetable and animal kingdom is the law of God on this subject, and it is a necessary law for the progress, the health, and the happiness of all that has life.

Celibacy is therefore a crime against God's laws; and men and women who practice it cannot be in full health—physical or mental.

It is pure chastity that is the great personal virtue of men and women.

But chastity is not celibacy; and there are few throughout the world, arising from the artificial marriages of the priesthood in all nations, who live the life of chastity.

True chastity consists in having no sexual intercourse except when God's affinity, or pure love and affection, exists at the time between the parties. It is only under these circumstances that a healthy child can be procreated; and not even with these favourable circumstances to commence with will a full-formed physical and mental and spiritual infant be born into the world, unless the mother during the whole of her pregnancy shall be careful in her diet and exercise, and be kept in a placid and happy state of mind.

And fully to reform the world it is necessary to commence with infants born from chaste parents, and who have been well cared for during the pregnancy of their mother, as well as being well cared for from birth through life.

The marriages of the priesthood and of legislators have destroyed all correct ideas of chastity, and instead thereof have forced falsehood, sexual disease, and the unspoken and hidden miseries of prostitution upon the world, by their insane opposition to the laws of God.

Your eighteen communities are an excellent foundation and good practical preparation from which to advance and proceed to a very superior state of communites of public property,—marriage according to natural laws of affinity,—a true formation of character before and from birth,—with the pure spirit of love and charity pervading the mind and every-day conduct of every member of such communities.

And these would become such a light to the population of the world, that—instead of eighteen communities, with a population of only 5,000 souls, in more than sixty years,—you would have in half a century all the more civilised portion of the world for your followers, if not, during the latter years of that period, the now uncivilised remaining portion also.

Were I a younger man than eighty-five years have made me, I would willingly join your societies, and endeavour to assist you *gradually* to change from what you are to what you might be—a shining light to the world.

In the pure spirit of charity and love for all the members of your eighteen societies,—

I remain, your friend,

ROBERT OWEN.

Sevenoaks Park, Sevenoaks.

England, April 6, 1856.

A NEW AGITATION OF NATIONS, TO INTRODUCE A NEW SYSTEM FOR THE GOVERNMENT OF MAN, TO RAISE HIM TO A HIGHER LIFE UPON EARTH, AND TO SUPERIOR CELESTIAL SPHERES IN HEAVEN.

THIS system will be

Without human-made laws.

Without despotic power for evil.

Without priests, lawyers, medical men, or military men.

Without a class to endeavour to buy cheap and sell dear.

Without money, a monied class, or any artificial circulating medium.

Without competition or contests for wealth, or for worldly honors, or for individual privileges.

Without a desire for individual distinctions of any kind.

Without slavery or servitude.

Without inequality of education, condition, or treatment.

Without any personal distinctions, except those created by age and by the varieties of natural capacity.

Without ignorance, pauperism, poverty, or the fear of poverty.

Without crime, or fear of human punishment.

Without anger, hatred, violence, jealousy, or any evil or inferior passion.

Without repulsive feelings, or disunion between man and man.

Without an inferior class.

Without physical or mental disease, or the fear of death.

Without the fear of hell or the devil.

Without any slavish or unpleasant fear of God.

Without, ultimately, one bad or inferior character.

Without the want of charity and kindness in any one, for all of our race.

Without human-made laws.

Without religious differences, hatreds, or wars.

Without civil or national wars.

Without standing armies, or navies for war.

Without difference of opinions creating a difference of feeling between individuals or nations.

Without a variety of languages.

Without inferior dwellings.

Without inferior clothing or furniture.

Without inferior surroundings in any of the departments of life.

Without inferior training or educating, to give inferior habits, manners, or conduct, to any one.

Without obstructions to prevent society giving a good and superior physical, intellectual, moral, spiritual, and practical character, before and from birth, to all.

Without the *causes* of evil.

Without misery or suffering, except from unavoidable accidents.

Without custom-houses, passports, or hindrances of any kind to prevent travelling freely over the earth.

Without any one being excluded from any part of the earth.

Without human-made bondage of any kind.

Without falsehood, in look, word, or action.

Without secrecy of any kind in withholding knowledge.

Without the few holding power for evil over the many.

Without merit or demerit for any conscientious belief.

Without merit or demerit for loving or disliking persons or things.

Without any one having any right over the opinions or conscience of another.

Without interference with individual rights.

Without any parties claiming an individual right to air, earth, or water, to the exclusion of others, equally entitled by nature to the natural use of them.

Without cities, towns, villages, isolated dwellings, streets, lanes, courts, or alleys.

Without other arrangements than social family commonwealths, —national commonwealths, — and the great nationally united commonwealth of the world.

Without individual selfishness.

Without social family-commonwealth selfishness.

Without national-commonwealth selfishness.

Without selfishness in the united commonwealth of the world.

Without private property or any desire for it.

Without limited national territories.

Without individual independence being interfered with, except so far as is unavoidable in a well-regulated society living in peace and harmony.

Without celibacy ;—it being contrary to the laws of God.

Without artificial or unnatural human-made marriages.

Without unnatural children, which are consequent on unnatural marriages.

Without prostitution ;—which is an unavoidable result produced by unnatural marriages.

Without unchaste desires ;—which will be effected by the sexes always uniting according to their God-made natural affinities.

Without one sex depending upon another, except for mutual affection and social aid.

Without disappointment of the affections.

This new system for the government of man will attain and secure the preceding results, by forming the character of all, from birth, on a newly developed true principle, and placing all within new surroundings, emanating from that true principle.

These proceedings will constitute a system of *Prevention of*

Evil, for the permanent government of the human race,—a system which, in fact, will give the full use of the world to each individual, so far as he can enjoy it, when made fruitful and beautiful, and when the character of his fellows has been made good, wise and happy.

Thus, ultimately, and at no very distant day, will society over the earth be without ignorance, poverty, disunion, falsehood, crime, or misery; but all will be surrounded from birth by new conditions, which must make *all* to become, in two or three generations, good, wise, united, healthy, prosperous in all worldly matters, and progressively increasing through every generation in excellence and happiness.

There is nothing stated in this article which may not be easily attained in practice by basing society on its true fundamental principle, and making the surroundings in accordance with that principle.

A thousand petty objections will be made by petty-formed minds, who are without knowledge of the laws of nature, or of what is or is not possible in practice. But the opinions of such individuals will be disregarded by the advanced minds and experienced men in the largest operations under the existing system.

Chemical discoveries and mechanical inventions, rightly applied, are already far more than society requires for its permanent happiness, and they can be increased without limitation.

The ultimate true division of the population of the world, and form of society, to insure the greatest amount of excellence and happiness to all, will be into divisions not exceeding three thousand souls, united in social family commonwealths, and these to be federatively united over the world.

This change to be gradually effected by means to be attained; which will be explained in the succeeding articles.

The social family commonwealths are adopted because they alone admit of the surroundings necessary to secure the happiness of the human race.

THE NECESSITY FOR A CHANGE OF THE SYSTEM OF SOCIETY, AND THE MEANS TO EFFECT IT.

It is useless to attempt to reform the present system of society, because it is based and has been constructed on a false principle, and therefore its practices have been injurious to the human race through the past existence of humanity.

It has been based and constructed on the imaginary notion that man forms his own qualities of body and mind, and in practice he has been made to be responsible to society for these qualities and their results.

All facts respecting humanity prove the ignorance and the endless miseries to the race, which this absurd imaginary notion has inflicted upon every past generation.

The facts of every age have proved—

That all the physical and mental powers of man have been, unknown to himself, given to him by the Power creating him in the womb,—and that from birth, and to some extent before, those physical and mental qualities are placed under the guidance and direction of the society by which the individual is surrounded.

That the surroundings of men and things determine the climate, language, religion, ideas, habits, manners, customs, occupation, and conduct, of every one.

That these surroundings influence to an illimitable extent for good or evil, all placed within them.

The science of the influence of these surroundings has been discovered; and in consequence, the means may be now made known to the human race, by which society may create new surroundings, which, without the knowledge in the early life of the individual, will compel him to become through life good,—intelligent,—attracted by, attracted to, and therefore united with, all his fellows,—wealthy beyond his acquirements and equal to his wishes,—his ideas true, and therefore always consistent,—and consequently so wise in conduct, as to be daily occupied in assisting to promote the permanent happiness of his race.

To effect this change, new surroundings will be required over the earth ;—because all existing surroundings made by men have emanated from the false principle stated—(that man forms his own qualities, physical and mental, and should be made responsible for them to his fellow men and to God, or the Mysterious Power which created him).

Under this new developement of man and society, there is but one course for the human race to adopt,—that is, by wise foresight, in peace and order, gradually to supersede all existing surroundings which are so opposed to progress and happiness, by new surroundings based on a true knowledge of humanity, and constructed throughout in accordance with the laws of God and nature, and ever consistent with them.

Being thus in the right path, we are directed how to proceed, in spirit, principle, and practice, to " reform the world."

The spirit is that of pure charity and love for our race.

The principle is, " that the character of man is formed *for* him."

The practice is,—to create and maintain such surroundings as will make all our race, good, united, abounding in wealth, enlightened, healthy in body and mind, and ever wisely employed in promoting the happiness of all around, within the circle of their influence, irrespective of all differences made by nature or education, including, while they last, differences of class, creed, and colour.

There may be differences among men respecting the mode of introducing this change of surroundings to the population of the world.

The following is proposed as the most natural, easy, and effective mode of gradually accomplishing this great change for all human-kind. If better can be devised the writer will be gratified.

Since No. 1 of the *Millennial Gazette* was published, hostilities have ceased between the belligerents of the West and East, and the world is at peace. This most happy event permits at the right moment the finest opportunity to adopt direct and decisive means, by the nations of the world, to effect the change for the system of falsehood and evil for the system of truth and goodness.

The best course to be adopted to effect this great and glorious change for man, will be for the present members of the Peace Conference in Paris, now that they have concluded a treaty of peace between their respective nations, to be formed into a committee for calling a congress of nations, to be held in London at as early a period as such a meeting can conveniently be convened,—each nation to be represented at the congress by two members selected by their respective governments.

The congress to take into their most grave consideration the best means of forming a Sacred Alliance of nations, federatively united to obtain and secure, by wise foresight, the permanent peace, progress, prosperity, and happiness, of the population of the world.

The following outline is proposed for the formation of this sacred alliance.

1st. That all nations be invited by the Peace Conference Committee to send their representative members to the congress, to form the Sacred Alliance of nations, federatively united to attain the objects previously stated.

2nd. That the Sacred Alliance shall adopt measures to effect the change from the false and evil to the true and good system of society in the shortest time practicable, without creating injury to any parties while the change shall be in progress.

3rd. That the Sacred Alliance shall, during the progress of the change from one system to the other, guarantee the internal and external peace within the territories now forming the state or empire of each nation.

4th. That during and after the change of system, the alliance shall guarantee to each one—man, woman and child,—in each nation being a member of the Sacred Alliance, that their present condition shall never be changed for one worse or inferior, and shall not be changed during their lives, except by their own expressed desire.

5th. That the change from the one system to the other shall

be effected by the creation, on new sites, of new surroundings, all made in undeviating accordance with the laws of God or nature, (or of God and nature,) and proved to be such by their continually recurring without change or variableness.

6th. That these surroundings will therefore be such as will insure to every one born and living within them, a superior formation of character—physical, intellectual, moral, spiritual, and practical,—a healthy, pleasant, and most convenient dwelling, with separate private apartments to each of both sexes from the age of fifteen,—a sufficiency at all times of the best and most wholesome food, unadulterated and well prepared to insure health, constant beneficial occupation, physical and mental, having reference to the natural qualities and acquired qualifications of the individual, — abundance of time for physical and mental recreations,—a fair full share, at the proper period of life, of the local government within their respective surroundings,—and as much individual independance as is practicable in social life— but an independence greatly superior to any which can exist under the present system of falsehood and evil. (The means, under this change of system, which will be always at the disposal of the Sacred Alliance, will be most ample to enable it to assure all the preceding results).

7th. That the Sacred Alliance shall gradually re-place the population of each nation, commencing with the working classes and their children, within these new surroundings ; but none to be taken without their strongly expressed desire to live within them.

8th. That these surroundings shall consist—

First, of social family commonwealths, never exceeding three thousand men, women, and children, in their natural proportions.

Second, of these united within their territorial bounds to form national commonwealths.

Third, of a union of these national commonwealths to form the great commonwealth of the world.

9th. That each social family commonwealth shall be governed on an equality of education, condition, and occupation, according to age and natural capacity.

10th. That each social family commonwealth shall have the following departments :—

1. The domestic.
2, The formation of character.
3. The creation of wealth.
4. Its preservation and distribution.
5. Recreations.
6. Government at home and abroad, or within and without the social family commonwealth.
7. A sufficient domain to supply the family, when at its maximum number, abundantly with the necessaries of life.

(These departments to be always kept at a high standard of perfection in practice.)

11th. The national commonwealth to purchase with the national funds, arising from the superfluous wealth created by the family commonwealths, all the present private property in land, on which the family commonwealths are to be established;—the national commonwealth becoming the sole trustee of the property of the land, for the benefit of all.

12th. No standing armies to be maintained in the great commonwealth of the united nations. But all in each family commonwealth to be trained in military evolutions, to the superior use of arms, and afterwards to be periodically exercised in them, until the great commonwealth of all nations shall form the human race into the true brotherhood of man over the world. But even *then* the young should be trained from early life by military discipline, to attain the civil advantages to be derived from acting in order with precision, when numbers are employed in practical operations.

When character shall be rationally formed from birth, and placed within rational surroundings, (and no other surroundings can form a rational character,) punishment of any kind will be unnecessary and therefore unknown.

PRACTICAL MEASURES TO INTRODUCE AND CONSOLIDATE THE MILLENNIUM.

THE practical mode by which to make man good, society rational, to unite the population of the world, and to train it to become wise, prosperous, and permanently happy, is now, through the experience derived from the past, become a science as fixed in principle, and as certain in practice, as any known science.

The character of the surroundings of humanity, forms the character of all within them. The path to the results stated is now plain and open, and the highest permanent interest of all will be secured by pursuing it without deviating to the right or to the left.

Make the surroundings good, and the population will be good.

It will be soon universally discovered, that the first step to make the population of the world rational and happy, will be to establish permanent peace over the earth among all nations and peoples.

This peace is to be effected by a federative union between all nations and peoples.

And a universal federative treaty may be now formed, which shall give to each nation and people a greater victory, without loss of any kind, than has ever been achieved by the most powerful and fortunate nation or people during the past history of the human race.

By this simple process, each nation and people will become far more than conquerers of the world under the existing system.

For if France under Napoleon the First, or Russia under Nicholas the First, had succeeded in extending their conquests over the earth—what would have been the position of either ?

They would of necessity have been surrounded by internal enemies, who would have left them no rest or quietness ; and they would have been in an irrational, dangerous, and uncomfortable state during the remainder of their lives, and their subjects miserable.

But by this universal Federative treaty, all enmity and opposition of interests will die their natural deaths,—all will soon see the advantages of remaining at peace,—and all will be enabled to enjoy it.

The present irrational obstructions between nation and nation will cease,—no custom houses will exist,—no passports will be required,—the earth will belong to every one,—all will attain that most desirable of political positions—that is, will become free citizens of the strongest, best governed country, with none to make them afraid.

The aspirations of the best men who have lived will thus be secured through future ages.   Each individual, by the new training, education, and position which will be given to each, will feel in reality that the world is his country, and that to do good to all his fellow-citizens is his true religion, and the only true one.

The articles of this universal federative treaty shall be given at or before the proposed Congress, in May, of " The Reformers of the World."

But one clause of this treaty must be at once obvious,—namely, that each nation shall effect its own interior reforms without interference of any kind from the federated nations, except so far as assistance and advice may be obtained at the request of any nation of the union.

The federative union will, however, soon destroy all jealousy about international interference ; for it will be discovered that there can be but one interest among the whole federation, and that interest will be to promote, to the highest point, the well-doing, prosperity, and permanent happiness of each state and people composing the entire federation.

The second great measure to attain and secure the permanent progress, peace, prosperity, and happiness of the federation, will be to make the scientific model of the true universal commonwealths known to the public in principle and practice ; how they are to be devised and executed,—and how each is to be governed so as always to produce harmony within each, and with all other commonwealths throughout the federation—which, sooner or later, will be sure to extend over the world.

The problem to be solved in devising these **commonwealths to** become universal through the great federative union of all nations, which will compose the great commonwealth of the world, is to ascertain what number of men, women, and children, in their natural proportions, can be associated together as one commonwealth family, to be the best and most easily trained, educated, employed, govern[1] and placed, so that each child born within the commonwealth shall be the best cared for, and done by, from birth to death. And in which the situation of the parents of children shall be well devised, to have the most healthy and best formed progeny both in body and mind, as a good germ or nucleus from which to enable the commonwealth to form a superior character for all from birth.

To combine all these considerations in the best manner to obtain these results the most advantageously, a commonwealth whose maximum shall be *three thousand* in number, formed into one family, under one arrangement, will give the solution required.

In a commonwealth so limited, based on the true principle, and consistently constructed in accordance with that principle, the following departments or divisions will be required, and to be so united as always to work harmoniously without one interfering to oppose another.

1st.—The domestic arrangements.

2nd.—Arrangements for creating and distributing wealth.

3rd.—Arrangements for governing the population within, and its relations with those without.

4th.—All these to be so arranged as to become aids in forming a superior character for all within the commonwealth,—every external object having a greater or lesser influence in forming the character of everyone.

As the well-being, well-doing, and permanent prosperity and happiness of each and all will depend upon the character formed for the population of the commonwealth,—this department will require the greatest care and attention in devising and executing.

It must commence in practical measures with the parents before the birth of their children, and continue from birth, during the life of each one, day by day, without ceasing; for the character of each is made better or worse each day through their lives. But this unceasing attention to the formation of the character of everyone will easily be effected by permanent arrangements which will accomplish the results almost unperceived by the individual.

The commonwealth, like the Indian mother, will be responsible for the character which shall be formed within it for all its members.

Thus easily will the character of the human race, as compared with their present character, become perfect,—wealth always good and superabundant,—their union cordial and permanent,—and the earth fertile and beautiful for the enjoyment of all.

No laws but the laws of God to govern each commonwealth and the great united commonwealth, in which ultimately there will be no city or isolated residence,—no street, lane, court, ·or alley,—all these being bad surroundings.

No priests, lawyers, medical or military men,—no buyers cheap and sellers dear,—all these being bad surroundings.

No churches, workhouses for paupers, prisons or punishments of any kind,—none being required, except for the commonwealth itself, if it could ever by possibility mistake its interests and its duties.

No slaves, servants, or inequality of condition of similar age, or oppression of one individual of any kind,—these being all ignorant, irrational, and bad surroundings.

With the true principles for its base, and consistent practice with that principle, and governed solely by the laws of God and nature,—how easy, simple, and prompt, might be the reformation of the world !

How easily might the human race slide out of the system of *evil*, into that of *good !*

How comparatively soon might the entire population of our globe supersede their present state of ignorance, poverty, disunion, fightings, quarrelings, and endless miseries, for a new existence upon earth, in which none of these evils could be known or experienced by one individual!

You have only to will it, and it will be done.

I have thus written, to endeavour to create this will in the population of the world. That it may be made to become an active reality, is the cordial wish and ardent desire of the spirit which has ever influenced my life and writings.

THE FEDERATION OF NATIONS A NECESSARY PRELIMINARY TO THE FORMATION AND FEDERATION OF THE SOCIAL FAMILY COMMONWEALTH ; WHICH, UPON FULL AND ACCURATE INVESTIGATION INTO THE WHOLE BUSINESS OF LIFE, WILL BE DISCOVERED TO BE THE TRUE SCIENCE OF SOCIETY, IN PRINCIPLE AND PRACTICE.

THE reform in practice of individual nations, and of the entire population of the world, must commence by the federation of nations, which is perhaps the happiest inspiration yet given by God to man, because it is destined to secure the permanent happiness of the race, by preparing the way for a rational practical brotherhood of the family of man through all future generations.

Three modes, after the most matured reflection, present themselves, by which these national federations may be effected.

The first is, a federative treaty, as an example to all other nations, between Great Britain and the United States,—upon terms of perfect equality.

In this case the United States would, to all intents and purposes, conquer the empire of Great Britain, which at this moment is the most advanced and powerful empire in the world. And this conquest would be gained by the United States without the loss of one life, or the expenditure of one penny.

On the other hand, Great Britain, with like advantages, would to all intents and purposes conquer the United States. These States possess domains capable of forming a rival empire in all respects to Great Britain.

The two, federatively united, would at once form an empire unequaled in the history of mankind, and constituting a combined power that could by force easily conquer the remaining parts of the population of the world.

But the reign of force now ceases for ever. Charity and love combined, directed by calm sound judgment, will now supersede force, and reign triumphant in its stead, and henceforth govern all nations for their progress in excellence and happiness.

The second mode of national federation is a federative treaty between all the present negotiating parties represented at the Peace Conference at Paris, adding to their number the United States of North America; and then for this federative union to invite all other nations on both continents to join in their federation.

It will be at once seen that each nation would thus gain immensely, and would lose nothing but their ignorance, poverty, disunion, and prejudices.

The third mode of federatively uniting nations is the one which I suggested to the United States when there and during the presidency of Mr. Munro, with whom I was to its conclusion upon the most confidential terms.

This was, that all the separate powers on the continent of America, North and South, should annex themselves to, and be received by, the United States, on terms of perfect federative equality, and that all the nations of the other half of the world should in like manner unite themselves to Great Britain:—and then, that the great federatively United American States, and the great federatively United European States, should federatively unite, and thus for ever secure the peace, progress, excellence, and happiness of all nations, including the entire population of the world.

Either of these modes would effect the desire of all hearts, which is to make a cordial permanent brotherhood of the human race. And this is the ultimate destiny of man.

Let the existing governments, for peace sake, have the choice between these three modes. But if the nations of the world do not desire this change, and do not influence the governments to adopt one of them, or one that will attain the same results, then are these nations too undeveloped yet to perceive or to adopt measures calculated for their well-being, well-doing, and permamanent progressive happiness.

These views and measures will be submitted to the Congress of the Reformers of the World, to commence on the 14th of May next, at noon, in St. Martin's Hall, London ; and when this shall have been done, if I live so long, my mission will terminate. It is useless to attempt to reform the present system of society ; for all attempts to reform it have failed, because it has been based and constructed on false principles, and therefore every such attempt must prove vain and useless.

No one who comprehends the laws of nature respecting humanity, and the natural construction of society, will ever imagine it possible to effect any substantial and permanent reform of the present system of society, based, as it is, on supposed facts which do not exist,—on imagined facts in direct opposition to those which came into existence when man was created, and which have continued with him to this day, without change or alteration,—proving them to be laws of God, intended ultimately to direct and govern man in all his proceedings through life.

The present system having been thus based and constructed in all its departments on error, and maintained by force, fraud, and falsehood, deserves no further attention from advanced minds, or those who are in the least prepared to assist in reforming the world.

I have now, it is hoped, put this now worn-out system for ever out of the way of progress, except to be considered as the old graveled roads were after the railways were discovered. As these were necessary to be maintained while the railways were being constructed,—so must this old system be kept in action while the new is in progress, gradually to receive within it the population of the world.

The new system will ultimately consist of scientific family commonwealths, not exceeding, in each, three thousand souls. These will be federatively united,—first, in each nation,—then, by degrees, from nation to nation,—until they shall include the population of the world in one great commonwealth, which will progress without ceasing from age to age, in every kind of excellence, until this globe shall be made a terrestrial paradise, and all men and women shall be full-formed and superior in all their qualities of body and mind, so as to fit them in the highest degree, when they put off this earthly form, for the higher spheres in the life to come.

To effect this great and all glorious change for humanity, there must be a permanent universal peace, and a spirit of charity and love created to guide, direct, and govern this change.

A slight reflection will assist all to discover that both of these events will be unspeakably for the advantage of all who now live, and of all who may live hereafter.

The first of the three modes which present themselves by which this change may be the most easily and justly made, in peace and harmony between all nations and peoples, is, as has been stated, to commence by a federative treaty between Great Britain and the United States of North America, upon terms of perfect reciprocity.

The advantage of such union would be soon experienced, and would be obvious to other nations to be so immense, that it would become a shining example to other nations, and would create a desire to unite federatively with these two nations, and to which union there will naturally be a ready assent of both.

If the rulers of the other most advanced nations are not yet sufficiently developed to make this federation now, through a general congress of nations,—a more extended federative union between them would be a useful practical commencement.

It is probable, however, that if the more civilized nations of the world would agree to call a congress of nations,—making no exceptions in Europe, Asia, or America, and inviting also China and Japan,—that at such congress the advantages of the most extended federation of nations would be made by discussion so evident to all, and so easy and beneficial to each, that a general agreement to form such extended federative union would be adopted.

An outline of a federative treaty and of an extended federative union between Great Britain, the United States, and all civilized nations, shall be given, to show how easily and beneficially nation may now unite with nation, to give peace, progress, and happiness to the population of the world.

These treaties, as will be ascertained by the articles of the proposed unions, will not prematurely interfere with the customs, laws, prejudices, or government, of any country, thus federatively uniting ; but they will gradually accustom all to more correct views and conduct in all their private and public proceedings, and prepare their populations to commence the language of truth, and to live a life of honesty.

When these federative unions shall have been formed, and something like true principles shall have been acquired, and a right spirit infused into these populations, they will be prepared to have explained to them the far greater advantages to be derived from the scientific family commonwealths, in which every one will be well cared for from and before birth to death, and in which the *cause of evil* will not be allowed to exist.

It will be found very easy to form arrangements to *prevent evil*. But when the causes of evil are unwisely allowed to enter any society, it will be found impossible to eradicate the evil thus created, except by withdrawing the cause producing it.

The scientific family commonwealths will be formed of surroundings to prevent the existence of any cause of evil entering them, and the common sense of all will fully comprehend the superiority of a system to prevent evil, over one which encourages the introduction and growth of evil, and then vainly attempts to cure small portions of it.

PROPOSED FEDERATIVE TREATY BETWEEN AUSTRIA, FRANCE, PRUSSIA, RUSSIA, SARDINIA, TURKEY, AND THE UNITED STATES OF NORTH AMERICA.

WE, seven of the leading powers among civilised nations, being desirous for the permanent peace, progress, and happiness of the human race, to terminate oppression and all other evils of man's producing, have united to form a federative treaty, to prepare the population of the world for this great and glorious change.

For these reasons we agree to the following articles,—

1st —That there shall be permanent peace and harmony between our respective nations.

2nd.—That they shall be henceforth for ever federatively united.

3rd.—That all the inhabitants of these seven nations shall have equal rights and privileges throughout the dominons of this federation.

4th.—That persons shall have unrestricted liberty of ingress and egress, and each shall be respected as a natural born inhabitant within the dominions of this federation.

5th.—That there shall be no interference of any of these nations within the territories of the others, except at the request of one or more of these nations, desiring or asking for the advice or aid of one or more of the federation.

6th.—That the existing territories of the members of this federation shall be guaranteed by the federation from all molestation from without by any other power.

7th.—That Sweden, Holland, Denmark, Spain, Portugal, Saxony, and Bavaria, shall be invited to unite in this league or treaty, in order to extend peace and prosperity to all nations and peoples, on principles of universal justice and good fellowship.

8th.—That when this federative union shall have progressed so far, all minor civilised nations shall be invited to join the league.

9th.—That when this extended union shall have taken place, (which may soon be expected, as it will be so strongly for the interest of every nation to become a member of this league,) rational, peaceable measures shall be adopted to induce China, Japan, and every other tribe or people to unite in this treaty, in order to form a commonwealth or brotherhood of the human race, composed of all nations and peoples, in order that the peace, progress, and happiness of the inhabitants of the earth may be permanently attained and consolidated on the most sure and substantial foundation.

10th.—That after a period to be named there shall be no standing armies within the federation; but that, as an essential part of educating or forming the character of the young, all to the age of fourteen shall be trained in military exercises, and in the use of arms, as long as any portion of the population of the world shall not become members of the federation.

11th.—That during the same period a steam navy shall be kept and maintained in full efficiency, to preserve the peace and safety of all the oceans and seas.

12th.—That measures shall be gradually introduced into the dominions of each member of the federation, to give one and the same language to all the children who shall be born after the signing of the treaty; and that this universal language shall be the Anglo-Saxon.

13th.—That all trained, educated, and employed within them, shall be governed solely by the laws of God and nature, and thus become full-formed men and women, knowing their own nature so well as to perceive the straight road to happiness for themselves and all placed within similar surroundings.

14th.—That new surroundings shall be so formed and combined as peaceably, gradually, and most beneficially for every one, to break up all present associations of the respective populations of each nation composing the league, by superseding them with the true scientific aggregate of surroundings, to be complete models of a working society, or a rational family arrangement to attain all the objects of human existence in a superior manner, to form the nucleus, germ, or family commonwealth.

15th.—That these family commonwealths shall be federatively united throughout the extent of the federation, so as ultimately to form by their union the true brotherhood of the human race and the great commonwealth of the world.

16th.—That these new surroundings to constitute family commonwealths shall not exceed three thousand in their maximum population, in order to give to each of its members the full advantages that society can prepare for them.

17th.—That the capital, skill, and labour, now worse than wasted most unnecessarily in standing armies, shall be employed to execute the new surroundings of the new family commonwealths, which shall be gradually increased in each nation, to be sufficient in number to accommodate the entire population of the federated nations.

18th.—That thus ultimately the nations of the earth shall be gradually formed by wise foresight, in peace, in order, and with the cordial consent of all, into limited family commonwealths, which shall be federatively united, without other distinctions, local or national, to form the great united commonwealth of the world.

19th.—That these family commonwealths, united in language, education, and interest, will be far more easily governed and kept in perpetual harmony, than can a single parish under the insane system by which the world has been mis-governed to this day.

20th.—That throughout this new federation of nations, those within each family commonwealth shall be trained, educated, and placed, under surroundings in which each one shall be taught to know himself, to comprehend the whole of society, and to be competent to take an efficient part in directing the new chemical and mechanical machinery, by which the domestic business, the creation and distribution of wealth, and the formation of character, will daily proceed in each of these family commonwealths over the world.

21st.—That each family commonwealth shall have sufficient domain to support itself amply in all the necessaries of life, and to have a surplus produce to exchange for what it may require beyond its own production.

22nd.—That each family commonwealth shall govern itself within its own domain.

23rd.—That the circulating medium of wealth within the federation shall be the notes of the united federation, guaranteed by the whole property within the united federation. These notes to circulate wealth until it shall be ascertained in practice that wealth can be pleasurably produced with ease and certainty beyond the wants and wishes of all, so that all may unrestrictedly use it as their wants require.

24th.—That each family commonwealth shall have but one interest, and each member to be without private property,—each being a producer and consumer upon equal terms according to age; and no other inequality to be known among them except that which nature makes in their natural qualities.

This is a mere first sketch and rough outline from which to form a well digested federative treaty.

THE MEASURES WHICH I HAVE BEEN IMPRESSED FROM MY YOUTH TO ADOPT THROUGH LIFE TO THIS PERIOD, TO PREPARE THE POPULATION OF THE WORLD TO CHANGE THEIR SYSTEM OF FALSEHOOD, IGNORANCE, AND MISERY, FOR THE SYSTEM OF TRUTH, WISDOM, AND HAPPINESS.

IN early youth I was strongly impressed with the conviction that " truth is always consistent with itself and in accordance with all " facts, which constitute the unchanging laws of nature." I was fortunately uneducated according to the notions entertained under the existing system of society. I had therefore the less to un-learn, and the fewer prejudices to contend against. I was taught only to read, write, and to understand the elements of arithmetic, in a common school, in a small town consisting then of about nine hundred inhabitants. But I was early fond of reading, and I read immensely ; and by this reading of all books which came in my way, as I read them was my real education commenced. I read promiscuously the leading novels of that period (1780),— Shakspeare,—Milton, — Harvey, — Young's night thoughts,— many religious works,—Universal History,—the Circumnavi-gators,—Lives of the Ancient Philosophers, and their Philoso-phies,—Biographies, &c., &c., &c. But I read all these differently from most youths. I had this standard of truth always in my mind when reading. I knew that " all facts prove that God, " (or nature,) and society make the character of every one upon " the earth :—God, through nature, giving all the natural qualities " at birth,—and society directing them from birth through life." Whatever, therefore, in my readings, was opposed to this cri-terion, left no lasting impression on my mind. What was in ac-cordance with it, was added to my stock of certain truths ; and thus my mind gradually became filled with ideas consistent with themselves and in accordance with all known facts. I therefore soon ceased to blame man for those qualities which God forced him to receive when born, and which society afterwards directed either ill or well, foolishly or wisely. Soon being convinced, by facts narrated in history, and by those existing around me, that society knew not human nature, or how to direct it for the good of the individual or the happiness of any society or any nation, I early commenced to contend against the popular notions of all classes, sects, and parties ; and I was soon called an infidel. But my readings and reflections opened to me the causes which ne-cessarily produced the errors and prejudices prevalent in all these classes, sects, and parties ; and, therefore, instead of being excited to anger for their educated mistakes, I was constrained to pity them for the unfortunate surroundings or circumstances in which they had been placed from their births. I was therefore impelled never to contend in anger for what I knew was truth ; but to place it in the best manner I could before the mind of others, and to treat all with the kindness which charity for their educated differences to my opinions compelled me to have for them.

This mode of proceeding, I soon discovered, had the effect in a *very large* majority of cases, of enabling me to draw out the *good qualities* of those with whom I came into daily or occasional communication, and very seldom any of *educated* evil qualities. For those who have an experienced knowledge of humanity know that man is not bad, but is divinely good, by nature; and that it requires only that he should be placed from birth within good circumstances and superior surroundings, to draw out those good qualities in all over the earth.

But society, so far, has been blind to the natural qualities of man, and therefore blind to the easy and simple means to insure his happiness.

By thus thinking and acting differently from my fellow-men I was enabled at the age of twenty to have the sole management of a new, difficult, and extensive manufactory, and the direction of five hundred men, women, and children, employed in it. The whole was new to me;—I had at once to enter upon my task without an hour's instruction from any one. In four years, under my direction, the character of this population was greatly bettered in its general conduct, the manufacture extended, and so much improved as to be eminently successful.

At twenty-five I had to create another new establishment, with similar success.

At twenty-eight a much more extended establishment, with a population of thirteen hundred was placed under my sole direction, and which was gradually increased until the population exceeded two thousand. And this establishment continued under my direction for more than a quarter of a century.

There it was that I commenced to put into practice my knowledge of the influence of circumstances over human nature in the formation of character.

I had a very inferior and immoral population to begin with. I pitied, without blaming or punishing them, for the very unfavourable circumstances in which they had been placed before they were brought from various distant places to the establishment.

This establishment was at New Lanark, in the county of Lanark, Scotland; and the existing circumstances there at that period were far from being likely to improve their condition. I did what all governments ought to do;—I gradually withdrew the unfavourable circumstances from around the adult part of the community, and created entirely new surroundings for the children of this population. These surroundings were unique in their character and results:—results never until then anticipated by any parties in any country. They were surroundings which created for the children a character totally different from that which had been given to their parents—a new character, which many clergymen and others who came to see and examine their proceedings said was so different from the character of other children, that it appeared to be a " new human nature." But it was only old human nature, *naturally* treated, by being surrounded by circumstances according with, instead of opposed to, its nature.

The result was such as ever will take place when human nature shall be placed from early life within surroundings in accordance with its nature. These children were, by comparison with the same number and age of any other children, high or low, in society, good, wise, and happy ; although the circumstances attending a large cotton-spinning population and establishment were far from being the best surroundings for these children, when they were obliged to leave each evening the new surroundings which I had created for them during the day.

These children, without the slightest merit on their parts, were of necessity made good in their tempers, manners, and habits,—wise in their conduct to each other, and to all around them,—and they formed by far the happiest population, for a succession of years, that I ever witnessed in any part of the world. It was happiness never seen to be enjoyed for so long a period before or since.

And yet, by the same true principles and simple means, wisely and peaceably applied to practice, might the population of the world be made more happy throughout all future generations.

And to effect this result requires now only common sense and common honesty in the nations of the more civilised portions of the earth.

Let not these nations longer complain of their governments. For governments are nothing without the nation ; and were there common sense in the nations, governments would act according to the will of the nation.

It was by carefully watching the progress and results of these new proceedings at New Lanark for upwards of a quarter of a century, that a practical knowledge of the science of society was forced upon me, so that I saw clearly the practical measures by which the population of the world could be yet made better, wiser, and happier, than these New Lanark children had been made. Yes,—even the population of the world, through all future ages ; and yet not one will ever be entitled to individual merit.

The animate and inanimate surroundings will effect this great result ;—a result which will commence as soon as society can be made to comprehend the now mysterious power of surroundings made on principles in accordance with nature, and which would be as simple and as certain as all nature's operations.

Why—now that the road is opened, the path known, and the

results certain—should man continue to be made an ignorant, poor, wicked, and miserable animal? Why? Because, with his false training and education, he is filled from his birth with prejudices of class, creed, sex, country, and colour, against his own happiness and the happiness of his race.

Knowing this, after I had ascertained the fact that man when enlightened could make man happy, I was impelled to direct all my means and powers of body and mind to endeavour to arouse men from their false mode of thinking and acting and of treating each other. I commenced by publishing my "*New Views of Society*," in four essays, which were published under the sanction of Lord Liverpool's administration, in 1812 and 1813.

By calling the attention of parliament to the cruelty and injustice practised on children by employing them, at so early an age and for so unreasonable a period per day, in cotton, flax, wool, and silk mills.

By holding large public meetings in the city of London in 1817, which caused universal excitement in governments and people.

By attending and memorialising the Congress of Sovereigns in Aix-la-Chappelle in 1818.

By encouraging and essentially aiding Lancaster and Bell in their preliminary attempts to educate the poor of Great Britain.

By visiting the learned institutions, the leading learned men of Europe, and their governments, from 1818 to 1821.

By holding great public meetings in the Rotunda at Dublin, and in the large towns throughout Ireland,—visiting at the same time the most liberal members among the Irish aristocracy, with the Protestant and Catholic hierarchy of their respective creeds, in 1822-23.

In 1824 I first went to the United States, and purchased New Harmony from the Rappites. But I found the population of the States far too undeveloped at that period for the practice of a full true and social life—of that life foreshadowed by Jesus Christ, the great medium and reformer of His day. This establishment, however, at New Harmony, afforded to myself and my family much valuable experience and assistance towards attaining my ultimate object,—which has been, and is, to change the present system of society over the world, in spirit, principle, and practice.

A favourable preparation for my reception had been made in the minds of the leading statesmen of the United States by one of the late Presidents—John Quincey Adams. When he was ambassador from the United States to our Court, I had published my four essays on the Formation of Character and a New View of Society; and he was so much taken with the important practical truths contained in these essays, that on his departure for the United States he requested to have copies of this work for his cabinet, the governors of each State, and others of the

most advanced statesmen of that day,—assuring me that they
should be faithfully put into their hands; and which on my
arriv.l in the United States I found had been done.

This, with the notoriety acquired through my public meetings
in London in 1817, and in Dublin in 1822-23, with the then
well-known successful experiment at New Lanark in Scotland,
gave me an introduction to all the first men throughout the
Union, and a welcome reception from them. Consequently, in
1825 I visited president John Adams, in the ninetieth year of his
age,—Jefferson, in his eighty-second,—and Maddison, in his
seventy-fourth year.

From these men, full of the spirit of the founders of the Constitution of the Republic of the United States, and signers of
the Declaration of Independence, I obtained their most matured
thoughts and the latest experience of their lives ; and from each
a strong and cordial approval of my " *New Views of Society*,"
which they had read and carefully studied.

With Mr. Jefferson I spent four days in close communion upon
the two systems of society ; and he afterwards openly avowed
himself a thorough disciple of the principles,—but added—" I
" have not had sufficient experience in practice to know how to
" apply them to effect the change which you contemplate."

With Mr. Maddison I spent eight days ;—four on my way to
visit his friend Mr. Jefferson, and four on returning from my
visit. The result was similar with Mr. and Mrs. Maddison ;—
the latter taking a deep interest in our investigations.

With Mr. Munroe, who was President on my first arrival in
the States, our intimacy was that of brothers ; the White House
was always open to me, when others were excluded. He,—his
cabinet,—the senate,—and all the judges of the supreme court
of the United States, attended my lectures, given from the
speaker's chair in the house of representatives, when Henry Clay
was the speaker, and who offered me the use of it. In these
lectures I fully advocated the new views of society, and they
were cordially received by audiences which seldom, if ever, so
attended the lectures of a private individual.

The present Earl of Derby, and his travelling companions,
Lord Waincliffe, Mr. Labouchere, and Mr. Dennison, were also
present.

Soon after, this same party were also present with me at the
inauguration dinner by the new President, John Quincy Adams,
who, during his presidency and to the end of his life, was most
friendly to me ; and when he became member of the house of
representatives, made a motion and strongly advocated it, for my
views of society to be fairly and fully investigated by Congress.

I had two modes open to me ;—one to have the motion made
by my son, Robert Dale Owen, who was then a popular member
of the house, and of the Democratic party, and to have the

majority of the house with them,—the other to give it to the ex-President and experienced statesman, John Quincy Adams, with the certainty of losing it. I preferred the latter mode, that I might have put upon the records of the house the testimony in favour of my views of one so experienced, sincere, honest, and deservedly esteemed by the best men of the Republic. Mr. Adams advocated the subject with great ability and earnestness ; but the motion was lost, as anticipated, although the minority was large and respectable. And my object was gained ; for even then the population of the union was too undeveloped, and made too selfish by their false education, for a system true in principle and too pure in practice for dollars and cents to comprehend. And it would have long so remained, had not the new spiritual manifestations come to the aid of those who, from the pure principles of charity and love for humanity under all its varieties, desire to reform the world. And to reform it, not by violence and in anger, but in peace and with wise foresight, so as not to injure any party or individual by the change,—although that change must be entire and complete in principle and practice.

After lecturing in several cities in the United States, I returned to Great Britain in the latter end of 1825.

In 1826 I returned again to the United States, and on my way to New Harmony in Indiana lectured again in the principal places through which I passed, and communicated much with the President, and also freely with Henry Clay, Mr. Calhoun, and Mr. Crawford—all candidates for the presidency.

In 1827 I came to Great Britain to prepare my partners for my leaving New Lanark, which I had much wished to do. But they were then unprepared with a successor, and I very reluctantly consented to continue until Mr. Charles Walker, who was to succeed me, could gain the requisite experience.

In 1828 I returned again to the United States, taking more of my family with me to New Harmony, which I intended for their future home.

In this case also, in going and returning by the route of New Orleans,—instead of New York, as formerly,—I lectured in that city and others ; and before my return to Great Britain in 1829 I made an engagement with the Rev. Alexander Campbell, the celebrated baptist minister, leader of the Campbellites sect, to discuss with him in the city of Cincinnati his religious views and my dissent from them in favour of my " New Views of society." The discussion to take place on a day fixed twelve months from the time of making this arrangement. And this year proved to be unexpectedly one of the most active of my life.

I had now two homes and two countries. On my arrival in Great Britain I was solicited by Mr. Rocafuesti, the Mexican minister then in London, to apply to the Mexican government, then a Republic, for the government of the provinces of Cohahuila and Texas. He and several other of the South American ministers were desirous that I should introduce my practical mode of governing as an example in Mexico, in the expectation that it would be afterwards extensively imitated, as were my new infant and other schools, on the then new principle of instruction by sensible signs, familiar conversations between the teacher and the taught, and without punishment or the fear of it.

Respecting this application to the Mexican government for the government of the provinces of Cohahuila and Texas, then belonging to the Mexican Republic, I wrote and printed a memorial, which I presented to our government and to the Ambassador of the United States in London, and both gave me great encouragement to proceed, and I determined to make the voyage to Mexico, and to negociate personally with that government.

Mr. Rocafuesti sent my memorial with various letters of recommendation of my views from several influential official parties, and I had strong letters from our government, especially from the Duke of Wellington, to Mr., now Sir Richard Pakenham, our Ambassador in Mexico, to use his influence, then very powerful, with that government, to the utmost, to forward my objects; and this he did with the most earnest good will, and, still more, with unexpected success. I had also letters from the American Embassy in London to Mr. Poinsett, the then highly talented American Minister in Mexico.

In a month after my memorial and letters had been forwarded to the Mexican government, I commenced the voyage in the British Packet ship for the West Indies and Vera Cruz and Tampico,— Captain James commander. My only cabin companion was Captain Deare, a most pleasant and excellent companion to as far as Jamaica, where upon his arrival he was immediately appointed to the Grasshopper—I believe a ten gun brig. Upon arriving safe at the Island of Jamaica I found there my excellent friend and most kind neighbour from Scotland, Admiral Fleming, with his fleet, having the command of the West India station; and he received me with open arms.

(To be continued.)

London :—Published by the Author at 16, Great Windmill Street, Haymarket : and sold by J. Clayton and Son, 223, Piccadilly ; Holyoake, 147, Fleet Street ; Truelove, 240, Strand; Goddard, 14, Great Portland Street, Cavendish Square; Farrer, 21, John Street, Fitzroy Square ; and all Booksellers.

ROBERT OWEN'S
MILLENNIAL GAZETTE;

EXPLANATORY OF THE PRINCIPLES AND PRAC-
TICES BY WHICH, IN PEACE, WITH TRUTH,
HONESTY, AND SIMPLICITY, THE NEW
EXISTENCE OF MAN UPON THE
EARTH MAY BE EASILY AND
SPEEDILY COMMENCED.

" The character of Man is formed *for* him, and *not by* him !"

No. 4.] MAY 15th, 1856. [PRICE 6D.

NARRATIVE OF PROCEEDINGS.

(Continued from No. 3.)

Admiral Fleming having the command of the fleet at this period at this station was to me a most fortunate circumstance, in aiding my intended proceedings in Mexico. He introduced me to the authorities in the Island,—invited the officers of the fleet to meet me at dinner,—and in the most friendly manner urged me to say whether he could in any way assist to promote the object of my voyage. I told him I had two difficulties in my way unprovided for. I had abundant letters of introduction and recommendation to all the authorities in Mexico except the ecclesiastical,—and I was uncertain whether I should find a vessel at Vera Cruz, on my return from Mexico, to be in time to convey me to New Orleans, to enable me to fulfil my engagement to meet the Rev Mr. Campbell for our discussion on the day appointed in Cincinnati. The Admiral replied—" I can effectually " assist you in the first, and perhaps when the time comes I may " also assist you in the second. Since the revolution in Mexico " there is but the Bishop of Puebla remaining, and he is now at " the head of all ecclesiastical affairs. I have long known him " intimately, having conveyed him some years since, before he " was made Bishop, from Old Spain to Mexico, and I will give " you a letter to him, which will effectually answer your purpose, " and it may be that I can send a ten gun brig with seventy men " to Vera Cruz, to wait your return and convey you from Vera " Cruz to New Orleans. A larger vessel cannot with safety pass " over the sand bar at the entrance to Belize going to New " Orleans."

The packet for Vera Cruz had to sail the third morning at

four A.M. The Admiral came at that hour with me in his long boat to put me on board the packet, and to take farewell of me, wishing, with all the officers of the fleet, great success in my novel undertaking. Without my knowledge until we were out at sea, the Admiral had put a large hamper of the choicest fruits of the Island on board for me ; and these were a great treat to the captain of the packet, his officers, and myself, during the remainder of the voyage to Vera Cruz, when many remained.

The seeds of the " New Views of Society" were soon in the Island and among the officers of the fleet.

The packet had to call and leave the mail for St. Domingo, and I went on shore with the captain ; and some of the British merchants who came to meet the boat at its landing, hearing the captain calling me by name, enquired if I was from New Lanark in Scotland. They said they had been present at my Great Meetings in London in 1817. They would like to introduce me to the authorities of the town, and to show me whatever I wished to see as long as I could remain. The captain remained as long as the service permitted, and we were much gratified by the attention of these gentlemen, taking us to all that was curious to us as strangers in the island. I was much surprised with their good taste in dress, their kind and polite manners to each other, the cleanliness of their persons, and their deference to strangers. I left some copies of my *New Views* among the British merchants, who appeared anxious to have them.

On arrival at Vera Cruz, preparation had been made to receive me and to forward my departure from so dangerous a place with the least possible delay ; and early the next morning I was on my way to the city of Mexico, in a litera drawn by two mules, and accompanied by two Mexican muleteers, each on a mule, and these men were to convey me safe to Jalapa. They knew nothing of the English language, and I as little of the Spanish, and yet we had a pleasant, safe, and interesting journey of several days, in which the men taught me as much Spanish as I could teach them English, and we became good friends by the end of the journey. They proved to be faithful and attentive muleteers, and conducted me safely through what I afterwards learned was a very hazardous journey—the road being infested with robbers and military marauders.

The ascent from Vera Cruz to Jalapa being about 4000 feet, it is necessary for travellers going from Vera Cruz to the city of Mexico, to remain some days at Jalapa, to accustom the lungs to breathe an air so much lighter, before proceeding to the yet higher plain on which the city of Mexico is situated. On arrival at Jalapa, I found the governor of Vera Cruz and several other travellers waiting there to take coaches onward towards Mexico ; and after four or five days I induced them, though afraid, to proceed, (the governor being opposed to the existing government,) and to the surprise of all, on entering Perote, we found ourselves in the midst of Santa Anna's army of 1500 men. This general was the commander-in-chief of the Mexican forces. On discovering our position, the governor and his friends exclaimed, " We are prisoners—what shall we do ?" They were greatly alarmed. I said—" Put a good face upon " this circumstance, and go at once to the general, and ask for " an escort forward, on account of danger to proceed unpro- " tected." " Yes," they said, " but who will venture to go to " him ?" I said—" if no one else will go, I will." Then one or two, not of the governor's party, said they would accompany me.

I was introduced to the general as an Englishman going in haste to the city of Mexico on important business. He received me politely, and enquired my object. I said—" I am going in " haste to the city of Mexico to communicate with the govern- " ment, and I wish an escort to Puebla." " When will you want " it ? " To morrow morning at five o'clock." " You shall have " it." Seeing his frankness, I. said—" General, where will you " be about six weeks hence ? I do not ask the question from idle " curiosity,—but I expect to be then on my return, and to have an " important communication to make to you." " I shall then be " at Jalapa," was his immediate reply, " and will be glad to see " you." The escort of six mounted cavalry was punctual at the hour, and we proceeded with them safely to Puebla. But what became of the governor and his party I know not, I suppose he retreated quietly from Perote.

On arriving at Puebla, where our escort left us, I presented my letters from Admiral Fleming to the bishop, with whom I had a long and very interesting interview.

The government of Mexico was at this time a very liberal one, and much opposed to ecclesiastical domination ; and I found the bishop was under great alarm for his own position. He had before the revolution an income of 120,000 dollars, and the government had unmercifully reduced his income so low as 80,000 dollars, and he did not know what they would do next to him, for he was now left the only bishop in all Mexico. He said what power and influence he had should be willingly used in my favor, on account of his great friendship for his old friend Admiral Fleming ; and I was again to visit the bishop on my return from the city of Mexico.

As my proceedings in this city of the ancient Mexicans were of a novel character for an uneducated, unpopular, unpatronised, and much opposed individual on account of his heterodox opinions against the present system of society, I must be somewhat less brief than I wish, to make the subject understood.

On my arrival in this city I was received by, and during my stay remained with, Mr. Exter, then one of the most influential and talented British residents in Mexico. He was much in the confidence of the government,—on good terms with the officials, domestic and foreign,—and much trusted and respected by all parties.

On the day of my arrival I called upon Mr. Pakenham our ambassador, and presented my letters from our government to him. Upon opening these letters, he said—" I am instructed to " give you all the aid in my power to forward your object with " this government, and I am very willing to do whatever I can " to expedite your proceedings." I said time was of importance to me, as I had an engagement to fulfil in the United States. He said he would see the President of the Republic that day, and would endeavour to obtain for me an early interview with him. At three P.M., on the same day, Mr. Pakenham called upon me at Mr. Exter's, to say he had seen the President and arranged an interview for me with him at twelve o'clock the next day, and he added—" as the President does not speak English, and you do " not know the Spanish language, I will accompany you, intro- " duce you to the President, and, if you have no objection, will " be interpreter between you." I said I was greatly indebted for so much kindness and attention.

The next day Mr. Pakenham called upon me at the hour appointed, and upon our arrival at the palace we were immediately introduced to the President. Mr. Pakenham opened the conference by a speech of considerable length, but which, being in Spanish, was while in delivery a blank to me. Mr. Pakenham, after our interview, said that in this speech he had explained what I had done through my previous life to promote the best interests of society, and especially what I had done to educate and govern the population of New Lanark in Scotland, and added the strong recommendation of our government to the Mexican government, to grant the object of my application to it, and then added from himself more, I fear, than I was entitled to.

The President replied, as Mr. Pakenham then explained to me, that his government had received by the previous mail, a month before, my memorial and many letters of recommendation so strongly in my favour, that he and all the members of the government regretted they could not give me the government of the provinces of Cohahuila and Texas, because the governor was elected by the population of the provinces,—but that the government had reserved to itself the full jurisdiction over one hundred and fifty miles in breadth along the whole frontier between the United States and Mexico, from the Pacific to the Gulf of Mexico, about two thousand miles in length, and that his government, after due consideration, had " come to the determination to offer " the government of this district to Mr. Owen, for him to establish " within it his government of peace, to be an example, as he says, " to all other nations."

When Mr. Pakenham explained to me this extraordinary offer, I was certainly taken by surprise; but immediately recollecting myself, and at a glance seeing what would be essentially necessary at the commencement of such a task, I requested Mr. Pakenham to thank the President and his government for their great liberality in making me so magnificent an offer, and for the trust and confidence in me which it indicated ; but to state that one obstacle presented itself, which, if not removed, would prevent my success, and which, without its removal, would frustrate all my intended proceedings to establish a model peace government. This obstacle arose from the Catholic religion being the only religion permitted by law to be established in the Republic ; and in the government which I knew could alone give peace to any population, there must be, not merely toleration, but full civil and religious liberty,—and unless that obstacle could be removed, it would be a failure, and would be useless for me to commence the task which otherwise I would willingly undertake.

This reply and explanation was given to the President by Mr. Pakenham,—when, to my yet greater surprise, the President said—" We thought this would be made an objection by Mr. " Owen, and we are prepared as a government to propose to the " next Congress to pass a law to place the religion of Mexico " upon the same base of liberty as it now exists in the United " States of North America." This being explained to me by Mr. Pakenham, I replied " that when that law was passed I would " willingly accept the government of the extensive district so " liberally offered to me."

After some general and complimentary conversation, this extraordinary conference terminated, apparently much to the satisfaction of the parties engaged in it.

I was now introduced to all the Mexican authorities as the future governor of this new kingdom of peace,—to the four ministers in the city,—and especially to Mr. Poinsett, the American ambassador and the celebrated American statesman,—and to the chief British residents and merchants. During my stay of five or six weeks in this capital, I received from all these parties kindness, attention, and hospitality, in which Mr. Pakenham, the British legation, consul, and merchants, were unceasingly prominent.

I knew that up to this period there had been a disagreeable, distrustful, and most unpleasant feeling between the British and the American United States governments, and a consequent jealousy between the officials of both countries in whatever foreign country they might be accredited. My great desire was to terminate this feeling, and to create a good understanding, and, if possible, a well-founded cordial friendship between them, as I knew ought to exist when their interests were so united, their language the same, and their relationship so combined.

Finding Mr. Poinsett to be a statesman of enlarged views, of high talents, great experience, ready to receive new ideas, and most favourable to my proposed establishment of a kingdom of peace between the two republics,—I stated to him what I thought a false and most injurious policy between his government and the British.   They were evidently now secret and almost open enemies, while it was their interest to be good friends, and to be cordially united. He said he was fully aware of the false position into which the two governments had drifted, and he would much like to see it changed.   I then said,—" As you see this subject " in the same light as I have long viewed it in,—if you will give " me letters to general Jackson and Mr. Van Buren, your " President and his Secretary, expressive of these views, I will " return home by Washington, and will see what I can effect " between the two governments, which ought to be one in feeling " and interest, for then they could influence the world for good." He readily assented, and after interesting and confidential conversation he gave me the letters I had requested.

About the time I anticipated to finish the object of my visit to Mexico, I received a packet from Admiral Fleming, informing me that he had sent the ten gun brig Fairy, Captain Blair, to Vera Cruz, to wait my convenience, and to carry me to New Orleans. The Druid, fifty gun ship, Captain Drury, also came at the same time ; and there was an invitation from the captain for me to remain on board the Druid until I should sail from Vera Cruz.

Pending the meeting of the Mexican Congress to pass the bill for religious freedom throughout the republic, upon the passing of which I was to return to Mexico and commence my government, I had arranged with Mr. Exter, my kind and most hospitable host, to take charge of my new affairs,—to aid him in which he had the promised assistance of Mr. Poinsett and some other friends, in addition to Mr. Pakenham, whose aid to me in this business was most valuable.

Leaving the city of Mexico, I proceeded to Puebla, being assured by the Mexican government that I should meet no obstacle on my journey to Vera Cruz.

On arriving at Puebla I called according to promise to visit the bishop, and was again cordially received. I was accompanied from Mexico by an interpreter, whom I had engaged to go with me to Vera Cruz, and I had by note asked the bishop if I should bring my interpreter with me on my second visit to him after my return, which was to be of a more confidential character than the first, which was more introductory and complimentary. He preferred to have my interpreter present. I told him of my proceedings in the city of Mexico, and of my intention to establish a kingdom of peace between the two republics, from the Gulf of Mexico to the Pacific Ocean—(and this would have included the best part of Texas and California) ; that the government were to pass an act through Congress to put the religion of the country on the same liberal principles as it was placed upon in the United States ; and that I much desired to reconcile the Heads of the Catholic and Protestant churches ; and I requested to know if he knew the real character of the present Pope at Rome.

To all that I said he was most attentive, and anxious to hear all I had to say, and he professed to be most desirous to assist me to the extent of his power, and said he not only knew the character of the Pope, but had been personally upon the best and most familiar terms of friendship with him, until he left the old world for the new, to be placed at the head of ecclesiastical affairs in Mexico. Hearing this, I asked him whether on my return to commence the government of the country which had been so unexpectedly offered to me, he would go from me, as a missionary and messenger of peace to Rome, and endeavour to persuade the Pope to agree to enter upon negotiations with the Church of England, to reconcile the two religions so far as to be on friendly terms, and not to oppose each other, but to allow each to proceed unmolested by the other, and neither to teach nor encourage feelings of repulsion between them,—and both to inculcate on all occasions the pure spirit of universal love and charity. The bishop seemed greatly pleased with this proposal, and said he would go, and would be highly gratified by being selected for so important and God-like a commission.

After much conversation on this and other subjects connected with these proposed changes, I left him apparently as well satisfied with our interviews as myself. I then proceeded on my journey to the coast, and on arriving at Jalapa found Santa Anna with his army, according to his promise to me when at Perote. I immediately called upon him, and was cordially received. He had been informed of my proceedings in the city, and wished me to explain fully the principles and practices which I intended to adopt. I told him I had written in manuscript the principles and practices in the most condensed form I could then put them, and if he wished I would bring them from my hotel at any time he would appoint, and we would consider them, principle by principle, and point by point in the practice ; and he named an early hour the next morning.

On attending at the time appointed, he was prepared with three intelligent looking officers of his army, all of whom spoke the English language correctly and fluently, and were prepared to hear what I had to explain to them. I had prepared twelve principles or sections for our investigation and discussion.

The first was the necessity of our nature to believe whatever was made to produce the strongest conviction upon our mind, and that consequently there could be neither merit nor demerit in belief or disbelief, because these were not acts of our will.

This statement aroused all their faculties into lively action, and Santa Anna especially combated the principle with great talent and ingenuity for a considerable period, and he was well seconded by his companions in arms. But the facts in support of the statement were too strong to be ultimately resisted, and at length he said—"You are right. It is true. Proceed to the "next." And we went with the same results through all the principles which I advocated.

By degrees this discussion created the deepest interest in Santa Anna and his friends, and at the conclusion their enthusiasm was at a great height, and Santa Anna said—" We have opposed you "to the extent of our powers. We acknowledge you are right, "and the great practical importance of what you have advocated. "I wish those principles were printed in Spanish, and circulated "throughout the republic. I am a thorough convert to them; "and whether I shall be at the head of the army or of the go- "vernment," (which he was afterwards,) "you may command "me to aid you to the extent of my power." He then invited me to dine with him; but I was pressed for time to proceed to my engagement with Mr. Campbell in Cincinnati; and the ship was awaiting my arrival on the day I had named. I there- fore excused myself on that plea; but I was very much pleased with the frank, straightforward manner of Santa Anna, and am convinced that, could he have gained sufficient power to act independently of the church and of factions in the state, he would have governed the republic better than any other Mexican I had been introduced to while in the city of Mexico; and I was introduced to every prominent character there at the time.

On my arriving at Vera Cruz, the long boat of the *Druid* was waiting to take me to that ship. The surf was high, and our boat at starting was nearly swamped. Dinner was prepared on board the *Druid*. Captain Blair of the *Fairy* had been invited to be introduced to me, and all the officers said they had instructions from Admiral Fleming to attend in every particular to my wishes. Captain Blair then said—" I regret that the cabin for the captain "in a ten gun brig, with seventy men, arms, ammunition, and "provisions, is necessarily so small that it admits of very poor "accommodation for two persons; but if you can put up with a ham- "mock for your bed, and such day room as it will afford, you will "be welcome to half the cabin accomodations during our voyage "to New Orleans, where I am directed to convey you as early as "possible." I was too happy to be so conveyed. Captain Drury, to whose kindness I was much indebted, put me on board the *Fairy* next morning early, and we sailed for our port, meeting on our way two severe north westers; but we passed the bar, and arrived in safety at New Orleans, where I took leave of Captain Blair and his officers, from all of whom I experienced the most considerate attention, and from whom I parted with reluctance.

I immediately set out for Cincinnati, and arrived there three days before the time which had been appointed just twelve months before. Mr. Campbell was there one day before my arrival.

Great formal preparation was made for this discussion between us, which continued for eight days, morning and evening. I had to oppose all the prejudices of the day; but the audience, brought from all parts of the Union, conducted themselves in the most admirable manner during its continuance. I had nothing to complain of,—except that Mr. Campbell, contrary to agreement, put the question unexpectedly at the conclusion,—whether they would continue to support Christianity. Every one knew what they must say; but I found throughout, day by day, that the feelings of the audience were much with me. The discussion fully answered all my purpose, and truth from that occasion, upon many important points, became widely spread abroad in the States and in Europe.

I remained several days afterwards in Cincinnati, to transact business, which occasioned me to pass daily from one extremity of the city to the other; and, considering the heterodox principles I had so openly advocated, it was surprising to me to experience the profound respect paid to me as I passed along the streets.

When this business was finished I hastened on to Washington, to commence my attempt to reconcile the two greatest nations in the world, who had been for years, up to this period, (1830,) opposing each other everywhere with very hostile, jealous, and rival feelings. I immediately waited on Mr. Van Buren, the then secretary of state, who had been by Mr. Poinsett's letters prepared favourably to listen to me. I explained my views of the real interests of the two nations, and day by day for about ten days we met and talked over all the objects of difference then existing between the governments, and I endeavoured to point out how easily, both parties being willing, the whole might be finally settled to the benefit of both nations. Mr. Van Buren said he had communicated my views to the President, and that now both agreed to the policy which I recommended, and that the General wished I would dine with him the next day. I did so,—meeting Mr. Van Buren and several relatives of the President.

After dinner, at a signal from the General, his relatives withdrew, and left Mr. Van Buren and myself alone with him. He then said—" Mr. Owen, your government imagines I am opposed " to them—but it is not so. I wish to be on friendly terms " with them and the British nation, knowing how much the " United States and Great Britain will be benefited by a well " understood cordial union; and if your government will fairly " meet us half way, we will soon adjust all differences now be-" tween us." I said—" I think I may promise on the part of " the British government that it will frankly meet you half way, " and I am sure the nation will be well pleased that it should be " so." He then became very familiar—explained in the most open manner his home and foreign policy, often in the exact words used to explain his views in the succeeding annual President's message to congress. It was then arranged that Mr. Van Buren should give me letters to the United States ministers in London and Paris, instructing them to follow the advice which I should give to them after I had seen Lord Aberdeen, the then foreign secretary in England.

With these letters I returned to England, and asked an interview with Lord Aberdeen, which he appointed for the next day. I explained fully to him what I had done to prepare for a cordial reconciliation with the United States, and what I had promised on the part of our government. He promptly said—" Mr. Owen, " I highly approve of the policy you recommend, and of what " you have done. If the American government will meet us " half way, we will meet it in the same spirit." I said—" I have " instructions with me to the United States' minister, from his " government, if I found you willing, to enter at once in this " spirit to settle by immediate negotiation all existing differences." He added—" I am quite ready to meet Mr. M'Lane on these " conditions."

I then went to Mr. M'Lane, the then United States' ambassador,—gave him the instructions from his government,—told him I had seen Lord Aberdeen, that the coast was clear for immediate proceedings,—and recommended him at once to commence negotiations, and to be sure to leave no point of difference unsettled, and if any difficulty arose that could not be settled between him and Lord Aberdeen, to inform me and I would endeavour to remove it. No difference of the kind did arise. Both governments became cordially friendly, and so continued from that time for several years, without any estrangement of feeling, and I believe until the dispute arose about the limits of Oregon.

On my arrival in England I expected Mr. Exter, my kind and talented host while I remained in the city of Mexico, and who was to bring important dispatches and transact much preparatory business for the government I was to undertake. When I left him he was full of these matters, and in close connection with the Mexican government. My first news was, that shortly after I had quitted the city, the government despatches were given to him, and he rode on horseback hastily down to Vera Cruz, where he speedily took his passage to England; but during his short stay in Vera Cruz, being over-fatigued with his rapid travelling, he caught the fever of the place, and died of the black vomit on the third day of his voyage.

I also soon after received intelligence that the Mexican government, faithful to its promise to me, brought into Congress the bill for religious liberty over the Republic,—but the ecclesiastical powers, hearing what was intended, employed the priesthood to exert all its means to oppose this measure in congress, and they succeeded in obtaining a majority against it ; and the liberal government, so friendly to me, was, in consequence of this defeat, out of power for eighteen months.

Thus were terminated the measures which had been taken to establish a kingdom of peace between the Republic of Mexico and the United States, and which, if they had come to a more successful issue, would have given a very different direction to the history of the Republics. The Texian war would not have occurred, nor the forcible dismemberment of the Mexican Republic.

It was my intention to have peopled this new and in many places wild district, with an intelligent and moral working class from the British Islands and Europe,—great numbers being anxious at this period to commence a true communistic life, which I intended gradually to introduce into this new social government of peace. These from Europe would also have been joined by multitudes from the United States, and by many from the old Mexican States.

It was my intention also to have made peace with all the Indian tribes, and to have invited them to settle, at first in their own way, within the new territory, and by degrees to accustom them to the true family commonwealth arrangements, for which they are already in some measure prepared.

It would have been a curious and interesting experiment for the world ; for I should have created a new and superior characte out of this heterogeneous mass,—with all of whom, under a system of strict justice and impartiality, administered in obvious kindness, to promote the happiness of all, I could not have failed of ultimate success.

However, it was not to be ; and other and very different measures were opening before me.

My early acquaintance with the working classes enabled me to see the downward progress they were making, in proportion as chemical discoveries and mechanical inventions increased to diminish the general value of their labour.

I noticed the increasing power that wealth, especially in the manufacturing districts, was acquiring over them, and how, gradually, the mass of them were sinking into real slavery, while retaining the name of servitude.

I was conscious that these proceedings must increase the demoralisation of all classes, and lead to social convulsions; and often did I endeavour to forewarn the governments of Europe of the danger which must arise from the continuance of these sufferings of the working classes.

The smallest measures proposed for their relief, and to stay this downward course, were strongly resisted by the wealthy and master class.

My Bill to give some small amelioration to the children and

others employed in mills and manufactories was resisted by the House of Commons, under the influence of mill-owners, for four years; and when it was passed, was so mutilated and altered from the original bill, which I had introduced through the first Sir Robert Peel, that it was of little or no value; and from 1819 to this day they have been contending about this "ten hours" bill.

Seeing how little the true interests of society could be understood by any class or party in the state, I concluded that no permanent benefit could be attained until the mass of the people could be better instructed, and enabled to comprehend their own position, and to understand that the progress of new inventions would ultimately benefit all society permanently.

I then devoted the next fifteen years to instruct, by writings in newspapers and other periodicals, and by lecturing, in Europe and America, the masses in the old and new world.

I was, however, much opposed in my progress in England by that warm-hearted, well intentioned, energetic, wrong-headed, late leader of the violent Democratic part of the working classes, Feargus O'Connor, M.P. He laboured to give them power, without the necessary knowledge to use it wisely; and I desired to give them power through knowledge, that they might make a right use of it; and I hope the fifteen years of such instruction have now given them power, through knowledge, sufficient to enable them to assist all classes to gain, in peace and with wise foresight, the rights of humanity for all of every rank and condition over the world. For all—prince and peasant—are grievous sufferers by the continuance of this false and evil system of society.

I published several works and wrote many articles for the newspapers, all bearing on the great change in society which I had ever in view.

During this period, and while Prince Metternich was the most experienced, influential, and leading statesman in Europe, I went to Vienna, in 1837, with strong recommendatory letters to him from Prince Esterhazy, the then Austrian ambassador in London, and who had known me and my proceedings from 1816, and was always kind and friendly to me.

On my way I visited Paris, and had friendly communications with the French government, under Louis Philippe, to whom in 1818 I had been introduced in an especial manner by His Royal Highness the late Duke of Kent.

While in Paris I gave a public lecture in the Hotel de Ville, to a crowded and most attentive audience, and as I proceeded in English, the well known and talented M. Considerant, a leading disciple of Fourier, translated what I said to the audience, and it was, even in Paris in those days, well received. I was made also a member of two of the public societies of Paris, and had the privilege of a sitting in the Royal Academy. But the government expressed some uneasiness at my increasing popularity in Paris.

From Paris I went to Munich, where Lord Erskine was then our ambassador, and to whom I explained the object of my journey, and who received me with great kindness and attention ; and I had an opportunity of disseminating my " New Views" among the leading men and authorities in that city

The king was absent at the time, at the beautiful summer residence of the court, and I took it on my way to Vienna. The residence of Berchesgadden is in one of the most beautiful districts I have seen in any part of the world.

Immediately on my arrival at the hotel, I sent a note to His Majesty, informing him of the object of my journey, and requesting an interview. This note was sent late in the evening. Early the next morning a messenger brought me an autograph from His Majesty, saying " although he was very much occu-" pied with state matters, he could not allow one so distin-" guished," (an idea quite new to me,) " to pass his residence " without seeing him, and he would have pleasure from the visit." No time for the appointment being mentioned in the note, I en-quired of the messenger if he knew at what hour I should go to His Majesty. He said—" Immediately,—and I have come to " conduct you to him." It was early morning—between seven and eight o'clock—and I was going to put on my hat to proceed with him,—but he said—" You cannot see His Majesty in that " coat "—(it was a morning frock coat), I had a dress coat in my portmanteau in the room near at hand, and I said I would change my coat and proceed to the palace. With great simpli-city he said—" I will wait until you make the change." I opened the portmanteau,—took out the coat,—and effected the change while he was present ; and then we proceeded to the chapel, where the king and his court were at mass.

We waited until the king returned to his apartments, and I was then introduced to him by the person who had brought the note, and who had come to conduct me to the palace. I was kindly received by His Majesty, to whom I explained my " New Views," and the benefits which would be derived by society from their introduction into practice. He requested I would put them in the form of a protocol, and send it to him before I left Berch-tolsgaden for Vienna. After about an hour's conference I went to my hotel,—prepared an explanation of my views in what His Majesty called a protocol,—took it to the palace,—and enquired for the person who had brought me the note in the morning from the king. I was told he would come to me immediately, and I had not waited more than two minutes in the apartment to which I had been shown, when he came, and I gave him the paper for His Majesty. He said he would immediately take it to him, for he knew His Majesty wished to have it.

Observing the attendants paying, as I thought, extraordinary attention to this person, who had been so familiar and kind to me, I enquired as I was going out who and what he was, and to my great surprise the reply was—" He is the Prince of Tour and " Texas, the King's Prime Minister."

The next morning I set out immediately after breakfast towards the Austrian frontier, about ten miles distant. I was travelling alone in an open carriage, driven by a postillion from the hotel where I had stopt; and when about three miles on my way through a most enchanting district, I passed a gentleman on foot, who as I passed took off his hat, which salutation I returned, as to an unknown stranger; but I observed the driver make a most reverential and long continued obeisance, and I asked him who the gentleman was. He said it was the King:— and I immediately stopped the carriage, alighted, and walked back about two hundred yards, and apologised to his majesty for not knowing him alone on foot so early in the morning. He said the Queen would overtake him soon, and that he was enjoying the beauty of the scene around him on so fine a morning. He had received my protocol, which contained much that was important, and which he would study with interest. After we had walked and talked for some time, admiring the unique scenery around us, he said he would not keep me longer from my journey, for I should be long detained by the examination of my luggage on entering the Austrian territory. Thanking his majesty for the attention I had received from him, I proceeded.

I was stopped at the Austrian barrier, and the officials were about to take out my luggage and minutely inspect it. I requested them to stop, and took out my dispatch from Prince Esterhazy to Prince Metternich, which the officials took into the office to their superior, and immediately returned with it, and closing up the carriage, very politely requested me to proceed, which I did without an article being touched, and I soon arrived at Nurenberg where there was a great difficulty in finding any one who could speak English. At length, however, a very respectable inhabitant of this fine old city, a publisher of some English works, was discovered, and he came to me, and I found him very intelligent, past the middle age, and well acquainted with all that was deserving of notice by a stranger, and he took me from place to place over the city, and never left me until my departure, except to go home for some of his own English publications, which, with great kindness of manner, he requested I would accept; and we parted like old friends, for I felt much indebted to him for the time he gave me, and the great interest he appeared to take in showing me everything worth seeing; and all parties seemed to pay him much attention. I cannot at this moment recall his name, although I have a lively recollection of his attentions to a mere passing stranger.

Arriving at Vienna over night, I had, according to Austrian regulations, to appear the next morning at the head police office, to say who I was,—where from,—what I came there for,—how long I intended to remain,—how much money I had with me to pay my way,—&c., &c. I accordingly went. I was asked my name, and then what I came for. I said I came to communicate with Prince Metternich. The official smiled, and said—" We " know all about it.—You may stay as long as you like, and do " as you wish." And thus pleasantly was this business over.

I then presented my letter to Prince Metternich, and was received in a friendly manner, and an early interview was appointed, when I was to explain my views and objects.

It must be remembered that at this period Prince Metternich was considered the most experienced and influential statesman in Europe. It was on this account I now visited him, preferring at all times to apply at once to the highest supposed intellect in authority. And it has always been my impression,—and after much experience with all classes this impression is confirmed,—that it will be much easier to reform the world through governments, properly supported by the people, than by any other means. Let the governments of Europe and America be made to see that it will be for their permanent interest and happiness that the population of the world should be taught and governed on true principles and consistent practices, and be assured they will lend their willing assistance and powerful aid to accomplish this ever-to-be desired result. And if the public cannot demonstrate this all important truth to the governments, it has no right to expect their co-operation. The onus, then, is with the public, to give this knowledge in the spirit of kindness and good will to the governments; and if it fails to do so, whatever blame there is in the matter must be attributed to the public. As one of the public I went to Vienna to see and speak the truth to the leading statesman of that day in Europe.

At the appointed interview, there were present with Prince Metternich, Baron Neumann the then secretary of State, and the Prince's private secretary.. The Prince placed himself on one side of a narrow table, and myself immediately opposite to him, so that I could distinctly observe every emotion upon his countenance at the memorial which I read to him, and the effect which my conversation produced on his mind.

I commenced by saying that the memorial I was about to read to him was a continuation of the two memorials which I had presented through Lord Castlereagh to the Congress of Sovereigns assembled in Aix-la-Chappelle in 1818. The Prince immediately said to his private secretary,—" We must have those " memorials. Go and see for them, and bring them to me." In about seven minutes the secretary returned with them. They were the originals, in my own hand writing, with a French translation. I requested to have the originals, and left the translation with the Prince.

I then proceeded, and stated—

That the present *Armies* of Europe required a greater expenditure and waste of valuable power, than, if applied differently and as wisely as they might be, would be sufficient to place Europe permanently in a state of peace and high prosperity.

That the *Ecclesiastical* expenditure, and its waste of valuable physical and mental power, would also, if differently and wisely applied, be sufficient to give high permanent prosperity to the entire population of Europe, and to insure a superior character to each.

That the *Law* expenditure and waste of valuable talent and labour throughout Europe, would, if differently and wisely applied, be sufficient to produce the same results.

That even the *Medical* expenditure and waste of valuable intellectual powers and physical labour, would be sufficient, if differently and wisely applied, to give permanent progress and happiness to Europe.

That these professions, as now applied, were opposed to the well-being, well-doing, health, and happiness, of all of every class, including these professions; and were so contrary to the common feeling and common sense of humanity, that they could not be continued except by the continual action of force and fraud.

That it would be for the lasting benefit and advantage of all governments and peoples, that this system should be as soon as practicable superseded by the new principles and practices which I recommended.

As I proceeded to read this memorial, I watched the impression which it made upon the mind of the Prince, and every sentence seemed to produce the effect which I had intended it should. When I had finished, Baron Neumann arose, and said something little relevant to statements which I had read. The Prince immediately stood up, and with much true dignity in his countenance and manner said—" Gentlemen, I have listened with attention " and deep interest to Mr. Owen's memorial,—and all which he " has stated is perfectly true. It is also true that we govern by " force and fraud—the only mode yet known to governments how " to govern. Here, in Austria, we govern with force and fraud,— " but with as little of both as is sufficient to keep the population " of the different districts peaceable and quiet; and our popula- " tion in Austria have as much enjoyment as this system of force " and fraud will admit." This, at that period, was correct; for the Austrians appeared to me to enjoy themselves more than any population I had seen. The Prince proceeded to say that he knew not how to govern a people except by force and fraud; and requested me to give him in a written document my views as to the changes which I would recommend. Our conversation, then, became more general; but from my whole intercourse with the

Prince, he left the impression strong on my mind, that he wished to govern in the best manner for the happiness of the people, with safety to the government.

I occupied myself in preparing the document requested by the Prince.

In the meantime Prince Esterhazy came from London to Vienna, and he immediately called upon me, and gave me an invitation to visit him in Hungary.

Mr. John McGregor, now M.P. for Glasgow, was then in Vienna, commissioned by our government to make a treaty of commerce with the Austrian government. We were together in the same hotel, and with Mr. McGregor, the American Consul, and myself, we formed a party to dine daily together. I received much valuable knowledge of detail from Mr. McGregor, who possesses more accurate knowledge of the statistics of Europe and America than any one I ever met with, and I was much benefited by his varied communications, and gratified by the interest which this little party took in my proceedings.

After presenting my document to Prince Metternich, and seeing what could be seen in and near Vienna, I hastened to prepare for my departure on my mission to other Courts of Europe.

But in justice to Sir Frederick Lamb, afterwards Lord Bouverie, the brother of our then prime minister, Lord Melbourne, I should have stated that immediately on my arrival in Vienna I communicated to him the object of my journey to Vienna, and he was frank, friendly, and hospitable to me while I remained in that city. I had often interviews with him, to explain more of the details of the change of system which I advocated. He made a dinner party for me, invited the French ambassador and his Lady, with other officials of the leading English families then in Vienna, to meet me, and his kindness far exceeded any expectations or claim I could have for it. He gave me letters on my departure to Lord William Russell, our ambassador then in Berlin, and to our minister then in Dresden,— as I intended to visit both these places.

Before quitting Vienna, and to prevent returning to these subjects, I left Mr. M'Gregor in full treaty with Prince Metternich, with whom he had to negotiate many particulars of detail long after I left him, and I did not meet Mr. M'Gregor again until we met by accident at the Board of Trade, of which he soon became the active secretary,—when he at once exclaimed—" What " did you say or do to Prince Metternich while you were in " Vienna?—for I was with him after your departure almost every " day for many weeks, discussing details of our commercial " treaty with Austria, and he always seemed quite impatient to " get over our business, that we might talk about you and your " New Views for governing society and giving a new character to " the human race, and he seemed infatuated with these subjects."

I regretted much when Mr. M'Gregor informed me that he was going to retire from the Board of Trade to become a member of the House of Commons. It was to leave an office which few, if any one living, could fill with equal efficiency and knowledge of the statistics and trade of Europe and America, to enter a career for which his natural faculties unfitted him, and in which his peculiar manner of speaking in public will ever be an obstacle to his progress and usefulness in parliament. It is to be regretted, as there are so few really practical men in the administration of this country, that his great experience should be so misapplied and lost to the nation. See his official report on the whole affairs of the United States, and others of his official documents respecting our commercial treaties with European states.

To resume my progress to make my views better known among the governments of Europe,—I went from Vienna to Dresden, where I was known by the officials of the court, and especially by the first minister of his Majesty the King of Saxony. Many years before this period I was visited by Baron Just, the long well known and highly esteemed Saxon Ambassador in London. He remained with me some time at Braxfield, my residence near New Lanark, and took much pleasure in minutely examining my proceedings there, and investigating the principles by which such satisfactory results had been produced as he witnessed in practice. He came and left, as many other distinguished foreigners did, expressing admiration at what had been seen, and which far exceeded any expectations they had previously formed of what could be done with such a population and such materials as I had to act upon and with,—and I thought no more of this visit from Baron Just than of hundreds of similar ones. But the Baron informed me before his departure that he was about to leave England and his post as ambassador to the court of St. James's, which he had so long filled. He was now advanced in years, and appeared in all he said and did to be a good, just, and benevolent man, desiring the happiness of his fellow-men in every situation in life.

Some time after his departure, to my surprise I received a packet from the then King of Saxony, inclosing a large gold medal with the likeness of his Majesty on one side, and " for merit" on the reverse, with complimentary letters from his Majesty, the Prime Minister, and Baron Just. These proceedings prepared me a favourable reception with the First Minister of the Crown, and we had several interesting communications. He agreed with me in the truth of the principles which I advocated, and as to the great benefits which they would produce if honestly and consistently carried into practice ; but he said—" I much fear " governments are not yet sufficiently advanced to understand " how to introduce the principles or to act upon them." I agreed with him, but said—" The fault is not theirs. As I desire the

" change; the onus is with me, to adopt measures to enable go-
" vernments to perceive the interest which they have to make
" the change, and until I can do so I must continue to devise
" measure after measure until I can effect this object." He approved of the course which I thus proposed to pursue, and
heartily and kindly wished me full success in my life time,—but
he thought the obstacles in my way were very formidable.

I then went forward to Berlin,—called upon our ambassador,
Lord William Russell,—his brother Lord John being then a
prominent member of the British cabinet,—but Lord William
was at Potsdam with the King. It seemed my card and letters
were immediately forwarded to our ambassador,—for the next
day I had a note from him regretting his absence when I called,
and appointing an immediate interview, as he had returned to
Berlin. I explained the object of my visit to Berlin, with which
Court I had had, through Baron Jacobi, the Prussian Ambassador
in London in 1815·16 and 1817, interesting proceedings, which
resulted in the Prussian national system of education.

I had previously published my four "*Essays on the Formation of Character and New Views of Society.*" This work
being on publication very popular among the higher classes, had
attracted the Baron's attention, and we became good friends and
had frequent interviews. He sent from me a copy of this work
to his Majesty the late King of Prussia, and after a short period
I received an autograph from his Majesty, saying how much he
was pleased with what I had written on the subject of national
education and upon governments, and that in consequence he
had given instructions to his Minister of the Interior to establish
a national system of education for his dominions; and it was established the next year.

I proceeded to inform Lord William Russell that in consequence of this old intercourse with this court I had written to
his Prussian Majesty on the evening of my arrival in Berlin, men-
tioning the object of my journey, and that the next morning before
ten the King had sent my old and much valued friend Baron Alexander Von Humboldt to communicate with me on the business of
my visit to Berlin, and that we were in friendly communication on
these matters. Lord William expressed himself much gratified with
this statement, and invited me to Potsdam, where Lady William
and her family were,—which invitation I accepted, and was
kindly and hospitably entertained, and was much pleased with the
unaffected and frank manner of her Ladyship.

We returned together to Berlin, where he made a dinner for
me, and invited the Prince of Prussia, who spoke English fluently, to meet me; and we had much conversation upon the subject of my visit.

With these proceedings and frequent visits to and from Baron
Humboldt I spent several days most usefully in Berlin. Those

only who have had opportunities of personal intercourse with Baron Humboldt can form any correct idea of the kindness, benevolence, and high intelligence with which he impresses all so favoured; and having known and witnessed his progress since we first met in Paris, in 1818, in the society of his friends Cuvier and Laplace, his progress has been observed with much interest by me, and I was on this occasion greatly gratified to have once more,—and, as I concluded from the advanced age of both, for the last time,—the pleasure of free and uninterrupted converse with him.

At parting at our last interview he said,—" You are here op-"posed by the Jesuits." This I knew,—not only in Berlin, but in Vienna, Dresden, Munich, and wherever I remained for any time,—for they were anxious to counteract the impression which my " New Views" seldom failed to make upon the minds of all seeking truth.

It had been my intention to visit St. Petersburg, the Hague, and other Courts; but the approach of winter and my affairs in England made it necessary for me to hasten home.

After my return I continued, by regular lectures, public meetings, and publications, to instruct the people, and gradually to prepare them for a better and higher state of existence than the painful condition to which the progress of science, misdirected under a false and evil system, had reduced, and was still lower reducing them;—for the longer this system of error in principle and practice shall be maintained, the greater will be the demoralisation and misery of all classes

To keep the subject of these New Views in the mind of the upper classes, I petitioned Parliament, session after session, with little intermission, from 1816 to the present time; and although these petitions were ably supported, often by Lord Brougham, sometimes by the Marquis of Lansdowne, and by Lord Monteagle, and by leading members in the House of Commons, they were always, although unopposed, ineffectual to stimulate an open and fair debate, since the administration of Lord Liverpool, who was a thorough convert to my views, and if he had not been on this subject strongly opposed by the church, then all powerful, he and his cabinet were ready and most willing that it should be thoroughly investigated and tested in practice.

The " New Views" and " The Formation of Character" had now become familiar subjects, even among the working classes, and although, for want of previous training in mental investigations, they took up these subjects imperfectly, and with little or no practical experience,—yet a new mind and new feelings were growing up among them, and the working classes of this generation have a very superior class of mind to those of former generations.

Leaving England now for a time, I went to sojourn with my

family in the United States, of which I had made them citizens, —knowing that liberal views, good moral conduct, talent, and industry, would there meet encouragement and reward, which could not be expected under a false and evil system as it existed and was supported in the old world. I was not mistaken in these conclusions; and it was fortunate that I returned to the United States at this period.

My eldest son, Robert Dale Owen, had now become a member of the House of Representatives in the Congress of the United States, after having been a member of the Legislature of his own state, (Indiana,)—and a subject of much interest to me and also my son had been for sometime before the House, and unsuccessful, although brought in and supported by the talent and interest of two highly respected and influential members. This was the establishment of the Smithsonian Institution, for which Mr. Smithson had left by his will a large sum in England, but which, if certain conditions were not fulfilled in England, should be applied as he directed in the United States.

Mr. Richard Rush,—son of the celebrated Dr. Rush, a signer of the act of Independence, and long United States' Ambassador in London,—came to England in virtue of this will, to claim the funds, and obtained them for the United States, with interest,— the whole sum to be applied according to the will. The principle and interest of these funds remained some years unused and unnoticed in the Treasury of the United States, until John Quincy Adams, ex-president, who knew all about the transactions connected with this affair, became a member of the House of Representatives of the Congress of the United States. and he introduced a bill to apply the funds, as directed, to establish an institution " to increase and extend knowledge among men ;"— but with all his extraordinary industry, high talent, and great experience, he failed.

Sometime after, the subject was again introduced by Governor Tallmadge of Wisconsin,—a then talented and popular member of the House of Representatives—or of the Senate, I forget which,—at Washington. He consulted much with my son upon the bill while it was in progress, and my son communicated freely with me on the subject, and we gave Mr. Tallmadge all the assistance in and out of Congress that was in our power ; but again it was without success :—the bill, like Mr. J. Q. Adams's, was lost.

Being thus made familiar with the subject, it appeared to me far too important to be lost sight of. Could the bill be passed, and the institution established and conducted according to the will of the liberal and far seeing donor it might be made of great permanent value, not only of the United States, but to the population of the world.

On pondering over the matter I considered its success deserv-

ing every effort, and I said to my son—" This affair is too im-
" portant to remain as it is. The government will lend no aid
" to take this large sum out of its hands, and a strong effort will
" be required to obtain it for its intended and proper use.   You
" stand pretty well with all parties in both Houses.   You can
" well defend such a cause in your own House of Representa-
" tives, and under these circumstances there is some chance that,
" with unflinching energy, industry, and perseverance in such a
" cause, you may succeed.   I know it is a most formidable task,
" especially for a young member,—but the satisfaction of suc-
" cess, if attained, will be so much greater.'

After some consideration he said—" I will attempt it, and will
" do all I can to deserve success."

He introduced his bill.   It was at every stage strongly opposed, and on the last day but one of the session he had almost
given up hope of success,—when on that morning he received a
letter from me, (I had left Washington for a few weeks,) strongly
urging him to strain every nerve among his friends to the last,
and never to despair.   This, he told me, aroused all his energies.
He went immediately among his most-to-be-confided-in friends :—
the bill had passed through every stage with almost a death
struggle to the third reading in the Senate, and only now required to be passed ; but there is on the last day of the session
such a crowd of bills to pass, and all are so eager to pass their
own, that to pass one on that day is most uncertain, and cannot
be done without an arduous struggle.   His friends were there,
true to their previous day's engagement,—and the bill was
passed.   A great victory certainly for a young member.

Having so far succeeded, he applied himself with great industry to make the funds available to the greatest extent for the
increase and diffusion of knowledge among men.

My son's mind had been trained and educated to be extended
beyond class, sect, or party,—and be desired that the Smithsonian
Institution should not be tinctured with either, as was evidently
the intention of its founder.   He took great care in preparing
the Institution itself, its plan, its building, and the materials to
be employed in the latter, as well as in the symmetry of its architecture.

He was also most anxious, (and I would say over anxious,) to
obtain for it the best and most competent secretary,—knowing
how much depended upon this official, for the ultimate success of
the object for which the Institution was established.   He had
been strongly impressed, I know not how, that the Rev. Mr.
Henry, president of the Princeton College, or University, was
the best choice that could be made for this office.   Not knowing
Mr. Henry, and well knowing Mr. Richard Rush, formerly Ambassador to London, and who had succeeded in obtaining in England the funds under the will of Mr. Smithson, and being con-

scious of his business habits, great talents, and high integrity, I strongly recommended him as the most fit person in the United States for secretary to that Institution. My son had the full influence of the appointment, and he used it to the utmost in favor of Mr. Henry,—and he was elected. He was and is, no doubt, well suited to preside over one of the old Institutions of the old, ignorant, and prejudiced system of society, as governed by the priesthood of this day in the United States; but not so well suited by his education and position to increase and diffuse superior knowledge among men. I therefore considered his appointment a great check to the progress of the most valuable knowledge among men; and I believe my son had soon reason to discover the mistake which he had made.

The building as it stands was decided upon by my son.

While this matter was in progress, the difference between the British government and the United States arose respecting the territory of Oregon, and a war spirit to a great height was created in the States,—but particularly in Congress,—supported by the press of all parties.

Seeing this, and that no party, on account of its great unpopularity, would venture in Congress or through the press to advocate peace between the two countries on reasonable terms,—I wrote and published in the leading Washington Journals a letter strongly advocating peace, and stating terms which I declared to be just to both parties, and that the government which refused them would be the cause of a war which all good men would regret, and which both nations would long have cause to lament.

The day previous to this publication, *The Union*, the Government Journal, and the speeches in Congress, were all for war. The following day, however, *The Union* came out in favour of peace, and the war spirit gradually diminished in Congress.

I was in communication daily with the government respecting my proposals, and finding a spirit in the Cabinet not unfavourable to my views, I came to England,—had an interview with Lord Aberdeen, still the Foreign minister,—and finding it would require but an impartial friendly interference to bring the two governments to terms of peace, I hastened back to Washington, where I found the parties in Congress nearly balanced between peace and war on the terms I had suggested. There was ever a difference between the two Houses upon the subject, and three members were appointed by each House to confer, and if possible agree upon this now all engrossing subject.

My son Robert Dale Owen was one of the three selected by the House of Representatives. He had now imbibed my views; and he strongly urged them at the conference between the two houses, and was successful in his advocacy for peace upon the conditions which had been stated.

I again immediately returned to England, where I remained

until I learned that the points of difference had been finally agreed upon by our government and the United States' minister, and then I returned to Washington,—thus crossing the Atlantic to endeavour to keep peace between the two countries in which I had so deep an interest, four times in less than five months.

In 1847 I returned to this country—the climate much better agreeing with my constitution than that of the United States.

Since my return I have endeavoured by lectures and various publications to prepare the public for an entire change of system, without which I have long known no permanent change for the happiness of the human race could be effected. These preparations have been increased year by year, until in May of last year I thought the public mind of this country was sufficiently developed to listen to the introduction of those principles and practices which, when adopted by society, will produce the Millennial State of Existence upon Earth.

I was not disappointed. The meeting which I called in May last was most gratifying and eminently successful, and gave me full evidence that when the governments of the civilised nations of the world can be convinced that the present system is based on falsehood and is necessarily productive of evil continually, and when they shall be therefore united in agreeing to change it for the true, good, and happy system of the human race, the people are preparing to second their efforts, and thus to give a New Existence to Man upon the Earth, and to introduce and maintain in practice the long promised Millennium.

That meeting prepared the public for the Congress of the Reformers of the World, which is to be held in St. Martin's Hall, Long Acre, to commence at noon on the 14th of May next, and to continue until the subject shall be fully and fairly discussed. For the time is come when a great revolution for good or evil is at hand;—for good, if right reason and sound common sense can be made to prevail;—for evil if the prejudices of falsehood, fraud, and despotism shall continue to be supported. And which of these results shall be the victor at this period in the history of the world, will depend upon the degree of development of the public mind.

This must be patiently observed. Nature requires its own time to mature all things,—whether mineral, vegetable, animal, or mind and spirit. She will not be prematurely urged on, before her due order in time. Therefore, if the mental faculties of man are now sufficiently developed, practical measures will be now adopted by governments and people, in cordial union, to commence the New Existence of Man upon the Earth, and thus to introduce the true Millennial state into the practice of the population of the world.

But if the mental powers of the advanced men of the world are yet too undeveloped for the entire gradual change from the system of falsehood and evil to the system of truth and good, then must nations yet wait the arrival, in the due order of time, of the period when nature shall have prepared the human race for this change, which sooner or later must come.

I have also at all times freely communicated my publications and proceedings to our own and the other governments of the civilised world, and while the Peace Conference was sitting in Paris I addressed the following letters to the Earl of Clarendon, and supplied each member of the Conference with copies of the *Millennial Gazette*, in which reference is made to the permanent advantages to be obtained by federative treaties between nations.

I am conscious that no great change for the permanent benefit of nations can be made without a union of these governments, and they must now so unite, or the people will unite against them, and thus again violence will be organised, and progress in knowledge, peace, and happiness will be delayed for a long season, and the reign of repulsive feelings over the attractive will be continued.

During the proceedings thus briefly and imperfectly sketched, of the continued agitation which I have excited to prepare the population for an entire change of system in principle and practice,—three subjects of more or less interest have occurred, to which it may be useful to refer, as they have been hitherto misunderstood by the public.

The first is the building of Orbiston, in Lanarkshire, in 1825.

The second is the establishment of the Labour Exchange in Gray's Inn Road, in 1832.

The third is the establishment of the community at Harmony Hall, in Hampshire, in 1839.

The first was commenced and finished while I was absent in the United States, by two of the most faithful and honest of my disciples, both over anxious for the improvement of society on the principles I had advocated and on the practice I had exhibited partially at New Lanark. These two were Mr. Hamilton of Dalziel, and Mr. Abraham Combe, the elder brother of Andrew and George Combe, but in many respects superior to both. Mr. Hamilton expended, I believe, upwards of twenty thousand pounds in this experiment, and destroyed his health,—for he died at an early period of life. Abraham Combe sacrificed his life prematurely to this well-intentioned, but ill-judged experiment.

Neither of these self-devoted men possessed practical knowledge equal to the task which they hastily and rashly undertook in my absence and without my knowledge. The building which they erected, and all their general arrangements, were constructed to prevent their success, and upon my return from the United States I told them they could never succeed with such arrangements; and I was never at this establishment for one day, and never interfered with it in any way.   Yet this was said to be one of my failing establishments.

Respecting the second experiment,—the Labour Exchange in Gray's Inn Road. I had published in my official report to the county of Lanark an outline theory of the society which I advocated, and in this report I explained the principle of exchanging labour for labour, by means of the labour note,—and that on this principle and by this practice wealth might be increased without the aid of metal money to an illimitable extent, even to saturate the world with wealth of the most useful and valuable description.

After my return from the United States in 1830, I commenced lecturing weekly on the Sunday, to explain in more detail my " New Views of Society," and to form a new and superior character for the human race.   It was at these lectures I introduced music at their commencement and termination, and by degrees a social tea party to precede the lecture. This I did, knowing that tea, music, and a lecture explanatory of valuable practical knowledge, were calculated to create more moral results than drunkenness in public houses.   And soon these lectures, so accompanied, created a large congregation ; and the two first places in which these lectures were given soon became too small, and Gray's Inn Road Institution, with its extensive accommodation for lectures to large audiences, and for various other purposes, was offered and strongly pressed upon my acceptance for occupation.

Soon the large lecture room, sufficient to accommodate an audience of two thousand, became regularly filled every Sunday, and disciples and apostles of the system increased week by week ; and it became necessary to form a committee from among these, to assist in the management of these increasing arrangements ; and by degrees an association was formed, on pure democratic principles, to promote in all ways the progress of the New Views towards their introduction into practice.

The committee elected as the executive organ of the association, who had studied my writings and attended my explanatory lectures, thought the time had arrived when the Labour Note system could be introduced into practice ; and they became daily more urgent that I should, as president of the association, give my consent for them to commence this change, in the buildings so convenient for the purpose of forming part of this establishment.

I told them, as a practical man, being accustomed to large practical arrangements, and knowing the necessity for an extended preparation before such a new mode of business could be commenced with order and under a well organised system, that it would require at least two years of continued attention to have the requisite arrangements completed to open such a business as this would be if properly conducted.

The committee could not understand the necessity for such preparation, and so many seemed to know everything that would be required, that it was decided by a majority of votes that the practice should be commenced with the least possible delay.

I said—" You will destroy or greatly retard your success for " want of due preparation on a scale sufficiently large for the " business which will arise to be transacted." And so it occured. The rush on the first day of opening the establishment was such as to endanger the lives of the parties on entering the establishment, and it was found necessary to put up strong barriers to be opened by guards stationed to admit only a certain number until they were attended to and dismissed.

The experiment, although thus introduced with great defects, was sufficient to show what could be done by experienced men of business on this principle. It continued gradually to overcome the great disadvantage of its premature commencement, and there was a fair prospect that eventually it would be very successful. But unfortunately the building was the property of an eccentric individual, almost bordering on a state of insanity, and we had also among us one who had been a dissenting minister, and who occasionally was permitted to lecture to our audience. The lectures were so popular as now to be profitable beyond covering their necessary expenses, and the business showed every sign of great success as it and the lectures were now conducted.

When matters were in this state, the dissenting minister, having no regard to the engagements to the cause in which he was permitted to become a member, secretly stimulated the proprietor of the building, (who had strongly pressed me to occupy it as I did,) to a state of real madness, by telling him that if he would take the building out of my hands, *he* could carry on the lectures, while, both together, they could conduct the Labour Exchange and make ten thousand a year profit.

This was too strong a temptation for the madman to withstand, and he and the minister got a number of ruffians together, and blocked up over night the entrance, and kept forcible possession of the premises. Some of my committee, without my knowledge and contrary to my wishes, opposed force to force; but when I heard of it, I prevailed upon them to desist. And I took a larger lecture room in premises in Charlotte Street, Fitzroy Square.

In preference to leaving the Gray's Inn Road Institution I offered the mad proprietor a thousand a year for a long lease, which the minister advised him to refuse—their prospects, as he said, being so great from the lectures and business. The result in a short time was to reduce the lecture audience from 2,000 to twenty, and to ruin the proprietor to such an extent that he lost the building altogether.

But this was afterwards called one of my failing experiments.

The third proceeding was the establishment of a community at Tytherley and Queenwood, in Hampshire.

My disciples and apostles in 1838-9 were becoming clamourous for the commencement of a community on the principles which I advocated. They thought they could raise sufficient funds to commence one, and that they possessed sufficient practical knowledge to conduct it. I was of a very different opinion; and would not commence until there were funds sufficient lodged in bank for that purpose.

My advice was disregarded. The parties commenced;—went forward without any practical knowledge of what they had to do; —came to a stand;—and then applied to me to relieve them out of their difficulties. I did so for that time; and as the first governor whom they selected had destroyed his health under a task for which he was unequal, they appointed another, and proceeded with his inexperienced assistance, until they again could proceed no further.

A second time they applied to me,—and then I went to the establishment, which, from want of the knowledge of governing qualities, had arrived at so much confusion as to make it impracticable to put it in the state in which it should be for ultimate success.

It was a Democratic establishment, governed at stated meetings; and there were several self-willed inexperienced members among them, who formed a party and out-voted some of the measures which I proposed, and which I knew were necessary for its success,—and I resigned all connection with it.

In less than two years they again brought it to a stand, and they could proceed no further with it, and gave up.

It has since been applied, as I intended it should be, for the formation of character for young persons, under the direction of Mr. Edmondson, who conducts the institution, from all reports, in a manner to give general satisfaction to the parents of all the children committed to his charge.

The outline of this establishment of Harmony Hall, on the estate of Queenwood, is favourable in many respects for the formation of a family commonwealth, when society shall be prepared for one on its true and only principles, which alone can ensure success.

COPIES OF LETTERS SENT TO THE EARL OF CLAREN-DON DURING THE SITTINGS OF THE PEACE CON-FERENCE IN PARIS.

(First Letter.)

MY LORD,—

Your Peace Conference has met at a critical period in human history. Old society is nonplussed, and cannot longer support itself. It has been fully tried through all past centuries, and is, at this day, over the world, a sad failure for all the purposes for which society should be constituted.

The means to make the population of the world healthy, enlightened, good, united, prosperous, and happy, without stay or retrogression, now abundantly exist, are known, and will soon be universally known. I ask your Lordship and the Members of the Peace Conference,—Is it probable,—is it possible, that the system can be longer maintained, which applies these same means to keep the population diseased in body and mind, ignorant of the most valuable truths,—to train them to be immoral and disunited,—to retain them in poverty or the fear of it,—and to make anything approaching to a rational enjoyment of life impracticable for any class in any country ?

No, my Lord,—this system of evil is doomed this year to die its natural death, and, if there be foresight and wisdom in your Conferences, you will prepare your governments and the public to effect this change, in peace, in order, and with wise foresight.

Do not hide your heads in the Peace Conference, and suppose that the thinking part of the public do not yet see things as they have been now expressed. Should you do so, you will act as unwisely as the ostrich, when it hides its head in the sand, leaving its large body exposed to view. I will first in a day or two send to each member copies of a preliminary address to the Conference, to open the subject of a *New System* for the government of the human race ; and in a few days afterwards I will forward for each member of the Conference an outline and to some extent the details of this new system.

It will be evident to your Lordship and the members of the Conference, that the principles which can alone permanently adjust the peace of Europe, will also permanently adjust the peace of the world. Your present Conference, wisely directed, may inaugurate this glorious change, and enable existing governments to direct it peaceably through its growth to maturity. If commenced aright, the subsequent measures will be plain sailing.

The two systems for governing the world will be before you :—the one true, the other false ;—the one good, the other evil ;—the one ignorant and foolish, the other enlightened and wise ;—the one gradually leading to utter confusion, and ultimately to a pandemonium ; the other to order, and ultimately to a terrestrial paradise. The one is a system of repulsion, the other will be of attraction.

If governments see their own interest, they will now openly adopt the one, and will gradually abandon the other.

Faithfully, my Lord, your friend and servant,

ROBERT OWEN.

Sevenoak's Park, March 1st, 1856.

(Second Letter.)

MY LORD,—

I forward to you by this mail a rough copy of my promised work, which I regret has been delayed in the press longer than I anticipated. Finished copies shall be forwarded from London for the members of the Peace Conference to-morrow or Tuesday.

It will be evident to the members of the Peace Conference, that no combination of powers can much longer maintain the present system of society in any country,—it is now so glaringly opposed to the interest of each nation, and to that of the population of the world. Its ignorance, evils, and consequent miseries, are become through the enlightened progress of the public mind too heavy to be longer supported or bearable.

But do not hastily conclude a definitive treaty of peace. A preliminary peace, to terminate at once all conflicts by land and sea, and to stop war expenses and feelings is the most desirable.

You have done well and wisely in admitting Prussia to your Conference ; but you can have no permanent peace for Europe without at the same time securing the peace of the world. And the peace of the world can be secured only by a Congress of the present acting powers, with the addition of the United States. The eight leading powers of the world, by pursuing a plain, common-sense rational course, could easily command the permanent peace of the world most beneficially for all governments, nations, and peoples.

I earnestly intreat you, my Lord, and the other members of the Peace Conference, not to let this golden opportunity pass, for terminating for ever the evils of the existing system, and for giving permanent peace and harmony to the afflicted population of the earth.

I have called a Congress of the Reformers of the World, for the 14th of May next, to assist you in directing public opinion in this great and glorious work for the redemption of mankind from sin and misery.

In these proceedings you will readily perceive I am aided by the great and good spirits of former days, who are deeply interested in the present measures to be adopted by the Peace Conference. I remain, my Lord, as ever,

A friend to you and the human race,

ROBERT OWEN.

Sevenoaks Park, March 16th, 1856.

(Third Letter.)

MY LORD,—

I have given instructions to my publishers in London to forward to your Lordship copies of No. 2 of my *Millennial Gazette*, which I expect will be completed to-day or to-morrow, and I expect they will be in Paris on or before Friday next. These copies are for the members of the Peace Conference now in Paris,—and in addition I enclose an article intended for No. 3 of the same Gazette, to be published on the 1st of May next.

These articles are written to prepare the public mind in all civilised nations for "The New Existence of Man upon the Earth,"—for the Millennial State, or cordial brotherhood of the human race. This is the great revolution, to be gradually and peaceably accomplished by wise foresight, beneficially for all nations and individuals. It is the destiny of the human race; and to resist it by human means will be a vain attempt.

The interest, progress, and happiness of the human race are involved in this change; and the meeting of the Peace Conference in Paris at this critical period is a presage of the forthcoming Sacred Federative Alliance of all Nations, for the general benefit of all, through future generations.

That you and your colleagues in the present Peace Conference may be efficient aids to forward this great work, is the cordial wish of

Your Lordship's friend and servant,

ROBERT OWEN.

Sevenoaks Park; Sevenoaks.
April 9th, 1856.

THE CAUSE OF THE PAST AND PRESENT IRRATIONAL CONTENDING STATE OF SOCIETY OVER THE WORLD.

THE population of the world has been hitherto governed by rulers, statesmen, and legislators, all too ignorant of human nature and of the unchanging laws of God, to know what was practicable or impracticable in the government of the human race.

These parties have been so trained and educated by their material and mental surroundings, that they believed it to be impracticable to govern men except by falsehood, fraud, force, and fear; and all governments known among men have been a compound of these errors and evils.

They all appear to have thought it impracticable to govern in the spirit of impartial justice, charity and love, or in accordance with God's unchanging laws of humanity.

To govern by falsehood, fraud, force, and fear, being directly contrary to the laws of God, required the most stringent, severe, unjust, and cruel laws of men,—laws which, however, required to be continually superseded by new laws, to be in their turn continually superseded by new attempts at law making; and this course has been pursued through all past ages to this hour. And these laws of men over the world require to be repealed at this day on account of their evil results in practice, as much as those which have been repealed age after age through every succeeding generation.

The want of knowledge, in rulers, statesmen, and legislators, of what is and what is not practicable, has been made strikingly evident by the results of the Peace Conference just terminated in Paris. No doubt these esteemed eminent statesmen on this eventful occasion acted up to the highest pinnacle of their knowledge, to endeavour to adjust a peace of considerable permanence for Europe and Asia, as far as European powers were concerned in that portion of the world. I ask in the name of common sense—what have they done by their united wisdom, and no doubt great desire to obtain this so much wished-for result by the well-disposed of all nations? In this treaty these statesmen have not expounded one principle for practice that can lead to a permanent peace in Europe, Asia, or any other part of the world. The whole treaty is based on the old undeveloped notions of statesmen,—notions which to this hour have kept the population of the world in a most irrational state of conflict, and which have given to all individuals the most repulsive feelings against their own humanity, and thus misery to a greater or lesser extent has been inflicted upon all born, trained, educated, employed, and placed, as all have been to this day.

That which is now practicable and impracticable to secure the peace, well-doing, and happiness of the human race, shall be more fully explained at the ensuing Congress of the Reformers of the World.

ROBERT OWEN.

Sevenoaks Park, Sevenoaks,
　　27th April, 1856.

London :—Published by the Author at 16, Great Windmill Street, Haymarket : and sold by J. Clayton and Son, 223, Piccadilly ; Holyoake, 147, Fleet Street ; Truelove, 240, Strand; Goddard, 14, Great Portland Street, Cavendish Square ; Farrer, 21, John Street, Fitzroy Square; and all Booksellers.

ROBERT OWEN'S
MILLENNIAL GAZETTE;

EXPLANATORY OF THE PRINCIPLES AND PRACTICES BY WHICH, IN PEACE, WITH TRUTH, HONESTY, AND SIMPLICITY, THE NEW EXISTENCE OF MAN UPON THE EARTH MAY BE EASILY AND SPEEDILY COMMENCED.

"The character of Man is formed *for* him, and *not by* him!"

No. 5.]   JUNE 15th, 1856.   [PRICE 6D.

THE CONGRESS OF THE REFORMERS OF THE WORLD.

THE first and second meetings of this Congress have been held in the Metropolis of the British Empire, the present Metropolis of the World.

These meetings will be had in remembrance by succeeding generations, as being the first meetings held in any nation or among any people to include in their object the principles and practices which will insure the permanent good of the human race through its future existence, and which will unite the population of the world as one family; and as exhibiting the plain and simple practical measures to be adopted step by step to effect this great revolution over the earth, and to effect it most advantageously for all of every rank, class, and creed, in peace, and with perfect order, because no one will be injured by the change, or prematurely hurried into it.

The practical measures by which to effect this change, when explained, are so simple and plain, that the wonder is how they could have been so long overlooked.

These measures are :—

First.—THE FEDERATION OF NATIONS :—

Second.—THE UNION OF THE PEOPLE IN FEDERATIVE SCIENTIFIC FAMILY COMMONWEALTHS :—

Third.—THE PLACING OF EACH FAMILY COMMONWEALTH WITHIN GOOD AND SUPERIOR SURROUNDINGS.

When understood, these three measures will be found sufficient to secure the permanent happiness of the human race.

These are the means, easy of practice as soon as the will can be created to put them into execution, by which the peace of the world is to be permanently insured,—men to be made to become good and wise, healthy and happy,—wealth to be made universally to superabound,—and the earth to be made fruitful and beautiful.

And what more can man desire while an inhabitant of this globe ?

This Congress terminates my mission upon the earth in this life. In the next stage of my existence, which for me is not far distant, I may in my spiritual state be perhaps permitted and directed to assist my present fellow mortals to carry these measures into full practice into all nations and among all people.

Let all classes in all countries now abandon their ignorantly educated objections to their own progress towards universal unity, excellence in all things, and permanent rational happiness.

The first meeting of this Congress was held in the Great Room in St. Martin's Hall, Long Acre, at noon on the 14th May, and was attended by 410 Reformers of the World. The second meeting was held on the evening of the 18th May, when about three times the number present in the first meeting were assembled.

These meetings were open and unrestricted, and all parties of all ranks were invited to be present and to take part in proceedings of the highest practical permanent interest to the human race through all future ages.

It was promised by the spirits from various quarters, through different mediums, that much harmony should prevail in these meetings, and that much permanent good should be effected by them. Yet, having prepared so great a number of resolutions to be proposed for the consideration of the meetings, and these resolutions being so opposed to the existing order of things over the world, and to the educated prejudices of the human race, much warm discussion was anticipated for many days in continuance, before they could be successfully carried, if carried they could be.

It was therefore an astonishment to the friends of these proceedings, and an agreeable surprise to all present, that resolution after resolution was carried, not only unanimously, but with considerable hearty good will.

Such is now, in the new times to which the world has attained, the influence of plain, simple, straightforward " truth without mystery, mixture of error, or fear of man"—the motto which I have adopted from my youth upwards.

These great truths for the future generations of men have gone forth at these meetings, and are now rapidly travelling by steam and telegraph to all parts of the world. Who shall now stay their continued course, or their influence on the human heart and mind ?

The deed is done. The path to progress illimitable in a right direction is opened. And man—universal man—shall be made good, united, wise, and happy !

My mission here, in this life, is therefore terminated.

It is left to my successors in this glorious cause for our race, to make the " federative treaties between the nations of the world," and to " unite the population of all nations in scientific family " commonwealths, whose maximum number shall not exceed *three* " *thousand*, and whose surroundings shall be all good and " superior," and to " unite these family commonwealths federa- " tively over the world, in order that there shall be but one in- " terest for ever among the human race, and that the earth may " become thereby the equal inheritance of all of every succeed- " ing generation, and the true Millennium be established for ever."

Rejoice ! All ye of the present generation ! That your children, and your children's children to the end of time, will be relieved from the errors and sufferings which you have expe- rienced, and that the Cause of evil will be for ever removed from among them !

It is by the measures herein stated, and by these measures only, that an elevated practical equality of the human race can be attained ; and without this equality there can be no permanent peace,—no language of truth—no real virtue or goodness,—no justice between man and man,—no unity and attraction between nations,—and no full-formed men and women, with their divine physical, intellectual, moral, spiritual, and practical powers highly cultivated and exercised to the point of temperance for each faculty and propensity, so as give full enjoyment of their divine nature to every child of man.

It is through this enlightened and just equality only, that the human race can be formed into one family, with one language, one interest, and one feeling.

It is through this divine equality only, that a cordial brother- hood of the human race can ever arise and be made permanent.

I now most earnestly put this all-important question to the human race :—

" Will you continue insanely to maintain the origin of evil, " with its disunion, repulsion, and other pandemonium practices, " —Or will you now exert yourselves to supersede this cause " of evil in principle and practice, by the cause of universal " truth and good, of union and attraction, and of every practice " consistent with the existence of a terrestrial paradise ?"

The one must continue to be maintained, or the other must be attained ; for to unite them is impossible.

The choice of individuals and nations is now, therefore, be- tween an earthly pandemonium, and a terrestrial paradise.

ROBERT OWEN.

24th of May, 1856.

THE FIRST MEETING OF THE CONGRESS OF THE REFORMERS OF THE WORLD, HELD IN THE METROPOLIS OF THE BRITISH EMPIRE, ON THE 14TH DAY OF MAY, 1856.

THIS meeting was called by six months' previous announcement, and in addition to the reformers of the world, the following were invited by special advertisement :—

The members of the British Parliament : --

The Foreign ministers at the Courts of London and Paris :—

The Archbishops and Bishops of Great Britain and Ireland, irrespective of the difference of creed :—

The Judges of all the courts in both Islands : —

The Authorities of the city of London :—

And the most experienced and advanced practical men in every department of life.

Especial invitations were also sent to Messrs. Kossuth, Mazzini, and Louis Blanc, requesting them to come and take part in these proceedings for the reformation of the population of the world. But these gentlemen are familiar only with the principles and practices of the present false and now worn-out system of society, to improve which without changing its fundamental principle and the practices necessarily emanating from that principle, they will, with the best intentions and transcendent talent, labour in vain, and waste their energies. It is much to be regretted that mental powers so calculated to arouse the feelings of the multitude, and to attract the attention of the world, should continue to be misdirected as they are.

The meeting of the Congress took place at noon, and was commenced by the election of the President, vice-President, and three Secretaries. These were unanimously carried. ROBERT OWEN for President, — JAMES WATSON Vice-President, — ROBERT COOPER, J. G. HOLYOAKE, and WILLIAM STEPHENS, Secretaries.

The President opened the meeting by stating the objects for which the Congress was called.

He said, speaking in a prophetic spirit,—

" This Congress in its consequences will in future be considered the most important public meeting ever held in any " part of the world. It involves broader, deeper, and more universal interests for the human race, than have been thus publicly advocated at any former period ; and it will be found to " advocate these interests on facts coeval with man, and on laws of " the creation unknown to change.

" It is the intention of the friends to this cause to base it on " self-evident truths, and to advocate it on self-evident deductions from those self-evident truths. Sophistry opposed to " them will therefore be harmless, and will be a broken reed in " the hands of the defenders of the cause of evil and of the

" practices which have necessarily emanated from it. All at-
" tempts therefore to bolster up a system which has done its
" work, and which is now far worse than useless, must fail.

" Its foundation being unsound, it has been undermined, and,
" without care and foresight in its supporters, it may prematurely
" fall, and crush many in its ruins.

" It will therefore be wise in these supporters of error and
" evil calmly to consider their present condition, to look before
" them, and to prepare a new structure for themselves while the
" present is standing, and to have it before the present structure
" tumbles with violence over their heads, or crumbles into dust
" through its own internal corruptions."

The President then requested Mr. Robert Cooper, one of the
Secretaries, to read the following preamble, published also in
No. 1 of this *Millennial Gazette.*

Preamble.

This Congress is held with the pure intention of benefiting
permanently the human race as one family, and ultimately, by
gradual practical means, to proceed in peace with foresight and
wisdom to adopt measures, uninjurious to any, to prepare the
population of the world to form themselves, nation after nation,
into one brotherhood, on the principle of a true and just equality
according to age,—this being the only principle which can insure
permanent peace and harmony throughout humanity. There
will however always be the never ending varieties of character
created by the natural combinations of the faculties, propensities, and powers, given at birth to each individual.

That these ever-to-be-desired ultimate results can never be attained except through the knowledge of truth respecting the laws
of human nature, and how to form all the arrangements of society
to be ever consistent with those unchanging and unerring divine
laws of humanity. These laws, when fully understood and
rightly appreciated, may be now applied to practice in such
manner that with the certainty of a law of nature these results
may be universally and permanently attained and secured for
humanity through all future ages.

That these all-glorious results cannot be given isolated to any
individual, any one nation, or to any partial division of the
human race.

That to attain these results, substantial arrangements must be
devised and adopted, which in their progress in practice will proceed from individuals to nations, and from nation to nation, until
the surroundings of the human race shall be complete to force.
by the irresistible influence of those surroundings, one and all to
become rational in feeling, thought, and action, and therefore
good, wise, healthy, united, wealthy, ever consistent, and happy.
It is one of the all-wise laws of nature and of God, that one

human being cannot be relieved and raised from the present state
of irrationality and insanity, except by measures that will equally
relieve and raise all to the same elevation of goodness, wisdom,
rationality, and happiness.   Hence the necessity for now adopting universal principles and practices.

That it is now evident to all who have powers given them to
observe, reflect, and reason accurately, that, from the earliest
period of human existence or infant state of humanity, to this
day, man has been without a correct and comprehensive knowledge of his own nature, and that in consequence society over the
world has been based on error, and constructed in all its parts in
accordance with that error.

That this fatal mistake has given a false character and a language of falsehood to man, and made society over the earth a
heterogeneous confused mass of the most gross follies and absurdities.   Hence the repulsive feelings, the quarrels, fightings,
and general disunion of the human race; when it is now evidently the interest of all not to quarrel, not to fight, nor to be
disunited, but to live within such surroundings as will make all
attractive to each other, so as to form one family or brotherhood
of united interests, and so to remain through futurity.   The unreflecting have believed, and until they shall see a new state of
things commence in successful practice will continue to believe,
the attainment of these Millennial results to be impossible ; but
those who by favourable circumstances have been enabled to
expand their mind beyond the petty circles of class, creed,
country, and colour, and to be competent to grasp at one view,
the entire of humanity, through the past to the present and
through the future, know that until the incubus can be overcome
and removed which deranges the faculties of the human race
and afflicts them with insanity, the true base on which society
should be founded and constructed cannot be adopted ; but that
when this base shall have been adopted, it will be a straightforward practical proceeding to advance society into the long
promised Millennial state.

This incubus, it must be evident to all who have acquired a
knowledge of God's laws of humanity, is the insane notion that
each one forms his own physical, mental, and spiritual natural
qualities, and makes his own local and general surroundings. While
the first indications of a sound mind acquainted with the facts of
history, past and present, make it evident how impossible it is that
the individual could know how he received these natural divine
qualities, or how he came to be so surrounded.   Yet with these
facts exposed to man generation after generation, society has
been from the beginning until now based and constructed on the
opposing supposition that each one decides upon and creates his
own natural qualities and his own surroundings, making him re-

sponsible for the influences which he is obliged to receive from the combined powers of these two forces.

Reflection, unbiassed by the local insanities of class, creed, party, country, and colour, must now make it evident that this incubus has caused the past and present insanity of the human race, and has produced all the evils which have affected mankind from the beginning even to the present hour. Remove this incubus—new base society on its true foundation—and construct it throughout to be consistent with that base, and the world will soon be reformed, and the true Millennial State enjoyed by all.

From that which has been now stated it must be evident that the first subject for discussion for a Congress called to consider the means by which the world is to be reformed, must be to deliberate and decide upon the base on which the human character should be formed from birth to death, and on which society should be constructed to be consistent with that foundation through all its departments, so as to become permanently prosperous, and the entire population continuous in progress towards higher and higher physical, mental, and spiritual excellence and happiness.

This all-important point once decided,—that society shall continue to be based on individual responsibility to society, as heretofore, or on the responsibility of society to individuals,—will at once decide the future proceedings of this Congress.

From men who meet for the purpose of reforming society over the world it will be naturally anticipated that they will decide in accordance with facts, and that these are universally known to give *all* power to society over the individual, and no power to the individual, except, perhaps, a small modicum to one in a million. The Congress will therefore decide that a reformation of the population of the world can be based only on the principle that God or nature and society form the individual, and that society should be responsible to the individual for that portion of his character which society forms. And as this portion includes the language, religion, habits, manners, conduct, the truth or falsehood of his language, the honesty or deception of his transactions with his fellow men, and in fact the truth or falsehood, wisdom or folly of all his sayings and doings through life, society must be so recreated as to make it responsible for the character in these respects of every individual committed to its charge. And under wise foreseen arrangements or surroundings every individual may be placed from birth to death under the immediate and direct charge of society.

The principle of non-individual responsibility, and the responsibility of society to the individual, with the practice of gradually creating new, good, and superior surroundings around all of the human race, being decided upon and agreed to as the foundation on which the business of the Congress should proceed, the investigation and discussion of the questions and business as stated in the programme will follow, and will call forth the highest qualities and powers of the, most advanced members of the Congress. But as the true criterion of truth is now known and can be always and in every case of difference referred to, there can be little chance of Congress, after a dull debate, coming to a false and injurious conclusion—for all false conclusions cannot fail to be ultimately injurious.

Some of the members of this Congress may not perhaps be familiar with the universal criterion of truth, and therefore it is here re-stated from many of the published works of the writer. It is,—" that truth in every case, on all subjects, must be throughout consistent with itself and in perfect accordance with every known fact." Truth must be one eternally throughout the universe, and admits of no inconsistency or contradiction to itself. All differences of opinion which may arise in this Congress being referred to this criterion or touchstone of truth, may be always truthfully decided.

These principles being decided, the great questions then to be investigated will be—

1stly.—What are the surroundings which will best form the character of the human race ?

2ndly.—What surroundings will enable the population of the world to create the greatest amount of the most valuable wealth in the shortest time with health and pleasure to its producers ?

3rdly.—What surroundings will be the best for the circulating of this wealth justly and beneficially to all ?

4thly.—What will be the best surroundings by which each social division and the aggregate of society over the world can be the best governed, beneficially for the governed and governors ?

5thly.—What will be the best social surroundings by which to combine into one, for each division of society, the four preceding subjects, to be the most effective for the attainment of the objects stated ?

6thly.—What will be the best mode of inducing governments and people to carry into execution the resolves of this Congress ?

7thly.—What practical measures will the Congress recommend governments and people to adopt, to gradually attain the permanent peace of the world ?

The writer from long consideration of this subject has come to the conclusion that the object proposed in the preceding paragraphs may be immediately the most easily commenced and attained, by Great Britain and the United States forming, upon perfect terms of equality, a federative treaty to unite the two nations as one, to constitute the two empires in their extended dominions over the globe as one, undivided in all their interests and great objects for promoting the true civilisation of the world. Thus will each give to the other a splendid empire, without a particle of loss to itself ; but as one light will give its light to another light without diminishing its own, so may the United States and Great Britain give each their full power to the other without any loss of power on the part of either. But soon both would discover that by this union the power of each would be far more than quadrupled. But even this will be but a small part of the ultimate benefit of this first divine transaction between rival nations. It will be an example that will be of necessity adopted by other nations. Such unions will possess so many important permanent advantages, that the example will be soon followed by other nations in their own defence. And Great Britain and the United States should hold out the hand of fellowship and friendship to the other states and nations, to federatively unite with them, until gradually, as other nations prepare themselves for such divine unions, the peace and union of the population of the world and its Millennial state shall be complete.

Mr. COOPER was then requested by the President to read the following address from him to the Congress, and while Mr. Cooper read this statement, the President frequently suspended the reading of it, and entered more fully into explanatory details, which appeared to interest the meeting very generally.

The Necessity for Rulers, Statesmen, and Legislators, to acquire a knowledge of what is, and what is not practicable.

WITH the aid of the sciences wisely applied it is practicable, under surroundings calculated for the object, to make men, by laws as fixed and certain as all the laws of nature, to grow up from birth to become good,—usefully intelligent,—united in feelings of love and charity to each other,—wise in their general conduct through life,—abounding in wealth for all desirable purposes,—healthy through life,—and in the enjoyment of high active happiness.

It is practicable by new surroundings to enable the population of the world to adopt effective measures to make the earth fruitful, healthy, and beautiful.

It is practicable by new basing society on the laws of God and nature, forming the character of all before and from birth by these laws, and governing the race in undeviating accordance with these laws, to make perpetually of the human race one family cordially united as one highly intelligent brotherhood, which shall progress from generation to generation in goodness, knowledge, and wisdom, ever living in peace and in the uninterrupted happiness of each, which will arise from the active endeavours of all to promote the well-being, well-doing, and progress of each towards the attainment of every kind of excellence.

All this is practicable, and will be attained when the rulers, statesmen, and legislators of the world shall acquire the knowledge to comprehend, and the moral courage to abandon, the false principle on which ignorance of human nature has hitherto based society, and to adopt the true principle of human nature on which society should be placed, and to make their practice and all their surroundings in accordance with that principle.

Here, then, is opened the plain straightforward road to universal happiness, and to a continual approach towards excellence in all human attainments,—to peace on earth and good will to man,—when the will of God shall be done on earth as it is in heaven,—and when the Millennial State of Existence will be for ever established.

But it is not practicable to attain any of these results in a society whose fundamental principle is opposed to nature and therefore false, and whose practices have all emanated from that false principle,—a principle which has divided the human race into contending classes and nations, with opposing feelings and interests, while, for the permanent happiness of all, there should be but one class, one nation, one feeling, and one interest, over the world.

Undeveloped man, in ignorance of himself and of humanity, would alone divide the population of the world into opposing classes and nations.

This has been necessary, no doubt, through certain preliminary stages of human progress towards man's mental developement to attain rationality to conduct him to the path leading to universal and permanent progressive happiness.

This period has arrived, or the knowledge by which to effect this glorious change for all the sons of men would not now be patent to any of the human race.

The time, then, for these opposing classes and contending nations is about to cease, to make way for the establishment of one class and one nation, to form a practical brotherhood of the human race—one in feeling and interest, and permanent as human existence in duration.

It should be therefore now made universally known as soon as measures can be devised and executed for the purpose, that opposing classes and contending nations are, and while continued must be, destructive to the best interests of all, and will now essentially retard progress to union, wealth, knowledge, goodness, wisdom, and happiness.

For these virtues and desirable results can never be attained with opposing classes and contending nations.

It will be for ever impracticable to attain them with

A Priesthood Class,—

A Lawyer Class,—

A Medical Class,—

A Military Class,—

A Naval Class,—

A Monied Class,—

A Buying and Selling Class for money profit,—

An Agricultural Class,—

A Manufacturing Class,—

A Trading Class,—

An Inferior Class,—

A Poor Class,—

A Governing Class,—

These classes while continued will prevent the creation of full-formed superior men and women, and will make all, as at present, but a small and irrational fraction of what a human being should be now formed to be. Society should now cease to form man to be a mere Ruler, Statesman, or Legislator,—a mere Priest, Lawyer, Doctor, Military Man, or Naval Man,—a mere Monied Man,—or a buyer and seller for profit,—a mere agriculturalist, manufacturer, or tradesman. These are all mere fractions of a rational being. Full-formed men and women can never be made by such a mal-arrangement of the human race ;—an arrangement which keeps all ignorant of their own nature and divine powers,—of society as it should be,—and of its real component parts,—all of which each man and woman should be trained and educated to comprehend, and thus each should be made to become in his or her own person a superior domestic assistant,—a superior creator and distributor of wealth,—a superior instructor or former of character,—and a superior assistant legislator, statesman, and governor. Thus only can men and women be full-formed, and be made to be equals in promoting each other's happiness, and in living a life of rationality in strict accordance with nature and with the laws of God.

It is in vain for man to strive against his nature and against the laws of his Creator and his Preserver through life. The present classifications of men over the world, and the present divisions of contending and opposing nations, can never produce good and superior men and women, or abundance of general wealth for all, or create among men unity and kind feelings, virtue, or happiness. As well may the religions and governments with these obstacles in their way endeavour to make the population of the world to think and act rationally, and to become truly good, as for them to attempt to make the earth fruitful and healthy without rain or sunshine.

Experience therefore now calls upon all rulers, statesmen, and legislators, to change their system of governing,—to abandon their own made irrational laws opposed to nature's laws,—and to become subject, with the entire of the human race, to the plain, simple, just, merciful, and all-wise laws of God,—laws abundantly effective to insure the permanent happiness of men as children of one family, under the government of a parent competent to govern them in peace, order, and harmony.

And it is full time that the rulers, statesmen, and legislators of the world, should now learn what is and what is not practicable for the good government of men, that no more time may be lost in pursuing impracticable attempts to govern men well and wisely in opposition to nature and to the unerring and unchangeable laws of God.

Were rulers, statesmen, legislators, and theologians, trained and educated to be rational, they would never imagine it to be practicable to have superior born children, or to make men and women chaste, truthful, good, rational, and happy, while united in *Marriage* by human-made laws opposed to God's laws. For when men and women are united by God's laws, it is only an ignorant impertinence and presumption to interfere by the impotent and puerile laws of men. In a rational state of human existence such interference will never be permitted or attempted.

Nor, when these rulers, statesmen, legislators, and priests, shall be rationally trained, and educated, employed, and placed, will they deem it practicable ever to make men truthful, honest, satisfied with wealth, or rational in mind and practice, under a system of *Private Property*.

Nor will they deem it practicable to make men speak the truth or the dictates of their nature, or to make them acquire the pure spirit of love and charity for our race, so as to become open, frank, and honest, under any of the *Religions* ever yet taught to man, except that simple, but yet all-comprehensive truth enunciated by Jesus Christ,—that the essence of goodness consists in love to God and man. This may justly be called the true religion :—not because Jesus Christ said it,—but because in itself it is eternally true. And where this love is not prominent in every act of life, there is no true religion, but merely a pretence and an empty name.

Now this love to God and man depends upon the formation of character from birth, and upon man's being placed through life within surroundings all made to be in accordance with the laws of God and Nature.

The all-important problem of the age, the great question of the day is—" How is the love of God and man to be attained " in practice, seeing that it has never yet existed upon earth ?"

It cannot exist in an individualised state of society, with Private Property, or with human-made Marriages.

It cannot exist with Inequality of Education and Condition, or with any Inequalities, except those of age and natural qualities.

It cannot exist under any of the present Arrangements of society in any part of the world.

It cannot exist with a Separate Class of Rulers, Statesmen, and Legislators.

It cannot exist with any artificial Division of Classes.

It cannot exist with Separate Nationalities, or with any opposing dividing influences among the population of the human race.

It cannot exist with human-made Laws, in opposition to the Laws of God and Nature.

It cannot exist with institutions based on imaginary notions opposed to the Laws of God and Nature.

It cannot exist with any artificial inequality among the human race.

How then, it will be asked, is this love to God and man—this only true religion for the human race—to be attained and made permanent among men?

Listen! O ye Rulers, Statesmen, Legislators, Professional, Monied, and Commercial Men, Agriculturalists, Manufacturers, Tradesmen, and all others of every class and degree! Listen to the Great Truths, by the practice of which alone you can be made to love God and man, and to be disciples of the only true religion, by the practice of which only you can become attractive, good, enlightened in real knowledge, healthy, united, abounding in wealth, wise in conduct, and happy by ever diffusing happiness to all around you!

This love of God and man,—this true religion,—is to be given to all from birth by forming their character and constituting society in strict and undeviating accordance with the Laws of God and Nature—Laws now made palpable to the common sense of the human race by all the experience of the past, and which experience continues to this day.

To prepare for this formation of character and construction and constitution of society, three things are necessary.

First,—The Federation of Nations, to establish permanent peace over the world.

Second,—The formation of Scientific Family Commonwealths in each nation.

Third,—The Federation of these Family Commonwealths over the world.

Without Peace the population of nations cannot progress.

Without Scientifically-formed Family Commonwealths, composed of good and superior surroundings, a good, useful, and superior character for man can never be given to him, nor can society be rationally constituted.

And without the Federation of Nations first,—then the formation of Family Commonwealths,—and then their subsequent federation,—there can be no union or happiness for man.

The practical process is simple. Nations, as it is their most evident interest, must agree to unite federatively so as to become one in interest and in practice, and thus to secure the permanent peace of the world. Each nation thus uniting, to gradually replace its entire population within new rational surroundings,—that is, common sense surroundings devised, in accordance with the laws of God and nature, to form scientific family common-wealths, not to exceed at the maximum population of each *three thousand* men, women, and children, in their natural proportions; and each one born within each family commonwealth to be well-cared for before birth and through life, by being placed, trained, educated, and employed, in such manner as shall form their character,—physically, intellectually, morally, spiritually, and practically—to be as perfect as present knowledge on these sub-jects will admit.

Then, for these family commonwealths to unite federatively in their respective nations, and afterwards to unite from nation to nation, until the population of the world shall be thus united into the great and universal commonwealth, so as in reality to form the family of man into one cordially united brotherhood of the human race, and so to be continued henceforward through all succeeding generations.

Thus, by the most simple, easy, and natural means, may every human being born on the earth be gradually formed to become rational and superior, physically and mentally, and the popula-tion of the world be governed perpetually in peace, while all are making a rapid progress in knowledge and towards every kind of excellence, in order to prepare them for the higher spheres in the spirit world and future heaven of man.

Who and what should now prevent the immediate commence-ment of this change for the permanent benefit of all classes and individuals in all countries?

It will be the greatest of all changes, with the least forcible or premature change of the existing system as at present carried on in all the nations of the earth, opposed as they may now be in colour, country, class, or creed.

And it may be now confidently stated, that there is no other mode under heaven, by which the population of any nation, or of the world, can be made permanently good, wise, happy, and rational, and the earth cultivated to become fruitful, healthy, and beautiful.

When this important document had been read and more fully explained by Mr. Owen,—he said the next proceeding, if agreed to by the members of the Congress, would be to submit a num-ber of propositions in the form of resolutions for the considera-tion and decision of the meeting. He then requested MR. WATSON, the Vice-President, to read the following

Resolutions.

1st.—That the permanent well-being, well-doing, and happi-ness of the human race, depend upon the character which society shall form for it.

2nd.—That the experience of the past has now developed the

means by which society may give any character, from the extreme of bad to the extreme of good, to all of the human race.

3d.—That it is of the highest interest to man now, that a good and superior character—physical, intellectual, moral, spiritual, and practical—should be given to the human race in the shortest time practicable.

4th.—That by prompt and decided measures society may now commence practical arrangements throughout all civilised nations to give to the rising generation of each nation, to a considerable extent, this good and superior character, and to prepare it to advance the succeeding generation to a full good and superior character, and thus to insure perpetual progress toward excellence and happiness through the future existence of man upon the earth.

5th.—That to effect this change in the character and condition of the human race, peace among nations is necessary.

6th.—That a permanent and substantial peace may now be advantageously made between all nations,—

First, by reciprocity federative treaties, which shall place all in perpetual security.

Second, by gradually placing the population of each nation within such surroundings as can alone enable society to give to each individual within those surroundings the good and superior character required.

7th —That the experience of the past, the discoveries in chemistry, the inventions in mechanism, and the progress made in a knowledge of the laws of nature, and especially of human nature, are now sufficient to enable society to devise and execute those good and superior surroundings which are alone competent to give to society the aid necessary to form this good and superior character for all.

8th.—That the surroundings required to enable society to give this good and superior character to all will also enable those within the surroundings to create annually—with health, pleasure, and high profit—so much real useable and valuable wealth, that wealth will cease to be an article of commerce, and will be always and everywhere so abundant, that all may freely enjoy it without money and without price, and being their own, will use without abusing it.

9th.—That these surroundings may now be so devised and executed, that through their means the earth shall be gradually so well drained, cultivated, made fruitful, and beautified, that it will in a few generations, as population increases, become a terrestrial paradise, and a fit abode for the good and superior fullformed men and women thus prepared to occupy and rationally enjoy in health and unity its illimitable pleasures, with the temperance required for their stability without creating satiety.

10th.—That to effect this change in human existence, and to

attain the Millennial state upon earth, in peace and with order, great patience, prudence, foresight, wisdom, and firmness, will be required in the population of each nation;—for nature requires time to perfect all her operations,—and nations will require time to prepare for and perfect these, the finish of nature's work upon earth.

11th.—That the first practical measure to prepare for this change in the character and condition of the human race will be for the population of each nation to memorialise its present government, to take this now all-absorbing subject into fair, full, and open investigation, so that it may be well understood and fully comprehended by the government and people, in order that both may begin to execute these new good and superior surroundings with knowledge and foresight of the measures which ought to succeed each other.

12th.—That as, on the great subject now under consideration the governments can do little or nothing without the aid of public opinion strongly expressed by the great majority of the people, these memorials should be presented to the governments from every city, town, village, and country district, within each nation, in order that the government should not be in doubt as to the extent and sincerity of the public voice for the change which they desire.

13th.—That when this desire of the great majority of the nation for the change shall be made evident to the governments, the latter shall appoint a committee or commission of the most known eminent persons in each required practical department of society, to devise and execute the good and superior surroundings in which gradually to place the population of each nation.

14th.—That to make the arrangements complete to enable society to take good care of every one born within them, from their birth, through life, to their earthly death, the maximum number in one aggregate or family union to form a commonwealth, should not exceed *three thousand* souls, of the average proportion of men, women, and children.

15th.—That these family commonwealths may commence with a population of *five hundred*,—be allowed gradually to increase until approaching *three thousand*,—and then a properly arranged party from this full hive should commence on a new site a new family commonwealth.

16th.—That these family commonwealths shall be federatively united on terms of perfect reciprocity, until the entire population of each nation shall be thus well cared for by society.

17th.—That the adults of each family commonwealth will have the full power to form a good and superior character for each one born among them, and it will be the evident interest of every such adult to lend their best aid to perfect each one thus committed to their charge—physically, mentally, and practically—to the extent of their acquired knowledge on this the most important department of life.

18th.—That, to proceed understandingly to effect, in peace, in order, and with foresight, this great revolution in human existence on the earth, the first step is for nations to agree to unite federatively on terms of just reciprocity, and all to abandon the insane idea of conquest ; and that by these means, plain and simple for practice, each nation, great and small in power and territory, will in fact, without loss, labour, or expense, become the conquerer of all other nations so uniting, until each one ultimately will to all practical purpose become conquerers of the whole earth, or, in other words, the whole will become one people, having all earthly powers under their control.

19th —That the second step will be to form the population of each nation into these new scientific family commonwealths, all of which to be formed of good and superior surroundings only— for as these are, so must men and women become.

20th.—That the third practical measure will be federatively to unite gradually each of these family commonwealths to all other similarly formed scientific family commonwealths over the world.

21st.—That for immediate practical operations, and to make a good and substantial commencement of this great work, this Congress shall petition both Houses of the British Parliament to have this subject taken into full, fair, and open investigation, and shall also memorialize Her Majesty, to request Her Majesty's powerful aid and influence to promote the same.

These resolutions having been read consecutively first, were afterwards considered separately ; and subsequently each one was proposed and seconded, and all were, one by one, unanimously carried. The whole were then put as one series of resolutions, to give more time for any parties who might be inclined to make any objections before they were finally passed by the Congress ; but after due consideration by 410 members, the whole were passed unanimously.

The following Resolutions, Petitions to both Houses of Parliament, and Memorial to her Majesty were then proposed and carried in like manner.

Resolutions continued.

22nd.—That the following be the petitions to both Houses of Parliament, headed in due form :—

PETITION OF THE CONGRESS OF REFORMERS OF THE WORLD, HELD IN THE LARGE ROOM, ST. MARTIN'S HALL, LONG ACRE, LONDON, ON WEDNESDAY THE 14TH DAY OF MAY, 1856, TO THE HOUSES OF LORDS AND COMMONS.

That your petitioners have investigated the principles, and have considered the consequent practices, of an entirely new system of society, for the new formation of character, and for the government of the human race.

That the advantages which this new system offers for the permanent benefit of the population of the world are so immense, that your petitioners are most anxious that the present generation may commence to make the change, and may derive immediately some of the innumerable meliorations which this system is calculated to effect through all succeeding generations.

That your petitioners, therefore, pray that your Right Honourable (or Honourable) House will take this now all-absorbing question into immediate full, fair, and open investigation, by your Right Honourable (or Honourable) House appointing a committee or commission for the purpose, or in any other manner which the wisdom and practical experience of the House may suggest.

And your petitioners will for ever pray.

Signed on behalf of the Congress by its President,

ROBERT OWEN.

23rd. That the following be the memorial to Her Majesty :—

TO HER MOST GRACIOUS MAJESTY VICTORIA THE FIRST, QUEEN OF THE BRITISH EMPIRE.

The Memorial of the Congress of the Reformers of the World, assembled in the Great Room, St. Martin's Hall, Long Acre, London, at noon, the 14th of May, to take into consideration the best means of changing the present system of falsehood and evil over the world, for the true and good system of society, which can alone introduce and maintain truth, union, permanent prosperity, goodness, wisdom, and happiness among men.

YOUR memorialists—conscious of the unabated anxiety of your Majesty to promote the best permanent interests, the continued progress in improvements, and the happiness, of numerous nations and peoples spread over the globe and now forming the British Empire committed by Providence to be ruled under your Majesty's government—desire the power and great personal influence of your Majesty with your Ministers of State, to induce them to take into their most grave consideration the easy practical means by which the present system of falsehood and evil, by which the population of the world has been and is governed, may be changed for the true and good system of society, by which the nations of the earth, for the permanent progress and happiness of all, should now be governed.

Your memorialists cordially and heartily unite in wishing your Majesty a long and happy reign, to see this great and glorious change in the condition of all humanity in full active progress in all civilised nations.

And your Memorialists will for ever pray, &c.

Signed on behalf of the Congress by its President,

ROBERT OWEN.

It was also unanimously carried, that Lord Brougham should be requested to present the Petition to the House of Lords, Mr. Roebuck to the House of Commons, and the President to present the Memorial to Her Majesty.

The Congress then adjourned to the evening of the 18th inst.

SECOND MEETING OF THE CONGRESS OF THE RE-FORMERS OF THE WORLD, ON THE 18TH OF MAY, 1856; ADJOURNED FROM 14TH OF THE SAME MONTH.

THIS meeting was held in the Scientific Institution near Fitzroy Square, and the Great Lecture Room of the Institution was densely crowded,—no standing room being left.

The first meeting had excited great interest, and those who could not attend that meeting on account of the early hour for which it was called were now present, and eager to hear what could be proposed for the reformation of the world while such conflicting opinions were advocated by the public.

Mr. Owen, the President of the first meeting, and who had great difficulty to reach the platform through the dense crowd which filled all the avenues to it, was received on arriving at it with much cheering and strong indications of the interest which his New Views of Society had created in the advanced minds among the public.

He requested the Chairman of the public meeting, which had previously been assembled in the same place to celebrate Mr. Owen's eighty-sixth birthday, and of which meeting the proceedings were still in progress, to allow him at once to enter upon practical business,—which was readily agreed to.

Mr. Owen then concluded the proceedings of the public meeting as related in a subsequent article.

He then addressed the meeting on the importance of applying every moment of the time of such assemblages as the one before him to give a right practical direction to the public mind.

" The members occupying the pulpit, press, bar, and both Houses of Parliament, had been so unfortunately trained and educated in the old system of falsehood in principle and consequent great error in practice, that they were all actively engaged in giving a wrong direction to public opinion, and in encouraging all parties

to continue a most injurious practice—a practice, although otherwise intended, most injurious to the self-interest of every member
of the human family, from the highest in rank to the lowest, and
from the youngest to the oldest,—all being under this system
grossly mis-placed, mis-trained, mis-educated, and mis-employed ;
and thus from birth is their self interest, progress in real knowledge, and enjoyment of permanent high happiness effectually
marred through the life of every one.

" In consequence of these fundamental errors in principle and
practice, the desires, wishes, and anticipations of all are sadly
disappointed in every sphere of life, from the beggar in his tat-
tered garments, to the crowned heads in the splendour of the
purple.

" Why, then in the name of common-sense, should this false
and most injurious system to all be longer supported by the suffering population of the world ?

" Let all direct their attention to decisive practical measures, to
peaceably supersede this monster of ignorance and iniquity, by
the true system of society—by the only system which could unite
the human race in a cordial well-understood brotherhood, raising
all to an equality through life, much higher, and far superior,
physically and mentally, and in material condition, to any attained by any class, rank, or station, in any part of the world,
under this old system, now in its dotage and incapable much
longer to maintain its own existence."

The attention of the audience was now riveted on the
speaker—their feelings were warmly expressed, and a great enthusiasm was excited by the irresistible truths which he so vividly
placed before them.

After a short pause, he said,—" I must now call upon my
" friends near me to aid in that which I wish to accomplish upon
" the present occasion, being fully impressed with the belief that
" it is the last time I shall appear on this platform, where in
" years past I have so often found myself as it were at home
" among my disciples and children, learning a new system of
" society to prepare them for a new existence upon earth and the
" enjoyment of a true Millennium.

" I have now resolutions to propose to this second meeting of
" the Congress of the Reformers of the World,— for all my true
" disciples are not petty reformers of petty measures of an old
" worn-out system, but they advocate a reform that will for ever
" substantially benefit every son and daughter of man, irrespec-
" tive of colour, country, creed, or class. I will therefore now
" call upon my disciple and friend, Mr. Fleming, to read for me
" the resolutions, petitions, address, and memorial, which I wish
" to submit to this Congress, that the plain path to the only
" practice which can permanently reform the world may be put
" on public record, that sooner or later it may be, as it must be,
" carried into universal practice."

Mr. Fleming then read the following resolutions, and Mr. Owen, after the reading of each, more fully explained his views in proposing them.

Resolutions.

First Resolution.—That to reform the world, and to insure the perpetual progress towards excellence and happiness of the human race, without intermission or retrogression, two attainments are necessary,—

First, a good and superior character—physical, intellectual, moral, spiritual, and practical—for each individual of every nation, people, and tribe, over the earth,—

Second, the annual production of good, useful, and valuable wealth, to exceed the wants and wishes of the population of the world.

Second Resolution.—That the means are now ample at the disposal of society, gradually to accomplish both these results throughout every succeeding generation

Third Resolution.—That by the cordial union of governments and peoples, these two results may be attained, by plain, simple, straightforward, practical measures, beneficial for every one over the earth.

Fourth Resolution.—That this character cannot be formed, nor the wealth produced, when nations are at war, or while they shall be governed on principles leading to practices of repulsion and injustice, or conquest and domination, and necessarily of demoralisation.

These resolutions were then put separately, seconded, and carried unanimously with much enthusiasm.

The following were then proposed and unanimously agreed to.

Fifth Resolution —That this supplementry Congress of the Reformers of the World do petition both Houses of Parliament, address her Majesty, and memorialise the Congress of the United States of North America, upon these all-important subjects.

Sixth Resolution.—That the following be the Petitions to both Houses of Parliament :—

THE PETITION OF THE CONGRESS OF THE REFORMERS OF THE WORLD, AT THEIR SECOND MEETING IN THE BRITISH METROPOLIS, HELD IN THE EVENING OF THE 18TH OF MAY, WHEN THE GREAT HALL OF THE SCIENTIFIC INSTITUTION NEAR FITZROY SQUARE WAS CROWDED TO EXCESS.

SHOWETH :—

That it is now evident to your Petitioners that society as at present constituted and organised can never produce unity, rationality, goodness, or happiness, among any portion of the human race.

That society ever has been and is now based on a gross and palpable falsehood, which is the origin of evil among men, and the sole cause of their disunion, crimes, and sufferings.

That this fundamental error is now the only cause which prevents society being made to become rational in spirit, mind, and conduct, and all its members permanently happy.

That were this fundamental error, which is opposed to all facts, superseded by the true fundamental principle, in accordance with all facts, and on which alone society should be founded and the character of all men should be formed, it would become an easy task for governments to new-make the human-made part of the character of all, and to new-construct society ; thus to make all men good, healthy in body and mind, intelligent in all useful knowledge, wealthy to the extent of their wishes, wise in conduct, and continually progressing in every kind of excellence and in happiness.

That it is the highest interest of all governments and people, now to unite to effect this change in principle and practice over the world, to terminate wars, and to prepare its population to use the language of truth only, instead of the language of falsehood, to become honest in mind and conduct, instead of being deceptious in the one and dishonest in the other, and thus to pave the way for all to be made from birth, by a new training, education, and mode of employment, rational beings, making themselves and others continually progressive in happiness.

That by these proceedings, now so pressingly required to calm the present alarmed and excited state of nations and individuals, a new existence among them would arise, by which the governments of these nations would be enabled to create new surroundings for educating and employing these people, and thus to make all become full-formed rational men and women, knowing and doing their highest duty to themselves and to all others.

That your Petitioners are also conscious that the existing classification of society over the world has emanated from the same false fundamental principle.

That while this classification shall be blindly maintained by the authorities in all nations, men can never be truthful, just, and honest to one another, but must continue as heretofore to think and act most irrationally, and to be deceptious and dishonest.

That, seeing these lamentable errors pervading society, your Petitioners deem the time to have arrived for nations to be frank and open with their respective governments, and to express to them the language of truth without circumlocution on all subjects involving the permanent interests of the people and their rulers.

That your Petitioners therefore state with the confidence of truth which no rational mind will attempt to dispute, that to prevent crime and misery will be a far wiser course for governments now to adopt, than to irrationally persevere in permitting, if not encouraging vice, crime, and misery to abound, and then, by futile laws of men and most unjust and injurious puuishments, to make a show of attempting to diminish these evils.

That your Petitioners know that the present classification of society is producing, and can only produce, disunion and every kind of evil to all ; and that even *two* opposing classes would continue to create ill-feeling and evil, so as to prevent the existence of truth, peace, justice, or honesty between them.

That this classification is artificial and unnecessary.

That true practical measures equal to the wants and permanent interests of society are now required ; and as governments can have no practical knowledge except that which is taught them by experienced men well acquainted with the practical operations of society in all its departments, your Petitioners state upon that knowledge, that the first step to obtain permanent substantial improvement and a rational and true state of society is for nations now to form federative treaties.

That by such treaties being justly formed, each nation so uniting would be an immense gainer, and would lose nothing.

That these federative treaties can alone insure peace among nations ; and that permanent peace is now required for the progressive improvement of the population of the world.

That steam, electricity, self-interest, and extended knowledge of human nature and of its true wants, have already prepared the way for this union among all nations.

That the time has therefore arrived for these federative treaties to be commenced, and gradually to be extended from nation to nation until all shall be permanently united as one people, with one interest only,—all cordially promoting the happpiness of each.

That these federative treaties would enable governments and peoples to unite on the true fundamental principle on which alone society should be based, and thus simultaneously to commence a new and rational system of educating and governing the human race, by forming in all countries over the world New and Superior Surroundings, which will constitute Scientific Family Commonwealths, not exceeding in each such family a population of *three thousand* as a maximum number.

That by these proceedings and by this simple arrangement a true and most advantageous classification of society would be established, all the business of life would be performed in a superior manner, union would become universal, and every one born within these new surroundings would be better placed and cared for through life than are now the children of any royal family, or of any class in any country over the world.

That your petitioners confidently state that they know the most ample means exist, if wisely directed and used, to give permanent progressive prosperity and happiness to the population of the world ; and that it is now the highest interest and duty of governments and people to unite in giving the right direction to these superabundant means to insure the permanent well-being and well-doing of the human race.

That your petitioners also know that if governments will not now unite to effect this happy change from error, falsehood, evil, and misery, to correct principles, truth, goodness, and happiness, —the day is not far distant when the people will be stimulated by their unnecessary sufferings and misery to take their own cause into their own hands and adopt the new and true principles and practices of governing for themselves.

That your petitioners are aware that this great and glorious change for man could be sooner, more peaceably, and much better effected by the governments taking the lead and uniting with the people thus to change evil for good over the world.

Your petitioners therefore pray that your Right Honourable (or Honourable) House will now have this ALL-IMPORTANT subject thoroughly investigated, openly, fully, and fairly, by a Committee of your Right Honourable (or Honourable) House, or in any other manner better devised to attain the object of your petitioners.

And your Petitioners will for ever pray.

Signed by order of the Congress,

ROBERT OWEN.

President at the second meeting.

May, 1856.

Seventh Resolution.—That the following be the address to Her Majesty :—

ADDRESS TO HER MOST GRACIOUS MAJESTY, VICTORIA THE FIRST, QUEEN OF THE BRITISH EMPIRE.

May it please your Majesty—

Your Majesty's memorialists, assembled in the second meeting of the Congress of the Reformers of the World, in the British metropolis, entreat your Majesty to take into your consideration the extent of gross ignorance, squalid poverty, extended injurious educated error, falsehood, and disunion, among so many of your Majesty's subjects, and the crime and misery thus produced, and now to learn from them, through the increasing knowledge acquired by the people committed to your Majesty's government, the great and all-cheering truth to your Majesty's amiable disposition and well known love for your subjects,—that the discovery has been attained by which these evils can be overcome, and by which permanent peace, prosperity, goodness, and happiness, can be insured for all conditions of the human race in every country over the earth.

That this subject, to make it effective for universal practice, requires only to be be thoroughly investigated.

That your memorialists therefore pray your Majesty to direct your Majesty's rssponsible ministers to bring this important discovery before the British Parliament, that it may be openly, fully, and fairly discussed, critically examined, and thoroughly sifted, so as to bring out all its immense benefits, which it is calculated to give not only to the subjects of your Majesty's extended empire, but also to the entire population of the world.

And your Majesty's memorialists will for ever pray.

Signed, by the President, by order of the Congress of the Reformers of the world, at their second meeting of the Congress, this 18th day of May, 1856.

ROBERT OWEN.

Eighth Resolution —That the following be the Memorial to the Congress of the United States : —

MEMORIAL TO THE CONGRESS OF THE UNITED STATES, FROM THE CONGRESS OF THE REFORMERS OF THE WORLD, ASSEMBLED IN THE BRITISH METROPOLIS FROM THE 14TH TO THE 18TH OF MAY, 1856.

YOUR memorialists—men and women of different nations, but chiefly of the British Empire,— members of the Congress of the Reformers of the World, address you as brothers of the same family, and as friends to the permanent peace and progress in knowledge, wisdom, and goodness, of the population of the world.

Your memorialists admire the foresight, wisdom, and spirit, of the founders of your advanced constitution, over all previous attempts to form one, and the same qualities of mind in the signers of your Act of Independence, and the devisers of national federative treaties.

These are measures, in the estimation of your memorialists, which it would be advantageous in the nations of the world to follow ; for universal mental liberty is now required, and self independence as far as practicable with superior social arrange· ments for the government of all people.

Your memorialists, as a first step in practice to obtain permanent peace among nations, most earnestly recommend the United States now to form a FEDERATIVE TREATY with Great Britain.

Such treaty, made on terms of justice and liberal reciprocity, would give to each—without loss, trouble, or expenditure—a splendid empire, and would increase the political power and beneficial influence of both more than fourfold.

Your memorialists deem these considerations of overwhelming interest to induce both nations cordially to unite in these wise measures to terminate all differences between both empires, and to remove for ever all causes of national jealousy or differences of any kind.

The advantages to be derived from a federative treaty between two such powerful empires would be seen by other nations to be so enormous, that the example would be irresistible, and all would desire to pursue the same wise course. Thus soon would nation unite to nation, until all would form but one great federation, which would include the population of the world;—when, indeed, swords might be made into ploughshares, and spears into pruning hooks, and peace and goodwill would pervade the spirit of humanity, and progress in all arts and sciences, in unity, wisdom, and goodness, would be rapid and illimitable.

Therefore your memorialists have confidence in the sagacity and wisdom of the Congress and population of the United States, to meet the government and people of the British Empire half way in the pure spirit of charity, kindness, and brotherly affection, to form this federative treaty, and to act with prompt energy to endeavour to carry these views into speedy execution, and thus to meet the ardent wishes and hopes of these memorialists.

Signed on behalf of the Congress of the Reformers of the World.

ROBERT OWEN.

President of the Congress, 18th May, 1856.

Mr. Fleming, on seconding the memorial to the Congress of the United States, expressed his great satisfaction with the entire proceedings of the evening, but could not allow them to conclude without stating the gratification which he experienced at the unanimity and cordial union of feeling which pervaded the meeting, in favour of the new proposed practical measures of their old well-tried leader, and their unabated confidence in his far-seeing judgment of what should be done to forward the great revolution which he has so long advocated, and which all things indicate is near at hand. He concluded by expressing the great satisfaction he enjoyed in witnessing the attachment and affection of this closely-packed meeting for his old friend, who had opened the path for so many improved innovations for the liberty of the subject, and in which during his long ministry he had led the way.

Mr. Owen then terminated the meeting by a farewell address to his old friends and followers, recommending them, as he always did, to continue united, and in every way in their power to persevere in aiding the cause of universal humanity.

On concluding he was cheered by the heartfelt applause of all present.

TEA PARTY AND PUBLIC MEETING TO CELEBRATE MR. OWEN'S BIRTHDAY.

A tea party and public meeting were held on the evening of the 18th of May, in the Scientific Institution near Fitzroy Square, to celebrate the eighty-sixth birthday of Robert Owen, who has devoted his life to prepare the population of this and other countries for an entire change in the system of society by which all nations and peoples have hitherto had their characters formed, and by which they have been governed.

Mr. Owen, who entered at eight o'clock, had great difficulty in making his way through the dense crowd to the platform, so filled that there was scarcely standing room to be found for the friends who wished to be near him.

He was received, as he always is at his public meetings, with the hearty cheers of all present. When he arrived on the platform, Mr. Holyoake was addressing the closely-packed audience of upwards of one thousand persons, the utmost number the Hall could contain.

Mr. Owen immediately hinted to Mr. Holyoake that it would oblige him if he would be very brief, as mere personal praise was now a sad waste of most precious time in such a public meeting, when business of the highest importance to the welfare of all, required to be transacted.

Mr. Holyoake immediately suspended his address, when Mr. Owen requested permission of the chairman of the meeting to propose resolutions. This being granted, Mr. Owen addressed the audience at some length with his usual effect at his public meetings, and all he said was responded to by the heartfelt applause of those present.

He then proposed the following

Resolutions.

First Resolution.—That the public of the civilised portion of society is become too enlightened not to see the cause of the past and present error and evil of society in the universal principle of disunion and repulsion, on which the character of all men has been formed, and all society constructed.

Second Resolution.—That the discovery of this origin of evil has disclosed the only remedy by which it can be overcome, and the principle and practice of good made to supersede it over the world.

Third Resolution.—That Petitions be presented to both Houses of Parliament, to adopt effective measures to remove from society the cause of evil to man, and to introduce the only cause which can make the human race good, wise, wealthy, and happy.

Fourth Resolution.—That the following be the Petitions to be presented to both Houses from this meeting :—

PETITION OF A CROWDED PUBLIC MEETING, HELD IN THE SCIENTIFIC INSTITUTION NEAR FITZROY SQUARE, ON THE EVENING OF THE 18th OF MAY, 1856, TO THE HOUSES OF LORDS AND COMMONS.

THAT your Petitioners are now enlightened on the true cause of the evils which they and their forefathers have suffered, and they desire this cause should now be peaceably superseded by the true fundamental principle on which the character of all from birth should be formed and society constructed to prevent the future existence of evil.

That by this simple change a new character with a new spirit of universal charity and love for our race will be given to man, and society, by being constructed to be consistent with itself and with that principle, will become rational and harmonious throughout the world.

That with this change there would be no ignorance,—no poverty,—no disunion,—no conflicts,—no crime,—no punishment,—no misery.

That these and all other evils directly emanate from the insane principle opposed to every known fact, that individual man forms his own physical and mental qualities, and therefore that he should be made responsible to society for those qualities of body and mind which his Creator and society have forced him to receive from his birth.

That while society shall continue to be based on this principle opposed to all facts, and therefore false, absurd, and wicked, men cannot avoid having their divine natural qualities so misdirected from birth that they cannot prevent their being made to become false, irrational, and wicked, as every class over the world has been made to be, and now is, to the great injury and misery of all.

That this fundamental error is opposed to the well-being, well-doing, and happiness of our nation and of the world, and is calculated to waste most valuable time in useless talking or debating about trifling matters of no lasting importance to ourselves or other nations.

That the time of our public assemblies should now be solely occupied in preparing the public mind for an entire change of system in principle and practice, and thus to make all human affairs consistent and harmonious.

That by this change from the system of falsehood and evil to the system of truth and good, all men over the world of every grade and rank will be permanently benefited to an extent beyond all present human estimate, because all will be made good and rational, and wealth will easily and pleasantly be made everywhere to superabound.

That your Petitioners therefore pray your Right Honourable (or Honourable) House to appoint a Committee of competent persons to openly, fully, and fairly investigate this now the most immediately important of all subjects, or to have it so investigated by any other means which your Right Honourable (or Honourable) House may direct.

And your Petitioners will for ever pray, &c.

Fifth Resolution.—That Lord Monteagle be requested to present the Petition to the House of Peers, and Lord Goderich to the House of Commons.

When these proceedings were finished, Mr. Owen again addressed the audience, and proposed, as they were all reformers, and as those who were present at the Congress of the Reformers of the World, which commenced at noon, on Wednesday last, the 14th of May, were also now here, that the meeting should resolve itself into a continuation of the Congress held on the 14th inst. in St. Martin's Hall, as so many were prevented attending on that occasion on account of the early hour at which it commenced. This proposal was unanimously agreed to, and the audience became the second meeting of the " Congress of the Reformers of the World."

THE USE, ADVANTAGES, AND BEAUTY, OF MAN'S FORMATION, WHEN HE SHALL BE FULLY DEVELOPED.

MAN's faculties can never be developed while society shall continue as at present based on a gross falsehood, and while his character shall be formed from birth on the same error.

As soon as the governments and people of the now separated nations in their apparent interests shall unite in basing society on its only true foundation, shall form the character of all upon that foundation, and shall make the practical surroundings of life to be in accordance with the same, the existence of man over the earth will become an uninterrupted life of health, pleasure, rational enjoyment, and perpetual progress in knowledge, wisdom, unity, and happiness.

His character will then be naturally formed, and in consequence he will always think and act according to the unchanging laws of God and nature. Truth will be his only language, and his love to God, through his daily practical love to all men, will be the universal conduct of every one from birth through life. For as soon as man shall be trained, educated, and placed, within such surroundings as will permit him to speak the truth only on all occasions, to be taught to know himself, and to discover the use, power, beauty, and divinity of his created nature, then will the physical, mental, and spiritual faculties and propensities of both sexes be ascertained to be not only good, but absolutely necessary to form a superior and happy character for the human race.

It will then be seen and understood that to elevate all of human-kind into full-formed rational thinking and acting men and women, *all* their organs, faculties, and propensities must be cultivated from their birth in each to the extent that nature will admit when the individuals shall be placed within superior human-made surroundings, devised to be in accordance with their divine nature, and when each one shall be so situated in society as freely to exercise all his or her faculties and propensities up to, but not beyond, the point of temperance,.

It is in this advanced phase of society only that the existence of the human race can be elevated, from its present gross irrational conditions, in which it is inferior to the life of various animals, to a rational, consistent, and superior state of existence upon earth.

How much is it to be regretted that man should continue so blind to his own interest and happiness as not to discover that society in the aggregate has attained the means—through the progress of material, mental, and spiritual knowledge, when those means shall be rationally used and applied—to insure the well-being, well-doing, and uninterrupted happiness of the human race !

Let common sense now begin to take the place of inexperienced, vague, inconsistent, and wild imaginations,—imaginations arising from the artificial surroundings made by men in various districts of the earth while ignorant of nature, of themselves, and of the knowledge how to form rational societies by creating rational surroundings.

Men everywhere, being ignorant of nature and of themselves, and while too undeveloped to investigate causes, imagined first appearances to be realities, and were in consequence led into many fatal mistakes, which have retarded their progress to the happiness which it is now evident they are ultimately destined to enjoy as a race of superior rational beings.

For example,—this mistaking of first appearances for realities induced our early ancestors for unnumbered ages to believe most undoubtingly that our globe was fixed and immovable, not round, but flat, and that the sun and our planetary system and all the stars moved daily round our earth, which they concluded was the centre of the universe. And those who first expressed their doubts openly of this creed of first impressions were called infidels, and were considered deserving of death for their infidelity to old established truths, as all believed them, but which time and experience have proved to be palpable and injurious falsehoods—errors of the human imagination and opposed to all facts.

These were *material* errors, which greatly retarded progres sin material knowledge. Yet these material errors have created but a small part of the sufferings of the human race, when compared with the sufferings inflicted upon all by the far greater mental errors of the imagination—errors arising from first appearances, without investigation or attention to facts always prominent and continually forcing themselves in all directions upon the observation of our faculties.

Men, from some wise purpose, which, no doubt, will be hereafter discovered, have been thus long blindly led to believe that they formed themselves individually, and that in consequence they were responsible to the power which created their divine nature, and to society which gave them the human-made part of their character ;—and that through this responsibility only could man and society be well-governed, or made to be good and rational. These absurd notions, opposed to all facts, are even now maintained by the authorities of the world ; while all facts, fairly and fully investigated, prove that these errors are the only means by which men and society could have been so long made wicked and irrational as they are everywhere made to be at this day.

How are all nations and peoples to be disabused of this error, so fatal to their rationality and happiness ?

Only by showing, in the spirit of universal charity, kindness, and love, the truth upon this all-important subject so fully and clearly to the authorities and instructors of the human race, that they cannot avoid seeing it and comprehending the magnificent and overwhelming beneficial results of this knowledge, to themselves, their children, and to the entire family of man, through all future ages.

The human race during its undeveloped or partially developed state has made the CREATED *responsible for its qualities to the powers which created it and which gave it those qualities without its knowledge and consent.*

Could insanity, perverting the human intellects to the greatest extent, exceed these errors, at present universally forced into the unresisting young mind and made to pervade it through life ?

No wonder that nations are unable to erect lunatic asylums large or fast enough to receive the lunatics thus made from their birth by society, previously made so by the same fatal errors of the human imagination—errors so gross as to be opposed to *all existing facts.*

It is now put to the proof whether the rulers and teachers of the human race are sufficiently developed in their rational faculties and reasoning powers to be competent to perceive these ever occuring and everlasting truths, on a right understanding of which the future progress of man in love, unity, wisdom, wealth, and happiness depends.

It will now also be proved whether this is the period destined by that Power whose mode of existence and operations are yet hidden from man, to commence the great and glorious change in the condition of the human race, from gross irrationality in mind and practice, producing endless evils to all, to a rational and consistent mind and practice, when ignorance, folly, disunion, poverty, crime, punishment, hatred, repulsion, and misery, shall be universally replaced by knowledge, wisdom, unity, wealth, goodness, attraction, love, and happiness.

It is now likewise to be proved whether there is sufficient common sense between the governments and people of the world to renounce a palpable fundamental falsehood respecting human nature, and to adopt and replace it with a fundamental truth equally palpable. And now gradually to abandon most irrational surroundings, all of which have emanated from that fundamental falsehood ; and to commence creating new surroundings—surroundings which will necessarily emanate from the fundamental truth, as soon as it shall be made to supersede the fundamental error.

(To be continued.)

THE SMITHSONIAN INSTITUTION.

In narrating the proceedings in the Congress of the United States previous to the establishment of the Smithsonian Institution, I stated that the second attempt to carry the Bill respecting it through the Congress, and which was unsuccessful, was made by Governor Tallmadge of Wisconsin. My Son Robert has since informed me that this is incorrect. The second attempt was made by Senator Tappan of Ohio.

CORRESPONDENCE.—A communication respecting the Architecture of " Homes of Harmony," with plans given by Spirits, which was forwarded from the United States of North America to be laid before the Congress of the Reformers of the World, will be inserted in No. 6 of this Gazette.

A birthday address received from my disciples and friends at Stockport will also be given in No. 6.

London :—Published by the Author at 16, Great Windmill Street, Haymarket : and sold by Holyoake, 147, Fleet Street ; Truelove, 240, Strand; Goddard, 14, Great Portland Street, Cavendish Square; Farrah, 21, John Street, Fitzroy Square ; and all Booksellers.

Robert Owen's
MILLENNIAL GAZETTE;

EXPLANATORY OF THE PRINCIPLES AND PRACTICES BY WHICH, IN PEACE, WITH TRUTH, HONESTY, AND SIMPLICITY, THE NEW EXISTENCE OF MAN UPON THE EARTH MAY BE EASILY AND SPEEDILY COMMENCED.

" The character of Man is formed *for* him, and *not by* him !"

No. 6.]   JULY 1st, 1856.   [PRICE 6D.

THE USE, ADVANTAGES, AND BEAUTY, OF MAN'S FORMATION, WHEN HE SHALL BE FULLY DEVELOPED.

(Continued from No. 5.)

It will now also be proved whether the human faculties are so far developed as to be enabled, when their attention has been especially called to the subject, to perceive that innumerable facts continually demonstrate the great truth—*that any human being may be forced from birth by the society which surrounds him to acquire any language, religion, belief, habits, manners, prejudices, local ideas, and conduct, without merit or demerit being rationally attributable to the individual. And also, that through this knowledge society may easily adopt practical measures, by creating new surroundings not difficult to devise and execute, by which all placed within them shall be made to acquire and speak perfectly a good language, and to express the truth only,—to receive the true religion and apply it to practice through life,—to believe that only which is in accordance with all facts,—to acquire superior habits and manners,—to be freed from local and general prejudices,—and always to be wise and consistent in conduct, so as to become a good, useful, and valuable member of society, and yet never to attribute to himself any merit, or claim any reward, except to be equal to his fellows at the various periods of life, when life shall be divided by society rationally for its business, progress, and enjoyment.*

If the human faculties have attained this state of development, or can now be assisted to enable them to acquire this advanced stage of progress, then may all nations, now so wonderously linked together by the combined new powers of the press, steam, and electricity, acquire the knowledge of the divine qualities of human nature, and how from birth to give a wise direction to those qualities, and begin to prepare for the introduction in practice of the New Existence of Man upon the Earth, and the attainment of the Millennial life so long promised to our race.

Peace has been attained by the great powers of the world. Let all now guard that peace until all nations shall be united by federative treaties, making all people into one nation, seeing and knowing that there is but one real interest for our race, which is, that all should cordially promote each other's progress in goodness, knowledge, and happiness.

People of the world! Are you sufficiently developed as rational beings to be prepared to induce your governments to enter upon this new state of existence, so easily attainable when you can abandon the false fundamental principle on which society is now based, and adopt the only true fundamental principle which can make you consistent in mind and practice, and give you perpetual progress and happiness.

The *use*, then, of man's formation is to enable him to acquire real knowledge, through experience and a calm comprehensive investigation of facts, and especially of those facts which enable him to know what manner of being he is,—what are the organs, faculties, propensities, qualities, and powers, which God and nature give to humanity,—how society from ignorance of this knowledge has misdirected these divinely given powers from the birth of every individual,—how they may now be all well-cultivated, directed, and exercised, so as to insure the health, progress towards excellence in all things, and happiness of individuals and of society.

The *advantages* of man's formation, when thus used, will be to make the human race rational, consistent at all times in mind and practice, and, compared with the race as it is at present, superior beings, occupied in making the earth a terrestrial paradise, and in training and educating each generation to exceed its predecessors in knowledge, wisdom, and goodness, and in attaining higher and higher progressive enjoyment.

When man's formation shall be applied to these uses, so as to attain these natural advantages, the *beauty* of the form in both sexes will far exceed any human forms ever yet seen upon the earth,—a high superior mind and spirit, beaming with love, goodness, and wisdom, will be expressed in every feature of the countenance and in every limb and gesture of the body,—all defects of body and mind and the causes of disease in both will gradually diminish, until they will cease to exist, and in succeeding generations will be unknown.

Rulers and Teachers of men! Can you now learn this lesson and permit the population of the world to become attractive, to love one another, to cordially assist each other in attaining every kind of excellence, and thus, one and all, to become united, rational, wise, and happy?

To effect this great and glorious revolution for humanity, the united will of the governments and people is alone necessary. The materials to effect this change exist abundantly over the earth, and wait only to be called into action.

ARCHITECTURE OF THE FUTURE.—DESIGNS FOR HOMES OF HARMONY, TRANSMITTED FROM THE SPIRIT WORLD.

(Note to Mr. Owen.)

TO ROBERT OWEN :

DEAR AND MUCH RESPECTED SIR,—

I send you several very imperfectly drawn (because very hurriedly done) diagrams, with an accompanying paper, to be presented by you, (if you deem it wise so to do,) to the Congress, &c., of the 14th May. I do this at the suggestion of my Spirit Teachers, under whose daily tuition I hope, by and by, to elaborate my especial part of an entirely new, more beautiful, and, in every way, more perfect system of architecture, than the world has yet known, cared for, or thought of. What I send you will give you but a very imperfect idea of this singularly beautiful and highly useful manifestation from the heavens ; but it is the best I can do at present, for I do it at short notice and in the midst of many cares and much struggle. Hereafter I may do better, as the advent of the spheres grows in breadth and strength, and as means (which give time and freedom from cares, &c.) come to me and mine.

Much of the time, for some three years, I have spent in elaborating these new ideas. Much more I shall doubtless spend in the future, with the serene hope that much good may come to humanity, (and through humanity *only*, to me and mine,) by these new labours.

With the highest regard for your self-sacrificing character, in labouring for universal man, I now submit these documents to your wise disposal.

S. C. HEWITT,
22, Tremont Street.

Boston, May 1st, 1856.

To Robert Owen and others, members of the Congress to be assembled in London, England, 14th May, 1856, to discuss principles and measures for the Reformatiom of the World.

GENTLEMEN,—

The hour has now fully come, when persons interested in important humanitary efforts should come together, associate, look one another in the face, communicate the purposes, plans, ends, and aims, which each and all have in view.

Among the many subjects which have occupied the attention of man in past ages, that of *structures* has been one of the most important. Little or no progress can be made until man shall be comfortably circumstanced. He needs, not only to look out on the broad landscape, to journey over the vast prairies, to wander among the silent groves, to seek shelter in the quiet arbour; but he also needs a comfortable, cheerful, harmonious place of abode—a HOME which shall be, at once, the sacred *locale* of his affections, the embodiment of his tastes, and, if not the symbol of his actual attainments, at least that of his aspirations and his more ennobling desires.

The past has been the age of struggle. Contest between man and man, nation and nation, has everywhere been exhibited. And it can hardly be said, even yet, that humanity has an abiding place, or a continual city. But a new order of society is now being ushered into existence. New forms of life and action will appear. There will be less of isolation—of mere *individualism* ; there will be more of association, of co-operation,—exhibiting the harmonious GROUP-LIFE. And finer offspring, also, manifesting the finer aspirations, will be produced through the aid of these finer conditions.

The new order of society will call for NEW ARCHITECTURE, corresponding to its wants, its aspirations. Now, nature exhibits *variety* It also manifests *unity.* In a very prominent way, and as one of her main features, nature presents CIRCULARITY OF FORM. Wherever the human eye beholds nature, it marks that interesting phenomenon. The forests, the earth, the planets, and, in short, all the heavenly bodies, (to say nothing of the human structure,) exhibit circularity of form.

It hardly needs to be said, that as the *human body* becomes perfect, it presents a more charming and agreeable rotundity of form. It is the house in which the man dwells, and as the man becomes rounded, all-sided, beautiful, in the maturity of his spiritual growth, his dwelling will exhibit a corresponding development.

In opening up, then, to the public mind a new style of architecture, naturally enough attention is turned to *circularity of form.* Within a few past years, not a few persons dwelling in

(Continued on page 11.*)*

PLATE 1.

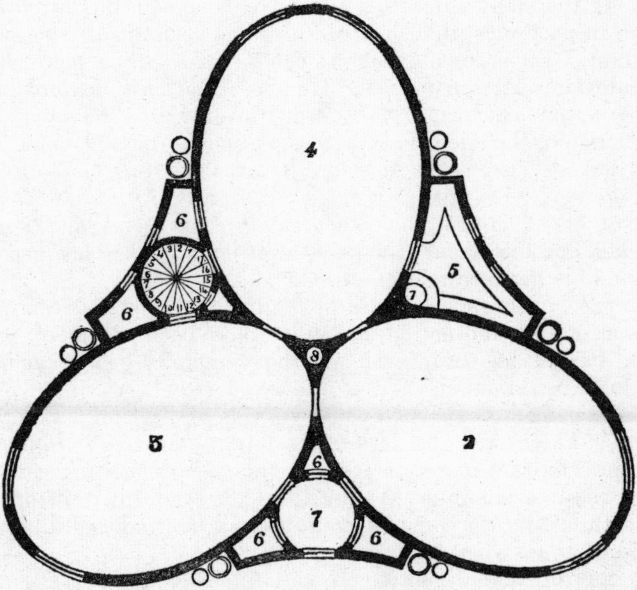

HOME OF HARMONY. GROUND PLAN OF 1st STORY.

Three Stories High—9 Rooms.

1. Front Hall—diam. 6 feet.
2. Parlour—25 × 18.
3. Sitting Room.
4. Kitchen and Dining Room.

5. Pantry.
6. Closets.
7. Chimney.
8. Flue for Ventilation and Heating.

PLATE 2.

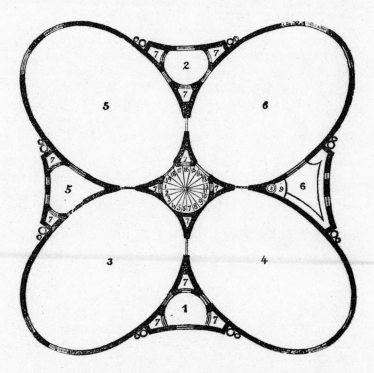

HOME OF HARMONY.—GROUND PLAN OF 1st STORY.

Three Stories High—14 Rooms.

1. Front Hall—6½ feet diam.
2. Back Hall   „   „
3. Drawing Room 25 × 18.
4. Parlour   „   „   „
5. Sitting and Dining Room, and Ladies' Dressing Room, —25 × 18.

6. Kitchen 25 × 18.
7. Closets.
8. Chimney.

1—19. Spiral Stairs from Kitchen, and Dining, and Sitting Room— 6 feet diam.
9. Gas Cooking Arrangement.

PLATE 3.

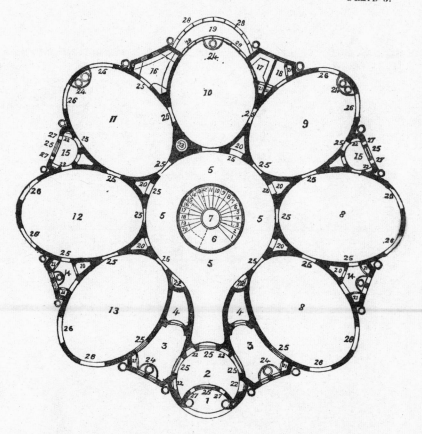

HOME OF HARMONY.—GROUND PLAN OF FIRST STORY.

1. Niche Entrance.
2. Entrance Hall.
3. Reception Rooms.
4. Wardrobes.
5. Inner Hall.
6. Spiral Stairs.
7. Opening for Light.
8. Drawing Rooms.
9. Music and Amusement Rooms.
10. Breakfast Room.
11. Kitchen.
12. Dining Room.
13. Family Parlour.
14. Ladies Dressing Rooms.
15. Side Entrances.
16. Pantry.
17. China Closet.
18. Musical Cabinet.
19. Conservatory.
20. Closets.
21. Cupboards.
22. Niches.
23. Chimney.
24. Toilets and Patent Wash Bowls.
25. Doors.
26. Windows.
27. Side Lights.
28. Iron and Glass.

(Continued from page 4.)

the American nation have been unusually unfolded as trans-
mitters from the Spirit World to the earth condition. Among
these persons there are able constructors, draughtsmen, inventors,
and diagramists ; and their mental powers, to some considerable
extent, have been directed to the study of architecture. Some
of the diagrams which have been transmitted are now forwarded
to this assembly for critical and careful inspection. Their simplicity of style, their beauty of form, their harmony with nature,
must attract the attention of intelligent persons in both the Old
World and the New.

These diagrams, this day presented, may be regarded in the
light of *rude efforts only,* intended to turn the attention of the
public mind to new forms, not only of structure for the individual or isolated family, but for unitary edifices ; also for the organisation of CIRCULAR CITIES. Persons who contemplate emi-
grating to the New World from the Old, would be advantaged by
considering the feasibility of organising their townships in such
ways that educational, religious, and commercial structures might
be located in their general centre. Religion is an element of
man's nature ; education is essential for all ; commerce is no less
important. Inasmuch, then, as all persons in a given territory
to a greater or lesser extent need these, they should be located at
equi-distant points—viz., the centre.

It were only needful to hint this subject to intelligent persons,
and they will instantly perceive the advantages which must result
from an arrangement of this character. The advantages, also,
derived from lighting and warming edifices thus located, can
hardly be over-estimated.

In presenting this subject to the consideration of this assem-
blage, it is felt that it may wisely take action in respect to the
general subject of architecture, without committing itself to any
particular plan at the present time ; and that the matter, as thus
presented, may take its place among the papers which appear on
this occasion for the consideration of this intelligent body.
And the hope is indulged that it will appear among its published
proceedings. Slight *diagrams*, corresponding to those accompanying this paper, might, with but trifling expense, find place
in the report. And should persons who inspect these diagrams
desire further information in regard to this branch of effort, they
will please address the undersigned, who will be most happy to
communicate further in respect to this subject, embracing teachings in reference to the best sites for edifices for the unitary villages, and also in respect to *materials* which may be economically
used for building purposes.

S. C. HEWITT.

No. 22, Tremont Street, Boston,
Massachusetts, U.S.A., May 1st, 1856.

REPLY TO MR. HEWITT.

My Dear Sir,—

I am glad to find that spirits versed in architecture have commenced giving knowledge to mortals on this subject. But the architecture for the New Existence of Man upon the Earth in the spiritual social state will require to be a united or combined arrangement for a federative family society of three thousand in number, and so combined into one arrangement as to be the most convenient for *all* the purposes of such united society.

More than thirty years ago I devoted, aided by a talented scientific architect, much time and great attention to devise such a combination, and I had it engraved and circulated to some extent. I will endeavour to procure a copy of the publication with the engraving, and send you one. Since that period, however, many scientific improvements connected with domestic buildings and arrangements have been made, and much new experience has been acquired by the erection of so many large hotels in the United States and elsewhere, which may yet be adopted to improve this first idea of combined social arrangements, and greater perfection may be now attained. I hope, however, that the spirits will continue to proceed onward in this good work. There is much to be admired in what they have enabled you to do.

ROBERT OWEN.

Sevenoaks Park, 24th June, 1856.

ADDRESS OF CONGRATULATION TO RORERT OWEN ON HIS 86th BIRTHDAY, FROM HIS FRIENDS AND DISCIPLES AT STOCKPORT.

Venerable and Respected Father,—

In your name, Robert Owen, we have the pleasure of meeting and taking tea together, in commemoration of your attainment of your 86th birthday. Our pleasure increases day by day and year by year as your life of benevolence is lengthened, knowing you have long dedicated yourself to the human race. You belong not to class, or sect, or country, or colour, but to mankind. If pride were an element of your character, you have reasons to be proud of your success.

How many reforms have you initiated, and how much reformation in our national institutions owes its existence to your influence,—to your constant unwearied endeavours for the physical, mental, and moral elevation of the human race. Every man who takes a fair and unprejudiced retrospect of the progress of public opinion in Europe and America, must acknowledge that

that mental freedom of which we are all so sensitive and proud
is immensely due to your influence on the governments and
peoples. We know what an engine of power is the press, and to
you is due the honour of having aided in conquering for us the
freedom of the " fourth estate." Through its medium you have
been enabled from time to time to develope a system of mental
and moral science, which must ultimately dispel the dark clouds
of superstition, with its train of hideous deformities and gross
persecutions, and substitute in its stead—" truth without mystery, mixture of error, or fear of man." You have taught us
the truth, than which there is none greater or more important—
" that the character of man is formed for him, and not by him."
Let this truth be deeply impressed on all our public teachers,
and reiterated until the nations and peoples are imbued with the
charity which its reception and incorporation in our habits must
induce, and the world is regenerated—its salvation is realised.

The world is better for you having lived in it. The factory
operative has need to thank the philosopher of Lanark for his
noble and generous example and self-sacrifice, in being one of the
first to propose, and the first to carry into practice, the reduction
of the hours of labour. The infant school, too, is greatly indebted to Robert Owen of New Lanark. *There* was established
the infant school from which Lancaster and Wilderspin drew
largely in their laudable endeavours to popularise the infant
school system. Indeed, it is of no use to attempt to catalogue your
services in a short address like the present. They are innumerable, and are mostly *appropriated* and *unacknowledged*.

The ocean has many tributaries, which disappear and are lost
in the vastness of its waters ; and there is a great ocean of reformation imbibing and absorbing the streaming contributions
from many sources, and Robert Owen is the grandest and noblest
stream of all, flowing majestically down the tide of time, irrigating and renovating the surrounding soil with his genial influence.
In due season the soil will produce fruit. The mental light scat-
tered over the world's wide domain will be radiated by numerous
disciples to all time, and in this sense " the mortal will put on
immortality."

Accept our warmest thanks and congratulations for your past
services, and let us hope you may live long and happily to bless
our race with your benign influence, and that you may further
encourage us by your noble example and sacrifice of self.

Signed on behalf of the meeting

JOHN HINDLE,

Chairman.

Stockport, May 14th, 1856.

THE NECESSITY NOW FOR THE UNION OF GOVERNMENTS AND PEOPLE.

WITHOUT the union of governments and people the population of the world will be in continual excitement and high agitation against the ignorance, despotism, injustice, and gross mis-rule of those who have the direction of public affairs, and governors and governed will be in perpetual contests, and both unnecessary sufferers.

It is the interest of the human race to be permanently cordially united. But there can be no cordial union between governments and people, or between governments, or between the people, under the existing system by which the character of all is formed and society is constructed.

The fundamental principle on which this system is based is not only false, as being opposed to all facts, but it is so repulsive in all its practical consequences that it becomes an insuperable obstacle to a cordial union among men in every division of society over the earth.

So long as each one shall be forced by false instruction from birth to believe that he forms his own qualities and powers, physical and mental, and his own conduct, there can be no real unity among men, nor can they attain to a state of rationality.

Men over the earth at this day, in consequence of this misinstruction from birth through life, are made to think and act in direct opposition to their own interest, well-being, well-doing, and happiness,—to speak the language of falsehood,— to be unjust to each other and to themselves,—and always to be acting a deceptious part in the drama of life.

From this false and repulsive fundamental principle, from which the present artificial state of society has arisen, proceeds the division of our race into contending classes with opposing interests.

It is by this artificial division of classes, opposing men to men throughout society, that the *few* by *their union* rule the many with a rod of iron, and make downright fools of them—sending them when they please like silly sheep to slaughter one another by hundreds, by thousands, and sometimes by tens and hundreds of thousands,—to waste and destroy much valuable property, and for no one interest of the millions who by their labour are forced to make good all this waste and destruction of wealth which might have been, and ought to have been, employed to instruct and insure the permanent happiness of governors and governed.

Is not the time yet come when the multitude can discover the cause of their disunion, and, in consequence, of their childish weakness and infantile submission to the most unjust and cruel laws and despotic conduct?

Is it a fact that this great multitude of human beings over the

earth must continue to be kept in this senseless state of stupidity,
degradation, and physical and mental weakness, through the want
of so much moral courage as would prevent their being frightened
out of all their common sense by a mere word—SOCIALISM:—
a word which their rulers and teachers have contrived to make
them dread more than all the armies of the world.   And why ?
Because SOCIALISM, or UNION, which are synonimous terms,
would, when rightly understood, reform the world, and make man
a rational, independent, and happy being, capable, in union with
his fellows, to assist to govern the human race a thousand times
better than it has ever yet been governed, or is now governed in
any part of the world.

Yes,—my wondering brothers of every clime, and colour, and
creed, and class,—this dreaded word SOCIALISM is destined to
redeem the human race from sin and misery, and to save mankind by THEIR UNION from ignorance, gross folly, poverty or the
fear of it, from despotism, mis-rule, and the cruelties of mis-
trained idiots, and from all the sufferings with which the insanities of disunion have afflicted and now afflict the human race.

Socialism, or union, is strength,—is power,—is wisdom,—is
knowledge of human nature and of society,—is charity, and love,
and universal attraction,—is the dread of despots, and of all
mis-rule,—and therefore ought to be more loved by the just and
good and by the multitude than their *now* useless and worthless
lives, given at any time by their mis-rulers to be slaughtered by
tens of thousands for nothing or worse than nothing—to support
despotic cruelties against some of the best men living, although
often mistaken in their theories and practical measures to reform
the world.

There can be no peace on earth, or happiness for mankind, except by universal UNION.   There can be no union while society
shall be based on the present fundamental falsehood.   There can
be no union in practice with the present class divisions of society.   There can be no union of society except through Socialism, in its full and pure action from the birth to the death of all
individuals.

Why do the mis-teachers and mis-rulers of the human race so
dreadfully dread Socialism ?   Because they know that it is the
only system which can cordially and permanently unite mankind,
and that the union of the millions when enlightened will finally
terminate the mis-teaching and mis-ruling of the few, so long
continued to destroy the wealth, knowledge, and power of the
many, and to keep them mentally blind to their own interests,
and as weak in intellects as infants.   To make the millions,
in fact, like the elephant of full growth and strength assisting to
burden himself, and then, ill-fed and ill-treated, driven by a
powerless child to his severe daily task.

Let the public in future, when the term *Socialism* is used by its opposers, translate it into its true meaning, which is *Union* of individuals and nations against mis-rule and false instruction, both intended to keep them and their children in slavery worse than Egyptian bondage, and then they will discover why so much pains and extraordinary measures have been taken by their false teachers and cruel taskmasters to frighten the millions by the word Socialism.

They have been thus frightened that the subject of union among the people might not be studied, and that its incalculable power to benefit mankind might not be undersood.

The mis-instructors and mis-rulers of the human race have with wonderful cunning and foresight, according to worldly wisdom, contrived to make two words suffice so far to keep the millions in all nations over the world as ignorant beasts of burden to these false teachers and most cruel and unjust rulers— rulers who rule only by force, fear, fraud, and falsehood, all based on the power of gunpowder, and on the absence of brains in the people, who have yet to acquire the first grains of common sense towards governing themselves.

Hundreds of millions of these stupid beasts of burden even at this day permit a few individuals, of themselves powerless, except through the devoted slavery of these beasts of burden, to sit in secret conclave and decide upon the fate of these beasts of burden, but in almost all cases to add more weight to the burdens with which they have been previously loaded.

And this is effected by the use of two mere words, which these mis-rulers and mis-teachers have made to act like charms upon the ignorant and credulous fears of their dupes. These two words are SPIRITUALIST and SOCIALIST, with which sectarians and the orthodox, as they call themselves, combine the term INFIDEL.

The mis-instructors of the human race by applying the word Infidelity as they do, intend thereby to create such unfounded prejudices in the minds of others, as to frighten poor weak isolated persons from speaking their honest convictions, or the truth, and they use every species of fraud and force or compel those whom they call Infidels to speak contrary to their convictions, or falsely,—or to be silent. All who thus use the word infidel are either very ignorant, or they have been trained and educated to think it right to act the part of demons upon the earth, and ere long will be publicly considered as such by the millions.

The second word, " SOCIALISM," means *material liberty* to be united in charity and love to all our fellows,—to have liberty to be well-trained and educated,—and to have a good and superior character formed for us, physically, intellectually, morally, spiritually, and practically,—to be placed from birth within common-sense surroundings, instead of surroundings directly opposed to common sense—in such surroundings as will at all times assist all to create with health and pleasure more wealth than all will desire to use,—instead of such insane surroundings as compel some to be idle against their will, and against their own health and interest, and against the interest and happiness of all society. Instead of such surroundings as give a false and most injurious direction to the physical and mental faculties of the human race,—such surroundings as force all from birth to think and act in direct opposition to their own interest and happiness, and to conduct themselves like insane children, devoid of physical and mental powers, wondering that, with such immense powers to attain high knowledge and permanent happiness, they should continue to remain in ignorance and in misery.

Men will indeed wonder when their eyes shall be opened to discover that they have been and are kept in this state by two words, one meaning mental, the other material individual liberty, —the one to think and speak the truth, the other to act the truth in union with his own fellows.

There is no truth more certain and important to know, than that until men become Spiritualists and Socialists there can be no chance for the population of the world to become rational in mind or conduct.

It is full time for the hundreds of millions who are now slaves and beasts of burden to the few who mis-instruct and mis-rule them, to learn the cause of their mental and physical weakness.

It is simply because they are so mis-instructed that they know not the truth, and so surrounded that when by chance they are enabled to discover or are taught the most valuable and important truths for them to know, they dare not openly express their belief in those truths, because their means of living would be immediately assailed by the priesthood of the world and their dupes—in some countries openly with violence, in others, in which violence cannot now be admitted, by every mean act in order to effect the worldly ruin of the honest and superior Spiritualist, or speaker of truth, and of the Socialist or advocate of union, love, and charity for the human race, and of the creation of new surroundings around all, which would admit of this union, love, and charity, in every-day practice, and would terminate for ever false teaching and mis-rule in any country over the earth.

Let the millions therefore seek out and cherish beyond all others the true Spiritualist. And in like manner let them seek out and cherish the true Socialist, so dreaded by those who mis-rule and live upon the labour of others, to whose labour they have no other right than that of force and fraud—the force of the sword and of gunpowder, and the fraud of the priests and of metal money.

It is full time that the great sinks of iniquity, corruption, force, and fraud, should be sounded to their lowest depths, opened up, and exposed to the light of day, in order that the multitude may see them in all their naked deformity; and were they once

seen and made publicly known, the millions would not only discover the cause of their own physical and mental weakness, through
their instructed disunion and ignorance, but also their strength
and irresistible power whenever they shall be permitted to be
taught true knowledge, so as to enable them to unite to terminate
the injustice and cruelties now inflicted upon the multitude solely
by their mis-instruction and by being mis-ruled by violence and
fraud.

This reign of evil spirits in human form, drifting year by year
the population of the world toward a real pandemonium,
governed and directed by falsehood, force, fear, and fraud, must
now be stayed in its onward course by the irresistible power of
the millions united to establish the reign of universal peace, of
charity, love, justice, and wisdom, and thus to turn the current
of society from rapidly running toward utter confusion, universal disunion, and a real pandemonium, carrying in its course all
classes, creeds, sects, and parties, in all countries, down this
strong stream of ignorance and blind folly.

Let the priesthoods and governors of nations look well before
them, and now take heed and ponder well upon the steps they
take in advance.

There is a yawning gulph before them, and into which they
will inevitably fall, to their own ruin and the ruin of their families, if they do not stay their course, pause, and listen to the
voice of experience and of their friend.

This experienced friend, at the close of a long eventful life,
now for the last time thus offers his advice to the priesthood and
rulers of the various nations of the world, and he calls upon
them, in the spirit of pure and genuine love and charity for our
race, to listen and give their most grave attention to that which
he will now declare for their permanent good, and for the eternal
happiness of the human race.

" From the beginning you have through inexperience known
only error, falsehood, and mis-rule, and these through every generation you have forced upon the population of the world, keeping it in wars and conflicts, civil and religious, and pervading it
with the spirit of disunion and repulsion.

" In consequence, the language and conduct of all have become the language of falsehood and the conduct of deception,
both now universally prevalent over the world.

" You are now, although many of you unwittingly, the immediate cause of these evils to all your fellows, to yourselves, and
to your offspring. And through these evils you are the cause
of all the ignorance, poverty, repulsion, disunion, vice, crime,
and misery, with which all nations are now overwhelmed, and
from which so much unnecessary suffering is experienced.

" You have neglected through all the centuries which have
passed to take any rational measure to form a good and useful
character for the nations of the world.

" You have adopted the most effective measures to force a false, inferior, and bad character upon all, and in which you have admirably succeeded.

" You have contrived measures to keep all in ignorance or mistaught.

" You cannot yet agree to train and educate the multitude in any rational principles, or for any rational practice.

" You have contrived to prevent their knowing themselves or their own physical and mental powers, to prevent their knowing how to create wealth for themselves, and to prevent their learning the jugglery practised upon them by your metal money, and how it continually afflicts them with slavery and poverty.

" You train and govern them by force, falsehood, fear, and fraud, because you know not how to train and govern them or your own children to be rational in mind and conduct, so as easily to be well-governed through their affections and a knowledge of their nature.

" You are yourselves ignorant of the practical operations by which a good, valuable, and superior character can, with the certainty of a law of nature, be given to the human race through all futurity.

" You ignorantly receive and teach dogmas opposed to all facts, and make the most unjust and cruel laws, opposed to the good, wise, and all merciful laws of God and nature.

" You have always opposed the divine laws of God, which are few, but efficient to unite man to man over the earth,—to make all good and cordially to assist and to love one another,— to enable all to progress continually in knowledge and wisdom,—to create at all times an abundance of wealth amply sufficient to supply the wants of all,—to give superior dwellings within superior surroundings in every direction, to the greatest distance they may wish to go,—laws, in fact, sufficient to direct and govern the human race well and wisely through all future ages without one human made law.

" In short, to express the whole truth as demonstrated by facts at this day, you have yourselves been from birth so mis-taught, mis-trained, and mis-governed, that a most inferior and injurious and false character has been forced upon you without your consent or even suspicion of the evil done to you ; but, in consequence, you have in your generation mis-taught, mis-trained, and mis-governed the coming generation, to the deep injury of all immediately connected with you.

" The greatest good which can now be done to you and the human race, is to discover and put into practice effective measures to stay these lamentable proceedings of early imbibed ignorance of ancient inexperience respecting human nature, the laws of God, and the only path which can lead to knowledge, goodness, wisdom, and happiness.

" You have been so trained, educated, and placed from your birth, that you have been made to dread *truth* and *union* in the *masses* more than all the most dreaded monsters upon the earth. It is therefore that you dread the Spiritualist who teaches the most important truths, and the Socialist who would unite the human race permanently in the spirit of love and charity, and in the practice of kindness in all the acts of life.

" But your false and disuniting system cannot stand the test of truth, or admit the practice of union.   You must therefore ignore, as you have done, the Spiritualist and the Socialist, knowing, as you instinctively do, that your system of falsehood, injustice, cruelty, and repulsion, cannot exist with truth and union being taught to the population of the world.

" But the principles of truth and union are now rapidly passing from mind to mind and from nation to nation, and no earthly power can now stay their progress until they shall pervade the mind of the population of the world.

" And as these principles proceed from mind to mind and nation to nation, the power and influence of the present false and wicked system must decline.   It is already on the wane, and in a short period, instead of possessing power with the more correctly taught millions, unless this system shall be abandoned by you, and the system of truth, good, and union shall be adopted and applied to the government of all people in all countries, it will become the scorn and ridicule of children as soon as they can be taught to acquire common sense.

" See its present weakness in its strongest hold, where I have lately put it to proof.

" The British Parliament is now the strongest hold of the existing false, disuniting, and irrational system for forming the human-made part of the character of man, and for governing the population of the world.   I gave Petitions from the Congress of the Reformers of the World, to the most advanced members advocating individual mental liberty in both houses.   They presented the petitions ; but no two members could be induced to move and second a motion to take this now all-important subject into consideration by the appointment of a committee of their members or in any other manner.

" This experiment will also be tried with the Congress of the United States, the second great stronghold of this system of ignorance, repulsion, and all manner of evil, and it will be seen if in that boasted assembly of free men there is sufficient moral courage and common sense to venture on the full, fair, and open investigation of two systems for the human government of the human race,—one based on notions of the imagination when men's mental faculties were undeveloped, and therefore not only unsupported by one fact, but directly opposed to all facts known through all past ages to the present,—the other based on facts never known to change since man was created to this day. The first of necessity producing continually falsehood and every kind of evil ; while the other will of like necessity introduce and maintain the language of truth only on all occasions, cordially unite all as one family over the earth, make peace universal and permanent, produce plenty at all times, and make the earth into a true terrestrial paradise, inhabited by full-formed men and women, knowing themselves and human nature, being taught from birth in the practice of making each other happy, and each being trained and educated to possess the attractive qualities which will enable every one to love his neighbour as himself,— taught also the theory, principles, and practice of a rational state of society, and no one inclined, or if inclined, enabled, to impose upon another."

You will now naturally say — this is indeed a new view of society, and very desirable,—but how is it to be attained ?

An answer to this question, so important for you to know and study, shall be given in the succeeding article.

And it is now the first lesson which all rulers and teachers of the people should learn to apply to practice, to save themselves and society from the direful effects of revolutions of violence, which the present system if longer continued is so evidently preparing, as a natural punishment to governments, teachers of the people, and the populations of the world, for continuing a system of mis-rule, mis-instruction, and most injurious practices.

It is by such punishments that nature compels man to change old errors of teaching and governing, and to adopt new and true modes of teaching and governing.

If you would avoid universal division, confusion, and national revolution, you must adopt the measures recommended in the next article.

TO THE GOVERNORS AND TEACHERS OF THE HUMAN RACE.

I WILL now explain how you may teach truly and govern wisely, so that in a short period there shall be no ignorant, bad, or inferior men and women, and no fear of revolutions of violence among any portion of the population of the world.

The teachers of the human race have been and are the various and opposing priesthoods of the world.

The present state of the populations of all nations proves that the priesthoods of these nations have been hitherto mis-taught and ill-taught. They therefore know not what true religion is, in spirit, principle, or practice. In consequence, the religions taught by these priesthoods have been religions of repulsion and of hatred of each other's dogmas and teachings ; while true religion consists in LOVE to HUMANITY without exception, and in CHARITY for all the DIFFERENCES which God, through nature, has made between men.

The *Spirit* of true religion is therefore *love to man, without limitation.*

The *Principle* of true religion is *charity* for the *human race,* without exception.

The *Practice* of true religion consists in this love to man and charity for the human race, and by which alone can love to God be evinced and proved to be sincere.

You—the priesthoods—who have been and yet claim to be the teachers of mankind, have now to unlearn all which you have been erroneously taught, in spirit, principle, and practice ; for it has now become too glaringly evident, even to the multitude, that you yet are strangers to the spirit, principles, or practice of the true religion.

If you desire to continue teachers of the population of the world, now about to be made rational or consistent in mind and practice, you must yourselves first acquire a knowledge of true religion in its pure spirit and genuine principle, and continually exhibit both in your every day practice.

All opposition, hatred, repulsion, jealousy, and ill-will, between the heads and leaders of the various priesthoods of the world, must therefore give place to the union of love and charity between them, as an example to those now made lower in station.

Are you, the heads and leaders of the so called Jew, Christian, Mahomedan, Hindoo, Chinese, and all other mis-named religions, prepared to abandon your repulsive feelings, hatred, and opposition to each other, and to agree to unite in teaching to the human race, irrespective of colour or country, the true religion, in its spirit and principle, and to exhibit your sincerity by the constant application of both in your practice, and to instruct your followers to pursue the same divine conduct ?

When you can do this, you will be prepared to instruct in the true religion, and to become teachers of common sense to the human race.

But until you have attained this human divine character, and exhibit it in your daily practice, you have no rational pretensions to continue the teachers of the population of the world.

This is to teach truly the true religion, and there is now no other teaching of religion that is not highly injurious to the best interests of the human race.

To GOVERN WISELY, Governments must know what human nature is, why it has been so far grossly mis-directed from birth, and how it may be well and wisely directed from birth to death.

All governments have been hitherto ignorant of human nature

—the material upon which they had to operate. Being ignorant
of the qualities of the material, they have been ignorant how to
work it, or what machinery to apply in accordance with its
divine, delicate, and wondrous texture. They have been always
unsuccessful in their efforts to produce rational or satisfactory
results. They have therefore been occupied in continually changing the machinery, and not succeeding, have for some time come
to the conclusion that the material was bad by nature, and in consequence have continued to use it roughly, and to spoil it in every
stage of their progress through all past ages to the present.

They seemed not to know, although the fact is so obvious to
common sense, that the material was of divine origin and therefore could not be bad by nature, and even until now they have
never suspected that the error in all their proceedings arose
through their ignorance of the true nature of the material as
they received it from its DIVINE CREATOR.

You—the rulers and teachers of the population of the world
—have not known, and you have yet to learn, that by placing
this material within wrong machinery—that is, in machinery opposed to its nature—it is injured, spoiled, and made unfit for the
purposes intended by its author and creator. And that when it
shall be placed within right machinery—that is, machinery in
perfect accordance with its nature—then the most useful, beneficial, and beautiful results will arise, to the gratification and delight of every one.

To those who have studied the organs, faculties, propensities,
powers, and qualities, of human nature, as these come from their
divine Creator, it is evident that they are thus created and
wondrously combined in each individual, purposely, when fully
developed or at their matured growth, to give happiness to each,
and to enable every one to contribute, by their variety of character, to the happiness of all. And that there will be no two
opposing interests throughout the population of the world when
it shall be placed, trained, educated, employed, and governed
rationally,—that is, in accordance with the unchanging laws of
our nature, and consequently governed by God's all wise and all-
merciful laws, instead of by men's foolish ever-changing laws,
made to counteract and oppose God's laws.

Were men not ignorant through inexperience, and blinded by
the accumulated prejudices of ages, they would now discover that
all God's laws are made in love to man ; while all men's laws are
made most unwisely and insanely in opposition to human nature
and necessarily in opposition to the happiness of the population
of the world.

You—the governors and rulers of the human race—have this
lesson now to learn, that while you govern by ignorant and cruel
and insane laws of men, you can govern only by force, fear, falsehood, and fraud, as you are all doing at this day. And that you

never can govern well and wisely until you shall be induced to
abandon all these laws, and to adopt for your practice the simple,
plain laws of God, all made in accordance with our nature, and
to guide man, when fully developed, to a high state of knowledge,
wisdom, happiness, and permanent enjoyment — in fact, to a new
rational state of existence upon earth, preparatory to a life of
greater excellence and higher delight in a future spiritual state.

When you shall have sufficient knowledge given to you to
know yourselves and humanity, and wisdom to enable you to understand and to act on God's laws, your task of governing will
become easy, until all necessity for especial governors will cease,
and the population of the world will govern itself solely on
God's laws.   And thus will the will of God be done on earth as
it is in heaven.

This change from the laws of men to the laws of God—from
all that is false in principle and most injurious in practice to all
that is true in principle and most beneficial in practice—would
be made much more easily and speedily if well-meaning inexperienced men, with strong feelings of hatred and anger against
injustice, cruelty, and oppression, would cease to attempt this
change by violence and in a spirit of revenge against the trained
and educated agents of these errors and evils—agents often as
much to be pitiéd as those who suffer through their ignorance ;
for these agents of wrong are frequently more miserable than
those whom they oppress.

It is for you, the governors and rulers of the human race, to
terminate these otherwise endless and useless contests between
yourselves and those whom you now govern and oppress.

Declare openly and at once that it is THE SYSTEM in which you
and those over whom you rule are involved that is the cause of
all the evil and apparent wrong which you are obliged under this
system of ignorance and falsehood to inflict upon the governed.
That while the population of the world continues so stupid and
insane as not to ask and demand from you a CHANGE OF SYSTEM
for the government of the human race, you must as heretofore
govern them, not by reason, kindness, and common sense, but
through coercion,—that is, by force, fear, falsehood, and fraud,
—the governors supplying the force and fear, and the priesthood
of the world aiding them by their falsehood and fraud upon poor
deluded humanity.

Were you and the priesthood of the world now to unite and
become honest and sincere in your desire to govern wisely and to
teach truly, you would simultaneously acknowledge that you had
discovered the cause of the past errors and miseries which the
false system in which all had so long been involved had compelled you to create, maintain, and continually encourage ;—that
you now saw how erroneously you had governed and taught the
population of the world, and that if this population would now

aid you to change this accursed system of error in principle and evil in practice, you would at once abandon your present mode of governing by force and fear, and of teaching by falsehood and fraud, and would adopt the true principle of governing by love and wisdom, and of teaching that only which is true in principle and beneficial in practice, and known to be such by its being always consistent with itself, in accordance with all facts, and uniformly beneficial in its practice.

By this open honest declaration your future progress would be cleared of all difficulties, and you would really become good governors and true teachers of the human race.

It would be most easy in practice to commence the change by forming Federative Treaties between Nations, in order first to obtain and secure permanent peace between them. And the priesthood of the world should unite in the spirit of love and charity to abandon all their insane dogmas and doctrines, which now divide them and derange their faculties, and should agree to instruct mankind to acquire the same divine spirit of love and charity, and to evince it in all their daily practice—not to a small local sect, but to all men of every colour, country, and creed.

By the adoption of the true fundamental principle on which to found society, the necessity for and advantages of union among the human race would become obvious, and as this principle is also the origin of universal attraction among men, union would be easily attained, so as to form for the first time cordially united Scientific Family Commonwealths, or a perfect scientific social society, by the union of which commonwealths upon the federative principle the population of the world would be easily united as one family, in which every one would be well cared for by a competent society during life, and by a society whose highest permanent interest would be to form for each from birth the best character that the natural faculties, physical and mental, would admit.

In these new-formed united scientific family arrangements, all according to age would be the most beneficially occupied for their own health and happiness, and for the permanent good of society; and all according to age would be upon a just and perfect system of equality, to the extent practicable, in education, employment, and condition, or position in society,

By limiting the maximum population of each of these superior Scientific Family Commonwealths to *three thousand*, with land sufficient around each for their permanent support, they could be most easily well governed; and being federatively united, the whole population of the world when thus arranged could be governed with less expense, trouble, disunion, and confusion, than continually occur under the present insane system of repulsion in any one parish in the British metropolis.

In fact, if you, the rulers and teachers of the population of the world, will now unite and agree peaceably to abandon the insane and diabolical principle of disunion and repulsion on which the human character is now universally formed and society constructed, and to adopt instead thereof the divine principle of union and attraction, on which to form character and construct society, you will thereby destroy the cause of evil among mankind, and will give a new and superior existence to the coming generation, who will become full-formed men and women, superior in mind and practice, cordially united and ever aiding each other to progress in knowledge, wisdom, and happiness, and in unceasing united efforts to make this earth, as under this change may be gradually accomplished, into a terrestrial paradise, and to secure the true Millennial state in perpetuity for the human race.

Can any sane man or woman refuse to aid in preparing society for this change ?

SPIRITUALISM AND SOCIALISM UNITED, THE CERTAIN FUTURE OF THE HUMAN RACE.

SPIRITUALISM and Socialism, when rightly understood in principle and fully comprehended for practice, will govern the population of the world. They will govern it by truth, unity, impartial equality, charity, love, and wisdom.

They will create a new elevated existence for man, and, notwithstanding the puny attempts to oppose their introduction, will establish in perpetuity the Millennial State upon earth.

For the time rapidly approaches when the eyes of all will be opened to perceive the glaring folly and wickedness of the present false, disuniting, and repulsive system, by which the character of all has been formed, and society over the world constructed.

Man desires happiness. The means to attain it for all are superabundant. And soon knowledge will direct the right application of the means to accomplish the desire of the human race.

The obstacles which prevent the attainment of permanent happiness and a life of high rational enjoyment to the world, are—

Ignorance of the laws of human nature :—Ignorance of the principle and mode of forming a good and superior character for all :—Ignorance how to create and distribute wealth in superfluity for all :—Ignorance how to devise and execute the surroundings to form this superior character and superfluity of wealth for all : —Ignorance of the principle by which alone the human race can be united and made attractive to each other.

It is the interest of all that these obstacles should be now removed.

Governments and people do not yet understand how to remove them. They have not been trained and educated to comprehend them.   They think and act in accordance with their training and education; and what they do is in accordance with the laws of their nature, as is seen at this day in all the various countries of the world.

Is the time arrived for the governments and people to assist me to remove these obstacles from among them, and thus to prepare the way for universal unity, impartial equality, knowledge, goodness, wisdom, progress toward excellence in all things, and the enjoyment of high physical and intellectual happiness ?

On the experience of a practical man, whose life has been devoted to the study and practice of these all-important subjects, I confidently state without fear of successful contradiction that the time has arrived when ignorance of the laws of our nature may be removed.   When ignorance of the principle and mode of forming a good and superior character for all may be removed. When ignorance how to create and distribute wealth superabundantly for all may be removed.   When ignorance how to devise and execute surroundings to form this good and superior character and to create and distribute this superabundant wealth for all may be removed.   And when ignorance of the principle by which alone the human race can be united and made attractive to each other may be removed.

Who then has an interest in preventing these obstacles to human progress and happiness being now removed ?

The same experience replies—" decidedly no one."

The most valued of the old vested interests of this false, wicked, most cruel, and now worn-out system of folly and insanity for governing mankind, are worthless trash compared with the solid and substantial advantages, progress, and enjoyment, which would arise from the removal of the cause of ignorance and the adoption of the new elevated existence of man upon the earth.

The old vested interests are sinks of corruption and misery, compared with the new interests which will be invested in all in perpetuity, and without inflicting injury upon the rights of any one.   While all old vested interests are held by the few in direct opposition to the natural and just rights of all.

Increased knowledge will make it evident that the present system of ignorance and error is substantially and permanently injurious to all ranks and classes in all countries.   But so deeply rooted are the prejudices of local surroundings over the earth, that they overlay or destroy the rational powers of all, and therefore all now view man and society through these local prejudices, and are governed through life by the habits of thought and action which they create, and hitherto no influences have been sufficiently powerful to overcome the prejudices of these local thoughts and habits.

These localities form the nationalities of the world, and thus each nation is impressed with the belief that its thoughts and habits are true and good, and are superior to all others.

This universal local prejudice of thought and habit can be overcome only by the introduction of the knowledge to be derived from spiritualism and socialism united. The one to create a new spirit of charity, kindness, and love in all :—the other to create an impartial equality in a new practice of united action throughout society.

Spiritualism has been but lately introduced. It has rapidly increased, is increasing, and ere long will overspread the earth.

The spirit, principle, and practice of spiritualism combine to produce unity of feeling, thought, and action ; and without this unity of feeling, thought, and action, socialism would remain beautiful in theory, but must fail in any attempt to apply it to general practice. It was, until united with spiritualism, a body without a soul—the true physical machine of society, devoid of its motive power. Now soul and body can be naturally and most beneficially united.

Spiritualism and socialism, the soul and body of human existence in happiness, will now prepare the physical, intellectual, moral, spiritual, and practical means, by which to make our earth the paradise for which it is evidently designed, and to place, train, educate, unite, and employ the human race gradually to become its good, wise, and happy occupants,—or, in other words, to become full-formed rational men and women, living in the enjoyment of their natural physical and mental existence, and no one to make them afraid of an all good and wise God, or of men, placed, trained, and educated, to be wise and good from their birth.

These are to be the certain results of spiritualism and socialism united.

The first term, or " spiritualist," is used by the orthodox to frighten parties dependent for their support on public opinion from investigating this extraordinary new source of spiritual knowledge, or, if they do investigate, and discover the truth from irresistible facts, which they are sure to do if they are unprejudiced persevering seekers after truth, to deter such parties from openly declaring their convictions. Or, when facts are too strong even for the orthodox not to acknowledge an invisible spiritual agency, then they would make their dupes believe that this agency is not from good, but from evil spirits, and that it is sent by a personage they call the Devil—a demon of their mis-taught imagination.

Now those who have patiently investigated this new, and to the present generation very extraordinary source of knowledge, know that it is calculated to effect more truth, goodness, love, and charity among mankind, and more moral courage and moral conduct, than all other kinds of teaching can accomplish. And that this new and wondrous aid was required to enable the true Socialist to reform the population of the world in principle and practice, and thus to change the entire system of society over the earth—in Religion, Politics, Law, Commerce, Domestic Arrangements, and Classification, and by this change to give a new character to the human race, by which the *mind* of all will be born again, that is, regenerated in mind and practice, so as to become full-formed men and women, knowing themselves and the principles and practices by which to assist to form a superior character for others and to create and maintain a rational organisation of universal society.

THE ORIGIN OF EVIL TO THE HUMAN RACE,—THE CAUSE OF ITS CONTINUANCE THROUGH ALL PAST GENERATIONS TO THE PRESENT,—AND AN EFFECTUAL REMEDY BY REMOVING THE CAUSE OF ITS CONTINUED PRODUCTION.

THE origin of evil is co-existent with the first creation of man, and is a necessary result of the undeveloped state of his reasoning faculties, of his inexperience, and of his ignorance of his own nature and all things around him.

He had to imagine what things were from their first appearances, and then the errors of these early impressions had to be corrected by subsequent experience and a knowledge of facts.

These first impressions, like those of present childhood, were deep and lasting, and many of them most dificult to be overcome by centuries of experience, and not a few of them remain even to this day.

Among these first errors of the imagination, and the most fatal of all to progress in wisdom and happiness, is the absurd and insane imagination that each of humankind forms his own physical, intellectual, moral, spiritual, and practical qualities, and that they are made good, indifferent, or bad,—inferior or superior, at the pleasure of the individual.

Now every fact connected with this all-important subject, from the creation of man to this hour, demonstrates that the individual possessing these divine qualities of human nature knows not how any of these qualities have been formed for him, or have been so wonderously combined, each with the other, to form him to be what he is—a feeling, seeing, hearing, tasting, smelling animal, with intellectual faculties superadded, and all kept in action by an internal spirit.

Yet to this day man knows not how any one of the organs of these senses of his intellectual faculties is formed, or is so combined as to be set and kept in motion through the life of each by the spirit within.

They are formed and combined for him by a power invisible and mysterious to him—by a power which creates, uncreates, and recreates continually throughout the universe, and which power is called God, or a name of similar import, by all nations and peoples over the earth.

And from this mysterious power, or God, all things necessarily proceed in a due order of progress in creation. And this progress, according to the best evidence given to man, is to result in the excellence, happiness, and harmony of all sentient existences throughout the universe; which universe includes all that exists.

To return to the origin of evil. It has been proved from facts that man was created with his physical and mental organs, faculties, qualities, and powers, without his consent or knowledge, and that he was thus created a universal know-nothing, influenced by internal instincts, whence derived he knew not, and by the action upon him of external forces, how created or from whence proceeding he knew not.

He imagined that he formed his own physical and mental qualities and powers, and that all his fellow men had the same wonderful capacity, and that each one was responsible to God and society for the actions of these qualities and powers.

This error is the origin of evil among men. It is the origin of all the inferior and bad passions,—of hatred, anger, violence, and conflicts,—of envy, jealousy, disunion,—of falsehood, crime, and human blame and punishments,—of continued ignorance of human nature,—of poverty and all its miseries,—of the present excitement among all nations, arising from their unnecessary sufferings and from the want of happiness among the population of the world, when the means of happiness for all everywhere abound.

The cause and the origin of evil being thus ascertained, its remedy by the removal of the cause becomes obvious.

Let the fact be now universally made known,—" That God " and society form the character and conduct of everyone before " and from birth, and that God and society are responsible to the " individual for his qualities of mind and body, and for the wise " or unwise direction of these qualities through the life of the " individual : — God, for the wonderful divine qualities of his " physical and mental formation before and at birth,—and " Society for the direction given to those wondrously combined " qualities and powers from birth to death."

By thus attributing to God the things which are God's, and to men the things which are men's, and adjusting all things in society accordingly, may evil be removed from among the population of the world,—everyone born be made good,—the family of man for ever cordially united,—wealth everywhere and at all times be made to superabound and be freely used by all,—the earth be made fruitful and beauteous,—and a new existence upon earth be prepared for all coming generations,—and a terrestrial paradise be thus made to arise, in which the human race will enjoy in security the substantial, permanent, rational, and natural happiness, for which the human faculties are so eminently adapted, and for which they are evidently destined by their Creator.

It should now be understood by governments, churches, and people, that it is vain and useless to talk about reforming mankind until the origin of evil and the cause of its continuance among all nations shall be removed. When this shall have been done, (and it may now be accomplished by the promulgation of truth upon this subject,) it will become an easy and pleasant task to governments, churches, and people, to adopt decisive measures to make all become good, wise, and happy.

And by a common-sense union between these parties, this great and glorious change may be now commenced in peace, with order, and so gradually, that no one shall be injured by it through its progress to its complete accomplishment over the world.

How simple will be the change to produce these wondrous re-results ! ! ! In principle, to abandon one universal falsehood, and to adopt one universal truth. In practice, to abandon the creation of insane surroundings in which to place humanity from the birth of each individual, and to create instead thereof common-sense surroundings, in accordance with the created nature of man.

This is all the difficulty now to be overcome—a difficulty which the inexperienced in practical measures say will require hundreds —thousands of years for its removal.

And yet, were there but a small amount of common-sense among the governments and teachers of the human race, to unite them in accomplishing this now obvious and easily to be effected change, it might be commenced this year in all the most advanced nations, and continued without stay or retrogression until its un-heard-of benefits should pervade the population of the world.

Should the governments and teachers of the people not yet have acquired sufficient common-sense to discover their interest and safety in now uniting with the people to effect this change quietly, in order, and with wise foresight,—then I will divulge to the people a simple process of proceeding, which shall enable them to effect this change for themselves, in peace, and without the aid of any of the unproductive classes, who will be left un-molested to take care of themselves only, while the productive classes will be taught how to take good care of themselves, and to give a superior character to all their children, whom they will place within common-sense surroundings of their own creation.

For nearly half a century I have patiently endeavoured to induce the heads of the governments and teachers of the most advanced nations to perceive the falsehood on which the system by which the world has so far been governed, is based and the wickedness and misery which it necessarily creates. And I trust that a sufficient impression has been made upon them to convince them that the system which has been so long the guide and practice of all governments and teachers is based on ignorance of the laws of nature—on a falsehood opposed to all facts ; that it necessarily deranges the faculties of all nations and peoples ; and that it can lead only to increased error, wickedness, and misery.

In my first publications, more than forty years ago, I stated that I felt for the population of the world the same interest as a physician feels for a patient in whose health and happiness he is deeply interested, but for whose complaints he knows it to be necessary, to effect this cure, to administer medicines against which his patient has been taught to have strong prejudices, and of which therefore he is very unwilling to take even the smallest quantity. Knowing this, the physician administers at first but small doses, and increases their strength by degrees as the patient is more and more prepared, and is less disinclined to take them.

I then promised to watch the progress of this most lamentable disease, and the effects which the medicine of truth produced on the patient, and gradually to increase the dose until a radical cure should be accomplished. My publications, lectures, memorials, petitions, addresses, and public meetings, given to the population in Europe and America, and works freely distributed and sent to all parts of the world, testify to the fulfilment of this promise, by the many unpleasant yet highly important divine truths which I have from time to time placed before all parties, and especially before the governments of Europe and America.

Feeling still the same deep interest in the health, well-being, well-doing, and happiness of my patient, I have reserved the strongest dose yet to be administered, if those which have now been given should prove deficient in strength to overcome this deep-seated disease of falsehood, wickedness, and misery.

I shall however endeavour as usual to make this strong dose palatable to all classes, sects, and parties, in all countries, who have attained the practice of thinking and reasoning through their own observation of facts as they perpetually exist around them. It is by these strong doses of truths in accordance with all facts known through past ages to the present, that spiritualism and socialism, fully understood, can be made to supersede the system of falsehood and evil by which the population of the world has been so long governed.

London :—Published by the Author at 16, Great Windmill Street, Haymarket : and sold by Holyoake, 147, Fleet Street ; Truelove, 240, Strand; Goddard, 14, Great Portland Street, Cavendish Square; Farrah, 21, John Street, Fitzroy Square ; and all Booksellers.

Registered for Foreign Transmission.

ROBERT OWEN'S
MILLENNIAL GAZETTE;

EXPLANATORY OF THE PRINCIPLES AND PRAC-
TICES BY WHICH, IN PEACE, WITH TRUTH,
HONESTY, AND SIMPLICITY, THE NEW
EXISTENCE OF MAN UPON THE
EARTH MAY BE EASILY AND
SPEEDILY COMMENCED.

" The character of Man is formed *for* him, and *not by* him !"

No. 7.]   AUGUST 1st, 1856.   [PRICE 6D.

THE PRACTICAL MODE OF CHANGING THE PRESENT FALSE, UNNATURAL, AND THEREFORE EVIL SYSTEM OF SOCIEEY, FOR THE TRUE, NATURAL, AND GOOD SYSTEM OF SOCIETY.

THE origin and cause of evil being ascertained, and the means by which to remove the cause for ever from society being known, it becomes the first and highest duty or interest of all govern-ments, churches, and peoples, to unite to have this cause re-moved in the shortest time practicable.

But as the human character from birth and society over the earth have been hitherto based, constructed, and conducted on this false, unnatural, and evil system, governments, churches, and peoples united cannot effect the change required until they agree to abandon this system in principle and practice, and to adopt in all its extent and purity the system of truth, nature, and goodness, in its spirit, principle, and practice.

It will now be said, as a matter of course, by those trained and educated, placed and governed within the surroundings arising from and created by this old unnatural system of falsehood and evil, that the governments, churches, and peoples are not pre-pared for such an entire change in spirit, principle, and practice. True, they are not prepared, nor will they ever be until they shall be taught the spirit, principle, and practice of the true, natural, and good system of society. But the more advanced minds of the world are so far prepared that they are compelled to acknow-ledge that there is something wrong at the foundation of society, and they desire and anxiously wait for and expect a change of system, but they know not whence or how it is to come.

Their carriage wheels of progress are deep sunk into the mud, and can proceed no further without sinking deeper and deeper.

All are lifting up their arms and eyes to Jove for help, and he

replies—" You will pray to me in vain until you put your
" shoulders to the wheels and use your natural strength and
" powers in the right direction. You want a good and superior
" character.—I have given you the means to attain one. Adopt
" those means.

" You want wealth. I have given you the most ample means
" to procure it at all times in superfluity. Adopt those means in
" practice.

" You want to be united. I have given you the principle of
" union and attraction, by which your race may be permanently
" united. You reject the principle, and like fools pray for the
" practice, while you cherish and give every encouragement to
" the principle and practice of repulsion. Adopt the principle
" of union, and you will have union.

" You pray for truth, goodness, and happiness. You tena-
" ciously cling to the principle and practices which must produce
" falsehood, evil, and misery. You must therefore change your
" entire system, and adopt the principle and practices which can
" alone produce truth, goodness, and happiness.

" I have given you the most ample means to attain great ex-
" cellence and high rational enjoyment, and until you adopt those
" means you shall remain in the mire and mud of ignorance,
" poverty, and disease,—in crime, its punishments, and utter con-
" fusion and disorder such as you now experience."

It is thus that God through nature speaks to all, and will continue to speak until his laws shall be obeyed and man shall be
made thereby rational and happy.

It may now be asked why, in the name of common sense, do
governments, churches, and peoples, continue to act the same
irrational conduct in which they have so long persevered, seeing
that they only make matters worse the longer they continue this
insane mode of forming the character of the population of the
world, of producing wealth, and of constructing society and
governing it.

Let us now come to the point. Do you, the governments, and
churches of the world, truly and sincerely wish to form a good
and superior character for the population of the world?

If you do, then at once adopt the only means by which such
character can be given to them, and make the proper surroundings for that purpose.

If you do not—have the moral courage to say so, and set the
wants and wishes of the people at defiance.

Do you really desire to enable the population of the world to
become permanently wealthy?

If you do—then at once abandon the insane practice of using
metal money, and adopt either a full national bank note, or the
just labour note as a preliminary measure.

If you do not—say so openly, and let the population of the

world know on what principle you act, and state honestly that you do not desire that the population of the world should become wealthy, or should know wherein real valuable wealth consists.

Do you truly desire to unite the population of the world for their permanent benefit, progress, and happiness ?

If you do—place, train, and educate them from birth on the only principle and in the only practice which can create unity among men.

If you do not wish to unite, but wish to divide them, and to set them in opposition to each other—then have the moral courage to declare your purpose to divide and conquer them to enable you to obtain your illegitimate purposes over them.

Do you really and truly desire to pervade the minds of the population of the world with the pure spirit of love and charity for each other ?

If you do—adopt and teach them the only principle by which that spirit and practice can be given to man.

Or if you do not desire them to acquire the divine spirit of love and charity by which alone the population of the world can be made to become good and happy, then say so, and the world will understand that you prefer to have the spirit of hatred, of indifference, and of uncharitableness forced from birth as at present into the minds of all.

Do you honestly desire the permanent peace of the population of the world ?

If you do—adopt immediately federative treaties as a preliminary, between the so-called great powers first, and afterwards between them and the minor powers.

If you do not desire peace between all nations—then openly declare your intention to conserve the principle of war for your especial benefit or amusement, and to keep the population of the world your beasts of burden without the power of reasoning or of self-action.

You see the day is come for a fair, full, and open understanding between the governing and teaching powers of the people and the population of the world—between universal despotism by the few over the many, and universal rational freedom and happiness for all.

But it is not your interest to endeavour longer to maintain this horrid, false, unnatural, cruel, and wicked system for governing and teaching the population of the world, if you could retain the power to conserve the misery which this wretched system has inflicted and now inflicts upon all, yourselves included. Substantial or permanent peace of mind and happiness for such governors and teachers can never be attained. With the new knowledge and powers which have now been acquired by the people, the contests for power between you and the population of the world must become more frequent and more severe,—you, the present governors and teachers of nations, greatly desiring thus to continue to govern and teach ; and the people wishing to effect an entire change in both.

The people are right in so wishing ; but as long as they attempt to effect this change by anger, abusive language, or violence, it is a proof that they are not yet prepared to conquer a rational change of system in a rational manner. The people, however, are rapidly acquiring a knowledge for the necessity of calm reasoning, firm resolve in principle, and the irresistible power of union, to carry all their righteous purposes to final permanent success.

You should, and if you can acquire sufficient wisdom and foresight you will for your own safety and happiness, anticipate these righteous purposes of the people, and gradually lead and direct them quietly and peaceably to attain them.

You reply—that trained, educated, and placed as you have been by society, you know not the practical measures, or how to introduce them, to attain the change from error to truth in principle, and from wrong to right in practice, and more especially you do not know how to create the spirit of universal love and charity, which is so essentially necessary in governors and governed, in teachers and taught, to effect this change with wisdom, without injury to any, and most beneficially for all.

I am fully aware of the unfortunate surroundings in which you have been placed by society from your birth, to prevent the possibility of you acquiring this knowledge, all important as it now becomes for your future progress.

I have promised to lead you step by step to the attainment of this knowledge, now so strongly required for your benefit and for the permanent benefit of the population of the world.

This is that knowledge now so necessary for you to attain, and to be openly given to all nations, tribes, and peoples over the earth ; and it shall be given with the simplicity of truth in succeeding articles.

NEW PRACTICAL MEASURES BY WHICH TO ENABLE THE TEACHERS AND GOVENORS OF THE NATIONS OF THE EARTH TO TEACH TRULY AND GOVERN WISELY.

THE priesthoods of the world have been hitherto the teachers of mankind, and they assume still to be their teachers.

And it will be well for them to continue to be so for a time, provided the spirit and wisdom of teaching can be given to them to enable them to apply both in their practice.

Teaching, or forming the character of the rising generation, is the most important acquisition to be attained by man and woman.

The preliminary measure to good teaching is, that the character of the teachers should be well formed physically. intellectually, morally, spiritually, and practically.   In all these qualities they should be models of examples to the taught, and from the birth of those to be taught, none others should be allowed to approach them.

Now the priesthood of the present day, most unfortunately for them, have been so placed from birth that they have been physically, intellectually, morally, spiritually, and practically, most unwisely mistaught and misplaced, and have thus been rendered totally unfit to teach men and women to become rational beings, or to know what manner of beings they are, or how to enable them to think, speak, or act.

As the human race have so far been taught by these priesthoods, it will be asked—Where, then, are we to look for teachers ?

For the reason just stated they are not yet to be found. They must be created and new taught.   And as soon as the priesthoods can be made conscious of their trained and educated incapacities for this divine office, they may be so far instructed generally, as at once to become useful preparatory teachers in the present generation, with little or no change in their respective positions.

They could from their churches, mosques, synagogues, and temples, teach the principle of truth, unity, attraction, charity, and love, and infuse into all the divine spirit to be derived only from that principle, and that spirit would be sufficient if given in its purity to prepare the minds of all to feel, think, and act rationally, provided the priesthood would set the example and be consistent in their practice with their preaching.

All the various systems called religion by their respective priesthoods they profess to base on love to God and love to man. But as God cannot be seen by man, love to that All-Creating and Directing Power can be evinced only by an undeviating love to all men in all our actions.   And as this love to man can arise only from knowing that he has been made to be what he is by God and society,—that knowledge should be the foundation of all their teaching.

This teaching, if consistent, would of necessity produce the divine principle of charity for all differences made by God in the creation of man over the earth ; and that charity would of necessity pervade all minds and prepare them to love that which God created.

The teaching of this principle which can alone create unity, attraction, charity, and love among the human race, is to teach the only true religion that ever can exist upon the earth, and it can be known only when exhibited in the every action of the priesthood, and in the daily conduct of those whom they teach. Without these, all the prayers, assumed piety, and dogmas of the various systems now called religion, among all nations, tribes, and peoples, are mere words, forms, and ceremonies, of no value whatever, but on the contrary are directly calculated to derange if not to destroy the reasoning faculties of the priests themselves and of all whom they attempt to instruct.

At present the priesthoods of the world exhibit in the strongest manner their total want of knowledge of the spirit, principle, and practical arrangements by which alone a truly good and wise character can be given to man.

As this knowledge nowhere exists among any of the priesthoods of the earth, it must be taught to the existing generation of priests of every name and opposing creeds and dogmas.

The lesson is a simple one-- it is in accordance with all known facts from man's creation to this day.   It will be easily acquired by the priesthood, and as easily taught by them to the laity.   It will immediately create a divine spirit of love and charity in the teachers and the taught, and the practice of both will be in accordance with the spirit and principle of this divine teaching. And soon will arise such a new character and conduct in the priesthoods and people, that heaven will be brought down upon earth, in which the will of God will be done as it is in heaven above.

This is the change which the priesthood of the world are now called upon to effect, and this is the lesson which they have to learn, to enable them to fulfil the mission of their high calling.

I am equally aware that the members of all existing governments have been most erroneously trained, educated, employed, and placed, and that they have been very imperfectly generated, their parents having been like themselves most unfortunately and ignorantly placed by society.   These evils by their positions none could have avoided, and they therefore require the charity and sympathy of all far more than blame, even for their worst qualities.

These qualities, by the introduction of new principles and practices and a new knowledge of themselves and of human nature, will be overcome, and their new position will be made safe, beneficial to themselves and the governed, and altogether prosperous and glorious.

But to attain this superiority of position they have a new lesson to acquire in spirit, principle, and practice.

This is, the spirit, principle, and practice to govern rationally —that is, to adopt new measures to train, educate, employ, and place the governed, to become full-formed rational men and women, knowing themselves and human nature, what society is, what it should be, and how to effect the change with wise foresight, in peace, with order, and without injury to any one.

All this you, the present rulers of the world, have now to learn, for you have been trained, educated, employed, and placed by society to govern unwisely, without foresight, not in peace,

without order, and to the great injury of all, including yourselves and your children.

To govern well and wisely you should be taught how to form
a good and superior character for all whom you govern,—how to
enable them to create wealth at all times in abundance for every
one,—how to be united and always at peace with all their fellows,
—how to devise and execute the surroundings which alone can
enable you and them to attain these results without injury to any
one, and with benefit to this and to every succeeding generation,
—and how to commence these new measures by forming federative treaties between the nations which you respectively govern.

By learning what these new surroundings should be, you will
discover the necessity for abandoning the existing inferior and
most injurious surroundings in which the population you govern
has been hitherto placed, and the necessity for a new arrangement and division of them within new surroundings, to form
scientific societies, or new federative family commonwealths, in
which alone the human race can be born, trained, educated, employed, placed, and united, to become full-formed men and
women, rational in feeling, mind, and practice.

In fact, to govern well and wisely will be an easy and most delightful task whenever you adopt the true principles of governing,
and apply them consistently to practice in the spirit of true religion or of universal charity and love.

It may be thus shortly expressed.

1st.—To adopt the true fundamental principle on which to base
society.

2nd.—To form a good and superior character for all the governed.

3rd.—To remove all artificial obstacles which now restrict the
creation of the most valuable wealth.

4th. —To unite the governed in feeling and interest.

5th.—To effect these results by applying the national or united
resources of the nation to create the new surroundings in which
alone the four preceding results can be attained.

6th. —These surroundings will new-form the population into
united scientific family commonwealths, to be federatively united
to all similar family commonwealths over the world.

7th.—These commonwealths not to exceed three thousand men,
women, and children, in their natural proportions, and thus to
constitute complete societies within themselves, so arranged that
those born, trained, educated, and employed within them, shall
be well cared for from birth to death, and be made to become full-
formed men and women, knowing the principles and practices of
society, and how to take part and perform their duty in every
division of it, and to be cordially united in all the required operations to secure for each other a superior existence for life—an
existence in which the individual will possess far more physical

and mental liberty, beneficially for himself or herself and for all others, than can be attained or enjoyed by any one under the existing false, disunited, and evil system.

And this is what the population of the world has ever sought to discover—individual independence or sovereignty, so united with social arrangements that both should be enjoyed in perfection with the least practicable interference one with the other.

Man and woman to be happy must be individually free and socially united to the race. This is now attainable.

TO THE PARLIAMENT OF THE BRITISH EMPIRE AND THE CONGRESS OF THE EMPIRE OF THE UNITED STATES OF NORTH AMERICA.

It is to you that the advanced minds of the world now look to lead the way to true knowledge, real liberty in mind and practice, and to the attainment of progression, excellence, and the permanent enjoyment of rational happiness for the population of the world.

The means to attain these results now abundantly exist.

You possess the power to apply those means to accomplish these results.

Circumstances have placed you to become the vicegerents on the earth of the Great Creating Power of the Universe.

Directly or indirectly you have the misery or happiness of the human race at your disposal.

Directly, you make laws for and govern your respective Empires. Indirectly, you may influence all other governments and people over the earth if your proceedings henceforth shall be based on truth and conducted with wisdom.

Men selected and elected as you have been must desire the happiness of yourselves, your children, and the world,—in fact, the happiness of the one cannot be separated from the others. You naturally and necessarily desire the permanent peace, progress, prosperity, and happiness of your respective populations. At present there is no secure happiness enjoyed by any portion of the population either of the British Empire or of the United States, but a vast amount of ignorance, poverty, disunion, crime, and misery, pervade both Empires.

How can these simple and obvious truths be reconciled? How are they to be explained so as to be made useful for immediate practice? Simply by declaring the whole truth to you, in the spirit of charity, kindness, and love. And this is now the task which I wish to perform and intend to accomplish.

You desire to make the respective Empires which you govern permanently prosperous and happy, and of course the populations of both rational in mind and conduct.

It has been said, and all facts confirm the statement, that the Great Creating Power of the Universe, which Power is the God of the Universe, has now placed at your disposal the most ample means to make each one of these populations intelligent, healthy, good, wealthy, united, wise, and happy.

Are they so?

No. There is not one individual as intelligent, healthy, good, wealthy, united with his fellows, wise, or happy, as by another system and arrangement of society *all* might be made to be.

You say truly that you do not understand this statement—you cannot comprehend how these results can be attained—you have never been taught these things, and therefore you know them not—your instruction through life has been to believe in a system the reverse of all which has been stated, and to acquire notions and habits quite opposed to all that has been said.

I know it. And I also know that you might far more easily have been taught from your birth to believe my statements and to act in accordance with them, than to believe and act as by the force of circumstances you have been compelled to do. And more easily, because all my statements are consistent with themselves and with nature or all known facts; while that which has been forced into your minds is thoroughly inconsistent one part with another, opposed to nature or all facts, and without a particle of truth for its foundation.

But to the proof, and to teach you a new and true lesson of life progress, and happiness.

Common-sense instruction in Common Things.

First lesson.

Men from various materials make an endless variety of things. Did you ever hear that the maker of any one of those things ever attributed merit or demerit to the thing which he had made? Would it not exhibit a total want of common-sense to do so?

Members of Parliament and of Congress reply.—" Yes."

Who created or made man?

Members of Parliament and Congress reply.—" The Great " Creating Power of the Universe."

How?

Reply.—" By giving him the qualities and powers of humanity, " at birth directly, and indirectly by the surroundings of nature " and the society in which he is placed—the surroundings and " society being also of God's creating."

Are the things made by man responsible to man and society for the qualities given to them by their maker?

Reply.—" No certainly—it would be opposed to common sense " to make them so."

Could any rational result arise from doing so?

Reply.—" Certainly not—but utter confusion of mind and
" conduct."

Now as all facts prove that the Great Creating Power of the
Universe, or God, creates every quality, power, and particle of
man, and that man knows not how he received them—I ask, is
God, the Creator, or man, the created, responsible for the qualities
which man is made to possess.

Reply —" It is certainly contrary to common sense to make the
" thing created responsible for its powers and qualities to that
" which created these powers and qualities."

No other answer could be given in accordance with common
sense.

Experience proves that men from birth can be taught to believe every kind of absurdity, however opposed to facts, to be
divine truth, as is now seen in all the nations of the earth. Now,
when the human mind, contrary to all facts and to common
sense, is made to believe as a truth not to be doubted that the
thing made is for the qualities given to it responsible to the Power
which gave it those qualities, and when society continues to form
and build up the mind of each on this absurd foundation, is it
bracticable to make such being rational or consistent in feeling,
thought, or action ?

Reply.—(After much reflection and searching in their own
mind for a common-sense reply, and being ashamed to give any
other).—" No, certainly ; it must be an impossibility."

Well then—your mind and the mind of all men have been so
formed ; and this is the reason why the population of the world
is to-day so ignorant, so impoverished, so disunited, so superstitious, and so inconsistent and insane, and often mad, in mind
and conduct. It is the cause of all conflicts and wars, of all
evil passions and crimes, and of the misery of the human race.

I hope you have now learned your first lesson—" That the
" made has no merit or demerit of its own, and cannot be res-
" ponsible for its qualities to its maker, and that the maker is
" responsible for what it makes."

Is it not most desirable that the human race should have good
physical, intellectual, moral, spiritual, and practical qualities ?

Reply.—" Yes."

Would it not add essentially to the happiness of all if all from
birth were so trained, educated, employed, placed, and directed,
that all should become superior—physically, intellectually,
morally, spiritually, and practically—compared with the present
formed generation, and should become at maturity full-formed
men and women, rational and consistent in all their sayings and
doings ?

Reply.—" Most certainly."

Would you, were you put in possession of the knowledge and
means to produce these results for the population of your respec-

tive Empires, now adopt those means and apply them without loss of time to practice ?

Reply.—" Can you doubt our desire to effect so much good if " we knew how to accomplish it ?"

Good—I know the onus lies with me to enable you to know how to succeed in this new mode of forming the human character. You have from the dates of your respective establishments talked much about educating the people, to make them good, intelligent, virtuous, prosperous, and happy. And from all your authentic records, it is now glaringly evident that you yourselves have never been trained and educated to be good, intelligent, or virtuous, or to know what the words goodness, intelligence, or virtue mean. You could not therefore teach the knowledge of these things to others.

Although the members of the Congress of the United States are on the subject of national education much in advance of the members of the British Parliament, yet facts demonstrate that both are yet totally without knowledge how to form a good intelligent and superior character for their own children or for any portion of the human race—that you are without knowledge of the principle and practice by which to commence to form a rational character for mankind, or to place, train, and educate any division of the population of the world to become good, useful, healthy, intelligent, or even rational, in feeling, thought, mind, or conduct,—far less how to pervade their minds from birth with the pure spirit of love and charity for our race.

And yet no man without this knowledge is prepared to comprehend either legislating or governing.

Hitherto you have wasted the time and means of both Empires while you have been talking upon the subject of education, for all the talking now upon your records is worse than useless, and is calculated only to lead the public mind in a wrong direction.

For this lamentable want of the most valuable knowledge which man can know, (that is, how all may be made good and rational from birth,) you are blameless and to be pitied,—for men can know only what they are taught and what they acquire afterwards by their own experience or by the inspiration of superior intelligence. And you have not been taught to know how to form a good and rational character; but you have been well-instructed how to form an evil and irrational one. Witness at this day the populations of your respective Empires.

In your religions, governments, laws, professions, commerce, domestic arrangements, and classification, if they are intended to produce goodness and happiness, there is not a particle of rationality or common sense to be discovered.

Your religions, governments, laws, professions, commerce, domestic arrangements, and the entire classification of society, are directly calculated to create all the selfishness, ignorance, evil passions, inconsistency, and gross irrationality which now pervade all classes in both Empires.

While, when you shall discover the true mode of forming a good and rational character from birth for all, it will be seen to be a plain, simple process, easy and most delightful in practice when the requisite surroundings for forming such character shall be adopted.

Within rational surroundings the character in early life will not be formed by books, but by the eye and ear. The eye to see and investigate outward material things, and the ear to listen to the replies of explanation made to the learning questioner by superior intelligent experienced persons, who can give such instruction in the spirit of love and charity arising from a correct knowledge of human nature and all its divinely given qualities.

For upwards of twenty-five years at the commencement of this century I exhibited such new mode of forming character, as far as the imperfect surroundings of your present wretched system would permit ; and even that imperfect experiment produced such beneficial and happy results that it aroused the attention of the advanced and most elevated men and women of all nations—all being freely admitted to examine those results for themselves.

All who came were astonished, pleased, gratified,—but none knew how such results could be obtained for the human race. While I was conscious that very far superior results could be obtained with the certainty of a law of nature for the entire family of man through all succeeding generations. And this, too, without making the individuals responsible to their makers, and without human punishments of any kind.

With the true principle of society for its foundation, all that will be necessary will be to have surroundings made in accordance with human nature and common sense.

Let us see now how we proceed, and what advance we have made.

First Lesson.—" The Creator, or Maker, responsible for the " qualities given to the created or made." Common sense.

Second Lesson.—" The divine qualities of man, created before " birth by God, or the Great Creating Power of the Universe, " and from birth directed erroneously or wisely by society and " the other external surroundings in which he is born and lives. " And through this knowledge, when society shall make rational " surroundings, all within them must become, without merit of " their own, good, wise, united, prosperous, and happy."

So far so good. We will now proceed to the

Third Lesson.—" Men have natural wants, and unless these " are supplied they cannot be good, healthy, intelligent, united, " or happy. But when these wants shall be supplied, as now " they might be, all must become good, healthy, intelligent, united, " and happy."

Members of Parliament and Congress interrupting —" Say
" you so ?   And do you really possess this knowledge ?   Why
" this is the very thing we now require, and of which at present
" we are most ignorant.   We shall be truly delighted to receive
" this invaluable information."

Well I will proceed to give it to you.   But do not anticipate
anything, or you will go in a wrong direction.   By proceeding
step by step gradually, we shall advance more slowly but more
surely, and the knowledge thus gained will be permanent.

I have said " men have natural wants which must be supplied
" before they can be made good, intelligent, united, and happy."

What are these wants ?   Good shelter,—good clothes,—knowledge of things,—of themselves, and of human nature and its laws.

Reply.—" Yes.—But how are these to be obtained?"

Patience, and you shall know all that is necessary for you to
know at the present time.

How are good dwellings, food, and clothes produced?

Reply.—" By labour."

True ; and best by skilled labour well directed.   Is it not so?

Reply —" Certainly."

Can idleness ever produce these things ?   Or Can skill and
industry produce them when the materials for their production are
withheld ?

Reply.—" No.   Idleness cannot create these things ; nor skill
" and industry, if the requisite materials are withheld from skill
" and labour."

Are dwellings, food, and clothes, wealth ?

Reply.—" Yes; while they can be sold for money."

And not otherwise ?

Reply.—" No ; they would become drugs of no value, as we are
" taught by our political economists."

And they would not be wealth, although hundreds of thousands were without good dwellings, food, and clothes, if they had
not money to purchase them, although they produced all these
things?

Reply.—" If they have no money they have no right to these
" things ; and the laws we make forbid their touching them."

Then metal money is real wealth, and not good dwellings,
food, and clothes, and those things called the necessaries of life ?

Reply.—" By our laws we make it so."

Then if all the gold and silver in the world disappeared and
none could be obtained, all wealth would be destroyed, and the
means of creating it would be lost, according to your made laws.
Would not this be the case?

Reply.—" It would be so, as we understand this subject ; but
" we acknowledge there is a mystery in the matter which we can-
" not explain.   We cannot tell how it is that the idle, who produce
" none of the necessaries or comforts or luxuries of life, have the

" money,—and those who can and do produce them can obtain
" only a scanty and very precarious supply of the most common
" necessaries, and sometimes none of them, and actually starve for
" want of sufficient to support life."

You have spoken truly and have given a strong case agains
your total want of humanity, or against your want of knowledge
how to make laws to govern any portion of the human race.

Reply.—" How so ? We labour day and night to make good
" laws, and at least they are intended to be just and humane."

You act as you have been taught, and as your surroundings
compel you to act ; but it is shown by increased knowledge derived from facts that you have been mis-placed and mis-taught
through life, that you know not how to make just or humane
laws, nor what real wealth is, nor how it can be always easily and
pleasantly produced in abundance and made to be ample at all
times for the human race.

Reply.—" How can you prove this case against us ?"

Thus. Every one born a century ago, when employed to produce real wealth, (which consists by nature not in artificial
money but in the necessaries, comforts, and useful luxuries for
man,) could produce, when by your laws allowed to do so, not
only sufficient wealth for himself and family, and as much in addition as when united with the production of his fellow producers
was sufficient to maintain in most wasteful luxury all the upper
classes, and in great comfort all the professions, with the wasteful extravagance of the church, the army, the navy, and the law,
and to provide drugs mostly applied to poison those ignorant of
the laws of health,—but also enough to supply the enormous
waste and destruction caused by almost continued wars and conflicts, commenced and continued for the amusement of the idle,
or to keep the mass of the people in brutal ignorance, that they
might destroy each other and the wealth which they had previously created. All this surplus wealth, thus applied to demoralise all classes, and wasted in war, was produced in the islands of
Great Britain and Ireland a century ago by less than *three millions* of men, and for a population not exceeding *fifteen millions.*
These *three millions* of producers of wealth were then aided by
old artificial power, derived from mechanism and chemistry, equal
to the labour of *twelve millions* of men producers.   Or there
was a combined manual and artificial power of production equal
to *fifteen millions* of men producers.   And at this period there
was far less poverty and demoralisation among the producing
classes than there is at this day, whatever bold but uninformed
political economists may say to the contrary.

But what changes have since occurred in the producing power
to create wealth in the British Isles, and in their population ?

The population has not yet doubled. It is not yet *thirty
millions.* While the producing power, manual and artificial,

has increased beyond human calculation, and now far exceeds *one hundred to one* of the population.

Similar changes have take place in the United States, and are proceeding with rapidity over the world, and are daily on the increase, especially in the United States and in the British Isles and Colonies.

Now I ask you, members of the Parliament of the British Empire and the members of the Congress of the Republic of the United States—What have you done with this enormous new power given to your populations to create virtue or goodness and happiness? Pray now answer me this plain question as now put to you.—What! No answer! Your silence is the best extenuation of the enormous errors which you and your predecessors have been unceasingly committing for one hundred years.

I will truly and faithfully answer this awful question for you.

You have, by your unwise and most foolish laws and system of governing, applied this newly acquired power from science to demoralise the world, and to make its population miserable. A power which, rightly applied, or applied in accordance with simple common sense, is far more than sufficient to insure the permanent goodness, wisdom, union, and happiness of the human race.

Reply.—" This is indeed a very grave charge against us and our " predecessors. But we fear the facts now prominent in both our " empires and over the world prove your statement too glaringly to " be longer attempted to be denied. But what is to be done ? " We see the present system is so worn-out that no administration " can longer govern under it. We must admit that it is opposed " to common sense and common honesty, and is too bad to be " longer continued. But what can we do ?"

Become as little children—knowing nothing and having everything to learn respecting making laws and governing.

Reply.—" Then you consider us regular know-nothings on " those subjects on which by our position we ought to know the " most."

Yes. On looking over your authentic records, which are most voluminous in words, but utterly barren of sound consistent ideas, or of any approach to common sense, these records demonstrate that you know nothing of the laws of human nature, —nothing of forming the character of men and women to make them good, wise, and happy—or good, or wise, or happy,—nothing of the natural, honest, and best means of creating and distributing wealth,—nothing respecting the only means by which men can be united in harmony to have their greatest pleasure in cordially assisting each other,—nothing towards devising and executing surroundings in which to place humanity from birth to have their physical, intellectual, moral, spiritual, and practical powers and faculties so trained and educated as to make them at maturity full-formed, rational, active, and happy men and women,

—nothing of the means to employ and classify them beneficially for themselves and for all society,—nothing of the laws of health by which to prevent disease and to live a healthy life of happiness. In fact, you have been taught those things which you ought not to have been taught, and you have been untaught in all that it is the most important for you to know.

Reply.—" Then we are unfit for the task of legislation ?"

Most unfit. But have any been trained and educated to be fit ? No—none. And you being in the office, and now made conscious of your erroneous instruction, will be as easily or perhaps more easily taught that which is true in legislating and governing, than any others.

On referring to the records of both your houses from their commencement, it is evident that the first principles of legislation have never been known by either house.

The principle to create union, to form character, to produce wealth, to make surroundings calculated to make men good, wise, and happy, has been to this day hidden from you, and in consequence more valuable knowledge for use and practice may be written on one sheet of paper, than is contained in all your authentic records.

And what are the subjects which now occupy both houses in your respective Empires ?

Not one of the least permanent value to your respective populations ; but the reverse. The subjects in which you take the most interest are those which are calculated to prevent union,—to prevent the formation of a good, useful, and superior character for men and women,—to prevent the production of the greatest amount of the most valuable wealth in a manner the most beneficial for all,—to prevent the formation of those superior surroundings which can alone make men good, wise, and happy, enable them to love their neighbours as themselves, or to have the only arrangements of society which can admit of the consistent practice of love and charity in the conduct of the human race.

No ! my friends—and you must forgive me for thus plainly speaking these all-important truths, because they are for your benefit and the lasting happiness of our race—it is a fact deserving your everlasting remembrance, that hitherto not one principle has been discussed in either of your houses that could lead to any permanent practical benefit to yourselves, your children, or the population of the world. A world which now only awaits wisdom or common sense in men, to make it an earthly paradise, and its population superior, intelligent, united, happy beings.

Stay, therefore, your present false principles of legislating, and adopt the true ones.

TO THE PRIESTHOOD OF THE WORLD.

OF all classes in society you now require the greatest sympathy from the other classes.

Your training, education, and position in society have unfitted you to obtain a living except by words, teaching to the population of the world, your own children included, errors producing the most lamentable consequences in practice to all classes from the prince to the peasant. And you are made the great stumbling blocks to union, to knowledge, to wealth, and to happiness.

You have been taught to preach and to teach doctrines which, while so taught, will prevent the creation of that spirit of universal love and charity which alone can cordially and permanently unite the human race as one family.

You have been taught to preach and teach those dogmas which, while so taught, must keep all classes in mental blindness, and physically and mentally in worse than Egyptian bondage.

You have been taught to preach and teach those notions opposed to all facts, which, while so taught, must prevent the possibility of a rational character being formed for man, or of his being made to become at maturity good, or wise, or happy.

You have been taught to preach and teach such doctrines as are calculated to keep the people in all nations slaves to yourselves through those false doctrines.

You and the population of the world are therefore greatly to be pitied that arrangements exist to train, educate, and place you under such circumstances as to make you as a class to produce more evil to yourselves and to the population of the world than all other classes united.

What then, you will ask, can be now done to relieve us and the population of the world from these enormous evils which the past ignorance and inexperience of society have forced upon us, and made us, and through us all classes, so grievously to suffer ?

Fortunately the world through the slow process of experience has attained to a practical period in its progress towards a rational existence, and as we thus advance, the means are discovered to overcome difficulties whenever they become too strong for human endurance; and your errors have now become too glaring and too destructive of human happiness to be longer permitted to cause to the human race miseries which have become unbearable.

The immediate remedy is for you to cease to preach and teach your senselesss and most injurious dogmas, and at once to commence to preach and teach those great and everlasting truths which will infuse into all minds the pure and divine spirit of love and charity for all of our race, and merciful feelings for all that has life, as well as pleasure in the contemplation of all nature.

The principles which will create this spirit and make it to pervade the human race admit of no dogmas—no anger, hatred, envy, jealousy, force, falsehood, violence, fear, or fraud.

No, my deluded brethren, those principles which create love and charity will never produce any of these evil passions or evil doings. They think of no evil—they will admit no evil; but they will indeed produce peace on earth and good will among men, make man love his brother as himself, and will for ever destroy all selfish feelings.

Thus and thus only, my dear hitherto misguided brethren, can you make the will of God be done on earth as it is in heaven.

Thus only can a new existence on earth be given to man.

Thus only can the population of the world be made to attain the millennial state of happiness promised to our race.

Thus only can you make man to be consistent and to think and act rationally.

Thus only can you induce the governments and people of the world to form federative treaties of peace to be permanent between all nations.

Thus only can you induce governments and people to unite in rational family commonwealths to carry on the rational business of human life, and thus with knowledge cordially to assist each other.

And thus only can you create that love and charity in these family commonwealths, formed by superior common-sense arrangements, that they shall federatively unite with each other until all the families of the earth shall become one united family, and shall form that brotherhood of the human race so long desired by all good men.

TO THE POPULATION OF THE WORLD.

The priesthood of all religions and the governments of all nations have so far united, although against their own real interests and happiness, to keep you ignorant, in poverty, and disunited, that you may be made subservient to their undeveloped minds and mistaken views.

By their training, education, and position, they have been deceived to their own injury, and they have in consequence deceived you to your greater injury.

The progress of science has now elicited facts which are calculated to open the eyes of the priesthood and governments of the world and of yourselves.

The system in which all have been involved is now worn-out,—it can be worked no longer by priests or governments.

It has been ascertained to be based on falsehood only, and to be continually productive of evil in practice, and that the evil is increasing in a continually increasing ratio.

It is true that the priesthood of all religions and the governments of all nations have made you beasts of burden and most ignorantly irrational in mind and conduct.

But your day and their true day is coming, when they will no longer err, and you will no longer be kept in worse than Egyptian bondage ; but you, the priesthood, and the governments, will unite to form one people, with one language, one interest, one cordial feeling of union, and to become one superior elevated class, divided only by age as nature directs.

Had you not been made and kept ignorant, disunited, in poverty, and beasts of burden, you could at any time have emancipated yourselves by uniting, when all the power of the world would have been yours, and you could have become free, independent, full-formed men and women, knowing yourselves and society, and how to practice in every department of it.

Such is now the prospect before you,—such will be your future destiny,—such is the progress and happiness which God, or the Great Creating Power of the Universe, is preparing for you and your children through all earthly time.

You ask how all this is to come to pass, seeing the helpless plight in which you now are, the few being your masters, many as you are.

It cannot be brought about by anger, hatred, and violence, by force or fear ; but it can be easily effected by a calm steady persevering conduct on your part, when you can be influenced by the spirit of love and charity, and when you can be made to acquire common sense in your measures to obtain your just rights ; —that is, when you can be made to acquire sufficient knowledge and moral courage to take your own affairs into your own hands, and to do your own business without asking others to do it for you, who are yet as ignorant as yourselves how it is to be done.

Your governments will do anything you unitedly ask them to do. But until you can thus unite they know you are too ignorant and too powerless to know what you do want or how to obtain it.

In consequence of this ignorance you are continually complaining of your governments, when you alone have the power to make them, without violence or confusion, what they should be.

The first measures required are, that the people of both Empires—of Great Britain and the United States—should form a federative treaty, as an example to all nations.

These two Empires are better prepared for such treaty than any others ; but the enormous benefits that would be derived immediately by both would be such as would induce all nations to unite, un: there would be a federation of all the nations of the world, and peace over the earth would be thus secured for ever.

The second measure for practice is for you to unite to ask
your governments to apply the national resources to create new
common-sense surroundings, into which gradually to remove the
whole population of every state and nation, in order to make it
possible, practical, and easy for all to lead pure Christian lives,—
that is, to exhibit in their every-day practice the universal spirit
of love and charity which Jesus Christ recommended, in order
that each may love his neighbour as himself.

I well know the so-called men of the world deem such a state
of society upon earth to be an impossibility—a mere imaginary
notion which never can be applied to practice.

This impression arises from the undeveloped and irrational
state of mind created by the human character being based by
society on a false principle, and being trained, educated, employed, and placed in accordance with that false principle, and
the entire of society in its construction and classification having
the same lamentable error for its foundation.

In consequence of this ignorance of scientific knowledge and
their undeveloped state of mind, our ancestors made the surroundings in which to place the population of the world to be such
that truth and honesty could not live within them, love and
charity would be laughed to scorn, and each one, instead of
loving his neighbour as himself, is opposed to him, and in most
cases acts upon principles of hatred to him.

This system of universal falsehood in principle and practice
makes the teachers to speak one thing, and all their lives to act
in direct opposition to their teaching,—and the taught naturally
to follow their example.

It is true therefore that under this system of falsehood, ignorance, injustice, and cruelty, and within the surroundings which
have necessarily emanated from this horrid system, it is impossible that men can have love or charity for each other, or can
love their neighbours as themselves; but on the contrary, this
system teaches and forces men to grasp at each others means of
existence, and thus often, in the midst of over-flowing abundance, the weak and unfortunate are made to starve for want of
the most common necessaries to support life.

Words are inadequate to express the ignorance, deception, injustice, cruelty, and inconsistent absurdities of this system,
which is called the wisdom of our ancestors.

No, my poor deluded friends, you never can under this system
become good, healthy, united, wealthy, or rational. You cannot
have universal love or charity, or love your neighbours as yourselves. It is a farce, and those who preach it know it to be a
farce, to attempt under this system to put those divine principles
of justice and happiness into practice.

And yet there is a beautiful system—a system of truth and
honesty, of justice and goodness, of peace and plenty, of unity

and happiness,—God's system of universal love and charity, in which all will love their neighbours as themselves. A system of common sense, in accordance with all the laws of nature—laws of goodness, mercy, and happiness.

And when you can be made to acquire one grain of common sense, you will ask your governments to change the one system for the other, and you will ask in such a manner as will insure their most willing consent to your wishes.

Whenever you unite to ask from your governments what is right, and in a right manner, you will be sure to obtain it.

Yes, my friends, there is a system to be attained, in which it will be practicable to have the language of truth and the practice of honesty,—to have the spirit of universal love and charity,—and for each to love his neighbour as himself,—and for all to be united, wealthy, and happy.

No longer believe those who tell you that this superior, rational, and natural state of society is impracticable. It is impracticable only while society is based on a false principle, and while men shall be trained, educated, employed, placed, and governed, on that false principle.

But when men shall be trained, educated, employed, placed, and governed on the the true principle of our nature, then will this false, unjust, cruel, and miserable system be no longer possible to remain in practice.

You, and the priesthood, the governments, and the legislators of the world, are at this day dupes to a false system, which makes you create evil and then become its ignorant and most irrational slaves. For evil is created and maintained solely by man's ignorance of himself and of the all-merciful laws of his nature.

Unitedly, then, ask your governments now to form federative treaties, and to apply present national resources to give you common-sense surroundings; and thus will you have for a generation or two full employment of the most advantageous description to yourselves and to the population of the world.

The question now is,—Will you continue to maintain a system which insures your ignorance, slavery, and misery, and which will give these evils to your children?—Or will you exert yourselves to obtain a system which will insure to you and your children, to the latest posterity, knowledge, freedom, and happiness?

Unitedly all power is with you. Divided you are powerless

You say, and say truly, that you wish to unite, but do not know how to effect it.

It can never be effected while your characters are formed on the belief that any of your faculties, qualities, or powers are formed *by* yourselves, and that you are responsible for them. But union will become universal among the human race when they shall be trained, educated, employed, placed, and governed, on the knowledge of the principle that "What man is he is formed

" to be by God and society, and that God and society are res-
" ponsible to all individuals for the character given to them."

And when you acquire common sense, you will listen to
no teachers who will not instruct you in this principle of union
and of nature.

TO THE CIVIL AND MILITARY PROFESSIONS OVER THE WORLD.

You occupy an important position under the present false principle and consequent mal-arrangement of society.

As the principle on which the system is based is false, all the
arrangements are false, and so is your position in those arrangements.

By being made merely men of a profession, you are injured,
and these professions being injurious to the population of the
world, you not only injure yourselves, but others also, to an extent of which you are probably little conscious.

In this system of falsehood, injustice, and cruelty, you are
placed half way between the depotism of the governing class and
the slavery of the untaught and ill-taught.

Were it not for the force, fear, falsehood, and fraud of your
combined professions, despotism, injustice, and cruelty could not
be now maintained in any part of the world, and the progress to
rationality and happiness would be permanent and rapid.

You are the centre links which keep this unjust and now most
unnatural state of society together—a system so unjust and unnatural as to induce men, while seeing their fellowmen starving
in the midst of plenty, to maintain such a system for the government of the world, in opposition to the true and rational system
by which society should be now conducted ;—proving to demonstration the want of practical knowledge in all parties, and of
how little use are what are called the learned professions.

All the knowledge you possess is applied to aid the despotic
few to keep the mass of the people in physical and mental bondage, and without your assistance this state of things could not
be long continued.

The advanced minds of the world know that the *Priesthood* of
the world claim to form and do form the character of the human
race,—and a wretched, inferior, and bad character they have
formed for them and continue to form.

Hitherto the priesthood have given no sign of knowing the
natural and therefore easy mode of giving a good, useful, and
superior character to any portion of mankind. They are not
practical men on this or any other subject; and to form a good,

useful, and superior character requires a knowledge of the entire practice of life.

Whatever may be said or intended by them, the effect of their preaching and teaching is to keep the taught in ignorance of their own nature, of the laws of nature, and of the real business of life,—to keep them in subjection to the priesthood and the ruling powers of the state, that both may keep them beasts of burden to create by their labour wealth for the priesthood and the ruling powers to spend in luxuries injurious to themselves and their families.

It is not the best interest of a single individual to be now trained to become a priest in any part of the world. It is a false and most useless position—a position most injurious to the individual and to all society. The apparent interest of the priest is opposed to the real interest of the human race. After this generation priesthood should be made to cease for ever, and every one should be trained and educated to be his own priest.

So with the profession of the *Law*—its members make and maintain laws to enable the few in place and power despotically to rule the many, and to hold them in bodily and mental slavery. For, except in name, there is, as all law matters are now conducted, little or no connection between law and justice. It is seldom asked what is justice in this case or that,—but always what is the law; and so admirably are codes of law made to confound common sense, that the law is easily made by lawyers to be doubtful upon most cases brought before them.

Whatever the best principled members of the law may intend or desire, the advanced minds of the world know that under the existing false, unjust, and cruel system of society, the training and educating and employment of lawyers make it their apparent interest to keep the people ignorant of their rights, divided in feeling, obedient to their laws, and slaves to despotic power.

Society may be constructed now to do far better without than with them. It will not be henceforward the real interest of one individual to be trained and educated for the law ; for every one will be so trained, educated, and employed, as to become his own best lawyer as well as priest.

So likewise with the *Medical Profession*. Although it appears to be somewhat more useful and necessary than the priesthood and law, yet it is only so on first appearances.

No parties know better than the intelligent members of this profession that the population of the world would soon become far more healthy without than with it.

The most advanced minds in the world know that the training, educating, and position of all medical men, are to give them an apparent interest that disease should generally prevail, and that individuals when diseased and employing them should not too speedily r over, or attain strong permanent health, except in the case of the Emperors of China, who make the physician's payment to cease as long as they are not in good health.

The most advanced physicians well know that disease is unnatural, and is created by the present false, unjust, cruel, and artificial state of society. That if all from birth were trained and educated to fully know their own individual constitution and the laws of health, and if the surroundings of all were made such as now they easily might be, and if men could act in accordance with those laws, disease would rapidly leave the earth, and in a generation or two would be scarcely or never known.

This subject, as well as those connected with the priesthood and the law, is becoming better understood by the masses, and soon it will not be the real interest of one individual to be trained and educated for this profession, and all men and women will be trained and educated to become their own medical advisers.

Except in an ignorant, artificial, unnatural, and insane state of the human mind, before it has been developed to become consistent and rational, there will be no *Military Profession*, or training and educating men to butcher each other and destroy and waste valuable property.

This is too insane and mad a profession to be much longer submitted to by the growing intelligence of the age.

To train and educate men to become insane and mad in their minds and conduct cannot be much longer held to be respectable by those who profess any religious creeds or dogmas, but especially by those who profess the Christian religion of universal love and charity.

What a farce for men to profess these doctrines, and then to go forth by thousands and tens of thousands to hack and maim and brutally murder those whom they have never seen, and who have done them no harm.

Let nations professing religion cease to train and educate men to hack, maim, and murder their fellows, and wilfully to destroy property, so much wanted by the poor, who are made such by this ignorant, unnatural, unjust, and cruel system which the conservatives of the world are so anxious to retain, as though it were possible that it could benefit themselves or their offspring.

How blind and stupid must those nations be, first to see laws passed, without making the least exertion legally to prevent them, which deprive themselves of arms, and then to proceed to vote money to create and maintain a standing army to make them and keep them cowards, useless to oppose invaders, and gradually to become slaves to force, falsehood, fear, and fraud!

Is such a system as this to be maintained by men calling themselves rational, but who so far appear not to have attained the first degrees of common sense, and prove how little they know how to govern themselves?

Whenever the human race shall be so far developed as to comprehend the difference between a system always creating disunion and a system always creating union, they will abandon the former, which keeps them in continual misery, and will adopt the latter, which will ensure the permanent happiness of all.

When they attain sufficient practical knowledge and common sense to prefer the system of union to that of disunion, they will understand how to make surroundings which in a healthy situation shall give them good dwellings, abundance of wholesome food, a new training and education for their children, which shall make them good, wise, and happy,—give themselves always for exercise useful and pleasant physical and mental employment, beneficial to themselves and to society,—unite them as one family, —and make them ever increasingly prosperous.

These first union surroundings will form Family Commonwealths, scientifically devised and constructed ; and by the gradual federative union of these scientific family commonwealths, first in each nation, and then from nation to nation until the population of the globe shall be included, all necessity over the world for priests, lawyers, medical men, or a fighthing class, will be made to cease, and then will the population of the earth become rational, peace will be universal and permanent, and every one will sit under his own vine and fig tree and there will be none to make him afraid.

THE FIRST LIFE OR INFANT STATE OF MAN.

IN this period man is ignorant of himself, inexperienced in all matters, undeveloped in his mental faculties and reasoning powers, and governed by his imagination.

He imagined that he formed himself, and that he was responsible to some other power or powers for the qualities which he possessed.

He therefore imagined that his fellowmen formed their own qualities of body and mind, and that if they did not form them as he thought was right, they were bad fellows and should be disliked and punished by himself or others banded together for that purpose.

This was the ORIGIN OF EVIL.

It necessarily created hatred, anger, envy, jealousy, and all the violent and injurious passions—created the dogmas, forms, and ceremonies of all the religions known in the world, leaving the practice of true religion to be commenced in t e second or matured period of human existence, a period yet to come.

Evil thus originated, causing first the violent and injuri us passions, then the false religions with the view to subdue or mitigate their evil consequences, but which inflamed and increased them and produced more private hatreds, and caused national conflicts and wars of the most cruel and savage character, and thus widely opened the floodgates of vice, crime, and misery, among all tribes and peoples while self-righteousness and the selfishness of individual power through wealth and station ruled the population of the world with despotic force, injustice, and cruelty.

During this imaginative or infant period of manhood, the leading men of the world imagined and taught that the earth was flat, and was fixed in the centre of the universe,—that the sun, planets, and stars moved daily around it,—and that these and all other things in the universe were made for man; and the accuracy of science was in this imagining period unknown for innumerable ages.

They imagined the earth to be a young creation, and but a few thousand years old.

For a considerable portion of this period they were governed solely by their imagination, which continually led them astray, and their minds and conduct were an excited mass of confusion and conflict.

During the progress of this long reign of the imagination, experience began to make a slow advance in developing the mental powers to observe facts, and by degrees to reflect upon them, but as these facts were opposed to their early imbibed imaginary notions, the natural conclusions to be drawn from them were resisted with the utmost tenacity by the religious and secular prejudices of the imagination, which had so pre-occupied the human mind as to make it desperate in their defence.

Thus commenced a war of life and death between young reason in its infancy and old imagination at maturity.

At first infant reason had small chance of progress against old established conservative imagination. It was snubbed, sneered at, or punished often even with death, for every advance which it made, and its early progress was in silence, fear, and terror.

All the authorities of the world were enlisted in favour of old imagination, full armed at all points, and all earthly power was at its command.

Old conservative imagination thus kept young reason under subjection. But experience quietly day by day and often by night brought new facts to the aid of young reason, and thus strengthened this rising power, ultimately to prepare for a deadly conflict, which experience knew would sooner or later give victory to reason, and utterly discomfit and destroy old imagination.

This conflict has now long continued. New facts have continually increased, and young reason approaches towards manhood. Experience with its facts is becoming man's sole guide, and is daily adding to its growing strength; while old imagination is at its wits' end. It finds all its resources of force, fear, falsehood, and fraud, begin to fail it, although force and false-hood are becoming desperate, almost frantic, to preserve its waning power and support its tottering frame.

But the advanced minds of the world see that old imagination is in the last stage of weakness—that, except when it is backed up by force and fraud, it will not now attempt to face reason or to meet it in open conflict.

Falsehood is so valiantly opposed by science, that it must soon quit the field, and even force begins to waver; and it is now doubtful whether it is not preparing to abandon old imagination, and to give its influence to reason, whose strength and power are every day more and more developing and upon the increase—a sure sign that the time approaches when it will unite itself with love and wisdom, and that this trinity of divine power, having charity for prime minister, will triumphantly govern the human race in perpetual peace, prosperity, and happiness.

Such is the history of the first period of infant humanity. Man undeveloped, inexperienced, and under the guidance of ima-gination, opposed to facts, to reason, and to common sense.

Hence the supposition that man forms his own physical and mental qualities—the origin of evil.

Hence the violent and injurious passions, the various religious delusions, their hatred of each other, and their continual conflicts and wars.

Hence the individual selfish system of society, creating Pri-vate Property and artificial and truly illegal Marriages of the Priesthoods, against the divine and everlasting laws of nature. Hence the Single Family training of children, to make them selfish and opposed to the interest and happiness of the public or the true commonwealth.

This has been and is the irrational period of human existence, which in the due order of nature is drawing near to its close, is about to give place to the second period or New Existence of Man upon the Earth—the long promised and looked for Millen-nial and rational state of humanity, in which all from birth will be imbued with the pure spirit of love and charity for our race, —when each will be trained, educated, employed, placed, and governed, in such manner, within new surroundings, that each must love his neighbour as himself,—when there will be peace and good-will among men,—when harmony will pervade the circumference of our globe,—and when the entire race will be prepared for a happy existence in a future life.

Let governments, religions, and people quit the region of false imaginations, and become practical in their feelings, thoughts, and actions. Let these now learn what is and what is not prac-ticable with each.

As matters now are all are thinking and acting erroneously. But there is a never-dying desire in all to think and act aright, however falsely they may be educated and placed.

All desire to be good and happy, and by a little rational reflection those who can reason accurately will be convinced that not one can be made good and permanently happy except under arrangements or within surroundings which will create and insure the goodness and happiness of all.

The approaching second period or phase of humanity will create and insure the permanancy of this goodness and happiness for all. To effect this change there must be a cordial union between the governments, religions, and people,—a trinity for the redemption and salvation of our race.

Governments cannot act in this great movement without the religions and the people.

The religions cannot act without the governments and the people.

The people cannot act without the governments and the religions.

But these parties must abandon their present irrationalities.

The governments must abandon their despotism.

The religions must abandon their dogmas and useless forms and ceremonies.

The people must abandon their anger, violence, and desire for revenge for past sufferings, which have been produced through their own weakness of intellect and want of practical knowledge and of moral courage.

By this trinity uniting to abandon their irrationalities, this Second Coming of Truth to effect this Glorious Change may be soon accomplished.

In this Second Period of Humanity, Truth in principle and Consistency in practice will ultimately be alone known over the earth.

In this phase of human life, society will be based on the *principle* derived from *all facts*,—

" That the physical, mental, and spiritual character of man is " formed before and from birth *for* him."

This principle can alone create union and attraction between the race,—can alone pervade the minds of all with the pure spirit of universal love and charity,—can alone make man love his neighbour as himself,—can alone make man wealthy, good, wise, and happy,—can alone make man a consistent and rational being, —can alone establish a cordial brotherhood among the human race,—can alone terminate the despotism of governments, the dogmas and hatreds of religions, and the ignorance and injurious passions of the people and of the entire population of the world.

This principle the governments, religions, and the people must unite to acknowledge openly, and to establish as the base of society.

This being accomplished, all future proceedings will be easy, pleasant, and delightful to all.

The next practical measure will be for governments to unite to form, upon principles of justice, federative treaties, on similar principles to those on which the federative treaties between the different states of North America are based. This will be permanently advantageous for all who now live, and for all who may live hereafter.

The next practical measure will be to introduce new surroundings, consistent with the new principle on which society is to be based.

These surroundings will comprise new arrangements for training, educating, employing, placing, and governing the populations of all nations previously federatively united.

These new surroundings will separate these populations into such manageable masses, that each one born within them may be so well cared for by his surrounding society that he shall be well trained, educated, employed, governed, and made to become good, wise, and happy, and to be an efficient agent to assist to make others good, wise, and happy : and these proceedings will unite all within these surroundings, and will insure the constant progress of each towards excellence and a high state of happiness.

These masses, to be manageable and best calculated for all the purposes of life, must not exceed *three thousand* as a maximum.

They will constitute the nuclei of society, instead of the single family with all its mal-arrangements and individual selfish results.

They will form united scientific social Family Commonwealths, in which the permanent good of all will be the ever-governing principle.

Each of these commonwealths will become an everlasting school and university, for the practical formation of a good and superior character through life for every one, and there are no other means by which such character can be formed for the human race.

Every attention should be given to form, combine, and execute these surroundings, to make them the most complete for all the purposes of a superior, good, and happy existence,—for as these are, so will be the men and women born and living within them.

These scientific Social Family Commonwealths must be also federatively united, in order to assist each other, and to form together but one great interest of humanity, when each will aid all, and all will aid each, and thus the happiness of each will be increased ten thousand fold.

And each family commonwealth must be governed solely by the unchanging, good, and all-merciful laws of God and Nature, and not one law of man must ever interfere with these all-wise laws of God.

In these divinely governed scientific social family commonwealths, the will of God will be done on earth as it is in heaven.

Their laws will be the laws of God.   Their religion will be the constant practice of doing good to all in the pure spirit of love and charity.

There will be no Private Wealth.

There will be no Illegal Marriages or giving in marriage,—God's marriages of affinity being alone legal.

All children will be cared for from birth, and will be trained, educated, employed, placed, and governed—physically, intellectually, morally, spiritually, and practically—in the best manner that the collected wisdom and means of society can devise and apply to practice.

All human Punishments will thus become injurious, and will be altogether abandoned.

The Training will be in the spirit of Love and Charity, to give to each the spirit of love and charity.

The Education will be an education of things, by seeing them, hearing them verbally explained, by the freest and fullest questions from the taught, patiently and kindly listened to and rationally answered in the spirit of love to give the knowledge sought for.

The Employment will be according to age, and beneficial for the individual and for society.

The Language will be that of truth only. No secrecy of any kind.

Individual freedom of speech and action, as full and perfect as is consistent with a rational and happy social state of man.

Perfect Equality according to age, in education, employment, condition, and position.

These practical arrangements are all essential to form man into a rational being, and to enable him to become good, just to all, united, healthy, wise, and happy.

May the governments, priesthoods, and people of the world soon perceive these eternal truths, and act upon them in the spirit of love and charity directed by wisdom.

INHABITANTS OF OUR EARTH, CITIZENS OF OUR GLOBE!

Men and brethren. I now address you, and probably for the last time, for I feel old age rapidly approaching, and I expect soon to be mentally as well as physically enfeebled. But attend to what I shall now write.

I have through life endeavoured to dive to the foundation of the causes of your misery and slow progress towards a permanent and happy state of existence, for which all your natural organs, faculties, propensities, qualities, and powers are so admirably adapted, and which they are every way created to attain.

And before I depart hence I wish to give you the benefit of my experience.

It seems to me certain that you are approaching a greater event than has previously occurred in your history.

You have from the beginning until now lived and been governed under a system which is now worn out, and which can proceed no farther. It has accomplished its mission and can work no longer. There are no men in existence who can work it. On the continent of Europe, in Russia and Turkey, in Asia, throughout the British Empire, and in the United States of North America, there are no men who can resuscitate it, or work a dying and now only injurious system.

The present system of governing in all the nations of the world is now by all advanced minds seen to be a farce, or too often a tragedy, and they are looking for a revolution which shall involve all nations and peoples over the world.

This must be a religious, political, commercial, and social revolution, which will entirely change the relations of men and of all things connected with the affairs of men.

The question of the deepest importance to all of every class in every country is,—Shall this great change be commenced and carried on through the irritated and violent passions of the suffering masses, or by the wise foresight and calm reason of the governing class, foreseeing and foretelling this tempest of trodden-down humanity ?

All things are gradually preparing for this change of system, from disunion and repulsion to union and attraction between man and man and nation and nation. The first being the undeveloped, inexperienced, and infant state of humanity; the second, the more developed, experienced, matured, and natural state of man, preparing him to become a full-formed rational being. The change from the one to the other is in progress, and is as certain as the change from infancy to maturity.

Knowing that this glorious change for humanity must come in the due order of nature, I have almost from my youth forewarned the heads of the governments and religions of the most advanced nations of the coming change, that they might not be taken by surprise and be unprepared for it. They are now I trust prepared to commence and conduct this change, which will be so permanently beneficial for you and for them.

Hitherto they could not commence it on account of your ignorant, inexperienced, and undeveloped state towards a rational and matured state of mind and feeling, and from the want throughout all classes of society of the pure spirit of love and charity for our race, of every colour, country, creed, and class.

This spirit, so long talked about, and the only spirit which can govern the world in peace and with wisdom, could not be introduced into the heart and mind of humanity, so as permanently to pervade the feelings of all, until the true formation of the human character was discovered and made generally known, and all blame thus withdrawn from the created being, so that effectual practical measures could be adopted to insure a good and rational character for all, and, through this knowledge of the irresponsibility of the created, to pervade the mind of each with this pure love and charity for our race, and by its exhibition in every act of our lives, to evince in the most certain manner our love to God, for the universal goodness and happiness which the Great Creating Power of the Universe thus creates.

I have now only to intreat of my disciples, spread as they now are among all nations and peoples, to endeavour to instil into all around them the true knowledge of the formation of character, and thus, on the surest base, to fill their minds with this divine spirit of love and charity for our race, and then the means of permanent prosperity, of universal union, of the true social system, and of rational happiness, will necessarily follow.

Your business, then, is, by your calm determined unity, to induce your respective governments to form federative treaties between all countries and to create new common-sense surroundings, that thus a superior character may be given to all,— wealth at all times be abundantly created,—universal union may be established,— and the peace and happiness of the population of the world may be secured for ever.

Farewell,

ROBERT OWEN.

Sevenoaks Park,
Sevenoaks, 18th July, 1856.

London :—Published by the Author at 16, Great Windmill Street, Haymarket : and sold by Holyoake, 147, Fleet Street ; Truelove, 240, Strand; Goddard, 14, Great Portland Street, Cavendish Square; Farrah, 21, John Street, Fitzroy Square ; and all Booksellers.

Registered for Foreign Transmission.

ROBERT OWEN'S
MILLENNIAL GAZETTE;

EXPLANATORY OF THE PRINCIPLES AND PRAC-
TICES BY WHICH, IN PEACE, WITH TRUTH,
HONESTY, AND SIMPLICITY, THE NEW
EXISTENCE OF MAN UPON THE
EARTH MAY BE EASILY AND
SPEEDILY COMMENCED.

" The character of Man is formed *for* him, and *not by* him !"

No. 8.]   OCTOBER 1st, 1856.   [PRICE 6D.

THE FIRST AND SECOND PHASE OF HUMAN EXIS-
TENCE UPON EARTH BRIEFLY STATED FOR THE
CONVENIENCE OF STATESMEN, MEN OF THE WORLD,
MEN OF BUSINESS, AND OTHERS TOO MUCH OCCU-
PIED, OR TOO INCAPABLE, TO GIVE THE ATTENTION
REQUIRED TO INVESTIGATE SYSTEMS OF SOCIETY
FOR THEMSELVES.

THE first phase of human existence commenced with the creation
of man, when his faculties were undeveloped and he was inexperienced. He commenced his first phase under the guidance
and government of his imagination, when, ignorant of facts and
devoid of common sense, he imagined that he formed his own
qualities of body and mind, and that he was responsible for them
to God and his fellow men. This supposition became the foundation on which society has been constructed and maintained
through the first phase of human life.

This fatal error is the origin of evil,—the cause of all violent
and injurious passions,—and of the disunion and repulsive feelings between men and nations,—and of all wars and conflicts of
past ages to the present. It is the cause of all religious dogmas,
doctrines, forms, and ceremonies, and deadly opposition to
each other. It is the cause of the preaching and teaching of
love and charity and at the same time practising hatred and all
uncharitableness. It is the cause of Private Property, and of
the illegal Marriages of the Priesthoods, against God's legal
marriages of Nature's affinities. It is the cause of all the evils
and disadvantages of single family arrangements, and of all the
ignorant selfishness thus produced,—of the absurd and insane
classification of society existing over the world,—of despotism
and slavery, and of all their endless demoralising results. In

short it is the cause of the present irrational and insane state in which all governments and people are at this day over the earth.

This first phase of sin and misery, of insanity and madness, will cease only when governments and people shall become sufficiently developed to see the enormity of this error of the imagination, and to abandon it and all its misery-producing consequences, and thus to prepare for the commencement of the second phase of human existence upon the earth.

This period, or second phase of human life, will commence when governments and people adopt for the foundation of socity the principle, derived from all facts past and present—

" That man has no power to form his own individual qualities " of body or mind, and that what he is, he is made to be by God " and society."

The knowledge that this truth is derived from and in harmony with all facts will naturally and of necessity create in men a new spirit, new principles of thought and action, and new practices over the world.

The new *Spirit* will be pure universal love and charity for our race, with all its natural and acquired varieties—the spirit taught by Jesus Christ, and never practised by any of his professed disciples, and now unknown, except in mere words, among every division of the human race.

The new *Principle* is the knowledge that man's divine and human character is formed *for* him by God and society, and for which God and society are alone responsible. This principle, now repudiated by all, must become universal, before man can be made to become a rational reasoning being, or can enter upon his second and superior phase of existence, and before his thoughts and actions can become sane and consistent.

The new *Practice* will be, through this new spirit and new principle, to unite the human race cordially to promote each other's progress towards excellence in all things, and in the attainment of happiness, and thus to form of the family of man during all future ages a real brotherhood of oneness in feelings, thoughts, language, interest, and practice ; thus establishing for ever the Millennium or true social existence of man.

In this second phase of humanity, or new existence of man upon the earth, all the old surroundings made by man and now existing over the earth must pass away, and all must become new, highly superior, and in outline and detail consistent, without deviation, with the new spirit and principle from which this second and new phase of existence will arise, based as on a rock, which will defy the storms of all future ages.

These new and superior surroundings will constitute those essential arrangements required to create and maintain the spirit of love and charity, to enable each to love his neighbour as himself, and to induce each to be ever actively engaged in cor dially promoting the true and permanent happiness of all.

In this second and superior phase or new life of man upon the earth, all existing cities, towns, villages, and single family residences will be gradually abandoned, and the population of the world will be formed into manageable masses. These masses will not exceed three thousand as a maximum, in order that every one from birth through life may be well cared for and may experience full justice from society, and that the entire business of life may be conducted in the best manner for each, and the most advantageously for all.

These masses will constitute the nuclei of society, and each mass will constitute a Scientific Social Family Commonwealth, with one language, one interest, and one feeling, all desirous to promote each others progress in excellence and happiness.

This arrangement of the population of the world will permit of new permanent substantial surroundings, that will secure to each the best dwelling, furniture, clothes, food, training, education, employment, health, amusements, and other superior surroundings, to give to each the highest individual liberty of thought, speech, and action, consistent with the permanent harmony of social society, based on a just practical equality of all, in education, employment, condition, and position through life, according to age, capacity, individual character, and natural powers.

To attain the most rapid progress and highest excellence and happiness of each,—

The *Government* must be the sole and pure laws of God, unadulterated by the laws of men.

The *Religion* must be that of doing good to all, in the spirit of love and charity, unadulterated by dogmas, forms, or ceremonies.

Marriages must be made by God. No unnatural children; but all the superior natural children of nature, of love, and of affinity.

The earth to be for the use of each succeeding generation.

All *Property* to be universally public.

Private Property to be unknown over the earth—all property made by God being universally public and intended for all.

Wealth to be produced by all, and to be equally enjoyed by all.

No one to be preferred to another over the earth, except as individual qualities naturally create preferences, which, however, will give no other privileges or advantages.

Society to be responsible for the character created for each one under its care.

God's *Punishments* to be the only punishment upon earth.

The present first or infant phase of human existence to be allowed to die gradually and quietly its natural death, and to cease its existence as the new and superior surroundings are completed.

Thus, without anger, hatred, or violence, without disorder or confusion, by wise foresight, may this second coming of truth, when the minds of men shall be born again, and all shall be redeemed from sin and misery, be introduced in peace, and for the everlasting benefit of all through every succeeding age.

OF THE INSANE HATREDS, VIOLENCES, CONFLICTS, WARS, SLAUGHTERS, AND MASSACRES, ABOUT GOD, THROUGH PAST AGES TO THE PRESENT.

The civil and religious contests which have raged among men for thousands of years are demonstrable proofs of the past and present insanity and madness of the human race, and that they are yet only approaching the confines of reason, to form them into consistent and rational beings.

Those called believers in God say that God knows all things throughout the universe and that He does whatever is done within it. That He everlastingly creates, uncreates, and recreates all things at His will and pleasure, and that without Him nothing is done, and that all that He does is done well and wisely, and that the power of the universe is in His hands.

Those who call themselves disbelievers in God, and believers in nature, say that nature is unknowing and unintelligent, but that it composes, decomposes, and recomposes all things throughout the universe, by laws of nature eternally existing and operating. That this eternal round of formation, decomposition, and reformation, is effected by nature blindly, without any conscious intelligence, and that there is no spiritual existence throughout the universe.

A conscientious difference of opinion always arises from a deficiency of truthful facts to decide the disputed question on one side or the other. This is the case with the difference of opinion as to whether there is a personal God, possessing attributes of perfection, who creates and governs all things within the universe—or whether unintelligent nature blindly and unconsciously effects these results, through what the unbelievers in God call inherent laws of nature.

Numerous facts favour both suppositions; but evidently not sufficient to convince *all* sincere truth seekers one way or the other.

So far facts are certain ; and hence through all past ages there have been sincere believers and disbelievers in the existence of God, prior and superior to, and independent of, nature.

Facts also prove, that the facts in favour of the eternal existence of a God of infinite power, wisdom, and goodness, are sufficient to convince many of its undoubted truths.

While facts also prove that there are facts sufficient to convince many that nature through inherent eternal laws effects all the results which are produced throughout the universe.

But there is also a third class of minds who with equal sincerity are convinced that God and nature are one—that nature is the outward and visible form to man, and that the motion, life, mind, and spirit, existing throughout nature, is its soul or God,—that it pervades nature, and is the soul of all that exists in the universe. Facts prove that there are facts sufficient to create in many minds a sincere belief and conviction that these latter suppositions are the truth on this yet doubtful question.

From this consideration of this so long disputed subject, several questions essential to the progress and happiness of the human race arise, which now require to be fully understood, and if possible to be settled for ever.

1.—How are human opinions formed?

Is not every individual *compelled* to receive and entertain opinions according to the strongest impressions made upon his mind, and which impressions while they so remain must appear the truth to him?

2.—For opinions thus formed, and often against the will and desire of the individual, can there be merit or demerit?

Common sense replies there can be no merit or demerit in any opinion, nor any rational cause for anger, hatred, or violence, from man to man, for *any* conscientious opinions upon *any* subject, civil or religious. Hence all angry disputes, conflicts, and wars, respecting opinions, are insane in their origin, and mad in their results.

3.—What difference can it make to God or nature, or to God in nature, what man believes or disbelieves?

If God or nature, or God in nature desires man to have any particular opinions upon this subject, the cause hitherto of so much hatred and evil among men,—Would not God or nature, or God in nature, produce facts sufficient to convince all minds of that which is true on this now deadly disputed subject?

Until the Superior Power of the Universe gives to men decided proofs of the nature of its existence, it is insanity in men to be angry and to hate each other on account of any difference of opinion respecting it, and it is madness to fight and slaughter each other for opinions which each cannot avoid having.

Do men not yet know that *any* Opinion, true or false, or *any* Character, the best or the worst, may be forced upon man by the surroundings or conditions, physical and mental, in which he is placed by society from birth through life.

If they know not this all-important practical truth, it is now time it should be known to all, and should be acted upon.

To learn how to devise and execute the new surroundings which can make all men good, wise, and happy, is now the great and all-important lesson which all from the highest to the lowest, from the most learned to the most ignorant, have to acquire, and until they are taught this lesson, to fully understand and comprehend it in all its bearings and consequences, other lessons will be of little value, and men will remain in the irrational, disunited, repulsive, and fighting state, in which they have been through all past ages to the present period.

ERROR FROM MAN'S CREATION THE SATAN OR THE DEVIL OF THE PRIESTHOOD, AND THE CAUSE OF EVIL, WHICH, UNDER THE NAME OF GOD, THEY HAVE ALWAYS WORSHIPPED.

THAT individual man creates his own qualities, physical and mental, and determines his religion, feelings, thoughts, language, habits, manners, position in society, or his own surrounding and his conduct,—and that, as these constitute his character, he is accountable for his feelings, thoughts, and actions, to his fellow men, and to the power which creates all his physical and mental organs, faculties, propensities, and powers,—is the foundation upon which society has been based and constructed, and upon which the character of all from birth has been formed.

Does the individual create one of the physical or mental qualities which he possesses at birth? No,—he knows not how they are created or combined to form him to become a human being.

Does he determine his religion? No. That is determined for him by the surroundings in which he is placed

Does he create his own feelings, thoughts, language, and associations of ideas? No. These are created for him, he knows not how,—but chiefly by the country and class in life in which he is born and lives.

Does he create his own surroundings? No. These are created for him, chiefly by society, past and present.

Does he determine his own conduct? No. All the previously mentioned circumstances combined create his will and determine his conduct.

Is it then in accordance with common sense to make the individual, thus created and formed, responsible to the power which creates all his physical and mental powers, and to society which gives the direction, right or wrong, to those qualities from the birth of infant man, by the inferior or superior, good or bad surroundings in which society places him? There does not appear to be one particle of common sense in this proceeding, or any approach to sanity in the conduct of society.

What are the natural consequences of these insane proceedings? To constitute an insane state of society over the earth, inconsistent, confused, contradictory, opposing, and conflicting, in every department of life and in every division of society in every part of the globe as society now everywhere exists.

What effect must such proceedings have in forming the character of each individual ? To give a wrong direction to the feelings, thoughts, and actions of all :—to create all the inferior and evil passions :—to produce a language of falsehood and conduct of insincerity :—to establish false religions, and ignorant, unjust, and cruel governments :—to introduce artificial arrangements of society, and complex, confused, and injurious divisions and classifications among men born with similar faculties and powers :—to prevent the introduction of truth, union, charity, and love, among any portion of the human race :—to encourage disunion, repulsion, civil and religious conflicts, contests, and wars, and to perpetuate them among all nations and peoples :—in short, such fundamental errors are directly calculated to derange the mind and conduct of all humanity, and to make it opposed to its own well-being, well-doing, and progress in real knowledge and happiness.

For proof of these results, see the population of the world at this day, existing in crime, contests, and misery, while possessing the most ample means, if wisely applied, to insure to all perpetual progress in real knowledge, in the spirit of charity and love, and in a never-ending happy existence here and hereafter.

But how are these good and happy results to be attained and secured ?

See the next article.

TRUTH, OR THE ORIGIN OF GOODNESS AND HAPPINESS.

How long has it been asked, and how long will it be asked—What is truth ?

Many times in my previously published writings has it been stated what the true criterion of truth is,—and no one, so far as is known to me, has ever objected to this explanation to the question.

I will now proceed to explain those truths which have been proved by this criterion to be the origin of goodness and happiness among men.

First, or Fundamental Truth.—That the Great Creating Power of the Universe gives to man every organ, faculty, propensity, quality, and power, which he possesses at birth, and that these are therefore of divine origin and are all good by nature.

Second Truth.—That these divine qualities and powers of

humanity are from the birth of each individual placed by the Great Creating Power of the Universe under the direction of men and women at maturity, formed into society ; and therefore, as these societies are in knowledge and experience, so will those trained and educated by them become. And thus is the entire character, physical and mental, of each individual, formed by the Great Creating Power of the Universe and by society through each succeeding generation.

Third Truth.—That the Great Creating Power of the Universe and society are responsible to the individual for the character, will, and conduct of each. And that, through this knowledge, society may from birth well form the character of everyone.

Fourth Truth.—That the inferior or superior, good or bad character of each individual depends upon the inferior or superior, good or bad surroundings in which the individual shall be placed from birth through life ; for as these surroundings are, so must be the character and conduct of those placed within them.

Fifth Truth.—That when one generation can be made to understand human nature and its unchanging laws, and to know how to form surroundings in accordance with that knowledge, then will society know with the certainty of the laws of nature how to insure from birth a good physical, intellectual, moral, spiritual, and practical character for everyone.

Sixth Truth.—That the means are now amply provided, by which society may create such new and superior surroundings, that by gradually placing all from birth within them, each one must acquire a good and superior physical and mental character.

Seventh Truth.—That this character can be formed only by personal verbal instruction in a knowledge of the qualities and uses of the things to be taught ; this instruction to be given at all times in the spirit of love and charity, ma...ng full allowance for the differences in the natural organs and combinations of the faculties and powers, physical and mental, of the taught.

Eighth Truth.—That the means, when rightly applied, abundantly exist to saturate at all times the population of the world with all real, useable, enjoyable, unadulterated, valuable wealth, that can be required for a rational and happy existence, without contests or competition,—and created by all with ease, health, and pleasure.

Ninth Truth.—That the wealth thus produced may be distributed justly and beneficially for all without the moral degradation of endeavouring to buy cheap and sell dear.

Tenth Truth.—That with these principles and practices the human race may be cordially united as one highly enlightened and superior family, each one forming a part of humanity, and each one deriving his great and never ceasing pleasure from contributing his full share to the happiness of all.

Eleventh Truth.—That the new surroundings required to produce these results in practice will gradually form our earth into a paradise, healthy, fruitful, and delightful, and the inhabitants into superior, rational, full-formed men and women, knowing themselves and human nature, governed only by the laws of God and nature, and all assisting to promote each others progress in excellence and happiness.

Twelfth Truth —That by the adoption of the preceding principles and practices, peace and order would be permanently established over the earth, on which the will of God would be done as it is now in heaven, and thus will my mission be terminated.

TO THE HUMAN FAMILY.

BROTHERS and sisters of the human race. of every colour, country, creed and class! Listen to one who has never deceived you, —to one who is deeply interested in your present and future progress and happiness.

You have been to this period passing through the infant and preliminary state of your earthly existence—a state of ignorance, disunion, repulsive feelings, contests, conflicts, sufferings, and misery—a preparatory state, necessary to prepare you for a more advanced future life, in which ignorance, disunion, repulsive feelings, contests, conflicts, suffering, and misery, will be unknown— a preliminary state in the progress of creation, necessary and unavoidable to attain for you future permanent happiness. A necessary preliminary, because the universe is governed and directed either by Supreme intelligence, goodness, and wisdom, or by an unavoidable necessity.

On either supposition the best has been done, is doing, and will be done, that the nature of things or the materials of the universe will admit. Upon either supposition it is evident you are destined to acquire real useable valuable knowledge, by the experience gained in each generation accumulating from one generation to another through past ages to the present.

It will be well therefore for your minds to be directed to take now a calm review of the knowledge which past experience has made certain, and in which there can be no mistake. This is the only sure course you can adopt to become rational in mind and practice, intelligent, good, and happy.

The experience of the past proves that *Union* is the *great lever* by which the human race can accomplish its destiny—which destiny is evidently to attain excellence in all human acquirements, and high permanent enjoyment.

Hitherto the progress of the race has been slow in its advance toward a satisfactory state of existence, and this delay has arisen from the fundamental falsehood on which society has been based since man was created—that is,

" That individual man creates his own physical and mental

" qualities, and is responsible for them to the Power which
" creates him and to society which gives the wise or foolish direc-
" tion to those qualities."

This fundamental error and most glaring mistake has made
man a most irrational being, and has induced him to adopt institution after institution which of necessity have divided man from
man and nation from nation, until men now begin to desire universal separation and individual sovereignty—or, in other words,
universal weakness, and the loss of the incalculable power to be
derived from universal union.

Individualism, carried to its full extent, will reduce human
power to its minimum ; while the union of the human race will
raise its power to the maximum.

In the former state the individual will possess the least power
and happiness, with the minimum of advantages ; while in the
latter case the individual would have his power and happiness
increased many thousand fold, and would acquire all the advantages that a highly progressed society could give and secure to
him.

It is on the knowledge of the difference to all humanity in
beneficial results, between disunion and union, that I have en-
treated and so earnestly recommended the governments of the
world to lose no time in forming federative treaties between all
nations, in order to commence in a state of permanent peace over
the earth the great revolution of the human race from disunion
to union ; and I trust, for their own and the happiness of the population of the world, that they will adopt this simple practical
measure by which to terminate the violent passions and insane
conduct of all parties.

If I cannot succeed in opening the eyes of the governments
of the world to their true interests and to yours, then I recommend you to form federative treaties among yourselves to unite
to create new surroundings on the principle of union and attraction, and to commence by federatively uniting the most useful
and necessary trades in such manner and under such arrangements as will enable you to supply each other on principles of
strict justice and equality with all you can require for a rational
and happy existence.

Without union there is no strength in the working classes.
They are mere ropes of sand, unable to effect anything for themselves ; while they are easily compelled to do everything for the
classes above them.

By union they would have the powers of society at their control. But until they know how rationally to use these powers for
the benefit of all in the spirit of charity and love, they will be
better without this power.

It is, however, gratifying to advanced minds to perceive the
gradual decay of the violent and contending passions leading to
contests and conflicts, and the increase of civil and religious

liberal principles, preparing the way for a spirit of universal charity and love, to insure the permanent interests of all in the federative union of the human race, and the ultimate cordial brotherhood of the family of man on a just and most beneficial equality according to age.

But you, my brothers and sisters of all colours and creeds, must not expect to attain this equality and union until one generation can have a new and superior character formed for it, based on the fundamental principle of union and attraction, and can have its mind formed of ideas and associations of ideas in accordance with that principle.

To commence this change in the principles and practices of the human race, the greatest of all changes yet known since man was created, will be the turning point in human progress from all that is erroneous and evil to all that is true and good.

The preliminary to this great change must be the introduction into the human mind of the pure spirit of universal charity and love, to be derived solely from the knowledge that the universal character of man is formed for him in every instance, by the Great Creating Power of the Universe at birth, and afterwards by society and by the surroundings created by nature and society.

There can be no union while individual man shall be made by his fellow men responsible for those qualities of body and mind which he knows not how to create for himself, or how they are created.

This grossly false notion is now the only obstacle to the rapid progress of our race to goodness, intelligence, wisdom, union, and happiness.

Let this obstacle be removed, and the mind of man will speedily be as it were born again,—he will become a new being, with a new spirit, a new mind, filled with new ideas and new associations of ideas, and his conduct will be in all respects different from what it has been and is.

It is only by this change that man can be redeemed from sin and misery, and made to become a consistent, sane, and rational being.

Should the ruling powers in churches and states unwisely and obstinately, in opposition to the forewarnings of all around, persevere in forcing this wretched system of falsehood and evil upon their respective populations, then will they force on a revolution of principles, which will hurl them from power and will create severe suffering to themselves, their families, and their populations ; but which revolution, by wise foresight now inducing them to make the required changes in time, may not only be avoided, but, instead thereof, they may secure to themselves, their descendants, and their respective populations, permanent benefits and substantial enjoyments such as no rulers of society have ever yet experienced.

Can any one observing the signs of the times doubt, that if governments will not give the people their just rights and the advantages now to be obtained in practice from the rapid and extensive progress made in the various practical sciences, by inventions, discoveries, and improvements, applicable to the every-day purposes of life, the working classes will combine to apply these immense new powers to their rightful purposes, and to prevent their being longer applied as at present to attain not only useless results, but the most unrighteous objects, such as only insane maniacs could think of adopting, supporting, and continuing.

Let the ruling powers in churches and states now take good council together, and be aware of the awful consequences to themselves of forcing the producing classes to federatively unite to obtain without the aid and co-operation of their present rulers the change of system which the increase of knowledge and of these new scientific powers requires—for assuredly this change must now be made by one or other of these parties, if they do not unite together to accomplish it in the spirit of cordial co-operation.

See you not, my brothers and sisters of every class, creed, country, and colour, the now irresistible necessity for universal union with all its illimitable permanent advantages, to prevent the continual increase of disunion rapidly extending among all nations, and which, if not stayed in its unnatural course, must force on the suspended conflict of nationalities against governments, and thus shed the blood of unnumbered thousands, and keep the population in worse than Babel confusion and in the horrors of civil wars which would cease only with the exhaustion of the means of contest.

Are not the people of Europe, of America, of Asia, and of Africa, now girding up their loins for this trial of strength, if governments do not wisely anticipate this pending storm, and dissipate it by openly and faithfully leading forward the people to change this system of universal error in principle and practice, for the only true system in principle and practice for the permanent good government of the human race ?

Can any parties now, with the facts before the world, claiming to possess common sense, hesitate between the system of disunion and that of union in the formation of society intended for the progress and happiness of mankind ?

I have endeavoured to place the two systems in their proper light fairly before governments and people. More I would do if I possessed the means. I would exhibit in practice a model of a full rational society, or one scientifically arranged family commonwealth, in which the happiness of each should be made to promote the high happiness of all,—in which there should be perfect union, arising from a just practical equality according to age, and every one being so surrounded that all his or her natural wants would be amply provided for in the best manner, and secured without contest or competition,—in which a good and intelligent character should be formed for every one,—in which truth alone would be their language, and each would always express the convictions and feelings which they were made to receive, and secrecy would be unknown,—in which all would be taught from facts to know themselves and human nature, and to comprehend society in principle and extensively in practice,—in which all would be actively engaged, and their occupations a never ending sort of pleasure and of rational enjoyment,—in which there should be *no inferior* or *injurious surroundings*,—and in which the happiness of all should be secured through life by all being made *good* and *wise* by those *animate* and *inanimate surroundings*.

Will the governments of the world now expend their national resources in murder, plunder, and demoralisation,—or will they expend them in creating New Scientific Family Commonwealths on such a model ?

We shall see.

DIALOGUES BETWEEN ROBERT OWEN, WHO ADVOCATES AN ENTIRELY NEW SYSTEM OF SOCIETY, IN SPIRIT, PRINCIPLE, AND PRACTICE,—AND A DEFENDER OF THE PRESENT SYSTEM, IN SPIRIT, PRINCIPLE, AND PRACTICE, AS THE ONLY SYSTEM POSSIBLE,—ASSISTED BY A MATERIALIST, OPPOSED TO THE EXISTENCE OF SPIRITS, WHICH HE CONSIDERS AN IMPOSSIBLE STATE OF BEING, OR AS NONENTITIES.

[In these dialogues, *O.* signifies Robert Owen,—*D.* the Defender of the present System,—and *M.* the Materialist.]

First Dialogue.

D. (addressing himself to O.) Why do you object to the present system of society, seeing that it has produced over the earth so much wealth, prosperity, union, civilisation, and happiness ?

O. I object to it for very many reasons.

1st.—Because it produces so little wealth, prosperity, union, civilisation, and happiness.

2nd.—Because it enforces upon all a language of falsehood and a conduct of duplicity and deception.

3rd.—Because it creates false and unjust feelings, violent and most injurious passions, and an erroneous direction of the best natural faculties of our common nature.

4th.—Because it instigates men to contests and deadly conflicts, opposing man to man and nation to nation.

5th.—Because it is based on a fundamental falsehood, which, entering into the whole character of man and construction of society, of necessity deranges the rational faculties of humanity, and thus compels the human race to think and act irrationally, insanely, and madly, to the deep injury of themselves and their fellow men.

6th.—Because it creates the most uncharitable feelings and consequent conduct from man to man over the earth, and induces every nation and people to form for themselves the most unnatural and artificial arrangements of society—arrangements varying in words and forms, but substantially the same,—giving the power of society to the few, to oppress the many.

7th.—Because it will, while continued, prevent the creation in any portion of the human race of the pure and genuine spirit of charity and love, without which there can be no true religion in practice, no real goodness, union, or happiness among men.

8th.—Because it presents an obstruction impossible to be overcome, until it shall be destroyed, to progress in goodness, wisdom, or happiness.

9th.—Because it will be impracticable while this system is continued, to make man truthful, honest, or sane in mind or practice.

And many more reasons against its longer continuance to form and govern society occur to me ; but those I have mentioned are sufficient, as it appears to me, to demonstrate its total unfitness for the future government of mankind.

D. If what you have stated can be proved to be true, you have given ample reasons for an immediate change of system over the world. But I deny your whole statement, and I assert that if it were true, to change this system for one so opposed to it in spirit, principle, and practice, as the one you advocate, would be impracticable, strongly impressed as society is in favour of things as they are.

O. The most palpable truths, and truths, too, of the highest importance to the present and future population of the world, may be denied, as you have denied my statements, and, however easy of practice they may be when understood, may be said to be, as you have asserted of these, impracticable. Now with these assertions on both sides no progress towards eliciting the truth is made. Let us therefore come to the point, and refer to facts which cannot be refuted or denied by any one in a sound state of mind.

D. Agreed. How do you propose to commence?

O. Let us first consider one by one in the order stated the truth or error of my objections to the present system of society. And let us afterwards discuss the practicability or impracticability of now changing the one system for the other.

D. I do not object to this course,—it is fair. Proceed.

O. I objected first to the present system of society, in answer to your question and statement, because it produced so little wealth, prosperity, union, civilisation, and happiness. You said, seeing it produces " so much " of each of these. I admit that the present system produces some wealth, some prosperity, some union, some civilisation, and some happiness.   My objection is that under the existing system the wealth, prosperity, union, civilisation, and happiness are produced to a very limited extent only, and very partially, and very precariously to any parties, when compared with what would be produced by the system with which I propose to supersede it.   Under the present system many who have been trained to produce wealth among the working class are withheld from producing wealth by being forcibly made idle, not being permitted to work, for want of materials and a demand for their labour ; while hundreds of thousands in all countries could be essentially benefited by their labour, and the real wealth of the world would be greatly increased by it Again, large numbers of the working classes who are occupied, are so injuriously employed that they produce much that is useless, much that is injurious, and much that is deteriorated and inferior ; while none are employed to produce the greatest amount of the most valuable wealth in the shortest time, in a manner the most advantageous for themselves and for society generally. While the working classes are thus so much mis-placed and mis-employed, the largest proportion of the middle class, called men of business, do not produce real wealth, but are occupied in extracting from the working class much of the limited wealth which they produce, while many waste much of their time in a most senseless and extravagant mode of distributing the wealth created by the working class, and become thoroughly demoralised by being trained to endeavour to buy cheap and sell dear.   Others of this class who have been what is called prosperous or successful in buying cheap and selling dear, live in idle luxury, producing no wealth, but consuming it wastefully.   While all the civil and military professions are not only entirely useless in producing wealth, but are in many ways great obstacles to its production, and wasteful consumers and often wholesale destroyers of it.

D. These are indeed heavy charges against the present position in society of the working and middle classes, and especially of the professions.   Surely these latter are of more use to society than you give them credit for.

O. I wish to give all credit due to these institutions now so much cherished and in many cases idolised by many over the world ; but my experience of the present system and its working throughout society compels me to know that these professions are the corrupted and the corrupting influences between the corrupting classes above them and the corrupted classes below them in society.   And that although the individuals trained and educated by society for these professions so destructive to honesty and happiness are blameless, yet is society worse than insane to foster and encourage the existence of such monstrous demoralising professions in the garb of sheep's clothing.

D. Hold! hold! Mr. Owen! you are surely libeling all these highly venerated and esteemed classes!

O. Yes, highly venerated and esteemed by those previously made mentally blind, and who cannot see anything as it exists. All things connected with their health of body and mind and progress of real knowledge of humanity or of a rational construction of society are carefully hidden from them, by being presented to their vision through a false medium which renders their vision of these matters worse than useless.

D. You express new and strange notions on these important subjects—so strange, indeed, that either you must be insane, or the past population of the world must have been so, and the present generation must be little improved in this respect; and you cannot surely be so wild in your ideas as to imagine that you are in the right and the population of the world, past and present, in the wrong.

O. I do think so,—and for this plain reason, that I draw all my conclusions from facts which never change, and which are always consistent with each other, without deviation, and which therefore prove each other to be true.   Thus, without merit of mine, have I been guided from my youth upwards to attend always to the unchanging facts of nature, which are ever consistent with themselves, and are therefore *the truth*, if truth is to be discovered by men.   And by this criterion of truth my ideas, associations of ideas, and my whole mind has been formed.   This process—of disregarding all theories, doctrines, and dogmas, not founded on ever recurring facts, and building up a mind solely in accordance with such facts—is new, and first appears in this generation; and all new knowledge appears first in the generation prepared to receive it by previous disclosures of knowledge derived from facts. And this is the first generation, prepared by previous scientific discoveries of facts, that could admit of these truths being openly declared and published to the population of the world.

D. This language is yet more wild and strange than any we have heard from you, for you now imply that all of our race has been and now is irrational in mind and practice, and you confirm deliberately the statements you have previously published that the world is a great lunatic asylum.

O. I re-affirm this statement, and for proof have only to refer you to the existing state of all religions, governments, and people, over the earth.   Can there be, by any parties professing to be in pursuit of happiness, stronger evidence of gross insanity than is exhibited at this day by the populations of Europe, Asia, Africa, and America?

D. This, Mr. Owen, is a bold statement to make in the middle of the nineteenth century, when the leading nations of the world are priding themselves on their advanced progress and high civilisation.

O. Name me the countries in which the religion, government, and people exhibit an approach to consistency in mind and practice, or to common sense in adhering to the unchanging facts of nature, from which alone can a rational state of society arise or happiness be attained.

D. Give me time to pass all nations in review through my mind. (After a pause.)　I must acknowledge my memory cannot supply me with one.　But objectionable as you make the existing system of society to appear, is it not the production of nature, and therefore the natural system of society?

O. Whatever has been, is, or shall be, is natural.　But it is also natural, and most natural, for men to discover one truth after another.　It was natural to believe the earth fixed and flat; and it is now natural to know that it is round and in rapid motion.　So it has been and yet continues to be natural to believe the present system of society to be the only system under which men can live, as they have known no other.　But now that another and the true system of society has been discovered—one that will for ever secure the continued progress and the permanent happiness of the human race,—this new system will become as natural as the old one has been, and the old will become obsolete and will be considered most unnatural.

D. But the present system can never be abandoned and the new adopted until the population of the world can be made to comprehend the error of the one and the truth of the other.

O. Of this I am fully aware, and I know that the onus lies with me to discover the means by which this change in the opinion of the leading minds of the world can be made; and in consequence of this conviction I have been continually occupied for many years in preparing society step by step, as its previously erroneous state would admit, to hear these new truths opposed to their old prejudices, and this has been the very difficult task which I have had to accomplish, and in which I am still engaged.

D. But can you seriously expect to effect such a change in the sentiments of the human race?

O. I do.　Firstly, because by the only criterion of truth known—that is, consistency with itself and with all facts—the new system advocated is the ultimate and true system of society. Secondly, because truth when unmixed with error is omnipotent over the human mind.　And thirdly, because the will of man cannot retain error when truth is made so obvious as to force conviction on the mind.　It does not therefore depend upon the existing generation whether they shall or shall not continue their present belief in the truth and durability of the present system; but it depends upon the facts which may be placed before them, and the consistent conclusions which may be deduced therefrom.

D. Do you really imagine that you can place such truths before the mind of the population of the world as to overcome its deep rooted prejudices, strongly impressed upon it from birth through every period of life, in favour of the absolute necessity of retaining the religions, laws, governments, classifications, marriages of the priesthoods, artificial or human laws, the practice of buying cheap and selling dear, the present mode of forming character, and all other existing institutions of society, including private property and single family domestic arrangements, with the direction of the instruction of children by their immediate parents ?

O. I do. Because all these institutions, arrangements, and practices, proceed directly or indirectly from one gross fundamental falsehood—a falsehood unsupported by one fact through all time, and opposed by all known facts now existing over the earth—a falsehood, too, which is the origin of evil among men, and the cause of all sin and misery, and of the false, inferior, and wicked character now forced on all of the human race. And because, in order to overcome all this error, ignorance, and falsehood, of which these old and deep rooted prejudices are composed, it is only necessary to make that fundamental error obvious to the public mind, and to make all its fatal consequences openly familiar to all, and an entire change of system, in spirit, principle, and practice, will of necessity soon follow.

D. You have immense faith in what you call truth, if you imagine that by the destruction or abandonment of one falsehood the old established habits of mind and practice can be for ever overcome.

O. I have that faith without the slightest doubt of the ultimate victory of truth over all error, and this change is at this day in rapid progress, and each advance makes the following more easy.

D. Can you, with the past history of man before you, and the present state of society, really imagine you can destroy the power of the priesthood over the world, and of the governments, each supporting the other ?

O. I do not desire to destroy either of these powers; but I desire to give a right direction to both—to withdraw from them the inclination and power to do evil, and greatly to increase their power of doing good.

D. Ah! How do you propose to effect this miracle ?

O. It will be done by no miracle, but through the application of plain, simple, common sense.

D. How applied ?

O By explaining to these parties that their power longer to produce evil must of necessity, by the irresistible progress of events, soon cease,—that it will be for their lasting benefit that it should speedily terminate,—and that it will be for their permanent interest and happiness that their united power should be now directed to produce good instead of evil,—and that to change the direction of their power from doing evil to doing good will be easy, pleasant, and highly profitable to themselves and the entire population of the world.

D. But you do not believe that the instruction of the priesthood of the world is for evil and not for good ?

O. Many of them have been trained and taught sincerely to believe that their teaching is for good ; as all men may be easily taught from birth to believe anything grossly evil to be divinely good. But their teaching is now such in all systems called religion as to produce evil only in all its consequences, and there is no other Satan or Devil on the earth but the erroneous teachings of the various opposing priesthoods, creating hatred and evil thoughts between the opposing religions and sects of the same religion, and thus all their teachings create the very uncharitableness and all the inferior passions against which they pretend to preach, and thus are they the real authors, through ignorance of God and of human nature, of all evil among men.

D. This is indeed new and strange doctrine respecting the priesthood of the world ; but if you will exclude the priesthood of our own religion I will admit what you say to be true of all other priesthoods and religions.

O. And do you not think that those who have been taught to have faith in the other religions, which you condemn, feel and think the same of their religion as you have expressed of yours ?

D. Yes, if they have been taught to be sincere believers in their respective faiths.

O. Then tell me between these opposing faiths who are to judge which is the true one, or whether any one be true ?

D. No one upon earth is competent to this task, so far as I know, except the heads of my religion, and because it must be the true one.

O. And you have no other criterion to guide your judgment ?

D. None whatever. But what do you say of governments ? Are they doers of evil as well as the priesthoods ?

O. The members composing all governments have had their characters substantially formed by the priesthood of their country ; and as no priesthood has any practical knowledge how to form a good, a rational, or a really useful character—for priests know only how to form a very artificial and false one—it cannot be reasonably expected that any existing government should know how to govern well and wisely, or rationally for their own happiness or for the happiness of those whom they govern. All countries therefore at this day are most unwisely and irrationally governed. Some, of course, more unwisely and irrationally than others ; but the best of them very unwisely and very irrationally.

D. How can this be, seeing that the people of some countries are prosperous and happy ?

O. Will you name those countries, or any one, in which the people are prosperous and happy ?

D. The United States and Great Britain. The population of both are surely prosperous and happy.

O. I know both pretty well, and I affirm that there is no substantial prosperity or happiness under either government,—admitting at the same time that they are perhaps the least irrational and wicked governments now existing.

D. These are indeed sweeping assertions. How do you make it out that the people in these two great empires are not prosperous and happy?

O. Because a large population of both are in poverty or the fear of it, and that which is called prosperity is an accumulation of wealth dishonestly obtained, either directly or indirectly. High prosperity, as it is termed, consists in great riches and an elevated position in society, and these constitute the desired happiness of all?

D. Well! and can you deny that where there is so much wealth and so much power arising from accumulation of great riches and high position in society, there is much prosperity and happiness?

O. Yes; I deny that great riches and high position can give substantial and permanent happiness to their possessors. They may give while new some pleasure; but this is temporary and very uncertain. And there must be always the conviction in reflective minds that great riches can never be honestly attained or retained. The surplus, beyond the supply of the rational wants of the individual, justly belongs to those who are destitute, or whose rational wants are unsupplied.

D. This is a new doctrine, and is wholly unsuited for the existing state of human society over the earth.

O. True. And why? Because all at this day are most erroneously placed, trained, educated, employed, and governed:— so erroneously, that error is called truth,—ignorance, knowledge,—wrong, right,—riches, prosperity,—and an inferior state, physical and mental, happiness.

D. Then do you seriously expect to improve—nay altogether to change—this state of things by abusing all parties in churches and states and in every class throughout society?

O. I do. Because all these irrational institutions richly deserve much severer terms of abuse. But remember I blame not; but I sincerely pity the poor individuals belonging to all these divisions for being so misplaced and misguided from birth, and thus forced to become the irrational and insane beings who are daily opposing their own happiness and the happiness of all their fellow beings.

D. On my word, your assumptions are intolerable. You deem yourself wonderfully clever.

O. You again mistake me very much—I feel my own deficiences more perhaps than others can or do.

D. How is this? I thought you considered yourself, by your abuse of all that is under the present system of society over the world, the wisest of men!

O. And if I did, that wisdom would be very limited. See my want of it. Without any merit of mine I have been forced to perceive the errors of the present system, and to discover another, consistent in all its parts with itself as a whole, and in accordance with all facts, therefore true, according to the best criterion of truth yet ascertained by men—a system calculated to give to all a good and superior character, illimitable wealth unadulterated, permanent progressive prosperity, and happiness—a system which will not injure one individual of our race, but which will be highly beneficial to all through futurity. Yet with these all powerful causes and influences to aid success, I have not succeeded in convincing my fellow men of these all important truths, and I do not know if I have made one disciple who fully comprehends the full import of the change which I so much desire to impress on the minds and for the practice of all. With my views of human nature, and feeling strongly my own deficiencies of mental power for my task, I know I am not entitled to any merit, not more than I give to all other men and women, conscious that we are all made to be what we are, not by ourselves, but by God through nature and the surroundings in which nature and society place us.

D. You are a strange and very unaccountable character. No one can tell what to make of you, and I do not wonder at some calling you mad and others insane.

M. But I have a word now to say to you. In some of your writings you express your belief in what is call Spiritualism, that you believe the new kind of rappings made on tables and other places by some invisible means to be made by departed spirits, and often by our friends and relatives who have been familiar with us during their lives upon earth. Do you still entertain these strange convictions of impossible things?

O. Yes. Every day brings forth new facts confirmatory of what you call impossibilities, and in my mind these so called impossibilities will prove such substantial realities as to aid materially to redeem our race from ignorance and the sin and misery which are the consequences of ignorance.

M. How you can be induced to believe in anything immaterial I cannot imagine.

O. I do not believe in anything immaterial, as you consider it. Immateriality, with you, is nothing, or nonentity. I believe spirits to be formed of more refined materials than those composing our visible earthly bodies, and the utmost refinement or essence of material existence to be that which constitutes the highest qualities of intelligence and power, or the pervading spirit or God of the universe.

M. I should like to hear a more full explanation of these new things which you say communicate their thoughts, knowledge, and feelings, to men while upon the earth, and thus disclose for our benefit the immortality of our spirit, and life in the celestial spheres.   But more of this in our next discourse or dialogue.

Second Dialogue.

M. (to Mr. Owen.) You have stated in a former number of the *Millennial Gazette*, that Spiritualism and Socialism united are to be the future destiny of the human race.   Now I believe Spiritualism to be altogether a delusion of the mind and a non-entity, and that no such thing as a spirit exists throughout the universe.

D. And I think that Socialism never can be practicable.

O. One subject at a time, if you please,—and we will first consider that of Spiritualism.   I have stated, and I now reiterate my belief in it, that Spiritualism and Socialism united, when fully comprehended and consistently applied to practice, are to be the future destiny of the human race.   But let us consider both separately first, and afterwards unitedly.

M. and D. We are agreed to pursue this course, and to commence with Spiritualism.

O. Whence do we derive that knowledge which we deem certain, and respecting which there can be no doubt in the minds of any?

M. From facts.

O. How ascertained?

M. By the concurrent testimony of witnesses of undoubted veracity, given in sufficient variety of persons, times, and places, to be unconnected, independent, and unknown to each other, and having no interest of any kind to serve by their statement.

O. And how many of such witnesses would be necessary to confirm new facts previously unknown to and disbelieved by almost all mankind?

M. To establish the truth of the existence of such facts the strongest human testimony is necessary.   It will require the testimony of a great number of men and women of sound understanding on other subjects, of undoubted veracity, wholly disinterested, unconnected with each other, and yet their testimony must be uniform and without disagreement respecting the facts stated.

O. Such testimony has been given in Europe, America, and other parts of the world in instances too numerous to be denied by any rational person who has investigated the subject, that new and various physical and mental communications have been made to these witnesses by invisible powers, unknown to them, and so far as they know by an agency unconnected with their personality.

M. Having given some attention to this certainly new and very extraordinary subject, I admit your statement to be undeniable so far.   But now to the proofthat these invisible powers communicating are the spirits of departed men and women, who have lived lately or more remotely on the earth.

O. I know of no other proof than the uniform testimony of this invisible agency that it is spiritual and often from spirits of departed relatives and friends of the witnesses ; and to convince the witnesses of the truth of their statements and of their identity, they communicate facts occurring in the lifetime of the departed, known only to the witnesses and the departed ; with other innumerable facts testifying to the truth of the statements made by this invisible agency.

M. But how can it be known that this invisible agency is not a delusive and deceiving material existence, acting by some means not yet discovered ?

O. What discoveries may be made in future it is impossible now to say ; but as the invisible powers uniformly say that they are spirits, and in many cases the spirits of the departed friends and relatives of the witnesses, with many tests to confirm their statements, the proofs thus given that they communicate that which they know to be true is much stronger than your imaginary conjectures that these are delusive and deceiving agencies.

M. But in many cases these agencies have been detected in giving false statements.

O. This may be true in some instances.   But in many others the apparently false statements have arisen from the ignorance of the enquirers, and frequently from the state of mind of the enquirers being most unfit to enable them to obtain communications from good and superior spirits.

M. Then it seems there are bad and inferior spirits.

O. The same evidence that testifies to communications from good and superior spirits, also gives evidence to communications from bad and inferior spirits.

M. How then can the witnesses know that the apparently good and superior spirits do not assume this character the more easily to deceive credulous witnesses of these communications ?

O. By testing their character as we test the characters of our fellow men, by their consistency.

M. But may not all these invisible agencies be evil, and come now in numbers over the earth under such false colouring as to deceive the very elect for wisdom of the human race ?

O. The evidence is all powerful to the contrary.   The teaching in the great majority of cases is for the permanent good and happiness of all, and in accordance with the largest experience of the best minds.

M. What is the object of the teaching of those you call good and superior spirits ?

O. By communications made to myself and to many others— " To reform the world,"—" The reformation of the population of " the world,"—" To redeem the human race from ignorance, sin, " and misery,"—" To prove the immortality of man in another and " higher life,"—" To terminate the present disunion among all na- " tions and peoples,"—" To introduce the pure spirit of universal

" charity and love among men, bring peace on earth, and establish
" for ever harmony between all of humankind, and unite them as
" one family."

M. These are high sounding pretensions, but we must remain
in suspense as to their inclination and power to effect these certainly most desirable results.   But I am a thorough materialist,
and do not believe that there is any immateriality or invisible
living existence in the universe. Everything existing is material,
and spirits are nothing—mere nonentities of the deluded imaginations.

O. You err in supposing that spirits are not material.

M. Who ever saw, touched, or felt a spirit ?

O. Many whose testimony upon all other subjects would never
be doubted.

M. I do not believe them.   I deem their whole statements to
be a delusion, and absurd in the extreme.

O. What does your disbelief amount to against such evidence ?
To nothing.   It can be of no value whatever as evidence or
proof against the most creditable positive personal statements of
facts.

M. Well,—admitting these statements to be undisputed facts,
—what good can arise from them ?

O. The greatest possible good to the future of the human race.

M. How so ?

O. By materially assisting to change men's minds from most
injurious falsehoods to most beneficial truths.

M. In what manner ?

O. By the uniform instruction of the superior spirits to acquire the spirit of unceasing forbearance, of universal charity for
all our differences, and of love without exception for the whole
of humanity ; and thus to prepare all nations and peoples to be
willing quietly and peaceably to change the present system of
falsehood, force, disunion, injustice, and cruelty, for the true permanent system of society—of truth, reason, union, justice, and
love.   Or to change the individual disuniting system, for the
social and attractive system, for the future government of the
world.

M. But the mass of the people everywhere are now strongly
opposed to spiritualism.

O. I well remember when the British population were opposed
to the introduction of the first mail coaches when they were promised to travel at the enormous speed (as it was then thought)
of seven miles an hour.   " Yes," it was commonly said, " it is
" easy to talk and promise that this shall be done, but it will never
" be accomplished." These masses have had their minds changed
on this subject, and they will have them changed on the subject
of spiritualism.

M. On what grounds do you make this statement?

O. On the declaration of truthful superior spirits, who say,—

" Disregard all present opposition to belief in the reality of spi-
" ritual intercourse with mortals.   We will adopt measures suffi-
" ciently strong to convince the most sceptical of the truth of
" our presence and communications."

M. And you give credit to these delusive statements as though
they were realities.

O. I have so far no reason to doubt them, for they are fulfilling their promise in so rapid and extraordinary a manner, that
the increase of converts appears almost miraculous.

M. But how will all this assist to introduce Socialism, or the
united state of society, to supersede the separate or individual
state ?

O By making it evident that the spirit of love and charity
is absolutely necessary to the progress and happiness of the
human race, and that this spirit of goodness and of justice can
never be acquired under the individual system.

M. But all our religions, governments, laws, commerce,
and in short all our institutions, are based and constructed in
all the departments of life upon the individual system ; and can
you expect that mortal man can change all these for a system in
all respects opposed to them ?

O. I do expect that mortal man, aided by immortal spirits,
will—and soon, too—change the individual for the social state
of universal human existence.

M. On what principle do you thus speak so confidently upon
this subject ?

O. Because I know it will be for the permanent high interest
of every one of the human race through futurity that this change
should be made now that all the materials for its accomplishment everywhere superabound, and spiritualism will create the
spirit of love and charity without which no progress towards
rationality or a consistent happy state of society can be made.
And Socialism will introduce the practical surroundings by which
universal union can be attained and maintained throughout the
earth while man shall live upon it.

M. Then you make no account of the present religions, governments, laws, modes of creating and distributing wealth, of the
character now formed for all, or of any of the modes now in
practice for forming character, or of any existing surroundings
in any part of the world ?

O. No, I do not. They can be of no estimation in a consistent and rational state of human existence ; but on the contrary they are the obstacles which now prevent the creation of
arrangements or new combinations of new surroundings within
which all with ease and pleasure may be made good, wise,
wealthy, and happy, far beyond what any minds formed under
the existing false, evil, and grossly inconsistent system can imagine
or believe to be practicable.

M. And to effect this change in man and society, you do not look for the aid of anything immaterial?

O. No I look for these to you and others impossible and impracticable changes in the condition of humanity to be brought about and finally accomplished by the spirit emanating from the highest refinement or essence of substantial materiality.

M. What do you mean by materiality?

O. I mean the elements of the universe, whether in the more or in the less combined, or in its pure uncombined state.

M. Then what is the composition of your spirits and angels?

O. They are composed of some of the more refined combined elements of the universe, too refined for our earthly and grossly compounded organisms in our normal state to perceive.

M. And what is your God?

O. The esence or combined element of the universe—the Creator or Father of all things which are created—eternal in duration, and infinite in extent.

M. Has it a conscious existence, intelligence, wisdom, and goodness?

O. God evidently possesses the intelligence, wisdom, and goodness exhibited throughout the universe. But who comprehends the original uncombined universal elements, eternal in duration and action, or the mode by which God operates in composing, decomposing, and recomposing all things, in all changes throughout the universe? No man or set of men; and, as I have previously stated, the greatest of all insanities is for men to quarrel about that which they cannot comprehend, and of which they know nothing, and for which they can do nothing,—while God or this Universal Power does everything for everything.

M. Then it is your conviction that man can do no good to God by his belief or disbelief in him or in his existence, or by worshipping or not worshipping this great and yet unknown Power?

O. Such is my most mature conviction; and that all that man can do rationally is to endeavour to improve and render happy all around him while he remains on earth, and to effect these results to the extent of the knowledge and power given to him by God and society, and to allow God to take care of his own honour and glory without the aid or interference of poor ignorant irrational man.

M. Then you abrogate all contests about Deity, and all prayer and worship of the Great Creating Power of the Universe and Father of all, as you call this unknown existence, the existence of which we materialists utterly deny?

O. I hold that all prayer and worship is, if possible, derogatory to Supreme Power, wisdom, and goodness. Prayer, as doubting those attributes, and worship, as supposing that supreme power, wisdom, and goodness, could be pleased or gratified by such weak and childish attempts to praise and glorify infinity or that which fills all space, which is eternal in duration, and which everlastingly composes, decomposes, and recomposes the eternal elements of nature throughout a universe illimitable in space and time, and therefore incomprehensible to mortal man and to all finite existence.   All prayer, praise, and worship of infinite power, wisdom. and goodness, will cease as soon as the human race can be made to become rational. and will be superseded by a consistent never-ending action through the life of each individual to promote the happiness of all upon earth, and to increase by thus acting the happiness of those spirits in the spirit spheres who continue to be interested in the well-being and well-doing of those whom they left upon earth.

M Well, this will be a change, if it ever should occur, which we materialists never should have imagined, and what the praying, praising, and worshipping religionists over the world will say to it may be easily anticipated.

O. Why, what will these well-meaning irrational-made persons say ?

M. That you are an atheist, an infidel, insane, mad, and the worst man that has ever lived upon the earth, confirming what one of them published of you many years ago.

O. What was that—it must be a curiosity ?

M. In a pamphlet published and widely circulated by a Rev. Mr. Smith, he said—" Carlisle and Taylor are as bad as the " devil,—but Robert Owen is fifty thousand million times worse."

O. I am obliged to him for this extraordinary compliment, and shall not forget it.

M. And you know, I doubt not, that the Catholic priests would not allow Messrs. Tussaud to put your likeness into their exhibition, although they willingly allowed them to have the worst characters known except yours, and now your present statement will confirm all religionists in these impressions.   And as you are become an avowed spiritualist, you can have no supporters among us materialists and infidels who oppose all spiritual existence.   Nor can you expect any from the believers in the superiority of the individual over the united system for the government of the human race, and you cannot anticipate accordance with your strange views from the followers of St. Simon, Fourier, Ann Lee, Johanna Southcote, Joseph Smith, Cabet, or even the spiritualists, from whom you differ in all their remaining sectarian notions respecting finite man's worship of infinity by words and ceremonies.

O. All this is true.   Yet must I continue to declare and publish the truth as it is made to appear to me, although I should not yet have one follower.

M. How, then, can you expect to change the existing system of society for another totally the reverse in spirit, principle, and practice ?

O. Because the system which I advocate is the reverse of the present in spirit, principle, and practice, believing that the present system is altogether false, and is continually productive of evil, artificial throughout, and opposed to nature.

M. But you acknowledge that you have all classes, creeds, and parties, in all countries, in direct opposition to your system. What chance, then, can you have for success?

O. The best of all chances. I know the humanity ever existing in every class, creed, and party, in all countries, and among all colours. It has so far been kept under, and compelled by ignorance, inexperience, and the want of mental development and moral courage in the human race, to lie dormant in the mass of mankind, and to be incapable of any united rational action by any division of society, in any country, at any period since man was created. But the accumulation of facts through past ages to the present, the increasing and increased development of the rational faculties and reasoning powers, the discoveries in science, especially within the last hundred years, have made the existing system, to those competent to comprehend systems, so irrational and absurd in spirit, principle, and practice, that none such can be found with capacity and effrontery sufficient to contend for its rationality, or to maintain that it will bear the test of investigation by those possessing the first degrees of common sense.

M. This is truly a pretty showing up of the present state of human existence over the earth.

O. And yet the past undeveloped state was necessary to produce the present, as the present half developed state is necessary to produce the fully developed and permanently happy state of all upon the earth.

M. And you expect this happy union to be attained by the union of Spiritualism and Socialism, when they shall be fully understood in spirit and principle, and shall be consistently applied to practice.

D. Well, we have now heard sufficient of the theory of both. I wish to be fully informed as to their consistent application to practice.

O. To this we will proceed in our next discourse.

Third Dialogue.

D. You say that Spiritualism and Socialism fully understood and rightly comprehended will be the future destiny of the human race. In our last dialogue you explained your views of Spiritualism. Will you now more fully detail to us what you mean by " *Socialism when fully understood and rightly com-* " *prehended ?*"

O. Most willingly: and you will find it deserve and tax the utmost extent of your capacities.

D. and *M.* We will give to what you have to say upon this subject our full attention to endeavour to acquire a knowledge of your views of this hitherto vexed question.

O. So far Socialism, as I have always entertained it in my mind, has been greatly misunderstood by the public, through the misrepresentations of its prejudiced opponents. They have made it to appear a demon of the darkest blackness ; while in reality it is an angel of the most beautiful and spotless whiteness.

D. and *M.* We shall be much surprised if you can prove the truth of your statement, and we are eager to hear your explanation.

O. Socialism, then, is the enlightened, cordial, and affectionate Union of the human race, made to be so united by a new training, education, and placing, to give to all attractive qualities from birth, which shall increase during life.

D. And pray how is this wonderful feat to be effected ?

O. By new placing all from birth within new common sense surroundings, and in which all will have a new training and education, given in a new spirit of charity and love—a spirit directed by a knowledge of the laws of humanity as given to it by its Creator :—by new-placing all, so that each shall be justly and therefore equally employed and governed according to age and capacity, in order that no one shall ever feel or complain that society has treated him or her partially in placing, training, educating, employing, or governing, from birth to death.

D. and *M.* We hold this condition of society to be unattainable.

O. In a society which has placed, trained, educated, employed, and governed all as *you* have been placed, &c., I am not in the least surprised at your conclusions ; for in such a state of society the results which I have given to you would be utterly impracticable.   The individual system of society, based on the supposition that each one forms his own physical and mental qualities, and that for these he is responsible to God, the Creator, and to Society, the director of them, is a system well calculated to train and educate men to become insane semi-barbarians,—and to this condition only have the most advanced nations of the world yet attained.

D. and *M.* What ! have you the effrontery to deliberately state that the most advanced people in civilisation over the earth are now mere insane semi-barbarians !   What proofs are there in existence to warrant any presumptuous individual thus to libel the whole of the existing enlightened generation ?

O. Sebastopol,—London,—Paris,— Vienna,— St. Petersburgh, —Madrid,—Pekin,— Constantinople,—Canton,— New York, — Washington,—&c. &c.—Great Britain,—France,—Germany,— Italy,—Russia,—Turkey,—Europe,—Asia,— Africa,—and America.   In short, look for proof to the present state of the population in all countries, from north to south, from east to west, over our lunatic globe.   If more detailed proofs are required—

look to the standing armies of the world,—to the ignorance, poverty, disunion, and contests of nations, and their conflicts in fact or in attitude.   Look to their repulsive feelings and artificially made opposing interests; and then survey the extent of individual and general misery which this concatenation of ignorance, error, and evil produces.

D. and *M.* It must be confessed there is great confusion, contradiction, ignorance, and counteraction to progress and happiness in what you have stated.   But this is the natural condition of human society, and it cannot be changed.   It has always been so from the beginning.

O. Not so.   The human faculties have been progressively in course of development, and consequent changes have taken place.   Experience has increased a knowledge of facts, until at length the sciences have given to the population of the world some real knowledge, just sufficient to prove the irrationality of all previous assertions and dogmas, made by men trained to be insane, and thus by very slow degrees to have brought it to a semi-barbarous irrational state.

D. And is this the utmost extent for which you give our present system credit?

O. It is the full extent that truth will warrant.

D. How can you prove this assertion?

O. With much ease.   The means to create a superior character, abundance of real wealth,—to unite all as one family,— to construct superior surroundings for all,—and thus to insure to the population of the world health, knowledge, union, wisdom, and happiness are now superabundant; and yet these means are not only unused, but are repelled as worse than useless.

D. This is indeed a very heavy charge against the existing system.   But how can any earthly power supersede it by another? Has not the individual system, selfish as it is, existed through all past time?

O. It has; and in the due order of nature it was necessary through certain stages of the development of our faculties, to progress them towards rationality.   These stages are passed.   A new era presents itself.   Ignorant selfishness and disunion, created by the individual system, are become too glaring in their evil tendencies to be longer tolerated in human society; and an advanced system of union of interests and feeling becomes absolutely now required, to prevent all society from falling into anarchy and confusion.

D. And to cure existing evils and prevent an increase of them, you propose to introduce what you call the social system?

O. Yes, this is the remedy which I propose, and the change which I advocate.

D. and *M.* You have given us the outline; but we require the details in full, to enable us to understand that which is so new to our mode of thinking, to our habits, and to all our previous instruction

O. I will endeavour to satisfy you, and I hope to convert you from the ignorant, opposing, selfish, and false system of individualism.

D. and *M.* Pray proceed. Tell us what is to be the principle, placing, training, education, employment, classification, and government of your social system.

O. The rational social system which I have so long advocated is based on the knowledge that the qualities of all things created are given to them by the power which creates them, and that consequently the physical and mental qualities of all of human kind are formed *for* them,—the seed, germ, or material of these qualities being created at birth by the Great Creating Power of the Universe, (whether called God or nature,) and being trained, educated and matured from birth by the society and natural surroundings in which the individual is born and lives. The good or bad influences of society act more or less upon all even previous to birth, the formation of character by society commencing not only from the germ of the fœtus directly, but indirectly from the characters formed by society for its progenitors through all succeeding generations.

D. and *M.* You are truly beginning at an early period; but we cannot object to the foundation on which you propose to raise your superstructure. Pray proceed.

O. The first, the highest, and most important business of life under this system will be to form the best character *for each* that the natural or created faculties and qualities of the individual will admit. This task being well performed, all other difficulties in the way of forming a permanently prosperous, good, united, and happy society over the earth will be easily overcome.

D. and *M.* Then you consider it to be absolutely necessary in your proposed state of society that everyone should have a superior character formed *for* him by society?

O. Yes. It is the foundation on which the superstructure of the new society is to be raised; and any society neglecting this duty I consider to be insane; and the British government and people, with their enormous means to enable them to give a good physical, intellectual, moral, spiritual, and practical character to every one born within their extended empire, I consider the most insane of all nations.

D. You surprise me! I have been taught to think we were the envy of surrounding nations, and the most advanced population upon the globe.

O. You, like all men, may be easily taught to believe anything, the most opposed to existing facts, as in the present case, to be true. The fact is, that Great Britain, with her enormous means of doing good to her population, and of elevating it to a high state of knowledge, wisdom, and happiness, has done little in these respects for the mass of the people, who are at this day kept in gross ignorance and poverty, and in slavish dependance upon a comparatively few wealthy, who have been miserably mis-instructed in real valuable useful knowledge, and have been filled with learned ignorance, called the " wisdom of our ancestors."

D. and *M.* Then you set little value on the present mode of instruction, if we rightly understand you ?

O. Very little indeed. It is, with few exceptions, almost the worst matter, given in the worst manner.

D. and *M.* How, then, would you train and educate children in your proposed system ?

O. In manner and matter the reverse of both now given.

D. and *M.* Explain—for we have no idea of your meaning.

O. I knew that, from knowing how and what you have been taught from birth through your lives thus far.

D. and *M.* We are now desirous of learning your new views on training, educating, and forming character.

O. I will now proceed. The first practical measure is to create the surroundings requisite to well train and educate children from birth. All existing surroundings are altogether unfit for this purpose. A new arrangement of superior conditions will be required, based on new sites, to accommodate the number that will constitute well organised, scientific, rational family commonwealths, to form the nuclei of society ; and without such surroundings a superior character for man and society cannot be given to any population.

D. and *M.* What constitutes the mysterious character of these surroundings ?

(To be continued in No. 9.)

London :—Published by the Author at 16, Great Windmill Street, Haymarket : and sold by Holyoake, 147, Fleet Street ; Truelove, 240, Strand; Goddard, 14, Great Portland Street, Cavendish Square; Farrah, 21, John Street, Fitzroy Square ; and all Booksellers.

Registered for Foreign Transmission.

ROBERT OWEN'S
MILLENNIAL GAZETTE;

EXPLANATORY OF THE PRINCIPLES AND PRAC-
TICES BY WHICH, IN PEACE, WITH TRUTH,
HONESTY, AND SIMPLICITY, THE NEW
EXISTENCE OF MAN UPON THE
EARTH MAY BE EASILY AND
SPEEDILY COMMENCED.

" The character of Man is formed *for* him, and *not by* him !"

No. 9.]   OCTOBER 15th, 1856.   [PRICE 6D.

DIALOGUES BETWEEN ROBERT OWEN, A DEFENDER OF THE EXISTING SYSTEM, AND A MATERIALIST.

[*Continued from No.* 8.]

D. and *M.* What constitutes the mysterious character of the new surroundings which you propose?

O. First.—Their arranged simplicity for aiding to perform the whole business of life in the best manner.

Second.—Their arrangements to enable society with ease and pleasure to create at all times their full share of the wealth required to abundantly supply the population of the world.

Third.—To enable the family commonwealth to well care for each one born within it, from and before birth through life, and to have equal justice done to all.

Fourth.—To admit of just equality, according to age and capacity, in education, position, and employment.

Fifth.—The greatest individual independence of both sexes, compatible with the best and most enlightened society.

Sixth.—To enable each commonwealth, not only to create with ease and pleasure their full fair share of the wealth of the world, but also to accomplish their fair full share to assist to make the earth fruitful and beautiful, in order that it may be gradually formed into a terrestrial paradise, open to all, and freely enjoyed by all.

Seventh.—All things within and without these surroundings, forming family commonwealths, to be the best that combined human knowledge can devise and means accomplish, in order that that only which is superior may be around each child from birth, and because the means now at the disposal of nations are ample for this purpose without farther competition and contests.

Eighth.—These surroundings will all be devised and executed with especial care by the collected wisdom of society, to be perfect for the easy attainment of all that a rational population can require; but most particularly to be constructed and arranged to insure the formation of the best physical, intellectual, moral, spiritual, and practical character for every one from birth to death.

D. But how can such characters be formed, seeing that none now exist as models, and that none have ever existed?

O. You appear not yet to know the great and all-important truth that—

" *Any* character, from the worst to the best, may be formed " by society for the whole of the human race, and that to know " how to effect the latter is the most useful and valuable practical " knowledge that can be acquired in the present generation."

D. and *M.* We readily admit it. But who can teach this knowledge to the present generation?

O. I will lend my aid, and by degrees others will assist; and it is now the first and highest duty or interest of society to acquire this knowledge, for it will require the aid and assistance of society when placed within these new surroundings and enlightened upon the subject, to fully accomplish this object.

D. and *M.* Will you now favour us with your knowledge how to form this good and superior character for all?

O. It is what I desire to do, knowing that so very little is yet known upon this subject in principle or practice, as evidenced by the character now formed for all in every nation and among all people. But to proceed. To form a good and superior character for all, the first measure absolutely necessary is to have these rational family commonwealth surroundings executed to receive the family which is to assist to form the new character for the children; and this family must be taught in what manner to act to give their assistance in forming the new character for the rising generation. The family entering into these new commonwealths must have the pure spirit of love and charity for our race, and must exhibit that spirit in all they say and do. They must cease to use abusive or unkind language, and to blame each other, attributing every defect to the false, unjust, and cruel system which they have left in the old world of individual selfishness; and they will be made conscious that as they are, so will the rising generation around them become. They will therefore never exhibit unkind looks, or use unkind language; but will always speak in a voice of love and with a manner corresponding with that overpowering and irresistible tone. And to *all* the questions of the young a rational reply should thus be given. The motive also of every action done to them should be fully explained in the same manner, and thus will the family assist essentially to form a rational character for all the young ones around them.

In these family surroundings there will be especial arrangements for infants from birth to three years of age ;—again from three to six ;—from six to ten ;—from ten to thirteen ;—and from thirteen to seventeen — at which last age they will be placed in the independent arrangements for men and women matured in the general knowledge of their society or family, and prepared to commence a knowledge of society generally by travelling and visiting other family commonwealths, in each of which, when vacant rooms permit their remaining for a longer or a shorter period, their services will be more valuable than the cost of their expenditure.

D. and *M*. But how would you have the infants to three years of age trained and educated ?

O. By unceasing love and kindness by those the most naturally fond of infants,—who know human nature the best,—who possess patience without limits,—who know how to observe the peculiarities of each,—who can give them the true spirit of love and kindness,—and who will form their tempers, habits, and manners, and teach them how to love each other and to acquire correct language.

D. and *M*. But who could be entrusted with this task ?

O. Not any inexperienced persons. But as these three first years of life are by far the most important for receiving lasting impressions, these infants should be surrounded only by the most experienced and best qualified, as previously stated, for this to these persons most pleasing and important task.

D. and *M*. Then you would have no young and inexperienced persons to come near them?

O. No, not on any account. These infants should not see any things or persons inferior. Every such impression would be an injury to the infants, whose impressions, as far as could be made practicable, should be all superior

D. and *M*. What would you do with the next period of three years ?

O. The same as the former in respect of being properly clothed, fed, and exercised in the open air, and also being treated in the same rational kind manner, and without partiality for any except those most defective by nature, to compensate for such deficiencies. But, in addition, these from three to six will be taken to see and examine for themselves, according to their ages and capacities, the objects within and outside the family surroundings, and by familiar conversation between the teachers and taught, everything should be explained to the full comprehension of the taught, and every child should be allowed to ask his or her questions upon all subjects in their own way, and should be answered in all cases as rationally instructed children ought to be By this natural process, at the age of six they will be better informed upon all useful subjects without books of any kind, than children now are taught with books at twelve or fourteen years of age.

D. Do you then exclude all parental instruction at this early period of life.

O. Parents, from their blind animal affections and want of knowledge of human nature and educated misdirection of judgment, are now the least fit of any properly trained instructors to form the character of their children and to train them to be unselfish. And although the infant for the first year would be under the new surroundings with the mother, she would be during that period assisted by an experienced matron in the care of such infant. But as the character of every child would be of great importance to the family commonwealth and to society, the wise forming of that character, being the first and highest consideration in a rationally constituted society, will never be left to the selfish partial animal affections of parents; but all the children of the commonwealth will be trained, educated, and treated, as brothers and sisters of one family, impartially and justly in all respects.

D. Why this would be a Spartan education!

O. No. But one much more humane and superior. Because equal attention will be given to well-form each one, physically, intellectually, morally, spiritually, and practically. We live in a different age of the world from that of Licurgus, who was doubtless the first legislator, educator, and governor of his time; and most of his principles for that stage of men's development were correct, and evinced an extraordinary advance in a knowledge of human nature.

D. Then you would have infants and children treated as rational beings from their birth.

O. I would have have them from their birth to be treated as beings to be made rational in spirit, feeling, and principle, and to be consistent with these qualities of mind in all their practice.

M. You propose to make man more perfect than he is in my opinion capable of becoming.

O. You have known and viewed man hitherto as a being formed from birth by society on a false basis, and by which all his physical and mental qualities have been grossly misdirected, and he has been forced to become most irrational in feeling, thought, and action. When his character from birth shall be based on the true principle, and he shall be trained and educated in accordance with that principle, man will become a new being in spirit, feeling, thought, and conduct. So much so, that the old being will wonder at seeing the new being,—a creature so totally different from himself in all his ideas and associations of ideas. For truly by this change the *mind will be new born, or born again*.

M. This is strange doctrine. But pray proceed with your new scheme for forming character.

O. I will. At six the children of both sexes, for they will not be separated in their education or general occupations, will commence to be instructed in an accurate knowledge of what manner of beings they are, physically first, and then mentally and spiritually. Physically, by accurate instruction in the anatomy of the human body, by the inspection and explanation of those artificial anatomical figures now so admirably constructed to be easily separated part from part and as easily reconstructed. The use of every organ and of its entire structure should be so explained as to be as well understood as present knowledge will admit. The causes of disease in every part of the body should be made familiar to the pupils, as well as the laws of health. For most true it is, that the most valuable of all knowledge is the knowledge of ourselves, or of how to attain to a superior rational sound mind in a sound body. Too much carefully devised instruction on this all-important subject cannot be given during these four years, from six to ten. And it should be remembered that what is useful and proper for one cultivated being to know, will be useful and proper for all rational beings to know and fully comprehend. In a rational, truthful, and superior state of human existence, such as is now contemplated, there will be no need for secrecy, which belongs solely to an irrational state of society.

D. What! would you teach children from six to ten anatomy?

O. And why should not children from six to ten be taught anatomy, when their minds are innocent and pure, rather than as at present at a more advanced age, when their minds have been made less innocent and pure? I was informed by a very honest and superior instructor of youth, who had a school well filled with the children of wealthy families, that being desirous to give his pupils some accurate knowledge of themselves he purchased a full well-formed skeleton in London, and brought it to Liverpool, enclosed in a case, with a door to shut it up when not in use for instruction. Upon its arrival he exhibited it to some of the elder boys from twelve to fifteen, who immediately wrote home to their parents with the information, and that they were too much frightened to sleep in a house with such a frightful object. This superior instructor immediately received several letters informing him that if the skeleton were not at once removed from the sight and out of the way of their sons, they should be immediately withdrawn from his seminary. These letters were not from the inferior and uneducated classes, but from those who could afford to pay £100 a year for the board and instruction of each child. This ignorance so disgusted the high-minded well-intentioned superior instructor, that he at once broke up his establishment and went to Switzerland. This is sufficient to show that in the once liberal and advanced population of Liverpool, as it was before it became over " righteous," the subject of education, or of forming a superior character, is a dead letter, as it is at this day over the world, even in the most advanced universities and other learned seminaries and institutions for training and educating the higher and wealthy classes throughout the most civilized nations, as they are now considered to be.

D. This is again one of your sweeping assertions. What proof have you in support of the truth of your statement ?

O. The existing character of the upper and wealthy classes in Europe and America. The conduct of these at this day being such as might be anticipated from the mode in which they have been instructed and the nature of their instruction. See the characters and conduct of the heads of all religions and all governments, and of the most wealthy over the world at this day :—a character and conduct forced upon them by their surroundings from birth through life.

D. And is not that character and conduct in their respective stations rational, good, and highly judicious ?

O. My most experienced convictions are, that the character and conduct of these unfortunate and injudiciously placed parties have been made by a most undeveloped population to be the reverse of rational, good, or wise, and I advisedly say so, because they have now the most ample means at their command to insure the permanent goodness, wisdom, prosperity, and happiness of the population of all nations and peoples, and they have not been taught by their instructors or any other parties how most beneficially to take one step in the right direction to accomplish this godlike result.

D. and *M.* We do not comprehend your ideas, and what you say is as an unknown language to us ; and we imagine that our impressions are similar to those which your language must make upon all classes in all countries.

O. I agree in your conjectures on this matter, and admit that it is with me to discover the means by which I can be understood by all parties, and it is with this view that I am now in conversation with you on the all-important subject of forming a superior character and conduct for the human race on principles as fixed and certain as those of mathematics.

D. and *M.* Well, we imagine you will find this a difficult, if not an impossible task.

O. However difficult it may be, I intend to persevere to the last in making the attempt.

D. and *M.* We will listen with patience to your additional explanations, how your new character is to be universally formed. You were going to state what was to be done in forming the character of your children from six to nine. Pray proceed.

O. Their instruction will be by inspecting the objects of nature, as well as of the human frame and its wonderfully complex and combined parts, mechanical, chemical, and spiritual, themselves comprising an encyclopædia of knowledge for human investigation. These children will now also commence their regular early duties for their family commonwealth in the several domestic departments, and will be made familiar with the mechanical and chemical operations which will be introduced to an extent little imagined at present to assist in performing and to a great degree to supersede all heavy, unhealthy, and disagreeable labour and employment, so as to simplify and diminish manual occupations in all the business of life, and to make it a pleasure and pastime, contributing to the health of body and mind. The forming and perfecting of the spirit, temper, and manner, will also be continued during this period, in order that the spiritual, moral, intellectual, and practical formation of character may be made to progress simultaneously.

M. What is the nature of the " spirit" here mentioned.

O. The spirit of universal charity, love, and kindness for our race.

M. What superior advantages do you expect to arise to the children from this instruction by personal investigation of the objects to be taught and explained to the pupils, and by verbal conversation, and by the children being freely allowed to ask their own natural questions ?

O. First, that the knowledge thus acquired will be understood, correct, and useful, and more valuable ideas and associations of ideas will thus be received by the taught in one year than is now given by book teaching in five or six years, and the latter instruction is always vague and confused in the minds of children so educated. Book teaching is artificial and opposed to the laws of nature; while to acquire knowledge by inspecting the objects intended to be taught, with verbal explanations in answer to the questions of the pupils, is the natural mode by which to give the most correct knowledge in the shortest time and in the manner most pleasant to teacher and to the taught.

D. Do you say this from theory or practice ?

O. From practice, commenced more than half a century ago, and continued for nearly thirty years with success beyond all previous anticipation.

D. Where was this experience acquired ?

O. At New Lanark in Scotland; where I invented the first Rational Infant School on these principles, and conducted the training and education of the children without punishment or individual reward,—both being highly pernicious. The religious public have attempted to engraft their instruction upon my foundation, and have made a compound of folly by so doing. They have mixed truth and falsehood together in such a manner as to make truth useless and falsehood more glaring. The Rational Infant School with its surroundings as I established it at New Lanark at the commencement of the present century was the first practical step ever made towards training human beings to become rational or consisient in *spirit,* mind, and conduct.

D. and *M.* Why we have never heard of this discovery which you now claim ! Why did you hide it under a bushel ?

O. I did not hide it from the enquiring population of the world. I opened it freely for the daily inspection of home and foreign visitors, and thousands for years from every quarter of the globe came to see what could not be seen in any other society over the world. A population of 2,500, originally ill-taught and ill-governed and very immoral, reclaimed and governed with order and regularity, all, when of age, active producers of wealth, or providing for those who did produce it. Governed and directed by persevering kindness administered with impartiality and judgment, and gradually without punishment, as some of the evil surroundings were gradually superseded by others comparatively good. Entirely new surroundings were created for all the children of this population, in which during the day all from one year old were placed.

D. And then so perverse is human nature, that I doubt not this population would be dissatisfied and discontented. What was the fact ?

O. No, it is the reverse. This population was daily occupied for the profit of a rich company in an unhealthy manufacture of cotton, and but small justice was done to them, compared with that to which all humanity is justly entitled. Yet for this modicum of rational treatment they on several occasions publicly expressed their entire satisfaction and contentment with their position and treatment, wishing only that all other workpeople could enjoy the happiness which they experienced for so many years. And the district in which they lived was long known as the " Happy Valley."

D. and *M.* How is it then that this discovery to make human beings gradually good and happy without punishment, the greatest of all discoveries yet made, is so little noticed by the public that we are totally ignorant that such a discovery was ever made and put into practice ? How is this ?

O. Because it was made and carried into successful execution by one opposed to all superstition under the sacred name of religion ; and because no clergyman of any denomination had anything to do with it, and the clergy were most jealous of its success, and took all the usual methods of the religions to prevent its notoriety and to falsify everything respecting its unheard-of success.

D. That was, I suppose, because you were considered the most dangerous of all atheists. Was it not so ?

O. I never was an atheist, but always knew and continually stated that all things were produced by the Great Creating Power of the Universe, or the rational God of all rational existences. But in what form and in what manner this mighty and all wondrous work is performed, I was and am ignorant, as are all, I believe, who have lived or who now live upon the earth.

M. Then the professors of spiritual religion have always been opposed to your theories and practice?

O. Those erroneously taught and placed, professing some of the superstitions called religion, have been generally, as was natural, opposed to all my teaching and recommendations for practice.

D. and M. No wonder, when you coolly propose to supersede all their doctines and dogmas, and all their instruction of the people, and in fact to change everything.

O. When it has been discovered from unerring facts that everything has been based on a palpable falsehood, the *only* remedy is to change everything.

D. and M. Well, you are the most cool radical reformer we have met with or heard of. But now proceed with your continued formation of your rational character, as you term it. You have carried us on to only nine years of age. Proceed, if you please. We are now interested.

O. Now that the instructed have received many ideas all consistent with each other, and when they have been taught to observe facts accurately, to compare them correctly, and to deduce natural conclusions from them,—they will commence being taught to draw objects from nature, to read and write, and to *understand* numbering, and the uses of these in the future business of their lives,—being informed that all books published, except those treating of the sciences, have been written by parties erroneously trained and educated from birth, and require to be tested by the only sure criterion of truth which men possess.

D. and M. Ah! Pray what may that all-sought-for discovery be?

O. That which I have often stated by my writings, which for so many years have been hidden by the arts of the superstitious from the knowledge of the public, on the plea that they were impracticable, when they are perhaps the most practical ever given to the population of the world. The criterion of truth to which I referred is—" That truth is always consistent with itself and in " accordance with all facts known or that can be known." That which will not stand the test of this criterion is not true, and should be publicly denounced as error or falsehood.

D. and M. We cannot object to your criterion of truth. It seems to us rational and true.

O. You perceive then that books which have been published can be of little use to aid in the formation of a rational, good, useful, and superior character, such as it will be for the interest of everyone should be given to all of humankind.

D. and M. We now begin to perceive this for the first time. But proceed.

O. In these years they will complete their domestic serving of the commonwealth, and in this period they will be taught by practice the ready use of the various tools, instruments, and implements required to be used in the trades, manufactures, and agriculture in the family commonwealth, and to understand the theory and the outline of the practice of the family commonwealth system of society, with its innumerable advantages over the unnatural, artificial, opposing, and inconsistent system of society so far in practice among all nations and people.

D. and *M.* Why you will leave us nothing of the system taught to us from our birth, and in which until now we have lived, and which we have thought to be the only one practicable.

O. No. This change of system will make a clear sweep of all existing human-made surroundings, so that those old things shall pass away, *and all shall become new.*

D. and *M.* Well I suppose we must listen to these strange sayings of yours, which most men will deem the ravings of a wild undiciplined imagination. Let us have more of your system, although it is to us yet very unintelligible.

O. And it will continue to be unintelligible until all your old notions based on falsehood can be superseded by consistent ideas and associations of ideas based on truth. I was explaining to you the formation of character and employment from nine to twelve years of age.

D. Yes, you were giving them more to do than many of our best educated attain when they finish their education.

O. Men trained and educated under the existing system have no means of knowing what man can and will do when he shall be trained, educated, employed, placed, and governed rationally, according to his nature. By the present system he is made a pigmy in mind, and irrational in spirit, feeling, and conduct. While under the system of society founded on truth, he will become by comparison a giant in mind, pure in the spirit of charity and love for our race, and always consistent in feeling and conduct.

D. and *M.* This is indeed a new comparison, which depresses one system to the lowest estimation, and elevates the other beyond our unregenerated conception.

O. Our descendants will view both systems in the light in which I have placed them. And in consequence of this change in the system, the youths trained, educated, and employed as I have stated, will at twelve years of age be superior in spirit, mind, useful knowledge, and practice, to any men under the present system when they leave the most learned and noted universities in the most advanced of modern nations.

D. and *M.* Well, proceed to explain your next class or stage in forming your new character for a new system.

O. The next class will consist of those from twelve to sixteen years of age. During this period they will be made familiar with the outline of all the sciences, and will assist in the daily occupations of the family commonwealth, always taking their due share in the agricultural and gardening operations. But as machinery will be as extensively used as shall be practicable in this department as well as in all the others, the manual work will be light and pleasant exercise, contributing to the health and enjoyment of all. Before the termination of this period they will be made familiar with all the materials used by or useful to society, and will be taught to know by inspection and to some extent by practice how these varied materials are combined or compounded for use.

D. and *M.* Then you repudiate the long established notions of the political economists, that the greatest division of labour, both of body and mind, is most profitable, and attains the highest perfection in the use of the materials.

O. I consider the division of labour as now applied by society to be destructive of the human being in spirit, mind, and practice, as a rational being, and as placing him much lower in estimation than the pin, thread, or other articles produced by such insane division of the physical and mental faculties of man.

D. and *M.* Then instead of sacrificing the man to the pin, you would sacrifice, if need be, the pin to the man.

O. I would not degrade rational humanity by such a comparison. And all such ignorant and unnatural, not to say insanely selfish proceedings, will be now without motive or excuse, when chemical and mechanical agency can be so universally applied that it may be made advantageously to supersede slavery and servitude over the world. These new powers are illimitable in their application to social purposes under the direction of the inventive faculties, when these faculties shall be rationally educated and shall be furnished with the aid and appliances to be derived from associated society in scientifically formed family commonwealths, and these commonwealths federatively united nationally and universally.

D. and *M.* You stretch your latitude and longitude to such extent over society, that we scarcely know how to follow you.

O. It is the confusion created in your mind by the gross errors and inconsistencies of the present system in which you have had your characters formed, which causes your perplexity. The system which I advocate is simplicity itself, compared with the past and present system by which so far character has been formed and society governed. The most advanced mind of this day is lost in endeavouring to comprehend a system based on falsehood and built up with all manner of inconsistencies to make it work on such an insane foundation; while every male and female at maturity will be familiar with the spirit, principle, and practice of the rational system, into which no inconsistency will be admitted.

D. and *M*. This will indeed be a change which we suppose none living deem practicable.

O. It is probable, as all have been trained and educated, and are unacquainted with its practice, that no one living can encompass the entire of another system differing so widely in spirit, principle, and practice.

D. and *M*. Then explain to us distinctly what you expect will be the spirit, principle, and practice of those at sixteen years of age, when trained, educated, and employed as you intend they should be.

O. They will be rational young men and women, prepared to enter upon the full business of life, filled with the pure spirit of universal charity and love for their race, imbued with the knowledge that their qualities of body and mind were formed for them, and with all the divine consequences necessarily flowing from that knowledge, and fully prepared to act in accordance with that spirit, and in unison with that knowledge, and thus to derive their highest pleasures and enjoyment from an active life devoted to increase the happiness of all others, and with minds so enlightened as to know in the best manner how to effect this all-important work. This is the ultimate destiny of the human race upon earth, and probably the great object of existence in after life, through every sphere of advance to the most perfect excellence.

M. All this is very fine talking, but you cannot seriously expect that it can ever be accomplished in practice. Besides, I have no faith in spiritual natures. They appear to me to be nonentities, and mere creatures of lively but superstitious imaginations. But proceed in explaing your new to-be-made men and women when they have attained their sixteenth year.

O. At this age their judgments will be so matured that they will be enabled, aided by their acquired criterion of truth, to judge accurately between truth and falsehood, and to detect all inconsistencies in matters placed before them. And now, when their judgments are sufficiently matured, and not before, the various religions, as they are called, now taught as the only true religion, will be impartially placed before them, that they may for themselves judge what is true and what is erroneous in each, and thus, putting all that is true together, and leaving out all that is inconsistent with known facts and therefore erroneous, they may acquire correct ideas of what constitutes a true, useful, practical religion, and what is mere superstition and conjecture unsupported by facts.

M. This appears to me, although a deeply imbued Materialist, to be fair, and only just to the rising generation, who should not be forced to receive mere notions of imaginations of men when they were inexperienced in a knowledge of themselves, ignorant of many facts now known, and their natural faculties developed but to a very limited extent. By this equitable mode of procedure it will be seen who will become Materialists and who Spiritualists.

O. I desire only that truth should have fair play, and should not be be unjustly prejudiced in early life, to warp, if not to destroy, the powers of judging without prejudice during their lives.

D. But would you not teach children and young persons any religion before they were sixteen years of age? Why they would be heathens and pagans.

O. Whatever you may call them, they would be far superior in mind and practice to any of the religionists as they now exist in any nation of which we have knowledge.

D. How could this be?

O By teaching them from their birth to love one another, and to make it not only easy for them to do so, but impossible for them to do otherwise.

D. That can be done only by instructing them thoroughly in my religion, the only true one, and therefore all others must be erroneous—for one only can be true.

O. Do all the members of your religion now love one another, and endeavour with sincerity to promote the happiness of each?

D. I cannot say they do, nor do I suppose that other religionists differ in this respect.

O. Then those that you would call heathens and pagans will differ from them in this essential particular. For professing no one creed or dogma now taught by any priesthood, they will have the daily practice of endeavouring to promote in all sincerity the real happiness of those around them, whatever may be their professions of any superstition which they may call religion.

D. What! you a Spiritualist, and renounce as you appear to do all prayer, praise, and worship of the Supreme Being, who fills the universe and creates and directs all things?

O. It is because I am compelled to be a Spiritualist and to believe in a Supreme Being, or an Existence which pervades the universe and creates and directs all things, that I denounce prayer, praise, and all ceremonial worship of any kind, to a Power so far above our comprehension, and so far beyond being affected in any way by what man can believe, say, or do.

D. This is most strange doctrine, and for which you ought to be burned alive.

O. And would that make what I have said to be truth or falsehood?

D. You teach blasphemy against God, and treason against all religions and governments.

O. I intend to teach the truth only, and truth, too, of the highest permanent importance to the human race now and through futurity, and to disabuse my fellow men of those gross errors and follies which have been hitherto, and which now are, the sole obstacles to their rapid progress in knowledge, wealth, wisdom, and happiness.

D. How can this be?

O. You say God is all powerful—creates all things according to highest wisdom; that He is the director of all things, and governs the universe and all within it well and wisely, and according to His will and pleasure?

D. Certainly, I truly believe all this.

O. Then why do you pray for anything to be different from that which Supreme knowledge and wisdom ordains? Is not this blasphemy or childish folly?

D. How so?

O. You by praying desire God to change His proceedings and to adopt your knowledge and wisdom, and you thus show that you have no faith in His knowledge and wisdom, or in His goodness. Is this blasphemy or folly?

D. I can make no answer to such a question. But *you* cannot reasonably object to praise superior Goodness, Power, and Wisdom?

O. Would you, a created being, receive any gratification by a mite, a pismire, a frog, or a tom tit attempting to praise you?

D. No. How ridiculous to ask such a question!

O. Is the difference between these creatures and you, greater than between you and universal knowledge, goodness, and power?

D. The difference is unnumbered millions of times greater between myself and Supreme Intelligence and Goodness, than between the creatures you have named and myself!

O. And you think that their attempt to praise *you* would be a waste of their efforts and time, and both of which would be far better employed in seeking their food, safety, and happiness?

D. Certainly.

O. And that to attempt to worship you by any forms and ceremonies they could devise and practice would be the very essence of folly in such creatures?

D. Most assuredly.

O. Then what possible good could arise from men ignorant of their own nature, ignorant of the incomprehensible Great Creating Power of the Universe, or how that all pervading Power operates to create, uncreate, and recreate eternally all things within a universe illimitable in space and duration, attempting to devise forms and ceremonies, and to call them worshipping acts, to gratify such an Existence, so far beyond the capacity of humanity to find out, except as seen by men in the wondrous operations of nature within the very contracted limits of their created senses and imaginations?

D. I must confess that it is impossible man can do any good to the Great Creating Power of the Universe. But by prayer, praise, and worship of the great and good God of all nations and peoples we surely do good to ourselves and improve our characters.

O. If so much prayer, praise, and worship of God during all the past of man's existence have made no better character for men and women than that now existing in all nations and among all people, then are they not only useless but most injurious to man and of no possible good to God. And it is a fanciful notion of undeveloped minds to imagine that any such puerile proceedings could give a good and superior character to the human race. The Power which has so mysteriously and wondrously created humanity, has so combined within it laws of its nature, that when men shall be sufficiently developed in all their faculties and powers to understand those laws and to act consistently in ac cordance with them, then will their characters be well formed, and they will become superior and rational beings, good, wise, and happy,—far, far beyond what prayer, praise, or worship of a Power incomprehensible to them can ever make them. The one never can produce the result sought for,—the other is sure to effect it, with the certainty of a law of nature.

D. This is to me the most extraordinary doctrine for practice that I have ever heard or read of !

M. I like the practice recommended, although I am a Materialist, and do not yet know what to make of your Spiritualism. It seems however to be a very practical Spiritualism, and not to have much of the old school of immateriality in it.

O. When men shall confess how little they know yet of themselves, of the laws of their nature, of the power which created them and those laws, and how little they yet know of the universe and its eternal operations,—then, by attending to the laws of their nature and of nature generally there will be some real progress in action towards making all men and women good, wise, and happy.

D. and *M.* And do you really believe that there are fixed laws of humanity which if now attended to and applied consistently to practice would make all good, wise, and happy, without prayer, praise, or worship, and by material means under the control of society ?

O. I not only believe, but know with the certainty of a law of nature that society now possesses the most ample means to compel every one to become from birth good, wise, and happy, and yet that this compulsion should be always pleasant and agreeable to the individual, and as little understood or perceived by him as the means are now understood or perceived which are used to make men and women Jews, Christians, Mahommetans, Hindoos, Pagans, or any other character over the earth, whether more or less savage or more or less civilised.

D. and *M.* Then you have no doubt that laws of nature exist, by which, consistently applied, any character not inhuman may be forced upon every one from birth?

O. Yes—so fixed or certain, that seven children born in the same place of the same parents might be taken from birth and placed in seven distinct districts of the world and forced to receive seven different languages, religions, habits, manners, tastes, prejudices, and a mortal or deadly hatred of each other when arrived at maturity. Or these same children might be forced to receive the same language, religion, habits, manners, tastes, prejudices, and be trained and educated so to love one another that each should be willing to sacrifice his life for any of the others.

D. and *M.* And to create more wealth than they would desire?

O. Yes—united rationally with others, as may now be easily effected by the adoption of right measures, they might always superabound in superior and unadulterated wealth.

D. and. *M.* But you have not told by what classes of ages this wealth will be produced, or how your new character is to progress from the age of sixteen.

O. To this knowledge I was about to lead you. The next class will be from sixteen to twenty-one years of age, and will precede the next class from twenty-one to thirty. From six to twelve years of age both sexes will be servitors in the domestic departments, and while so occupied they will acquire an accurate knowledge of many materials and how to apply them in the best manner for use. From twelve to thirty years of age they will be actively employed in the production of wealth of such description as will best accord with the localities of the commonwealth of which they be immediate members. It is anticipated that when the scientific powers shall be applied in every department of life to the extent practicable, and when the best and therefore the most durable articles shall be produced, made, and manufactured, —less than six hours per day of pleasant healthy exercise of these classes, thirty years and under, with such combined arrangements as public property and mutual aid will easily admit of, will be ample to keep society overflowing with the best qualities of all kinds of the most useful and desired wealth.

D. and *M.* Surely you miscalculate the powers of these ages to satisfy the wants and desires of society with wealth for all the purposes for which it is now required?

O. No parties have been trained to consider to what extent the labour, skill, and capital of society are now mis-applied. Less than one-tenth of the labour, skill, and capital now employed by society would produce under public property with united arrangements for the general benefit of society a far superior condition of life for all, and would place every one in a position to be envied by all now under the existing system of private property. In fact the difference would be so great as to baffle all comparison.

D. and *M*. Your statements more and more confuse our ideas, and we cannot follow you in this extensive change of practice. But what of your next class ?

O. The next class of age will be from thirty to forty, and these will be occupied in superintending the various operations and business of the commonwealth, in the arrangements to best preserve the wealth produced by the younger classes, and in distributing it daily for the use of all the members of the family commonwealth.

D. and *M*. And from forty years of age ?

O. The class from forty to fifty will be the governing class of the commonwealth, whose business will be to see that every department shall be kept at all times in the highest state of order, cleanliness, and perfection, for the object of the department, and to anticipate the necessity for repairs, so as to *prevent* all deterioration or falling back in any way   They will also correspond and communicate personally with other similiar commonwealths, and will regulate the exchanges of productions with them, in order that the granaries and storehouses of all may be continually replenished and kept fully supplied.

D. and *M*. And who makes the laws by which to govern these communities of commonwealths ?

O. The laws are already made by the Creator of man ; and the class from fifty to sixty will have to see that those laws are applied on all occasions to every day practice, and that they are never interfered with by any regulations made by any classes of the commonwealth.   But this class will also have leisure and experience to enable them to see if any improvements can be made in any departments, and to investigate all suggestions made by others for this purpose.

D. and *M*. And of those above sixty years of age ?

O. These will be the highest aristocracy in the commonwealth, having their time wholly at their own disposal, while those from fifty to sixty, or the second order of the aristocracy, will be occupied only from one or two hours daily.

D. and *M*. But who are to be the instructors of these classes ?

O. The immediate instructors of each will be the next class in advance ; but all the more advanced classes will be general instructors in the practice of the laws of nature.

D. and *M*. Are the laws of God and nature known by which the human race may be permanently united and made good, wise, and happy ?

O. Yes ; and by which the true Millennial Existence may be commenced and made to extend rapidly over the earth.

D. and *M*. And do you in sober seriousness believe that there is another system for the government of mankind and for creating a new worldly character for the human race, and by which *all* shall be securely placed permanently to enjoy greater advantages and more happiness than *any one* now living ?

O. I not only believe, but know, with the certainty of a law of nature, that the system which I advocate is the true and only system of nature,—that everything now tends to introduce it into practice,—and that when fully and consistently introduced it will accomplish all which has been stated, and more than undeveloped minds can yet comprehend.

D. And without prayer, praise, or worship of God ?

O. These are infant notions of undeveloped man. Their best object has been to make men good, wise, and happy. They have never done so and never will. They are calculated to weaken the mind, to make it superstitious, and to give false and inadequate ideas of the wisdom, goodness, power, and consistency of the Great All-Pervading Eternal Essence which without ceasing creates, uncreates, and recreates all things within the universe.

D. Then how is this good and superior character for the human race to be formed ?

O. By placing the race within new surroundings to be created by man—and these surroundings to be consistent with the laws of humanity and of nature generally.

D. Can such surroundings be now made ?

O. With ease. All the required materials abundantly exist, with full mental, manual, mechanical, and chemical powers to arrange and put them together in working order.

D. Who should make these surroundings ?

O. If governments are wise they will now form a really holy alliance to effect this glorious change for man over the world. If they should be so unwise as to neglect this golden opportunity for themselves and their immediate posterity, then will the people form federative unions of brotherly love upon terms of perfect equality as to birth, training, education, employment, and position or condition, and except these means, there are none under heaven by which mankind can be united, redeemed from sin and misery, and made from birth to become good, wise, and happy.

M. And this all-pervading eternal creating, uncreating, and recreating Essence—the great cause of all things, is immaterial according to the general notions of mankind, and I suppose also according to yours ?

O. Once for all let it now be understood, in order that disputes about mere words may cease, that immateriality is a nonentity. Could space be deprived of all existences you would have immateriality or nothing. But the earth, atmosphere, minerals, vegetables, animals, men, spirits, angels, and the Creating Essence of the Universe, are all of them *something*. They are the eternal elements of universe, combined or uncombined. When combined, men call them *material*, as far as human power can discover their combinations. When the limited powers of man can no longer detect their combinations, they give them another name—immateriality or nothing. When in the invisible state to man's senses, they are as much material as when visible to them ; and of all follies none can exceed the centuries of excited differences among *trained* men about these two words—material and immaterial.

M. Then, according to your views, men have for so many ages been made enemies to each other about nothing ?

O. Yes. And they are so to this day to an incalculable extent.

D. and *M*. Well, you have contrived to confuse our minds on many subjects, and we find it extremely difficult, not to say impossible, to imagine a system in spirit, principle, and practice, so opposed to the one in which we have been trained, educated, and have received our ideas, habits, and modes of thinking and reasoning.

O. I know it, and therefore I have had the patience and perseverence to reiterate the subject again and again in every variety of forms of expression that have from time to time occurred to me.

D. and *M*. It would assist us to form a better judgment upon this new combination of spirit, principle, and practice, which you call a new system of society to introduce the true millennial state of human existence, if you could give a brief summary contrast between our system and yours.

O. I will endeavour to satisfy your wishes, and I think it may tend to make the subject of *Systems of Society* better understood in detail, and more easy to comprehend as a whole of that which is so new to all parties.

To examine and compare entire systems of society is indeed new to all parties—new it spirit, principle, and practice, as a combined whole for the government of the human race.

The *Spirit* was taught in its purity by Jesus Christ—

" Charity which thinketh no evil of any one. Love for all of " the human race, as the work of the Great Creating Power of " the Universe, or God."

The *Principle* is—

" That the faculties, powers, and qualities or character of man, " are formed *for* him."

This has never been taught by any one so far as I know.

The *Practices* which will necessarily emanate from the union of this pure spirit and principle in accordance with all facts, past and present, are unknown and unimagined by any parties who cannot combine this spirit and principle as the foundation on which to construct society and form the character of all.

D. and *M*. We admit your statements to be plausible, and certainly always consistent. But they are most outrageous against all apparent interests and prejudices, and indeed against the entire system in spirit, principle, and practice, of the populations of the world as it is now governed. **From whence** and how, then, did you derive the knowledge of the system which you so perseveringly, through evil and good report, have advocated during your long life ?

O. From the same source whence all knowledge is derived, and by new combinations of existing facts—the source and mode whence and by which all new discoveries are made by man.

D. and *M.* But as you say character is formed *for* everyone, you can claim no merit should your discovery prove to be true and to be as beneficial for practice as you state.

O. It is in my estimation and most thorough conviction impossible that anything or person created can have personal or individual merit. But all things created have a diversity of qualities, and by our comparisons may appear to be better or worse of their kind. And until all ideas of self importance, of individual merit, and of self interest, shall die their natural death by conviction of their absurdity and false foundation, man cannot be made to have right spirit, true principle, or consistent practice, necessary to his progress or happiness—that is, he never can be made to think and act rationally, or to become a reasonable and rational being.

D and *M.* We wait your brief summary contrast of the two systems.

O. I will now give it.

A brief summary of the past and present system of society contrasted with the future, for forming the character of man and governing the human race.

The past and present system of society for forming the character and governing the population of the world is but one and the same throughout, however varied in appearances. It is founded on the supposition that individual man forms his own qualities of body and mind, and their direction through his life, and that therefore for what they are and what they do he should be made responsible to the Power which creates those qualities and to his fellow men who give the right or wrong direction of them. This is the only system of society hitherto known and acted upon by the population of the world.

Experience now demonstrates that this foundation is opposed to all facts and therefore false,—proceeding from the undeveloped imaginations of men before they had acquired any knowledge of the qualities or laws of their own nature.

The future system for the government of the population of the world is based on the knowledge that God, the Great Creating Power of the Universe, compels every individual to receive the physical and mental qualities which he possseses, with their combinations varied in everyone ; and that the direction of these qualities constituting humanity is given by the society in which the individual lives from his birth. And that therefore God, the Creator, is responsible to the individual for the physical and mental qualities and their peculiar combinations which are thus forced upon the individual without his consent or knowledge, and Society is responsible to the individual for the direction given by it to those qualities from birth through life.

These two different foundations constitute two totally different modes of existence for the human race.

The one imaginative, inconsistent, false, irrational, contradictory, unjust, cruel, and leading constantly to error and misery,—creating all the violent and injurious passions,—keeping the human race in perpetual conflicts, public or private,—and gradually progressing towards a pandemonium state of existence, with a Babel of languages and interests, as now seen and felt, but not understood, by all nations, tribes, and peoples.

The other rational and consistent in spirit, feeling, thought, and action, leading daily to more and more knowledge derived from facts, which change not for man, and which are therefore the true words of God ; and there are no other words of God which can be relied upon for the government of the human race.

The one based on falsehood, requiring all kinds of falsehood in principle and injustice in practice for its support, and without which it could not now exist for another year.

It must have a *Priesthood* to fill the minds of the population in all countries with such imaginations opposed to facts as to confuse and destroy their rational faculties, and to create a false medium through which they see everything in nature so distorted that they see nothing in its natural state, and are thus made incompetent to reason, or to draw just conclusions from the most common and palpable facts perpetually before them.

They therefore make *Private Property* of the earth, which justly belongs equally to the living generation for its use, and thus they grievously injure all, by laying the foundation for everlasting conflicts, for all the demoralising effects of wars, and the endless miseries which they produce.

Making land private property renders it necessary that a general system of Private Property should be established ;—to protect which again the most injurious, unjust, cruel, and absurd *Laws* of men, opposed to the laws of God, are required, and also surroundings of various kinds inimical and destructive of the well-being, well-doing, and happiness of all.

By these insane proceedings,—of making the earth and other kinds of wealth Private Property—each one is compelled to take care of himself, opposed by all others ; instead of all being made willing and to have their greatest pleasure in aiding and promoting the happiness of each.

This error alone makes a difference against the happiness of all, of many thousands to one.

The system derived from facts, or the everlasting words of God, makes all property Public, to the exclusion of all private property, and makes all to have but one interest, thereby destroying the animal selfishness which private property creates. Thus terminating all motives to war, and to the destruction of life and property, and all its demoralising influences.

The imaginative system gives merit and demerit for belief and disbelief of opinions, thereby showing that the population of the world is still ignorant of the most obvious laws of God respecting humanity.

God's law is, that man, as created, *must believe* according to the strongest conviction made upon his mind,—and this he cannot avoid believing. There cannot therefore be merit or demerit in the individual for any belief whatever.

Again,—God's law is, that man has been so created that each individual *shall love* that which is the most attractive to his peculiar constitution or organisation of body and mind,—both being the production of the spirit of God within him; and that he *must dislike* that which has been made to be the most repulsive to him. And therefore he can have no merit or demerit for loving or not loving any person or thing.

Then again,—God's law is, that each one in body and mind *must* be most powerfully influenced in language, ideas, associations of ideas, religion, habits, manners, and conduct, by the kind and qualities of those surroundings, created by nature and made by man, in which the individual is born and in which he lives through life. And as these are all formed *for* him by God and society, he can have no merit or demerit for any one of the effects which they produce upon his peculiar constitution—the constitution or organization being itself forced upon him without his knowledge or consent.

D. and *M.* We cannot deny any of your details, or oppose any of the parts separately as you have now stated them. But as your conclusions are wholly at variance with all that we have been taught to believe to be the most sacred of all truths, you must be in error, although we know not in what the error consists. Your strange principles and teachings in accordance with those principles would overturn and change the principles and practices of society as now existing over the world.

O. I know it, and that this result is now inevitable. The wisest of men will fail to detect an error of fact in that which I have stated, or to prove inconsistency in any one of the conclusions which I have placed before you. It is at once admitted that you and the human race generally have been taught that notions the reverse of my statements are the most sacred and eternal truths—so divine as never to be doubted or thought to be subjects for human investigation? But, my friends, do you not now see, from what I have previously said, that you and the population of the world could with yet greater ease have been made to know that these so called divine and most sacred truths were gross falsehoods, as they are, and were errors so fatal as to destroy the rational faculties of the human race, and to give a false and most miserable direction to the reasoning powers of every one born and trained within a system so opposed to facts and to common sense?

D. and M. Well! This is indeed more strange to us than all the most strange things narrated in the history of the human race, or even in romances! Such a change would be in fact a revolution over the world in the mind and practice of all nations and peoples of every colour, country, creed, class, and party.

O. Yes. I admit it. And that there would not be one stone left upon another of the existing surroundings in which humanity now exists in any district of the earth.

D. and M. And can you in your sober senses contemplate the possibility of such a revolution ever taking place?

O. I not only contemplate such a change in all human affairs, but know that there is no power on earth which can much longer prevent its commencement, for which the most sublime and substantial preparations have been made and are daily making. This is the Millennium, which is to be far advanced in spirit, principle, and practice, as so long foretold, before 1857 shall come and go.

D. and M. How wild you talk! Who in these days believes the ancient prophets, or regards any of their visionary sayings?

O. Whether their sayings were visionary or inspired by spiritual influences no one can prove one way or the other. But existing facts, now prevailing over the world, indicate that this revolution of revolutions is near its commencement, and that probably the present generation may witness its early progress.

D. and M. How you talk! Where are there to be found men or women so mad as to venture to teach openly doctrines so repugnant to all the varied existing prejudices of nations and peoples?

O. Thousands, nay millions, are now daily preparing for this now looked for commencement of the Millennium, which is to secure the permanent high happiness of the human race.

D. and M. What can induce the human race to agree to effect such a total change in all their ideas, feelings, and habits?

O. A similar cause to that which has induced so large a portion of the human race in this generation to change their ideas, feelings, and habits of travelling by sea and land, will produce the entire change of a false, unjust, and cruel system for governing the population of the world, for a true, just, merciful, and very superior system,—and in a manner also very similar. The old system will be kept in repair while the new is in progress of creation; and thus will one aid the other until the entire change shall be completed.

D. and *M*. How can you, with your long practical experience of man and society as they are, be so visionary as to suppose it possible to bring about in less than some thousands of years such a change as you contemplate?

O. Why, my good friends, many changes previously supposed to be impossibilities have occurred in this generation !

D. and *M*. What are these ?

O. Navigating the ocean against wind and tide,— deemed to be, until this generation proved the contrary, an utter impossibility.

Lighting private houses and large cities with gas,—long deemed by this generation an utter impossibility.

Travelling by land forty instead of four miles an hour, and much more safely, — deemed by this generation an utter impossibility.

Taking a correct likeness by the sun in a few seconds,— deemed by this generation an utter impossibility.

A cordial union between the English and French nations,— deemed in this generation to be an utter impossibility.

And many other such changes, unnecessary to enumerate.

D. and *M*. This is all very true ;—but the change which you propose is so enormous and complicated—so opposed to all our prejudices, and to the apparent interest of every superior class in every country, that it is downright madness, in our opinion, for any one to imagine such a change to commence in this generation.

O. You appear not to understand what the change is, or how it is to be effected.

D. and *M*. If we are in error on these points, pray explain your views in these respects.

O. I will. The change is of one false for one true principle and the necessary consequences in practice,—which will be from arrangements to support individual interests, to arrangements to support universal united interests.

D. and *M*. Shortly stated indeed. But what parties are now interested to commence and progress with such a change ?

O. The heads of the governments and of the priesthoods of the world, who are at this moment the most opposed to it.

D. and *M*. We request you to explain this enigma.

O. There will not be much difficulty in complying with your request. The explanation will soon force itself on the public mind—perhaps in the following manner.

Governments and people are upon the point of discovering that no mode of governing, either by the despotism of the most despotic governments, or by the despotism of republics, can much longer govern anywhere under the existing system. It has become so glaringly absurd in its creeds and classes and their necessary practices, that all reflecting minds see clearly that no single government can now support itself and continue the system. The British government, bad as it is, is at this day perhaps the best and strongest of all modern governments. Yet withdraw Lord Palmerston, perhaps the most acute modern statesman, and how is another working government to be formed? Withdraw Napoleon III. from the throne of France, and who is to govern it under the existing system?

Single governments under the existing system cannot longer support themselves against the rising knowledge of the nations whom they govern. The governments must therefore unite to protect themselves against the excited premature rising of those whom they govern. The next move therefore will be for the Nations to unite. The governments will then see that they are again checked, and that it will be vain in them to attempt longer to coerce their populations to submit to be governed under a system so false, unjust, cruel, and opposed to common sense. The governments will therefore feel the necessity for an immediate change of the present system.

The priesthoods of the world are also sinking so rapidly in public estimation, that they cannot much longer be supported in their present divisions and hatred of sects against sects. The heads of all these opposing creeds must unite for their continuance and support upon some universal principles and practices. Governments and priesthoods must therefore look around them and investigate what principles and practices they can adopt to maintain for a time their present position. This investigation will lead them into the right path, and the peace of all nations and their progress in knowledge and wisdom will be established and will permanently progress, until the population of the World by the most simple and straightforward means shall become good, wise, and happy, and the true Millennial state of man upon earth shall be established for ever.

D. and *M.* This would be indeed a change most desirable for all. But by what practical steps can such a revolution in the minds and practice of governments, priesthoods, and people be effected?

O. By governments forming national federative treaties, and the people forming family commonwealths, and the priesthoods uniting among themselves and teaching only the principles of love and charity, and showing the practices in their own lives.

D. and *M.* And what power is to induce these parties to act thus rationally, when they are now acting so irrationally?

O. A strong necessity will be one aid, and the progress of well-understood Spiritualism will make that necessity operative, and will materially hasten the change.

M. Then you persevere in the belief of this modern Spiritualism! What good can it do against so much strong prejudice in opposition to it?

O. It will overcome all opposition, convert all, and induce all to become really good in spirit, principle, and practice.

D. and *M.* **May you** prove a true prophet!

O. I reason from existing facts.

D. and *M.* **You** have been labouring all your life to prepare the public for this change of system;—but what progress have you yet made towards accomplishing your object?

O. A great and most substantial progress. The advanced minds of the world are now compelled to believe that the physical, intellectual, moral, spiritual, and practical qualities or character of all men are formed *for* and not *by* them,—and that society, through this knowledge rightly applied, may make demons or angels of all of the human race.

Also; that man is so created that he *must believe* that which has made the strongest conviction upon his mind, and consequently that there is no merit or demerit in the belief or the disbelief of anything.

And that he is so created that he *must like and love* that which is made to be the most agreeable and pleasant to his individual organization, and *must dislike* that which has been made the most disagreeable to his organisation, and consequently there is no merit or demerit in loving or disliking any person or thing.

And these three fundamental truths are the only foundation on which the character of the human race can be formed to pervade it from birth with the spirit of universal charity and love for all of human kind.

D. and *M* These are indeed great and all important truths, if they could be brought into general practice. How do you propose to do this?

O. As a preparation I called the Congress of Delegates last year to inaugurate the commencement of the knowledge in *spirit, principle,* and *practice,* which will produce the Millennium. And this year I called a Congress of Delegates of the reformers of the population of the world.

D. and *M.* And of what use were these meetings?

O. Of incalculable practical consequences— they enabled me to promulgate *universal ideas* and *causes,* and to show their superiority over *local ideas,* and the superiority of attending to the causes of all things, instead of wasting human energies continually about effects, without referring to their causes.

D. and *M.* And what next?

O. I intend to call a Congress of the advanced minds of the world to effect in peace, with order, and with wise foresight, the great revolution of revolutions, to change the existing false, unjust, cruel, and absurd system for forming the character of the population of the world and for governing the human race, for the true, just, merciful, and rational system, by which the character of all will be new formed, and the population of the world will be rationally governed in peace, and will be made to attain perpetual progressive and endless excellence and happiness.

D. and *M.* Where and when is this Congress to be held.

O. If my life on earth shall be spared so long, it shall be held in the British metropolis on the 14th of May, 1857.

THE NEW SYSTEM TO SUPERSEDE THE OLD.

MR. OWEN states that as it is impossible to improve the condition of the human race under the present false, repulsive, unjust, cruel, and absurd system of society and classification for forming character and governing the affairs of men. He will call a Congress of the advanced minds from among all classes, to consider the means by which the existing system of society as now in practice over the world may be gradually superseded, with wise foresight, in peace and order, by the true, attractive, just, merciful, and rational system, with a new classification and a new formation of character, to give a new spirit, new principles, and new practices to all of the coming generation, and thus to raise man from an irrational animal to become a consistent, rational, and superior being in mind and conduct throughout life.

Under this system, derived from nature alone or the unchanging words of God, the Great Creating and Governing Power of the Universe, the laws of God, which change not for man, will reign supreme over the earth, on which the will of God will be done as it is in heaven.

Man will therefore be trained, educated, employed, and placed, to become consistent in spirit, principle, and practice,—consistent in thought and action, and, compared with man as now existing over the earth, a superior rational being.

The moulds in which the character of all are cast are composed of the surroundings in which each one is placed by society from birth through life. Hitherto these moulds have been in all nations and among all people composed of the most inferior, injurious, and incongruous materials, making them most defective and irrational moulds or surroundings. And this must continue to be the character of all moulds while they shall be formed under the existing system of falsehood and repulsion.

To make man a consistent and rational being, in spirit, principle, and practice, he must be cast from birth in a new mould, emanating from the system based on truth, attraction, justice, mercy, and always consistent with the unchanging laws of the Great Creating Power of the Universe. This will not be a Chinese, Japanese, Hindoo, Jew, Mahommedan, Christian, Pagan, British, French, German, Russian, Italian, American, or any other existing mould; for all these are incapable to form man into a good, wise, rational, and happy being.

A new mould, different from any of these, must now be made,

in which in part to recast the present generation, and entirely to new cast the succeeding generations.

The new man to be thus new cast will be formed with a new mind, a new heart, and a conduct new in every particular. Self will be lost in the universality of the race, when all with knowledge and wisdom will cordially and with the highest pleasure and gratification endeavour to promote the excellence and happiness of each.

Under this change of system there will be no insane differences about God. It will be known that God does everything for man, and that man can do nothing for God, who is altogether independent of man's sayings or doings, believings or disbelievings. All notions to the contrary will be known to be most derogatory to the Supreme Creating Power of the Universe, which has so wondrously created man and all things, and continues them in eternal progression. By this progression the present irrational or first undeveloped state of man will terminate, and the new rational period of man's existence upon earth will commence, and will progress until the earth shall be made a paradise, and man a superior rational being.

It is a law of progression on this earth, and perhaps throughout the universe, that evil or pain and suffering should be first produced, in order that good may be afterwards more strongly felt and exquisitely enjoyed. Infinite wisdom and goodness may know that this is the course by which the greatest amount of permanent happiness can be secured to all created sentient ex istences.

Let men therefore now open their eyes and see the wondrous change which the Great Creating Power of the Universe is evidently preparing for the human race ; and let them not vainly attempt to oppose, but rejoice that man has attained the period when this glorious change is about to commence and to be made manifest through the communion which he is now enabled to have with good and superior spirits who have previously lived upon the earth.

These are now our fathers who live in the spirit heaven, and who are deeply interested for the happiness of their children. They tell us that the existing moulds in which men are cast have performed their task,—that these must now be laid aside, and new moulds must be made in which to cast new men, who shall by comparison be perfect in spirit, mind, and conduct, and whose thoughts and practice shall be true, good, and always consistent and rational.

Thus will the millennial state of man's existence be commenced, and be progressed until the knowledge of the Lord shall cover the earth as the waters the sea, and the terrestrial happiness of man shall be complete, when men shall cease their irrational contests about what God is and how He exists and acts, and shall have their thoughts directed to what man is and how he is to be improved and to be made to become rational in mind and practice, and to have a new spirit of universal love and charity. Then will evil and suffering among the human race cease, and God's wisdom in the creation of man be known, and His goodness be acknowledged by all.

But to commence this change of the entire system of society some parties must undertake the initiative and show the nations of the world how it is to be accomplished.

It is to be attained only by universal principles and practices; —the principles in accordance with nature, and the practices always consistent with the principles.

All men desire happiness; and happiness must be made universal or it cannot be permanently secured to any.

The following, when made to become universal, will secure the permanent happiness of all, by placing the human race under the sole government of the laws of God and nature, or God in nature—of that Power

" Whose body nature is and God the soul."

To effect this great and glorious change from the false and repulsive system of society to the true and attractive, the following are proposed for gradual universal adoption.

The *Union* of *humanity*,—irrespective of colour, country, class, or creed.

The Peace of the world,—by insuring justice to all.

The Union to be the sole proprietor of all property. No private property. All to be equal users and enjoyers of it.

Free soil, purchased from present possessors by and for the Union.

Free Men, Women, Speech, and Action, as far as is practicable with superior social society.

Equality of education, and of condition according to age, as far as practicable with the variety of natural organisation.

The Character of each to be formed from birth to be as superior, physically, intellectually, morally, spiritually, and practically, as original organisation will admit.

The Surroundings or external arrangements of all to be as superior as present knowledge will admit.

The only Laws to be the ascertained and universally admitted laws of God and nature.

All Arrangements and Regulations to be in strict accordance with those laws.

The Union alone to be answerable for the the character formed for each individual.

No human Punishments or finding fault with individuals.

Individual Freedom provided for to the utmost extent which is practicable in a superior social organisation of society.

The population of the world to be separated into the most convenient masses, for health, for the formation of a superior character, for the best creation of wealth, for the most individual freedom, and for the greatest pleasure and enjoyment of all.

The business of life conducted according to age,—each age to have its appropriate employment and occupation.

All differences between individuals and betweeen aggregate masses—while differences can exist—to be finally adjusted by previously appointed arbitrators.

It should now be universally known that Ignorance is the sole Cause of Human misery.

Ignorance produces disease of body and mind,—poverty or the fear of it,—disunion and repulsion,—and inferior, injurious, and irrational surroundings.

It produces Private Property.

It leads men to attempt to force opinion and affection by superstitious and insane human laws, opposed to the laws of Go- and nature.

It creates false religions and governments, which rule the population of the world by fear, force, fraud, and falsehood.

The union of humanity will prevent these miseries, and will remove the cause of evil from the human race for ever, and will establish the true millennium and brotherhood of the family of man.

But as words without actions cannot effect this change in the condition of the human race, I am strongly impressed to prepare means to set the ball in motion at the top of the hill, with the hope that, in defiance of all the obstacles which the ignorance and consequent injurious habits of thought and action of this old, false, repulsive, and most irrational system has placed in the way, it will continue to roll on, and will overcome every obstruction, until it reaches its ultimate destination, and thus over the earth will supersede ignorance and disunion by wisdom and universal union.

With this view I call a public meeting of the most advanced minds of the world, to be held on the 14th of May next, in St. Martin's Hall, London, to consider the best means of peaceably superseding the present false, by the true system of society for the government of the human race, and also the best means by which to induce governments and people to commence simultaneously to create those new rational surroundings for all, which will give a good, valuable, and superior character to each, and will enable them, with health, pleasure, and high enjoyment, to produce annually a large superfluity of beneficial wealth for all, by uniting all in one interest and ultimately in one language.

CONCLUSION OF THE FIRST VOLUME OF THIS GAZETTE.

THE supplementary number will conclude the first volume of the *Millennial Gazette*, which was commenced and continued to prepare the most advanced nations first, and afterwards the population of the world, for an entire change of the present false and wicked, for the true and good system of society, by peaceably superseding the one by the other.

But let it be held in everlasting remembrance, that the system of society by which the population of the world has been hitherto governed can never make men good, united, wise, or happy, or rational and consistent in mind and practice. This system is opposed to all facts,—is based on a palpable and most lamentable falsehood, the origin of evil among men,—is unnatural,—and therefore it leads all from the right path to unity and happiness.

But let all rejoice that there is a true system, derived from and in accordance with all facts, consistent in all its parts, and perfect as a whole, directly calculated to make all good, united, wise, natural, rational, and happy, consistent through life in mind and practice, and which will produce a permanent terrestrial paradise. It is the system for which the past and present phases of society have been necessary preparations, and without which preparation this happy future would be unattainable.

But let it be held in everlasting rememberance, and be deeply impressed on the minds of all, but especially on the minds of those who desire to reform the people and governments of the world, that a system based on a falsehood respecting human nature must be an unnatural system, and can be maintained only by stringent, ignorant, unjust, and cruel laws of man, opposed continually to the good and wise laws of God and nature—to those laws which are always merciful and beneficial to humanity, and which are abundantly sufficient for the permanent effective and good government of the human race.

Also that a system based on falsehood produces individualism, which is the bane of human existence, because it necessarily generates selfishness, weakness, disunion, opposing interests, private property, single family training, most injurious classifications of society, demoralisation, and ignorance of human nature; and requires, in consequence, human-made marriages, and all their endless evils when there is not the same means of separating as of uniting.

While the system based on truth will produce universal unity, and consequently strength to overcome all difficulties, and will accomplish what are now considered impossible results for the permanent benefit of the human race, and will speedily make the earth a terrestrial paradise, inhabited by superior rational beings, living in harmony, speaking the language of truth only, and ever progressing in knowledge, wisdom, and happiness.

Every sincere attempt, however, to improve the condition of humanity, should be encouraged,—even isolated individualism itself, because some useful knowledge will be derived from it as from Shakerism, though both equally emanate from the present universal ignorance of the material of human nature, or of the means to manufacture it to become in every instance good, wise, and happy, ever progressing towards higher and higher excellence.

Humanity will remain in a very low state of development while it cannot discover the difference between the false and the true system for forming the character and governing the human race,—between the weakness and irrationality of individualism and all its demoralising and evil results, on the one hand, and Socialism or unity, and its strength and endless moralising beneficial effects and beautiful results on the other.

Surely the time is near at hand when the advanced men of the world will discover the *true* system for forming the character of every population, and for governing them, through that new formation of character, in unity and happiness.

And when the entire population of the world can be made to comprehend the immense incalculable difference for their happiness between an ignorant, false, individual, repulsive,—and an enlightened, true, united, and attractive system of Society.

[*For the conclusion of this first volume see the Supplement.*]

London:—Published by the Author at 16, Great Windmill Street, Haymarket: and sold by Holyoake, 147, Fleet Street; Truelove, 240, Strand; Goddard, 14, Great Portland Street, Cavendish Square; Farrah, 21, John Street, Fitzroy Square; and all Booksellers.

Registered for Foreign Transmission.

Supplement to No. 9.

ROBERT OWEN'S
MILLENNIAL GAZETTE;

EXPLANATORY OF THE PRINCIPLES AND PRACTICES BY WHICH, IN PEACE, WITH TRUTH, HONESTY, AND SIMPLICITY, THE NEW EXISTENCE OF MAN UPON THE EARTH MAY BE EASILY AND SPEEDILY COMMENCED.

"The character of Man is formed *for* him, and *not by* him!"

No. 9A.] OCTOBER 15th, 1856. [PRICE 3D.

THE EXPECTED-TO-BE LAST LEGACY OF ROBERT OWEN TO THE HUMAN RACE.

APPROACHING my 87th birthday, I feel conscious that the termination of my earthly existence is near, and is to be daily expected. I desire therefore to make the best use of the hours which may yet remain to me, in order to benefit you, my poor deluded and undeveloped fellow men.

With this view I leave you this last legacy, with the request that you will receive and study it as the words of one who through a long life has been made to endeavour to discover the cause of so many evils which continually produce to you ever-recurring misery, when your organization and natural qualities and powers are so wondrously created and combined, that when they shall be developed and rightly directed they will produce progress in goodness, excellence, and happiness to all, and to the increase of which there can be no assignable limits.

It is a beautiful dispensation of Providence, or Law of Nature, that parents, or the more matured by age and experience, are the agents by which to develope and rightly direct those natural and divine qualities which are created for and given to every one at birth —a mode of creation so mysterious as to be yet hidden from every child of humanity. Strong affections are therefore given to parents, that as they advance through experience in real knowledge they may have great pleasure in developing or in seeing developed the natural faculties of their children, to attain the progressing advance of goodness, excellence, and happiness. And development will gradually through experience carry this principle of parental affection to its ultimate destiny, and will make all parents to deem all children their own, or as their own. And thus will individual animal selfishness be made to terminate for ever.

Acting upon this principle, and viewing the rising generation as of one family, I leave, then, to you, as the strongest remembrance of my affection, this my last legacy.

Without prejudice or partiality I have viewed and considered the well-intentioned endeavours of all parties over the world to institute measures, in peace or by war, to improve your condition, in part, or as a whole.

Hitherto I have sought in vain to discover one rational measure calculated to go to the root of the recurring evils which afflict humanity ; but I perceive that all at this day are continually cultivating with their best energies the supports to the origin of evil, and are blindly encouraging its growth to the highest luxuriance.

It is an ungracious task to discover and explain the mistakes of any parties,—but it falls to my lot, if I am to do you any permanent and substantial good, to first point out the mistakes of the best intentioned in their endeavours to improve your condition in part or as a whole.

What are those endeavours ? You may ask to what endeavours I refer. I refer to those which have for their object to obtain Free Trade over the world—or the Six Points of the Charter—or partial local Education on existing principles and practices—or some petty improvements in Churches and States —or an Italian, Hugarian, Polish, French, Spanish, or European Republic—or Red or some other imperfect Socialism—or pure and universal, or divided, Despotism—&c., &c.

My poor deluded and deluding children !—What, in the name of common sense, could any of these or kindred measures do for you, but increase your disunion, repulsive feelings, your general poverty and misery ?

Free Trade, carried to its full extent or highest perfection, would, by its desire to buy in the cheapest and sell in the dearest market, demoralise the population of the world to the greatest possible extent, and utterly destroy the best and finest sympathies of humanity; and universal covert warfare, with its consequent miseries, would be its ultimate result.

What of the Six Points of the Charter ? And of Republics ? Have not these Six Points been now well tried in the United States of North America, where they have established the pet republic of the world, and where also Free Trade exists between the respective states and territories ? And what is the result at this day ? The natural one—disunion, repulsive feelings among all classes, competition carried to the extreme, the rich in all ways exhibiting through a wasteful and injurious extravagance a bad example to all, and while oppressing the poor, assuming a wordy profession of humanity, and religious zeal without any useful or intelligent practice of it.

The attainment of goodness or impartial justice with Free Trade and the Six Points of the Charter is impossible. There is not one of the Six Points that could be of any use in a rationally constituted state of society.

Would an Italian, a Hungarian, a Polish, a French, or an European Republic produce more prosperity, as it is called, or more happiness, than has been acquired by the pet republic of the world ?

And now for Despotic rule. Have any of the ancient or modern despotisms shown to the world an example to be followed, of justice to and happiness in their population ? Or is there now in the most perfect known of what is called Constitutional Monarchy, as now practised in the British Empire, anything for the population of nations to desire and adopt ?

Then as to improvements talked of in Churches and States. To what can they amount? Or of what possible utility can they be to any portion of you, while they continue to be based on the false repulsive principle, the origin of evil ?

But as all attempts at associating men for their happiness have failed, it is now seriously proposed to "individualise" the whole of our race, and to obtain that by isolation, which has not been attained by attempts at association on the principle of repulsion. While the first advance to common sense will demonstrate that it is only by founding society on the principle which will gradually lead to universal union and prosperity, that happiness, the desire of all, can be universally attained and secured.

As to improvements in any of the Religions of the world, they have surely been sufficiently tried to demonstrate how utterly incompetent they all are to form a good and superior character for you, or to give you real prosperity and happiness. They are, on the contrary, *the* obstacles to the formation of a good and superior character for all, and to the attainment of real prosperity and happiness for all. It is evident that churches and states, based as they ever are, and all attempted or proposed improvements emanating from the same false foundation, are not only useless, but that they waste the best feelings and faculties of our nature in vain, and to the injury of all of every colour, country, creed, and class.

Yet do I deem it not only useless but unfair for any parties to denounce things as they are,—for when everything is based on and partakes of the original error, there is nothing so easy as to find fault with parts of a system which in all its parts and as a whole is grossly erroneous,—unless the objector has something better to propose, or a perfect remedy to offer to supersede existing evils.

This I now propose to do.

I have been permitted to overcome all partialities for colour, country, creed, or class, rich or poor, or for those called by society good or bad, and to consider you as one family, and, as parents naturally do, to feel a greater interest in the weak and erring, with a view to compensate for their natural defects. My intention is, materially to benefit those now living, and to benefit in a much higher degree every succeeding generation.

Whatever may have been said or written, there is throughout the universe but one truth on all subjects, and therefore but one mode of making the family of man united, good, wise, and happy.

This mode of proceeding is—to adopt the true principle, consistent with all facts, on which to base society,—which principle is " the responsibility of society for the formation of the character of every one from birth."

This is the principle from which will emanate universal unity and co-operation among the family of man. It is the principle from which will proceed universal attraction among our race, and which will make it easy for each one to love his neighbour as himself. It is the principle and the only principle which will or can create universal love and charity. It is the principle by which gradually *all* will be trained and educated to become at maturity good, wise, and happy. It is the principle that will create rational and superior surroundings, in which to place all of you, and your children for ever. It is the principle which will terminate war and all feelings of contention. It is the principle which thinketh no evil, and which will destroy the origin of evil. It is, in fact, the pearl of such value that no wealth can purchase it, for it will at all times saturate the world with superior wealth. It is the little grain of mustard seed which will ultimately cover the earth with its branches, and protect you and your children through futurity from all harm.

I have said that this principle will gradually lead to universal unity and a permanent cordial brotherhood of our race. But to attain this result the principle must not be merely acknowledged and accepted; it must be made active in every department of life.

To effect this there is but one true and rational mode of proceeding.

The authorities of the world in churches and states must first unite among themselves on this principle or origin of good among men.

The rulers of states must then form Federative Treaties upon principles of impartial justice to all, and thus place the world at peace to commence a rational system for forming character, creating wealth, uniting, and governing you through futurity.

To effect these results the next proceeding required will be to commence the construction of common-sense surroundings simultaneously in all nations and districts. on new sites, to enable you to be well placed in manageable masses, without which those results are unattainable.

These arrangements are necessary—

1stly.—In order that every one from birth through life may be well cared for by society, and may receive from it such a rational training and education as shall make them, physically, intellectually, morally, spiritually, and practically, superior to any trained and educated under the insane systems called education which have drawn forth and cultivated all the most animal or inferior qualities of humanity, and have discouraged or depressed all the best and finest qualities of your common nature.

2ndly.—To enable you, with health, ease, and pleasure, unitedly to keep the population of the world at all times saturated with unadulterated superior wealth, and to distribute it justly and most beneficially for you and your descendants.

3rdly.—To enable you practically to unite as children of one family, and to grow into one cordially associated brotherhood of your race, on conditions of practical equality according to age. This is the only possible mode by which true liberty, real equality, and rational fraternity can ever be attained in practice. As these words have been and are now generally applied, they have no meaning but as clap-traps for the ignorant masses.

4thly.—To enable these separated masses to lay out and cultivate the earth so as gradually to form it into a terrestrial paradise, inhabited by a population made to become good, united, wise, and happy, by simple, plain, practical measures—measures as certain in their results as are all the other fixed laws and operations of nature.

5thly—To overcome and destroy for ever in you the unnatural principle of repulsion and opposition, now forced into your minds by the error which has created the origin of evil. And instead thereof to infuse the pure principle of universal love and charity.

6thly.—To induce you for ever to abandon all ideas of effecting these divine objects by ignorant physical force, the utmost success of which has never yet given to you in any part of the world permanent substantial good,--while your united moral force would, by simple demonstration of your union, obtain in peace and harmony all that you can desire in your earthly existence.

Cease, then, my children, to direct your attention to obtain relief from your ignorance and consequent sin and misery by brutal merciless physical force, the most demoralising of all powers? I earnestly and affectionately intreat you to turn your attention and yield your mind to acquire knowledge of the principle of union and attraction, and how to apply it at this period rationally to practice for your united advantages through all coming ages.

These are some of the many great and glorious results which will necessarily arise from the adoption in practice of these superior rational surroundings, and to the creation of which I now so urgently press your attention.   I am,. however, well aware of the undeveloped and irrational state of mind created in you by the false principle of repulsion which has been forced upon you, and by the insane surroundings which have of necessity emanated from that false principle—surroundings in which all of you have lived from your birth, by the unceasing impressions of which upon all your organs and faculties you have all been influenced. I do not therefore expect that you can make a rapid progress in the knowledge and practice of the rational system of society until you can be placed within these new rational surroundings, and hence the importance, which cannot be too highly estimated, of speedily covering the world with these new surroundings, or commonwealths of united families, combined to give the maximum of individual liberty, prosperity, and happiness, compatible with the permanent existence of society in order and harmony.

But who is to devise and execute these wonder-working surroundings to new-form man and society, and to introduce and establish the true permanent Millennium and unite our race as one family?

I will devise the outline and much of the detail of these new surroundings, as they may well be called,—for they will effect far more permanent and substantial good and happiness for our race, than all the so-called divines with their wordy teachings through all past time.

But the ultimate finish and execution of these at present unknown and unthought-of new practical combinations should be made by the united experience of the most advanced scientific and practical men to be now found, irrespective of country, in all the essential departments of life, in order that each of these commonwealths may give to each one placed within them the maximum of comfort, benefits, and happiness, with the minimum of inconvenience and disadvantage.

It is well that the great ones and the little ones, so called, have lately witnessed what wealth, power, and position can give, in the pageantry of the coronation of the Emperor and Empress of all the Russias.   And were not these two personages, the envied of all, on that day filled with anxiety and overcome with fatigue by forms and ceremonies, courtly indeed, and attractive to undeveloped minds among the great and little, but which to those who are now approaching a rational state of mind must appear frivolous, useless, wasteful, and irrational, in the highest degree? How tired of them must the Emperor and Empress have been when the day ended, and when their hard and unhealthy task was brought to its termination!

And now that this much-talked-and-written-about ceremony is over,—what is the position of these two envied personages ? It must be a life of deep and harassing responsibility ; a living for others far more than for themselves, and daily liable to many annoyances.

Such must be the life of all despotic rulers ; and the better the men and women holding these responsibilities under the existing false and now worn-out system of ignorance and irrationality, the more unsatisfactory and painful must it be to them.

Knowing humanity and the influence of surrounding circumstances over it, I know that there are few more to be pitied at this day than the Emperors and Empresses of Austria, of France, and of Russia, with the despotic Kings and Queens of Europe, and the Sultan of Turkey. While under a change to the true and rational system of society, the happiness of all these would be increased a thousand fold and made permanent. The time however for these parties to see things in this light is not yet come, although it may be much nearer than any of them now anticipate.

It is also fortunate that at this juncture of extraordinary events the congress of the most advanced of the modern philanthropists, and of men desirous to discover the means to ameliorate the condition of the poor and working classes in all countries, is taking place. Fortunate, because I am quite sure that this meeting will prove to them, that, with the best intentions and under the immediate patronage of the best disposed and most constitutional king in the civilised world, they will fail to discover any permanent practical measure that can produce relief to the poor and working classes under the present system of absurd competition, opposition, and war of creeds and classes. The attempt will be utterly vain and hopeless.

To put an end to these vain attempts to make something true and good out of a system radically false and wicked, I have called a Congress of the advanced minds of the world, to consider the best means of changing this misery-making system of falsehood and repulsion, for the system of truth and attraction. It will commence in St. Martin's Hall, Long Acre, London, on the evening of the 14th of May next, at eight p.m., and will be continued day by day until the business to be proposed shall be concluded.

ROBERT OWEN.

Sevenoaks Park,
21st September, 1856.

TO THE PRESIDENT OF THE PHILANTHROPIC CONGRESS NOW HOLDING IN BRUSSELS.

RESPECTED SIR,

I yesterday forwarded by post to you for the Congress two copies of No. 8 of the *Millennial Gazette*. To day I send two more of the same number, and two of No. 7, to more fully explain No. 8, and four slips of proofs of No 9, and on Monday next I will send the remaining proofs in order to place before the Congress an entirely new system for governing the population of the world in permanent peace, goodness, prosperity, and happiness.

This system is the true system of nature.

It will give a new, good, useful, and superior character to a½.

It will perpetually supply a superfluity of superior wealth for all.

It will unite all as one family, in language, interest, and feeling, and will produce real liberty and true practical equality according to age, and the fraternity which all good men desire,—and there are no other means under heaven by which " liberty, equality, and fraternity," can be attained.

This change of system may be easily effected in peace, by wise foresight, by the cordial union of governments and people,—and without this union both will soon become severe sufferers.

May I request you to obtain a fair and full investigation of the system by the Congress?

Most respectfully yours,
ROBERT OWEN.

September 26th, 1856.

THE PLATFORM ON WHICH TO FORM A GENERAL ASSOCIATION OF ALL NATIONS TO EFFECT IN PEACE AND WITH WISE FORESIGHT AN ENTIRE CHANGE OF THE EXISTING FALSE, REPULSIVE. UNJUST, CRUEL, AND IRRATIONAL SYSTEM OF SOCIETY, BY WHICH THE POPULATION OF THE WORLD HAS ITS CHARACTER NOW MISFORMED FROM BIRTH, AND BY WHICH IT HAS BEEN AND IS NOW MOST ERRONEOUSLY GOVERNED, UNDER EVERY NAME AND FORM OF GOVERNMENT,—FOR THE TRUE, ATTRACTIVE, JUST, MERCIFUL, AND RATIONAL SYSTEM FOR FORMING THE CHARACTER AND GOVERNING THE HUMAN RACE.

THE true and rational system of society can be based only on the knowledge of the fact that the character of man is formed *for* him by the Great Creating Power of the Universe, or God, and by the qualities of the surrounding persons and things in which he is placed and lives; but his language, religion, habits, manners, ideas, and conduct, are given to him by the society and locality which surround him, and society has the power to make these good or bad, inferior or superior, for every one.

Reflection upon the subject will make it evident that the human race has a deep and lasting interest in the good and superior formation of character for the entire population of the world. And until arrangements shall be made to give this good and superior character to all from their birth, on principles as fixed and certain as those of mathematics, it will be vain to expect that any other measures will produce unity, general wealth, prosperity, and happiness, to any portion of society.

As God creates at birth all the natural faculties and qualities of each, and society cultivates those qualities for good or evil results, all responsibility for the formation of character and conduct of the individual necessarily devolves upon society. And the means amply exist to enable society to insure a useful, good, and superior character for all of our race.

The formation of this character depends entirely on the knowledge of society how to place, train, educate, employ, and govern, the individual from birth to death; and to attain this knowledge society must acquire the science of the surroundings which form the human character.

With this knowledge, united with the experience and means now acquired by the more advanced nations, it will be practicable to create new surroundings in accordance with the true fundamental principles of society, by which to new place all, without chance of failure to give to each from birth the good and superior character, and to enable all to acquire with ease and pleasure the best and most valuable wealth at all times in superfluity, to unite cordially with their fellows over the earth, to establish universal peace to be permanent, and make each one powerful by union, wise, and happy.

The natural and easy mode by which to effect this change in a business like manner and without prematurely disturbing any portion of society as now existing will be—

Firstly.—By existing governments making national federative treaties to establish permanent peace between all nations.

Secondly.—By each nation simultaneously commencing to make the new surroundings on new sites; these new surroundings to be made in accordance with the true fundamental principle on which society should be based, and on which the new character is to be given to every one placed within these new surroundings.

Thirdly—These new surroundings will form in each nation scientific societies or rational family commonwealths, whose maximum number will not exceed three thousand, in order that every one born and educated within them should be well cared for by his society through life.

Fourthly.—That all born within them should be treated, trained, educated, employed, and governed, impartially as children of the same family.

Fifthly.—That each one should be trained and educated to have their physical, intellectual, moral, spiritual, and practical qualities cultivated in the best manner known by the most advanced in practical knowledge on this most important of all subjects.

Sixthly—That within each commonwealth all property shall be for the free use of all its family members. That the exchange of wealth between these federative families be at first by Labour Notes, and until it shall be discovered by experience that under this system wealth of superior quality and unadulterated can be created by all these united federated commonwealths so pleasantly and abundantly, that like air and water it will cease to have commercial value, and will be always obtained without money and without price.

Seventhly.—That as the perfection of this change of system will depend upon the perfection of the new surroundings, these should be completed from the outline and detail of the inventor of these surroundings, in accordance with the new true fundamental principle of society, by the union of the best known practical scientific men in each department of life, and this to be done in order that all nations may be supplied with perfected models of these to-be-wonder-working surroundings, which are to secure the permanent unity and happiness of the human race.

TO THE PRESIDENT OF THE CONGRESS FOR THE IMPROVEMENT OF SOCIETY NOW HOLDING AT BRUSSELS.

RESPECTED SIR,

I now inclose for the use of the Congress a more full platform or statement of the practice by which the change from the false and worn-out system to the true and good system of society may be speedily and easily carried peacefully into execution, by a well-understood confidential union of the governments and people, each cordially aiding the other.

I also forward by this mail copies of No. 1 to No. 6, inclusive, of the *Millennial Gazette*, having already sent Nos. 7. and 8, and I now also send a full proof of No. 9.

There will appear much of repetition in this Gazette,—but truth is always the same, and great repetition of these new truths is required to overcome the old false associations of ideas, forced by the surroundings of each upon all

If the subject will not carry its own excuse for the trouble which I give, no words of mine can suffice or have influence.

I have the honour to be, Sir,

Yours respectfully and faithfully,

ROBERT OWEN.

Stockton Lodge, Hampshire,
September, 29th, 1856.

THE PLATFORM FOR THE CHANGE OF THE OLD FOR THE NEW SYSTEM OF SOCIETY.

1.—The new and true system for the government of the population of the world is based on the knowledge of the facts which demonstrate that " the character is formed *for* every one, and " not, as universally imagined under the old false system, by the " individual for himself."

2.—That God, the Great Creating Power of the Universe, creates the material of man perfect as a material, and gives it to human society to cultivate, manufacture, or form into an inferior, indifferent, or a superior being.

3.—That it is the interest of all of our race that every one should be made to become as superior as the material or natural organization of each at birth will admit.

4.—That society now possesses the most ample means to ensure this character to every one, and will be enabled to effect this all-important result when it shall acquire the knowledge how to apply those means to make the surroundings or external machineries which are necessary to obtain this great object of the life of man.

5.—That to create these new surroundings or machineries to make or manufacture this superior character for all, should immediately engage the best attention and most energetic measures of governors and governed in all nations.

6.—That the rational preliminaries to the formation of these new machineries for manufacturing a superior character for the human race, will be for the governments of all nations to unite to form national federative treaties, by which each nation would acquire the advantages of all other nations, without sacrificing one of its own advantages. This would secure permanent universal peace, and enable every nation and people to commence simultaneously to construct these new and wonder-working machineries to manufacture a good, useful, and superior character for all from birth, and to insure also prosperity and happiness through life, and thus destroy the cause or origin of evil among men.

7.—That these new machineries cannot be made to give these

great advantages in perfection to more than three thousand as a maximum, and therefore it will be necessary to draw off by degrees the present much injured population of large cities and towns, and to form isolated situations, that they may acquire and possess the advantages of a rational society, without being injured by over crowding by streets or lanes, or having to construct the machineries to be too complex to obtain the required objects in their united perfection.

8.—That these new machineries or surroundings will not only give this superior character to every one, but will also enable each to aid to create more superior unadulterated wealth than they will desire to consume, having the free and unrestrained use of whatever they may want or wish for.

9. These new machineries will also distribute the wealth justly and most beneficially for every one, so as to enable them to partake of it according to their requirements.

10.—These machineries will unite the members of each separate mass, which may be called "Scientific Family Commonwealths," in one language, interest, feeling, and action

11.—These machineries will unite the separated masses or individual family commonwealths so as to form federative unions, all having one language, interest, feeling, and common action, thus gradually forming the population of one country after another into a cordial and well organized brotherhood, and establishing the true Millennium, or perpetual harmony to the human race.

12.—That the family commonwealths, individually and unitedly, be governed in all their proceedings solely by the all-wise, just, merciful, consistent, and rational laws of God and nature, and for ever supersede the foolish, unjust, cruel, inconsistent, and therefore ever-changing laws of undeveloped man.

13.—That the present monetary system of the world, the unseen and unsuspected tyrant and demon of society, shall be immediately superseded by honest Labour Notes in the preliminary commonwealths and between them, until these preliminary commonwealths, or family independent unions, shall be superseded by the full scientific family commonwealths, when labour notes and all schemes for representing wealth will cease, being no longer required in a rationally constituted society, in which superior wealth will always superabound, although freely used without restraint by all.

14 These preliminary commonwealths, or independent family unions, are intended to be constructed with surroundings which will gradually train the heads of families to united general operations, but which will admit of independent family residences, so nearly united as neighbours, that their children can be trained and educated together as children of one family, and fitted in all respects as they advance in years to become occupants of full-

formed rational family commonwealths, fitted in spirit, principle, and practice, for the true Millennial state of earthly existence, and well prepared at death to enter the superior spheres of the spirit world.

15.—That it is the first duty of the government of the most powerful and advanced nations, to obtain the best plans and models of the new rational surroundings which should constitute the preliminary independant family union, and also of the full-formed scientific family commonwealths. And in which also to create full-formed superior men and women, true in spirit, principle, and practice, having all their faculties, propensities, and powers, trained, educated, and exercised to the point of temperance for each of these, as perfect as present and future ac-quired knowledge will admit.

16.—That to govern society on its true fundamental principle, carried into practice through the federated union of scientific united family commonwealths, in which every one shall be se-cured from birth to death in the full enjoyment of the best of every-thing for a rationally constituted being, will be a small expense of labour, time, and materials, compared with the present waste-ful, extravagant, and most absurd and irrational mode of em-ploying men and materials. The Millennial and universal happy state of earthly existence will be obtained and maintained at less probably than five per cent of the cost required to maintain this monstrous, ignorant, and brutal state, by which the world is now so wretchedly misgoverned and mistaught.

ROBERT OWEN.

September 29th, 1856.

TO ALL CLASSES, SECTS, AND PARTIES, IN ALL COUNTRIES.

FELLOW MEN,

A great discovery has been made. It may be called the Science of Sciences,—because it is the science through a know-ledge of which the happiness of our race will be permanently es-tablished to the end of earthly time.

It will insure a good, useful, and superior, physical, intellec-tual, moral, spiritual, and practical character for every one.

It will cordially unite the human race as one enlightened and affectionate family, filled with the spirit of universal love and charity.

It will enable all without contest or competition to super-abound at all times in unadulterated superior wealth.

It will make metal money no longer necessary to create wealth, and it will disclose the injustice and cruelty of the present mo-netary system to the mass of the population of the world, and will also show how in various ways it is injurious to the upper classes.

It will for ever destroy the false principle on which society over the world has been based and constructed, and on which the character of all has been formed from the beginning to this day. This false principle is the origin of evil, and is now the sole cause of its continuance among men. When this most lamentable error shall be abandoned by our race, and shall be superseded by the true fundamental principle on which society should be alone based, then will universal happiness be attained by our race, and there will be none over the earth to make any one afraid, for all will be united as one enlightened family in love and charity, in interest and in language.

To attain this state of permanent progressive happiness for all, the practical measures are plain, and with the right spirit among you will be easy of execution.

The Priesthood of the world as long as their services can be useful must abandon all their doctrines, dogmas, and creeds, and teach only the divine, because true, precepts of love and charity—precepts derived from the knowledge that all the qualities of man are formed *for* and forced upon him. And the priesthood must also, in *all* their practice, make this love and charity evident to all, and thus become a shining light to the population of the world. As they now teach and practice they are far worse than useless, and are a most injurious example to society.

The Governments of the world must unite to form just national federative treaties, which it is now highly for your interest to have accomplished with the least loss of time. Observe and remember the great overwhelming fact for good or evil as it may be used by you,—" That as are all the natural qualities of man " at birth, and his surroundings made for him by society, so " must he become for good or evil, for misery or happiness, and " that society has now the full power to decide the one or the " other for the future of all of our race."

You of course naturally desire that all should be made from birth to become as good and happy as their born qualities of body and mind will admit. How is this all-important result to be secured permanently for our race?

There is but one mode, and that is by making surroundings in which to place all of our race through futurity within such surrounding arrangements as will be efficient for the purpose. And as the means now abundantly exist to form these new arrangements or surroundings, it becomes your highest interest and strongest duty to your children to decide that they shall be adopted and carried as speedily as practicable into execution, simultaneously in all nations over the world.

You ask how can this be done. It may be done easily, by the

cordial union of governments and people, now become so necessary for the safety, peace, prosperity, and happiness of both.

The governments to make the national federative treaties, and thus they will open the world to all, giving the use of it to you and your children—the perpetual rightful owners of it.

You ask again how can this right be attained and used beneficially for all.

The governments and people should now cordially unite to make these wonder-working surroundings, to accomplish which the populations of nations and of the world must be divided into masses the most easily to be arranged to attain in the best manner all the objects of human life, or, in other words, the highest permanent happiness for all, so that not one human being shall ever be neglected or not well cared for by society from birth to death.

These masses will be from one thousand as a minimum to three thousand as a maximum, and then the arrangements or surroundings in which to place each of these masses, which may be called scientific family commonwealths, may be made such as shall give to each one within these scientific family commonwealths the advantage of being from birth to death under the eye and care of this family immediately, and as each family will be federatively united with all other similar families over the earth, generally under the eye and care ultimately of the entire population of the world.

By this simple general arrangement over the earth it will be practicable to secure to each of our race in perpetuity for life the use and enjoyment of more wealth and power, than under the existing false and cruel system has ever been possessed by the most mighty conqueror who has slain his millions and destroyed the labour of yet more millions.

Such is the future, and it now depends upon the progress which can be made in developing your good and rational faculties how soon that future shall be made to become the present.

You have only to acquire the knowledge of the science of surroundings and of their practical application to the business of life, and as soon as you can be prepared to attend to the lesson it will be found an easy task.

More for the present will be unnecessary.

ROBERT OWEN.

London, October 1st, 1856.

NOTICE.

A public meeting of the most advanced minds of the world of both sexes, to consider the best peaceable means to change the present false, unjust, cruel, and most irrational system of society, as it now exists over the world, for the true, just, merciful, and rational system of society, and to effect the change through its entire progress without injury to any and most beneficially for all, will be held in St. Martin's Hall, Long Acre, London, on the 14th of May, 1857. It will commence at eight, p.m., and will be continued day by day until the business to be proposed shall be concluded.

And it is stated, in the most positive terms that language will admit, that a comparatively few of the most advanced, energetic, and practical men and women, united heart and soul in the cause, could now accomplish this great and glorious change for the human race ;—because it may be demonstrated that the true, just, merciful, and rational system, will be highly advantageous, physically and mentally, through all future ages, for the entire family of man, of every colour, country, class, and creed,—and equally so for prince and peasant.

ROBERT OWEN.

Sevenoaks Park, Sevenoaks,
  September, 1856.

N.B.—All attempts to reform the present system of society, through all past ages, have in every country, under every form of religion and government, woefully failed, and at this day society in all nations more requires reformation, or a thorough change, than it has done at any former period.

All attempts to reform the present system, except by an entire change in spirit, principle, and practice, will equally fail and be vain and useless.

This notice is also recommended to the most grave consideration of the rulers of all nations, states, and peoples, and to the heads of all religions over the world ; because it is become imperative, for their safety and future permanent interest, that they should now unite among themselves and cordially with the people.

It will be proposed that this change of system shall be effected as the old gravel roads were peaceably and most beneficially superseded gradually by the new iron roads, by which the population of so many nations are deriving incalculable varied advantages.

This first volume of MILLENNIAL GAZETTE will be succeeded by a second, also to be published in parts, and in each number a portion of the life of the writer will be given.

The first part of the second volume to commence the first of January, 1857.

ROBERT OWEN.

Registered for Foreign Transmission.

ROBERT OWEN'S
MILLENNIAL GAZETTE;

EXPLANATORY OF THE PRINCIPLES AND PRACTICES BY WHICH, IN PEACE, WITH TRUTH, HONESTY, AND SIMPLICITY, THE NEW EXISTENCE OF MAN UPON THE EARTH MAY BE EASILY AND SPEEDILY COMMENCED.

"The character of Man is formed *for* him, and *not by* him!"

No. 10.]　　　　JANUARY 1st, 1857.　　　　[Price 6d.

THE TWO SYSTEMS FOR FORMING THE CHARACTER OF AND GOVERNING THE HUMAN RACE :—THE ONE BASED ON THE IMAGINARY SUPPOSITION THAT EACH ONE FORMS HIS OWN QUALITIES—PHYSICAL AND MENTAL ; THE OTHER BASED ON THE KNOWLEDGE OF THE FACT THAT THESE QUALITIES ARE FORMED *FOR* EACH ONE OF OUR RACE.

[Explained in Questions and Answers.]

Question.—You say there are two systems by which to form the character of, and govern the human race. Can you explain these two systems so as to be clearly comprehended by the population of the world in such manner as to become useful for universal practice?

Answer.—I will endeavour to do so. This is the object which I have in view in commencing this conversation with you; and knowing, as the human race has hitherto been governed and its character formed, how difficult it must be to imagine another system of society, opposed in spirit, principle, and practice, to the one in which we have been trained, educated, and have lived from birth, I will endeavour so to explain them as to overcome this great difficulty, arising from prepossession of ideas and of habits in accordance with those ideas.

Q.—You have undertaken a most formidable task, for you have a world of deep-rooted mental prejudices and physical habits to overcome.

A.—I have unshaken confidence in the omnipotence of truth, when unmixed with error and freed from mystery.

Q.—I admire your faith in the omnipotence of truth. But

you must acknowledge that to this period its progress has been slow,—and is not the general language of the population of the world at this day the language of falsehood ?

A.—It is. The language of the population of the world is of necessity the language of falsehood, because the system in which we live is based on falsehood, and does not admit of the language of truth, without creating great excitement, disorder, and confusion.

Q.—And if you are now about to give us truth without mystery, mixture of error, or fear of its consequences, do you not apprehend arousing the anger of the population of the world against you ?

A.—I always expected, but never feared it. For I had full confidence in the *shield of truth* when declared in the *spirit of love and charity for our race.*

Q.—I perceive now the ground which you have taken. Pray proceed to explain the two systems for conducting the terrestrial affairs of humanity.

A.—I will, and I will call one, the first, or the past and present,—and the other, the second, or the future. The first, the animal, selfish, undeveloped system, is based on unobserving, unreflecting notions, opposed to all facts, and is therefore false and artificial. The second is derived solely from facts, and is therefore true, rational, and natural. The *first* is founded on the thoughtless supposition that each one of our race forms himself, physically and mentally, and in consequence of this notion men have made each responsible to his fellow man and to the Creator of his natural organs, faculties, propensities, powers, and qualities, for what each one feels, thinks, and does. The *second* is based on a knowledge of the fact that the Creator of man gives him his natural organs, faculties, propensities, powers, and qualities, and forces him to receive them at his birth, and that these are cultivated from his birth by society and the surroundings in which he is placed through life. It consequently gives all responsibility to the Creator for man's natural or born powers, and to Society for the cultivation of all the physical and mental qualities from the germ before birth and through life. Or, in other words, the *first* system is constructed on the supposition that each one forms himself to be what he is, in feeling, thought, and action, and is responsible to God and man for what these may be made to be ; while the *second* will be based and constructed on the knowledge that what man is he is compelled to be, by God and society, and that he is irresponsible for his feelings, thoughts, and actions. And it is only on this base, and on the irresponsibility of the individual, that man can be made good, wise, and happy,—to be pervaded with the spirit of universal love and charity,—or be made to love his neighbour as himself,—to speak the language of truth, in look, word, and action,—to be honest in all his dealings with his fellow men,—and to walk uprightly before his Creator, or God and nature—or God in nature, as the term may best accord with your impressions of the Great Creating Power of the Universe—the to us yet mysterious power which is eternally changing the forms of the elements of nature, by composing, decomposing, and recomposing them, according to a will in that power incomprehensible to man, or by eternal unchanging laws, necessarily existing, and the origin of which is equally mysterious to our finite comprehension.

Q.—Before you proceed, pray explain what you mean by the universe.

A.—All that exists ; including past, present, and future.

Q.—Are there limits to it ?

A.—It must be boundless in space, and illimitable in extent and duration.

Q.—Whence your knowledge, that you thus express your ideas upon this mysterious subject so decidedly ?

A.—The human mind is so constructed by the power which creates it, that it feels a consciousness of the impossibility of limits to space or time, and yet it cannot encompass the ideas of the Infinite and Eternal, although conscious that both must be facts. But upon these subjects, in the present state of human knowledge, it is weakness of intellect for men to dislike one another because of a difference of opinion respecting them.

Q.—I agree with you that to do so is childish and absurd. And now proceed further to explain your two opposing systems for the government of the population of the world. You said that man could be made to become good, wise, and happy, only on the knowledge that his character, physical and mental, is formed *for* him, and that he is not and cannot rationally be made responsible for the qualities given to him, to the power which gives them, or for the inferior or superior cultivation of them from birth, to those who have the power to enforce the inferior or superior cultivation upon all, from the sovereign to the beggar.

A.—Yes—and as this is the chief stone of the corner, with which the builders of society have so long refused to build, and without which no sound or substantial work for man can be constructed or made to be beneficial and permanent, it now behoves all to examine it well, to see that there is no flaw or defect in it of any kind. By such examination it will be discovered not only that it is a sound and perfect stone for the foundation on which to construct the whole of society for ever, but also that it is the mirror of truth, which will reflect all things in nature as they are, without mystery, mixture of error, or fear of man, so far as the powers of humanity have been created and developed to extend into the universe, and to acquire knowledge of the powers of its elements.   It will also make evident how little men yet know of truth, and what an immensity of knowledge is yet to be acquired.

Q.—But by introducing this new foundation on which to construct society, you demolish the entire structure of society which our ancestors through all past ages have taken so much pains to build up and to fortify with so much care, caution, and foresight.

A.—It is true our poor deluded and undeveloped ancestors have so loved and cherished this old system of their early inexperienced imagination, that to prevent it soon falling to pieces they have fancied they had made it impregnable and immortal, as the multitude even now deem it, by fortifying it with artificial religions, governments, laws, commerce, classifications, and numerous other artificial institutions to support these, until they have now so far heaped error upon error upon a false base, that it can bear no more, and all are now afraid that the entire structure is about to give way and to bury them in its ruins.

Q.—And what do you say should be done under these circumstances ?

A.—That not a stone of this old rickety structure should be prematurely touched, or it may indeed suddenly tumble to pieces and bury us by its premature destruction.

Q.—Then you have no desire to destroy immediately this old system of society, although you deem it so false and injurious to all ?

A.—Quite otherwise.   It is like an old house, which, although tottering on its foundation and decayed in its walls and timbers, is still a shelter from storms and some protection from petty thieves ; and therefore I would prop it up and support it while the new house was building, upon a new and true foundation, even upon a rock so solid and firm, that it should remain good to the end of time without flaw or rent.

Q.—Then you disapprove of revolutions of violence, of raising nationalities against existing governments, or of supporting any of the local prejudices of nationalities or what are esteemed patriotic virtues?

A.—Patriotism is another name for prejudices against, and injustice to, all other countries.   I would therefore create new surroundings which should gradually terminate all local nationalities, and make the population of the earth into one nation, with one language, interest, and kind feeling for one another, and thus by degrees form all of our race into one enlightened family, all cordially loving and assisting each other to excellence in all things, and to progressive happiness as knowledge and excellence increased.

Q.—This would be indeed a very different revolution from the revolutions of violence so ardently advocated by so many well-intentioned ardent spirits now active throughout many nations.

A.—It would be so.   And I lament the waste of so much valuable energy, if well employed, and of such abundant means, if rightly applied, now misdirected in the pursuit of that which if successful would not succeed to give peace, rationality, or happiness to the world.   These self-sacrificing men are novices in a knowledge of human nature, and undeveloped in those faculties which, if developed, would enable them to comprehend what society should be, and how to construct it to become beneficial to all and permanent in a rational progress to universal happiness.

Q.—Then you expect that no good can arise from these national conflicts and revolutions, even should their promoters become the successful parties?

A.—Were these parties to succeed to the extent of their wishes, and to destroy all present governments, they would soon have the populations in a worse condition than they are at present.   The existing differences of opinion and feeling among them would keep them in perpetual agitation, and party would endeavour to destroy party as on former occasions, and all the hideousness of this old false and cruel system would soon be in full activity among the ambitious in every nation.   An entire change of system can alone now benefit the human race.

Q.—Then you expect no good results in the present age from revolutions of violence?

A.—None.   Reason, directed by the spirit of charity and love, and not the sword, with its inhumanities, can alone effect a permanent beneficial change for the population of the world.

Q.—But how can the voice of reason be heard and made to prevail, although declared in the spirit of charity and love, against the selfish individual spirit which now governs supposed individual and class interests ?

A.—By the whole truth respecting humanity and society being openly declared to the population of the world, and advocated with calm energy in the spirit of love and charity.

Q.—Who at this period, when the public mind is engrossed with the desire of accumulating money, and of increasing individual selfish aggrandisement, will attend to any declaration of truth, although made with calm energy in the spirit of charity and love?

A —Those who perceive these important truths, and who can comprehend their inestimable value to the human race through futurity, must discover the means to arouse public attention to the investigation of this subject, and to enable it to understand that its deepest, highest, and most valuable interests through time and eternity are involved in it.   This has been the mode by which every strange new truth has become known to mankind.

Q.—But the public say your new truths are of a different character to these material truths, as they call them to distinguish them from yours, which they say are immaterial and impracticable.

A.—My ideas are as material as any of those mentioned, and, when comprehended in their full extent by the public, will be found to be far more easy of practice than longer to continue the present system of society without creating national confusions and great individual misery. The system which I advocate is derived from a knowledge of facts, is based on unchanging facts, and will be constructed of facts all in conformity with the base on which it is founded.

Q.—How do you make your views of society to be a system of facts, derived from, based and constructed upon facts, and all consistent one with another throughout the whole system ?

A.—It is derived from a knowledge of the facts which prove that man is a created being, possessing definite qualities, given to all of his race, but varied in each individual in the combination of those qualities,—the qualities and their combinations not being the choice of the individual, but being forced upon him at birth. That these qualities are such that each human being *must* believe anything to be true or false according to the strongest impression made upon his mind and feelings, and *must* like and love that which is made to be the most agreeable and lovely to his own impressions or feelings, and *must* dislike or hate that which is made to be the most disagreeable and repulsive to him, and made so either by nature, or by artificial or acquired causes. That man is therefore a being who must receive his qualifications of body and mind, and must believe or disbelieve, or feel love or hatred, according to his individual organisation and his artificial instruction by society and the surroundings in which society places him from birth through life. Thus is the second or future system of society a system, derived from and based upon material facts, which have changed not since man was first created, and which to all appearance will continue unchanged to the end of his race upon earth. While the first or past and present system of society over the world is derived from an undeveloped and inexperienced imagination, before man had acquired the power to observe facts accurately or usefully, and in consequence the entire system is one of imagination, based on falsehood, incongruous, and made up of opposing parts supported by false reasoning, force, fear, and fraud.

Q.—Then you abandon all expectation of improving the present system or of uniting it in any manner with your new views of society, or what you call the second and future system for the government of the human race ?

A.—I know that the first or old system, in consequence of being falsely based, is so erroneous in each of its parts and as a whole, that it cannot be united with a system based on truth, and it has become too glaringly false in principle, and too corrupt and injurious in practice, to be longer maintained by the advanced minds of the world.

Q.—Is it for these reasons that you have called a Congress of the advanced minds of the world to meet you on the 14th of May next in London ?

A.—Yes. And at that meeting I hope to convince those who may be present, and through them the population of the world, that the time has actually arrived for the commencement of the millennium in practice in all nations and among all peoples. For—in the name of common sense, when the most ample means to secure the permanent happiness of the human race have been attained and secured—why should they not be applied to satisfy the ever existing desire of all who are born and live upon the earth ? If the change should not be effected at this eventful period of our existence, when good and superior Spirits have come to our aid, and declare that these new Spiritual Manifestations are made to hasten the period for the reformation of the world, when it shall be governed by wisdom, charity, and love, it must arise from the strong root of insanity and madness with which falsehood has so long afflicted all of our race, and I have not rightly read the signs of the times, and have miscalculated the period for man to be made a rational being and for the millennium to commence.

Q.—Have you doubts on this all-important subject?

A.—None whatever. I have unshaken confidence in the irresistible power of truth, when without mystery or mixture of error it is openly and fully declared, without fear of man, and when it is also aided by the good and superior Spirits who are now so deeply interested and actively engaged in promoting this the greatest of all human changes while men live upon the earth.

Q.—But do you think the advanced minds of the world will come to meet *you* on the 14th of May next,—you of whom one reverend gentleman in a pamphlet has published his opinion that you are fifty thousand million times worse than the devil, and when it is currently reported that the Jesuits, or some parties, advisers of the late Madame Tussaud, prevented her, after she had made full preparation to place you in her exhibition of celebrated notorious characters, admitting you there, because you were too bad to be a companion there even for the worst men and most notorious characters of the last and present centuries?

A.—All this I am told is true. Yet in the face of these proceedings I expect the best and most advanced minds of the world to meet me in St. Martin's Hall, Long Acre, London, on my next, and probably, if I live so long, my last birthday while visibly in life on this earth. But should I not then be in life, my Spirit if practicable will be there to assist those who will take my place on that occasion.

Q.—But what should induce the advanced minds of the world to attend your meeting on the 14th of May next ?

A.—The certainty in their minds of the false base on which this old system is based, and its utter worthlessness now for good to the human race. The conviction also that an entire change of system for governing man has now become a first necessity,—a change of system in spirit, principle, and practice,—one that can and will make the human race to become rational in feeling, thought, and action, and unite all for the permanent happiness of each,—one which shall give peace to the population of the earth, and train and educate all, by new placing them within rational surroundings, to make a rapid progress towards attaining excellence in all the essential affairs of humanity,—one that, without injury to any, shall new place all, under such new and improved conditions, that all remaining within the old conditions will gladly, when opportunity shall offer, exchange the old for the new and the only system which can produce in practice the " Liberty, Equality, and Fraternity," so long the anticipation of advanced minds,—and a system which can produce them in peace, with order and wise foresight, so that during the change from the system of falsehood and evil to the system of truth and good there shall be no conflict of interests, no confusion, nor any premature proceeding

Q.—And how, in the name of common sense, with present appearances over the world, can you expect this change to be effected in less than a thousand years?

A.—Inexperience in a knowledge of human nature and of society may suppose a thousand years to be required in which to effect this to them a change of such incomprehensible magnitude. But the advanced minds in a knowledge of humanity, of society, and of the system by which the world is now so misgoverned, see things through a different medium, and calculate the progress of terrestrial events upon other data. You forget that all that is required to effect this change to its full extent is mere matter of simple practice. It is but to abandon a glaring falsehood, opposed to all facts, which is the origin of evil—the notion that man forms himself individually,—and to adopt for the base of society the divine truth, supported by all facts, that the qualities and powers of all are formed *for* them, and that they can have no merit or demerit for them, and that now these qualities and powers can be, by society, greatly improved and increased for every one. In consequence, that a useful, good, and superior character may be ultimately forced, in a pleasant manner, on every one, from birth through life. That wealth can now be produced annually with great pleasure to all to be at all times superabundant for all. That, with this character and creation of wealth, the human race may be united as one enlightened and affectionate family. And that these results are to be attained with the certainty of a law of nature by nations creating new surroundings for their respective populations on new sites—new surroundings, calculated on scientific princples to produce with the greatest certainty each of the results stated. It is an easy matter of practice to change a glaring falsehood for a glaring truth, and it will be yet more easy when it shall be known that falsehood is the origin of evil to man and of misery to the human race, and that truth is the origin of good to man and of happiness to the human race. It will be an easy matter for practice, when society shall be based on this divine truth, to form surroundings which shall pleasantly force the useful, good, and superior character on all of our race. When society shall be so based it will be easy of practice to combine with the surroundings for forming the useful, good, and superior character for all, other surroundings which shall enable these characters so formed to unite cordially as one family, superior in all human attainments, and with health and pleasure to each to create continually more good, unadulterated, and superior wealth, necessary for the health and enjoyment of all, and desired by all, than the wants and wishes of all will require. You see, then, that this science of society—this revolution of revolutions—is to be obtained now in practice by changing a false fundamental principle for the true one on which to base society, and by changing injurious surroundings, emanating from that false principle, for beneficial surroundings, necessarily emanating from the true principle.

Q.—What! do you mean to say that the entire system of the world, in spirit, principle, and practice, is to be supersedsd in peace and order by merely changing a fundamental falsehood for a fundamental truth, and injurious for beneficial surroundings, and that these superior surroundings could now be made by man from the materials and means now under the control of the government and people of all nations ?

A.—Yes. And that this change will and must be made, although in its ultimate operations it would not leave one stone upon another of this old, worn-out, and now misery-producing system.

Q.—If what you now say should prove to be true, this new system which you so perseveringly advocate must surely expand the reasoning faculties mightily, for you can see much further into a millstone than my powers of mental vision will aid me to penetrate. But on what do you ground your confident expectation that this great and overwhelming change should speedily commence ?

A.— Upon all the great signs of the times.

Q.—What are these ?

A.--The extraordinary discovery of inventions to promote the union of nations, by railways, steam navigation, electric telegraphs, &c.,—the excitement in the United States between the free soilers and pro-slavery parties,—the unsatisfactory results, to all parties engaged, of the Russian war, its immense destruction of life and waste of wealth, its demoralising effects upon all engaged in it, and its now palpable irrationality to improve the condition of any portion of the human race,—the present excited state of all the nations of Europe, fearfully looking forward to political changes, the results foreseen by none, but dreaded by all,—the peace of France and of Europe depending upon the uncertain life of Napoleon the Third,—the dead-lock and apathy in Great Britain from the want of men who know how to use and direct the immense means and power of the British Empire beneficially for itself and the populations of the world,—the rapid spread of the Anglo-Saxon race over the world, and the incalculable power which it might use to secure the well-being, well-doing, and happiness of all nations and peoples, by peaceable means, advantageous for the population of the world, —the practicability of now forming federative treaties between nations, and the interest which all have that these treaties should be now entered into, to secure the permanent peace of the world previous to the commencement of the new surroundings which are to enable all of the human race to become good, useful, united, wise, and happy,—the discovery of a new mode of placing, training, educating, employing, and governing, the human race, so as, on principles as fixed as the laws of nature, to make all better and generally superior to any placed, trained, educated, employed, and governed, under the existing mal-arrangements of the human race,—the submarine telegraphs preparing to unite the most advanced nations in daily communication with one another,—the utter helplessness of all statesmen to govern any population to its satisfaction under the now worn-out existing system of society,—the now palpable injustice, cruelty, and inefficiency for good government of the present falsely based system of society, and the impossibility of the best intentioned parties well governing any population under it, because, on account of its false foundation, the language of the world must continue to be the language of falsehood, and its conduct that of deception, while the permanent interest of all of our race requires that the language of the world should be the language of truth only, in look, word, and action, and the conduct that of undeviating honesty in all to all,—the publication of these new truths, and their silent reception by governments and peoples,—

Q.—Hold! You have given a sufficient list of the signs of the times to warrant your conclusions, and I see you could easily add to it. But it is unnecessary. You then, I see, persevere in believing that the millennium is a practicable state of earthly existence, and is now attainable ?

A.—I do. In addition to the signs of the times which I have stated, I may add the new Spiritual Manifestations, which have commenced at this period in the United States, and which are rapidly spreading over the world in a manner so extraordinary, in defiance of the strong opposition from vested interests and conservative minds.

Q.—But on this point you and all Spiritualists are considered by the world to be deluded, insane, or mad, or that the Spirits communicating are evil ones.

A.—The conservative population of the world must continue to believe as it does until a stronger evidence shall be forced upon it. But that evidence is daily extending and increasing in power, and, ere long, will become universal. The true Spiritualists have no anxiety on account of any present disbelief in the truth of these mysterious and wonderful Spiritual Manifestations.

Q.—I will patiently wait the development of this mystery, knowing that truth will ultimately prevail.

A.—You may safely do so. For if the universe is governed with wisdom and goodness, all things within it must proceed in the best possible manner.

Q —But many contend that knowledge, wisdom, and goodness, have nothing to do with the government of the universe, and that all that is done is effected by a law of fixed necesssity, unavoidable, and irresistible ; and is an eternal succession of cause and effect, without beginning and without end.

A.—It is true there is the appearance of an eternal action of cause and effect throughout the universe, so far as man's knowledge of the universe yet extends. But there is also as strong evidence of knowledge, wisdom, and goodness, throughout all creation, far surpassing human conception, and it is difficult, and with many impossible, to conceive these attributes of power, exceeding human capacity to comprehend, without being impressed with the conviction that they emanate from an Eternal Intelligence, pervading space, which the human mind in vain attempts to grasp—a Divine Spiritual Intelligence, far beyond man's utmost stretch of thought or comprehension.

Q.—But there are physical and mental pain and suffering, which are apparently incompatible with infinite power, wisdom and goodness.

A.—Admitted. And therefore there is a limitation either to the power, wisdom, or goodness, of this Divine Intelligence. Wisdom and goodness are however so evident throughout man's knowledge of the universe, that it is natural to conclude that they are carried to the utmost extent that the eternal elements of creation will admit.

Q.—There is in all connected with the unceasing circle of creation, a mystery beyond my comprehension.

A.—Everlasting Power, which composes, decomposes, and recomposes the elements of the universe, into the endless variety of forms and their endless variety of powers and qualities, physical, or mental, must remain a mystery to our race until new discoveries in the laws of nature, or of that power whence these mysteries proceed, shall dispel it, if this knowledge is to be acquired by the inhabitants of this planet. In the meantime it is most unwise in men to have estranged feelings for each other on account of a difference of opinion, or on account of their impressions respecting these hitherto hidden mysteries.

Q —This conclusion I readily admit. It is obvious common sense, and will create the spirit for onward progress and an increase of real knowledge, and this spirit will open the way for the population of the world to change, in peace and with wise foresight, the present false and wicked system for governing men, for the true and good system, which will secure the unceasing progress and happiness of our race, and will unite all as one family, ultimately with one language, feeling, and interest.

A.—Amen. So be it !

DIALOGUE BETWEEN ROBERT OWEN AND ONE OF HIS OLD FRIENDS RESPECTING WRITING HIS LIFE.

Old Friend.—You know that your oldest friends have been long urgent with you to write your life, knowing that were you to die, no one, from your independence of action from your childhood, could execute a task of such interest to the human race ;—I say to the human race,—because your life has been during many years devoted to devise measures for the improvement and happiness of all, making no distinction of colour, country, class, or creed. Your life is now so advanced that its continuance must be uncertain, and your friends desire above all things to have a faithful history of your proceedings from your earliest years of recollection. They are now the more earnest in continuing this request to you, because they believe that a full history of your life would tend more than any other measure you could adopt to facilitate the great change in human affairs which you have so long advocated. Will you now accede to our request?

Robert Owen.—I am always desirous to meet the wishes of my old friends and faithful disciples. I have so long delayed my consent to your earnest solicitations, because I have been continually actively engaged in living my life—in pursuing a mission which has been impressed on my mind from my earliest years, and which, hopeless of accomplishment as every one of my friends endeavoured to make me believe it, never ceased to inspire me with the never-wavering conviction of ultimate success. And so this conviction remains,—but always increasing as my age increases. I am now engaged in the most important part of my progress in this work, and can now scarcely withdraw my attention from the present and the future of this mission, to recur to the past which is ended, while more is required from me and can yet be accomplished by my remaining active exertions.

O. F.—But surely it is time you should cease these active exertions and now sit down quietly to recollect and write your life. What can now be so important to you, to the interest of your family, and for the benefit of society?

R. O.—If I thought it would be more for the benefit of society generally that I should *write* my life, than that I should progress in my mission to its final accomplishment, I would not hesitate to comply with your wishes. But my im-impression is otherwise,—knowing that there is much important work yet to be done before the population of the world can be prepared to change a false system of society for the true, although that false system is hourly producing incalculable misery to the millions, which the change would terminate. While therefore anything remains to be done which I can do to forward this great and good work, I am unwilling that my attention should be in any way withdrawn from it.

O. F.—But what can you now do at your age in conflict with a world taught to be prejudiced from the birth of every one, and so strongly in favour of their present false system, productive as it is of all manner of evil to the people and governments of all nations?

R. O.—I can continue to write, and to circulate among leading minds in various countries what I write explanatory of the falsehood and evil of the one system, (the present,) and of the truth and goodness of the other, (the future,) which is destined to supersede the present in the due order of the development of man and progress of terrestrial creation. With this view, also, I have called a Congress to be held in St. Martin's Hall, Long Acre, London, on the 14th of May next, of the advanced minds of the world, who take an interest and who are active in promoting the unlimited happiness of all our race.

O. F.—But how can you expect to make any impression upon society at this time, when all nations and all parties in all nations are all at sixes and sevens and know not what to do to sustain their present local views and interests?

R. O.—It is because I know they are all as it were at sea without rudder or compass, and are driven about by every wind that blows, that I am most anxious to give to each a sound rudder and correct compass, not only to prevent their shipwreck and to calm their fears, but to enable them to steer direct into a safe harbour. It is therefore that I think the writing and publishing of my life of far less importance than now to place the whole truth respecting the system of ignorance, falsehood, and misery, and the system of wisdom, truth, and happiness, before the leading minds of the world in so clear a manner that the difference between the two systems may be glaringly seen by them, as well as the impossibility of uniting the spirit, principle, and practice of the one, with the other. And also to enable them to perceive that the present system, as it is in nature, may now be made to become the immediate parent of the true and good system, and to foster it as parents take charge of their offspring and endeavour to leave a valuable inheritance to them.

O. F.— You will write to the leading minds of the world in vain. They are not prepared for any such sweeping change as you suppose. They have not yet commenced to think about two systems so opposed to each other, and yet that the one shall willingly introduce and sustain the other in its progress towards maturity. This very morning the *Times* newspaper, deeming itself the mouthpiece, not only of Europe but of the civilised world, has a leading article to dissuade its readers from ever thinking it possible that a system of equality among mankind is practicable,—and equality is one of the main features of your proposed new system.

R. O.—The *Times* knows nothing, or pretends to know nothing, of the system which I advocate. It has a bribe of more than a hundred thousand pounds a year from the public to support this wretched thing which is called a *natural* system of society,—when its foundation and entire superstructure are opposed to truth and nature. What does the *Times* know of the practical equality among the human race which I advocate? It is blinded by the learned ignorance of the present system, through which alone it has yet attempted to look at man and society. I have never advocated the possibility of creating a physical and mental equality among the human race, knowing well that it is from our physical and mental varieties that the very essence of knowledge, wisdom, and happiness, or rational enjoyment is to arise. The equality which belongs to the new, true, and rational system of human existence, is an equality of conditions, or of surroundings, which shall give to each, according to natural organisation, an equal superior physical, intellectual, moral, spiritual, and practical treatment, training, education, position, employment according to age, and share in local and general government, when governing rationally shall be understood and applied to practice. It is doubtful whether any editors of newspapers, now the great instructors of the human race, or the professional instructors in the schools, colleges, and universities of the world, have any clear ideas or correct notions of what is or is not practicable respecting human nature, of which these so learnedly ignorant men of the present system of society appear to have but the minimum of real knowledge. Their acquaintance with human nature has been derived through successive generations solely from the undeveloped imaginations and inex-

perience of our early ancestors, and it has required the accumulation of fact upon fact, increasing through each generation, to
enable the discovery to be made at this period, that our ancestors
were in error and totally ignorant of what manner of beings they
were. In now looking over the earth among all peoples and
nations, it is too evident that to-day this ignorance of ourselves
has been wondrously preserved, and that by the mass of the
human race, and with very partial, if with any, exceptions, the
populations of the world are now as ignorant of themselves as
were our first parents, if not more so, in consequence of the
errors added to the errors of every succeeding generation on this
now-perceived-by-the-few-to-be the most important of all knowledge.

O. F.—Why this is the strangest of all your strange teachings ! You make nothing of human knowledge and the accumulated wisdom and experience of the world through all past
generations !

R. O.—Yes, I do make much valuable use of the past experience of the *facts* of the world and of human knowledge, as far
as it has progressed in discovering facts in the various sciences.
It is from this knowlenge that I have derived the great and all-
important truth—

" That the character, physical and mental, of all men and
" women, is formed—not, as hitherto imagined in opposition to
" all facts through all ages, BY themselves—but by the Great
" Creating Power of the Universe and by society, FOR them ;
" and that for the character thus formed it is the essence of in-
" sanity to make the individual in any way responsible."

From this knowledge I have also discovered the greatest of all
truths for man to know—

" That any character, from the worst to the best, may, with
" the certainty of a law of nature be given by society to all of the
" human race,—and that through this knowledge every one
" may be made to become at maturity, good, wise, and happy."

O. F.—Why, if you are correct with your conclusions, it is
indeed the most valuable of all human knowledge yet acquired,
a knowledge far more to be desired than the discovery of the
philosopher's stone. But what are the inferences which you draw
from these two facts—if facts they be,—,' that the character of
" man is formed *for* him, and that society may now adopt
" practical measures to make all future generations, without
" any exception, good, wise, and happy ?"

R. O.—*Firstly.*—That this is the knowledge that the most
advanced minds of the world in all ages have sought for,—but
until this period without success.

Secondly.—That this knowledge will confound the ignorance
of those deemed the most learned in all past generations.

Thirdly.—That this knowledge will introduce the Millennium,
to commence in this generation.

Fourthly.—That it will introduce the Millennium over the world, by peaceably and quietly superseding the existing ignorant, false, wicked, and insane system of society, by the wise, true, good, and rational system of society, for the government of the human race as one family.

Fifthly.—This new system of society will develope the true religion, government, laws, classification, and institutions of society, for the population of the world.

Sixthly.—That it will cordially unite all of our race as brothers,—create a practical equality of position, education, and occupation, according to age and capacity,—and establish for ever true liberty, just equality, and real fraternity.

Seventhly.—That it will by uniting man to man and nation to nation establish peace for ever among the human race.

Eighthly.—That this knowledge discloses to our race the origin of evil, and that evil produced solely from man's ignorance of himself.

Ninthly.—That by enabling man to know himself, the origin of evil to our race will be destroyed for ever.

Tenthly.—It proves the false foundation whence all human laws have proceeded—their ignorance, inutility, and constant failure, in consequence of being always opposed to the good, wise, and unchanging laws of God and Nature.

Eleventhly.—It demonstrates the cause of the past insanity of the human race, and its cure.

Twelfthly.—It will enable the existing rulers of society to adopt decisive measures to commence to make the human race through futurity sane, wise, good, united, and continually to increase in knowledge, excellence, and happiness.

O. F.—If you are right in these inferences and conclusions, then indeed is the knowledge that the character of man is not formed *by* himself, but *for* him, the most important of all human knowledge, when united with the knowledge of the practical measures by which to create the new surroundings which can produce, with the certainty of a law of nature, the results which you have stated.

R. O—Through this knowledge I know that the governments of what is called the civilized part of the world, have the most ample power and means at their disposal, by uniting cordially with the people of their respective governments, now to commence the practice of the science by which to insure the progress and happiness of the population of the world while living on the earth, and after death through a life immortal.

O. F.—Surely these governments, if they were convinced of the truth of what you state, would use all the influence they possess to secure the progress and happiness of the present and future population of the world, including their own offspring.

R. O.—Yes,—and by so doing to attain a higher degree of

happiness for themselves, than the possession of all earthly power and wealth could give them.

O. F.—But how are they to be made conscious of possessing this unheard-of power and influence?—for without this knowledge they will continue to act as they have done and are now doing.

R. O.—I know they will, and my present writings and practical proceedings are with a view to convince them of this great fact—a truth of the highest importance to themselves and the people of the world, and yet more to our children of succeeding generations.

O. F.—How do you mean to turn the current of the public opinion of governments and people?—for in such a change as you propose, both must unite to effect it.

R. O—For this purpose I have called a Congress of the advanced minds of the world, to be held in London on the 14th of May next, that I may explain these matters to them, discuss them, and have their assistance to discuss the best peaceable means to effect the change, and to give the sanction of their names to princes and people, and thus prepare them to take an active part to accomplish the permanent progressive happiness here and hereafter of the human race.

O. F.—But your friends say your life, if written and published by yourself, would attract more interest than your new, and to the world strange system which you advocate.

R. O.—I know it, and have long known it. The population of the world have been tired out by so many false and delusive systems of reforms upon the present erroneous formation of the structure of the human mind and of society, that it now turns with disgust from them all, concluding that all attempts to improve society must prove equally fallacious, and they ask only to be amused, for which they are willing to pay a great price according to their individual means. But that which is really required is sound instruction on a true foundation.

O. F.—Then you will continue your *Millennial Gazette* and disappoint your friends who have so long waited for your promise to be fulfilled?

R. O.—I will compromise this matter with them, and will divide the next volume between the advocacy of an entire change of system, and my life.

O. F.—If this will satisfy you, I suppose your friends must be satisfied.

R. O.—I deem the making plain to the public of the immense difference for good to the human race between the old, false, and evil system, and the new, true, and good system of society for forming the character of and governing the future generations of men, to be an object of the very highest interest to humanity, and in which the happiness of all are deeply involved.

O. F.—But how can you expect the public to take the same interest in this subject as you do, to see it in the same light, and to give to it the same pre-eminent importance ?

R. O.—By the same means that all other new and important truths are forced upon the public against its will and strongest prejudices.   All new truths, however beneficial to our race, are distasteful and hateful to the pre-occupied mind and self-satisfied convictions of the public. This is a law of nature, and need to suprise no one having a knowledge of our nature, and must be met by the proper surroundings.

O. F.—And you think you can create those surroundings ?

R. O.—I will make the attempt, even with my limited means. With larger means I could be certain to secure full success.

O. F.—What ! at your advanced age—with imperfect sight and hearing, and now a feeble frame to support any great physical exertion ?   It is true your spirit is willing, and your mind yet more clear and strong than could be anticipated of one who has had so active a life from early childhood to his eighty-sixth year.   But of these you may be deprived any hour before your intended meeting on the 14th of May next, and then is to become of this Congress, from which you anticipate such great results ?

R. O.—The objections you make are natural.   But it is only to a man far advanced in age, when the desires of earthly life have died their natural death within him, and one who has had confidential acquaintance with all classes, and great practical experience, not only in directing great commercial and manufacturing operations successfully for many years, but in governing for forty years a numerous population in all its details, and who for thirty years of that period new educated all the young, and to a great extent new formed the character of the old, creating a better and happier working population than could at that time be found in any nation or among any people.   And although a few well-disposed proprietors of similar large establishments have attempted subsequently to follow the example thus set, they have failed to produce the same extent of beneficial results, or to give for so long a period such a character to the children, or so much happiness to a community of 2,500 souls.   And because no other population has ever yet been educated and directed on the same principle and spirit, continued without deviation for so many years,—and no other principle and spirit can produce similar results. It is true, however, my life now hangs by a slender thread, which may break at any moment, and in the body I must in that case be absent at the Congress.   Should this occur, I will endeavour to provide one younger, more active, and more competent, to perform the new and arduous duties which will be required of the person who shall be called upon to preside over or to advise the progress of a Congress so new in the history of the human

race, and far more important to the present and future population of the world than all previous Congresses—all having hitherto been of a local character only.

O. F.—You stretch your latitude and longitude of thought
and action to such extent, that I am not competent without much
more consideration than time will now permit, to give a rational
opinion upon your strange anticipations.   But I do not see how
you are to induce a sufficient number of the most advanced
minds of the world to attend your proposed Congress.

R. O.—That must be yet my business to find such minds, possessing sufficient moral courage to disregard the opinions of an
ill-educated public, whose ideas and associations of ideas, except
on matters of fact demonstrable to the senses, or on principles
of science demonstrable from facts or self-evident deductions
from self-evident truths, are of little or no value.

O. F.—Yes,—but where will you find men and women for
your Congress, with sufficient mental powers and moral courage
to brave the irrational public opinions now pervading all nations?

R. O.—I know the love of truth in some men and women
creates a moral power within them which elevates their minds
to the greatest extent of self-sacrifice.   And what can more deserve that sacrifice than measures to change a false, wicked,
and irrational system, which has created and inflicted endless
evils on the human race through all past ages to the present, for
the true, good, and rational system of society over the earth—a
system which will gradually train all to become good, wise, and
happy,—to progress rapidly towards excellence in all things,—
will terminate all apparent incongruities and inconsistencies, and
will make the earth and its inhabitants one harmonious whole,
governed, as intended by its Creator, in the spirit of charity, by
knowledge, love, and wisdom, securing permanent peace among
men, and insuring mercy, as far as practicable, from man to all
the animal creation.

O. F.—You have a most sanguine spirit, and are yet as strong
and confident as ever, although through your life you have been
opposed by the prejudices of all classes and by the public opinion of the world.

R. O.—I have ever had undiminished confidence in the power
of truth to overcome all error and opposition, when openly, fully,
and faithfully declared, in the genuine spirit of charity and love
for our race, and persevered in sufficiently long to give time to
overcome the natural conservative principle of error in humanity.

O. F.—May you be right !   But I fear your task is next to
an impossibility.

R. O.—Fear not, my old friend,—I am accustomed long
since to overcome imagined impossibilities.   There is nothing
that is true, good, and permanently beneficial for the human
race, which cannot be attained by perseverance, when pursued
in the true spirit of charity and love.

O. F.—But who for the years required can persevere in this spirit of charity and love in a cause, however true, good, and beneficial to our race, when continually opposed by the ignorance and prejudices of a race so opposed, through want of knowledge and through mis-instruction, to its own well-being, well-doing, and happiness?

R. O.—The task, taught as all have been by a system having a gross falsehood for its foundation, and that falsehood pervading every part of it, counteracted only by the inroads which science has slowly made upon it—is most arduous; and I must confess that at times the gross ignorance and prejudices of some have put my patience to severe trials, and I am not sure that I have always exhibited to my opponents the full measure of charity and kindness to which their unfortunate surroundings when calmly considered justly entitled them from one advocating illimitable love and charity for our race.

O. F.—Considering the deep-rooted errors inflicted by a false system on all of our race, yourself included, perhaps your friends, if your opponents will not, will make allowance for your short comings in this respect.

R. O.—I am quite conscious of having been on many occasions too severe in my expressions in writing and speaking, to be justified by the ever considerate true spirit of charity and love, and I will endeavour in future to make practice always consistent with this spirit.

O. F.—All your friends will rejoice if you succeed,—for we must acknowledge it is the most powerful of all arguments you can use, for it is always true that practice is better than precept.

R. O.—Having sufficiently discussed these matters, I must now attend to my promise, and prepare to proceed with the history of my life.

O. F.—You know how anxious your friends have long been on this subject, and how much they have feared you would postpone it until your strength would fail you for the task.

I have this day received a communication from superior Spirits by an experienced medium in the United States. It is headed "AN ADDRESS TO THE WORLD," and it contains principles and practical instructions which are greatly in advance of the most advanced liberals, so called, of the present day, and as it will instruct the most progressed, and even my most experienced disciples, I will publish it for the advantage of the public.

10th November, 1856.

CORRESPONDENCE AND SPIRITUAL COMMUNICATIONS.

THE following letter, prospectus, and address, I have just received from parties in the United States, whose lives are devoted to the great cause of humanity, irrespective of colour, creed, country, or class. The address is the most advanced in principle and for practice, and contains more valuable common sense and right reasoning than I have yet seen from any party, visible or invisible, and it is in many respects the document which of all others that most deserves the profound consideration of the advanced minds of the world.

I am however compelled to differ in opinion from that part of the address which ignores all expectation of aid from governments in the change of a false and evil system for the true and good system for forming the character and governing the human race. I differ, because I know the change will be for the highest and best permanent interest of all governments and of every member of each government. I differ, because where there is error in man, the cause is not in the individual, but in the ignorant, false, and evil system of society, by which the individuals erring have been surrounded before and from birth. I differ, because where there is error, the parties should not be blamed, but in the unceasing spirit of charity and love instructed,—and this instruction, if persevered in and true, will never fail to convince, when taught with judgment, or in accordance with a knowledge of human nature under the various surroundings in which it is placed. I differ, because it is unwise to cause distrust or anger in those who require to be taught that which is true, to relieve them from error and from that which is injurious to them, as all error is sure to be,—and all governments are at this day in this predicament. It is for these reasons I am reluctantly compelled to differ so far from the address—an address which in all other respects I deem beyond price in silver and gold. And for the great truths which it contains, my best thanks are due to the superior Spirits who dictated it, and to the medium through whom it was received, and by whom it was sent to me.

ROBERT OWEN.

To JOHN M. SPEAR and ELIZA J. KENNY,

My most esteemed friends in the great and good cause of truth,—

I received here yesterday your letter, prospectus, and address from superior spirits. These I intend to publish in the next number of the *Millennial Gazette*, and more or less of them I expect will be published in the *Yorkshire Spiritual Telegraph*. In my publication they will be preceded by the prefixed introduction, which I hope will attract the attention to their valuable teachings of the most advanced minds in Europe and over the world.

The next number of the *Millennial Gazette* with these documents I expect to have published the 15th of December next, and of course copies will be sent to you. I hope these proceedings of mine will be satisfactory to the good and superior Spirits who aid us.

I hope many advanced men and women from your side of the Atlantic will attend the proposed Congress to commence on the 14th of May next.

With sincere regard and kindly affection,
I remain,
Your friend,
ROBERT OWEN.

Sevenoaks, 11th Nov., 1856.

Letter from John M. Spear and Eliza J. Kenny.

Melrose, Mass., W. S., Oct. 16, 1856.

ROBERT OWEN,
  DEAR SIR,—

    I had the honour to receive an invitation from you to attend the Congress of Reformers of the World held in London, May 14th, 1855, but it was not in my power either to accept the invitation, or to acknowledge its receipt, but am happy to say that I have been labouring for many years, that the object for which said Congress assembled might be realised. It gives me great pleasure to tell you that I am at present engaged in aiding the practical unfolding of a new social state, as transmitted from the Spirit world, wherein God, as revealed throughout all nature, *alone* shall be recognised as lawgiver.

In my humble opinion, it is entirely futile to look to any existing nation or government for the recognition of those principles, fundamental laws, which *must* form the *basis* of a true society upon this earth. The axe must be laid at the root of the tree, by selecting a spot of land dedicated to freedom, truth, right, whereon shall dwell those persons *seeing* and *feeling* that all *patching* of the *old* is useless, and that an entire, radical, fundamental change, a new beginning of all things, a perfect unfolding of all nature's laws must be, and that they are no longer to be merely acknowledged by the lip, but to be incarnated in every thought, word, deed, that outer elaborations may correspond to the perceived, received, principles within ; that no one is to be hindered from doing anything and everything, harmonious with nature, requisite for the perfection of the same.

A perfect social state cannot be expected at once, composed as it must be of those who have been denied the elements and sources of growth, knowledge, power, because surrounded by ignorance, or hemmed in with an iron grasp. But much, *very* much, may be expected by a true combination of these persons, thus emancipated, by producing beautiful offspring, having symmetrical bodies, sound minds, high moral, religious, spiritual, celestial natures, trained prior to and succeeding birth in harmony with the laws of their being, working with, and not any longer contrary to nature.

Time would fail me, would your patience and leisure allow me, to tell you of the varied and multiplied plans, purposes, for the outlining of a new social state, as transmitted from the noble men and women, who have entered into finer, and consequently higher conditions of life, through their well chosen and inestimable medium, John M. Spear. These manuscripts are now in process of publication; I will enclose with this a " Prospectus," which will give you a clear idea of the nature and character of the prospective volume.

I have also the pleasure of forwarding you this day, the accompanying " Address to the World," which will give you a specimen of the addresses we are daily receiving from the spirit life, also somewhat unfold to you the work in hand.

It will give you unmeasurable happiness to be thus assured, that the great object, for which you have so nobly devoted your long life, is at last to be realised, by the founding of a colony, here in the new world, which shall, by the blessing of Almighty God, be the deliverer of all nations, kindreds, tribes, tongues, upon the face of the earth, from their present inharmonious, warring, hopeless condition; thus beginning at a single point, so shall eventually be described that mighty circle, which shall enclose *all*, in one common brotherhood, one family, having one purpose, one Father, speaking one language. Thus and thus only shall come that blessed hour when the will of God shall be done on earth as it is done in heaven.

For this purpose I have dedicated all I have, am, or hope to be, while my life shall be continued on the shores of time, and when my work has ended here, may I awake in a higher sphere, with all my faculties still consecrated to the elevation, redemption of those I shall no longer behold with mortal eyes.

JOHN M. SPEAR.

Mrs. A. E. Newton and other dear friends, unite, in sending you best wishes, for your present and future peace and happiness,

Allow me to subscribe myself,

Yours in serving a common humanity,

ELIZA J. KENNY.

P.S.—I am located here for a few months, my permanent place of residence being Salem, Mass., W.S.A.

AN ADDRESS TO THE WORLD.

" Mountains interposed make enemies of nations.
Lands intersected by a narrow frith abhor each other."

How sad to the contemplative mind is the present condition of the
inhabitants of this earth.   Almost every person, town, clique,
clan, nation, is seeking its individual interest separate from the
good and interest of all.   " Mine and thine" are written in legi-
ble characters upon all things.   There is no common weal, no
deep and abiding interest in man as man, irrespective of nation,
complexion, sex ; hence, vast sums are requisite to sustain a few
millions of people.   That which man needs now to know is how
best to combine his interest with the interest of others, and how
to render labour attractive and consequently agreeable.

It is felt to be wise to present, in a brief form, an outline of certain essential things, which when understood, observed, will tend
in a large degree to unite man to his fellow man.   In entering into
a subject of such intense interest, there are many minor points
which cannot, in the nature of things, be presented.   Should that
work be undertaken, a volume, rather than a brief paper would
be requisite.

Man has certain natural wants.   Unless these wants are supplied, he is a restless, uneasy, dissatisfied being.   He wants the
following things.   First, a soil on which he can stand, to which
he has a clear, incontestable, permanent right.   Secondly, he
wants a comfortable and convenient shelter erected on that soil.
Thirdly, he wants certain essential sustenances, and comfortable
garments.   Fourthly, he wants what may be justly termed, in its
broadest sense, *home*.   Fifthly, he wants around him, within convenient distance, agreeable and attractive society or neighbourhood.   Sixthly, he wants certain surroundings which shall in
their tendency promote his bodily health, mental growth, and affectional unfolding.   Seventhly, he wants to be entirely free from
any fearful forebodings, in respect to any future life to which he
may be destined.   Give him these, in a high, pure, broad sense,
he is in the enjoyment of what is absolutely essential to his purest
and divinest conditions.   Give him any six of these, cut off the
seventh, and to that extent he is unsatisfied, longing, struggling,
to obtain that which he has not.   Now the mind of the intelligent reader should look at these points as a whole, that it may
be seen, that they not only embrace the essentials, but that all
and each are needful.   Looking now out upon the world as it is,
with ease it will be discovered that almost everybody is deprived of one, and some of nearly all of these, and it is because
of a lack of these essentials, that man preys upon and devours
his fellow man—'tis a reaching for something which he has not
secured.   Could these natural wants be supplied to man, indi-

vidual wars, tumults among nations and colonies would not be. All efforts to promote universal peace and good will among mankind will, in the very nature of things, fail, until man's natural wants are supplied.

There begins to be a desire among a few philanthropic persons to annihilate war, to induce the nations of the earth to beat their swords into ploughshares, their spears into pruning-hooks, to produce that state of things. when nation shall no longer lift up sword against nation, nor longer learn the art of war. No writer yet has ever estimated the evils which come of war. But whence spring wars and fightings? War is declared between two nations; that declaration is simply an outbreak. The two nations were just as much at war before declaration as after. *Internally* the strife had commenced and the war declared. Wherever an effect is, behind it there lies a cause. Look into a neighbourhood —the cannon may not be there, the sword may not be seen, the fort may not be built, and yet *war* is there; or, enter into a closer relation, the domestic; the parties may not blow out each other's brains, cut off one another's heads; or in any way, with brute force, mangle each other, and yet war is there—'tis a contest between parties—it is a strife to gain something which one or the other has not. Let that domestic circle have a *home*, in a pure sense war could not enter its doors,—let all needful sustenances, garments be at hand as they were wanted, let all the surroundings be consonant with bodily health, mental growth, affectional expanding, and there is nothing to war about. Cut off either of the parties from one of these essentials, no matter which, and war is in that domestic circle. Little things sometimes are useful as illustrations of greater things. Supply a neighbourhood with all these essentials, and war could no more enter there than it could invade the portals of heaven itself. In fact that neighbourhood is heaven. But let some of the neighbours enjoy certain things which are essential to the well being of all, contention, strife, war appear, and these neighbours in some way will attempt to devour one another. The same law obtains in respect to colonies, provinces, states, nations. The American nation, as such, at this present moment, is as much in a state of civil war, as it ever can be. The mere breaking out of a flame on the roof of an edifice is not essential to call it a fire; it may burn internally, consume all the essentials of a dwelling and not be seen on the roof. One may have an internal cancer that is eating out the vitals, 'tis not essential to constitute it a cancer, that it should be seen.

Whence comes war in the American nation? Ans. An entire disregard of the principles upon which it professes to be founded—namely, that man has certain inalienable rights, among which are life, liberty, the pursuit of happiness. Grant man these to their fullest and broadest extent, and he could ask no more. Take his life, deprive him of liberty in any of its forms cut him off from pursuing his happiness in his own way, and he lacks something ; and this lack forms within a restlessness, a longing for, a desire to obtain, and when borne for a certain length of time, until the yoke becomes too heavy, one of the following results appear. First, the oppressed are crushed to the earth, groans, tears, anguish which no tongue can describe, are experienced, or, secondly, the oppressed determine at all hazards to throw off the yoke, and then war, rapine, blood are ; nation is arrayed against nation ; ordinary labours are laid aside ; everything is made to bend to that single point,—emancipation. Commonly the weaker is crushed, or, some slight arbitration may be ; the cause is not removed, and sooner or later, of necessity, there will be another outbreak. 'Tis perfectly futile then to undertake to smooth over things of this character. The parties look for peace, but there is none ; they look for union, but there is none ; they look for harmony, but there is none. In the nature of things there never can be until man's essential wants are supplied. What then, the philanthropist may ask, is to be done ? Shall not efforts be made to promote peace ? Unquestionably. But whosoever undertakes that work needs to ask the parties, what do you want? and when those wants are gratified, the peacemaker may go to bed and sleep until the crack of doom —there is no more for him to do. Until these points shall be made clear to the mind, there cannot be a reasonable expectation of permanent peace in the domestic circle, the neighbourhood, province, state confederations or nations at large. It may be as well then now, as at any future time, to look at the subject of war and peace in this plain, common sense light. It will be seen that if war is settled by mere arbitration, that the settlement cannot be permanent. Why ? Because there is not an internal peace, there is not a divine equanimity ; something is longed for which the parties have not. It were useless longer then to dwell on the *surface* of things, it were wiser to come to an intelligent understanding of man's essential wants, and in the ratio that these are supplied, will internal peace be secured ; eruptions will not appear on the surface.

It may be said that a work of this radical character must proceed very slowly. True. All thorough reformations will be opposed by the existing state of things. In short, parodoxical though it may seem, an effort of this kind to produce peace, will be tantamount to a declaration of war. Philosophically one said, " I came not to send peace on earth, but I came to kindle a fire ;" and that fire is kindled which shall burn the rubbish, separate the dross from the silver, the pure from the impure, the loving from the selfish, the true from the false, the good from the evil, but, what of that ? In view of the end to be reached, namely, permanent and universal peace, these incidentals are little more than the cobweb—comparatively of no consequence—developers they are, helping one to see the true state of things, opening blind eyes, occasionally perhaps breaking a heart, severing tender cords, but as long as the elements of disunion are within there is no union—man sleeps, and beneath him the fire is burning that some time, perhaps in an unexpected moment, the devouring flame appears. Who would risk going to bed at night, knowing that there are flames in the cellar below, which at some time would envelope the whole edifice, and yet this is precisely where the world is at this moment. The weaker nation may not venture to declare war, the stronger will do so, as certainly as one man will try to take advantage of another. In one case it is individualism, in another nationalism. Nations struggle for a season, become weary, lives are destroyed, property confiscated, millions of hearts broken, the combatants retire for a little time, enter into some sort of negociation, peace is declared; externally, all seems quiet, but internally the fires are burning, and why? Because man's essential wants are not supplied. Turn the subject over as the statesman may, investigate it as the philanthropist will, it all comes back to that single point, something, somewhere, by somebody is wanted; and growing out of that, there is struggle or effort to obtain it. If another has it a struggle to grasp it and so wars are. The true friends of peace are they who contemplate causes, who form broad, comprehensive plans to remove these causes. In efforts however of this character, to some extent, certain old institutions must be jostled; the foundations on which nations are based must be inspected, broad and practical plans must be presented; 'tis not enough that one see the evil, but there should be an ability to remove it and to substitute therefor that which shall strike at causes, and shall introduce a new state of things, wherein shall dwell harmony, peace, union, love.

Remedies, unless they are broad enough to cover the whole ground are, to say the least, delusive, raise expectations, which not being realized, leave persons often in far worse conditions, than prior to the proposed remedy. The skilful physician, the intelligent surgeon studies first, with care, the condition of his patient, obtains clear views, as far as may be practicable, of causes, and wisely endeavours to remove these. They know full well that if bad matter be left in the system, it will spread, corrupt, and poison, and perhaps eventually endanger the life of the patient. Now evils are not simply to be palliated, but are to be removed entirely from the body politic, else corruption, disease and death, politically speaking, will sooner or later appear. In looking out then upon a subject of this character, it may not be altogether unwise to propose the following interogations. First, is it likely that the oppressors themselves unaided by others will see the wrong they are doing and break off at once therefrom, and commence in a right direction? Secondly, is it likely that the oppressed and downtrodden classes will themselves be able, by any united and systematic effort to intelligently and systematically throw off the yoke under which they are suffering? Or, finally, is it requisite that there should be a third class, who are in comparatively easy conditions, and who can balance between the oppressors and oppressed, and point out clearly the thing or things to be done? Such is the delusive nature of oppression, that the oppressed often hug their chains, and any effort to remove them will be resisted. Interested in continuing things as they now are, the oppressor of course, would not welcome any effort, which, sooner or later, would, in his judgement, affect his personal interest, so that often the person or persons who attempt a labour of this kind may expect to be misjudged by the oppressed on the one hand, misunderstood by the oppressor on the other, so that he works, as it were, between two fires. Now that one may perseveringly engage in a labour of this sort, several qualities are requisite. First, an unfaltering trust in the triumph of Eternal Right; secondly, a deep and abiding interest in the welfare and general progress of human kind; thirdly, an internal prompting which says " Woe is me unless I engage in this effort." These three considerations will lead to that condition of mind usually called prayer. The petitioner, in substance *feels* or says " Show me, oh, show me the work I can do, give me wisdom and strength and I will perform it." In such a case all the emotional faculties are called into exercise—it becomes a work of the heart, and there one stands in an impregnable position—such an one can neither be called off by flatteries, nor intimidated by dangers, but steadily moves on, faithfully, lovingly and intelligently doing the work of each opening hour, each dawning morn or each quiet night, perpetually having a great purpose and so there comes to the labourer a strength of character, an energy of action, a firmness of purpose, corresponding to the work. One of the first things then, which is essential to man's redemption, is to call out, wholly consecrate a class of persons of the character described above—true, such are rarely found. Sometimes a *planet* needs to be explored to find a single person, having that nobleness of life, devotion of heart, purity of thought, divinity of aspiration, that he or she will lay down a life, and yet the pages of the past record the appearance of persons of this unusual character—they are the lights of the world—they shine perhaps dimly in their time, but as man grows up to them, sees their greatness, comprehends the grandeur of their labours, reads the history of their efforts, the world garnishes their tombs and sepulchres, rears its lofty monuments, does homage to them as the benefactors of their day, weeps that they were not better known in their time. That which the world now most needs, and there is little hope of its redemption until that can be done, is, as it were, to generate a new world's Redeemer—one who elementarily shall be able to command the love of a Jesus, the boldness of a Paul, the fidelity of a Daniel, learning of an Aristotle, morals of a Socrates, education of a Plato, intellect of a Webster, eloquence of a Brougham, and the religion of a Madam Guyon. All these elements seem to be essential that one may be suited to the emergencies of the present hour. Such an one would martial his forces, gather around him his armies, call to his aid the distinguished persons of *his* time, nay, would command the interest and call out the influence of distinguished persons of *former* times. Concentrating this power upon a single body, such an one would go forth armed with the panoply of love, truth, wisdom, become a grand organizer, place persons where they belonged, show them how to combine their efforts, how to actualize their ideas, discover the laws of attraction and affinity, so that labours would be natural and agreeable. Looking at a subject of this sort, one asks, how can a work of this magnitude be executed ? The answer is, the friends of man must unite. Persons in comparatively easy circumstances, persons who can change their position, location, who can devote their energies to a work of this sort, should plant themselves on a spot dedicated to freedom, to the interests of humanity, to all that is high and holy within, cultivate their finer faculties to highest possible extent. Search should be made in different nations for persons having within themselves the right elements ; these should come together, found a colony ; these should construct a model society, should create a state of things, wherein it would be practicable, for such an one to be generated, born, reared, expanded, cultivated. Separated, to some extent, from unfavourable influences, seeing the world as it is, knowing its wants, something might through that single instrumentality be accomplished, that would not only aid man in the present, but would advance his interest in the future. The world's reformers then must, sooner or later, see the need of starting a work of this character. Unquestionably the American nation is the place above all others to commence a work of this sort. Domain can easily be had, economically purchased in central positions. Whoever then shall see that this is the work to be done will focalize their efforts in that particular direction. At first, efforts, of necessity, will be of a rude and simple character, yet having the right elements, commanding the heart, head and hands, the little tree may be planted, watered with tears, call forth an intense interest, bring out the diviner and emotional faculties, lift the soul up to God, cultivate the affections, and the enterprise shall be, as it were, a dear child struggling into birth ; and when the hour shall come then plans of a broad, philanthropic and buisness character shall be unfolded, then easy and natural steps can be taken. Already a single person has journeyed somewhat extensively in the New World, teaching these doctrines, unfolding these principles, declaring practical plans, calling out eminent persons. The Old World and the New need to combine their efforts. At a favorable moment some few choice persons will leave the New World, land on the shores of the Old, with a view of interesting persons of different nations in this branch of labour. Sir, the Spirit World looks to you; it knows your untiring fidelity; it rejoices that such an one has lived to ripe old age; it sees you busily arranging your papers; preparing your departure to a higher and diviner state. It forwards this paper to you at this moment, leaving it to your judgment to incorporate it among your published documents, or, to read it to such parties, as in your judgment, will comprehend and appreciate teachings of this philanthropic character. The Spirit World takes this opportunity through a leading communicating mind to express its confidence in your judgment, its reliance on your fidelity, its consciousness of your desire to aid man as man.

It moreover takes this opportunity to state, that persons of an intelligent and moral cast are influencing your mind, leading you onward in the steps you are now taking. Should this document, Sir, meet your approval, should it in your judgment, be wise for some choice persons to visit the Old World with a view of interchanging thoughts, feelings, actions, unquestionably you will find highest delight in facilitating an effort of that character. At all events an epistle from your pen will be welcomed by the person to whom this paper was directly transmitted.

Letter and Spiritual Communication from Samuel Clarke.

Beaverton, Boone Co., Ill., U.S., Oct. 14th 1856.

DEAR SIR,—

I never heard your name nor the right foundation of the principles that you are advocating to the world until a few weeks ago I came into my house at noon and there lay your *Millennial Gazette,* but the cover not removed, and as I took it into my hand to open it a divine spiritual influence dropt over me, as if a mantle of light and harmony was cast over me by some invisible power. It vibrated through my entire system, and by that I knew I held something holy and true in my hand. I opened and great was my delight there to find the principles plainly laid before me, which I had been trying to advocate in public for sometime past, with spiritualism combined, having been a medium some ten months, speaking in public, languages that I do not understand, and sometimes no person present understood not even one word. I have seen spirits and had them touch me, have seen the most beautiful visions, and healed the sick by laying on of hand by the same invisible power.

I openly and with spirit help publicly lecture for the advancement of *union* and *spiritual truth*, which I am persuaded must go hand and soul together, for one is the body and the other the spirit. It is the very God-sent truths that will redeem the inhabitants of this sinful earth, made full of sin and shame by man himself, by the wrong direction of the free will God has given us for our individual existence and for our progressive happiness.

When I look around on this broad and goodly land, and see the strife and wretchedness that general robbery or individual interest hath brought on us, and is still making things worse and worse, it makes my very spirit fain within. Then I rouse up again with renewed vigor, and battle with sectarianism and individual interest. The enemies of those blessed truths call me insane, but cannot face the same truth in public. They have tried every way to put it down, but cannot. They are sorely troubled because of the signs that follow truth. They have told the people that the day of signs and miracles is a long time past, —but that is not so, for if we follow God's natural laws, the same results will be brought about now that was performed eighteen hundred years ago.

The believers in Spiritualism in the United States now number more than two millions. The manifestations are spreading fast, and numbers are daily convinced that departed spirits do communicate with us in the body, or that there is a certain connection between us here and our spiritual friends and relatives gone before to a higher state of perfection. Our growth in numbers is fast, but without union or a general brotherhood in outward matter we cannot be happy or harmonious and permanently established in a more perfect state. And before the will of the Creator can be done on earth as it is in heaven (or in other words that the material must be governed by the same laws of unity as the spiritual,) we must be all united in one common brotherhood, and our material governors and lawmakers must act the part of fathers, that the good of one may be the good of the whole, and the whole as one. I am well persuaded that in the spiritual existence there are laws to that effect, and that we shall find it out when we are changed from our mortal bodies and enter our spiritual bodies, which is at the time we call death. Death is the wrong name—it is life, or a resurrection from death unto life.

I will conclude by thanking you for your kindness in sending me your *Millennial Gazette*, hoping you will continue sending its numbers (the last was No. 7) to me. But I should love to see and hear thee, oh thou noble champion of truth. One favour I ask. If you are taken to the purer spiritual life before me, then throw thy holy influence on me, to convince the sceptical, and to help me speak the truth, impress me with your ideas. This you can do on a medium, by and through the laws of unity which exist between individual spirits of pure harmony. **Ripe-**

ness is near on you for the change, but your great and benevolent mind will have a more powerful influence in the cause of humanity, and a happy and busy time will it be for you, when you will be employed for more powerful and greater efforts in the same cause of love and truth, though invisible to the material eye of the worldly man.

Courage then, my father, my brother in truth and love. Your work in this cause is not ended when you go above, but on streams of light the thoughts of thy mind will be showered down, to help us loose the chains with which poor men are bound.

Please answer this by publishing or otherwise, which will be a favour to me, as I have relatives and friends in England.

I remain yours in truth,

SAMUEL CLARK.

To Robert Owen, Esq.,
      Sevenoaks Park, Sevenoaks,
           London,
              Old England.

Excuse all errors, for I never had an education at school. Was born in old England and lived there eighteen years.

Mr. Robert Owen,—London, England.

You have pain in your right side, extending from the liver to your kidney, rather acute, just above the hips, and so in your spinal column, the calf of your leg aches—with a curious sensation about the ears.

The above is the pain you are suffering or have suffered.

S. CLARK, *Medium*

[It is true I had this pain in the right side and the sensation n the left leg.—ROBERT OWEN]

[*See Supplement for advertisements of Congress, &c..*]

London:—Published by the Author at 16, Great Windmill Street, Haymarket : and sold by Holyoake, 147, Fleet Street ; Truelove, 240, Strand; Goddard, 14, Great Portland Street, Cavendish Square; and all Booksellers.

Registered for Foreign Transmission.

Supplement to No. 10.

ROBERT OWEN'S
MILLENNIAL GAZETTE;

EXPLANATORY OF THE PRINCIPLES AND PRACTICES BY WHICH, IN PEACE, WITH TRUTH, HONESTY, AND SIMPLICITY, THE NEW EXISTENCE OF MAN UPON THE EARTH MAY BE EASILY AND SPEEDILY COMMENCED.

" The character of Man is formed *for* him, and *not by* him !"

No. 10A.]   JANUARY 1st, 1857.   [PRICE 6D.

A NEW YEAR'S GIFT OF INESTIMABLE VALUE TO THE POPULATION OF THE WORLD THROUGH FUTURITY.

NOTICE.

[*Editors of Periodicals, and those who disinterestedly desire to promote permanently the happiness of the human race, irrespective of colour, country, class, or creed, will assist to circulate the following.*]

A CONGRESS of the advanced minds of the world, to consider the best immediate practicable mode of gradually superseding the false, ignorant, unjust, cruel, wicked, and most irrational system of society, opposed to the righteous laws of God and nature, and which hitherto has been the only system known to man,—by the true, enlightened, just, merciful, good, and rational system of society, in strict accordance with the all-wise laws of God and nature, will be opened at noon precisely, on the 14th of May next, in St. Martin's Hall, Long Acre, London, the present metropolis of the world, — when will be explained the outline of the change which is highly to benefit all of the human race through futurity, and to injure none, even while passing through its first or transition generation, preliminary to the attainment of its full change, which will be the commencement of the long-promised millennium.

This work is too important,—involving, as it does, the everlasting well-being, well-doing, and happiness of all nations and people,—to be explained, discussed, and understood for immediate practical action in less than many days. The Congress will therefore be continued day by day, from ten a.m., to three p.m., until this great work of reformation for the lasting advantage of all of humankind shall be brought to a satisfactory termination.

Different days will be appropriated to explain and consider the interests of the leading classes as now existing throughout society, and how those interests are to be promoted by the change from the false and evil to the true and good system, for new forming the character, physically and mentally, of the human race, and for governing it on principles of impartial justice and universal attraction.

In order that this subject, which includes the permanent good of all parties in all countries, may be well practically understood by all, the following invitations are given to the respective divisions of society, as addressed, to be present on the days named, when the interests of their respective classes will be explained, examined, and discussed.

In a Programme of the intended business of the Congress, and which will be published previous to the 14th of May, the day which will be devoted more especially to the consideration of the subjects immediately connected with the classes invited, will be stated for the benefit of those whose time will not admit of continued attendance at the Congress.

It is hoped that the interests involved will appear too important to be unattended to by any class thus invited.

ROBERT OWEN.

December, 1856.

A CARD

To the conductors of the Periodical Press, and to the popular Writers of the civilised world.

GENTLEMEN AND LADIES,—

You have now much influence for good and evil over the public mind, and the path will be opened to you by which you may greatly increase your powers for good, and may allow your influence for evil to die its natural death.

I therefore invite you to meet me in St. Martin's Hall, London, at eleven o'clock, A.M., on Tuesday the 12th of May next, previous to the Congress of advanced minds to commence at noon on Thursday the 14th of May, when I will explain to you how you may apply your powers to assist to form a superior, good, wise, and happy character for the human race, yourselves of course included, and may thus become most efficient agents to gradually and peaceably terminate this false, ignorant, unjust, cruel, irrational, and now thoroughly wornout old system of society, for forming the character and governing the human race.

Your true friend, ROBERT OWEN.

Sevenoaks Park, Sevenoaks, England.

December, 1856.

TO THE SOVEREIGN POWERS OF THE CIVILISED WORLD.

The glorious period has arrived when the crysalis state of man shall cease and his miseries terminate.

Hitherto the germs of his rational faculties have been in a state of continual effervescence, preparing to develop his spiritual, moral, and mental powers, to enable him, at the time appointed by nature, to burst his crysalis shell of ignorance, and to come forth in all the true powers of humanity, a good, wise, and happy being, cordially and permanently united with all of humankind, and merciful to the greatest extent practicable to all.

Your safety and well being, and the future progress and happiness of your offspring, are deeply involved in this change, glorious to you and to all humanity through every succeeding age.

I therefore invite you to send your most talented representatives, possessing firm integrity of character, to assist at the London Congress of advanced minds, commencing on Thursday the 14th of May next, at noon, in St. Martin's Hall, Long Acre, London, to consider the best peaceable practical measures to change this crysalis or infant and preliminary state of human existence, for the full, true, and physically and mentally harmonious life—a life which will perpetually increase in these respects and also in knowledge, goodness, wisdom, and happiness.

Well may you rejoice that this long looked for and much desired period has come in your day, and at this juncture, to prevent untold miseries to yourselves, your children, and the myriads yet unborn.

ROBERT OWEN.

Sevenoaks Park, Sevenoaks,
December, 1856.

A CARD

To the leading Statesmen of the civilised world.

GENTLEMEN,—

I invite you to attend the London Congress of advanced minds, to meet on Thursday the 14th of May next, in St. Martin's Hall, London, when I will solve to you the great problem, which for past ages has occupied the attention and deep consideration of the best of your class in all countries,—that is, —" The practical measures to ensure perpetual progress and " happiness to the human race, and to unite them as one family " in a never ending cordial brotherhood, in which all shall be

" made to become through life good, wise, and happy, and peace
" shall for ever prevail over the earth."

The time for the commencement of this glorious change for
all is near at hand.

Your true friend,
ROBERT OWEN.

Sevenoaks Park, Sevenoaks,
    December, 1856.

TO THE ARISTOCRACY OF BIRTH, TALENT, AND WEALTH, OF THE WORLD.

Gentlemen,—

A great change is coming over the world, which will give you
substantial and healthy enjoyments of life, instead of the superficial appearances of them.   By this change you will have truth
instead of falsehood, affection instead of flattery and mercenary
service.   You will have substantial rational enjoyment of the
use of all wealth, without dishonesty to others, without conflict,
contests, or competition, and a superior character for all of you
and your descendents.

I therefore invite you to attend the Congress of advanced
minds in St. Martin's Hall, London, to commence on Thursday the 14th of May next, at noon, when I will explain to
you how the true aristocracy of birth, talent, and wealth, are
to be attained and permanently maintained through all succeeding generations.

Your true friend,
ROBERT OWEN.

Sevenoaks Park, Sevenoaks,
    December, 1856.

A CARD

*To the Members of the Civil and Military Professions in
Europe, Asia, and America.*

Gentlemen,—

I invite you to attend the Congress to be held in St. Martin's
Hall, Long Acre, London, to commence at noon, on Thursday
the 14th of May next, when I will explain to you a new mode
by which to form from birth a new and very superior character for the human race—a character which, after the pre-

sent generation, shall gradually supersede the necessity for the continuance of any one profession.   And I will then also explain the means by which your present position shall be permanently improved and elevated, to an extent now unimagined by any of your class.

By this change your present difficulties and annoyances shall be overcome and no more experienced.

Your true friend,
ROBERT OWEN.

Sevenoaks Park, Sevenoaks,
 December, 1856.

A CARD

To the Clergy of all ranks and denominations.

MOST REVEREND SIRS,—

Having called a Congress of the advanced minds of the world, to consider the *best peaceable practical means* to *change* the *existing ignorant, false, unjust, cruel,* and most *irrational system* of *society*, for the true system for forming the character of and governing the human race, I deem it a first duty to the character and position you have held so long, and continue to hold among the nations of the earth, to invite you, in the pure Christian spirit of charity and love for our race, to attend this Congress, which will commence at noon on Thursday the 14th day of May next, in St. Martin's Hall, Long Acre, London,—at which Congress I will explain to you the plain, simple, practical means, by which you may immediately greatly improve your present position,—which position the signs of the times indicate to be precarious, without some substantial change in the cast of society.

This invitation is given to the leading minds of the Jewish, Christian, and Mahommedan, and all other priesthoods, with a view of explaining to them at such meeting the means of uniting them in a sincere bond of union and of brotherly love, in the spirit of undefiled universal charity and kindness.   Also the easily-to-be-executed scientific means to accomplish in practice the real object for which all priesthoods were originally established,—that is, to make the human race good, wise, and happy.

You will all be delighted to learn, by the explanations which will be given, that the means have been discovered by which all hatred, jealousies, and unkind feelings, between the members of different religions and different denominations of the same religion, may be made to terminate for ever, and all may be induced hereafter to teach and to preach, only and on all occasions, the great advantage of, and now the strong necessity for, the daily and hourly practice, in all sincerity, of an unfailing spirit of love and charity, to be always evident in the tone of voice and conduct, in such manner that no one could mistake the true character of the spirit within.

This Congress is called with the intention to change the destiny of the human race, from its present most irrational state in all departments of life, to a new existence, in which all from birth will be made to become rational and consistent in mind and practice, and ultimately good, wise, united, and happy.

Desiring your peace and prosperity in this world, and immortal happiness hereafter, I remain, most reverend sirs,

Your true friend,

ROBERT OWEN.

Sevenoaks Park, Sevenoaks,
    December, 1856.

A CARD

To the Professional Teachers of the human race in all nations.

GENTLEMEN,—

I invite you to attend the Congress of advanced minds, to commence at noon, on Thursday the 14th of May next, in St. Martin's Hall, London. This Congress is called to change the destiny of the human race, from its present language of falsehood and conduct of deception, to a new condition, in which its practice will be the language of truth only, the conduct honest without exception.

This glorious change in the condition of humanity will arise from a new formation of character from birth. The easy practical mode of its attainment I will explain to you at the meeting now proposed, to enable you to take, as you ought, a prominent part at the Congress mentioned, because the true formation of character is the highest and most important object to be attained in the most advanced state of society.

Desiring that your arduous yet most important duties may be made most efficient to establish goodness and happiness among all of our race, I am faithfully your true friend,

ROBERT OWEN.

Sevenoaks Park, Sevenoaks,
    December, 1856.

A CARD

To the leading Members of the Money, Commercial, Manufac-
turing, and Trading interests of the civilised world.

GENTLEMEN,—

I invite you to attend the Congress of advanced minds, to
commence at noon on Thursday the 14th of May next, in St.
Martin's Hall, Long Acre, London, at which I will explain to you
a plain and simple mode by which to terminate your risks and
difficulties respecting the acquisition of wealth, and by which
means you may in perpetuity attain, without risk, all the highest
substantial enjoyments which wealth can give.

This invitation is given that by the knowledge which will then
be developed, you may be prepared to take a beneficial active part
in the Congress to change the destiny of the human race, from
its present ignorant, false, and most irrational state, to the
true permanent condition of humanity, in which from birth all
will be made to become rational or consistent in mind and practice, and ultimately, without exceptions, good, wise, and happy.

You will all rejoice to learn the beautiful simplicity by which
the results stated will be attained in practice.

Desiring your permanent prosperity and happiness, believe me
to be

Your true friend,

ROBERT OWEN.

Sevenoaks Park, Sevenoaks,
    December, 1856.

TO THE LEADING PRACTICAL AGRICULTURISTS,
HORTICULTURISTS, GARDENERS, SURVEYORS,
DRAINERS, CIVIL ENGINEERS, ARCHITECTS, BUIL-
DERS, AND MEN OF SCIENCE IN SOUND, HEATING,
LIGHTING, VENTILATING, AND COOKING, OF ALL
NATIONS.

FELLOW MEN !—

I invite you to attend the Congress to be held in St. Martin's Hall, Long Acre, London, to commence at noon on
Thursday the 14th of May next, when I will place before you
the outline of the model of new surroundings, in which ultimately to place all of our race, varied in some particulars according to climate and natural localities. Surroundings in which
it will be easy in practice to form all born and living within

them to become superior, practical, full-formed men and women, who through life shall become good, wise, united to their race, rational, and happy.

You will then see the great necessity which exists to reconstruct the new combinations of surroundings over the world, on new sites, leaving the existing random and Babel arrangements of society to die their natural death, like the old graveled roads as they were superseded by railways.

By this change, most simple in principle and practice, the entire population of the world will be ultimately, when the surroundings shall be completed, more easily well-governed and made wise and happy, than any single parish of three thousand souls can be under the insane teachings and surroundings now existing in all the nations of the earth.

You will also discover that there will be plenty of the most useful and beautiful work to execute for some time to come, although all nations and all provinces in each nation were immediately to make the arrangements to commence the change.

Your true friend,
ROBERT OWEN.

Sevenoaks Park, Sevenoaks,
   December, 1856.

A CARD

To the more advanced minds of the Operative Classes, Masters, and Workmen, of every description, who can attend from all nations.

FELLOW WORKMEN,—

I invite you to meet me in the Literary, Scientific, and Social Institution, John Street, Fitzroy Square, London, on Sunday the 17th of May next, at ten o'clock in the morning, in continuance of the Congress of advanced minds which will commence on the 14th of the same month in St. Martin's Hall, Long Acre, London,—and I will then explain to you the practical means by which you can much improve your own condition, secure the prosperity and independence of your children, and elevate their characters so as to become in the next generation and through all succeeding ages, on an equality with the best and most valuable of the human race.

It is for want of this knowledge that more than nine-tenths of the human race are no better than slaves or servants to bad and most injurious surroundings, which keep them and their masters, and the remaining tenth, in worse than Egyptian darkness.

Many of you know the time and attention which I have given to solve this great problem for the human race, now happily accomplished, to secure the well-being and well-doing of all, and to harmonise in future the proceedings of all governments and peoples.

Your old true friend,
ROBERT OWEN.

Sevenoaks, Kent. England,
December, 1856.

A CARD

To the Members of the Parliament of the British Empire, and the Members of the Congress of the Empire of the United States of North America.

Gentlemen, Senators, and Legislators—the British Parliament and United States Congress—the two most free public assemblies in the world, and who have great influence over the present destinies of our race, and may have much greater influence over all coming generations.

I invite you to attend the Congress of advanced minds, to be commenced at noon an the 14th of May next, in St. Martin's Hall, London, when I will explain to you the plain, straightforward, simple practical measures, easy, with your means at command, of immediate general execution, by which universal peace shall be established for ever between all nations and peoples, and by which in the next and succeeding generations all of humankind shall be cordially united as children of one enlightened, well trained, educated, employed, placed, and governed family,—all members of which, according to age, being one in spirit, principle, and practice. And thus will you become the favoured means of establishing the harmony and happiness of the world unbroken through all future ages. And in these results there will be no mistake.

Your true friend,
ROBERT OWEN.

Sevenoaks Park, Sevenoaks, Kent.
England. December, 1856.

A CARD

To the Spiritualists and Socialists of the world.

FRIENDS,—

Your future prospects are glorious,—but having had your characters formed under an ignorant, false, unjust, wicked, cruel, and most irrational system of society, -always opposed to true

c

humanity, your antecedents in life have been unfavourable to create union of mind or action, and without these there can be no general and permanent happiness for any portion of our race.

The good and kind Spirits who have disappeared from our sights who come to communicate with us through *media* and to give us the best knowledge which they have acquired in both worlds, by retaining for a longer or shorter period, while in the second world, the early imbibed prejudices of the first, have tended so far rather to increase than decrease disunion among Spiritualists. See the present various sectarian and sceptical divisions among Spiritualists. While the early and continued habits acquired by the Socialists, so called, tend to keep them also divided, so as to prevent mental or practical union, or cordial co-operation in the business of life. See the St. Simonians, Fourierites, Icarians, Ballouites, and Allhusenites, &c., &c.

Without union in mind and practice the population of the world must continue, as heretofore and now, a Babel of irrational contention and confusion.

I therefore invite you to meet me on Sunday the 24th of May next, at seven o'clock in the evening, in the Literary Institution, John Street, Fitzroy Square, London, when I will explain to you the only means practicable or possible by which universal cordial union can be attained and made permanent among our race.

Your true friend,
ROBERT OWEN.

Sevenoaks Park, Sevenoaks,
  December, 1856.

A CARD.

To the Republicans and Democrats of the World.

FRIENDS AND FELLOW REFORMERS,

You ultimately desire the peace of the world,—a good, useful, and superior character for all,—a just practical equality for all,—abundance of unadulterated wealth for all,—and a permanent cordial union among the human race.

Now Republicanism and Democracy, or any political change under the existing false and evil system of society, will never effect these objects, which with you are the ardent desire of all good and enlightened men. No republic, ancient or modern, presents an example to be followed. Those who formed the constitution of the United States were among the most practical disinterested men that the false and evil system has produced in any age of the world,—and democracy under the present ignorant and unnatural system for forming character and governing the population of the world, could not improve upon their well considered results as a republic. Yet what is, at this day, the state and condition of this pet republic, and what kind of character has it given to this new and latest Democracy?

It is not by fierce democracy or republicanism that the population of the world can ever be made to become good, wealthy, united, wise, and happy, or rational in mind or practice.

I invite you as brother reformers, having the same great object in view, to attend the London Congress of the advanced minds of the world, to consider the best peaceable means to change the false, cruel, and insane system of society, as now existing over the world, for the true, good, and happy system for our race, and I will then, on one of the days especially appointed for this purpose, explain to you how, in a peaceable and rational manner, without calling any of the bad and inferior passions of humanity into action, all your great and good objects may be easily obtained and secured for ever.

Your true Friend,
ROBERT OWEN.

Sevenoaks Park, December, 1856.

A CARD.

To the Atheists and Sceptics of the World.

FRIENDS,—Men of mind, of thought, and who desire to discover the truth upon important subjects.

You have been trained, educated, and surrounded from your birth, by a false, irrational, and opposing system. You have discovered its falsehood, irrationality, and opposition to human happiness, and have therefore come to the conclusion that the universe has no supreme eternal intelligence, and you feel no fellowship for those who are compelled by the laws of their nature to differ from you on this subject.

You deem the ignorance, evil passions, and miseries of the human race, evidence of the want of goodness, wisdom, or power in the eternal cause, or in the laws which govern the universe, and which perpetually compose, decompose, and recompose all the elements within it, and you therefore conclude that man as he now exists upon the earth is the most advanced sentient existence yet created.

To dissipate all opposing feelings between man and man, and to prepare the way for a happy future existence of our race upon the earth, I invite you to attend the London Congress of advanced minds, to consider the best peaceable means to change the present false system of society for the true, when, on a day especially appointed for this purpose during the Congress, which will commence on the 14th of May next, in St. Martin's Hall, London, at noon, I will explain to you the great evils which have arisen through past ages to the best of the human race, in consequence of the difference of opinion upon the subjects previously mentioned, and on others which as yet cannot be referred to known ascertained facts, and respecting which it is therefore most unwise in any party to create anger or irritation on account of this difference of opinion, which ought only to engage a pleasant, useful, and friendly investigation of matters not yet agreed to, for want of demonstrable facts, but which disagreement of opinion, in a true and rational state of society, will not create a particle of angry or unpleasant feelings between any parties who may be compelled by their convictions to hold or imagine one set of opinions on these subjects more true than another set. When men shall be made to become wise, these irrational feelings will be unknown.

Your true Friend,

ROBERT OWEN.

Sevenoaks Park, Sevenoaks,
    December, 1856.

THE FUTURE NEW RATIONAL AND HAPPY STATE OF SOCIETY. AND THE CONGRESS OF MAY, 1857.

In the future new rational and happy state of society, it will be always *consistent* with itself and with *all facts.*

It will be universally known that the Divine Principle of the universe, by whatever name called, is the Power acting through or in nature, which does all that is done ; and all men should be trained to have love and charity for each other, and to wait with patience until more facts shall have been discovered to disclose to humanity this Divine Principle and the mode of its operation, —if ever discoverable by humanity.

In the meantime all that is necessary for man to be taught by society is the unchanging laws of his being and of all humanity, —how to be happy himself and to make others so, in order that all mankind may permanently live in harmony and may rationally enjoy their existence.

In this new state of existence, and new system of society, it will be known that nature and society immediately form the character of everyone, and that now society may form a good and useful character from birth for all of every colour and country, and by common-sense arrangements may continually create more wealth for all than will supply their utmost wants and wishes, when the human race shall be rationally placed, trained, educated, employed, and governed.   And it will be for the everlasting highest interest of all that the entire of the human race should be so placed, trained, educated, employed, and governed.

The progress latterly made in general knowledge and in the practical sciences, is now abundant to create the surroundings by which all may gradually be so placed, trained, educated, employed, and governed, and humanity be thus elevated to a new phase, in which all will be secured in a superior happy existence, peace will be perpetual, and harmony will for ever reign over the earth.

In this new phase of existence for the human race, the following changes will arise.

There will be *real liberty* for everyone, a *true cordial fraternity* throughout the entire population of the earth, and a *just practical equality*, according to age and capacity, in education, condition, and position.

All will know that man's physical, intellectual, moral, spiritual, and practical qualities, or his entire character, is formed *for* him.

All will know how, with the certainty of a law of nature, this character may be well formed, so as to be always beneficial, and never injurious to society and to himself.

The surroundings of the population of the world will be always superior, and ever improving as knowledge increases.

The classification of society will be of ages, and there will be no other class.

The population of the world will be separated and re-aggregated into the most manageable masses, for each one to be the best cared for from birth, the best trained and educated, employed, and governed.

Such masses will consist of men, women, and children, in their natural proportions, from one thousand, to three thousand as a maximum.

These masses will form united family commonwealths.

These united family commonwealths will be federatively united in close and cordial bonds of union with each other over the world :—a cordial federation of all nations having previously been made.

Consequently there will be one nation, one people, one government, one code of laws, one language, one religion, one classification of ages, one classification of employments according to age, and one universal desire and action, to promote each other's excellence and happiness, irrespective of colour, country, creed, or class, or of any difference, physical or mental, while these continue during the progress of change from the old to the full new system of society over the world.

The one nation and one people will occupy the whole earth as their for ever entailed estate.

The government will be of age, easily to be arranged to be

made fully effective for all purposes of governing a population, all made to become from birth, good, wise, and with all their natural wants fully supplied, and therefore always happy.

The code of laws will be the unchanging laws of God and nature, uninterfered with by any of the ignorant and absurd laws of men.

The language will be the Anglo-Saxon, now so widely spread over the earth.

The religion will be the worship of God and nature, by promoting to the extent of our power the excellence and happiness of our race.

The classification of the population of the world will be by age.

First class.—Infants to one year of age.

Second class.—Infants from one to *three* inclusive.

Third class,—from three to five inclusive.

Fourth class,—from five to ten inclusive.

Fifth class,—from ten to fifteen inclusive.

Sixth class,—from fifteen to twenty inclusive.

Seventh class,—from twenty to thirty inclusive.

Eighth class,—from thirty to forty inclusive.

Ninth class,—from forty to fifty inclusive.

Tenth class,—from fifty to fifty-five.

Eleventh class,—from fifty-five to sixty.

Twelfth class,—sixty and upwards.

These classes will form the natural inequality or true division of the population of the world,—made to be so by superior training and education from birth, physically, intellectually, morally, spiritually, and practically,—knowing society by regular classified experience through all its stages, as they had previously advanced from age to age.

These classes will be placed within surroundings entirely new, according to the divisions of age, but each surrounding will be purposely devised to promote the excellence and happiness of each, to the highest points that the knowledge and means of society when united will admit. The world will therefore be composed of human surroundings, new in their combinations, and ultimately to exclude one injurious or inferior surrounding over the earth.

The first class, or infants during the first year, will be with the mother, assisted by one well instructed and experienced in infant training. No inferior surrounding to be seen by the infant.

The second class from one to three to be in the first infant training school. This school to be superintended by superior persons in a knowledge of the infant wants, and of the means to supply them without punishment, and always to exhibit the spirit of pure love and charity in voice, manner, and action. This class, in addition to being carefully trained in good temper, habits, and manners, will be taught, by inspection and replies to their questions, the use of many of the surroundings in which they will be placed, while their physical, mental, and moral health will be especially attended to. These two years may be made most important in the life of everyone, and if properly directed and superintended will prevent all after difficulties in forming their subsequent character. No parties appear to have any clear conception of the importance of these few years in forming the future character. It may be a true or false foundation,—and who can estimate the difference in value to the individual and to society?

The third class, from three to five, will require similar attention as to physical, mental, and moral health, and to temper, habits, and manners. In this period, knowledge of their surroundings will be extended, and beside their uses, the formation of many of them made by man will be examined by and explained to them. They will also be made familiar with some parts of nature in the gardens, fields, and woods, being in all their walks accompanied by one or more who could give a true explanation to their questions, or say at once that an explanation was unknown or could not yet be given to them until they had acquired more knowledge.

The fourth class, from five to ten, would be equally cared for in respect of physical, mental, and moral health, temper, habits, and manners. But when trained, educated, and treated as described in the three previous classes, there would now be little or no trouble, for they would have been made to become rational children, ready and willing to do whatever could be shown to them to be right and consistent. During this period they would be gradually taught the lighter operations in gardening and horticulture, with the science of botany, and the art of drawing from nature. They would also be gradually taught the lighter domestic operations, and commence to serve the older classes at their meals. Also to become familiar with the u e of such tools as were not beyond their strength and capacity. And they should be now familiarized with seeing the general operations in the workshops, foundries, manufactories, and field operations, all of which should be plainly and fully explained to them, giving each one full liberty for his or her own questions always to be rationally and pleasantly answered. This will also be an important period in the formation of a rational and good character. At the end of this period, without being previously prematurely troubled with reading, writing, or accounting, these children at ten years of age will have a superior character formed, and will possess more real and valuable knowledge than three fourths of the human race now acquire during their lives.

The fifth class, from ten to fifteen, will occupy a period of great progress in the formation of a superior rational character. The processes commenced in the fourth class will be continued in this, in which reading, writing, and numbering will commence, with a full understanding of their use and relative importance. They will in this class be taught the rudiments of all the sciences, and they will be informed of the extent known in each of them, and during this period the peculiar genius or talent of each will be developed, so as to be subsequently beneficially cultivated and applied for the advantage of society, and for his or her own gratification and happiness. In this period they will also become active operators in the general business of their family commonwealths, and by its termination, their judgment, corrected by experience, will be somewhat cultivated to know something of themselves, of humanity in general, and also of natural objects and of the laws of nature, so as to enable them advantageously to commence the sixth class.

The sixth class, from fifteen to twenty, will study with advantage the past history of their race, will perceive their infant and undeveloped state,—their fightings, their opposing religions and wild superstitions, with their irrational notions of themselves, and their consequent irrational laws, governments, classifications of society, and modes of creating wealth. And they will be taught by their own experience the irrational and absurd notions and practices of all tribes and peoples in their ever failing attempts to form a good, wise, and happy character for the rising generation. The cause of their innumerable mistakes, errors, and miseries, will become glaringly obvious to those now made rational full-formed men and women, who will pity the sufferings which their predecessors have for so many generations experienced. These new formed rational men and women will however be so well informed as to know, that all that has been, is, or shall be done throughout the universe, has proceeded, proceeds, and will proceed, from the highest intelligence, eternally existing, or from an eternal law of necessity, adapting all things to their existing state,—and therefore that the past has been necessary to produce the present, as the present is to produce the future,—and consequently, on either supposition, that the best has been, is, and will be done throughout the universe, that the creating elements will admit. They will not, however, quarrel about that which is yet hidden from their finite powers,—but will wait adtiently for new devolopments and more light to direct their knowledge aright. In the meantime these rational made men and women will plainly perceive their true path to more knowledge, to rationality, and to happiness. They will know all the wants of their nature, and that true permanent happiness can be attained only by these wants being satisfied. They will know that now all the means amply exist to satisfy these wants at all times for all, and they will know how to apply those means to satisfy their wants in such manner that all will be not only satisfied but permanently highly gratified. During this period they will attain their full rights of men and women, having their separate independent apartments and full rights of individuality. Being thus prepared, they will most advantageously enter upon the seventh class.

The seventh class, from twenty to thirty, who will continue to pursue their progress in the acquisition of the most useful knowledge for practice. This process, with the continued formation of their character, will cease only with life. This class will also be the period for acquiring greater knowledge in the various departments of the business of life, and for taking an active part in all these operations, and in assisting to keep all things within the circle of the family commonwealth in the best repair and highest order They will in this period also acquire an accurate knowledge of the working machinery, which will be introduced into every department of life to the greatest extent practicable, and thus make science the slave and servant of man, instead of, as at present, making men, women, and children, the slaves and servants of science and of dead materials. The misery created in the civilized world, during the last half century especially, by the misapplication of mechanical and chemical science, is beyond human faculties to estimate. The power of these sciences, rightly understood and properly applied to diminish manual operations, is illimitable, and it is gross folly alone now to retain slaves, or to experience the many disadvantages of servants and of all servitude. In this period of life the parties will take an active share in all the manual operations of society, and will be enabled to apply their power to any work which may be required for the benefit of the family commonwealth. With the proper application of the sciences to the every day business of life, four hours application of each per day, to the business of the family commonwealth, will be abundant to over supply its wants, and to keep everything connected with it in high order. The mechanical and chemical power may be kept in action eight hours per day, and superintended by two relays of persons each for four hours. All occupations with such trained and educated companions will be considered as holiday pleasures, necessary for health, and the remainder of each day will be used by all according to their respective tasts and inclinations. Four hours of manual, and eight hours of mechanical daily time, will be required only while the family commonwealths shall be in progress of formation, and to its completion in full working order ; after which, three hours of manual and six hours of mechanical will be more than sufficient to amply supply all the wants of the human race, so that, except the desire of all for an increase of knowledge, the desire itself being a pleasure, all their wishes, as all will be made to become rational in mind and practice, will be gratified to their full extent, and in a manner much superior to anything known under the existing ignorant, false, wicked, unjust, cruel, and most irrational babel state of contending society, not one division or portion of which will withstand unprejudiced or common-sense investigation.

The eighth class, from thirty to forty years of age, will be occupied in all the higher and more difficult departments and business of life, and of instruction for all the junior classes. But the whole business of these family commonwealths, and of their federated union, will be so simplified, that, trained and educated as all will be under this true, rational, and good system of society, it will be an enlightened amusement to every class as they advance to the most matured age.

The ninth class, from forty to fifty, will be engaged in visiting all the federative family commonwealths, giving and receiving knowledge of practical utility as they proceed on their way; and in each commonwealth they will be willingly and affectionately received as members of the family, and treated as such, remaining in each as long as they deemed it necessary, useful, or pleasant, and at the termination of their travels returning to their birth-born commonwealth, unless they prefer to join and end their days in some of their visited commonwealths. As property would be common to all, luggage of any kind to be cumbersome would be unnecessary, because all their wants would be readily supplied in every commonwealth.

The tenth class, from fifty to fifty-five, will be the governing class. The oldest in tha fifty-fifth year to he the acting father of the commonweaith, and the four next of age to him to be his friendly counsellors and assistants. But these in their respective offices will have little to do,—for all will proceed with the regularity of time itself, each assisting all, and all assisting each. No elections, no selections, no contests, except who shall most promote the happiness and rational enjoyment of these commonwealths.

The eleventh claas, from fifty-five to sixty, will constitute a board of elders, to whose final decision every difficulty which may occur in the commonwealth will be referred. This will also be an office of pleasure to fill and sustain for five years.

The twelfth class, sixty and upwards, will be the aristocracy of the new, true, good, and rational system of society, and will have no official duties to perform, but to enjoy their existence according to their own feelings. It is anticipated that when these commonwealths shall be established, and the children of these superior made and happy parents shall commence to form the new rational generations of the human race, life, upon the average, will extend as readily from one hundred to one hundred and forty, as under the present destructive system of life it now extends from sixty to one hundred.

Through every class, justice and common sense require that both sexes should have equal rights ; except that the weaker sex physically, in consequence of being the mothers of the human race, will be treated with more tenderness and consideration, and will through life have the choice of the most desired companions.

All children will be considered to be the children and subjects of the commonwealths, and of priceless value, when trained and educated to become rational and superior citizens of the commonwealth.

The mind, speech, publication, and freedom of action will be unlimited, except when injurious to others.

The right of man over man, or of sex over sex, will not exist in any form, as soon as society shall have passed through the intermediate generation between the irrational and evil and the rational and good state of society, when the surroundings shall be full and perfect.

The intermediate generation will require its own new surroundings, adapted to effect the change from the existing ignorant prejudices, ideas, habits, manners, and conduct, to the elevation of the true and good system, in the most gradual easy mode that will be practicable, to attain this all glorious result in peace and with the least annoyance to all parties and individuals.

All must perceive the impossibility of placing such opposing materials as the present generation has been made to become, on an equality, and to unite them cordially under the same surroundings.

A preliminary and transitory arrangement will be required, in which to place the working classes of the world, to enable society to train and educate their children in mind and manner for the superior state of existence, and to create or build up the surroundings required for the full and perfect rational state of human existence over the earth.

The children trained and educated in the transition and preliminary state will be at maturity so superior in mind and conduct to any existing class in any country, that all will desire that their children should derive the advantages which will be given to all children even in the transition state, and thus with the children of every class, by desire of their parents, be trained and educated together, to form the first members of the new and superior state of humanity upon the earth.

This is the only peaceable and rational mode by which a change from all that is false and evil to all that will be true and good can be accomplished.

It will now require the united wisdom and experience of the most advanced practical men in present society to devise and execute the best surroundings to constitute the transition or new training and educating state, to attain excellence for and give permanent happiness to the population of the world.   This work should be done by the governments of the civilized nations, calling to their aid their most advanced scientific and practical men in every required department of life for the new state of existence, and requesting them to unite their knowledge and experience to form the most complete transition surroundings for a new training and educating model family commonwealth, which they can devise and construct from an outline of one which shall be given to them as some guide to combinations for future progress so new to them.

By a comparison of these models of a transition commonwealth made in different countries, a second model, combining the best parts of each, may be obtained, for all nations to adopt as far as climate and other localities will admit.

To make the proposed change familiar to the population of the world, I have called a congress of the advanced minds of the civilized nations, to consider the best peaceable means by which to change the existing false and evil system of society over the world, for the only true and good system of society which can exist upon earth,—for there is only one truth in all things within the universe. As the subject is so extensive as to include the entire business of human existence in its most perfect and happy state, the congress will be continued from day to day until the departments of which the new system will be composed can be fully explained to the various sections of society as now existing, and time given afterwards for these advanced minds to fully discuss the whole subject, and come to their well-considered calm conclusions, so as to enlighten upon sound data the population of the world, now anxiously expecting deliverance from the false, cruel, and Babel confusion, of artificial made opposing interests and feelings among all of our race.

The Congress will commence, as a preliminary meeting, on the 14th of May, precisely at twelve o'clock in the morning, and will be afterwards continued from day to day at the hours then to be agreed upon, until the business of the Congress shall terminate. It will be held in St. Martin's Hall, Long Acre, London, and different days will be appointed by advertisements in the London newspapers, when it will be the most advantageous for each class of society to attend, when subjects involving the interest of their class will be explained and discussed. And it is hoped that the most advanced minds and experienced in practical knowledge will then attend, and give their best thoughts and powers in aid of the measures for the benefit of all which will be then proposed.

It will be obvious now to all who reflect, that a subject which involves the well-being, well-doing, and happiness of every one who shall be born through futurity, cannot be explained in its outline and details to the existing various classes throughout society in less than many days, and each day devoted to the benefit of certain connected classes, and the whole business of the Congress so arranged and methodised, that the falsehood in principle and the necessary evil consequent in practice of the one system, and the truth of the principle and necessary good consequent in practice of the other, shall become easy of comprehension to those who attend, and through their means to the public in all nations. Also that it may become obvious to all, that rude force and coercion can never effect any permanent good for humanity, but that love and charity, directed by calm experienced wisdom, will when united constitute a power to which the population of the world will willingly yield obedience, and will readily admit to be governed by civil military discipline according to age, in every class into which society when made to become rational will be divided.

The progress and happiness which may be now attained for the human race through the means which the advance in material and mental science has placed at the disposal of society when united, are almost too much for the human mind in its present disordered and excited state calmly to contemplate. But all may be assured that the good time coming is near at hand, and that this generation shall see its commencement and shall experience some of its innumerable advantages and enjoyments.

Let all hope, and none fear for the future.

ROBERT OWEN.

December 9th, 1856.

INTRODUCTION TO THE LIFE OF ROBERT OWEN.

WHAT are the motives for any one to write his life ? Egotism,— money profit,—to amuse, or to instruct the public.

Inquisitor.—Well—you, Robert Owen, are now about to write your own life. Which of these is the motive which now impels you to commence this task ?

Robert Owen.—I have always had a great distaste and reluctance to write my own life, because of the egotism, nauseous to all readers, which it necessarily involves, and I have therefore put it off from time to time, expecting to terminate my earthly career, and then the task would devolve upon others, and I should be saved the disagreeable feeling of doing that which has always been repugnant to my mind and sense of propriety.

Inquisitor.—Then why do you commence it now ?

R. O.—Because I have so often promised my friends and professed disciples that as soon as I should cease to live my active life in promoting the great object of my earthly existence, I would sit down quietly and endeavour to meet their wishes.

Inquisitor.—Did those promises satisfy your friends?

R. O.—No. They said—You have acted so much alone and independently in many of the most interesting events of your life, that no one except yourself could truthfully narrate them, and you have been influenced in your proceedings by motives so different from those of other men, that none but yourself could divine them. Then they added,—You have always expended so much in all your distasteful and repulsive publications to the public, and in circulating those publications in order that they might be known and to a certain extent forced upon the notice of those who would otherwise remain ignorant of the spirit, principles, and practices of the new system for forming the character and governing the human race, that you should now write something that would interest and amuse the public, according to its present character, and which will therefore sell and bring you some profit, to pay you for former losses and expenditures in your publications and their circulation.

Inquisitor.—And what could you say in reply to such disinterested and friendly advice?

R. O.—That it was true. I have acted very much alone and independently of all parties—often in opposition to the well-intentioned representations of my relatives and friends, who could never fully comprehend my views, although they always did full justice to my motives; but they believed my efforts, however well intended and true in the abstract, could never be made in this age to influence the public to action, or to induce it to give the subject, so opposed to all past and present notions and prejudices, sufficient attention to be understood.

Inquisitor.—And were they not right in giving you such sound advice?

R. O.—They were right according to their impressions, which were at the time also the general impressions of the public; but it was well I disregarded the advice so given, or I should never have accomplished the many important practical measures from which the public are now deriving benefit, and from which, when they better comprehend them, they will derive much more.

Inquisitor.—But you have not answered the profit and loss consideration of your publications. Your friends were surely right in saying that your life would interest and amuse the public, and would bring you a profit, instead of the continued loss which you have sustained.

R. O.—Wealth, beyond the decent necessaries and healthy comforts of life, has had no charms for me, except for its use in aiding me to promote the change of system which I have undertaken to effect, if not in my lifetime, soon after I shall have passed into another state of existence. No money consideration could divert me from this object, because it appears to me far to transcend all other earthly subjects, uniting all reforms in one plain practical measure,—while all other proposed reforms would be useless, defective, or impracticable. Besides these considerations, much surplus wealth, as now used, is often highly injurious to its possessors, and generally the more wealth, the more annoyances and evils. Surplus wealth creates an unnatural, unjust, false, and most injurious state of society. I have always had through life as much wealth at a time as it was useful for me to possess, and so it continues.

Inquisitor.—But would not an increase to your wealth enable you to carry your new views of society into practice?

R. O.—No. No amount of wealth could introduce this change into practice if it is not based upon truth, and if it is not to be permanently beneficial for the human race ; while no amount of wealth or human power can prevent its introduction and universal adoption, if it is based on unchanging truth in principle, and if its practice shall be permanently advantageous to all of our race, as I contend it is in principle and will be in practice.

Inquisitor.—If egotism and profit by money cannot influence you, surely to amuse and instruct the public are sufficient to induce you to listen to the advice and wishes of your friends and disciples, of whom you have many more than the public give you credit for.

R. O.—I know I have,—but the old false system puts them in a position to make it unsafe to their means of existence to avow openly their accordance with my views. Very many have injured their worldly prospects by so doing, without aiding the good cause. I have urged upon many to be silent when by their open professions they would only injure themselves and families, and would not promote the cause for which they were going to sacrifice their means of support for themselves and families.

Inquisitor.—But your life would amuse the public, which amusement in the present unsatisfactory state of society over the world is greatly required, and is so much in demand that the public are willing to pay a high price for it. And your object, you say, is to increase the happiness of all parties.

R. O.—It is so. But others, who desire money, and many who require it, can better amuse the public. The hours yet spared to me should be employed to promote substantially the permanent happiness of our race, to the extent that my knowledge and experience will admit.

Inquisitor.—But from what is already known of your life by the public, it is probable much useful instruction might be derived from it, and many imagine it would make more converts to your new views than any work you have written.

R. O.—So I have often been told by my friends, and as there appears some truth in these representations, I will (irksome as the task has always been to me, and now at my advanced age and with my increasing infirmities more onerous than ever,) prepare myself for the performance of the most disagreeable duty I have ever undertaken, and that from the conviction that no one can be in a position to write his own life truly and beneficially for the public.   The public are yet too ignorant to comprehend a life truthfully written.   A system based on falsehood cannot stand the test of truth, or comprehend that which when understood will be discovered to be beyond price.

Inquisitor.—Will you then in writing your life give the public falsehood for truth ?

R. O.—No.   I will give the full extent of truth that a system based and constructed on falsehood will admit.

Inquisitor.—How do you mean to proceed with it to give the truth and avoid the falsehood ?

R. O.—Knowing that the germs of my physical, intellectual, moral, spiritual, and practical qualities were all formed for me before I was born, and from birth directed well or ill, wisely or unwisely, by society, I shall consider myself as one whose mind and entire character has been formed for him, and for which he has no merit or demerit, and I shall consider Robert Owen as a third person, whose life I am writing and reviewing.

Inquisitor.—Then the result of new basing society on this fact, or knowledge as you call it, is to withdraw all merit and demerit from the individual, and to make him irresponsible for his feelings, thoughts, mind, and conduct?

R. O.—It is, because it this in accordance with all facts known since the creation of man, and because it is in accordance with all facts existing at this day.   And also, because it is the great truth which can alone open the path of wisdom to man, enable him to know himself,—how his character is formed for him,—and how it may with the certainty of a law of nature be well-formed for every one before and from birth,—and how the population of the world may thus be made to become in the shortest period practicable united as one family, and good, wise, and happy.

Inquisitor.—Why this would indeed be to introduce the millennial state of existence upon earth.   Surely there must be some mistake in your first principle, or in your deductions from it, or you could not have been now more than half a century in convincing rational beings of that which would secure the permanent happiness of their race ?

R. O.—You forget that any ideas, however erroneous and absurd they may be, can be forced into any minds, even as being divine truths never to be doubted, and that all the ideas hitherto taught to the human race have been based upon a falsehood, which pervades the mind and conduct of all.

Inquisitor.—You do not intend in this sweeping assertion to include the knowledge derived from the sciences or facts ; that would be to confound truth and falsehood.

R. O.—The sciences are always in accordance with themselves and with all other facts; but in many cases men of science, so called, although they know some facts of one or more sciences, have this knowledge so mixed up in minds previously trained and educated on a false base, that their scientific knowledge is often a confused mass of truth and falsehood, of which they make little valuable use, compared with the powers which the sciences can give for the general benefit of mankind. It is the knowledge of the true formation of character that can alone give the right direction to the application of the sciences for the use of the population of the world, and this knowledge will show that the sciences are in opposition to all human religions, governments, laws, and institutions, based on the supposition that man forms himself or his own qualities, and all know that on this supposition the religions, governments, laws, and institutions of the past have been based, and that these have hitherto formed the character of the human race.

Inquisitor.—Then you do not think scientific men are to be depended upon as instructors of the human race.

R. O.—No, I do not. They can teach some valuable facts in the material sciences which they have mastered, but out of those sciences they are frequently mere children in mental knowledge or the knowledge of themselves. They presume much on the little they have been taught to acquire in material science, and are not unfrequently strongly prejudiced in favour of some of the injurious dogmas of the old systems of society.

Inquisitor.—If you have this inferior opinion of men of science, who, as such, are men of facts, and come the nearest to your views in many respects,—to what class in the whole range of society do you look for the advanced minds of the world to attend your Congress on the 14th of May next?

R. O.—Not to any class. The existing classifications of society are gross errors. They of necessity cultivate some of our inferior faculties inordinately, at the expense of the superior. They oppose class to class, and even the members of the same class to one another, creating jealousy and often hatred between them, because their apparent interests are at war with each other. And this now most unwise division of the human race into classes makes the children of humanity into small portions of men and women, shorn of their fair proportions, and with the better parts left out.

Inquisitor.—Why you go in direct opposition to the established doctrines of the *doctrinaires* of the politico-economical school, who teach that the division of labour is the perfection of society and the best means to increase wealth and knowledge.

R. O.—I know that this is one of their pet doctrines. But it is like all their other dogmas, which they call a science, a mere superficial view of man and society, neither of which have their

minds yet been opened to comprehend.   Since the discovery of
the enormous, incalculable power to supersede manual labour, to
enable the human race to create wealth by the aid of the sciences,
it has been a gross mistake of the political economists to make
humanity into slaves to science, instead of making, as nature intends, sciences to be the slaves and servants of humanity.   And
this sacrificing of human beings,—with such exquisite physical,
intellectual, moral, spiritual, and practical organs, faculties, and
powers, so wondrously combined in each individual,—to pins,
needles, thread, tape, &c., &c., &c., and to all such inanimate
materials, exhibits at once the most gross ignorance of the nature
and true value of humanity, and of the principles and practices
required to form a prosperous, rational, and happy state of society, or the true existence of man upon the earth.   These wise men
of the present day seem in no manner to comprehend the difference between manufacturing human beings to become full-formed
men and women, with *all* their organs, faculties, powers, and
qualties, cultivated to their natural perfection, and well forming
pins, needles, or thread.

Inquisitor.—Why, to what are you going to lead us, if you
thus impugn the wisdom of our foremost practical men, as they
are called ?

R. O.—Only to common sense, and to a knowledge of common things, which, in the first generation rationally taught and
equitably placed, children of ten years of age will acquire and
comprehend far better than the most matured political economists or so-called practical men of the present day have yet
attained to.

Inquisitor.—What do you mean by the common sense and
common things, that will hereafter be so easily acquired ?

R. O.—I mean by common sense that it consists in observing
common universal past and present facts, and in making the
most natural use of them for the permanent benefit of our race.

Inquisitor.—This needs explanation.

R. O.—I mean that it is a fact so common as to have been
universal through all past time, that every natural organ, propensity, faculty, quality, and power of man, is made and forced upon
each one at birth without his knowledge or consent; and that
this may be seen to be the case by observing the past and present
conditions or surroundings in which each one has been and is
placed, and hence Medes and Persians, Chinese, Japanese,
Greeks, Romans, Trojans, &c.,—and hence the English, French,
German, Russian, Turk, &c., &c., of to-day.   It is simple common sense, then, to perceive and conclude that all of human-
kind are formed to be what they become by having their natural
powers and qualities, which were formed for them by the Creating
Power of the Universe, acted upon by the surroundings in which
they are placed from birth by matured society.   And that, *as are*

*the natural qualities of each one at birth, and as are the sur-
roundings in which he is placed,—so will the individual be.*

Inquisitor.—Well, so far it must be admitted this is but
plain common sense, deduced from the most common facts, and
so common that it must be known to every reader of history and
observer of common facts, now universal among all the varied
nations, tribes, and peoples of the world. But what of that?
Everyone who reflects must know this, and what do you make of
it?

R. O.—That the readers of history and observers of existing
facts have been hitherto so surrounded from birth as to be prevented from acquiring common-sense.

Inquisitor.—How dare you to accuse the learned men of this
advanced age of the world of want of common sense? They
will require you to prove an assertion so opposed to present universal belief.

R. O.—It is very easy to prove it. The simple facts stated
exhibit at once the cause of all the varieties in human character,
and make it glaringly evident that it is impossible for individuals
to form their own physical, intellectual, moral, spiritual, or practical character. This conclusion is the most obvious to common
sense, as soon as any one has been so formed and placed as to
acquire the first rudiments of common sense.

Inquisitor.—Well,—it does seem so, and your statement shall
be granted, and admitted to be a truth as old as man. But what
can you make of this common sense view of humanity,—" that
" men's natural qualities are made by the Creating Power of the
" Universe at birth, and that they are cultivated by the surround-
" ings, endless as these appear to be, in which from birth they
" are placed by society?" Everyone who reflects must know
this. It is but common sense drawn from facts which are universal and known to all accurate observers. What use can you
make of them, which men of science and of learning have not
already made of them?

R. O.—It appears to me that the most important practical results may be derived from this common-sense view of the true
universal formation of character of the human race.

Inquisitor.—This is a mystery to me, and appears to be so to
all others through all past ages. Pray explain what probably, by
a common-sense explanation which can be understood by the
public, may really prove of practical utility to our race.

R. O.—I will. To those who have studied the use of the
natural organs, faculties, propensities, powers, and qualities of
humanity, it is most evident that each one is intended or formed
and combined, when properly trained from birth, and each duly
exercised to the point of temperance for every faculty and propensity, to give health and pleasure to the individual, and to
diffuse happiness to all around him.

Inquisitor.—Yes. But how are these results to be obtained for any portion of the human race?

R. O.—They are not to be obtained for any separate portion of the human race. But they can be easily attained and secured for all through futurity.

Inquisitor.—This would be indeed knowledge worth knowing, and would be the science of all earthly sciences. Make this intelligible and practicable to governments and people, and for their own happiness and that of their children they will overcome their present prejudices in favour of things as they are, and will adopt those views which will realise such splendid universal permanent results. I am truly impatient now to have this discovery of discoveries made plain to me and to the population of the world.

R. O—Have patience, and your desires shall be satisfied. Have you observed how very desirous the priesthoods of the world have always been to have the education of children under their control and direction, and how much they have been opposed to all other parties having any influence in this matter?

Inquisitor.—Yes,—I have seen quite sufficient of this spirit in this country among Christians of every sect, and among Jews and Mormons also.

R. O.—And have you reflected upon the cause of this strenuous exertion to obtain possession of the young mind?

Inquisitor.—I suppose it is because each sect and division of society has been taught by their respective surroundings, as you would say, that their sect or division alone possessed a knowledge of what they call divine truth upon certain mystified subjects, and that all other sects are in error upon these to them all-important matters, and they therefore wish if possible to make the population of the world to be of their opinion. This is the only view I can take of this universal principle to make proselytes to the opinions of each sect.

R. O.—You are right in your conclusion so far as you have stated, for the priesthood of the world well know that they can easily force their creeds into the young mind, however absurd other sects and divisions may deem those creeds, and that when once the young mind can be pre-occupied with any creed, it is often difficult and generally impracticable to make a Jew a Christian, a Christian a Jew, or a Mahommedan a disciple of Confucius or of Bramah, or the reverse.

Inquisitor.—But this is no new knowledge. It has been known through all past ages, and the priesthood in all countries have had the moulding of the young mind to suit their respective ideas, and thus have they kept the world, and been themselves kept, in gross ignorance how to train the human race, to make it good, wise, and happy. While the means by which they profess to endeavour to produce these results are the very surest means to make the population ignorant, wicked, and miserable, and to keep all nations and people disunited and most irrational in mind and practice—in fact, to make man the most inconsistent of all tribes of animals, ever striving to act in direct opposition to his own nature—a nature which, if understood and rationally trained, educated, employed, placed, and governed, would be discovered to be superior to all other natures known upon earth. And instead of the ignorance and misery which now pervade the earth, all would be enlightened and happy to an extent beyond present human imagination.

Inquisitor.—But how are all to be thus trained, educated, employed, placed, and governed ?

R. O.—By the science of surroundings being made familiar to all, and being applied to practice.

Inquisitor.—The science of surroundings ? Why this is a science I never heard of before! It must be some outlandish idea of your ultra notions of all things. Who ever heard of the science of surroundings ?

R. O.—You, like all the world, make a most lamentable mistake upon this subject. The science of surroundings may be termed the science of practical common-sense.

Inquisitor.—But who can understand what you mean by surroundings ? It is an enigma to all your readers, and each one asks the others what you mean by it.

R. O.—I am now aware of this difficulty, and while the term brings thousands of ideas to my mind, such as the innumerable circumstances which surround the various classes, creeds, and colours over the globe, forming the opposing characters of the world, making so many of them irrational, inconsistent in mind and practice, insane, idiots, or mad,—I have also in my mind other combinations of circumstances, conditions, or " surroundings," which when properly executed for practice will compel all to become good, wise, and happy,—rational or consistent in mind and practice, and all to become united as one family or one man.

Inquisitor.—To have such surroundings would be a miracle and more than mortal can imagine. It will be vain to teach powerful sovereigns,—wise statesmen,—wealthy capitalists,—priests,—lawyers,—medical, military, and commercial men,—especially free traders,—and all who think they have vested interests in the present order, or rather disorder of things. The task, with these prejudices against you, is hopeless. It is an utter impossibility.

R. O.—The term impossibility has little influence upon my proceedings. So many impossibilities have been made possible and practical, that the term means only that the thing spoken of is impracticable in the estimation of the person so applying it. I have already overcome many things said previously to be impossible, and I hope to overcome some others, and among them to make the public understand what surroundings mean, and how to create new ones and to apply them universally in practice to secure the permanent progress and happiness of our race.

Inquisitor.—Why how can you, an old man, so advanced in years, living so quietly near Sevenoaks as to be almost unknown to be in the neighbourhood, expect now to make any additional impression on the public ?

To be continued in No. 11.

COMMUNICATIONS AND REPLIES.

Letter from B. Beardsley.

Willett, Cortland Co., N.Y., U.S.N.A.

FRIEND OWEN,—

Three Nos. of your *Millenial Gazette* have arrived to my address by our regular mail. I have read them myself, and circulated them among the friends of investigation and progression, in the vicinity of my residence. Although a stranger to your person, and heretofore unacquainted with your particular views or desires, yet, from the oft-repeated charges, sounded from the self styled orthodox speakers and writers of the past half century, I should, if led by them, have been compelled to have esteemed you atheist,—infidel,—outcast of God and man, the personification, embodiment, and incarnation of evil and villany, vice and corruption. Judge, then, how pleased I am when from your own pen I am enabled to hear you speak the untrammelled voice of benevolence, " Peace on earth and good will to man !" Can I any longer doubt whose pen is dipped in gall,—whose tongue utters slanders ? Dark are the realms of orthodoxy— darker their deeds. Poor suffering humanity throughout the world will bless you for your labours in the cause of truth whenever and wherever your ungarbled writings may meet the eyes of true reformers, progressives, or spiritualists.

Enclosed is one dollar from H. K. Reed, who has read the three numbers, and desires such further numbers of the *Millennial Gazette* as that will pay for to be forwarded to his address at Willett. I have but the poor man's good will to reward you with for what you have furnished to me. Hence this acknowledgement to a benefactor of the race, and to me in particular. Had

I thousands to bestow, I should think them well bestowed in purchasing such eye salve for the diseased of the rulers and the ruled. Our age is the period of time when the ancient of days, or the man of wisdom, is to cast the fourth beast and the false prophets into the lake of fire, or arguments of conclusive irresistible truth, prepared for the self-willed deceivers of the human race.

Accept, dear Sir,
The sincere good will of, Sir,
Your much obliged co-labourer,
BELAH BEARDSLEY.

Prospectus received from John M. Spear, whose letter is given in a previous page.

THE undersigned propose to issue a work to be called " *The Educator.*" It will consist mainly of teachings or suggestions from the Spirit World, presenting new, interesting, and eminently practical views of social life, commerce, government, education, agriculture, the promotion of health ; also novel suggestions of a philosophic and scientific character, with available hints in respect to the growth, culture, and expansion of the mortal body, and of the human mind.

The undersigned feel that the issue of this volume will not only aid the Spiritual movement of the day, but also that it will incite to a more thorough inquiry into grand primal principles, and that nobler views of God and of humanity will be presented than have ordinarily come from either the pulpit or the press.

The volume will contain about 700 pages, octavo form, will be embellished with several engravings and diagrams, and will be prepared for the press by A. E. NEWTON, editor and proprietor of the *New England Spiritualtst.*

It will be printed on fine white paper, with clear type, firmly bound, and will favorably compare with the most carefully prepared publications of the day. It will be afforded at two dollars per copy. Persons desirous of procuring copies of this work, will please append their names, with the number of copies they will take, and return the same to the undersigned at MELROSE, Mass.

ELIZA J. KENNY,   ⎫ Committee
JONATHAN BUFFUM.   ⎬   of
THADDEUS S. SHELDON.   ⎭ Publication.

Oct. 6th, 1856.

Replies to Correspondents in the United States of N. A.

William Offord, Lebanon, S. Village.—Letter announcing his safe arrival, &c., received. Thanks for his kind services on his arrival, with best wishes for the continued happiness of himself and family, and of the eighteen family unions. Send some good men and women from them to the London Congress, to commence on the 14th of May next.

Otto Kunz, Pittsburgh, Penn.—Many thanks for your valuable communication and its inclosures. They are very interesting, and especially as they evidence that superior spirits take so much interest in the new social movements. I wait the conclusion of the spiritual report. I wish you could attend the London Congress, to meet on the 14th of May next. You see the good and superior friendly spirits are interested in the proceedings on this side of the Atlantic for man's regeneration. When the conclusion arrives, I may perhaps be induced to publish the whole.

Belah Beardsley, Willett, Courtland co., N. Y.—The golden inclosure received, and new numbers sent to him and his friend Reed.

J. L. Rock, Decatur, Van Buren County, Michigan.—Letter received.

Samuel Clark, Beaverton, Ill.—Received with thanks for the communications. Your letter is published in the *Millennial Gazette* of January 1, 1856.

Received Spiritual newspapers.—*New England Spiritualist*, Boston. *Christian Spiritualist*, N. Y. *Spiritual Messenger*, Cincinnati. *Spiritual Universe*, Cleaveland, Ohio. *The Medium*, Conneaut, Ohio. Also the *Boston Investigator*. With many thanks. Sent to each of the above the *Millennial Gazette*, including the New Year's Gift of Inestimable Value to the Population of the World.

In 1830 I published a small work containing my proceedings in the city of Mexico, with the then Republic of Mexico, and some other matters. If any one has yet a copy, or can procure one, and send it to my address, (Sevenoaks, Kent, England,) I will willingly pay all expenses incurred by so doing.—R. O.

London:—Published by the Author at 16, Great Windmill Street, Haymarket : and sold by Holyoake, 147, Fleet Street ; Truelove, 240, Strand ; Goddard, 14, Great Portland Street, Cavendish Square; and all Booksellers.

Registered for Foreign Transmission.

ROBERT OWEN'S
MILLENNIAL GAZETTE;

EXPLANATORY OF THE PRINCIPLES AND PRAC-
TICES BY WHICH, IN PEACE, WITH TRUTH,
HONESTY, AND SIMPLICITY, THE NEW
EXISTENCE OF MAN UPON THE
EARTH MAY BE EASILY AND
SPEEDILY COMMENCED.

"The character of Man is formed *for* him, and *not by* him!"

No. 11.]   AUGUST 1st, 1857.   [PRICE 5s.

REPORT OF THE PROCEEDINGS OF THE CONGRESS OF ADVANCED MINDS OF THE WORLD, FROM THE 12TH TO THE 25TH OF MAY.

PREFACE.

I CALLED this Congress to prepare the governments and people of all nations for the greatest change which has ever been made in the history of the human race; to change falsehood for truth,—ignorance for knowledge,—poverty for wealth,—division for union,—ill-will, anger, jealousy, hatred, and all repulsive feelings, for charity, kindness, love, and all attractive feelings, —in other words, to change evil for good, suffering for pleasure, and misery for happiness, over the world.

In fact, to change a system for governing society, of continued inconsistency, contradiction, and counteraction, for one of never-ceasing consistency and perfect harmony, in spirit, principle, and practice. In short to change a pandemonium for an earthly paradise.

But to effect this great and glorious change for the human race, it is absolutely necessary that all the laws of men should be now superseded, by the All-good, all-wise, all-merciful, and all-efficient laws of God;

the laws of men being the creators of all vice, crime, repulsive feelings, and physical and mental sufferings of all of human-kind.

And also to terminate the reign of superstition upon earth, now called the religions of one name or another, for the universal religion of Truth or of Christianity, which consists alone in applying the spirit of love and charity for all men to practice in every action of their lives, irrespective of all physical, intellectual, moral, spiritual, and practical differences, so as to prove by our conduct that we love our neighbours as ourselves. And this is to be the PRACTICAL PUBLIC RELIGION of mankind, leaving all free to think and express any additional PRIVATE or PERSONAL thoughts respecting the Great Creating Power of the Universe, or what they may call their sectarian religion, or to have no religion if they cannot comprehend or feel the all-importance of acting to their fellow men in ever consistent accordance with the pure spirit of universal love and charity.

For by the laws of nature all minds should be perfectly free to express their convictions, without hindrance from any of their fellow men, singly or united.

And lastly to prepare an undeveloped, and while undeveloped, unbelieving generation in the new Spiritual Manifestations, to try these spirits, and to listen to the instructions of those spirits who when tried prove themselves to be truthful and superior.

ROBERT OWEN.

1st of June, 1857.

ROBERT OWEN'S RECOMMENDATION TO THE RULING POWERS OF THE CIVILISED PORTIONS OF THE EARTH TO CALL A CONGRESS.

THERE is a short, plain, easy, practical course to adopt, by which the present irrational turmoil, ignorance, and confusion may be speedily overcome and peaceably superseded, by the union of the governments and people; and without this union, based on principles well understood and openly acknowledged by both parties, all attempts at petty reforms either of governments or people will be a useless waste of time, talent, and capital.

To proceed in earnest to stay and overcome the present evils of society, a Congress should be called, of the ruling authorities in churches and states of the civilised portions of the world:—

1st.—To consider how best to form Federative Treaties between these nations, allowing each nation, for a sufficient time, to retain its present language, laws, religion, and government; but each to be open and free to all other federated nations, as to its own natives.

2nd.—To consider how best to form the population into the most convenient manageable masses, to perform the most advantageously all the business of life, in the best manner for the permanent benefit of each of such populations.

3rd.—To consider the principle on which society within this extended federation should be based, and whether it would not be for the permanent well-being, well-doing, and happiness of each one within the federation, that society should be based on the universal fact " that God or Nature forms before birth the " peculiar physical a d mental qualities of each one," and that from birth, Society gives a rational or irrational direction to those qualities; and that, with the knowledge and experience now acquired, society may easily be taught to give a rational direction from and in part before birth to all of human-kind.

4th.—To consider whether human-made laws have not hitherto given an irrational direction to the physical and mental qualities of the human races, and thus created all the evils of an irrational state of existence hitherto experienced by mankind.

5th.—To consider what the unchanging laws of God or Nature respecting humanity are, and whether, if now adopted and consistently acted upon, they would not create a rational state of human existence upon earth, and secure the well-being, well-doing, and happiness of every one.

6th.—To consider whether the population of these confederated nations could not be congregated in such masses as would be the most convenient to well-form their characters from birth, physically, intellectually, morally, spiritually, and practically; to enable them in the best manner to produce a superfluity of superior wealth at all times for all, and to produce it with pleasure and advantage to producers and consumers; to unite them cordially in one interest; and to place them within such superior surroundings, material and mental, that the influences upon each one within them should be always for good, and never for evil.

7*th*.—To consider how the most speedily to instruct the population of each federated nation in a knowledge of the important science of the influence of surroundings, by which the causes of good and evil to all may be ascertained with the certainty of a law of nature; this instruction being now the most essential part of a rational system of education, to form a good and useful practical character for men and women.

8*th*.—To consider the best mode by which to have these superior combinations of the best devised surroundings carried into execution.

9*th*.—To consider the necessity for and the advantages which would arise from this Congress of the ruling authorities in churches and states, calling to their aid an assistant Congress of the advanced men of the age in practical knowledge in the arts, sciences, and practical businesses of life, to whom the authorities could apply for information upon every point of doubt or difficulty respecting practice.

10*th*.—To consider how to acquire a knowledge of the probable amount of new scientific power introduced within the last century, and which may be applied to aid and supersede manual labour when useful and desirable.

11*th*.—To consider how this almost incalculable and illimitable power, can be the best applied to promote the permanent prosperity and happiness of the population of all nations.

12*th*.—To consider how the peace, prosperity, and happiness of these federated nations can be permanently established; and how these more civilised nations may best assist the less civilised portions of the population of the world to be instructed to fit them to unite with the more civilised federated nations; in order that peace and harmony may become universal.

This recommendation is in the first instance most earnestly pressed on the immediate attention of the governments and people of Great Britain and the United States of North America, as their institutions, and their habits arising therefrom, are the best adapted to enable them to take a lead in this now all important change for the population of the world.

ROBERT OWEN.

Sevenoaks Park, Sevenoaks,
        England, June 27th, 1857.

REPORT OF THE MEETINGS AND ENTIRE PROCEED-
INGS OF THE CONGRESS OF THE ADVANCED
MINDS OF THE WORLD, WHICH TOOK PLACE IN
ST. MARTIN'S HALL, LONG ACRE, AND IN THE
LITERARY AND SCIENTIFIC INSTITUTION, JOHN
STREET, FITZROY SQUARE, LONDON, FROM THE
12TH TO THE 25TH OF MAY, 1857, CALLED BY
ROBERT OWEN TO CONSIDER THE BEST POSSIBLE
METHODS AND PEACEABLE MEANS FOR GRA-
DUALLY CHANGING THE PRESENT MOST IGNO-
RANT, FALSE, UNJUST, CRUEL, AND EVIL SYSTEM
OF HUMAN SOCIETY, FOR THE ENLIGHTENED,
TRUE, JUST, MERCIFUL, AND GOOD SYSTEM, EX-
PLAINED AND ADVOCATED BY MR. OWEN, FOR
FORMING AND DEVELOPING MEN'S PHYSICAL,
INTELLECTUAL, MORAL, AND SPIRITUAL CHA-
RACTER, FOR PRODUCING, DISTRIBUTING, AND
ENJOYING ALL DESIRABLE WEALTH, AND FOR
PLACING, EMPLOYING, AND GOVERNING THE HU-
MAN RACES IN PERFECT HARMONY WITH THE
DIVINE UNCHANGEABLE LAWS OF HUMAN NATURE
AND THE UNIVERSE.

First Meeting, May 12*th, in St. Martin's Hall.*

On this day, at noon, the *Conductors of the Periodical
Press, and the Popular Writers* of the civilised world,
met, previous to the commencement of the Congress, in
order to have explained to them by the venerable Reformer the
important objects for which they were invited to attend, when
the following address was clearly and distinctly read by Mr.
Daniel Cotter, and fully explained by Mr. Owen.

ADDRESS OF ROBERT OWEN TO THE MEM-
BERS OF THE PERIODICAL PRESS AND
TO POPULAR WRITERS, ATTENDING, AT
HIS REQUEST, A MEETING IN ST. MAR-
TIN'S HALL, LONG ACRE, LONDON, ON
THE 12TH OF MAY, 1857.

GENTLEMEN,—

I have requested your presence here at this time,
to explain to you the result of the experience acquired through a long life devoted to the investigation of the causes of human evils and the permanent
remedy for them.

Among the causes of great good and evil, the Press
in all countries stands vividly prominent. The causes
of its good and its evil are familiar to me, as they
must be to all who reflect upon the subject. But, as
the past is irrevocable, our time will be best occupied
in attending to the future, and especially to the
present.

United, you wield a power beyond the means of
calculation, to immediately benefit the population of
the world, and to hasten that period when all shall
be well instructed in the most useful knowledge; shall
have their characters (physical, intellectual, moral,
spiritual, and practical,) well-formed for them from
birth; shall have the most valuable wealth abundantly
created and distributed most advantageously for all;
when the human race shall be, by the attractive qualities given to each, united as brothers and sisters of
one good and enlightened family; and when all shall
enjoy a high degree of substantial happiness, by all
doing at all times the will of the Great Creating
Power of the Universe, by acting in accordance with
the unchanging laws given from the beginning to
humanity.

You, gentlemen, are now called upon to make yourselves well versed in the knowledge of the principles

and practices by which, with ease and pleasure, a good, valuable, and happy character can be given to all from birth ; by which wealth—real, substantial, useable, and enjoyable wealth, can be, with health and comfort to all, abundantly created and wisely distributed; by which such attractive powers shall be given from birth to all, that each will of necessity love his neighbour as himself, and man will be united to man over the earth in brotherly affection ; by which universal peace and progress will be made permanent; and by which the surroundings in which to place all from birth shall be constructed and maintained to produce with the certainty of a law of nature all the preceding results.

By attending to the daily proceedings of the ensuing Congress of the advanced minds of the world, these now all-important subjects for all nations and all peoples shall be unfolded, day by day, in such manner that, by due attention, all will be enabled fully to comprehend them ; and when you shall so comprehend them, you will be enabled to instruct the people of all nations, by the best mode of instruction yet discovered, that is, by making the right use of the periodical press and popular publications ; but of these the daily newspapers may be made the most useful and valuable, in rapidly distributing the knowledge now so necessary for the peace and happiness of all nations, governors and governed.

You have now some freedom, but by your union that freedom and your powers for doing good, in spreading truths essential to the well-doing and well-being of society, may be greatly increased.

I am not ignorant of the limitations to your greatest influence for effecting immediate good to your fellow men, arising from the prejudices of the public by whom you are supported. But as soon as by your united efforts you can overcome this ignorance, how superior, by the change of the entire system of society, in spirit, principle, and practice, would the uncontested permanent situation of each of you become !

Through the necessity which you experience to attend, under this wretched old system, to your individual existence, in uncertain comfort or enjoyment, you are now compelled to be slaves to an ignorant public opinion ; when you might by your union become the highly respected creators of public opinion, and the instructors of the human race, to raise them from their present degradation of mind and practice.

The most important office in society is that of forming the character of the population. When this is ill-formed, all manner of evil and misery are the necessary results ; when it is well-formed, goodness and happiness may be more easily made to become universal.

In fact, the time is not far distant when it will be discovered that to govern is to have the surroundings complete to form from birth a good character for the entire population—for such surroundings will of necessity include the whole business of life. And the daily newspapers may be made the best " schoolmasters abroad."

By diving to the foundation of true knowledge, based solely on facts devoid of all imagination or supposition, you will discover that the direct road to the universal permanent happiness of the human race is now opened, and that when once entered upon it is a plain and pleasant path to pursue, until, with the certainty of a law of nature, the desired object shall be gained.

You will find that all which is required in practice, is now to apply the enormously superabundant means at the disposal of society, to create the surroundings required to well-form character, produce valuable wealth abundantly, unite all cordially, and to combine these into one arrangement to act harmoniously in all its parts and as a whole.

This is the circle required for the union, progress,

and happiness of our race; and this circle must be complete in all its parts, or it will not work.

A superior character.

Abundance of superior wealth.

A cordial union of humanity.

Perpetual progress in knowledge.

These are the substantial ingredients to attain and secure happiness for all of our race.

These results are now attainable with the certainty of a law of nature, by the formation of a new combination of surroundings, now easily to be carried into execution in all lands and among all people, if you will set your minds to acquire this most valuable knowledge, and to convey it on the wings of the press to all nations and peoples.

Say not that this is a difficult task.

I am not a learned, but I am a plain, simple, straightforward, practical man, a lover of truth and of the happiness of my race, ever willing to make any sacrifice to make both universal. These qualities, by due attention, all of you may acquire, and you may thus become efficient to induce governments and people to commence in earnest, with knowledge and foresight, to make these new divine surroundings, which, as soon as understood for practical purposes, with their natural results, it will become a labour of love and high enjoyment to all to realise.

You will have to impress deeply on the public mind of the world, that effective surroundings may be now easily executed and combined, to satisfy with the certainty of a law of nature every rational desire of humanity; and that this all-glorious and greatest of all changes for humanity may be now carried into universal practice, in peace, and without prematurely disturbing the existing order of society in any country or among any people.

I am now ready to listen with attention to any observations which may occur to you arising out of what has been stated. But before sitting down, I desire to state that I have long been and now am most thoroughly convinced, that our divine and mortal character is formed for each of the human race, and being most conscious that mine has been formed for me, I know that it would be most irrational in me to claim any merit for what I have done or may do.

Second Meeting, May 14th, in St. Martin's Hall.

ROBERT OWEN in the chair.

On this day the proceedings of the general Congress of the Advanced Minds of the World, convened by Mr. Robert Owen, were commenced, to acquire, consider, and demonstrate the knowledge and the power, the principles and the practices which are now required to remove all the errors, evils, tyrannies, and oppressions, which afflict, degrade, and crush mankind,—to introduce an entire change of the existing irrational system of human society,—to improve and develope the physical, intellectual, moral, and spiritual nature and condition of humanity over all the earth, and to secure to all men their natural and just rights and liberties,—their divine right to the best means of subsistence,—to the best possible instruction, and to the best possible laws and institutions.

The venerable Social Reformer (now entering upon his eighty-seventh year, but still remarkably spirited and buoyant, and enjoying his usual vigorous energy and self possession,) delivered an opening address to the Congress, of which the following is the substance. Mr. Owen commenced by saying—

Were the objects intended to be accomplished by this Congress of less importance to the present and future progress in real knowledge and substantial permanent happiness of the population of the world, I would apologise for the position which I have now assumed—that of the teacher of the human race. Had I found one of my fellow men with the natural and acquired qualities in mind and practice to receive and act upon the knowledge which my natural organisation, my surroundings, and my long extensive experience in varied practice, have forced upon me, through a life, this day of eighty six years, I would have solicited such individual to have occupied my place on this day. For in my early years (as I told the sovereigns of Europe assembled in *their* Congress in Aix-la-

Chapelle in 1818,) I considered worldly honours, wealth, present popularity, and future fame, " the mere playthings of infants." How much less do I now value these things, when experience has proved to me, that they are far worse than useless,—that they are highly injurious to givers and receivers.

The time for names, persons, and all personalities, will soon expire. Individuals will be nobodies, and will be nowhere considered to be of any desirable importance, or to be distinguished from their brother men.

Truth will be hereafter held in estimation among men of every colour and clime. This is eternal and unchangeable; individual forms are ever changing.

I will explain the difference between *truth* and *persons.*

It is a *Truth,* eternal in the nature of things, that one and one make two. It stands a truth eternally, by itself, unaided by any name; and would not be made more true, were it to be declared to be such through the trumpet voice of Nature to the Universe by Deity itself, or the aggregate Power of Eternal Existences.

Nor would it be less a truth, or less valuable were the same Power in the same manner to declare it to be a falsehood.

Nor would it be less true or less valuable, if declared to be a truth by the supposed Evil One of the so-called religious World.

I have made this statement with the view to terminate all individual notions of the importance of names, and to open the minds of the population of the world to the necessity of abandoning the authority of all names, and of transferring the importance to truths which change not for man, nor for any power within the universe.

It is *truth,* regardless of all names, and *truth alone,* that can set the *nations free.*

And now that " truth without mystery, mixture of error, or fear of man," can be thus declared, freedom will soon spread its wings and fly unchecked over and to the uttermost parts of the Earth.

Mr. Owen then called on Mr. Robert Cooper to read the following address for him to the Congress—

ADDRESS OF ROBERT OWEN ON OPENING THE GENERAL PROCEEDINGS OF THE CONGRESS OF THE ADVANCED MINDS OF THE WORLD.

FRIENDS—men of mind and good intentions—for superior minds desire the happiness of all.

I have a pleasure not to be expressed by words in meeting you on this eventful day—a day which will be held in everlasting remembrance by all future generations, as the day on which a new dispensation for our race, to secure its happiness through time and eternity, was openly proclaimed through this Congress to all nations and peoples.

And all ere long will rejoice with me that this worn-out dispensation, based on gross falsehood, opposed to all unchanging facts, and of necessity leading to every kind of evil, is about to die its natural death, at a good old age, in peace, and without arousing the indignation of nations, so naturally excited against revolutions of violence and bloodshed.

It will be true wisdom in all to allow this old system to be gradually superseded, with order and foresight, as the old roads of the world are now quietly and gradually dying their natural death, and giving way to the new railways and electric telegraphs to convey new knowledge of progress more rapidly over the world.

To insure the permanent happiness of all, it is necessary,

First.—That a good, useful, and valuable character should be given to all from birth through life.

Second.—That substantial wealth should be amply provided for all, by means pleasant and agreeable to all.

Third.—That all should be united as one superior family, each possessing the pure spirit of universal love and charity, and applying it to practice through every hour and action of their lives.

Fourth.—That the surroundings of all, to make these results certain to each, should be as perfect as the existing knowledge and means of society can accomplish.

And this knowledge and these means are now so far advanced, through the progress of material science, that surroundings of great beauty and excellence may be devised and executed so as to secure high happiness and enjoyment to all.

This Congress has been called to make this new

dispensation known, and, for the benefit of all, to teach it to the human race in the shortest time practicable, in order to speedily terminate this old dispensation, with the ignorance, falsehood, poverty, disunion, crime, and punishments, which it so universally generates among all nations and peoples. And thus to prepare the way for the reception of the new spirit, principle, and practice, which of necessity will arise in all, through the introduction of the new dispensation.

It will be said, and truly, that the character of the existing generation, like that of all former generations, has been formed for it; and it will be asked, how, then, is this new charcter to be formed, and how are the new superior surroundings to be created, and how is the new dispensation to be introduced?

To understand this part of the subject will require the best attention of those accustomed to form character on a large scale, and of those accustomed to create conditions or surroundings of extensive combinations for creating wealth.

Because to change the one dispensation for the other in peace and without confusion, will require new surroundings, in which gradually to change the old mode of forming character and of creating wealth. And it will be found that the surroundings which can alone attain these two results, must include all that can be required to constitute a perfect science of society in practice, to secure the permanent union, prosperity, and happiness of the human race through futurity.

This new dispensation will put an end to the absurd, contradictory, and confused laws of men, *all* emanating from a fundamental falsehood, in opposition to all know facts since the creation of man,—for the Great Creating Power of the Universe has created man and all his natural qualities without his consent or knowledge, and continues so to create him; and that he may become rational, or good, wise, and happy, he must be governed alone by God's eternal and unerring laws of humanity.

These laws are—

First.—That man *must* believe according to his strongest convictions; and that therefore there can be no merit or demerit in any belief whatever.

Second.—That man *must* like and dislike according to the organization created for him; and that therefore there can be no merit or demerit in loving or hating.

Third.—That man is and must be influenced by all the surroundings within which he is placed through life. If these are calculated to produce rational, good, wise, and happy influences, man will of necessity become rational good, wise, and happy. If, on the contrary, the surroundings in which men are placed through life are calculated to produce irrational, evil, foolish, and unhappy influences, then must men of necessity become irrational, evil, foolish, and unhappy.

In this old dispensation, arising from the false foundation on which the human-made part of the character of men has been formed and society constructed over the world, the surroundings in which almost all, if not all, of the human race have been placed, are irrational, evil, and foolish, and are calculated by their influences to make the population of the world, as all are at this day, irrational, evil, and foolish, and to give to those who are the least injured by these irrational surroundings, only a low degree of uncertain happiness.

Under the new dispensation, arising from the true foundation on which the human-made part of the character of man will be formed and society constructed, the surroundings in which all will be placed through life will so influence the population of the world, that all must become, of necessity, without merit or demerit to any one, rational, good, wise, and happy. ·

To prepare the way to effect these results, with the certainty of a law of nature, this Congress has been called, and it is now in your hands.

After the delivery and careful discussion of the subjects of these addresses, &c., Mr. McBean, the reporter engaged by Mr. Owen, addressed the Congress, and concluded by submitting the following resolution, which was cordially carried; and the whole proceedings were then referred to a select committee, to calmly consider them, and in due time to report the result to Congress.

Mr McBean's resolution was—

" That the first solemn subjects which present themselves for the most careful consideration of this Congress are, first— How shall men at present be effectually taught the knowledge of the duty of acquiring, possessing, and exercising the powers, the privileges, the rights, and the liberties, which belong by nature, and by virtue of the social compact, to human beings? And second—What are the principles and the practices which are essentially necessary to promote and secure the permanent peace, the progressing prosperity, and the perpetual good of the human races, in the present and through all future generations; and which shall ultimately unite the different populations, communities, and nations upon the earth, into one grand harmonious confederation, speaking the same language, pursuing the same interests, and possessing the same convictions, sentiments, feelings, and aspirations."

This day's meeting adjourned at four o'clock, until the next morning at eleven.

Third Meeting, May 15th, in St. Martin's Hall.

ROBERT OWEN in the chair.—On this day the *Delegates from the Civilised Governing Powers, Statesmen, Legislators, Members of Parliament, of the United States Congress, and of other Legislating Assemblages*, were more especially invited to be present, when the true principles of governing and legislating according to the unchanging laws of nature—laws as far superior to men's laws as wisdom is to folly—were submitted and explained.

Mr. OWEN opened this day's meeting by saying, that the great change in the condition of all humanity from error and evil to truth and goodness can be effected only through the spirit of charity and love, applied to produce universal peace, order, and harmony throughout all the affairs of men.

Peace, order, and harmony, among the nations of the earth, or among any people, can be attained only by introducing and maintaining, in their full extent, the pure and undefiled

C

principles of love and justice. The laws of ignorant and undeveloped man have created the repulsive feelings between men and nations, deluged the earth with human blood, caused crime, and thus far given a false direction to the rational faculties of all, so as to inflict universal misery on the mass ; but when the laws of humanity—of nature—of God, will be introduced and consistently acted upon, and form feelings of universal attraction, charity, and love, they will insure the peace, order, and happiness of the human race, and crime and misery will be no more.

You desire to know what these laws of God, of nature, of humanity are, which can accomplish these great, glorious, and happy results. Among those laws of God which have an immediate and direct influence upon the well-being, well-doing, peace, and harmony of the human races, the following may be enumerated as some of the most important for man to know and act upon :—

First Law.—That the Divine Great forming Power of the Universe — God, Nature, or by any name, it matters not, for the Power itself is the same, eternal, unchanged, everacting—gives to every one without his consent or knowledge, at birth, the germs of all the physical, intellectual, moral, and spiritual qualities which they possess.

This Power, then, gives to all men without their consent or knowledge, at birth, the germs of all the physical, intellectual, moral, spiritual, and practical qualities which they possess. They are the same general qualities in each ; but ever diversified in their combinations in individuals, consequently, for these qualities, and their varied combinations, it would be most irrational to make the compelled receiver of them responsible.

Second Law.—That the germs of all these qualities are influenced, trained, educated, and matured, more or less, by all the surroundings in which the individual possessing them may be placed, and that there is a constant action and reaction going on between these germs of internal qualities and the external influences acting upon them, and the action and reaction of these two forces compel the individual to be that which he thus becomes during every period of his life upon the earth, and that the kind and quality of the surroundings which produce the external influences, have a power in early life almost irresistible over the internal power in forming the character of every one.

Third Law.—That every one is compelled to believe according to the strongest convictions made upon his mind.

Fourth Law.—That all are compelled to like that which has been made the most agreeable to their individual organisation, and to dislike that which has been made the most disagreeable to it. And for these likes and dislikes it is error alone that could make the individual responsible.

Mr. Owen, before he sat down called upon his assistant, Mr. Robert Cooper, to read the following address to the Congress.

ADDRESS OF ROBERT OWEN TO THE MENTALLY ADVANCED STATESMEN, LEGISLATORS, AND LAW MAKERS OF THE WORLD.

GENTLEMEN,—

I have requested your presence here to-day, to hear from me an explanation of my experience in solving the problem "How the human race can be most "easily the best governed, to secure the permanent "happiness of the human race."

The result of this experience is, that the population of the world, in its present divisions, or as a whole, can never be made good, wise, or happy, on the base on which, to this day, the human-made part of men's character has been formed, and all society, past and present, has been constructed—*that* foundation being an ignorant falsehood, directly opposed to all facts, past and present.

This ignorance and this falsehood have been made to pervade the character of man, and every variety of society which he has yet tried in order to become good, or to create happiness in practice; and were this base to be maintained, such must be the result to the end of time.

See the confusion of intellect and of practice at this day in all the nations of the world, not excepting those deemed the most advanced. In all these nations, a false spirit, principle, and practice, has been made to reign triumphant. And to attempt to solve the problem, upon a false base would be vain, useless, and, now, a sad waste of most valuable time.

All who have any pretentions to rationality will at once abandon this satanic foundation ;—for it is the father of all lies and of all evil.

It is therefore full time that a new dispensation should arise and a new life commence.

But while it is impossible to solve this problem on a false base, it will be most easy to solve it upon the true base for forming character and constructing and governing society. With the knowledge that the immortal and mortal character of man is formed *for* him, and that the means exist, ready for use, to well form the character of everyone, by making the practical surroundings such as are calculated to form that character, and which, through the aid of the advanced sciences, will be now easy of execution, the problem how to attain universal happiness for our race will be solved ; and the incalculably beneficial results will be witnessed as soon as this principle and practice shall be extended to all nations and peoples.

The adoption of immediate measures for this extension should now be the all-absorbing object of all governments and peoples. For it is impracticable to devise surroundings to form a good and superior character for all, physically, intellectually, morally, spiritually, and practically, without those surroundings include the means of creating and distributing wealth in the best manner for all, and of uniting the human races as one family, superior in mind and manner, and pervaded with the pure spirit of universal charity, love, and kindness ; the interest and happiness of one, being the interest and happiness of all. For isolated individual selfish happiness is and ever will be unattainable.

This new dispensation, built on the foundation of the universal fact " that the divine and mortal character of man is, and ever must be, formed for him," opens a new path to the statesmen of the world, by which, with the certaintity of a law of nature, when rightly pursued, all men may be permanently made intelligent in mind, rational in conduct, and through life may be compelled, by the irresistible combined influences of mental and material surroundings to be good, wise, and happy.

You have therefore a new and delightful lesson to learn, and a new practice to adopt, which will secure to you and your children's children, to the latest posterity, an unceasing enjoyment, of which now you can have no adequate conception.

Mr. McBean, after the full discussion of all the subjects brought forward by the president in his addresses, came forward and said—" The love of humanity, and the most firm faith in its inherent goodness," and powers of progress, have always been, and still are, the distinguishing characteristics of Mr. Owen's social philosophy—for the complete regeneration of society. Mr. Owen, during his long life, has continued to make a noble stand to reclaim, and save mankind from ignorance, superstition, division, despair, misery, poverty, and the fear of want—both by endeavouring to call forth the divine powers of human nature, and by reforming the political and social state and structure of society. He has, in opposition to all priestcraft, appealed to, and successfully defended the inherent capabilities of human nature, and has clearly shown how to prepare, educate, train, and apply its Divine powers and principles, to the Reform of the existing state of things, in the family, and in the state, and in every sphere of social life.

The philosophy of human destinies has thus, through his powerful advocacy, taken a decided tendency towards pure philanthropy—a tendency which is leading the way to a renewed state of society in every country ; and which may and must become the sound basis of powerful united efforts, of new energies, of continued exertions, and of hopeful views of human destinies upon the beautiful and fertile earth, the Divine and equal property of every human being.

The entire proceedings of the day having been duly debated, and referred to the committee to calmly consider and report the result to Congress,—the meeting was adjourned at three, P.M., to ten, A.M., next morning.

Fourth Meeting, May 16th, St. Martin's Hall.

ROBERT OWEN in the chair.—On this day the delegates and representatives of all the *Religions of the World* were more especially invited to be present ; when the true foundation of all these religions was explained to them, and more particularly what Christianity has been and is, and how it is to become the unopposed universal religion of the human race.

Mr. Owen, the President of the Congress, on rising to open the proceedings of the fourth meeting, said—" This in some respects must be perhaps the most important day of this Congress, because the great interests of the human races is deeply involved in this subject being fully and rightly understood. Hitherto the religions of the world have created the repulsive feelings of humanity, and deranged the faculties of the contending nations of the earth.

" By arousing these feelings and creating this derangement, they have been the most effectual barrier to prevent any portion of mankind being trained to become rational in mind or conduct, or to attain to the knowledge of the Divine spirit of universal love and charity either in principle or practice. While the only religion which is true, and that can be of benefit to man, is the pure undefiled practice of love and charity in every action of our lives, proceeding from that divine spirit, which has now, by the dispensation about to commence, to be given to all from their birth, and thus to establish and for ever maintain goodness, wisdom, peace, and harmony among mankind, and cordially unite all races and colours of humanity.'

Mr. Owen, before he sat down. called on Mr. Cooper to read the following address to the Congress—

ADDRESS OF ROBERT OWEN TO THE REPRESENTATIVES OF ALL THE RELIGIONS OF THE WORLD, BUT MORE ESPECIALLY TO THE CONFUCIANS, BUDDHISTS, JEWS, CHRISTIANS, AND MAHOMMEDANS, ALL NOW INCLUDED WITHIN THE BRITISH EMPIRE.

MEN AND BRETHREN,—

IGNORANCE of your Creator's laws of humanity has from the beginning led you all, contrary to your best and permanent interests, into false paths, to seek for goodness and happiness. And in these false paths, which have seduced you into the wilderness of falsehood, you are lost amidst contending errors; and instead of religion cordially uniting you as one family, in universal love and charity, as true religion must unite you, it has under divers names divided you, and caused an artificial spirit of repulsion over the world, filling it with hatred and disorder, when true religion must cause and continue attraction and harmony among all of the human races.

You, ignorant of yourselves, of how you obtain the qualities which you possess, physical, material, or spiritual, or for what object you are so formed to exist in the universe led you to think that you, the created, can do good to, and glorify the Great Creating Power of the Universe! An atom claiming to be a mountain would not err to so great an extent as the religious world err in supposing that man, an atom in creation, could by any of his puny efforts of voice and genuflections, or by ceremonies of any kind, do good to the Great Creating Power of the Universe.

Your desire, no doubt, is to make man good, wise, united, and happy. You have all taken, however, the direct road to make them evil, foolish, disunited, and dissatisfied.

While another road would enable you to make every man in spirit, principle, and practice, a rational being, good, wise, united, and happy; full of charity and love for his race, not in word only, but applied continually to practice in every action of his life.

And this is that *Christianity* which is alone *true*, or which can ever become *universal, and unite the human races as one family of superior enlightened men and women, having one language, religion, interest, and feeling, to promote each other's happiness.* Anything short of this is a waste of words, time, and talents about religion ; and the sooner these false religions can be peaceably superseded by the true religion, the sooner will it be practicable to make men and women rational beings, happy themselves, and having their greatest pleasure in promoting the happiness of all others within their influence. It is not those who say—" Lord! Lord!" all day, or all day or night, who will be saved from misery ; but those who do the will of the Great Creating Power, by assisting to extend goodness and happiness over the earth. These are they who shall attain to the true joys of heaven, and who will acquire that inward peace and satisfaction which in no other way, the world can give or take away.

The first practical step which you can take is to acquire the true spirit of universal love and charity, which, when you have acquired it so as to apply it to continual daily practice, will unite you all as brethren of a superior enlightened family, and you will not accept of any other distinctions than those of age ; for human-made distinctions tend continually to divide man from man, and to destroy all feelings of *true Christianity* between them.

Your best occupation now will be to acquire a practical knowledge of the science of surroundings, and to teach it in your temples, synagogues, churches, mosques, meeting houses, and all places for religious teachings ; because through this knowledge all who shall be born after this science shall be well understood and carried into practice, may be made, with the certainty of a law of nature, good, wise, united, and happy, as each will be pervaded, in proportion to their growth from birth, with the true spirit of universal charity and love, which they will without ceasing apply in their every day practice.

In the name of common sense, why all this waste of mind, time, and treasure, over the world, to cause and continue repulsive feelings between men and nations, and to produce evil continually, where, without these false religions, no evils would exist?

But let the world beware of doing injustice to those who could not prevent these religions being forced into their minds. For these errors they are blameless ; and not one professing religionist over the world should be in any manner injured, in mind, body, or estate, for becoming and being what society has forced him to become and to be.

Nor is there the least real necessity for such injury to be inflicted upon any one of them. For the path will be now open, when real enjoyable wealth will be so easily and pleasantly produced in superfluity for all, that there will be no necessity to diminish the emoluments, however large or enormous they may appear, of any one of any religion as now practised over the world. And the true spirit of *truth* or *pure Christianity* must create so much charity and love for them, as to prevent all other kinds of injury in mind or person.

After these all-important subjects had been duly debated and carefully considered, and had been in like manner as the former subjects referred to the committee appointed by Congress to report their sentiments upon them, Mr. McBean came forward and addressed the Congress. Mr. McBean said :—

Individual man no more exists for himself, than by himself; for his real progress and destiny are intimately connected with the progress and destiny of humanity. But what is humanity without its physical and spiritual brotherhood—without its infinite father, God ? What are the sciences of human progress—of the formation of human character, without their primary, and most precious objects—without the bright and cheering hopes of immortality ? Man's whole nature and powers are not supplied, exercised, and exhausted in possessing, partaking, studying, and subduing the portions of the physical universe, falling within his reach. He has higher wants, larger affections, and greater powers, than the mere physical universe can meet, and exercise. Man came, and comes from God. His closest connection is with God ; and he can find peace, progress, joy, and real mental life only in the knowledge of his eternal Father—in learning, and in obeying the will of God.

To learn to know to do the will of God is man's highest end, for it is the employment of his highest faculties and best affections on the sublimest subjects and objects. Man has much for which to love and be grateful to God—but for nothing as much as for the power of knowing his will as expressed in all the Divine operations and laws of the universe, and in obeying himself—the sublime source of all-being. Let us, then, strive to rise up to behold these great and grand truths in all their brilliant freshness and divine universality ; and as Mr. Owen has shown us this day, to throw down all the walls of separation between science and superstition, must necessarily be the first grand step in this glorious work of human emancipation—in this good work of the regeneration of human society.

This meeting was adjourned at 3 o'Clock P.M., to the Literary and Scientific Institution, John Street, Fitzroy Square, to the next morning at 11 o'Clock A.M.

Fifth Meeting, May 17th, held in the Literary and Scientific Institution, John Street, Fitzroy Square, commencing at 11 a.m.

ROBERT OWEN in the chair.—On this day the *Producers of Wealth* of every description, from land as well as from all other materials and sources, including employers and employed, masters and operatives, were more especially invited to be present, in the Literary and Scientific Institution, John Street, Fitzroy Square, when the true practical principles by which the greatest amount of the most valuable wealth could be obtained in the shortest period, with the most health and pleasure to the producers, and permanent advantages to every member of society over the world, were fully and clearly explained by Mr. Owen, who opened the meeting by saying—To produce wealth of the best qualities in abundance for all, with pleasure to the producers, is the first duty of a rational society, and should be the first object of all governments, statesmen, and legislators.

Upon this department depends the life and happiness of the population of the world, and when society shall be rightly or wisely constructed, all will be engaged for some period in every day in this their first duty to society, but a duty which may be made most healthy, pleasant, and even delightful to every one engaged in its various operations. When the sciences shall be applied under the dictates of common sense to supersede manual labour, the creation of wealth will become a mere exercise for health, and a pastime of enjoyment of the human races.

The existing arrangements for producing the wealth of the world for the use of man are the most decisive proofs that society everywhere is yet in its earliest infancy respecting the true formation of character and right construction of society.

Until the principle on which society should be based shall be known, well understood, and shall be consistently applied to practice, it will be vain to look for or expect any common-sense arrangements in any one of the departments of life.

Mr. Owen then requested his friend Mr. Cooper to read the following address to the Congress—

ADDRESS OF ROBERT OWEN TO THE PRODUCERS OF WEALTH—EMPLOYERS AND EMPLOYED.

FRIENDS AND FELLOW WORKMEN,—

You are the *substantial substance*,—the *bone* of all society.

Without your active exertions society must die, or only a few exist upon the scanty uncultivated productions of the earth.

Up to this period, society, through want of knowledge, has placed employers and employed in a grossly false position, a position most injurious to each other, and yet more injurious to the entire of society.

To place you in your true position is now one of the first duties of the statesmen and legislators of all nations, and until this shall be done, there cannot be peace on earth, common sense, or security for the safety of any government, or for the happiness of any class.

But what is wealth, and wherein does it consist? The things which constitute wealth are—

1st.—The *necessaries* of life.

2nd.—The *comforts* of life, and

3rd.—The *beneficial luxuries*, to give health and varied pleasureable sensations to all men; for without the happiness of all none can be truly happy.

In what do the *necessaries* of life consist?

In food, clothes, and shelter, of *ordinary qualities*.

In what do the *comforts* of life consist?

In *good* food, clothes, and shelter, combined with good instruction.

In what do the beneficial luxuries of life consist?

In having at our pleasure the best food, clothes, and shelter, and the requisite surroundings to form the best character from birth for all, so as to remove all bad and inferior surroundings from us, and to prevent any such coming to us.   And every bad or inferior person is an evil surrounding.

Is it practicable for society, with the means now at its disposal, to attain these three kinds of wealth for all men, in peace, and with permanent benefit to all.

Yes,—by foresight and common sense, rightly applied, these three kinds of wealth may be gradually attained, most beneficially for every individual and class in existence.   But they cannot be attained under the present false principle on which society ever has been based, and with the mal-formation of society consequent on its erroneous foundation.

The Producers of Wealth, to effect this change in a short time, in peace, and most advantageously for all, must unite, employers and employed, to abandon the false foundation and mal-formation of society, and must agree among themselves to make arrangements, first to secure for all the *necessaries* of life without contest or competition.

This may now easily be accomplished if the producers of wealth can agree to abandon the *false principle* on which society has been based—a principle, or rather notion of the imagination, opposed to all facts ; and if they will openly, fairly, and fully declare their fixed determination to adopt and act consistently on the true system, on which alone all society, for the interest and happiness of all, should be based.   And this is the only real difficulty which you, the producers of wealth, have to overcome, to constitute a true, ever-prosperous, and happy state of existence upon earth ; for whatever you, the producers of wealth, shall determine to adopt, on principles in accordance with nature, (the only right principles to govern the actions of men,) all society

must adopt ; for society exists only by your exertions.
When you have on this principle made your arrangements to secure the *necessaries* of life for all
without contest or competition, now so easily to be
effected, the arrangements to secure for all the comforts of life will be more easily attainable for all ; and
then, by this arrangement, good instruction, which
includes good training and education for all, shall be
given to all. And without that instruction from birth
which can insure a good, useful, and valuable character for all, there can be no claim to common sense in
the whole business of life ; for it is now practicable
to form arrangements of surroundings, by which,
through means unperceived by the individual, to give
with the certainty of a law of nature a good physical,
intellectual, moral, spiritual, and practical character
to everyone born with a natural healthy constitution
or organisation.

And if these new combinations of surroundings
shall not now be made by the union of the employers
and employed in producing wealth, it will be evident
that they have not attained sufficient common sense
to understand their own interest, or how to pursue
the plain path to permanent prosperity and happiness.

With the aid now to be obtained by society from
the practical sciences, to make new surroundings to
have a perpetual supply of superior wealth for all with
the certainty of the seasons, will be an easy and pleasant task for a rationally trained and educated population. And this will be obtained with so much system and foresight, that no one will have any occasion
to waste time or talent, or to be in any way anxious
to consider how they shall be fed, clothed, sheltered,
trained, educated, employed, placed, and governed, in
the best manner for each and all of our race in perpetuity.

By the new combinations of superior surroundings,
based and constructed on the laws of nature, all these

essentials of a future happy existence upon earth will be provided for all, as all requisites are provided for the flowers of the field and for the other innumerable kinds of life, by nature from the earth.

And this might have been done long ago for the human races in perpetuity, if their rational faculties had been sooner developed, and especially the faculty of common sense.

For if this faculty had been developed at an earlier period, it would have occured to all to enquire, if man in the infant state of his existence and progress in knowledge, when so little aided by the powers of the sciences and arts, could maintain himself and his family, and most wasteful ignorant governments,— what could he not do by the aid of these sciences, when rightly applied by society for the benefit of all ?

In this country at this day, were common sense used in the right application of scientific power, the natural powers of each man would be increased more than one hundred fold, and the increase to this scientific power is illimitable. In my lifetime it has increased in these islands from one to one compared with the working population at the commencement of this century, to much more than one hundred to one. Or as though each workman had more than one hundred hardy, willing, well-taught slaves to work for him.

And if the faculty of common sense had been fully developed in our population, instead of this enormous new power being wasted in most irrational wars, and mis-applied in individual injurious indulgences, each workman would now be living in a palace, with more healthy and superior surroundings than any monarch now possesses, or than any prince, king, or emperor can possess under the existing false or insane system.

Open your eyes—examine, and reflect upon the facts around you ; and then ask—where is the common sense of the British population ?

When you can use common sense, happiness will be easily attained in perpetuity for all.

When Mr. Cooper had read the above address, Mr. Owen came forward, and said,—Now, my friends, I shall be most happy to listen with the utmost attention to any questions or observations, which may occur to you, arising out of what has been stated and brought forward in the address which you have now heard read.

Mr. Murray, representative of the Boot-closers of London, and other workmen, addressed the meeting at some length, to whom Mr. Owen replied in very forcible terms.

Mr. McBean came forward to the platform and said :— Mr. Owen has been for upwards of sixty years the most profound advocate, and successful student, and practiser of the science of political economy, of the comprehensive science of human legislation,—of the great and sublime science of the formation of human character. It must now be admitted by all classes of all countries, that Mr. Owen has been the most extensive discoverer, and the most energetic and perfect describer of the fundamental causes which perpetually generate, produce, and continue misery, poverty, suffering, discord, and weakness in human society ; as well as the most clear and beautiful demonstrator of the true methods, and the never-failing means by which,—without injury to any person or class,—those causes and all their baneful consequences may be gradually and effectually removed, and by which the valuable interest of the human races may be permanently advanced and constantly secured.

Mr. Owen has clearly and successfully demonstrated that the period has arrived, and that the means are become obvious, by which, without fraud and force of any kind, men may be trained, placed, employed, and governed in harmony with the Divine laws of their compound nature; and by which all kinds of riches and wealth may be produced and procured in such abundance, and so advantageously for all, that the wants and the wishes of every human being on earth may be more than satisfied.

Mr. McBean concluded his interesting observation on Mr. Owen's statements, by submitting the following important resolutions, to the meeting, which were carried unanimously,—namely,—

First.—That this Congress of Advanced Minds—true representatives of every human interest, want, and right—producers of wealth, employers, and employed—after having attentively heard Mr. Robert Owen this day, 17th May, 1857, clearly and fully explain the beautiful, the lovely and the practical principles by which the greatest possible amount of the most valuable wealth, the accurate knowledge of truth, natural virtue, pure morality, and human happiness can be obtained and secured in the shortest possible period, and in the surest possible manner, and with the most pleasure, health, and benefit to the producers and the requisite distributors, and with permanent advantage to every member of human society over all the earth, do thoroughly recognise, and solemnly resolve, that it is the primary duty of each of its members to acquire, communicate, and diffuse as much as possible the knowledge how to frame, develope, and adopt the practical arrangements, and the beautiful surroundings which are necessary to originate, promote, secure, and realise all these grand physical, intellectual, moral, and spiritual advantages to all mankind.

Second.—That this Congress, also, clearly recognise the solemn importance of the comprehensive truths just now explained by Mr. Owen, and cordially pledge themselves individually to maintain and proclaim, that the primary duties of philosophers, philanthropists, teachers, statesmen, and legislators, of all states and nations, are to acquire the knowledge and the power to form human character, in harmony with the Divine, physical, intellectual, moral, and spiritual laws of man's nature, and of the universe,—to place the whole people in their true position,—to give to each man and to all men their rights and liberties,—to secure the necessaries, the comforts, and the beneficial luxuries of life, both physical and mental, as explained by Mr. Owen, to all ; for until this be accomplished, and until every human being is cared for from birth, there cannot be permanent peace, progressive prosperity, and solid security for the health and happiness of any class.

After all the subjects embraced in the foregoing addresses, remarks, and resolutions, had been fully debated, and, as in all the previous cases, referred to the appointed committee to report to the Congress, the meeting was adjourned, to meet again at 7 p.m. in the same place.

MR. OWEN'S BIRTHDAY MEETING, MAY 17TH.

The meeting to celebrate Mr. Robert Owen's eighty-sixth birthday, was held on Sunday evening in the Literary and Scientific Institution, John Street, Fitzroy Square. Mr. Brinsmead, president of the Institution, in the chair.

At 5 o'clock, P.M., Sunday, 17th of May, 1857, a Social Tea Party, which was numerously and respectably attended, took place in the hall of the institution, to celebrate the great philanthropic reformer's eighty-sixth birthday. At 7, P.M.,

Mr. Brinsmead, the president of this famous free platform institution was called to the chair, who delivered a most instructive and apropriate address ; after which G. J. Holyoake, Esq., of 147, Fleet Street, came forward and proposed the following resolution, which was most affectionately received by the crowded assembly :—" That this meeting warmly congratulates Mr. Owen on the attainment of his eighty-sixth year." Mr. Holyoake, in a neat, telling speech, illustrated by various examples, the continued constancy and perseverence of Mr. Owen in the cause of suffering humanity ; and referred to the evident success which has followed his unparalleled exertions, as manifest in the improved tone of society, in the improved and improving condition of large portions of the working people compared with former times, by the partial adoption of even a few of his practical plans and principles in many new public establishments, and arrangements in the country.

John Scott, Esq., C.E., Belfast, in seconding the resolution, observed,—

In coming forward to second the resolution now proposed by Mr. Holyoake, I fully concur with all that he has said respecting the character and doings of a man whom every one that knows, must admire, respect, and love. Being but a young performer on the stage of life compared with Robert Owen, I have only had the pleasure of an intimate acquaintance with him in the latter part of his life ; yet every one who is familiar with the history of the civilised nations of the world, must be aware that he has spent the whole of a long life in constantly striving to improve the condition of his fellow men. I am sorry to say that in the autumn of life, he has been deserted by many of his formerly professed friends and associates ; and it is the more to be regretted when the cause of their forsaking him is, that, having obtained satisfactory and unrefutable evidence that man continues to exist after the present life, and that departed spirits communicate and converse with men in the physical body on earth, when the requisite conditions and laws of spirit intercourse are fulfilled and complied with, he believed the truth, and honestly avowed his convictions.

Now, I am not aware what amount of evidence Mr. Owen has received of the truth of spirit-teaching ; but this, I can say, that if he has obtained a tithe of the proof which I have of its truth, he cannot but believe in it, unless he would prove false to his own convictions ; as it generally happens without exception, that all who examine the subject honestly and attentively, become convinced of its truth. Ever since Mr.

D

Owen avowed his belief in the truth of spiritual science, it has been repeatedly stated that his belief in spirit existence and spirit-teaching, is mere mental hallucination in consequence of impaired intellect resulting from his advanced age. I can find no appearance of any defect in his intellectual powers; indeed, so far from exhibiting any signs of mental aberration, he is more vigorous in body and mind, and as acute and discriminating in mental perception, as he was many years ago; and for every friend he has lost on account of his advancing progress in the knowledge of man's Divine and Spiritual nature, he has gained two, as good and equally sincere.

A more pitiable state of mind than that of those who cling tenaciously to the wish and the hope that this life is the only one in which man will retain individual personality, and that the grave will cover alike knowledge and ignorance, virtue and vice—those who are so mentally paralysed and imbecile, as really to believe in such views, are entitled to our solemn sympathy; but while we pity those who have no pity on themselves, let us not fail to condemn the apathy and indifference of mind of those who rest contented with the degrading idea, that man is little or nothing more in value than a moth or a worm, and that he will come to a similar end. The defection and opposition of persons holding such grovelling views of human nature, may retard the progress of social and spiritual science for a time, but as well might they expect to arrest the mighty planets in their ceaseless courses, as to stop the advancing progress of the knowledge of truth and duty, so ably advocated by Robert Owen; they are only so many drags withdrawn from the rapid running wheels of his Divine progress, and he is now leaving them far behind, while his youthful spirit continues to pursue with increasing ardour and expanding benevolence, his onward eternal march.

Mr. Owen has stated that he does not expect to attend another Congress on earth; now, however much I agree with him in many points, I do not agree with him in this, for although the old case in which he now resides may not be tenantable much longer, as it has nearly served its designed purpose, of developing the rudimental germs of his spirit, preparatory to its birth into the spirit spheres; he will then enter upon more extensive fields of usefulness, and will continue to visit, in company with others who have gone before him, as many meetings of the friends of freedom as he can conveniently attend, to assist by suggestions, mental impressions, and direct communications, in carrying on the grand work which has been his chief aim throughout his physical life—that of regenerating the world, and co-operate with congenial associates and with others he may leave on earth, for the progressive and permanent improvement of the whole human races.

Sixth Meeting, May 17th.

Mr Owen was called to the chair, and the adjourned meeting of the Congress resumed its proceedings at 7 p.m. Mr. Owen briefly recapitulated his forenoon remarks, and called upon Mr. Cooper to read the prepared morning address " *to the producers of wealth, employers and employed.*" After which several parties proposed various important questions, and made different pertinent observations, which were all clearly and satisfactorily re-stated by Mr. Cooper, and completely answered by Mr. Owen.

At the conclusion, John Scott, Esq., C.E., delivered a short address on Social and Political Science ; and the meeting terminated at half-past nine o'clock, with the understanding to meet at noon next day, as before in St. Martin's Hall, Long Acre.

Seventh Meeting, May 18th, in St. Martin's Hall, Long Acre.

ROBERT OWEN in the chair.—On this day more especially were invited to be present the *Heads of Universities, Colleges, Academies, Schools*, and all whose profession it is to assist to well-form the character of human beings from birth, to have explained the causes by which the character of all has been to this day, most unfortunately for all, mal-formed, and why the language of falsehood and conduct of deception has been made of necessity to become universal; and when the means were made obvious, by which all may materially assist to form a good, useful, and superior character for all, and introduce over the world the language of truth and conduct of honesty, without a motive existing for falsehood, in look, word, or action, or for deception in conduct.

MR. OWEN opened the proceedings of the seventh meeting of the Advanced Minds by saying—To teach man is to form the character of humanity. A New Dispensation is about to commence when "old things will pass away and all will become new." There will be a new formation of the human character over the world, based on a new principle and formed in a new spirit, so that the man thus new-formed will be in spirit, principle, and practice, a being altogether different from the humanity formed under this old and now worn-out dispensation for forming character and governing man. The human-made part of the human character has been based from the beginning on an error fatal to the rationality, goodness, and wisdom of all nations and peoples—evil or great imperfection could alone emanate from a foundation so false, so contrary to all facts, and so highly injurious to all men. A new base for the foundation of society is about to be established to give the pure spirit of universal charity to all from their birth, and retain it for daily application to practice through life, and thus to secure the permanent harmony of the world. In fact it will be now soon discovered that the required surroundings to form the character of every human being to become good, wise, and happy, that is, to be consistent in principle, spirit, and practice, will be to make the surroundings required for the whole business of life, to learn and to teach, will be the chief business of every one to the end of our physical existence upon earth.

Mr. Owen then called on Mr. Cooper to read the following prepared address to the Congress :—

ADDRESS OF ROBERT OWEN TO THE HEADS AND ADVANCED MINDS OF THE PROFESSIONS, AND OTHER TEACHERS OF THE HUMAN RACE, WITH OR WITHOUT ANY SECT OF RELIGION.

MEN AND WOMEN,—

DID you and the population of the world know the importance of the task which you have undertaken, and were you qualified for it, all would esteem your position the highest that could be given to men and women ; for the goodness, progress in real knowledge, permanent prosperity, and happiness, of all, depend upon your task being well performed.

To give to all men a good physical, intellectual, moral, spiritual, and practical character from birth to

maturity of mind and practice, would be to secure
the permanent high happiness of the human races.

And this may be done, with the certainty of a law
of nature, and with ease and pleasure to teachers and
taught, as soon as society shall be based on its true
principle, and shall be constructed in undeviating consistency with that true fundamental principle.

But while society shall be based on the false principle on which alone it has been hitherto founded, and
you and your pupils shall be placed within the surroundings, mental and material, in which you have
been placed by the generations which have preceded
you, it will be an impossibility to form a good, or rational character, or one possessing even common
sense. Hence the bad and inferior character given to
all, and the confusion throughout society.

You are greatly to be pitied for the task which
society thus imposes on you under such injurious surroundings. You are required and expected to form
a good character for your infants, pupils, and students,
without having given to you any of the essential materials to enable you to do that which is desired.

When society shall know what is requisite to form
a good character for man, and shall supply those requisites, the great business of life will be accomplished ;
for it consists in framing and arranging those surroundings, material and mental, which by their natural
influence will compel all placed within them to acquire a superior character, physical and mental—in
fact, to acquire the character of a superior being,
compared with all those whose characters have been
formed within any of the surroundings now existing
in all nations and among all people.

All present surroundings are essentially injurious to
all men ; for they are eminently calculated to
force all to acquire a false, bad, and inferior character,
and to make it impossible that one true Christian
could be made by them.

Where now is there one upon the earth who always

expresses, in look, word, and manner, the simple truth which he is obliged to feel; and whose mind is pervaded with the true spirit of universal love and charity for all men? And yet this, and this alone, applied to the whole practice through life, can make real Christians.

And these are now to be made, and will be made, with ease, pleasure, and delight, under the new dispensation, based and constructed on nature's everlasting, good, consistent, and beautiful laws.

Will you now aid in assisting the population of the world to abandon peaceably the old worn-out dispensation of error, and gradually, without injury to any, to attain this new glorious dispensation, which is to secure goodness, wisdom, unity, and happiness to all?

The path is plain and open, and under the new dispensation will be easily pursued by all who enter it.

Society will be based on its true foundation, and truth alone will be the language of the population of the world. Insincerity in word or action will be unknown.

A superior physical, intellectual, moral, spiritual, and practical character will be given to all from birth, and the germ of man will be greatly improved before birth.

The production of useable and enjoyable wealth will be a pleasure and a pastime for health and exercise to all, and this wealth will be produced annually in such superfluity, that all will freely partake of it without money or price or hindrance of any kind.

Temperance in *all things* will be the continued practice of all.

Equality according to age will be discovered to be the only mode of attaining and maintaining permanent peace, prosperity, and happiness among the human races.

And all will perceive the necessity for new combinations of superior surroundings, devised, with foresight and knowledge, to possess the influences on humanity to make it to acquire the results previously stated. And society is now in possession of the most ample means to have these surroundings executed in a very superior manner.

You will now perceive the high importance of your position, and the responsibility attached to it.

Thus, in the due order of nature, will *truth* or pure Christianity reconcile man to man, overcome all evil, establish the reign of peace and harmony, and happiness will prevail and reign over the earth for ever.

Say not that these heavenly results are unattainable on earth. They are so only under the Satanic system of individual selfishness, ignorance of the laws of humanity, and obstruction to the practice of universal love and charity for all men, the divine principles taught by Jesus of Nazareth, or the Great and Glorious *Truth* which was the *First* Coming of Christ among men.

The *Second Coming* is the yet greater and more glorious Truth, given in this our day, of the science by which to make the *First Truth* universal in practice. And thus will be fulfilled the promise to the Jews of the Coming Messiah to overcome and conquer the world of evil; and to the Christians, of the Second Coming of Christ to overcome and conquer all error. Thus will be united Jew and Gentile and all the nations of the earth, into one family of good, wise, and happy, full-formed men and women, having one language, interest, and feeling, all superior in their individual qualities, yet no two the same, but the combined distinct qualities of all contributing to constitute the one great humanity of the earth.

May you all by calm reflection be enabled to see the importance of this revolution in mind and practice, and effectually aid its advent.

Mr. Owen rose and said :—My dear fellow beings, I shall now be most happy to listen with all possible attention to any observations which may occur to you as important as arising either out of my remarks this morning, or out of the prepared address which my friend Mr. Cooper has just read to you.

Mr. McBean, the reporter, then came forward, and submitted the following resolution which was unanimously agreed to—namely :—

" That this Congress having heard Mr. Owen's clear and comprehensive views and explanations of human nature, and of the science of the formation of human character, are more and more convinced that all men are the equal children of the same supreme source of all existence ; that all men are equally divine beings, and sons of God—having equally divine rights and wants; and that all the sciences and truths of the universe are equally divine, and should be taught to all mankind as the elements and subjects of education.

After the principles and views brought forward on this day were fully discussed and referred as in all the former cases, to the appointed committee to report to Congress, the meeting adjourned at 4 P.M. to 11 A.M. next morning.

Eighth Meeting, May 19th, in St. Martin's Hall,
Long Acre.

ROBERT OWEN in the chair.—On this day were more especially invited to attend, the present *Distributors of Wealth,* including *Bankers, Merchants, Wholesale and Retail Traders, money and wealth changers* of every description ; to have explained to them the gross mal-formation of society which renders any one of these occupations necessary,—except that of mere carriers. It was shown also that, in a rational formation of society not one of them would be useful or required ; and that this immense mass of industry and highly misdirected talent, capital, and powers, would be added, most advantageously for each of these occupations and for the public, to the superior-made producers of real wealth, — the increase to which, by these means, would be enormous, while the production thereof would be made a pleasure to each individually and would produce much more.

These classes, it was shown, consume wealth to an incalculable extent, produce none, and are greatly in the way of those who, were it not for their obstruction, could produce much more.

Mr. Owen opened this day's proceedings by saying—That when society shall be based upon its true foundation, there will be no necessity for any class of distributors. These classes are now a dead weight upon the producers of wealth ;

they are also, by being thus placed by society, made to become demoralised and a grievous injury to all classes, themselves included.

The formation of this class vividly exposes the ignorance and the undeveloped state of mind of our early ancestors, who thus constructed society; making it now evident that they were totally devoid of any correct knowledge of their own nature, or how to construct a rational system for the business of life, or a social state of existence, in which the duty, the interest, and the happiness of all should be permanently and cordially united.

The New Dispensation now about to arise will accomplish this result, and will regularly train all for the coming Millennium.

Mr. Owen then requested Mr. Cooper to read the following address to the Congress—

ADDRESS OF ROBERT OWEN TO THE VARIOUS DISTRIBUTORS OF WEALTH, FROM THE MOST TO THE LEAST EXTENSIVE IN BUSINESS OPERATIONS.

A FALSE base and construction of society in principle and practice has placed you in a false and most injurious position for yourselves and the population of the world.

This false base and consequent false construction of society have of necessity produced an inferior and miserable fighting era, of long duration in the history of the human race ; of repulsion, opposition, competition, contests, and wars ; and which may be considered the infancy of humanity, in which, by these apparently injurious means, man has been forced into strong action to acquire knowledge, through experience, to fit him by great contending exertions for a much higher and more perfect state of existence— a new existence of attraction, peace, goodness, wisdom, union, and happiness.

The period for the commencement of this new era, or dispensation has arrived, and this will gradually and naturally supersede the infant period of human life.

During this first period of existence, all the arrangments and proceedings of society, although necessary for the infant state of humanity, have been, and they still are, calculated to divide man from man, to repress real knowledge of our nature, and to keep all greatly demoralized. While the new dispensation, which nature is everywhere providing for its general introduction, will cordially unite man to man, give great accession to his knowledge of humanity, and make him to become through life good, wise, and happy.

In this new dispensation none will be instructed to endeavour as a business of life " to buy cheap and sell dear ;" but all will be taught the true essential business of life, that is, to aid in giving a good character to all, and in producing the best wealth in the best manner for the free use and enjoyment of all, without the necessity of buying with money or price to be fixed for it ; for under wise arrangements superior wealth will be produced with pleasure to all, so abundantly that there will be everywhere a supply beyond the wants or desires of all.

No real Christian can be a buyer or seller for money profit. Jesus of Nazareth, the first preliminary Christian, and the founder of Christianity, turned the money exchangers and buyers and sellers for a money profit out of the temple. He taught that there should be no private property among his followers, and he and his immediate disciples had no private property.

Buying and selling for a money profit, whatever may be the apparent sanctity of the buyer and seller, demoralise the man, and unfit him to become a Christian, or to acquire and practice the essential qualities of Christianity, of universal love and charity, or to " love their neighbours as themselves." In a truly formed Christian society, these essential qualities of Christianity will be the unassuming and unpretending character of all. They will be given to each

from their birth, without merit to the receivers of
them.   And upon this principle—" that any cha-
" racter (Jew, Christian, or Mahomedan,) may be
" forced from birth upon any one," or that of a producer,
a distributor, a fighting man, an idler, or an useless
person, as well as that of a true Christian.

You cannot be blamed, but are to be pitied, for the
useless and demoralized character which society, by its
erroneous and injurious surroundings, has made it necessary that you should acquire.   In a society based
on its true principle, constructed and governed by
sound reason or common-sense, there will be no necessity for a class of mere distributors of wealth.
Other arrangements will be adopted, and new surroundings will be made, to save all this talent, falsely
directed industry, and misapplied capital, and to give
them a much more valuable, moral, and pleasant
direction, for the individual and for society; and by
which all motives to deteriorate the quality of any
kind of wealth will be for ever removed.

Be assured that a buyer and seller for a money
profit must be demoralised in his general character,
and cannot be a Christian, except in mere name. There
will be no buying and selling among true Christians.

Do you ask why the early Christians ceased from
being associated and from living on public without
private property.   It is because Jesus and his immediate followers had a mission to introduce a knowledge
of the principles of real Christianity, and to foreshadow
some of its practices.   But he said, " this is not the
" full coming of truth or real Christianity, the time is
" not yet come for it, in all its beauty and glory in
" practice.   My mission is to introduce it by declaring
" its essential principles for practice ; but the time is
" not yet for that full practice."   In the due order of
nature, when the Great Creator of all things in the
Universe shall have made the necessary pre-
requisites, there will be a second coming of truth,
or of Christianity, in the fulness of time, when will be

declared, not merely to the Jew and Gentile, as then known, but to all the children of men, how those first announced divine virtues of love and charity are to be given to all without exception, and the means, through the progress of science, by which they will become the every-day practice of all. The announcement to the world of these great and glorious results, and of the means by which they can be and will be applied to universal practice, overcoming and conquering all previous error and evil, is the coming of the Messiah, promised to the Jews, and the second coming of Christ, foretold by Jesus of Nazareth, the most advanced medium, or mediator between man and the Great Creating Power of the Universe, or God, that has appeared among men.

" What ! then," you will naturally ask, " is now our " duty ?"

It is to assist with all your strength of body, mind, spirit, and means, to change the false, cruel, and wicked system of society, now existing over the earth, for the true, merciful, and good system, for the government of the human race. And to effect it by reason and in peace, and not by abuse and violence.

When Mr. Cooper had read the above prepared address, Mr. Owen rose and said—My dear fellow-men,—I have firm confidence in the penetrating and persuading powers of the pure piercing knowledge of truth, to produce, promote, and perpetuate immovable conviction,—to enlighten, strengthen, and beautify the human mind ; I therefore cordially invite all parties here to present their questions, and to propose their objections, in order that I may endeavour to answer and remove them.

John Scott, Esq., C.E., Belfast, then came forward and addressed the meeting very successfully for a short time ; and concluded by giving notice, that on Thursday, the 21st inst., he would, if an opportunity occurred, address the Congress on the philosophy of political and social sciences.

The subjects of Mr. Owen's remarks and those contained in the address having been carefully considered, duly debated, and referred to the Committee, the Congress adjourned at 4, P.M., till 11, A.M., next morning.

Ninth Meeting, May 20th, in St. Martin's Hall, Long Acre.

ROBERT OWEN in the chair.—On this day the heads and members of the *Profession of Arms* were more especially invited to be present, to have explained to them the false arrangements of society which have made and continue to make their professions necessary, and the means by which this necessity may be gradually diminished, until it shall no longer exist, and a very superior and much more useful and pleasant occupation of their time and faculties will be provided for them, greatly to their benefit and to that of the public.

Mr. Owen opened the proceedings of this day by observing —The first step towards a rational permanent reform of the population of any country has yet to be taken, and until that difficulty shall be overcome, it will be vain to attempt any other measure for the advance of society from its present low physical and degraded mental condition.

While society shall remain based as now on a glaring false-hood, unsupported by one fact through the whole history of the human races, and opposed by every known fact bearing on the subject, all must be trained, educated, and placed, to become not natural men and women, but artificial and most irrational beings.

All are thus made to contend against their beneficial instincts, and to have their minds filled with false ideas, and with the most incongruous and absurd associations of them, and filled also with the most wild and often the most injurious imaginations, so as to make their lives more miserable than that of any tribe of animals upon the earth which live in their natural state. While, if men were governed and directed by common sense, they would be beyond all comparison the most happy of earthly existences.

When will the time come when humanity shall be taught to know so much of itself, as to ascertain that it is formed of physical, intellectual, moral, spiritual, and practical qualities in each of the human races, without the consent of the individual, who is compelled to receive them, and the peculiar combination of them which distinguish him as a separate being from all other living existences ?

And when will men acquire so much common sense, as to construct society to be in accordance with this divine principle on which alone the human character should be matured and society formed through all its ramifications ?

Until this period shall arive, all of humankind must continue the contending, disunited, superstitious, and fighting irrational animals, which they have hitherto been and are at this day.

I now again openly denounce this false notion for the foundation of society, and advocate the immediate adoption of the only true principle on which society can be founded to make the human race good, wise, united, practically religious, and happy through life.

In proportion as the population shall unite to form one family, will their power increase to effect material changes of great magnitude, in cultivating the soil, in obtaining an immense water-power, and in irrigating land to a considerable height above tide levels. Also in various sciences to attain new great results on the earth, to navigate the seas and oceans on large islands, and to cross the British and Irish Channels on dry land, and, if useful, to remove mountains and to fill up valleys.

These and many other great results will be attained by the population of the world abandoning the evil and repulsive principle for the foundation of society, and adopting the good and attractive principle, and reconstructing society to be throughout consistent with this base.

Mr. Owen, before he resumed his chair, requested his deputy, Mr. Cooper, to read the following address to the Congress—

ADDRESS OF ROBERT OWEN TO THE PROFESSIONS OF ARMS, FROM THE COMMANDER-IN-CHIEF TO THE PRIVATE.

GENTLEMEN, AND MEN OF ALL FIGHTING GRADES,—

As far as Christendom extends, and I now especially address myself to those within this extended and all-powerful circle, you call yourselves Christians; you are engaged by governments calling themselves Christian governments; and you are paid by nations calling themselves Christian nations.

The time is come when the veil must be raised, and the whole truth, or Christianity pure and undefiled, must be openly declared to all men and nations, that it may become the unopposed attractive religion of the human race for ever.

The truth then is, that the armies, the governments, and the nations, calling themselves Christians, are only so in name, without a particle of its substance, in mind, feeling, or practice.

This cannot be longer continued, for the period is near at hand when all the nations of the earth shall become Christians in deed and in truth.

There can be no Christianity in union with the spirit of war; nor can war and violence ever make a Christian, whose essential qualities are universal charity and love, in every day practice.

As soon as pure undefiled Christianity can be perceived and introduced in all its divine qualities, with its beautiful and glorious results, it will spread like wildfire over the earth, and will speedily burn up the last remains of this false, wicked, cruel, and repulsive system, in order that all old things may (entirely) pass away and all may become new, good, and highly beneficial to man.

You will naturally ask,—" Are we to be disbanded and thrown helpless on society ?"
No. In the change from the false to the true Christianity, not one shall be injured, but all will be essentially benefited by the change.

The governments must now turn Christian, in reality, and not merely assume a false name to cover all manner of evil doings.

They will see and feel the necessity of at once uniting to adopt an entirely new system, in spirit, principle, and practice.

The *spirit*, that of Christianity, which is love and charity in practice for all, without exception.

The *principle*, " that man's character is formed by " God and society, and not by himself."

The *practice*, to form, on this spirit and principle, a good character from birth for all, by placing all within Christian surroundings, which by their influences will well train, educate, employ, and govern all, in peace, union, and happiness.

You will again ask for the practical steps by which this change from evil to good, from false to true Christianity, can be peaceably effected ?

It will be the most easily accomplished by the existing governments forming each regiment under its own officers into members of a scientific Christian society, to retain military discipline for as long a period as may be necessary. Each regiment to be associated as a family, and placed within buildings and appendages of proper surroundings, to enable them by their own powers, aided by all the means which science can now give, to maintain themselves as Christians, and to enjoy life rationally, as becomes men and women enlightened to become Christians in language and conduct; that is, to be consistent in mind and practice.

One of the essential surroundings for each regiment will be to have land sufficient around their associated dwellings and buildings, to enable the regiment of real Christians to create food in abundance at all times for themselves, and a surplus to exchange for other necessaries, comforts, and beneficial luxuries.

By this simple process, the present extravagant, warlike, dangerous state of society, to all parties, will be gradually and peaceably changed, from being opposed in spirit, principle, and practice, to true Christianity, to being the real supporters of pure and undefiled Christianity, and thus will all nations soon be induced willingly to adopt and thus secure the permanent peace of the world for ever.

The government of each of these new associated military Christian families, to assist to attain and maintain universal peace, will soon gradually fall into the natural mode of governing by the gradations of age, as I have in various publications explained in detail; and this is the natural and superior mode by which all will be governed in the spirit of real Christianity, as was the population of New Lanark far more than a quarter of a century with the happiest effect.

The present military life is a life of many evils and dangers. The Christian military life will be one of usefulness, goodness, pleasure, and happiness.

At a subsequent period of the day I will explain how the Christian military life is to be obtained and to become universal.

Mr. Owen as usual having invited and afforded the opportunity for the full discussion of his views on these subjects, several parties proposed different important questions, which were all satisfactorily answered by Mr. Owen, after which Mr. McBean came forward and proposed the following resolution, which was cordially carried :—

" That this Congress, after having attentively heard Mr. Owen's clear and comprehensive views and explanations (this 20th of May)—in reference to the profession of arms—resolve to urge with all their powers and energies, upon their fellow men everywhere—upon all public and private teachers —upon the statesmen and legislators of this, and of all other countries, the supreme importance of acquiring the most accurate and practical knowledge of the sublime science of the " formation of human character,"—in harmony with the divine laws of human nature and the universe, and recognise the duty of all men to have themselves and their fellow men placed in their true natural and social position—in possession of all the just rights of men—in the position to be useful and beneficial to themselves, and to all mankind."

The whole proceedings having been duly debated and referred to the Committee to report to Congress, the meeting adjourned at 4 P.M., till 11, A.M., next morning.

Tenth Meeting, May 21st, in St. Martin's Hall, Long Acre.

ROBERT OWEN in the chair.—On this day more especially were invited the *Republicans and Democrats* of all nations, to have explained to them the utter hopelessness of ever expecting a peaceful, useful, or happy state of society, were the population of the world to be put under their sole government, and to show and demonstrate to the world that the individual system of selfishness and ignorance of the laws of humanity, would destroy them, as they have destroyed all that is desirable in the government and institutions of the United States, the most perfect republic ever yet established in the world. And to point to them that the same would be the fate of every republic established upon the ignorant selfish principle of individualism, and upon a false base for the formation of the character of the population of the world. And

E

to have the true formation of character and construction of society explained and made plain to all whose minds are prepared to comprehend these subjects.

Mr Owen opened the proceeding of the tenth meeting of the Congress of the Advanced Minds of the World by saying —I am well aware there are many talented and good men who desire to improve society by Republican Institutions under a Republic based on the principle that man forms his own qualities of body and mind, and that he should be made responsible to his fellow men and to his Creator for the conduct emanating from these qualities, physical and mental. My matured convictions are, that upon a foundation so grossly false, and so ignorant of humanity, no rational government can ever be constructed, or can man be trained and educated to be made to become consistent in mind or practice. Hence the decline and disappointment of all old governments during past ages—hence the absurdities and incongruities of all existing governments, and the irrational conduct of all people at this day. To have a good and wise government, society must be based on its true fundamental principle, and constructed in all its parts to be consistent with that foundation.

The false base if maintained will lead to a pandemonium— while the true foundation of society will lead to the Millennium.

Mr. Owen, before he sat down, requested his friend, Mr. Cooper, to read for him the following address to the Congress.

ADDRESS OF ROBERT OWEN TO THE ADVANCED MINDS OF THOSE WHO DESIRE TO CHANGE GOVERNMENTS TO BECOME REPUBLICS ON THE INDIVIDUAL PRINCIPLE OF SOCIETY.

BROTHER REFORMERS,—

Of your good intentions to your fellow men, in desiring to change Monarchies into Republics, I have no doubt. You strongly perceive and feel the many evils produced by the present system of society under despotic monarchies, and you think many of these evils would not exist under a republic constituted as you desire, and in which there should be what you call equality.

Now, all old republics have become so venal and corrupt, that they could not sustain power of such character.

" True"—you will say—" but we do not look to old " but to the latest modern republics.   See"—you will add—" the new Republic of the United States, with " its rapid increase of population and growth of ma-" terial prosperity."

The people under this republic have all the parts of the charter for which you contend, and its constitution was framed by men of high aspirations, and considerable experience and endowments for the task, as far as political knowledge was then known ; for when they made it they had no ideas respecting two systems for the government of the human races—one false in its foundation and through all its ramifications most ignorantly selfish, leading continually to evil and misery from one point of the world round its whole surface ; the other, to be based on now self-evident truths or universal facts, and consistent with that truth throughout its entire formation and perpetual government.

These talented and disinterested men did the best possible, with the limited knowledge then known of the formation of character, construction and governing of society, or of the means by which all could be united and made to love their neighbours as themselves, and by which the unchanging government of charity, love, and wisdom could be established over the world.

This all-important knowledge, when they were considering and when they completed the constitution of that Republic, was hidden from these high-minded and wise men for their day and time.

The two men who took the lead in concocting and bringing into practice the constitution of the United States, since so shamefully misconstrued and abandoned in its most essential principles, were Thomas Jefferson and John Adams—the latter of whom was the second, and the former the third president of the United States.

It so happened that I visited these old colonies of our empire, but fortunately no longer colonies of despotic power, as they were under George the Third, who obstinately treated them not as men, but as slaves to his power and influence with parliament. I was desirous to acquire the most advanced political knowledge that could be gained from men of wisdom and experience, and my first visits were to John Adams, to Thomas Jefferson, to James Madison, and to James Munroe,—the two latter, the fourth and fifth presidents. General Washington, the first president of the republic, had died before my first visit to the United States.

At this period John Adams, with his mind clear strong, and distinct, was ninety years of age; Thomas Jefferson, equally so, was eighty-two years of age; James Madison seventy-four; and James Munroe sixty-six; the last was the acting president when I arrived.

These men were honest, and had the permanent good of the Republic deeply implanted in their hearts and minds.

Owing to my antecedents, better known and far more highly appreciated in the United States than at home, I was at once admitted to the unreserved confidence of these men, when they had attained the highest pinnacle of their ambition, and when their minds were calmed from political contests, and could therefore reflect with advantage upon past events, and make the best use of their experience.

To these may be added Chief Justice Marshall, and all the then judges of the Supreme Court of the United States. These were men selected for their high attainments and sound judgments, to whom the first president had entrusted the full legal power of the constitution.

It was with these men (one of the latter of whom was a near relation of President Washington,) that I delighted to commune, mind to mind and spirit to spirit, on the great destinies of the human races through future generations.

These men, all advanced in years, had lived sufficiently long to see some of the early effects of their own deeply hazarded and well-considered work. Presidents Adams, Jefferson, Madison, and Munroe, admitted to me that they were greatly disappointed with the working of the constitution which they had risked their lives to establish. The young of the most wealthy and influential families were acquiring habits of luxury and intemperance to an alarming extent; and they said with great feeling, that if this wealth, luxury, and intemperance should go on increasing, they should despair of the republic attaining the objects which they had in view when framing the constitution for it.

These men were all straightforward in their minds, simple in their manners and habits, and devoid of all ostentation. They possessed to a great extent the kind of character which society, for its own interest and happiness, should now make arrangements to give to the whole of the human races. They were men of advanced minds, as well as advanced in age, and of great experience in those eventful times.

When I told them that I had anticipated their well-founded disappointment in the character of the rising young republicans, they enquired upon what grounds I had founded my anticipations. I said that the formation of their characters had been false and erroneous, and the construction of society, or the surroundings in which they had been placed, had been most injurious to them, and that these will continue as long as society shall be founded on the false base on which it has hitherto through all time been constructed and governed.

This statement greatly surprised each in succession, as I visited them; especially John Adams and Thomas Jefferson, to whom I made my first confidential visits in the United States, being desirous of first knowing the extent of their knowledge and experience, and the circle or expanse of their minds under the existing system of society ; concluding (as I found,) that they were politically the most advanced minds which it had produced.

I then explained my views of an entirely new state of human existence, in spirit, principle, and practice, as I have so often endeavoured with but very limited success to make it understood by the general or ordinary mind of the world.

But it was not so with these men. Their former experience of contending for new principles and measures with other strong minded opponents, had prepared them to listen to and reflect upon any new principles, opposed to their former views. They (as was the case at an earlier period with the Rev. Mr. Turner of Newcastle, Mr. Wellbeloved of York, and Dr. Marsh, then Regius professor at Cambridge, and afterwards Bishop of Peterborough,) could not resist the truth of the laws of nature on which the new dispensation which I have advocated, and which I now again proclaim to the world, is founded, and is built up in perfect accordance with those unchanging laws of nature.

After a full explanation of my views to the four Presidents of the United States, they regularly, one after the other, admitted the truth of the fundamental principle on which the new dispensation must be raised. But one and all said, we do not see how these principles, true and beautiful as they are, can be applied to practice.

I then stated in what manner I had then for thirty years applied them to practice partially in Manchester and at New Lanark, with a success far exceeding my most sanguine expectations, and that the practice when fully introduced without the interference of any part of the old dispensation, no doubt necessary for the early and undeveloped state of society, could be far more easily maintained in practice than the present can now be much longer continued.

They said you have had so much practical knowledge of the application of these new principles to practice, that our want of experience must yield to your experience.

A singularly fortunate event occurred on my visit to the second President, John Adams. I had taken with me Robert Watson, as my travelling servant. He had been employed at New Lanark, from a boy, upwards of twenty years, and had witnessed the changes I had made in the whole establishment. and knew the perfect state in which I had left it in 1824, when we set out for the United States, and during part of that year in Washington he had been frequently at the President's residence, called the White House, and had seen Mr. Munroe, and had been with me on a visit of many days at Ex-President Jefferson's, and also at Ex-President Madison's. He was intelligent, and this journey had much enlarged his knowledge, and he was very desirous to increase it.

Mr. Adams, while I was with him, was confined to his own room, in which he received his visitors, who at meals went below to partake with the family. Mr. A ams had an old superior confidential man servant, who appeared to be on the best terms with his master. Robert Watson had made friends with this fine old servant, and had told him that he had seen all the Presidents then alive, except Mr. Adams, and he should very much like to be able to say on his return home that he had also seen Mr. Adams. The old servant communicated this conversation to Mr. Adams, who said—" I shall have pleasure in seeing him,— bring him to me." Watson was thus introduced to the President who, as Watson afterwards told me, shook hands with him frankly, requested him to be seated, and then began to enquire into all the particulars respecting the practical proceedings at New Lanark, which Watson was too happy to communicate. The President took great interest in the details which Watson gave in reply to the many questions which he asked, and the interview continued for two hours, when I returned to the President's room, and Watson retired.

The President then said to me—" I have been " much gratified by this visit of your servant. He " has given me the full details which I wished for from " an actual receiver of the benefits of your wonder-" working system, and I cannot but approve of your " system, both in principle and as applied to practice."

There was at this period a friendship established between the Ex-President, the existing President, Mr. Munroe, and his successor John Quincey Adams, the son of President Adams ; and I had every reason to suppose that the Ex-President, whom I had thus visited, communicated his ideas and impressions to all of them; for from that period I had the full confidence of the United States government, through the administrations of Mr. Munroe, Mr. John Quincey Adams, General Jackson, and Mr. Van Buren ; the interesting particulars of which will be given in detail in my life which I am now engaged in writing.

I am therefore well acquainted with the Republic of the United States of North America, and in some measure also with those of South America ; and I hesitate not to declare that they are incompetent to govern society for the benefit of any population over the earth. There must be a new principle and a new practice, before any form of government whatever can produce unity, goodness, wisdom, and happiness, permanently among men.

I therefore recommend you to apply your minds to acquire a full knowledge of these new principles, and of their consistent application to practice for the government of the population of the world.

Mr. Owen having offered the usual opportunity for the full discussion of the subjects brought forward in his remarks and address on this day, John Scott, Esq., C.E., Belfast, agreeably to his previous notice, came forward and said—Mr. President and gentlemen of the Congress. The duty of acquiring. possessing, and exercising the powers and rights which belong to humanity, is the subject to which I now solicit your best attention.

1.—The desire for the possession of power is one of the primary attributes of the human mind. There are various kinds of power, which it is our solemn duty to acquire, accumulate, hold fast, and properly exercise. Power over ourselves, power to conceive and utter our thoughts, to love and learn the knowledge of truth, to overcome difficulties and withstand trials—power over pleasure and pain—power to awaken, enlighten, and elevate our fellowmen, and follow our convictions, who can prize too much? Who can prize too highly the power to love and acquire the knowledge of truth and duty—the power which calls forth the intellectual and moral resources of mankind—which communicates new impulses to society—which throws into world-wide circulation new and stirring thoughts of progress towards perfection—which gives to the human mind a new consciousness of its growing faculties—and which rouses and fortifies the human will to an all-conquering energy and purpose of well-doing?

2.—Power is the chief element in all the commanding qualities of humanity; it forms the foundation of fortitude, faithfulness, courage, and constancy. Power enters into all our actions, into all our physical, intellectual, and moral energies. It is by power that we form and develop ourselves—conceive, take cognizance of, and utter our thoughts—originate, direct, and regulate our physical and mental movements—press the physical elements, objects, and animals around us into our service; and it is by power, that we must exercise a beneficial influence, and a benevolent sway over our fellow men. It is by and through the acquisition, possession, and proper application of intellectual and moral power, that we can enjoy and exercise our rights and liberties;—that we can benefit and bless our fellow men;—that we can reach and realize every object and purpose of our existence.

3.—To acquire, possess, and exercise a noble, quickening influence, and a great and good sway over our fellow men, form the grand test and the accurate measure of true greatness. It is our high and holy duty to acquire through well doing—through the constant cultivation and proper development of ourselves—a noble power-giving sway over our fellow men—a sway which will bring them into intellectual and moral concert, sympathy, and likeness, with ourselves; and which will give them the conscious possession of the power of self-direction, and of free and fearless thought and action. To acquire the power to be able to improve the outward physical condition of our fellow men, is chiefly important, as it forms a means for inward mental growth; as it enables us to breathe into them the love of the knowledge of

truth—the love of their rights and liberties, and to strengthen them in their purposes of virtue, of freedom, of independence, of self-reliance, of self-government, and of self-development.

4.—We are not, therefore, to seek influence, or to acquire and possess power, merely, in order to enjoy and monopolise it for ourselves—merely in order to subject others to our will, and mould them after our views and wishes, but with the grand view to communicate and impart it to our fellow men, that they may possess it—that they may freely exercise it for themselves and others. Every man in proportion to his progress in intellectual and moral development, acquires a measure of power which may become the source of light and energy to others. In the humblest condition of society, men are found acquiring and possessing powers by which they call forth silently, the intellectual and moral energies of their fellow men ; in the lowliest and most labourious walks of social life, men are often found possessing a force and an elevation of mind by which they exercise a beneficial sway and a quickening influence over the minds of their fellow men, to which no limits can be fixed or prescribed. They conceive and utter thoughts, which are felt in distant nations, and which shall go down to future ages, to move, enlighten, and bless mankind. These are the true great and good men of their age. These are the grand sovereigns of the human races. They inherit and display a Divine grandeur. They possess and communicate a greatness and a goodness, which shall be more and more felt and recognised as the successive ages of duration will roll onward.

5.—The time is fast coming, its signs are now clearly visible, when the grand Divine attributes of true greatness and real goodness, will be seen to belong eminently, and only to those, who, by their intellectual and moral developments, and love of the knowledge of truth,—who, by the excellence of their characters, persevering exertions in behalf of human progress, and deeds of philanthropy, patriotism, and benevolence, impress and leave imperishable and ennobling traces of their virtuous motives and actions on the face of the earth, on the institutions of society, and on the improved and improving condition of their fellow men. Among these legitimate sovereigns of the human races will be ranked the free fearless, and faithful lovers of the knowledge of truth and duty—the true philosophical inquirers into the real nature of things, who penetrate into the hidden arcana of matter and mind, of body and spirit—into the absolute forces and phenomena of the universe ;— who open up new fields to the intellectual and moral faculties of mankind ;— who constantly help their fellow men to gain free, enlarged liberal habits of thought and action, and a new consciousness of their own ever-growing powers—of their Divine origin—of their equal rights and liberties ; who constantly aid their fellow men to comprehend, that an ever-expanding knowledge of truth and duty is the Divine patrimony of the human races ;—who rise up above the degrading errors and pernicious abuses of their times ;—who are moved by a pure holy zeal for the progress of the knowledge of truth, to frown the causes of evil and crime out of existence, to assail and besiege the vicious views, and the iniquitous establishments around them, sustained by fierce superstitions and by the force of inveterate prejudices ;—who rescue great truths from surrounding corruptions, and present new views of them, in fresh and attractive forms, which secure for them at once, enlightened and earnest conviction ;—who by these means unfold to men higher forms of excellence and virtue than they have yet conceived or attained ;—and who give to their fellow men a victorious faith founded on the knowledge of truth, and higher and more hopeful prospects of the perpetual progress towards the possession and enjoyment of the rights, liberties, and perfection for which men were formed. Among these legitimate sovereigns of the human races—these princes of human progress towards higher degrees of perfection, will be classed the philanthropists, the patriots, and the statesmen, who rise up to the discovery of the true physical, intellectual, and moral interests of the people—who constantly and courageously seek, without fear or favour, the practical recognition. and the actual realization of the public good ;—who accurately understand and boldly maintain, that a nation's mind is more precious, valuable, and important than its material wealth ;—who unfold, develope and direct the people's energies and enterprises without making them sordid slaves of physical labours, and passive participators of wealth-worship ;—who devise and originate social institutions, which secure to men the possession and enjoyment of their natural rights, and the free exercise of their proper civil liberties, and by which society may be progressively carried forward in the march of improvement ;—who confide with a sublime, courageous constancy, in righteousness, justice, and moral virtue, as the solid foundations of political policy, of public power, and of social prosperity ;—and, above all, who constantly inculcate the knowledge that the people of any particular country are but members of the great human family, bound to all other nations by Divine ties, by bonds of similar interests and of equal rights, and by the indissoluble laws of universal equity, and perpetual benevolence.

6.—The distinguishing characteristics of the powers and influences which these great and good men acquire, possess, and exercise over their fellow men, are, that they awaken in them kindred powers and principles ;—that they form in their minds similar motives, and call forth their faculties into new action ;—that they strengthen them to follow their own convictions of truth and duty, and that they render all those on whom they are exercised more free and noble—more conscious of self-energy and self-respect—more intellectually and morally independent,—and more opposed to every form of despotism and usurpation.

7.—There have been, and there are still, other classes of men, very different from those described, as the legitimate sovereigns of the human races ;—classes of men, who, constantly seek to acquire and exercise powers and influences, not to quicken, enlighten, and elevate their fellow men, but to subject and subdue them ;—who eagerly grasp at every kind of power and influence with the view to rule and reign over their fellow men, and give forth their views and wishes in the form of laws ;—who constantly exercise all their powers and influences to rob and spoil their brethren of their most precious rights and liberties—of the free use of their best faculties—of self-respect—of self-direction, and compel them to bend to their pernicious fashions, vicious views, and enslaving wills ;—and who by terrors, tortures, prisons, penalties, and the fears of varied pains, degrade their fellow men into servile slaves—into abject mechanical repeaters of visionary views which they can neither try nor trust. The character and influence of almost every political, social, and moral institution upon the earth have been, and are still, calculated to degrade and make men abject, fearful, and servile in mind ; and the passive supporters, by their means, of forms of governments and systems which fail to promote the public good. Immense multitudes of the men thus injured and wronged are unconscious of the turpitude of the crimes committed against them, and of the inherent dignity, grandeur, and moral worth of their nature, formed to grow and prosper by its self-forming and self-directing energies. But we have the strongest and the clearest proofs of the degrading influences, of the nefarious usurpations of the few, who seek power exclusively for themselves, in the intellectual and moral consequences of the imposition of their wills and wishes on the many ; and of the debasing and enfeebling results of their abuse of power, in the public denial, by class laws, of the essential equality of men.

8.—The great majority of men, however, never form adequate ideas of the moral turpitude, of the flagrant crimes and injuries chargeable on those, who constantly aim at imposing their own wills on society, and at establishing dominion over their brethren. The great crimes committed against human society —the crimes of robbing and depriving the majority of its members of their civil and social rights and liberties—of the rights and liberties belonging by their nature to rational responsible beings—still fail to move the deep abhorrence which are their due ; and which if felt would fix on the usurpers the brand of indelible infamy. There still exists, among the great majority of men, a mournful obtuseness of intellectual perception and of moral feeling in regard to many of the crimes which are constantly committed against human society ; and in particular, in respect to the crimes of political and social degradation—the crimes of robbing and depriving men of their civil and social rights and liberties.   The wrong doings of those who continue to raise their voices, and to level their influences against the recognition of the civil rights of the people, have never yet drawn upon them that sincere abhorrence and that solemn indignation which their callous crimes against human society justly merit. Multitudes of the people seem still to betray the righteous cause of human freedom, and to court political bondage by their stupid admiration of successful usurpers and hereditary despots.   The political wrongs from which the people have suffered and are suffering most, in body and mind, are yet uncondemned—are yet unpunished.

9.—It is true, that certain portions of the public press have long taught, and are constantly teaching the people to pour out reproaches on the authors of these crimes against human society.   But these reproaches are yet little more than mere sounds, and unmeaning commonplaces.   They are, in the great majority of instances, merely formally repeated.   When we read, or hear them, we must feel that they want depth and strength. They are not sincere and solemn.   They are not bold, burning convictions breaking forth from fearless, indignant spirits, with powerful tones of reality before which the guilty would cower. The true intellectual perceptions and the moral feelings which ought to exist in regard to the crimes of political and social degradation—in regard to the great crimes of robbing and depriving men of their rights—are almost to be formed.   Multitudes of men possess no distinct consciousness of the moral turpitude of these crimes, which are so extensively committed against human society ; and the people who encourage and contribute so much to their growth and to their perpetuation, are indeed responsible for their consequences, and merit in part to suffer from the miseries which they produce and spread.

10.—Despotism, whether usurped or hereditary, and in every form, should be abhorred, as one of the most grievous crimes against human society—as one of the greatest wrongs and insults to men.   But towards hereditary despots we must mingle some compassion with our indignation.   Nursed and trained up in gross delusion—worshipped from their childhood—never approached in a free, familiar manner, nor spoken to in the fearless tones of truth—taught to look on the great bulk of their fellow men as kinds of inferior beings, to regard their own supremacy as a fixed social law—the false position, as well as the unnatural condition of such persons, almost deny them the possibility and the means of acquiring clear intellectual perceptions, healthy moral feelings, and manly virtues ; and they must, therefore, be pitied as well as condemned.   There are different distinct orders of hereditary despots, abusers of power, and conspirators against the rights of humanity, who must be pitied as well as censured and removed from their present position.   Still in pitying the various kinds of hereditary despots, abusers, of power, and conspirators against the rights and liberties of humanity, let us not cease to censure and condemn every form of despotism, and every manifestation of treason against public freedom, as among the greatest wrongs from which men can suffer. Has not the time for the complete removal from human society of every form of despotism arrived? Can every form of treason against the rights and liberties of humanity—against public freedom—be taken away too sudden or too soon? Have not hereditary despots, abusers of power, and their servile minions, long enough chilled social intercourse, defeated the Divine designs of society, and pillaged and wrung from honest labour its industrious earnings? Have they not long enough squandered and wasted the wealth of nations on themselves, and on their worthless, perverted, polluting parasites and minions, and added to all their other wrongs and insults, that of the most flagrant ingratitude towards their humble benefactors? Have they not long enough chained down mental energy, fettered the powerful press, and crushed the freedom of the public mind with corrupting creeds? Have they not long enough, both retarded and resisted the progress of the knowledge of truth and duty, filled prisons and dungeons with the best promoters of human freedom, with the best advocates of political liberty, and murdered the best patriots and philanthropists they could find? Then let their pernicious influences come to a complete end, sudden and soon.

11.—The people of different nations appear now, to be acquiring some accurate conceptions of the ennobling nature of political freedom, and to be making a corresponding intellectual and moral preparation, for the full recognition and free exercise of their civil rights—for the full possession and free enjoyment of their political liberties. But, as a people, we are yet scarcely ripe for the full and free reception of the great political good which we are anxiously seeking. We are, it is much to be feared, still too ignorant and too corrupt for the reception of the fullest measure of political freedom. It is to be greatly regretted that our many intellectual and moral defects forbid us yet to be politically free. Are not multitudes of the people still grievously and grossly ignorant—still deeply and deplorably vicious? Have not many of them completely thrown off all the convictions and restraints which enlighten and ennoble the human mind? Do not many of them deny and deride the very idea of the existence of God, and every view of man's connection with, and dependence on, the supreme source of being? Do not many of them despise and reject the truth of human immortality and all the great truths which are the sources and seeds of all true rational liberty, and of all real greatness? Do not many of them look upon human beings as mere worms, who are soon to cease to exist—to rot and perish for ever? Would

it not, then, be sheer infatuation to expect, that such men are
actually prepared to receive and exercise the fullest measure of
political rights? Would it not be, indeed, next to complete insanity to hope that such men could solely work out the political
and social emancipation of their brethren? Or that the dearest
rights of humanity could be perfectly secure in the possession
of such men? The very names of freedom and liberty are
tarnished by their touch; and it would be great folly indeed to
suppose that the political rights and liberties of men could be
safe and secure, or healthy and vigorous in their keeping. Our
political rights and liberties will not come to us through such
men, or by accident, nor will they ever be the gift of a few public leaders; but they must grow up in a cultivated mental soil,
and from sowing the sound seeds of intelligence and morality
plentifully in the minds of the people. They must grow up
from the for ation of deliberate convictions—from the diffusion
of generous principles, and from the solemn purposes of being
free. The people must become politically free, from their own
intelligence, moral courage, energy, wisdom, and purity of purpose. The people who do not possess the intelligent, earnest
principle of freedom in their own minds, are not yet ready to
be free.

12.—A most important part of this subject now offers itself
for our serious consideration. If an intellectual cultivation and
a moral preparation are absolutely required for the possession of
political rights, and for the exercise of social freedom, how, it
may be asked can the people of this and of other countries become actually free? How, under the many forms of despotism,
corruption, ignorance, and division, can the people grow ripe
and ready for the full possession and the free exercise of their
rights and liberties? Is it to be hoped that men will learn in
the schools of social slavery, and among the scenes of political
degradation, the intelligence and the moral virtues, which can
alone work out their complete deliverance? In this, and in
different other countries, the very means and instruments which
should be constantly employed, to instruct the people in the
knowledge of their rights, and to form an enlightened and generous love for political freedom, are continually pressed into the
service of error and corruption; and to secure and support class
privileges, and to maintain various forms of the abuse of power.
How, then, shall an intelligent, wise, moral freedom be generated and diffused in every country? How, then, shall the people of all nations become politically free and self-governing?
Let us carefully endeavour to ascertain and to look at the full
force of all the difficulties which we have to overcome; for no
advance can be made by overlooking the many obstacles with
which the progress of the recognition and realisation of our
political rights and liberties have to contend. We will not, at
present, however, attempt to exhaust the answers to all these

questions now proposed ; and we will only very briefly suggest, what seems to us, to be the chief means and methods, by which the cause of genuine freedom, obstructed as it is, must now be advanced.

13.—In this, and in all other countries, those men who are inspired with the sublime and lofty sentiments of freedom and justice—who comprehend, that, there are great solemn human rights which precede civil laws, and on which all laws should be founded—must begin, in their individual characters, to communicate their knowledge of truth and justice, their enlightened views and liberal principles, to individual minds around them. The cause of genuine freedom and justice cannot, as yet, be advanced by men in large masses. But, in almost every country there are those who are inspired with the sublime and lofty love of liberty and justice—men who feel their own and their fellow men's political degradation and social wrongs ;—men who, indeed, abhor every obstruction to the progress of individuals, communities, and nations, and every form of the abuse of human powers Let such men constantly spread around them, their own sincere love of the knowledge of truth and duty, their enlightened views and generous principles, and their mental powers and love of freedom, by every possible means, and through every practicable channel. Let them give free and fearless utterance, to their own love and convictions of the knowledge of truth and duty, to their lofty love of rational liberty and justice, and to their sublime sentiments of magnanimity and of intellectual and moral greatness, in private conferences, in public assemblies, from the platform, and through the powerful press : and these are means and modes of expressing and communicating the kindling and quickening knowledge of truth and duty,—of removing ignorance,—of repressing wrong,—of vindicating innocence,—of humbling the haughty,—of publishing the rights and liberties of men,—and of forming the love of freedom and justice; which, it is presumed, have never yet been brought into full active operation.

14.—Let them especially communicate and teach the love and the knowledge of the great truths, which form the very foundation of all virtuous freedom, of all true intellectual and moral liberty ; namely, that the sense and love of right, or the perception and love of duty, in every healthy developed mind, are to be listened to and regarded above, and before all other guardians and guides ; that this sublime sense of duty, this sovereign perception of right—God's greatest gift to men—is more powerful to reward and punish than all other outward laws and sovereigns ; and that they alone are worthy of the name and vocation of men who give themselves up, solemnly and deliberately to obey this internal lawgiver, through all pleasures, perils, and pains. This is the essential essence of the real elements of true freedom ; for no man is wholly and absolutely free but he who constantly acts independently of every outward influence, he who invariably resists every external usurpation, that he may freely follow his own convictions of duty, and obey the dictations of his own sense of right. These are the principles and the lessons, which should, and which must, be constantly taught, to the people of all countries. As yet they are but very imperfectly comprehended, and very inadequately appreciated, even by the highest advanced people, of the most favoured countries. Their full application, and their complete appreciation, remain to be made and developed. They who have been completely developed by the conscious presence and experience of these vital and all-comprehending truths and principles, must everywhere exert themselves to promote and propagate the most accurate knowledge of them ; and every one who can convert a fellow being to these principles, has broken already the principal links of the chains of every despotism.

15.—It is chiefly in the diffusion of the knowledge of these sublime truths, and lofty moral sentiments, that we place our hope of human freedom ; and we have this grand hope, and we do not, and we cannot, despair of its ultimate achievement; because we know that there are those who are ready whenever opportunities offer, to be their sincere promoters and constant propagators. We do not, and we cannot, despair of the ultimate achievement of human freedom, for there are Divine powers of self-diffusion—all-enduring. all-subduing, and all-defying energies—in these sublime truths and moral principles. The conscious knowledge of the mind kindling and ennobling energies, which reside in these truths and principles, is the chief foundation of our immovable trust, that in proportion as the pure vital knowledge of them is diffused and implanted in the minds of men, they will cease to rely on all descriptions of force, for the achievement of human freedom. The promoters of human freedom, of justice, and benevolence, are learning to scorn the use of all kinds of force, to forward their cause ; and they are becoming more and more convinced that their true vocation is to consecrate themselves wholly to the grand work of awakening their fellow beings to the consciousness of the powers, rights, and purposes of human nature—to generate in the public mind the heroism of intellectuality, and the bravery of magnanimity, of moral courage and self-government. And we are firmly convinced that, at this moment, there are intelligence, wisdom, and virtue enough in this, and in many other countries, to break down. dissolve, and dissipate every form of despotism, tyranny, and oppression, were the possessors of these intellectual and moral qualities. as confidingly united, as conscious of their own might, and as constantly and zealously engaged in pouring and communicating themselves. through every possible channel, into the public mind, as they should be.

16.—The promoters of human freedom—those who feel con-

F

vinced that human life (man's time and powers) should not be wholly usurped and consumed by corroding cares for mere physical subsistence—those who enjoy the happiness won through successful struggles with various vanities, follies, and foes—the happiness of intellectual power and moral victory—the happiness of wide-spread philanthropy ; the happiness of the boundless hope of perpetual progress towards perfection,—should raise themselves up above their age ; and fortified with the consciousness of their high vocation, they ought to become both to their own and future times, examples of human virtue, energy, and greatness. In regard to the opponents and abuses—despots, tyrants, usurpers, and abusers of power in state and church, and all the corrupt institutions of human society—which must be constantly assailed, in order to advance the cause of human freedom—the strains in which they ought to be described and denounced, should be truthful, exalted, strong, stern, and withering. There is constantly going on in human society a conflict between present evil and future good. The cause of truth, of justice, and humanity, has thus constantly to struggle and wrestle with strong foes and persisting wrongs. All human improvements are won by great intellectual efforts, moral powers, and constant struggles. And human freedom is thus constantly resisted and placed in peril, from the fact that all existing evils and abuses, struggle strongly for perpetuity, and can only be completely broken down, dissolved, and dissipated by great intellectual efforts and all-conquering moral powers. The promoters of human freedom should, therefore, feel that interests of infinite moment, of incalculable importance, are constantly in jeopardy, and placed under their charge, and that they must bind and exert themselves to advance and defend them, with all possible boldness, fervor, and perseverance. We must not, therefore, conclude that the love of truth, justice, moral excellence, virtue, and human freedom, has but one voice—that of pity and soft entreaty. This love can, and must, speak in powerful and piercing tones. All the great periods of human history, which have been distinguished by rapid developments and improvements of the human mind, have been particularly signalised by the free, fearless uttering of truthful, exalted, strong, stern, and withering denunciations against all forms of despotism and the abuse of power. At all such great and momentous periods, men gifted with great intellectual and moral powers, with the lofty sentiments of virtue, and the burning love of human freedom ; men who clearly see the dark harsh gloomy offsprings of ignorance and superstition holding undisputed sway over the minds of hundreds of millions of the human races, who are constantly languishing under the immense numbers of false faiths, a variety of erroneous creeds, unnatural, unwholesome systems of political government, and unhealthy man destroying social institutions—at such periods, we say, that men possessing the powers and energies of men, are especially summoned and commissioned by their own generous magnanimity, to speak against all forms of the abuse of power, error, and evil, with an indignant energy of thought and utterance, which cannot fail to move and shake the corruptions of nations.

17.—We adore, admire, and venerate the supreme intelligence, wisdom, and goodness of our Father God, who has ordained that human freedom, human improvement, and human happiness shall be wrought out and secured, by the intelligence, wisdom, magnanimity, courage, virtue, and benevolence of men. And we should constantly rejoice to know, that the love of the knowledge of truth, of duty, of justice, and of human freedom, can be monopolised by no particular persons or parties ;—that the love of the knowledge of truth, duty, justice, and freedom, can be no more confined to a single mind, or party of men, than the beautiful light of the solar centre be shut up in the pompous palaces of princes. It is, however, a great question at present, how men may be effectually instructed, and be put in perfect possession of the pure knowledge of their proper civil rights and liberties. This field is still almost untrodden; but if we read aright the signs and wants of the times on which we are entering, the day for fully exploring it draws nigh. And while entertaining this cheerful hope, we should constantly rejoice, for the many glorious and grand efforts, which the cause of human freedom has already called forth;—for the magnanimous and intrepid promoters and defenders who have energetically gathered round it in different ages—for the toils, the sufferings, the patience, and the perseverance, by which it has been upheld, and advanced,—for the awakening, the quickening, and the thrilling influences, which come to us from the heroic and courageous example of those, who were the faithful examples of human freedom in times gone by; which come to us from the great and good example of those, who have often demonstrated, by their pains, prisons, and even physical lives, the strength of truth, justice, and virtue—as also their power in suppressing and uprooting ignorance, despotism, and tyranny. We should constantly desire, that these pure influences, coming to us from the great and good examples of men, enriched and signalised by their eminent gifts and great powers, would enkindle and quicken in us, an unquenchable love of truth, justice, virtue, and human freedom ; in order, that we may become able to fulfil the high functions of inspiring our fellow men with the consciousness of their birthrights, and the glorious destination of human beings ; in order, that we may become more and more able, to labour effectually, to remove all existing errors, and evils, by the mild and gentle, yet great and awful powers of truth, justice, and virtue ; by the victorious triumphs of the sentiments of magnanimity, moral courage and hope, which will enliven the depressed and the degraded, and which despots, tyrants, usurpers, and abusers of human power, will not be able to withstand.

The subjects of Mr. Owen's and Mr. Scott's addresses having being duly debated, and referred to the committee to report to Congress, the meeting adjourned at 4 p.m. till 11 a.m. next day.

Eleventh Meeting, May 22nd, in St. Martin's Hall.

ROBERT OWEN in the chair.—The eleventh meeting of the Congress sat in St. Martin's Hall to receive and adopt the report drawn up by the committee appointed to present the result of their deliberations on the proceedings of each day from 12th to the 21st of May. Mr Maughan, on behalf of the said committee, in introducing the report, desired to say a few words. He expressed the pleasure attending these meetings of this Congress had afforded him. Robert Owen's principles, which he had once opposed, he was convinced contained those societary truths which could alone restore society to happiness and harmony. They do not deal with symptoms merely, but go to the root of the evil at once.

The enemies of Mr. Owen's views, were so far from misconception, for they adopted them, and advocated them without knowledge of their source, or in many instances knowing it. The whole of their proceedings showed that they appreciated the truth of Mr. Owen's fundamental axiom, that the character of man is formed for him, and not by him.

The main difficulty experienced by many otherwise well diposed to receiving Mr. Owen's views, arose from the idea of non-responsibility. This was not true in the absolute sense, nor does Mr. Owen teach it in this sense, for he says—society is responsible to the individual, while the individual is not responsible to it. What can this mean, but that those who are more enlightened than their fellow men, who have power to make the laws, and the arrangements of society, and especially those of them, who see clearly the evils society suffers from, and their causes—are responsible for their removal, and that this is a responsibility from which men should not shrink? No man can be held to be responsible in a matter over which he has no control, and we have only to examine the extent to which we can exercise real control to find the measure of our responsibility; you have no right to punish any man for the character he has under the influence of bad surroundings, which he neither formed, nor can extricate himself from. When you hold a man responsible for his character, you must show that he had full control, that he was able from birth to choose, and that he was endowed with wisdom to choose rightly, in the midst of ignorance and inexperience. A strange apathy has crept over mankind, they have eyes and see not, and ears and hear not, they have mouths—but to how little purpose do they speak ? We, who say we see, ought also to speak to good purpose. We, who say we know the principles of societary reform, ought to be the foremost in carrying them out. Our apathy and disunion is a disgrace which we ought to remove far from us.

Mr. Maughan was then called upon by Mr. Cooper, chairman of the Committee, to read the following report, which, upon being duly moved and seconded, was unanimously adopted.

REPORT OF THE COMMITTEE APPOINTED BY THE CONGRESS OF THE ADVANCED MINDS OF THE WORLD, CONVENED BY MR. ROBERT OWEN, TO PRESENT THE RESULT OF THEIR DELIBERATION UPON EACH DAY'S PROCEEDINGS, FROM THE 14TH TO THE 21ST OF MAY, 1857.

YOUR Committee—though composed of persons differing in opinion in many respects—avail themselves of this opportunity to express their unfeigned satisfaction that they have had the privilege of assembling under the auspices, and of listening to the sentiments of the venerable convener of this Congress.

They beg to offer him their sincere congratulation that at the advanced age of eighty-six he still enjoys so large a measure of health and vigour, and that with faculties unimpaired he is still able clearly to unfold principles which have been the study and practice of his life ; principles which have for their object the benefit of the human family.

When they take a retrospect of his long life, and consider his valuable services in the cause of humanity— labouring in all seasons, among all classes of society, and in many countries of the world, to diffuse a knowledge of the Fundamental Principles by which the happiness and permanent welfare of mankind may be secured—they cannot but admire his consistency and perseverance, and appreciate the evident success which has attended his exertions, manifest in the improved tone of society, the improved condition of a portion of the people, and the partial adoption of his plans and principles.

They hope that he may be long spared, and that those who have attended this Congress may yet have many opportunities of listening to his philanthropic teachings, and his benevolent aspirations for the good of all men.

Your Committee notice with pleasure the calm, philosophic, and impartial spirit which has pervaded the meetings of this Congress; and that though many differences of opinion were expressed, there was no acerbity displayed; all the speakers appeared to be animated with the prevailing desire to promote the happiness and welfare of their fellow men. The urbanity of the venerable president contributed in no small degree to this result, and presents a brilliant example to public teachers in general.

Your Committee have listened with attention and great interest to the explanations of the principles of social regeneration Mr. Owen propounds for the adoption of mankind; they perceive and acknowledge the pressing necessity there is for some vital change in the mode of training, educating, and placing the human family, to rescue them from the false, hollow, and degrading system which now contributes so extensively to debase and malform the character of all. They agree with Mr. Owen, that " Humanity, in all " born of man, desires from birth to death to be happy ;" that " all, through past ages, have been, through a " law of necessity, trained, educated, and placed, so as " to prevent the possibility of any one of our race being " happy through life ;" that " all have been generated " in ignorance, and therefore have been imperfectly " born ;" that " all have been trained, educated, em-

" ployed, placed, and governed, on false principles;
" and in consequence man has hitherto been malformed,
" physically, intellectually, morally, spiritually, and
" practically ;" and that " society over the earth has
" been and now is grossly misconstructed."

That " this has been the early period of humanity,
" through which it had to experience the evils of its
" infancy and childhood, and of the ignorance conse-
-" quent thereon ;" that " this has been the period of
" hitherto unavoidable individual Satanism, or worse
" than mere Animal Selfishness ;" and that " the
" experience which has now been acquired of the
" inestimable knowledge and value of the spirit of
" humanity, united with the discoveries which, through
" the progress of science, have been made of the
" elements of nature, and of the enormous incalculable
" powers which, when wisely directed, these elements
" can be made to give each individual, to secure his
" well-being, well-doing, and happiness through life—
" will now terminate this period of the infancy, error,
" and suffering of humanity ;" and that " the reign
" of goodness, wisdom, and happiness will commence,
" by man being born, trained, educated, employed,
" placed, and governed from birth rationally, in strict
" accordance with the laws of his nature, instead of
" irrationally and in direct opposition to all the now
" easily ascertained laws of his nature." ·

They fully concur that it is only by obedience ·to
the natural laws of well-being—wherever those laws
may be found recorded—whether they be called Laws
of God or Laws of Nature, that these results can be
attained, and that there is no other path to permanent
happiness, elevation, and well-being for all, but simple
unwavering obedience to them.

They are happy to be able cordially to subscribe to
the opinions expressed by Mr. Owen in his opening
address :—

" First.—That a good, useful, and valuable cha-
" racter should be given to all from birth through life.

" Second.—That substantial wealth should be amply
" provided for all, by means pleasant and agreeable
" to all.

" Third.—That all should be united as one superior
" family, each possessing the pure spirit of universal
" love and charity, and applying it to practice through
" every hour and action of their lives.

" Fourth.—That the surroundings of all, to make
" these results certain to each, should be as perfect as
" the existing knowledge and means of society can ac-
" complish."

And they recommend to the study and adoption of
their fellow men Mr. Owen's advice to the " Repre-
" sentatives of all the Religions of the world," contained in the following extract from his address to
them. He says:—

" The first practical step which you can take is to
" acquire the true spirit of universal love and charity,
" which, when you have acquired it so as to apply it
" to continual daily practice, will unite you all as
" brethren of a superior enlightened family, and you
" will not accept of any other distinctions than those
" of age; for human-made distinctions tend con-
" tinually to divide man from man, and to destroy all
" feelings of *true Christianity* between them.

" Your best occupation now will be to acquire a
" practical knowledge of the science of surroundings,
" and teach it in your temples, synagogues, churches,
" mosques, meeting-houses, and places for religious
" teachings; because, through this knowledge, all who
" shall be born after this science shall be well under-
" stood and carried into practice, may be made, with
" the certainty of a law of nature, good, wise, united,
" and happy, as each will be pervaded—in proportion
" to their growth from birth—with the true spirit of
" universal charity and love, which they will, without
" ceasing, apply in their every-day practice.

" In the name of common sense, why all this waste
" of mind, time, and treasure, over the world, to create

" repulsive feelings between men and nations, and to
" produce evil continually, where, without these false
" religions, no evils would exist ?

" But let the world beware of doing injustice to
" those who could not prevent these religions being
" forced into their minds. For these errors they are
" blameless ; and not one professing religionist over
" the world should be in any manner injured in mind,
" body, or estate, for becoming and being what society
" has forced him to become and to be."

The address delivered by Mr. Owen on Sunday
Morning, May 17th, at the Literary and Scientific Institution, John Street, to " The Producers of Wealth,
Employers and Employed," your Committee specially
commend to the attention of those classes of Society,
as containing the essential principles on which the
well being of society must be based, to secure those
beneficial surroundings so necessary to the formation
of a good and true character for all. The document
is too long to be incorporated in this report, and they
must refer the Congress to the address itself, which
has already been placed in their hands.

In the evening Mr. Owen's 86th birthday was celebrated by a large party of his friends, who took tea
together, after which Mr. Owen addressed a considerable audience with his accustomed spirit, clearness, and
urbanity.

On Monday, the 18th, Mr. Owen addressed the
educators of mankind ; and your Committee are with
sorrow compelled to subscribe to the statement Mr.
Owen thus makes of the present condition of mankind. He says :—

" All present surroundings are essentially injurious
" to all of our race ; for they are eminently calculated
" to force all to acquire a false, bad, and inferior cha-
" racter, and to make it impossible that one true
" Christian could be made by them." And they ask
with him, " Where now is there one upon the earth
" who always expresses, in look, word, and manner,

" the simple truth which he is obliged to feel; and
" whose mind is pervaded with the true spirit of uni-
" versal love and charity for our race?"

Your Committee sincerely hope that by the means
and instruction of enlightened educators, mankind
may be able to realise that—

" The path is plain and open," and that " under
" the new dispensation" it " will be easily pursued
" by all who enter it."

" That society will be based on its true foundation,
" and" that " truth alone will be the language of the
" population of the world;" that " insincerity in word
" and action will be unknown."

That " a superior physical, intellectual, moral, spi-
" ritual, and practical character will be given to all from
" birth, and that the germ of man will be greatly im-
" proved before birth."

That " the creation of useable and enjoyable wealth
" will be a pleasure and assistance for health and ex-
" ercise to all; and that this wealth will be produced
" annually in such superfluity, that all will freely par-
" take of it without money or hindrance of any kind."

That " temperance in *all things* will be the con-
" tinued practice of all."

That " equality according to age will be discovered
" to be the only mode of attaining and maintaining
" permanent peace, prosperity, and happiness among
" our race."

And that " all will perceive the necessity for new
" combinations of superior surroundings, devised with
" foresight and knowledge, to possess the influence on
" humanity to make it to acquire the results previously
" stated. And that society *is* now in possession of
" the most ample means to have these new surround-
" ings executed in a very superior manner."

That your committee heard with great interest on
Thursday Mr. Owen's address to those who desire to
change governments to become republics on the individual system of society. His account of his visit to

the United States of America, and of his interviews with
the originators of the Republic was most interesting.
Speaking of the United States of America, Mr. Owen
says—

" I am well acquainted with the Republic of the
" United States of North America. and in some mea-
" sure also with those of South America ; and I hesi-
" tate not to declare that they are incompetent to go-
" vern society for the benefit of any population over
" the earth.   There must be a new principle and a
" new practice, before any form of government what-
" ever can produce unity, goodness, wisdom and hap-
" piness permanently among men."

Your committee, while unequivocally maintaining
with Mr. Owen the rights of the people to political
equality, concur with him that mere political institutions on the *individual system* are inadequate to secure
the permanent happiness of mankind.

The principles Mr. Owen so inflexibly maintains in
relation to " Individualism, the formation of the indi-
" vidual character, the necessity of human actions, and
" the non-responsibility of the individual," have, as
might have been expected, elicited considerable discussion and difference of opinion.   Some of the committee endorsing Mr. Owen's principles fully—some,
while agreeing with him in many of his views, dissenting from him upon others ; indeed, there may be expressions used by Mr. Owen and in this report, in which
each member of the committee might not be able individually to concur, while he might yet agree with
their general spirit.

Resolutions have been proposed, seconded, and resolved on unanimously (there being but one or two
dissentients to some of them,) having in view to
pledge the members of this Congress to some active
practical measures to make Mr. Owen's principles
more widely known, and to enforce them on the attention of the government.

Communications and propositions were read from various friends, of a nature highly flattering to our venerable president, which were not within the scope of the powers of the Congress.

In conclusion, your committee would earnestly hope that the present proceedings may not be suffered to drop fruitless, but that they may be the precursors of a more systematic and universal organisation of the advanced minds of this and all other countries, that they may be brought into active communication with each other, so that the principles of societary truth may be circulated to the utmost extent among the families of mankind ; and they sincerely desire that the aspirations of Mr. Robert Owen for the well-being of his fellow men may be speedily realised, and that " A new " dispensation is now about to commence, when ' old " ' things will pass away, and all will become new ; ' " and that " There will be a new formation of the " human character over the world, based on a new " principle, and formed in a new spirit, so that the " man thus new-formed will be, in spirit, principle, and " practice, a being altogether different from the hu- " manity created under this old and now worn-out " dispensation for forming the character and governing " man."

Signed on behalf of the Committee,

JOHN MAUGHAN, *Hon. Sec.*

May 22nd, 1857.

The above report having been cordially agreed to, Mr. Owen and Mr. McBean addressed the Congress in relation to the grand primary principles and practical arrangements which are necessary to introduce the new dispensation of the sublime science of the formation of human character. The proceedings were then adjourned at 4, P.M., till 11, A.M., next morning.

Twelfth Meeting, May 23rd, in St. Martin's Hall,
Long Acre.

ROBERT OWEN in the chair.—On this day Mr. Owen, with his usual mental vigour and moral urbanity, gave minute and detailed descriptions of the different classes of the population of the United Queendom by the exhibition of cubes. A large tabular statement of their relative proportions, of which the following is a copy, was exhibited daily during the sittings of the Congress.

The different classes of the population of the United Queendom, and their relative proportions, including their families, arranged according to their relative magnitudes, as stated by Colquhoun in his " Resources of the British Empire."

---

1. { *Royal Family and Lords Spiritual and Temporal* - - }   *About* 1 *in* 5,936.

2. { *Dignified Clergy, (under Bishops,) and most successful of Class 5* }   *About* 1 *in* 280.

3. { *Baronets, Country Gentlemen, &c., with large incomes* - }   *About* 1 *in* 72.

4. *Army and Navy* -   -   *About* 1 *in* 18.

5. { *Learned Professions, Bankers, Merchants, &c.* - - }   *About* 1 *in* 15.

6. *Paupers, Vagrants, Criminals, &c.*   *About* 1 *in* 9.

7. *Shopkeepers, Small Freeholders, &c.*   *About* 1 *in* 6.

8. *Working Classes, Servants, &c.*   - *About* 3 *in* 5.

Whole Population in 1857, nearly 29 millions.

Mr. Owen, by means of the cubes representing the relative proportions of these different classes, entered most elaborately into the exposition of the present irrational constitution, condition, and various arrangements of human society over all the earth ; while the greater part of the time of the meeting was taken up in giving practical answers to important primary questions proposed by Mr. McBean,—questions bearing on the best possible methods and peaceable means for gradually changing the present most ignorant, false, unjust, cruel, and evil system of human society, for the enlightened, true, just, merciful, and good system, explained and advocated by Mr. Owen, for forming and developing men's physical, intellectual, moral, and spiritual character, for producing, distributing and enjoying all desirable wealth, and for placing, employing, and governing the human races in perfect harmony with the Divine unchangeable laws of human nature and the universe.

At the conclusion of the meeting Mr. J. P. Hazard, of America, made the following remarks, which were well received.

About 1810, or at least as late, fabrics were manufactured in the United States which then cost 4s. per yard—(I shall adhere to sterling in these statements,) but which could now be offered at wholesale for about 10d.

At that period the whole operation of manufacture was by manual labour, aided by very primative machinery. Such has been the improvement since that period, that machinery requiring the attention of only one man and one boy, performs at the present time the labour which then occupied about 700 women. Such, too, has been the improvement in style of results, that the article then sold at wholesale for 4s., would not now fetch 8d.

It is worthy of remark, too, that the material used in these manufactures are very little, if any, reduced in price.

It may be worthy of remark, that betwixt the years 1839 and 1849, wages in the manufacture of the above character of goods doubled. Nevertheless, the goods could be made at one quarter of the cost of labour in the yard, at these higher prices paid the labourers than at the minimum rate of wages.

Proofs are abundant, that the profits of labour to its employers, masters, is far greater at high rates of wages than at low ones.

The slave labourer, doubtless, consumes a larger proportion of his production than other labourers do. Indeed, so contrary is this system to a law of creation, that slave labour cannot endure the competition with free, neither can slaves be even supported by their labour, (as a grand rule), unless they have fertile lands to work upon, and consume in their destructive system.

The stone dyke that is made in Scotland by labourers who are intelligent men at two shillings and sixpence per day, costs as much per rod as that of the same sort which is made in America by labourers at seven shillings and sixpence per day. These facts can be easily derived from observation, and the reason for it becomes apparent the moment we have a conception of the real sources of ability in man to make exertion most effectively for himself or his employer.

Mr. McBean then addressed a few observations to the Congress respecting what the followers of Mr. Owen—those agreeing with his enlightened grand comprehensive views—can do, and should do to promote and diffuse the knowledge of them—and to soon reduce them into practice.

Mr. Owen said that nothing short of the government of all countries taking up and trying his principles and plans would please him; after which the Congress adjourned its sitting at 3 p.m. to the Literary and Scientific Institution, John Street, Fitzroy Square, at 11, a.m., next day.

The proceedings of the foregoing twelve meetings formed a distinct part of the business of the Congress.

The desire to confine the report within certain fixed limits, —the incomparable importance and length of Mr. Owen's prepared addresses, rendered it necessary to omit many remarks and explanations of much value.

G. N. B. McBEAN,

Reporter to the Congress of the

Advanced Minds of the World.

May 23rd, 1857

REPORT

OF

THE THIRTEENTH, FOURTEENTH, AND FIFTEENTH,
MEETINGS,

OF

THE CONGRESS

OF

THE ADVANCED MINDS OF THE WORLD, &c., &c.,

CALLED BY

MR. ROBERT OWEN,

HELD IN THE LITERARY AND SCIENTIFIC INSTITU-
TION, JOHN STREET, FITZROY SQUARE, AND IN
ST. MARTIN'S HALL, LONG ACRE, LONDON, ON 24TH
AND 25TH MAY, 1857, TO FURTHER CONSIDER THE
BEST PEACEABLE METHODS AND MEANS FOR
CHANGING THE PRESENT MOST IGNORANT, FALSE,
UNJUST, CRUEL, AND EVIL SYSTEM OF HUMAN
SOCIETY, AND FOR INTRODUCING THE ENLIGHT-
ENED, TRUE, JUST, MERCIFUL, AND GOOD SYSTEM
OF SOCIETY, FOR FORMING MEN'S CHARACTER,
PRODUCING WEALTH, AND GOVERNING THE
HUMAN RACES.

---

*Thirteenth Meeting, May 24th, in St. Martin's Hall,
Long Acre.*

SOCIALISM, SECULARISM, AND
SPIRITUALISM.

MR. OWEN IN THE CHAIR.

The Thirteenth Meeting of the Congress was held on
Sunday morning, in the Literary and Scientific
Institution, John Street, Fitzroy Square, for the purpose of hearing and discussing Mr. Owen's address to
the so-called *Socialists, Secularists,* and *Spiritualists ;*
and with the view to unite them, to co-operate, in every
locality of the Empire,—in petitioning Parliament for
the immediate adoption of these comprehensive plans,
consistent principles, and beautiful harmonious prac-

tices, so long and clearly developed by Mr. Owen, and which would put an effectual end to the highly irrational state of things, in this country, and ultimately all over the earth.

MR. OWEN commenced this day's proceedings by saying—

" This must be one of the most memorable days in the history of this ever-to-be-remembered Congress.

" The spirit, the principles, and the practices to be stated, considered, and debated on this day, must, when published, go far to unite man to man and nation to nation over the earth, and to dispel the worse than Egyptian darkness of ignorance that has hitherto overwhelmed the minds of the highest authority in all churches and states through every progress of the history of humanity, from the first formation of man to this hour.

" They will expose the undeveloped state of the minds of all our predecessors, and the causes, thence ensuing, of the errors, crimes, and miseries of the human races, past and present.

" They will enable all to attain the knowledge of the means by which, in a short period, these errors, crimes, and miseries may be overcome, and, instead thereof, truth, goodness, and happiness may be made to become universal over the earth, and thus will the true practical Millennium be established.   Are you,— Socialists, Secularists, and Spiritualists,—prepared in spirit for this great and glorious change for all humanity?

" Are you prepared to put off your filthy rags of superstition, contention, and of presumtuous, unkind feelings for each other; and in the true spirit of universal love and charity to bear with each other's sincere convictions, and to allow to all others the liberty of expressing their thoughts, as you expect and claim the liberty to express those thoughts which you, like them, are compelled to receive and to believe for the time to be true?

G

" Unless you are thus prepared, you have no just title to be called rational beings.

" The first thing, therefore, that I claim from you who say you are Socialists, is, that in all your practice you exhibit to every one the Spirit of universal love and charity for all human beings without which there can be no true Socialism.

" MEN of thought and reflection,—

" On this occasion I have promised to explain what is the only true universal practical religion for the entire population of the world.

" Men of mind, who know the past history of man and his present position over the earth, are conscious that not one of the existing religions, as now taught and practised by the human races, can ever become universal, or unite men to make them good, wise, permanently prosperous, and happy. And a religion which can accomplish and retain these results, can alone ever become universal ; and without a religion which shall pervade the hearts and minds of all, which by its truth, wisdom, and consistency, can compel, as it were, all, at all times to practice it, it will be vain to expect what is now called religion among the Chinese, Japanese, Buddists, Jews, Christians, or Mahommedans, ever to become universal.

" To discover a universal religion is the first step to unity among men, and to a permanent peace for the population of the world ; and it must be attained before practical measures can be adopted to construct the surroundings which can alone make all placed within them, to become united, good, wise, permanently prosperous, and happy.

" What, then, you will now ask, is this *true religion*, which is to be accepted by all nations and peoples ?

" It is the substance of all religions, without their useless forms and ceremonies.

" It is the daily, the hourly, the unceasing practice of love and charity for all men, irrespective of colour, country, creed, or class ; or a never ending desire to

promote the permanent happiness of all men, through
the life of each.

" This will be now soon attainable.   The shell and
spell of ignorance are broken ; and life, liberty, and
knowledge will have free range over the earth, directed by wisdom, in peace and harmony.

" This great change, the wonder of all nations and
peoples, will be effected through the medium of the,
to many, strange and yet little understood *Spiritual
Manifestations.*

" The spirits of just men made perfect, will assist,
guide, and direct the way to the full and complete
reformation and regeneration from ignorance to wisdom of the races of man, thus preparing, through a
new practical religion, a new earth, and a new sphere
in heaven for those thus reformed and thus regenerated.

" There are Spirits now around and about us, Spirits,
who, through the aid of superior intelligence and power,
have been purified and perfected, who are now deeply
interested in forming and carrying forward various measures in different parts of the world, to bring about this
great and glorious change for humanity—this new dispensation, and permanent happy existence of man upon
the earth, to prepare him at once for the higher enjoyments of superior spheres in heaven.

" But to attain these results, certain practical measures are necessary, which can alone emanate from
the true fundamental principle, which enables man to
know himself, how he should assist to form the character of his successors, and how he should construct
society, and thus make the principles and practices of
all men to be consistent with the laws of nature, and
in harmony working together to consolidate the unity
and permanent happiness of the human races.

" This and this alone is true Socialism.   This is the
Socialism I have been so long in preparing the world
to receive in spirit, principle, and practice.   And so
long,—because individual selfishness fills all minds with

notions directly opposed to the spirit, principle, and practice of unity among men, or of common sense in the construction and practice of society, in the formation of character, and in the government of the population of the world.

" Individualism also imagines, in direct contradiction to common sense and to all facts, that the individual state of society, is the best calculated to increase the wealth of all and the general wealth of the world. While this system is the sure way to keep the great mass of the human races in poverty, and all in the fear of it, and to *prevent* to an immense extent the production of wealth for all, and thus also to *prevent* the formation of *surroundings* in which to place all, and which would prevent both the existence and the fear of poverty in any nation, or among any people over the globe.

" Socialism, or a rational state of human existence, is based on the *fact*, " that God or nature forms the " spirit or divine character of man previous to birth, " and that society, by its irrational or rational sur- " roundings, forms and directs the human-made part " of the character of everyone."

" The character of all who have lived upon the earth has been thus formed by the action and reaction of these two distinct parts upon each other.

" When men can be made to understand these simple truths of nature, and to comprehend all their immediate and remote consequences, they will discover how plain and pleasant paths will be opened to them, to make the rising and all future generations good, wise, united, wealthy, and happy, to which, after one or two generations, there will be no exceptions. And these results will be attained with the certainty of a law of nature, and to the permanent high gratification of the human races.

" Against this new and glorious dispensation of the Great Forming and Governing Power of the Universe, it will now be vain for ignorant and undeveloped man,

to oppose his puny efforts.   Truth, in spirit, principle
and practice, must now soon reign triumphant over
all error, and make man a wise, consistent, and rational being, in mind and practice, and thus, and thus
alone, can the will of God, or harmony on earth, be
attained, as it exists in the spheres of heaven, and
among all the heavenly bodies throughout the Universe,
(which is space and all within it,) infinite in extent
and duration—if any finite mind can comprehend
the term.

" But the secularists and the so-called religionists are
at present north and south poles to each other, causing
an opposition in mind and feeling, the reverse of love
and charity for each other.

" This must not longer continue. It is the cause of
hatred between them, and is deeply injurious to both,
without benefit to either.   Where there are hatred,
anger, and ill-will between parties, on account of a
difference in belief or opinion, there can be no knowledge of our nature, no foundation laid for the
admission of common sense into minds which have
been so unfortunately trained and educated by an
equally ignorant society and injurious surroundings.

"The first introduction of a true and useful knowledge
of ourselves, informs us that we *must believe*, and *cannot avoid believing*, according to the *strongest impressions*
made on our minds, and that therefore there never
was—there never can be, merit or demerit in any
belief, true or false.   It is most irrational for men to
be angry or displeased with each other, or to suppose
that there is or can be merit or demerit in any belief
whatever, even in affirming or denying the existence
of a supreme intelligence, a framer and director of
all things within the universe.

" Of what possible consequence can it be to the
All Ever-acting Power throughout the Universe, what
an insignificant atom upon the earth believes respecting
its existence or non existence ?

" Or can the lowest degree of common sense, or the

first indications of rationality among men, imagine that man can do any good to that power, or act in opposition to it?—Call it what you please—God.— The great first cause,—nature,—necessity—or adaptability—&c., &c., &c.?

"These unfortunate theological derangements of the human intellect, are only the defects necessarily arising from the undeveloped state of the rational faculties of humanity, and will be entirely unknown as soon as the rational reasoning faculties of man can be fully developed; when, of all the errors and follies of men, none will appear more absurd and injurious, than an estrangement of feeling between men on matters of which, all at this day, are profoundly ignorant, and which can do no good, but must cause endless evils, without a rational object to be gained.

" Let it be deeply impressed on the minds of all, that true religion consists in the practice, in thought, word, and action, throughout life, of love and charity for all mankind, and in being merciful in conduct, as far as is practicable, to all that has life; that anything short of this is a name only, and not the reality or substance of religion.

" It is *this practical religion* which can alone set nations free; which can saturate the earth with wealth, to be used and enjoyed by all; which can unite man to man over the earth; which can give a good, useful, and valuable character to all men; which can put the spirit of peace within the minds of all, and insure the permanent peace of the world.

" Let it also be equally remembered, that it may sink deep in your minds, that individualism is another term for covert hatred, competition, contests, wars, poverty, degradation, and misery for the mass. That it is the mere infant, ignorant, and undeveloped state of humanity. But that it has been so far a necessary evil, and the preparatory nurse for the true, divine, united, social system, which through futurity will well care for every child of man from birth, and will introduce and for ever maintain the promised millennial state of existence upon earth.

" And as these truths will overcome and conquer all evil, and will constitute the happy life of peace among men, they thus prove themselves to be the true Messiah of the Jews, and the second coming of Christ, to establish the *practice* of *Christianity* among all nations and all peoples.

" Let it be now known to all, that individualism and true Christianity can never co-exist. No one acting on the system of individualism can be a Christian, except in name. Individualism is, and ever has been, the Anti-Christ, or *opposer* of *truth* over the world, in *principle* and *practice*, in forming the character, and in governing the human races. The disciples of Jesus of Nazareth, the first Christian, were all Socialists, as far as their practical knowledge of worldly matters then extended ; and to be a Christian indeed, that is, in mind and practice, it is necessary to become a Socialist, in the true meaning of the term. A true Christian and a true Socialist are two names for the same thing.

" And the terms mean, one, who in spirit, mind, and practice, has love and charity for every human being, who loves his neighbour, as shown by his practice, as himself ; who heartily and cordially desires and endeavours to promote the best permanent happiness of every one, without excepting even the worst made human character ; who desires to be on an equality with his fellows, but not higher in rank, station, privileges, or enjoyments, than his equals in age, and one who will sacrifice his life before he would deny the truth on any of these *all-important* subjects.

" Such and such only can be a Christian, a true Socialist ; and it is the worst of all falsehoods to call any system Christian which encourages and maintains anger, hatred, contests, wars, and the repulsive feelings caused by the individual undeveloped system, opposed to the good system for forming a good character, and for producing at all times in all places abundance of superior unadulterated wealth for all, or forming common sense arrangements of superior surroundings, in which to place all succeeding generations.

" This falsehood must be now abandoned. It is too glaringly untrue and opposed to all facts, to impose longer upon a public who have been taught to begin to think and reason upon what they every day see around them.

" It is full time for the world to acquire realities and substance instead of mere words and imaginations.

" I therefore now declare myself, from the fullest convictions, to be a Socialist, such as I have now described, and to be opposed to the Satanic system of individualism.

" But what am I now to say to those sincere and well meaning men who call themselves Secularists ?—men who deem themselves superior to other men who do not believe, as they do, in the non-existence of some imaginary notion, or word in their mind, which they call God ?

" Now let us look full in the face of this subject of endless contests, wars, hatreds, misery, insanity, and madness among the human races through all past ages ; and let us endeavour to discover to what it amounts, and to what it leads.

" Suppose first that there is a Personal God, with all the qualities given Him by the religious, or by believers in such God or Gods over the world.

" With such qualities, could it in any way effect Him whether men believed in His existence or not ?

" If He desired man to believe in His existence, could He not enable and compel him to do so ? and thus prevent all religious wars and hatreds ? Could He not, if He desired it, terminate or prevent all differences of opinion on this subject ?

" The law of God, of nature, of humanity, call it what you please—is, that man cannot believe contrary to his convictions, which, by his constitution or organization, he is compelled to receive.

" As soon as society can be made to become rational,
and shall be governed by common sense, there will be
no merit or demerit given for any belief or disbelief on
any subject whatever.

" Of what consequence can it be to any one what
another believes respecting a supposed cause of which
at this day all are profoundly ignorant or without any
certain knowledge ?

" The impressions which I am compelled to have
respecting Deity, are, that there must be power to
produce the life, motion, and mind which exist, not
only in the mineral, vegetable, and animal structures
in and upon our earth, but in every changing form of
material existence throughout the universe ; that no
facts known to man to this period enable him to
discover what that power is ; what form it possesses ;
or how it acts, to produce the wonders of nature
even within the ken of humanity ; and that for this
knowledge we must patiently wait until those facts
can be discovered. That that Power has no dependance upon man ; but that man and all things depend
on that Power.

"Now whether that Power is called God, Nature, the
Great Spirit of the Universe, the Essence of matter,
or by any other name that men may devise to desig-
nate what they cannot comprehend, it matters not to
man, and until more facts shall be revealed to him, by
new discoveries of the laws of nature, it is most vain
and useless for him to waste his time, faculties, and
feelings in insanely tormenting himself and his fellows for no rational purpose.

" Our business, in our present state upon earth, is
with facts, which we can investigate and comprehend,
to enable us to make each other good, wise, and happy,
which is man's mission on earth, as is evident by the
desire of all to attain these results.

" But the question now is—How are these results to
be attained in practice ?

" The reply is,—Solely by practical measures, derived from facts and the past experience of the human races.

" And to bring the human races to *this practical result* has been the great object of my long public life, and now especially of this Congress.

" I now earnestly recommend to all my fellow men to abandon, for a time at least, all theoretic or mere imaginary notions respecting a First Cause, God, Nature, Spirit, materiality, or immateriality, as being far worse than useless, until we have more tangible facts on these subjects, which, without more facts being developed respecting them, will be as useless as endless.

" Now, that which is first wanted and above all things required, is the direct practical means to make all men good, wise, united, healthy, and happy, and society consistent in all its parts and as a whole; or a perfect science of society, to insure the continual progress of the human races towards every kind of excellence.

" To attain these results, we must know the facts respecting the material of man from his birth and through every step of his existence through life.

" A knowledge of these facts we acquire by the study of the past experience of humanity, under all its various surroundings in different parts of the earth, and through the successive periods of change from the beginning of the history of man to the present hour.

" By this course we discover, that man is born without his knowledge or consent, with the germs of all his physical and mental qualities. He is therefore *forced* to possess them—let those qualities and powers be called good or bad; and the possessor of them cannot deserve merit or demerit.

" He is also born at a *particular period* of human history,—in a *particular place*,—and within *particular surroundings*,— all without his knowledge or consent; and for which he can have no merit or demerit.

" Now these surroundings in a more or less open manner force him to acquire a language, a religion, manners, habits, ideas of right and wrong, prejudices, his likes and dislikes; and for these, all forced upon him, he can have no merit or demerit, and cannot with justice be made responsible to God, to man, to nature or to society. Nor is there the least utility in the attempt to endeavour to make him and his fellows believe that he has or can have merit or demerit for his natural or divine qualities, or for the direction given to those qualities by the surroundings in which he comes into life and is retained during his existence.

" His undying desire is to be happy; and by this most irrational proceeding of attributing merit and demerit to him, he is of necessity made to become irrational in mind, feeling, and conduct, as all at this day have been forced to become. There is not at this hour a nation or people on the earth who are rational or consistent in mind, feeling, or practice. All are thus made forcibly to become so insane, as madly to pursue a road which they expect will lead to happiness, when what they are in search of can be found only in the opposite direction.

" Are the human races to be blamed for thus being forced to become in mind and practice inconsistent or absurd, or insane or mad?

" Not in the least. But the Acting Power of the Universe (call it what you please,—God, Nature, the Essence of Nature, the Great Spirit, &c., &c., &c.) forces humanity to feel pain when it is not in the true path to happiness, and to have that pain increased until the right path shall be found and pursued without deviation.

" Hence all experience pain of body or mind. All desire and long for happiness; yet no nation or individual has found it. Hence the disappointment of man, and the misery of all nations and peoples.

" But let all the sons of men now rejoice and be exceeding glad, for the discovery has been made, by which, as the population of the world has been to this hour forced to become through the entire infancy of society, inconsistent, absurd, insane or mad, and unhappy, it will hereafter be forced to become consistent wise, sane, rational, and happy.

" It has been discovered that there are two distinct and opposing systems for the formation of character, producing and distributing wealth, and governing the human races,—two systems—one repulsive, the other attractive; one evil, the other good; one based on individual *ignorant* selfishness, the other on united enlightened selfishness, embracing the permanent high happiness of the human races ; one leading direct to all manner of error and its fatal evil consequences, the other leading direct to truth and good, or to the pure and undefiled Christianity of universal love and charity in the mind and continued practice of the human races through futurity.

" This is the true Messiah of the Jews; the true Second Coming of Christ, or of the Great Truths which, at the First Coming of Christ, as declared by Jesus of Nazareth, the world was too undeveloped then to bear, and therefore was it then withheld ; and now this is the very earliest period in the history of humanity, when man has been sufficiently developed to listen to those great and divine truths, on which the future happiness of the population depends, and which few only can yet comprehend in all their bearing and ramifications throughout society when thus wisely constituted.

" Forty years ago, this year, I most publicly denounced all the superstitions of the world; and All Religions as now taught and practised are lamentable superstitions, calculated only to derange the reasoning faculties of humanity.

" I have now declared as openly to the world the great truths, which, as soon as carried into practice, will introduce the Millennium to the human races,—with this difference, that instead of its duration being for one thousand years only, it will continue until time shall be no more and humanity shall enter upon eternity.

" In this state, names, persons, personalities, and all individual considerations, will terminate; all will be one with Christ or Truth; and each will become all, and all each, to form one humanity over the earth, and all invidious distinctions will terminate for ever; no one claiming merit or any kind of superiority over another; but the cordial union of all hearts and minds will form and maintain universal harmony on earth, as it exists in the higher spheres in heaven.

" Some of you will ask, or desire to ask,—" How do " you know that there are different spheres in heaven, " or that there is a heaven?"

" This is a very proper question to be asked by those who cannot yet believe in a future state of conscious existence, after we have ceased to live visibly on the earth; and I will now answer it.

" The evidence of my senses, applied with all the acumen and judgment which I possess, has given me the following facts and consequent convictions, as strong as convictions can be made on my mind.

" 1st.—That there are certain individuals of both sexes and of all ages, who possess the qualities, unconscious to themselves what those qualities are or how they obtained them, by which various kinds of communications are made by unseen and unknown influences, and sometimes in opposition to the strongest will of the persons possessing these extraordinary qualities; and these persons are called mediums.

" These communications are made, according to the peculiar combination of the qualities mentioned, by tipping of tables, by raps upon them or on other furniture, on the floor or other parts of the house; and through these communications by means of tippings or rappings when particular letters of the alphabet are pointed to, intelligent communications are made, entirely without the will or knowledge of the medium; and often these communications are most deeply interesting to the persons to whom they are especially addressed.

" Through other mediums, the communications are made by their being compelled to write, without knowing what they write, and often to write in opposition to their own previous views and opinions.

" In many cases, when questions are asked for a good or rational purpose, correct and highly intelligent replies are given.

" When the questions are asked of these invisible and unknown influences—' What are you ?'—the reply by tippings, rappings, or writings is, through all mediums, in countries the most distant apart,—
" Spirits, who have lived upon the earth, and who are
" now in the world of spirits, having acquired power
" thus to communicate with you, although to you we
" are invisible.

" If you ask—' what or whose Spirit are you?'— The unknown influence will often give the name of a near and dear deceased relative, who, in reply to other questions asked, will give an accurate account of many particulars respecting that individual, which you know to be true, and some unknown to you until proved by subsequent enquiries.

" Now all this is as certain as that the sun rises daily, and is confirmed by the experience of thousands possessing sound judgments and high integrity of character.

" But that which probably cannot be tangibly demonstrated is—that these invisible influences are the identical spirits of men ; that is real men ; or if they are real spirits—real men—indeed our real brethren, that they are always truthful in giving their earthly names, or in other communications which they often appear anxious, and sometimes very anxious to give to particular persons.

" I can now only give opinions derived from my own experience of these yet natural but extraordinary events, and these opinions should be taken for what they are worth and no more.

" It is frequently found difficult by some persons to

obtain any communications through the mediums to whom they apply. At other times, to some persons, perhaps those who are not really seeking for truth, the most absurd and ridiculous replies will be given, there being little or no cordial feeling or sympathy between the enquirer, the medium, and the influence purporting to be some particular spirit or spirits.

" But when there is a real sympathy between the enquirer, the spirit said to be present, and the medium, the communication is generally easily effected, straightforward, truthful, useful, and sometimes highly important.

" There is often much deficiency and ignorance on the part of the enquirer, and sometimes of the inexperienced medium, how to proceed in the best manner to obtain truthful answers.

" Hitherto no discovery has been made, by the learned and scientific opponents of what is now called Spiritualism, of the Cause which produces the intelligent and superior replies to the questions asked of these invisible influences, nor any explanation approaching to common sense.

" I have received communications from various influences calling themselves the Spirits of departed friends and relatives, in whom when living I had full and perfect confidence in their integrity, and as each made their communications to me in the character, strongly exhibited, which they possessed when living on the earth, I am compelled to believe their testimony as thus given ; and as these communications have a good and high character in testifying now to the active exertions made by superior Spirits to assist developed men now to reform and regenerate the human races, I think their direct and uniform statements respecting themselves, are far more worthy of credit, than the random suppositions of those who are evidently ignorant of the whole subject of Spiritualism, and who by their previously acquired prejudices are strongly opposed to admit the existence of spirits, against any evidence that can be testified by human means to the contrary.

" But as this is yet a subject which is generally so little understood, and which in irrational made minds excites only irrational feelings of anger or ridicule, let it remain in abeyance until experience shall give us more facts and knowledge on this complex subject, and let us apply our attention to practical measures of deep and lasting interest to all of our race. This is *now our* business; and the Spirits, by the unchanging laws of their *will-power*, shall ceaselessly take care of their own, and certainly perform their duties to us.

The foregoing address, which was particularly well read for Mr. Owen, by Mr. R. Cooper, was listened to by the crowded audience with marked attention, and great interest; and the comprehensive views and grand principles contained in it, having been freely discussed by several of the audience, they were calmly and clearly defended by Mr. Owen, who, in adjourning the meeting till 7 p.m. in the same place, proposed, that a Committee should be then formed, to report upon the proceedings of that day; when Charles William Gregory, Esq., London; John Scott, Esq., C. E., Belfast; and Mr. McBean, the reporter engaged by Mr. Owen for the Congress, were appointed, with power to add to their number, to draw up a report, and which document will be found subjoined to this day's proceedings.—*(Vide p.* 111.*)*

The Fourteenth Meeting.

THE ADJOURNED MEETING ON SUNDAY MAY 24TH, AT 7 P.M., IN THE LITERARY AND SCIENTIFIC INSTITUTION, JOHN STREET, FITZROY SQUARE, ON SOCIALISM, SECULARISM, AND SPIRITUALISM

ON Sunday at 7 P.M., the adjourned meeting of the Congress of the Advanced Minds of the

World, was held in the Literary and Scientific Institution, John Street, Fitzroy Square. The hall of the
Institution was completely crowded, and the greatest
possible attention and interest were manifested by the
audience. The Socialists, Spiritualists, and Secularists,
having been especially invited to be present by Mr.
Owen, to hear *true Socialism in spirit, principle, and
practice, explained, and the only true universal practical
religion, and the cause of the new spiritual manifestations which are being made in different countries
at the present period, clearly stated, these respective
bodies were well represented at the morning and
evening meetings.*

Mr. Owen opened the meeting by observing,—

" I announced to you this morning truths of the
highest import, to the permanent well-being, well-
doing, and happiness of all of human kind. Many,
I may say all, of the truths, were in direct opposition
to the prejudices and errors which have been forced
into the minds and upon the habits of the human
races.

" I have purposely stated these Truths in the most
broad and distinct manner, to rivet the attention of all
to the earnest and most considerate thought and reflection upon them, that they may discover whether
my statements and New Views of Society are true or
false , whether they are intended for good or for evil.

" In these statements I denounced all the laws of
men, including every code, given by legislators and
statesmen through all past ages, of the laws of the
United States and of Great Britain, as being the
cause of all vice, crime, prostitution, poverty, and
misery among the populations subjected to these laws.

" I now reiterate and confirm all I then stated to the
audience present, and I wish all that I did state to be
given to the world, that all may judge for themselves
whether I speak the language of truth and sound reflection, or that which is contrary to facts, which have

H

been ascertained to be unchangeable by the power of the human races.

" But I not only denounced all human-made laws, as being the sole cause of inflicting the continuance of ignorance, vice, crime, poverty, prostitution, and misery on mankind ;—I also advocated the rejection of all these by the people, and at once to supersede them firmly by the quiet and peaceable adoption of God's Laws—the eternal laws of nature, which change not for man, or for aught he can do :—Laws of wisdom, goodness, mercy, and beneficence to all men and which, when they shall be introduced and consistently acted upon, will make all to become good, united, wise, abounding in superior wealth, and permanently happy."

" These laws will direct surroundings in which all should be placed from their birth, to enable society to make them united, enlightened, good, wealthy, wise, and permanently happy."

Mr. Owen on observing that great numbers were present in the evening who were not in attendance at the morning meeting's discussion, requested Mr. Cooper to re-read the long address which had been read and debated during the morning sitting of Congress, which Mr. Cooper again did in an efficient manner.

When Mr. Cooper had concluded the reading of the address, Mr. Owen in his own peculiar and characteristic manner, expressed his undying confidence in the power of the pure knowledge of truth, to produce lasting conviction, enlighten and strengthen the human mind ; and therefore, he invited all parties present, to come forward and ask questions, or make such remarks as they might deem proper. Several parties in the audience availed themselves of the opportunity of proposing questions and starting objections, all of which were beautifully and clearly answered and explained by Mr. Owen.

Mr. McBean in expressing his cordial concurrence

with all the views and explanations advanced and given
by Mr. Owen on that and former days, said,—

" The grand science of the formation of human character—
the most important, sublime, comprehensive, and useful of all
the sciences, because actually composed of all the other Divine
branches of the knowledge of truth, should include and recognise all the divine powers of humanity,—should support and
unfold the different faculties and elements of human nature—
the varied powers of man. This science composed of all the
other sciences of the universe, must provide for the physical, intellectual, moral, and spiritual wants and aspirations of men,
must be in perfect harmony with all the Divine qualities and
laws of immortal humanity,—in harmony with the eternal forces
and phenomena of the universe,—in conformity with the unchangeable laws of God.   It is very well, but it is not
enough to provide for men's physical and secular wants,
because their intellectual, moral, and spiritual powers and requirements must be also carefully developed, and constantly
cared for—must be cultivated, exercised, and satisfied. In order
to give a vital and a virtuous potency to the influences of the
external surroundings—which are to be employed and brought
into active operation to constitute the science and the art, for
the formation of human character—these external influences
and surroundings must be all devised and directed by the
matured intelligence, arranged by the confirmed wisdom, and
applied by the purified goodness derived from the accumulated
experience of the humanity of the past and the present.   The
causes must be adequate to produce the effects desired—the
effects can never be superior to the causes employed to produce
them.   And I therefore, cordially agree with, and endorse Mr.
Owen's views and principles, because I look upon them as
meeting the whole wants of human nature."

Mr. Brinsmead, then came forward and stated his
doubts and disbelief respecting the doctrines and
doings of spirit teachings, and wished for spirit manifestations there and then, before the large audience; when
Mr. P. B. Randolph, an American believer, in spiritual
science, and spirit intercourse, addressed the audience,
and submitted several pertinent remarks illustrative of
Mr. Owen's views of human immortality and tending
to show that men perpetually progress in knowledge,
power, wisdom, and goodness, and continue to assist,
impress, and hold the most intimate and familiar intercourse with their fellow men, subsequent to their leav-

ing their physical bodies. Mr. Randolph spoke in a most energetic and impressive tone, and concluded by declaring, that spirit teaching would ultimately regenerate human society.

Mr. Robert Cooper then came forward, and said,—

Mr. Owen,—No man living has a higher appreciation of your character, your labours, and your practical plans, than myself. I will succumb to no one in the strength of my attachment to you. I am as *you* have made me, and I am quite persuaded you will ascribe the observations I now feel reluctantly compelled to urge to the right motive. I speak in the name not of myself merely, but of many old devoted followers who now sit around you, who have proved, by a *life* of devotion to you and your cause, their sincerity and their constancy.

Sir, I submit that according to *your own* standard of truth, and I know none better, " Spiritual Manifestation," so called, must be, to use a strong phrase of yours in relation to the old system, " founded on a *gross* error."

Your definition of truth is as logically complete as it is morally sound. You have affirmed to-day that " Truth is ever consistent with itself, and with all known facts." Now, I hold, most respectfully, that the theory of " Spiritual Manifestation" is neither consistent with itself, nor with known facts.

First, you have told us that these spirits are deeply anxious to improve the condition of humanity. I apprehend they cannot be *very* anxious to perform this laudable work, or why have they remained silent and idle through so many thousands of years of ignorance, slavery, and suffering ? Why only " manifest" themselves in the middle of the 19th century ? Does the spirit act *consistently with itself,* when, being solicitous to promote the happiness of the world, it has never attempted the task till our day ? The spirits have not been so consistent as yourself, Mr. Owen. The spirits of the old prophets, whom you allege have appeared and expressed such lively anxiety for the welfare of the human race, have taken a *long* time to make up their minds to " practical operations !"

Besides, if these spirits were fully impressed with the dignity of Truth, and the elevation of Philanthrophy, would they present themselves in such "a questionable shape ?" Would they content themselves by thumping tables, and tipping in all sorts of "holes and corners ?" Why not present themselves in a manner so evident to our senses as to obviate all cavil ? Mr. Randolph has said spirits will only appear in secret, and not before public audiences. I ask why not ? To be consistent with themselves—with the wish to benefit " *all* classes"—they *ought* to appear before *all.* The larger the numbers before whom they might "manifest" themselves, the more likely they would improve the condition of all."

Is the idea of Spiritualism consistent with itself, when every condition required and every agent employed is material ? The " medium," a being of flesh and blood like ourselves, is material ; the table is material; the atmosphere which conveys the sound of the " tips" is material : and yet, though everything connected with the phenomenon, as Spirit-rappers themselves describe it, is material, the phenomenon itself is " spiritual ! !" Is that being consistent with itself ? Take away the medium, the recipient, the table, and the atmosphere, and where would be your " tips ;"—where your " spirits ?"

Sir, the supposition that " Spiritual Manifestations," are direct communications from those who have been *dead* ages, years, months, days, or even seconds, is inconsistent with *many* " known facts." It is a KNOWN fact, that when any organ of the body is destroyed, *its function ceases.* If I destroy the organ of hearing, all hearing ceases. This we *know* is a fact. If I destroy an organ of muscular action, all power of motion ceases in that portion of the body ; cut off the muscles of the lower extremities, we *know* the person cannot walk. That is a *known* fact. Destroy the palate, can you taste ? Destroy the olfactory nerve, can you smell ? If, then, when an organ is destroyed its function ceases, it is " inconsistent with known facts" to assume that when the organ of thought, intelligence, consciousness, is destroyed, namely, the *brain, its* function does not cease.

According, therefore, to your own admirable definition of truth, Mr. Owen, it is a " *gross* error," to fancy you are conversing with dead friends when you hear tips and scratches on tables or under tables, in walls or on walls, in secret or in public.

These phenomena, allowing that they are strange, must be differently interpreted than by assuming they are the communications of defunct people.

Mr. Randolph says he repudiates all priestcraft—the priests delude the people. Why then does he and you, and the Spirit-rappers as a party, imitate them ? Why like the priests, do you ascribe that which is wonderful—that which cannot yet be fully explained—to a SPIRIT ? Why follow the example of those whom you have said a thousand times are the sources of all error ? This very day you have told us, with a dignity and courage that excited our admiration, that *all* religions were founded on a *gross* error, that was " inconsistent with itself and *all* known facts." I most cordially agree with you, Mr. Owen : *all* religions are founded on such an error, *the religion of the Spirit World included.*

Would it not be wiser, more philosophical, more worthy of " *practical* minds," first to know all that *matter* can do, before you talk of " Spiritualism" and "Spirits ?" What do we yet understand of *electrical* phenomena? My opinion is, when we are better informed on the subject of electricity—its nature, its causes, its effects , its action, especially on animal life and cere bral sympathy—the "gross" fallacy of Spirit-rapping will be exploded.

I was proud, Sir, and so were the large majority of this assembly, to hear you say such phenomena as "Spiritual" manifestations should be held in abeyance till better understood, and we should direct our efforts to practical measures. May you live long, yet, Mr. Owen, to direct those practical measures, which, I firmly believe, can alone secure practical liberty, practical virtue, and permanent happiness to humanity.

Mr. J. P. HAZARD, of America, desired to reply to Mr. Cooper; but as there was no time to hear his rejoinder, which will be immediately introduced into this report, Mr. Owen, himself, briefly replied to Mr. Cooper, after which the meeting separated.

Mr. HAZARD's following reply to Mr. Cooper's speech above given, was addressed to Mr. Owen :—

London, 24th May, 1857.

MY DEAR AND HONOURED FRIEND,—

I hope you will excuse, I know you will, the category in which I have ventured to place you.

Should you precede me to the world of Spirits, you may, I hope, from thence perceive my heart's relation to your own better than it could now be described. I trust you may then, too, perceive a desire on my part still to listen to whatever you may feel disposed to communicate.

I was sorry that the late period of Mr. Cooper's eloquent speech upon the subject of Spiritualism this evening, precluded possibility of reply on the part of some persons *especially* interested in that portion of the programme proposing its consideration.

I rose to attempt one, but was over-ruled by the clock.

In reply to remarks made by yourself, and also to those on this subject by Mr. Randolph, Mr. Cooper stated that he was not of that number who spoke or had written upon this subject blindly. He had given it personal attention, and was therefore prepared to meet it with a knowledge of its facts.

He stated, also, that at a *seance* where Mr. Owen had (as Mr. Owen believed) just previously to his (Mr. Cooper's) entrance to the room, received a communication from the Spirit of Benjamin Franklin, by agency of "raps," the alleged manifestations ceased upon his (Mr. Cooper's) admission to the apartment, and declared the thing an entire failure. Mr. Cooper "would not *now* state," but if I mistake not his significance, it was a plain confession of his conviction of fraud on part of the medium, and *more* than an implied charge of a most serious character upon her.

Mr. Cooper further stated it to be a known fact that when human muscle had been stricken in death, its power ceased. When the eye or other organ of sense became lifeless in the body, it became in fact a nonentity. That the brain, deprived of its present form of life ceased to act, and consequently to think, to be, He, therefore, concluded all belief in spiritual phenomena as palpably absurd. That to attribute facts and incidents of any sort to agency of any parties who had been former possessors of these organs and faculties, was contrary to fully ascertained laws of human existence.

He likewise adduced the self-evident proposition, that all truth must be consistent with itself; that no two truths or facts can possibly conflict; that therefore the present theory must fall before the *ascertained established* fact (as he appears to suppose), that in all the world's experience, no phenomena of a similar character have *before* occurred.

Mr. Cooper also believes it necessary that man should comprehend the entire laws of matter, and become thoroughly conversant with *its* capabilities, capacities, and powers, before we can be justified in attributing any phenomena, of any sort, to spiritual agency.

He daily charges those whom investigation of this subject has forced upon them a belief (a knowledge I may say, for it makes no demand on men's faith,) in the spiritual origin of its phenomena, with having themselves invented the idea of referring it accordingly.

He also finds a singular, a vitiating inconsistency in the interest which spirits profess to take in human welfare, and their failure to exert their power in its behalf. Thousands of years (adds Mr. Cooper) having elapsed before they accomplished any thing, or even expressed a desire to do so. Mr. Cooper triumphantly asks why they have not done so before—seeing they have such powers.

He evidently believes, also, that there is a most unsavory significance in the circumstance of these manifestations being confined to private and small parties. That one of the conditions of their occurrence should preclude the possibility of their presentation to large assemblies in public.

It would be a vain impossibility for me to quote Mr. Cooper's thoughts in his own clear and eloquent terms. I have, therefore, not attempted it further than in a few instances of brief phrases which I happen to remember as he uttered them. It is quite possible I may not have fully understood Mr. Cooper; but I have endeavoured to do so, and to faithfully cite his positions herein. Should there be any omissions of essential points, (and as I cite from memory alone, I fear there may be,) I should be most happy to receive from Mr. Cooper, a detail of his positions and arguments, to which I pledge myself in as full a response as my abilities will admit.

I desire, however, to submit this reply before leaving town, which will be necessary for me to do immediately on the close of Congress to-morrow evening. Messrs. Baring, Brothers and Co., will forward to me any thing they may elicit.

Having attended all the meetings of the Congress in which you at present preside, I have been afforded too full and satisfactory opportunities of witnessing Mr. Cooper's ability to seize upon the strong points of what may be passing before him, to entertain any doubt of his capacity as an observer, and further, in the inflexible impartiality and high respect for truth and justice he has so ably and beautifully manifested in the peculiarly difficult duty assigned him in that Congress. I have all the guarantees I could desire of his entire sincerity in the views and statements he has submitted this evening.

But, in regard to the *knowledge* he may possess in these premises, I am no further qualified to judge, than by his own exhibition of proofs upon that subject, as contained in his own words. I am driven irresistibly to conclude from the general tenor of these, that his definition of knowledge is most essentialy different from that entertained by the great majority of thinking minds.

In the first place it would appear, that Mr. Cooper went to see something which Mr. Owen states he had seen. Mr. Cooper, however, arriving too late, or under circumstances adverse to his objects, did not see anything at all. The whole thing, while Mr. Cooper was present, " was an entire failure." Now, how in the name of common sense, allow me to ask, was Mr. Cooper or any other person to derive any pertinent knowledge from this experience ? How, I would ask, has this avowed failure, on his part to obtain any knowledge of the facts of the case, qualified him a judge in the premises—more especially to sit in judgment upon the opinions of those who honestly declare they are in possession of the facts which Mr. Cooper declares he has not in his possession, nor has any conception of. That Mr. Cooper is in possession of honest opinions upon the subject— none who have heard him express them can doubt. But the sort of logic that would admit such as these in lieu of such as claim to be based upon experience. and not upon failure is, to say the very least, highly questionable.

I am quite sure that one who had spent his life in a mine, having only heard of the beautiful stars of the heavens, would not be competent testimony in opposition to the opinion of others who had been more fortunate. And should such an individual emerge from his cavern during some cloudy night, whatever might be his disappointment upon looking toward the skies, *no* expression thereof could possibly be construed as proof that others had been mistaken. His *ignorance*, in however strong terms the declaration, would hardly be accepted as the boundary of all that might be known upon the subject of the existence of stars.

It is in vain to reply that the declaration of the existence of these manifestations is the voice of a small minority. It is the

voice of an *immense* majority of investigators, and their numbers are millions. Nor are these millions of those who are
most likely to be the victims of authority, or of superstition and
tradition. They comprise a large proportion of independent
enquiring minds, who have gone forth in obedience to a love of
truth, and believe they have not searched in vain. I have never
known an individual who has adopted these errors (if they be
such) at the dicta of others, but only in obedience to the irresistible testimony their facts offer to the human *senses*. I have never
found an individual who had given sufficient attention to the
subject to enable him or her to become familiar with what it has
to offer, who entertained a doubt of the facts themselves, and
only comparatively very rare instances of doubt of their spiritual origin. Of some forty or fifty writers in America who have
published their views at length in opposition to this great subject; all, with one exception, agree to the genuiness of the facts;
their opposition being based upon the narrowness of pious prejudice, the smallest possible to be conceived. I do not speak
from hearsay, I have read all the works to which I refer. The
exception to their agreement exists on the part of a clerical gentleman, who opens his work with the startling announcement
that he has never given the subject a moment of practical attention. All the others declared themselves to have been investigators.

In regard to Mr. Cooper's apparent influences upon the proceedings to which he alludes. The very fact that the raps
ceased on his entrance to the room is *prima facia* evidence of
the genuineness of what had preceded it in Mr. Owen's presence. I think that Mr. C. will find that all persons familiar
with the subject will so consider it. I should not hesitate at all
to engage to intercept and cause entirely to cease, for the present, any spiritual manifestations of the character now under
discussion. In most cases this could be effected instantaneously.

Mr. Cooper perfectly well knows there are many chemical and
other experiments and processes, the success of which depending on delicate or easily disturbed conditions, are very subject to
imperfect results, or entire failure even, in some chemical experiments the success is not once in a hundred attempts, or
séances if you please. But *one* success is enough : a century of
failures is of no avail against it.

Mr. Cooper obviously presumes that the millions who have
examined this subject, and who have been forced by the power of
its testimonies to differ from him upon its merits, must be la-
boring under some strange delusion, some unaccountable hallucination. This may be so, but the onus of proof lies on the
opposing side, and when it is offered it will claim due consideration.

I feel very doubtful if any man can *prove* that this human organisation of ours is *not in reality* a mere instrument most cun-

ningly devised to mislead and deceive its possessors. However clear the converse may appear to some, I believe the proof of it, at least to such as deny the evidence of the senses in any case, would be a very difficult task to most minds.

But such a mode of reasoning (or rather of suspicions,) weighs equally against *all* human testimonies. If the senses of these intelligent millions to whom I refer are not reliable, where are the millions to be found whose senses are reliable. If the investigation of this subject begets incompetency, where is the evidence of it, and what other class of investigations may not be as rationally supposed to effect the same results? Moreover, if this subject hallucinates those who approach it from one side, what is there that so fully protects from similar influences the very small party who meet it on the other? Is the rule of strength reversed? Is "a cloud of witnesses" nothing but a cloud? Does not the mode of reasoning adopted by Mr. Cooper go as far to show that *he* is mistaken in supposing he did *not* see what Mr. Owen states he saw, as it does to prove anything else? How could, by the ordinary mode of handling testimony, it be expected that Mr. Cooper should see that which transpired in Mr. Owen's presence, if Mr. Cooper was absent at the time, as he states to have been the case. The reason Mr. Cooper did not witness a continuation of those phenomena upon his arrival, will be very clear to all conversant with the subject, and will become so to himself, I doubt not, should the subject receive his earnest and persevering attention.

The evidence of our senses being the sole foundation of those facts on which we base all our reasoning; must be considered trustworthy, otherwise all logic is at an end, and Mr. Cooper is wrecked upon his own argument with all the rest of us. Mr. Cooper cannot be ignorant of the serious responsibility of its true character, which so many assume in charging dishonesty of purpose upon their fellow men without sufficient proof. He cannot but be aware that, particularly in connexion with so-called spiritual media, there is a prevalent recklessness on this point. The most degrading allegations are made respecting parties by comparative strangers to them, who at the same time ought to know that many who have better opportunities of judging those parties have only testimony to their integrity. I have the fullest confidence in Mr. Cooper's intentions, and know he would not thoughtfully cast an insinuation or imputation without possessing what he considered pretty full proof in support of it.

If this question is to abide the decision of mere presumption of fraud and imposture, I have only to remark that the tyranny of suspicions or jealousy, is not (as many appear to suppose,) the healthful exercise of a rational faculty, but the recognition of an usurped authority, the deranging influence of a base passion, ending to the subversion of every ennobling faculty of our nature, destructive of those higher elements on which anything that is worth preserving within us can be based. My own experience (happily as I conceive,) has clearly demonstrated that men in the main mean well, and that those who doubt it, who act on the promptings of suspicion will deceive themselves ten times when an open manly confidence in their fellow men would deceive them only once. If this proposition be not true the notion of benevolence and providence, of the power that formed all we see, is a bald, naked, unprotected lie.

As to media themselves, I have only been familiar with these during the last four years. So far as I am capable of judging, I am forced upon the conviction that they are not inferior in integrity of purpose to any class whatever, with which I am acquainted. Many, very many, of our most highly respected citizens in America are media. The most respected and intelligent families in our cities, those enjoying the very highest position in social life in Boston, and other cities furnish many of this remarkable class. Men whose names are famous in science, governors of States, members of Congress—men eminent in literature, revered as religious teachers, are not only spiritualists, and in numbers, but also media.

That some media may not have attempted fraud, and even successfully I am not prepared to say. For although I have never myself witnessed anything on the part of any one of them which led me to any conclusions to their disadvantage in this respect, I cannot feel authorised to adopt the course of many of our opponents, by declaring my own failure at detection, to be triumphant proofs of the fallacy of any testimony of a more positive character, which the experience of other individuals may enable them to offer.

In his theory of the effects of physical death upon the really vital principle of man, it appears to me that Mr. Cooper simply begs the question, which is—Has man the power to manifest himself from beyond the grave or not? There is assuredly no proof to the contrary, while there is an unspeakable amount of incident offered as testimony of the affirmative by those who believe it to be entirely genuine, and which opponents have failed entirely in the effort to set aside. I thought also that Mr. Cooper might mean, by some of his remarks in this connexion, that spiritual beings, if such there be at all, would necessarily, from their spiritual character, be incapable of physical or any tangible demonstration to man.

If such be the case, the entire question is at once settled. But no testimony supporting such a position has ever been adduced, within my knowledge, although a great deal has been offered, and is daily offering, in support of the contrary opinion. The assumption that spiritual bodies are immaterial bodies appears to me highly contradictory of all we know of existences of sentient beings, and like all other assumptions unsupported by proof must pass as very insignificant coin. How much less then, should they conflict with unrefuted testimony, even admitting such testimony not entirely adequate to the establishment of such forms of existence.

Mr. Cooper finds this theory to be false because, also, it is in direct antagonism with truth itself. The truth, in his estimation on this point, re-affirming his opinion of the world's previous inexperience and ignorance of such phenomena as are now supposed to transpire. He leaves the proposition to find its support in his own declaration.

I have very rarely become intimate with any family in any country, in which I have not found one or more members to declare, the contrary of Mr. Cooper's views has been the experience of one or more of such family within the memory of the living generation, to say nothing of family tradition (of perhaps less reliable character,) of similar events in its past history.

All records of all peoples testify to a constant succession of events which have ever engaged the public to a most lively interest in this feature of human experience. A debating ground in these premises which human knowledge, and even human ignorance has vainly endeavoured to demolish. I believe there is not a shadow of such inconsistency as Mr. Cooper indicates. I maintain that human experience ignores entirely the position he has assumed, and assumed without one particle of support. I further maintain that even admitting that the first so-called spirit manifestations of which we are cognizant did occur within the last ten years, it proves nothing whatever of his proposition.

Surely Mr. Cooper does not mean that because spirits may never have appeared to man they never can do so. Where is there any proof of such an impossibility? As well might it be maintained that nothing new *to man* can transpire. And it equally follows that nothing new *ever did* occur. The ignorance of man, however blank, can prove nothing. It may cast its shadow upon them, but it is in light, and not in darkness that knowledge and truth are revealed.

Mr. Cooper suggests the propriety of understanding the laws of nature and the powers of matter before we attribute any facts to spiritual sources.

Men must be governed by the facts before them, they must assign phenomena to what appear to be their real sources. To say we will listen to no convictions which lead us to spiritual solutions would be no less adverse to the principles of a true inductive philosophy than would be an abandonment of all facts referable to physical causes until we had exhausted the spiritual.

If we find one obstructs the other, let us separate them by all means, if indeed it be within our power to do so; but neither the necessity nor possibility of such a divorce has yet been demonstrated.

In Mr. Cooper's iteration of the charge with which spiritualists have so often been burthened, that they themselves refer, and most unnecessarily, these phenomena to spiritual agency, and that its investigators are responsible for such a christening, appears to forget the fact that the announcement of spirit agency is *one* of the phenomena. The little girl at Rochester to whom this announcement was made at the commencement of the present series of these spiritual manifestations, was perhaps as much surprised as others. She asked the question I believe in utter ignorance of the source of those sounds which had grievously annoyed her for about forty-eight hours. The announcement then made is confirmed by all intelligent experience on the subject since. So far as my knowledge extends, the reply is still the same to the same question. I have probably heard it asked hundreds of times with the same result.

The inconsistencies alleged by Mr. Cooper are such as have ever attended the progress of human advancement. The new dawn has ever abounded in apparent inconsistencies, which time and more knowledge ever prove to be merely imaginary. When two facts appear to conflict, it is in the theory of them we must find the difficulty. Knowledge leads to simplicity in which its perfection lies.

The circumstances, real or apparent of human conduct, are rather qualities of its actions than refutations of their reality, and in the absence of proof that no inconsistencies prevail in the Spirit World, that men take none to that from this, we have no particular reason for supposing they may not still characterise the conduct of some of the inhabitants of that sphere. I confess, however, I have not been able to detect the kind of inconsistency to which Mr. C. particularly referred. Until he has shewn that spirits have hitherto done nothing for man, or have not done all they could under existing circumstances do, his accusation must rest upon mere authority. I see no difficulty in supposing that Spirits may often influence men on earth in a manner of which we are entirely unconscious, and that conditions of the past have been less favorable for tangible and general manifestations than those of the present day. That conditions in America at the present period are far more favorable to these phenomena, whatever may be their source or character, must be fully obvious to all observers in these premises. What is obviously true of locality, may (as I conceive), be equally so of time.

We know that the condition of man in this world, has been one of change—we hope, of progress. A constantly varying condition of circumstances attend him. We also know, that if there be a spiritual world, the intelligences of this world bear some kind of relation to the powers of that. It, therefore, follows, there being a constant change in this world; that the relations betwixt the two must change in some degree every moment. Is there then any difficulty in supposing, that in the ripeness of time, a period has at length arrived through the operation of this ever-shifting relation betwixt the two worlds, wherein circumstances governing their means of communication have become more favorable to their purposes than have before existed, for perhaps an indefinite period? Is not this a more Christian, a more rational, a more ennobling conclusion, than one that simply jumps into the awful necessity of condemning the countless millions of our fellow beings who may have really gone to a spiritual world, as mere machines of empty professions and base practices? Besides, at what period would Mr. Cooper have had these manifestations to commence to be consistent with the views he here offers of consistency—unless the first spirit rapped or manifested in some way to man for his benefit, a serious accusation must lie at his door? All things must begin, and doubtlessly do so at their natural periods. To suppose otherwise, is to condemn the world, and the universe as a mere confusion.

Mr. Cooper, in supposing that these manifestations are confined to private circles, is in the main correct. Nevertheless, he labors under a most gross error of fact. If his position in this respect were true, it would only prove what is true of all other things, that certain conditions are necessary to certain results. A very little dust defeats the end of the daguerreotypist. The slightest flaw in a wire destroys all the magnificent powers of a harp. One degree of heat constitutes all the difference (in results) betwixt an effete acorn and a noble oak.

In the city of New York, there is an association of respectable gentlemen embracing some of the best minds and hearts in that city. I would mention also its scientific members literary and professional, if I were not well assured the mere senses of the great mass are as good instruments of their kind as any we have. This body of men denominates itself, the " society for the diffusion of spiritual knowledge."

These persons having satisfied themselves by their own experience of the reality of these manifestations, and that human life is very often made happier by a knowledge of this truth, have nobly combined by a devotion of time, talent, and money, for the purpose of bringing its advantages within the reach of all, so far as lies in their power to do so. Broadway, in New York, is very much what Regent Street is in London. In one of the most public and central parts of this great thoroughfare, and consequently in one of the most extensive, this society has for (I believe) *over* two years provided large apartments on a first floor, (second there), together with a spirit medium, who is in constant attendance. Thither all may go without fee or reward and witness the manifestations for themselves, propound their own questions, and make such investigation as they desire. There is no privacy; I have often been there—a looker on. The rooms have always been fully attended. The raps are constant when questions are asked; and I found these were almost invariably either mental, and known therefore to the interrogator only, or written secretly on paper. Thousands and tens of thousands visit this establishment. The flood pouring into and out of it is constant. We have one other medium in America, whose immobility of temperament is such as to enable her to retain the calmness under almost any circumstances which is necessary to the objects of spirits who may desire by these means to communicate with man. To attempt such results where calmness cannot be maintained, would be as vain as for a man to write legibly on a runaway horse. At least, such has been the result of my experience in the investigation of the subject.

Mr. Cooper, like many others, attributes these phenomena to some physical cause not yet understood. Supposing they have reality for agreement sake.

I would answer that the manifestations, be they from whatever source, declare they are from spirits of men who have lived on earth. Now, is nature, or is matter a liar, will logs of wood speak untruths? Human agencies may make them do so, or Spiritual agencies may do the same doubtless. But, if matter is the agent as is constantly urged, that resort is cut off.

I have addressed these lines to you, my dear sir, leaving to your own judgment, what shall be done with them.

I am sorry I could not be more brief. But you will readily perceive that this subject is at present in a condition, in England at least, which involves a necessity of going over much ground.

I would thank you to preserve these remarks for me, as I may desire to make extracts for other purposes.

If you can make any use of them, please consider yourself at full liberty to do so; and that I am, most sincerely, your affectionately attached friend,

JOS. P. HAZARD.

Robert Owen, Esq., London.

The following is the report of the Committee referred to in page 86 of this report—

REPORT OF THE COMMITTEE APPOINTED BY THE TWO MEETINGS OF CONGRESS OF THE ADVANCED MINDS OF THE WORLD, CALLED BY MR. ROBERT OWEN, HELD IN THE LITERARY AND SCIENTIFIC INSTITUTION, JOHN STREET, FITZROY SQUARE, LONDON, ON SUNDAY, THE 24TH MAY, 1857.

YOUR Committee, consisting of Spiritualist members of the Congress, agreeing with Mr. Owen's physical, intellectual, moral, spiritual, and practical views, and with the principles and practices founded on these views, have listened with the utmost attention and interest, and with the most sincere desire to acquire the knowledge of truth only, to his addresses and explanations, to the *Socialists, Spiritualists, and Secularists,* on the morning and evening of the 24th of May, 1857 ; and unanimously recommended the most careful investigation of all these subjects, instead of prejudging the value or non-value of any of them, taken separately, without examination.

Your Committee, composed of believers in human immortality, and that men perpetually progress in knowledge, power, wisdom, and goodness, and continue to hold the most affectionate and familiar intercourse with their fellow men, subsequent to their leaving their physical bodies, cordially endorse Mr. Owen's views and principles, and view them as completely meeting the whole wants of human nature, and feel great pleasure in drawing particular attention to the following extracts taken from the addresses delivered on that day :—

" That man is born without his knowledge or consent, with the germs of all his physical and mental qualities. He is therefore *forced* to possess them—let those qualities and powers be called good or bad ; and the possessor of them cannot deserve merit or demerit.

" He is also born at a *particular period* of human history, —in a *particular place,*—and within *particular surroundings,*—all without his knowledge or consent ; and for which he can have no merit or demerit.

" Now these surroundings in a more or less open manner force him to acquire a language, a religion, manners, habits, ideas of right and wrong, prejudices, likes and dislikes ; and for these, all forced upon him, he can have no merit or demerit, and cannot with justice be made responsible to God or man, to nature or to society.

" Where there are hatred, anger, and ill-will between parties, on account of a difference in belief or opinion, there can be no knowledge of our nature, no foundation laid for the admission of common sense into minds which have been so unfortunately trained and educated by an equally ignorant society and injurious surroundings.

" The first introduction of a true and useful knowledge of ourselves, informs us that we *must believe, and cannot avoid believing,* according to the *strongest impressions* made on our minds, and that therefore, it is most irrational for men to be angry or displeased with each other for their different individual convictions and feelings.

" Men of mind, who know the past history of man and his

present position over the earth, are conscious that not one of the existing religions, as now taught and practised by the human race, can ever become universal, or unite men to make them good, wise, permanently prosperous, and happy.

" Our business, in our present state upon earth, is with facts, which we can investigate and comprehend, to enable us to make each other good, wise, and happy, which is man's mission on earth, as is evident by the desire of all to attain these results.

" To discover a universal religion is the first step to unity among men, and to a permanent peace for the population of the world ; and it must be attained before practical measures can be adopted to construct the surroundings which can alone make all placed within them to become united, good, wise, permanently prosperous, and happy.

" What, then, you will now ask, is this *true religion,* which is to be accepted by all nations and peoples ?

" It is the substance of all religions, without their useless forms and ceremonies.

" It is the daily, the hourly, the unceasing practice of love and charity for our race, irrespective of colour, country, creed or class ; or a never-ending desire to promote the permanent happiness of all, through the life of each.

" This will be now soon attainable. The shell and spell of ignorace are broken ; and life, liberty, and knowledge will have free range over the earth, directed by wisdom, in peace and harmony.

" This great change, the wonder of all nations and peoples, will be effected through the medium of the, to many, strange and yet little understood *Spiritual Manifestations.*

" The spirits of just men made perfect will assist, guide, and direct the way to the full and complete reformation and regeneration from ignorance to wisdom of the race of man, thus preparing, through a new practical religion, a new earth, and a new sphere in heaven for those thus reformed and thus regenerated.

" There are now around us superior Spirits, who, through the aid of superior intelligence and power, have been purified and perfected, who are now deeply interested in forming and carrying forward various measures in different parts of the world, to bring about this great and glorious change for humanity—this new dispensation, and permanent happy existence of man upon the earth, to prepare him at once for the higher enjoyments of superior spheres in heaven.

" But, to attain these results, certain practical measures are

I

necessary. which can alone emanate from the true fundamental principle, which enables man to know himself, how he should assist to form the character of his successors, and how he should construct society, and thus make the principles and practices of the human race to be consistent with the laws of nature, and in harmony working together to consolidate the unity and permanent happiness of our race.

" This and this alone is true Socialism. *This is the Socialism I have been so long in preparing the world to receive in spirit, principle, and practice.*

" Let it be deeply impressed on the minds of all, that true religion consists in the practice, in thought, word, or action, throughout life, of love and charity for all of our race, and in being merciful in conduct, as far as is practicable, to all that has life ; that anything short of this is a name only, and not the reality or substance of religion.

" It is *this practical religion* which can alone set nations free; which can saturate the earth with wealth, to be used and enjoyed by all; which can unite man to man over the earth ; which can give a good, useful, and valuable character to all men ; which can put the spirit of peace within the minds of all, and insure the permanent peace of the world."

Your Committee feel great pleasure in directing particular attention to all Mr. Owen's Addresses delivered by him on the 24th May, 1857.

CHARLES WILLIAM GREGORY,
Of the City of London,
Chairman of the Spiritual Committee.
JOHN SCOTT, of Belfast, *Hon. Secretary.*

London, May 25th, 1857.

REPORT OF THE CONCLUDING MEETING OF THE CONGRESS OF THE ADVANCED MINDS OF THE WORLD, HELD IN ST. MARTIN'S HALL, LONG ACRE, LONDON, ON MONDAY, EVENING, MAY 25TH, 1857.

At the conclusion of the sittings of the Congress of the Advanced Minds of the World, called by Mr. Robert Owen, to consider the best possible plans, principles, practices, and peaceable means to change

the present most ignorant, false, unjust, cruel, and
evil system of human society, for the enlightened,
true, just, merciful, and good system of society, so long
and clearly explained, and advocated by him, (Mr.
Owen) for forming men's physical, intellectual, moral,
and spiritual character—for producing, distributing,
and enjoying all desirable wealth, and for placing, employing, and governing the human races, in harmony
with all the divine laws of human nature, and the universe, (which sittings took place both in St. Martin's
Hall, Long Acre, and in the Literary and Scientific
Institution, John Street, Fitzroy Square, London, from
the 12th to the 25th of May, 1857), the members
held a public meeting in St. Martin's Hall, Long
Acre, London, at 7 p.m., on Monday evening, May
25th, 1857, which was both numerously, and respectably attended,—Mr. Owen, the venerable President of the Congress in the chair.

Mr. Owen opened the proceedings by briefly explaining that he had called this meeting at the conclusion of the protracted sittings of the present
Congress, to take farewell of his friends —to shortly
recapitulate the best possible principles, practices,
plans, and peaceable means, to change the present
most ignorant, false, unjust, cruel, and evil system of
human society over all the earth, for the enlightened,
true, just, merciful, and good system of society, clearly
explained and long advocated by him (Mr. Owen), for
forming men's physical, intellectual, moral, and
spiritual character, for producing, distributing, and enjoying all desirable wealth ; and for placing, employing,
and governing the human races, in harmony with all
the divine laws of human nature and the universe ; and
to give the members of this Congress, and to all who
might be disposed to unite and co-operate with them
in every locality of the Empire, an opportunity of
petitioning Parliament, for the immediate adoption of
these comprehensive plans, consistent principles, and
beautiful harmonious practices, which would put an

effectual end to the present highly irrational state of things in this country, and ultimately all over the earth.

Mr. Owen went on, to point out the changes which would probably occur before the termination of the present century. He said,—

" The Evil Principle on which society has been based from the beginning until now, will be peaceably superseded by the Good Principle, which will change the falsehood, deception, and repulsive feelings, to this period so universal, and necessarily emanating from the Evil Principle, to the universal language of truth, conduct of honesty, and attractive feelings among all of the human races.

" There will be permanent peace over the earth, attained by all nations being federatively united on principles of justice and humanity.

" A rapid change will be in progress to give one language to all, to form one interest and one feeling of love and charity for all colours and races, and to produce perpetual joyous harmony throughout the population of the world.

" There will be no buying or selling wealth of any kind for a money profit; superior wealth will be annually produced in great superfluity for the human races, and all will freely partake of it without money and without price.

" All, for the great benefit of each, will have their natural physical, intellectual, moral, spiritual, and practical qualities, cultivated as well and as highly as the combined knowledge and means of society will admit; and a universal good, wise, and happy character will be thus formed for all, without exception.

" The sciences will be made the slaves and servants of the human races.

" There will be a just and enlightened equality according to age in the condition, training, and education of all.

" The population of the world will be lodged, fed,

clothed, employed, and placed, in a superior manner within superior surroundings, to the exclusion of all inferior.

" The population at the termination of this period will be actively engaged in extending the City of the New Jerusalem, which will extend over the earth, and in which there will be no streets, lanes, courts, or alleys—all these being inferior or injurious surroundings.

" Telegraphic communications may when necessary be made over the extent of this City, when it shall cover the earth and be divided into its natural family townships, with populations not exceeding three thousand.

" The inhabitants of this new City will be occupied, according to age, in producing superior wealth in a superior manner, in aiding to form superior characters for all within their influence, and in enjoying their existence ; each having all their faculties and natural qualities well trained and educated, according to their well disciplined wishes and desires.

" The City will be the home of all, and each may remove from one part of it to another at pleasure, and everywhere will be provided, in return for their superior services, with superior accommodations, and all wants fully supplied, each one everywhere meeting only his brothers and sisters, upon an equality with himself according to age.

" And I now put forth these statements to the public, that the eyes of all may be opened to the immense unnecessary evils and sufferings of the human races under the existing system of falsehood, force, fear, and fraud, and to assist all to come out of this evil course, which is leading the human races down to a pandemonium,—while the new and true system which may be now adopted will lead direct to an earthly paradise.

Mr. Owen proceeded and said, that he would now state, what he believed would probably take place before the termination of the present century.

" Nations will be united federatively over the world, and there will be permanent universal peace. The first federative treaty will very probably be made between Great Britain and the United States.

" All will be placed from birth within good and superior surroundings, and thus all will have their characters well-formed from birth, physically, intellectually, morally, spiritually and practically. All will be made to become good, wise, and rational, and, when compared with the present generation, superior rational beings.

" All will be so surrounded from birth, as to be well fed, lodged, clothed, placed, employed, and governed.

" The earth will be new laid out to form, over its whole extent, one City, to be composed of separate townships with their required appliances; and each will be a paradise of a township, connected with all other such townships over the globe, until they will form the earth gradually into this one great city, which may be called the New Jerusalem, or the united earthly Paradise.

" The spaces between the townships will be laid out in gardens, groves, fertile fields, to be as beautiful a, human knowledge and scientific means can make them

" The City, containing all the inhabitants of the earth will be occupied by a thoroughly developed and regenerated race of human beings, governed solely by God's Laws, speaking the same language, and that, the language of truth only ; having one interest and one feeling, to promote each other's happiness; all filled from birth with the spirit of universal charity and love for one another, and applying those divine qualities to their every-day practice through life.

" Vice, crime, prostitution, and misery, will entirely cease. Anger, ill-will, or abusive language will be unknown.

" Individual selfishness will cease, and isolated interests will be unknown.

" An elevated equality in condition and education, will be universal.

" Each age will have its peculiar employments, rights, and privileges, and these will be the only distinctions, contests, competitions, quarrels, and jealousies, among men and women will cease for ever.

" Arrangements will be formed to produce wealth of superior qualities, so abundantly, and so pleasantly to its producers, that all will freely partake of it according to their wants and wishes. And it will be made to abound at all times in every part of the extended city of the New Jerusalem.

" Telegraphic communications, when necessary or useful, will be made daily to every township composing this coming great and glorious habitation of the human races.

" The use of every township, and of all the earth, will be equally the right of all, and all will be thus free men of this city and equal partners in all its possessions.

" Each will travel when and where inclination may direct or health require, and in return for their superior educated services, will everywhere be supplied with all they may desire to have or to enjoy.

" The travelling over seas and oceans will be on well constructed large Islands, formed by men, and navigated by the aid of steam, if better and superior motive powers may not in future be discovered and brought into use. Thus travelling will be always performed on dry land, unless the means for superior safe arrival by *aërial navigation* may be discovered and introduced into practice; and this discovery, under the new dispensation of unity of mind and interests, may, indeed, be reasonably anticipated ; for under the united system of truth and goodness for forming character and governing the world, men will be enabled not only to remove mountains and fill up valleys, when useful, but to do far greater things than these.

" Under this New Dispensation, old things will rapidly pass away, and all will become new—even men and women will be new formed from birth, and all in external form and internal feelings and mind will be-

come beautiful, and both will be in perfect harmony; and
then the human races and all nature will also gradually
grow into harmony, and thus attain their foreseen destination, when the happiness of humanity will be complete, and upon earth man will have no more to desire

" It will be asked—on what foundation I make these
predictions? The reply is, on my knowledge of human nature, of the interests of the human races, of
the illimitable powers of the sciences, and of what
man can do for man, when cordially united with all his
fellows, and when the world shall be at peace.

The spirit-quickening animation, the sublime pa-
thos, the intellectual force, and the mind-kindling
moral power and grandeur with which Mr. Owen delivered the above address clearly demonstrated, that
his mental vigour is constantly increasing, and continually undergoing progressive development.

" The meeting," he said, " if it thought proper,
might request that he (Mr. Owen) should be heard
and examined at the *Bar* of *both Houses of Parliament*." After several other valuable explanations and
practical suggestions, never to be forgotten, Mr. Owen
before he sat down called on Mr. John Maughan to
move the *first* resolution, namely,—

" That this meeting views with apprehension the rapid moral
and social declension of society, and is of opinion that radical
and comprehensive measures must be speedily adopted or permanent suffering will be entailed upon all classes"—which on
being seconded by Mr. McBean in a short comprehensive speech
was carried unanimously.—

Mr. MAUGHAN on rising to move the resolution,
said—

" We know how to value newspaper statements of prosperity.
We have looked behind the glare and glitter of the shops to the
condition of those on whom the shops depended—the working
and producing classes. We asked what was their condition? Did
it keep pace with external appearances of improvement? The
extension of the commercial and manufacturing system has
been accompanied by a disproportionate deterioration of the
working classes of society, for the employed were becoming the
serfs of the employers. Uncertainty and doubt attended the

lot of the working man. To remedy this state of things the people must be rendered independent of daily wages by such a re-organisation of society as would at least secure them food clothing, and lodging of good quality with certainty. That emigration was no remedy, if it could even be considered a palliation. The system led to falsehood and fraud, and left the lower classes in that horrible condition depicted by Dr. Letheby in his Report to the Common Council on the condition of the poor. He adverted to the condition of women who existed in a state of serfage—could not hold property—could not dispose of themselves in many instances : he adverted to the fact of the notorious deficiencies in their education—large numbers being unfitted for maternal and domestic duties. Women held the most important position in the rank of humanity. The character of mankind was largely dependent on their capability of training the infants they bring into the world. The remedy for the evils of society must be sought by a recurrence to the first principle. We must bring societary science into harmony with natural law, and give to all without exception the best training and the best conditions, and then and then only shall we have a society peaceable, truthful, virtuous, and happy."

Mr. McBean on coming forward to second the resolution, said—

" Let us carefully keep in view the interesting occasion, and the grand objects of the protracted meetings of this Congress, which is now about bringing its important public deliberations to a happy conclusion for the present. and if we do so, I am certain that this influential and respectable meeting will clearly comprehend that the resolutions which it should adopt and pass this evening, should collect and express as much as possible the essential essence of all that Mr. Owen has taught us on this important occasion—perhaps the most important that ever occurred in human history. This meeting must now clearly comprehend and perceive the pressing necessity there is for the immediate full and fair recognition of all human RIGHTS, secular, social, civil, and spiritual; and for the immediate introduction of a grand practical system of educating, training, placing, employing, and governing every human being from birth in harmony with the unchanging NATURAL RIGHTS, WANTS, and LAWS of human nature—in conformity with the eternal laws of God— in order that the best possible physical, intellectual, moral, and spiritual character shall be conferred on, and developed in all men, with the certainty of a law of nature ; and also, that we require, as a grand first step towards the immediate realisation of these glorious benefits, that until a UNIVERSAL religion, resting on, and arising from self-evident truths, shall be discovered by all, and deemed worthy by all men, to be supported by all men—that till this period shall arrive,—no class, party, or person in the *state* shall be any longer taxed for the support of the existing contradictory religions, with which we do not agree, and from which we do not, and cannot receive any benefit whatever. We must commence and teach our fellow men their own importance, and that they have natural rights, and what these rights really are ; and that they have Divine natural wants which must be met and supplied. We must teach our fellow men that it is their duty to acquire the most extensive and accurate knowledge of all their powers and rights ; and that it is their highest prerogative as men, to possess, exercise, and enjoy all their physical, intellectual, moral, and spiritual *powers*, *rights*, and *liberties*. The knowledge, the power, the wisdom, and the will to do good which we may happen to possess, we must teach and communicate to our fellow men. By giving our fellow men the accurate knowledge of all their Divine duties and rights, we shall give them the will and the power to obtain and exercise them.

ROBERT COOPER, Esq. Notting Hill, in a lengthy and eloquent speech, moved the second resolution ;—namely—

" That this meeting considers that the plans proposed by Robert Owen, Esq., formerly of New Lanark, are the best adapted to meet the growing evils of society, and that therefore a memorial be presented to Her Majesty and petitions to both Houses of Parliament, praying for an immediate enquiry into these plans, and that Mr Owen be heard at the Bar of both Houses — which on being ably seconded and supported by Mr. James Rigby, in a practical speech, perfectly explanatory of Mr. Owen's comprehensive principles and gigantic plans for human amelioration, was carried unanimously."

JOHN SCOTT, Esq , C.E., Belfast, moved the third resolution, namely,—

" That the following petitions be presented to the Houses of Parliament—that to the House of Commons, by Viscount Goderich : that to the House of Lords, by Lord Belper : and that Mr. Owen present the memorial to Her Majesty—which on being seconded by Charles William Gregory, Esq., London, was carried unanimously."

Mr. Scott read copies of the petitions to be presented to both Houses of Parliament, and of the address to Her Majesty, the Queen, and memorials to the Lords of the Treasury—(copies of which will be found subjoined to this report.) In urging the necessity for their adoption, he clearly pointed out the duty of every member of the Congress; and submitted several valuable practical suggestions to the meeting: and concluded a short, but interesting speech by observing,—" I may add, that while cordially concurring in the prayer of this petition, I have no faith in the success of any petition to the Houses of *Lords,* and *Men,* unless such petitions are seconded and supported by the united power of the people. If the people will unite on the broad basis of true Christianity, which is the love and practice of wisdom, virtue, and benevolence; if they will join their forces, unite their powers, and settle their mode of operation in peace and harmony, they will bring to bear on the lavish squanderers of the public wealth, which is obtained by the sweat and blood of the people, such a " pressure from without," as the most accomplished conspirators against the rights of the people, and the most cruel and callous usurpers and despots in State and Church will be powerless to resist.

MR. GREGORY, on coming forward to second the third resolution, said,—

" He had much pleasure in seconding this important resolution, and he sincerely trusted that Parliament would afford Mr. Robert Owen a fair hearing for explaining his plan for changing this period of crime and misery to a state of virtue and happiness."

MR. CORFIELD moved the fourth resolution, namely,—

" That a Committee be now formed with power to add to their number for the purpose of devising such measures as may lead to a systematic organisation of those persons who believe Mr. Owen's societary views to be true, and to secure a wider diffusion of them among mankind—which was ably seconded by Mr. Donovan, and carried unanimously."

After these resolutions were passed, Mr. Owen came forward again, and said,—

" What the Advanced Minds of the World have now to do, to change the present false and evil system for governing the populations of all nations and peoples, for the true and good system, by which to introduce and maintain real virtue among all, and to put them in the direct road to attain excellence and high permanent happiness.

" *First.*—They must supersede all human-made laws, by the All-wise, All-good, All-merciful, and just laws of God and Nature. Man's irrational laws ever have and ever will require changing :—God's laws never ; they were the same yesterday, to-day, and for ever. They are abundantly sufficient to lead all to goodness, wisdom, unity, wealth, and happiness.

" The abrogation of all men's laws, and the adoption of all God's laws respecting humanity, will become a solid foundation on which to construct a consistent, superior, and permanently happy state of society over the world.

" *Second.*—These laws of God or Nature have then to be consistently applied to form the character of every one from birth, so as to unite in perfect harmony the Divine or God-made part of man at birth, with the human-made part of man from his birth. By this union and process all will be made to become good, united as one family, wise, ever prosperous, healthy, and happy.

" *Third.*—These laws have next to be applied to reconstruct society to be in harmony with them and with the new superior character formed under their direction and guidance. This reconstruction of society will be formed of new combinations of surroundings, each of which will be purposely devised to have a good and superior influence upon every child of man placed within them.

" These new surroundings to be so combined as to insure a good and superior character for every one from birth to death, in accordance with their original organization,—to enable all to produce with pleasure to themselves their full share of the wealth required for society, and to distribute that wealth justly and wisely for all.

" The surroundings to produce and permanently

maintain these results will constitute a scientific nucleus of society, and will include within each nucleus a population not exceeding three thousand as a maximum number.

" These scientific nuclei of society will be so arranged as to contain, within each, all the appliances for everlasting self-support, and for the highest state of earthly enjoyment.

" *Fourth.*—These townships to be federatively united with each other, on terms of perfect equality and reciprocity, as soon as each township shall be constructed and organized.

These superior surroundings will not admit of a street, lane, court, or alley, in any township constructed in accordance with the laws of God or Nature.

" These new scientific societies or townships should be made to gradually supersede all existing villages, towns, and cities, and all isolated residences; all these being now inferior or bad surroundings.

" *Fifth.*—But preliminary to these full and more perfect scientific societies or townships being formed, preparatory villages of union and mutual co-operation should be constructed, in which parents might live in separate dwellings, while their children were being trained together as of one family, and educated to become rational beings in mind and practice, without interfering too much at first with the long established habits of the parents and older persons. These villages however should be constructed and governed in strict accordance with the laws of God and Nature. But parents in their day and generation must be allowed to live in these villages in separate dwellings, while their children are being trained and educated to become members of rationally united families.

" *Sixth.*—As soon as the members forming these villages and townships are perfect in the knowledge of the laws of God and in their right application to practice, such parties, whenever they shall meet with difficulties, or shall be at a loss how to proceed, will have only to refer to these laws, and in every case which may occur they will direct how all should act to overcome the difficulty in the spirit of charity and love—these laws being all powerful for the good government of the human races, under all circumstances.

" I have in my various publications given many details for the right formation and conducting of these preliminary villages of union and mutual co-operation; and to these I must refer you.

" Before the termination of the present century, all nations and peoples will be federatively united on principles of justice and equality.

" Great Britain and the United States of North America will first federatively unite; the innumerable advantages that will arise from this union will induce all other nations and peoples to partake of them, by federatively uniting with this first great united power; and then peace over the earth will be permanent and universal.

" The existing evil surroundings of the human race will be superseded by new combinations of surroundings, of a divine heavenly character, which will transform the earth into one City, composed of superior dwellings, gardens, groves, fertile fields, and pleasant retreats from the extremes of heat and cold. Yet a City without the evil surroundings of streets, lanes, courts, or alleys. This universal city, or New Jerusalem, to be divided into districts of townships, no one of which will exceed three thousand inhabitants; each township having its proportionate surroundings of gardens, groves, fertile fields, and pleasant retreats.

" These townships to be federatively and socially united over the entire city, and their productions, free to all.

" Each one in every township over the city of the earth, or the New Jerusalem, to have their physical, intellectual, moral, spiritual, and practical faculties, propensities, and powers, trained and educated from birth in a superior manner, so as to make all, according to their natural organized constitution, to become good, united, wise, and happy, through life ; and all to exercise their physical and mental natures in beneficial and pleasant occupations, up to the point of temperance for each faculty, propensity, and power which nature has given to them.

" There will be one language, one religion, one interest, and one feeling throughout this city.

" The Anglo-Saxon language, improved to the utmost, will be taught to all in its purity from birth, and the language will also be the language of truth only in look, word, and action.

" The religion will be that of Christ, or *Truth*, of love and charity through the every-day practice of everyone.

" The interest will be the equal benefit of all throughout the City, and the never ceasing desire, applied actively to practice, to promote the highest permanent happiness of each and all.

" The City will be free to all, and the citizens may change their locality to benefit their health or please their taste.

" The English and Irish channels will be crossed on dry land.

" The seas and oceans will be navigated on islands instead of in ships.

" The arts and sciences, especially mechanism and chemistry, will be the willing, faithful, and talented slaves and servants of the human race, performing whatever is unhealthy or disagreeable for men to do.

" Old things will pass away, and all the surroundings emanating from the satanic system of selfish individualism, falsehood, and deception, will be superseded by entirely new surroundings, emanating from the true, the good, and divine system, which seeks to promote the high permanent happiness and progress in excellence of each.

" The earth will remain its Creator's, and the rent

will be paid by the rationality, industry, and harmony, of its principal tenants or occupiers.

" These results will arise of necessity, by the change of the false base on which society has been hitherto founded, on which to form character, produce and distribute wealth, devise surroundings, and govern the human races, for the true base, on which alone a rational and happy life for man can ever be attained."

At the conclusion of this grand prophetic address, which was listened to throughout with the most profound solicitude and attention, Mr. Owen spoke of his mission on earth, in his present bodily form, as being gradually drawing to a close, and that possibly he might not have many other opportunities of addressing his friends in public. Then a resolution, expressive of the most affectionate regard, and of the fond hope that he might yet be able at some future times to appear in public ; and—That the Congress could not separate without expressing their high approbation of the unceasing urbanity, dignity, and firmness, with which he (Mr. Owen) had presided day by day over the proceedings of this all-important Congress, without tendering him their best thanks, and wishing the remainder of his already long life, may be spared in its present health of body and vigour of intellect, to aid to introduce into practice the spirit and principles which he has advocated in this Congress and through his public life, and of which they have so cordially approved—was carried unanimously and with prolonged acclamation.

Thanks were also unanimously voted to Mr. Robert Cooper for his patient, arduous, and impartial attention and conduct as Mr. Owen's reader during the protracted sittings of this Congress, after which the meeting separated.

The following are, the Address to Her Most Gracious Majesty, and the Petitions to both Houses referred to on page 122.

ADDRESS TO HER MOST GRACIOUS MAJESTY THE
QUEEN OF THE BRITISH EMPIRE, FROM THE
CONGRESS CALLED BY ROBERT OWEN OF THE
ADVANCED MINDS OF THE WORLD, HELD IN ST.
MARTIN'S HALL, LONG ACRE. LONDON, FROM THE
12TH TO THE 25TH OF MAY OF THIS YEAR.

WE, Members of this Congress, having heard, day by day,
during this period of our sittings, full explanations from the
unanimously elected President, Robert Owen, of the new system
which he now advocates for the immediate adoption of the government and people of this country.

We, also, at his request, having stated all our educated objections to his system, and having endeavoured to defend the
present order of society in opposition to his new views for
forming character, and governing mankind; but having been
convinced by Mr. Owen that we were in error, and that we
reasoned from a false foundation, and that the system which
he advocates is strictly in accordance with all the laws of
nature, and that it will prove when applied to practice, permanently beneficial for all your Majesty's subjects in every part of
your Majesty's dominions.

We therefore pray your Majesty to direct your Majesty's
ministers and government, to take this now all-important subject
into consideration, and to have it so investigated as to prove it
to be either erroneous or true, and if it is found to be true, that
legislative measures may be immediately adopted to bring it into
beneficial general practice. And, we your Majesty's most faithful
subjects, will be ever grateful, and endeavour to preserve the peace
and harmony of your Majesty's wide spread empire.

Signed by the Chairman of the day.

TO THE RIGHT HONOURABLE THE LORDS OF HER
MAJESTY'S TREASURY.

THE memorial of the Congress of advanced minds for considering the best peaceable mode of changing the present false and
evil system for the true and good system of society by which to
new-form the character of all from birth, and reconstruct society
through all its ramifications, in order to make man good, united
to his fellows, wise and happy, and society prosperous, consistent, and each part working in harmony with every other
part, forming thus a perfect science of society to create, consolidate and perpetuate human happiness.

K

Your memorialists have to state, that this Congress was called and presided over by Robert Owen, that it was held in St. Martin's Hall, Long Acre, from the 12th of May, to the 25th, both inclusive, that during this period, the President at great length, explained his views of the all-important subjects brought before the Congress, and that your memorialists were unanimous in approving the principles of the practical measures which he recommended, deeming those principles and practices competent to relieve society from all its present numerous and severe evils.

That your memorialists are of opinion, that these principles and practices require only to be known to be immediately sanctioned by all the rational authorities of the world, and that the best way to make them speedily and generally known, is to examine Robert Owen at the bar of both houses of parliament, by which means the whole of this all-important subject may be fully brought out in its outline and detail.

Your memorialists therefore pray that your Lordships' will use your great influence and power to have Robert Owen, the President of the Congress, so examined with the least delay practicable, and your memorialists will for ever pray, &c.

Signed, by order of the Congress, and with directions to forward to your Lordships a copy of the proceedings of the Congress during all its sittings.

ROBERT OWEN,

President of the Congress.

St. Martin's Hall, May 25th, 1857.

TO THE HOUSES OF LORDS AND COMMONS.

THE Petition of Members of the Congress, called by Robert Owen, of the advanced minds of the world, held in St. Martin's Hall, Long Acre, from the 12th to the 25th of May, 1857, to consider the best practical peaceable mode to supersede the present false and evil system, by the true and good system for governing all human affairs, and for giving from birth a useful and superior character to all of human kind.

Your Petitioners have attended this Congress day by day for twelve days in succession, during which we have heard Robert Owen, the President of the Congress, explain the outline and much of the detail of an entirely new system of society, in spirit, principle, and practice, and which he states to be the only true and good system for the government of the human race. He courted objections from all parties to his new views of society, in its spirit, principle, and practice. Objections were made, and were fully discussed and fairly met by the President of this extraordinary Congress.

Your Petitioners thought the objections were well replied to and truthfully answered ; and if, after a more full investigation, this new system, which may be called a new dispensation for the government of the population of the world, should prove to be as truthful as we now deem it to be, we hesitate not to affirm, that in practice it will prove to be the greatest boon that the human race has yet received from man.

Your Petitioners therefore are strongly of opinion that it should be subjected to the most full scrutiny and investigation of Parliament, in order that, if it be an error or delusion, it may be stayed or stopped in its progress by all the legal powers of the state and the authority of Parliament, while if, by a thorough investigation, this now most exciting subject should prove to be as true and good for practice, as the President of the Congress and your Petitioners now believe it to be, the sanction of the Government and of the Parliament may be given to it, in order that, through its general adoption, crime may be made to cease, and poverty and misery to terminate.

Your Petitioners therefore pray, that Robert Owen may be examined on this all important subject at the Bar of your Right Honourable House, and your Petitioners will ever pray.

Signed for the Congress, this 25th day of May, 1857.

ROBERT OWEN,
President of the Congress.

As stated at the conclusion of the report of the first part of the proceedings of the congress, on page 79,—the supreme importance and length of Mr. Owen's prepared addresses, as well as that of Mr. Scott's long speech, and Mr. Hazard's long letter in reply to Mr. Robert Cooper's speech in reference to SPIRIT TEACHING, rendered it necessary to omit many valuable remarks, and interesting explanations in support of Mr. Owen's views, advanced by several gentlemen attending the Congress.

GEORGE NICHOLSON BRUCE McBEAN,

Reporter to the Congress of the
Advanced Minds of the World.

London, 26th June, 1857.

MANIFESTO OF ROBERT OWEN TO ALL GOVERN-MENTS, NATIONS, AND PEOPLES.

BE it known to all men, that the great discovery has been made, by which the destiny of the human race will be changed, from ignorance and misery to wisdom and happiness, and by which the all-good and merciful laws of God and Nature will be made to govern the world, instead of the insane and cruel laws of infant undeveloped man, in opposition to those Divine Laws.

But this change is not to be effected by contests between peoples and governments; but by the people acquiring new knowledge, to enable them by moral power to induce the existing governments, by their firmness, numbers, and unity, to abandon all the inconsistent and ever-changing laws of men, and to adopt the ever-consistent and unchanging laws of God and Nature, which are alone applicable to humanity, and which alone can be applied to train, educate, employ, place, and govern man, so as to make him become rational, good, wise, united to his fellows, and happy.

The laws of God and Nature are—

" That the created receives all its qualities and powers from " its Creator, and that the Creator is alone responsible for the " qualities and powers thus given to and possessed by the " created."

" That man is created without his consent or knowledge, " and receives the qualities and powers of humanity from his " Creator, and that the power creating the general qualities and " powers of humanity and the peculiar combination of them " in each individual, is alone responsible for the thoughts, " feelings, and actions of all."

" That man is made by his Creator to believe in obedience " to the strongest impression made on his mind and feelings, " and to like or dislike, love or hate, in obedience to the " effects made by material and external objects on his peculiar " created nature or organisation, forced upon him at birth."

" That it is not only absurd, but gross insanity, to attribute " merit or demerit to man for his convictions or his feelings, " or for any of the qualities of humanity which he has been " compelled to receive from his creator."

" That all human laws are grossly absurd and insane, be- " cause they are all based on principles in opposition to nature, " —that is, on the supposition, that the created man makes " his own qualities and powers, and creates by his will his own " convictions and feelings."

These insane suppositions now govern the world by human-made laws, and they have hitherto governed mankind; while every fact known since man was created is opposed to these suppositions, and proves their falsehood and ignorance.

It does not therefore depend now upon governments to make this change from evil to good over the world; but it depends upon the knowledge, unity, and moral courage of the people, to be determined to be henceforth governed by the Divine Laws of God and Nature, instead of the insane laws of men, opposed to those Divine Laws.

Therefore, while the people are content to be governed by human laws, and reject divine laws, let them cease to blame their governments; and let them now look to themselves as the true cause of all their physical and mental degradation and suffering.

The laws of God and Nature will insure wisdom, union, and happiness to man.

Human made laws are useless, or create falsehood, crime, disunion, injustice, and cruelty.

The happiness of our race will be in the power and at the disposal of the people of all nations, as soon as they can acquire common sense and moral courage to make a right and wise use of that power; for they have but to will the change, to insure its accomplishment.

Sevenoaks Park, Sevenoaks,
    10th July, 1857.

SECOND MANIFESTO OF ROBERT OWEN.

BE it universally known, that the well-being, well-doing, and permanent happiness of the human race, is now easily and speedily to be obtained, by the united active moral force of the people upon their governments, to induce the latter to abandon all human-made laws, and to adopt the unchanging Divine Laws of God and nature.

And, in conformity with those Divine Laws, to make new surroundings, calculated to give a good, useful, and superior character to all from birth,—to create at all times abundance of wealth for all,—to distribute this wealth justly and wisely,—and to unite all cordially in one general interest and kind feeling, regardless of colour, country, creed, or class, or of any other differences.

These New Surroundings may be now easily and speedily created. All the means to accomplish them exist in great superabundance.

It now depends upon the people, when this All-glorious change for the inhabitants of the earth shall commence, and to them I now commit this great task.

ROBERT OWEN.

Sevenoaks Park, Sevenoaks,
12th July, 1857.

A NEW LIFE AND MODE OF EXISTENCE FOR MAN, ATTAINED THROUGH THE GLORIOUS CHANGE FROM THE FALSE SPIRIT, PRINCIPLE, AND PRACTICE, OF THE NOW WORN-OUT OLD SYSTEM OF SOCIETY, FOR THE TRUE SYSTEM, IN SPIRIT, PRINCIPLE, AND PRACTICE, FOR FORMING THE CHARACTER OF ALL FROM BIRTH IN A SUPERIOR MANNER, CREATING ABUNDANCE OF WEALTH, AND GOVERNING THE HUMAN RACE IN HARMONY OVER THE EARTH.

THAT the present system is entirely worn-out and dead for all useful purposes has been made evident to the world by the Congress on Education, held last week in Willis's Rooms and in the Thatched House Tavern, under the auspices of the Church, assisted in part by the Government, and conducted by the foremost men of the old expiring system for forming character and governing men.

The first practice, under very unfavourable circumstances, of the new system for forming character and governing man, was exhibited at New Lanark in Scotland more then half a century ago.

That practice was then more than a hundred years in advance of the knowledge of the Church and Government, as put forth by the foremost men in both at this Congress.

Under the new life and mode of existence, children of both sexes at ten years of age will have far superior knowledge how to form character, create wealth, and govern society beneficially for all ranks and classes, than was even glanced at by any of the most learned members of this to-be-celebrated Congress:—to-be-celebrated, for exposing the weakness in Church and State of this old worn out system of ignorance and evil, when advocated by the most learned and advanced minds formed under it, even when aided by the greatest advantages possessed by Church and State.

Few will deny, that under the British Government and Church of England the freedom of thought, speech, and writing, is in fact now to a greater extent and better secured, than it has been at any period in the history of the human race in any nation, ancient or modern.

If, then, under the most favourable circumstances yet attained under this old, false, and wicked system, so little practical knowledge of forming a good character, of producing abundance of wealth, and of well-governing humanity, has been acquired, after so many centuries of contests and bloodshed,—I ask,—Is it not full time that a system so utterly devoid of truth, and of any useful knowledge of human nature,—how to train and educate it,—how to form arrangements to supply its natural wants and requirements, physical and mental,—or how beneficially to place, employ, and govern it,—should be now superseded, gradually and naturally, by the true and good system, based on a knowledge of human nature, its requirements for health, peace, union, and active enjoyment, in accordance with the laws of its nature ?

" Yes,"—all who think and reflect will say, " but how can " such a change be effected—seeing the present prejudices, " from early training and habits, forced upon our race from " birth ?"

This HOW is the great stumbling block to the peace, unity, and happiness of the human race ; and it now requires but one united effort of the advanced minds of the age to overcome it. And what a glorious victory would be thus gained for humanity through all future ages !

And yet it appears to me a victory easily to be won, and I will now explain how the advanced minds of the age may attain it, in peace, and with high benefit for all of human kind.

Let these foremost men and women of the present day instruct the public in the genuine spirit of love and charity for our race—a charity and love to be derived only from the knowledge " That the character of man is formed FOR, and " not, as the present system insanely supposes, BY him,—" in this spirit let the wise men, not only of the east, but also of the west, of the north, and of the south, teach all the people the invincible power of determined passive resistance to error and evil, with the fixed purpose to keep and maintain the peace of all nations.

The cause of all error and evil is the ignorance of human nature whence all the codes of laws of men have emanated ; and every law of man is directly opposed to the laws of God and Nature ; and therefore do these laws produce contention, sin, and misery, continually. While the laws of God and Nature will produce throughout all time the concord, peace, prosperity, and happiness, which will necessarily arise from the Divine Spirit of love and charity being made to pervade the mind and feelings, and to govern the actions, of all men.

To overcome and abandon ignorance, sin, and misery, and to attain wisdom, goodness, and happiness, we have but to supersede, in peace and quietness, all the laws of men, by the all-wise and all-efficient laws of God and Nature; and thus for the human race to be for ever governed by the Divine laws of God and Nature, instead of the ignorant, absurd, ever-changing, foolish laws of men.

The laws of men lead gradually towards a pandmonium.

The laws of God and Nature lead towards a progressive paradise.

The Divine laws of God are—" That man must believe ac-" cording to the strongest conviction made upon his mind, " and for which belief therefore he has no merit or demerit."

The law of man is—That man must believe according to his ignorant and foolish imagination.

The divine law of God is—" That man must like and love " that which is the most agreeable and lovely to his peculiar " organisation, or to the faculties and qualities given to him " by the Power or Powers which created him."

The law of man is—That men and women shall like and love according to his gross laws of ignorance of what human nature is, or of the laws which govern it.

The law of nature is—" That the *Creating Power* gives all " the qualities possessed by the *created*, and for which it is " most irrational to praise, blame, reward, or punish, the " *created.*"

The laws of man make the *created* responsible for the qualities forced upon it by the power or powers which created those qualities.

Hence the utter confusion of mind of the human race through all past ages to the present

Hence the deadly hatred and bloody contests between men and nations, made to be madly insane by the folly and absurdity of their early training and instruction on a gross fundamental error, teaching all to imagine that they themselves form all their own physical, intellectual, moral, spiritual, and practical qualities. While they know not how any one of these qualities has been created for and given to them, and while they are also to-tally ignorant of the laws of God and nature respecting hu-manity, or how to direct those divine qualities of humanity to obtain the high happiness and enjoyment which they are evidently formed to give, and which, as soon as men can be trained and educated to become rational beings, they will give and secure to every one of our race.

And this great and glorious change for all humanity will be attained as soon as the advanced minds of the age will unite to set the example and teach the people to unite in an unchangeable determination to be no longer governed by the demoralising, unjust, cruel, wicked, and grossly inconsistent and absurd laws of men ; and openly declare it to be their fixed unchanging purpose to be governed henceforward alone by the laws of God and nature.

The path of contest and evil which you have alone hitherto pursued is here set before you ; and I now open to you the path of peace and good will, of charity, love, and happiness.

If you have free wills,—choose now which you will henceforward take,— the path to all evil, or the path to all good.

Why, in the name of common sense, do *three hundred millions* continue to pray, petition, and beseech a dozen families, now ruling with a rod of ignorance the so-called civilised world, to give these *three hundred millions* liberty to think, write, speak, and act, in accordance with common sense and the rights and laws of their common nature, while these three hundred millions have only peaceably to say to those families—

" We will no longer be governed by your most erroneous " and unwise laws ; but we will henceforth and for ever be " governed alone by the all-wise, all-good, and all-efficient, " unchanging and unchangeable laws of God and nature ?"

" And we now abandon all the ignorant superstitions of " men, which have been hitherto called religion, and we will " adopt the universal religion for man,—the religion of God " and nature, which consists solely in the never-ceasing prac- " tice, equally in each individual, of love and charity to all, " of every colour, country, creed, and class, and of all other " differences made in us by the great mysterious power which " has created us."

" And we will also, as God and nature always (when we are " not falsely placed, trained, educated, employed, and go- " verned,) impels us to do, speak alone the language of truth, " in look, word, and action, as we are compelled to receive " and entertain it according to the laws of the nature given " to each of us."

Now who will say, in defiance of the laws of God and nature, that the human race has not the right thus to think and to act ?

I claim this power as my just right, and I thus now act in accordance with that right.

But it should be held in everlasting remembrance, that, to form the earth into a terrestrial paradise, all that is necessary is, to combine new scientific surroundings to well-form the character of the human race, to produce abundance of wealth for all, and to well-govern all. And that the most ample means now exist at the control of society to attain these results.

The Friend of man,
ROBERT OWEN.

Sevenoaks, 4th of July, 1857.

WHAT THE ADVANCED GOVERNMENTS OF THE CIVILISED WORLD SHOULD DO TO PREPARE FOR THE NEW DISPENSATION OF HUMANITY ABOUT TO COMMENCE.

UNDER this change from the infant, undeveloped, evil, and suffering dispensation, to the more matured, more developed, good, and enjoying dispensation for the population of the world,—what conduct would it be wise in the governments of the more advanced nations now to adopt, and especially those of Great Britain and the United States of North America, to set the example to all other nations and peoples?

There are but two modes, the one to succumb to the advanced mind of the world in mental, scientific, and practical knowledge,—the other to lead and direct it in the right course.

It is beyond all comparison better for all governments and people that the governments should lead it, and should conduct the change in peace and with wise foresight.

But there must be no halting between two opinions. The true or the false, the evil or the good, must now be decided upon, or universal confusion of mind and action is before us and near at hand.

The true and the good system for the government of the world requires to be introduced by a bold decision, and prompt declaration, by the power or powers which shall first adopt it, in order that it may not be misunderstood by any part of the population of the earth.

The government or governments which shall commence the glorious change should put forth a manifesto, addressed to all nations and peoples, that it or they had accepted the new dispensation or millennial state of existence, and that it or they intended to adopt it in spirit, principle, and practice, and that it may be thus shortly stated

That it is based on facts, or universal self-evident truths, or self-evident deductions from self-evident truths.

From these emanates pure, undefiled, universal Christianity, or the unceasing practice of love and charity for all of our race, to the full extent of the meaning of those terms.

Pure universal Christianity leads direct to the desire to adopt practical measures to promote the well-being, well-doing, and permanent happiness of all of human-kind, and to mercy as far as practicable to all that has sensitive life.

This desire will lead at once to the creation of new surroundings over the earth, scientifically devised and combined to produce in perpetuity with the certainty of a law of nature, the preceding results.

These scientific new and superior surroundings will insure a superior physical, intellectual, moral, spiritual, and practical character for every one born, trained, and living within them, and an abundance at all times of superior wealth for all, attained with high health and pleasure by the consumers, who will superintend the operation of its production. To produce superior wealth in abundance at all times for all, and to insure a superior character for all, are all that will be required to commence the millennial state of man upon the earth, and gradually in peace and with wise foresight to form the earth into a terrestrial paradise.

For to accomplish this high state of permanently progressive happiness for our race, the most perfect scientific and beautiful surroundings will be required, within which to place all of our race from birth.

The present age has attained the means, and the knowledge to apply those means, to accomplish this simple, yet great, glorious, and everlasting change for man; and when the means and knowledge have been given to man, it is a sure sign that the time has arrived in the due order of nature for the infant, evil, and suffering Dispensation to be superseded by the matured, good, and universally happy Dispensation. Or for the crysalis state of humanity to cease, and for man to be new-born with his full powers of excellence for high permanent enjoyment.

ROBERT OWEN.

Sevenoaks, July, 1857.

THE INDIVIDUALITY AND SOCIALITY OF THE HUMAN RACE.

THE authorities and teachers of the human race have kept the mass of the population of the world through all past ages so ignorant and degraded, that their rational and reasoning faculties have not been developed to enable them to know any of the laws of their own nature, to comprehend what society should be, or to know how to attain the knowledge of these subjects now all important to every one of our race.

All have been so mal-treated, mis-trained, mis-educated, mis-employed, and mis-placed through life, that all require not only to be new trained, educated, employed, and placed, but also to be untaught the gross errors of irrationality which from infancy have been forced into the mind and upon the habits of all.

To teach from birth all that is true, good, and right, to all, as soon as they can be rightly placed within rational or common sense surroundings, will be an easy and most pleasant task. But to unteach a life made up of false ideas, erroneous, combinations of ideas, and of bad habits, emanating from those false ideas and combinations of ideas, is the most difficult of all tasks for man successfully to perform.

Yet this must be accomplished before man can be permanently benefited, or can be elevated to his destined rank in the creation.

Why do I say his destined rank in the creation ?

Because the germ of his existence contains qualities and powers which, when they shall be placed within proper surroundings to bring out those qualities and powers in accordance with their nature, will make man of necessity to become a rational, good, wise, and happy being, so superior to that which he has been made to become by ignorance of human nature by society, that the new man, physically, intellectually, morally, spiritually, and practically, will scarcely appear to be of the same species as the animals hitherto called men.

But by whom is this new direction to be given to all the native qualities and powers of humanity ?

It must be given by those who have been enabled to discover how to new form the mind and habits from birth of the human race, in such manner that from that period the mind, so to speak, shall be born again, so as to see all things through a new mental medium, be enabled to ascertain truth from falsehood, right from wrong, and good from evil, and to feel, think, and act right; so as highly and permanently to benefit itself and all of human kind, and to assist efficiently to make earth into a terrestrial paradise.

How will such discoverers, if such there be, proceed to perform their task ?

By simplifying the whole business of life,—teaching from facts the knowledge of ourselves, so far as yet known, and bringing that knowledge down to the present very limited capacity of the mass of the population of the world.

And this will be done—

First.—By considering what man is by nature at his birth.

Second.—By considering what, through ignorance of his nature at birth, he has been hitherto forced to be.

Third.—By considering what, with the present acquired knowledge of humanity, he may now be made to become.

This development shall now be attempted, for the benefit of the common mind of the world.

First.—What is man at his birth ?

He is a germ or compound of physical, intellectual, moral, spiritual, and practical qualities and powers, all of which united constitute humanity or human nature, and which distinguish it from all living beings upon the earth.

At this period he is for a longer period more powerless than any other animal, depending for immediate existence upon those around him.

The germs of these qualities and powers in infancy and childhood are so passive and impressive, that they will readily receive the influences of the surroundings, whatever these may be, in which they shall be placed, even from the wolf surroundings, to the most perfect that human knowledge and means can conceive and execute.

The proof of this is in all the past history of man, and in his present state in all nations over the earth.

Consequently any infant may be put from his birth within the most savage, or within the most civilised surroundings now known, and, without his consent or knowledge, may thus be made to become the one or the other.   And for becoming the one or the other it is most irrational to make him, in any way, responsible to the Power creating the germ, or to the surroundings, including the society, in which the germ may be placed through life.

Second.—What, through ignorance of the native qualities and powers of these germs, has man been made to become through all past ages to the present hour ?

Ignorance has supposed that this germ makes its own natural or human qualities and powers and the surroundings in which it is placed and from which it receives all its influences to form its humanly matured character.

From these conclusions, both contrary to all facts, man has been made to become every variety of an inconsistent irrational animal, opposed to his own happiness and to the happiness of his fellows, always making laws for his government opposed to the unchanging laws of his nature, and thus inflicting misery on himself and others, exhibiting on all occasions a total want of knowledge of his own qualities and powers, or how they should be cultivated and placed to make him to become rational and happy.

Hence the existing contests and irrational confusion of mind and practice over the world

Hence man has been made to this period to be the most inconsistent and irrational of all animals,—for all other animals seek their happiness by acting consistently according to the laws of their respective natures ; while man vainly seeks to attain happiness by opposing Nature's wise and good laws, by his own artificial and absurd laws ; and Nature's laws, if adopted, would insure both his physical and mental happiness.

Third.—What, with present acquired knowledge of humanity may man now be made to become ?

Knowing to some extent the natural qualities and powers given to the germ of humanity ; knowing also to some extent the influence of physical and mental surroundings upon these germs from the birth through the life of each individual ; a knowledge is acquired of the lever by which, rightly applied, man may be compelled to receive or attain the qualities given to angels, (except their wings,) and to gradually form the earth into a terrestrial paradise.

But this mode of compelling man from his birth through life to become superior, physically, intellectually, morally, spiritually, and practically, will give only pleasure to the individuals so compelled, through every step of progress in the formation of their new rational and superior character.

The whole science of this operation is known, and will be easy of execution as soon as the union of governments and people to carry them into practice can be accomplished.

But why should this union be longer delayed, when it would contribute so essentially to the permanent happiness and high enjoyment of all governments and peoples ?

Because society is based and constructed on the individual, repulsive, and most ignorantly selfish system ; when, for the permanent improvement and rational happiness of all, it should be based and constructed on the united, attractive, and enlightened system for the government of the population of the world.

To make this subject yet better to be understood,—let us consider man as an individual opposed in feeling and interest to his fellows ; and as an individual cordially united in feeling and interest to all of his race.

As society is now constituted, man is individualised, and is to a great extent trained and placed to be opposed in feeling and interest to a large proportion of his fellow men, at home, and over the world.

And as he is trained, educated, and placed to be opposed to them,—they are equally trained, educated, and placed to be opposed to him.

This mutual opposition of feeling and interest between the individual and society, destroys the great powers of progression in society, and the means of giving and securing prosperity and happiness to all of our race.

The power of individuals opposed to society (except in a very few cases, perhaps one in a million,) is as nothing ; while the power of society over the individual is all-powerful and overwhelming.

Let us now see what the individual can do for society, and what society can do for the individual.

Under the existing false and evil-producing system for the government of the world, the individual can do little for society except to expose and denounce this system of error and ignorant selfishness ; while society can do little for the individual until it shall determine to change the fundamental error on which it has ever been based, and the surroundings which have emanated from that false principle.

What, then, when society shall be based on its true principle, will the individual require from society, as his just right, for his own benefit, and for the permanent good of society itself ?

The individual will require to be placed within such new surroundings from birth, as will cultivate in the best manner all his natural qualities and powers, and will allow him to exercise all of them through life to the point of temperance for each physical and mental faculty.

And that which is now the best for one individual, will be the best for all of our race through futurity.

The surroundings should also be such as will enable the individual to aid to produce in the best manner his full share of the wealth required by society, and to make the earth into the terrestrial paradise previously stated.

And surroundings to effect these results may now be easily executed by united society.

For to form a superior character, and to produce abundance of superior wealth for all, and to make the earth into a terrestrial paradise, will constitute the business and the whole work of society, when Nature's laws shall be made to supersede the ignorantly opposing laws of undeveloped man.

ROBERT OWEN.

Sevenoaks Park, Sevenoaks,
   15th of July, 1857.

URGENT REASONS FOR THE GOVERNMENTS AND PEOPLES OF ALL NATIONS TO CHANGE OPENLY AND IMMEDIATELY THE LAWS OF MEN, MADE WHILE THEIR RATIONAL FACULTIES WERE UNDEVELOPED, AND WHILE THEY WERE IGNORANT OF THEIR OWN NATURE.

Contrast between the unchanging Divine Laws of humanity, and the ever-changing laws of men, opposed to the Divine laws of their own nature.

First.—The unchanging Divine Laws of humanity are—

That these laws compel men to believe in obedience to the strongest impression made at the time on their mind, and that therefore men cannot have any merit or demerit for their convictions, true or false.

The laws of men say—

" You must believe in accordance with and in obedience to
" *our* dictates, and if you do not and will not say that you do
" believe according to our written laws, you shall be punished
" and be made an outcast from our society."

Second.—The unchanging Divine Laws of humanity enact—

That humanity *must* like and love, dislike and hate, according to the impressions made by persons and things on the peculiar and distinct organisation or natural constitution of each individual ; and that, for thus liking, loving, disliking, and hating, man has no merit or demerit, being compelled to have these feelings.

The laws of men are—

That men and women shall like and love, dislike and hate, persons and things, according to the laws which *we* law-giving men make from time to time ; and when men and women disobey these our laws, and like and love, dislike and hate, in opposition to these laws of our land, state, and government, they shall be severely punished, or shall be made outcasts from our society.

Thus by men's varied ignorant and insane laws, as they now exist in all nations, opposed to the divine unchanging laws of humanity, sin and misery are created,—vice, crime, and suffering are made to be universal,—man is forced to become an irrational fighting animal, more inconsistent and opposed to his own nature than any other animal, filled with most injurious passions, which oppose man to man and nation to nation over the world,—and utter confusion and disorder are created wherever man exists, to the destruction of his superior rational faculties and of all chance of happiness.

For these cogent reasons I earnestly entreat all governments and peoples now openly to abandon all the laws made by man, and to be governed through futurity by the all-wise, good, and efficient laws of humanity, which will gradually develope and bring forth all those superior qualities in man, which will insure his universal permanent happiness.

ROBERT OWEN.

Sevenoaks, 15th July, 1857.

TO THE GOVERNING AUTHORITIES OF THE CIVILISED WORLD.

THE time is rapidly approaching for a great change to come over the civilised portions of the earth—a change to be effected either by physical or by moral power.

I most earnestly intreat you, while you have the means under your control, to adopt immediate measures to prevent the necessity for the former, and to make the change under the direction of the latter.

The present system by which the nations of the world are now governed, is become so glaringly false and ignorant in principle, so unjust and cruel in practice, and so un-Christian in spirit, that it will be impossible for governments, however despotic, to maintain it much longer by any power to be derived from force and fraud. Nor is it the interest of any party in churches or states, from the highest to the lowest, to attempt to retain this wretched system, calculated to force all to become false and deceptious in spirit, principle, and practice, as is the case at this hour over the world. While the true system for the government of the human race, now easily to be established by the union of governments and people, would insure the rapid progress towards the permanent excellence of character and permanent happiness of the family of man, of all shades of colour, and of all other physical and mental differences.

This change may now be made in peace and with perfect order; but if you allow this awfully important period to pass without wisely applying it to make the change from the one system to the other rationally, with foresight, and in safety to all parties,—then may the population of the world look for the change to be made by rivers of human blood, and with utter confusion in all empires and kingdoms.

I have given you in this publication my expected-to be last legacy to the human race; may it tend to open the eyes of all parties to the great good or great evil which is about to change the destiny of the family of man, most probably in the present century —possibly in a few years.

Your Friend,
ROBERT OWEN.

Sevenoaks Park, Sevenoaks,
     1st August, 1857.

The following is a copy of Petitions to both Houses of Parliament—one sent for presentation to Lord Belper, for the Peers; the other to Lord John Russell, for the Commons—dated 13th July, 1857.

THAT your petitioner has made the most important discovery yet made since man was created, for the permanent good government, well-being, and happiness of the human race—a discovery by which all of humankind will be made to become from birth, without punishment, good, wealthy, wise, and happy.

Your Petitioner therefore prays that your honourable (or right honourable) House will appoint a Committee or commission to investigate this all-important subject, or that the Petitioner shall be examined at the bar of your honourable (or right honourable) House, in order that the discovery may be soon known to the public, and that the practical changes which it requires may be gradually made, in peace, with wise foresight, and with the least loss of time.

And your Petitioner will for ever pray, &c., &c.

ROBERT OWEN.

PRELIMINARY STATEMENT,

EXPLANATORY of the reasons for establishing a society on a new base, to redeem the entire family of man from its present ignorance, poverty, disunion, sin, and misery, and to secure to it permanent progress towards excellence in all things and in promoting the happiness of all.

These results can be attained by creating a new spirit and principle to guide and govern the practice of all from birth to death.

The new spirit is that of universal love and charity applied to practice in all our conduct to our fellow men. This spirit, so to be applied to practice, can be created only through the knowledge of the great fundamental principle on which the character of all from birth must be formed to make it rational, and on which society through all its ramifications must be constructed.

This divine principle is " that the character of each one is " formed for him, and that through this knowledge such " character may be well-formed, from birth through life, for " every one of our race."

That the character is formed for each without his consent or knowledge, is known from the universal fact that the being or thing created can possess those qualities only which the creating power or powers give to the created. Man being created by God, Nature, and society, can possess those qualities only which those powers force upon or give to him.

With this knowledge of the laws of our nature for the foundation on which to proceed, the simple, straightforward road to universal progress and happiness is fully opened and made certain in the result.

This fundamental knowledge of our nature and of the true powers which form our character, physical, intellectual, moral, spiritual, and practical, when openly taught to the public in the spirit of love and charity, will enable society to become, at first, so far rational as to perceive the necessity for, and advantages to be universally derived from, the adoption of immediate decisive measures to give a useful, good, and superior character to the coming generation ;—thus to terminate as speedily as possible the existing ignorance, poverty, disunion, sin, and misery, forced upon our race through the false foundation on which society has formed the characters of all, thereby rendering society itself a mass of confused inconsistencies, destructive of the rationality, well-being, well-doing, and happiness, of our race.

But as society can form and will force any character upon all, even from the worst to the best, it has, through inexperience and the yet undeveloped state of the superior and rational faculties of our created nature, formed a most inferior and injurious character for all, making it strongly prejudiced against all great and important truths, except those forced upon it by the discoveries in the various sciences—therefore some new and most decisive measure of a strong character is immediately required, to overcome these lamentable prejudices, and to new-form the mind and new-construct society.

Decisive measures of a strong character are necessary, because these ignorant prejudices of our undeveloped superior faculties are deep-rooted and manifold, notwithstanding that these prejudices are obviously opposed to unchanging facts, perceived by those trained to observe accurately and to draw just or self-evident conclusions from such facts.

Some of the most fatal of these prejudices to the rationality and happiness of our race may be enumerated thus :—

1st Prejudice.—The notion that the created being or thing can possess qualities not given by the Power creating it.

2nd Prejudice.—That man, being created with all his organs, faculties, propensities, qualities, and powers,—physical and mental, without his consent or knowledge, yet forms his own character, and is made to be by man responsible to society for these divinely created qualities and powers, all of which are good by nature when not mis-directed and counteracted by man's ignorant and absurd laws.

3rd Prejudice.—The prejudice arising out of the great circle of superstitions, whether Chinese, Hindoos, Jews, Christians, Mahomedans, or Pagans.

4th Prejudice.—The prejudice of country and of the particular locality in which we live.

5*th Prejudice.*—That of class.

6*th Prejudice.*—That of particular creed.

7*th Prejudice.*—That of sex.

8*th Prejudice.*—That of political party.

There are many strong minor prejudices of local and family habits, &c., but those stated are sufficient to show the almost unconquerable difficulties to be overcome in changing an entire system in spirit, principle, and practice, when supported by such a formidable array of opposing obstacles. Yet will truth without mystery, mixture of error, or fear of man, aided by strong conscientious will, exercised by individuals, be found equal to this great and apparently impossible task.

To this end a society must be formed, of men and women with strong minds and willing hearts, determined, if necessary, to sacrifice their lives individually or generally, in order to emancipate the human race through futurity from its present ignorant and degraded mere animal condition, (without its advantages), to the rank of intelligent, rational, consistent, and happy beings, preparing themselves for a yet higher sphere of existence when they change this life for one more advanced and far superior, in which goodness, wisdom, and happiness, will attain still higher perfection.

This society may be called " The Society of Martyrs," for the redemption of the human race, from a false system of society, creating falsehood, repulsive feelings, sin, and unceasing misery over the earth.

And as soon as a sufficient number, willing to be members of such a society, shall forward their names to me, I shall call a public meeting to announce its objects and purposes to the world, and thus to bid open defiance to falsehood, error, superstions, and all the laws of men.

The qualifications for membership to the society of Martyrs to be—

First.—The abandoment of men's laws, leading to repulsive feelings, sin, and misery.

Second.—The adoption of the Laws of God and Nature, always leading to goodness, wisdom, rationality, and happiness.

Third.—The adoption also in *daily practice* of the true universal religion of love and charity for our race, and the abandoment of the endless superstitions now practised in all nations and among all people.

ROBERT OWEN.

August 5th, 1857.

M'GOWAN AND CO., PRINTERS, LONDON.

Registered for Foreign Transmission.

ROBERT OWEN'S

MILLENNIAL GAZETTE;

EXPLANATORY OF THE PRINCIPLES AND PRACTICES BY WHICH, IN PEACE, WITH TRUTH, HONESTY, AND SIMPLICITY, THE NEW EXISTENCE OF MAN UPON THE EARTH MAY BE EASILY AND SPEEDILY COMMENCED.

"The character of Man is formed *for* him, and *not by* him!"

No. 12.]   OCTOBER 1st, 1857.   [PRICE 6*d*.

A BRIEF STATEMENT OF A CHANGE TO BE EFFECTED THROUGHOUT THE WORLD, IN SPIRIT, PRINCIPLE, AND PRACTICE, AND IN ALL THE DEPARTMENTS OF LIFE :—INTENDED FOR THOSE TOO MUCH ENGAGED IN BUSINESS, PARTY, OR IN SECTARIAN POLITICS OR PLEASURE, TO ATTEND TO A MORE FULL EXPLANATION, OF A SUBJECT THE MOST IMPORTANT TO THEIR HIGHEST PERMANENT INTEREST.

THE change is from the government of mankind under the laws of man, to their permanent government under the laws of God and Nature.

The population of the world to this day have been governed by the laws of men. These laws have been all based on an error, fatal to the rationality of the human race, to its common sense, virtue, and happiness.

Our early undeveloped ancestors imagined, as they did that the sun moved daily round the earth, that the created, and not the Creator, originates and makes its own qualities; and this gross impossibility they have transmitted from generation to generation, even to the present; and hence the gross irrationality of all nations and peoples at this day, although such progress have been made in material science.

This fatal error, transmitted through many generations, shows the overwhelming influence of early impressions, to compel the strongest educated prejudices to take possession of the mind, so as to destroy the reasoning faculties for any rational purpose, and even for so many thousands of years to prevent their making the simple discovery that the thing made could not make itself or any of its qualities.

From this fatal error have originated men's laws ; and men's laws, being of necessity opposed to the ever-existing all wise and all-merciful laws of God and Nature, have been the sole cause of all the sin and misery of the human race through all past time ; and they are to day the only cause of the crimes and sufferings of mankind.

For these laws compel all to speak the language of falsehood, to be criminal against nature, and to be most irrational in mind and practice.

To make all good, wise, united, and rational in mind and practice, they must be governed alone by the unchanging laws of God and Nature ; and then will all gradually become in accord and harmony with God and Nature ; and thus will the wish of God be done on earth, as it is in heaven.

This ever-to-be-desired result will be attained by the unchanging laws of God and Nature respecting humanity. For when these Laws shall be consistently applied to practice, they will compel all to become good, wise, united, wealthy, rational in mind and conduct, and happy beyond any thing yet known upon earth ; and the desire of all hearts will be thus attained and secured, and the Millennium will commence, and will continue to progress until it shall be permanently enjoyed by all.

To introduce the knowledge by which to terminate over the world ignorance, sin, and misery,—and to establish for ever the reign of wisdom, goodness, and happiness, is the discovery which I claim.

And I am now prepared to explain to the governing powers of society the practical measures which will be required to attain these results, and gradually thus to place the population of the world under the immediate government of the laws of God and Nature.

In due time a public meeting will be called to consider how first to form a society to carry these measures into execution, peaceably and progressively, in the shortest time.

ROBERT OWEN.

August 10th, 1857.

REASONS FOR PROPOSING TO ESTABLISH IN ALL
CIVILIZED NATIONS, SOCIETIES OF THE MOST
ADVANCED OF BOTH SEXES, TO CHANGE THE
PRESENT FALSE, EVIL, AND DEGRADING SYSTEM
FOR THE GOVERNMENT OF MANKIND, AND TO
PEACEABLY SUPERSEDE IT BY THE TRUE, GOOD,
AND ELEVATING SYSTEM FOR PRODUCING SUPE-
RIOR WEALTH IN ABUNDANCE, FOR FORMING THE
CHARACTER, AND FOR GOVERNING THE HUMAN
RACE, IN SUCH MANNER AS TO MAKE ALL RA-
TIONAL AND HAPPY, AND TO UNITE ALL AS ONE
ENLIGHTENED AND AFFECTIONATE FAMILY.

IT is evident to those who accurately observe and
study the signs of the times, that a mighty revolution
over the earth is at hand :—that the present system
is worn-out, and has become unequal to the good or
rational government of the world,—and more especially since the progress made in the discovery of
material knowledge in the science of mind, and in
the true principles of training, educating, employing,
placing, and governing mankind.

The evils and sufferings created by this worn-out
system, constructed and governed by the laws of men,
are become so grievous and unbearable, that the
mass everywhere desire a change.

Many energetic and well-meaning patriots in various nations desire to effect a change by physical
force,—to take the power from one party to give it to
another, who, acting on the same erroneous laws,
would soon recur to governing as the former, by falsehood, force, and fraud.

All previous physical force revolutions have, through
ignorance of our nature, terminated in the tyranny
of physical force ;—and what is to-day the result of
all these physical force revolutions ? The establishment of stronger physical force governments. And
such will ever be the result.

Even the pet republic of the United States, as well
as the British government, the two most advanced
nations existing, are now governed in opposition to

the advanced minds of the world and to common sense.

While moral force, based on truth, or the laws of God and Nature, and made to be consistent in its operations, would succeed with the certainty of a law of nature— and succeed, too, in the shortest time, and with the least evil in its progress.

But moral force, based on the laws of God and Nature, proved to be true by their uniform consistency with themselves and with all facts, has never yet been attempted; because those laws, which constitute true morality, have never been understood.

To change this false and evil system for the true and good has been left to be accomplished at this eventful period, in the present generation—a period when not only Europe, but the population of the world, will be degraded to mental slavery and Cossack ignorance and dependance, or will be elevated to the rank of rational, independant, enlightened, good, and wise men and women, inhabiting the earth made to become by their industry and wisdom a terrestrial paradise.

To prevent this degradation and to attain this elevation, truth, in spirit, principle, and practice, must be applied, to create the moral force which can alone accomplish this task—which can alone regenerate the world, and create full-formed men and women, speaking and acting the truth through life. And these will form a new population, which will attain and secure happiness for themselves and all future generations.

From the practice of the laws of God, in spirit, principle, and practice, will arise true morality, or pure undefiled religion,—for both are one, and they consist in the daily practice of love and charity for all,—in loving our neighbours as ourselves,—loving our enemies,—doing good to those who hate and despitefully use us.

This also is true Christianity, based on eternal truths, which are the same yesterday, to-day, and for ever.

This morality and religion are attainable only by the abandonment of all the laws of men, and by the adoption of all the laws of God and Nature respecting humanity.

But the authorities in Churches and States are yet too ignorant willingly to abandon their cruel and vicious laws; and hitherto the governed have been too ignorant to comprehend what morality is, or its irresistible power when wisely applied.

This knowledge will now be given through the new spiritual manifestations, to those of both sexes who have moral courage to receive and to act it out in their lives.

These men and women must unite, and must agree to form themselves into a society, to be entitled

" *The British and Foreign Life and Death Society, to give and secure Happiness to the Human Race.*"

To effect this change in the condition of mankind, there is but one mode possible, and that is for the members of this Society to openly abandon the ignorant, false, unjust, and cruel laws of men, by which all are now governed, and as openly to express their determination to constitute new associations of men and women, to be governed alone by the now ascertained laws of God and Nature respecting humanity. And to abide by this determination; and in its defence when opposed, as it will be, by human-made laws, to willingly suffer the penalty of death, in preference to submitting to those laws, which alone continually create falsehood, deception, repulsive feelings, wars, conflicts, crimes, degradation, and misery.

To effect this great and glorious change for man, lives must be sacrificed in resisting error and evil; but these lives will not exceed the lowest number that will be required to attain and secure the desired object.

The lowest number to be sacrificed will be secured by the most conscientious men and women, having sufficient moral courage, offering themselves as willing victims to the cause of human redemption from sin and misery.

The early Society of Friends sought to attain the same end by the means now proposed, and many of their lives were sacrificed, and their sufferings through the ignorance and superstition of their poor deluded well-meaning fellow men were severe and long-continued.

These self-sacrificing men and women were nearer to the discovery of the all-good and wise laws of nature, than any who have attempted to follow them.

They desired universal truth in language, and honesty of conduct. They desired universal love and charity. They desired universal equality. They desired universal simplicity in their dress, houses, and furniture, and faithfulness in all their transactions with each other.

All these they desired, because many of their leaders were as mediums, inspired to know and feel that all these were necessary in practice to the attainment of the happiness of our race; and they were the advanced minds of their age.

But the time was not yet for the development of the knowledge of these principles, and their application to practice, by which these and greater results could be attained. This discovery, apparently in the due order of creation, has been left to be made and acted upon by the present generation.

But the early Society of Friends have given and left to the world a great and glorious example of self-denial for the good of the family of man.

This example, in its full integrity, and without flinching, must be adopted by those who become members of the

" *LIFE AND DEATH SOCIETY,*"

to be governed consistently by the laws of God and nature, which laws are alone capable of making man rational, good, wise, united, and happy.

It should, however, be known, before any become

members of this society, that the laws of God and nature cannot be introduced and practised under a system based on Private Property and Opposing Interests.

The laws of God and nature require a system of truth, without guile in language or deception in conduct, and undivided interests, with superior social arrangements for all according to age.

These arrangements are shadowed in part by the superior London Clubs; but the whole system of domestic arrangements for both sexes and all ages would be yet more complete than are the best of these clubs.

And these superior domestic arrangements for all, would be combined with other new surroundings, by which to unite the practical operations of the whole business of life, in which every 3,000 of the population of the world would govern themselves, according to age, as one family; for by this arrangement the greatest amount of individual liberty, compatible with order and permanent individual and public advantages, could be attained.

For more particulars see my MILLENNIAL GAZETTE for the 1st of August this year,—also the HISTORY OF MY LIFE—the first volume of which, with a copious and valuable Appendix, is in the press and will speedily be published.

ROBERT OWEN.

13th of August, 1857.

LIFE AND DEATH SOCIETY.

To attain the millenial state of existence upon earth it is necessary to combine into one system Spiritualism, Socialism, and true practical Christianity or universal religion; and this system may be justly entitled—

" The Rational System for the future government of the " population of the world in accordance with and under the " guidance of the laws of God and nature."

But Spiritualism, Socialism, Universal Religion, or practical

Christianity, and the laws of God and nature, are in spirit, principle, and practice, in direct opposition to the system by which the population of the world has been governed to this day, which system is justly entitled to be called the " Irrational System of Society," for forming character, producing wealth, uniting, and governing mankind.

Experience now makes it evident that, in the order of progressive creation, the irrational, undeveloped, or infant state of humanity must precede and prepare the means by which to attain its rational, consistent, and happy state.

And it appears to be in the due order of nature that the change from the irrational and conflicting, to the rational and harmonious state of human existence should take place about this period; but that, to effect the change from the one to the other, lives must be sacrificed, either by fierce physical force, with great slaughter, or by passive self-sacrificing moral courage.

The latter will be by far the most effective, and probably with far less loss of life and demoralising proceeding.

This is the great change from evil to good which now requires the establishment of the " Life and Death Society," for the redemption of the human race from sin and misery, emanating from the irrational impression made on all the past, that the created, animate or inanimate, creates its own qualities and powers, and that man, a created being, should be made responsible for those qualities and powers which he has been forced to receive without his consent or knowledge from the powers creating those qualities.

The change now proposed from the irrational to the rational system of society will completely accomplish all, and much more than all, that the reformers of parts of an irrational system have desired to effect, and which proposed practical changes, if effected under such an imperfect and undeveloped system, in spirit, principle, and practice, would produce little or no good.

The period is happily passed for wasting more precious time in these petty proceedings on false principles.

The system of evil and of good are now placed front to front, and there must be a death grapple between them before evil can be forced to quit the field and to resign its dominion over the race of man.

To shorten this great death struggle, the earnest men and women must now come forth and enrol themselves as members of the Life and Death Society for superseding the laws and governments of men by the laws of God and nature—by those laws which can alone make men good and wise, and give permanent peace and happiness to the population of the world.

The laws of God and nature have never ceased to speak to the minds and feelings of each child of humanity, in a voice continually unvarying through every succeeding generation, until now, when, by the pain which the disregard of these divine laws inflicts upon our race, it demands to be heard and to be obeyed.

For now the advanced minds of the age perceive and strongly feel the innumerable evils arising from man's most foolish and absurd laws respecting belief and love, disbelief and hate, in direct opposition to the all-wise, all-good, and all-merciful laws of God and nature on these all-important faculties of our created organisation.

Hence these advanced minds with moral courage and fixed purpose equal to the task will now congregate in such practicable masses, as will form the best separate societies or families to perform the most advantageously all the business of life, and to enable them so to organise all their operations and arrangements, that they may be directed and governed, not by men's laws, but by the laws of God and nature.

When the public shall have had time to reflect upon this subject, now far more important than all other subjects united, then a public meeting shall be called, to consider the best peaceable practical means by which, without real injury to any, the crime-creating and most mischevious and unnatural laws of men may be superseded by the laws of God and nature,—the only laws which can create universal love and charity, unity, goodness, wisdom, and happiness among men, and terminate the insane contests and wars and repulsive feelings which make this earth a pandemonium, when, with so much ease and pleasure, under the laws of God and nature, it might be made a terrestrial paradise.

ROBERT OWEN.

August 15th, 1857.

LIFE AND DEATH SOCIETY.

THIS is an earnest appeal to the advanced minds of the age, who desire to attain and secure the permanent happiness of the population of the world, and to attain it by changing the present false, evil, and repulsive system, for the true, good, and attractive system of society, for forming the character of and governing men ; and who, to effect this great and glorious change, are willing, if required, passively to sacrifice their lives to secure its attainment.

c

To accomplish this result, the laws and superstitions of men, as they now exist in all nations and among all people, must be openly abandoned, because of the errors and evils which they continually create and inflict upon their insane-made victims.

And instead thereof, all must agree to be governed by the unchanging, all-wise, and merciful laws of God and Nature, and the pure practical principles of universal religion or true Christianity.

True Christianity consists in love and charity for our race, and not only in loving our neighbours as ourselves, but in loving our enemies, and doing good to those who hate and despitefully use us ; and a true knowledge of ourselves will produce this result.

By this change the world will secure perpetual peace, plenty, goodness, wisdom, and happiness; the true Millennial existence upon the earth ; and the will of God and nature will be made to be done on earth, as it is in heaven.

It is evident that God and nature have made the germ of all human faculties with the ultimate view to attain happiness ; and that now all things are wonderfully prepared to assist society to accomplish this long-looked-for result.

But my friendly opponents, Malthus, Mill, Ricardo, Place, Torrens, &c , men of great talents and good intentions, did much for a time, by what they called the modern school of political economy, to destroy all common sense on this subject, and to make the attainment of general permanent happiness an impossibility.

With great ingenuity they mistified their own minds and those of their followers with the words " *over population*,"— " *labour*,"—" *capital*,"—" *supply and demand ;*" ringing perpetual changes upon these words, without ever understanding the import of one of them.

They were all men of theory, devoid of all practical knowledge, in consequence of their having been taught from birth in a false system ; and through their energy and industry in inculcating their entangled imaginary notions on the passive recipient mind of the public, these words, meaning nothing but wild imaginary conceptions, had a great influence for a time over governments, and over a part of a very influential portion of society.

So far from their unnatural theories being true, the great want of the world has ever been, and is now, a want of a greatly increased population, well trained, educated, employed, and placed, from birth.

For this population there will be an increasing demand

until the whole earth shall be highly cultivated, and the rivers and seas exhausted of their supplies.

Until this period, such a population will with ease and pleasure be enabled annually to over-supply all its wants many fold in a superior manner, each using every kind of wealth to the full extent desired, without money and without price.

The real capital of the world is now far in advance of the requirements of society, and ever will be so in a properly educated population.

This capital exists

First.—In the fixed labours derived from the brains and hands of all past generations, as possessed at the present day by the population of the world.

Second.—In the experience derived from all past ages.

Third.—In the present state of the cultivation of the earth.

Fourth.—In the knowledge of mining, and of minerals with their uses.

Fifth.—In the roads, canals, shipping, and knowledge of navigation.

Sixth.—In our knowledge of the extent of the earth and seas, and of the past, although very imperfect, history of our race.

Seventh. — In the machines for carrying on the active business of the world. But especially does the capital of the world consist,

Eighth.—In the brains and hands of the existing generation, to give life and motion to the fixed capital.

Consequently, in a population placed, trained, educated, employed, and governed, in accordance with common sense or the laws of nature, there can never be any waste of capital, or of superior labour, which is the highest degree of capital, nor can there be any waste of wealth of any kind.

As to demand, it is always one and the same through every succeeding generation. It is for the supply of all our wants in a superior manner, in accordance with the individual natural qualities given to each at birth, and the education given by society,

The supply to meet this demand can be always produced with the regularity of the seasons, with high delight, by a population rationally placed, trained, educated, employed, and governed.

Gold, Silver, and Copper, are parts of capital, as metals for their respective uses, required for the business of life; but as money capital, and applied to represent real wealth, they are an evil, the extent of which no words are equal to describe or express, and well may such money be called the root of all evil.

A writer on the exploded subject of over population has within these few days obligingly sent me a copy of his work, entitled the "*Political Economist,*" in which my name and views are mentioned, and the latter are attempted to be disproved. The title and contents inform me that the industrious author, to enable him to become a teacher of mankind, has yet to acquire a knowledge of human nature, of society, and of the practical business of life, of which he appears at present to be without useful information, though learned in applying words without knowing their value and import, to mystify himself and his readers.

Were it not for ignorance and erroneous government, capital and labour would always exist to create supplies far beyond the most extended demands of the population of the world, without any being over worked, and without vice or crime.

The most valuable capital, to an amount which baffles all calculation, which might be applied to advance the progress and increase the happiness of the human race, is now insanely wasted over the world, by the misdirection of the brains and hands—

1st.—Of the Priesthood and all engaged in the various forms and ceremonies of the opposing superstitions called religion, as now in practice over the earth, and as now used to destroy the rational faculties of all, and to keep the world in ignorance, discord, and misery.

2nd—Of the Armies and Navies of the world, who are now trained and employed to waste and destroy capital upon the most magnificent scale, by murder and destruction of property, proving to what extent by training and habit men may be made with ease to think and act insanely and madly.

3rd.—Of those engaged in making and executing the Laws of men, on the insane notion that the created being or thing creates its own qualities and powers. This notion, so opposed to all facts, past and present, is quite sufficient to derange the faculties of the past and present race o fmen.

4thly.—Of medical men, as now trained, and placed, and employed,—not to have an interest in *preventing* disease, but in its continuance and spread through the earth.

5th.—Of dealers in money and traders for a money profit, who, necessary as they are under a system of falsehood, deception, and repulsion, would be far worse than useless in a rationally constituted society.

6th.—Of the aristocracies of the world, and all who are

tormented by being so placed as to live, unfortunately for themselves, a life of idleness or of uselessness.

But the greatest of all waste of capital of the most inestimable value arises,

7th.—From the ignorance and undeveloped state of the higher faculties of humanity, which faculties have been kept in a dormant state in consequence of society being hitherto based on the insane notion that the created being or thing could by any possibility create its own qualities and powers.

Ask any manufacturer or maker of anything, if any thing he manufactures or makes gives itself any of its qualities,— and the endless absurdities arising from the fundamental error on which society has so far been based must become obvious to all possessing common sense and moral courage to express their true convictions.

For surely, if one truth can be more obvious to the mind than another, it must be the fact that all things created throughout the universe must possess the qualities given to them by the power or powers creating them, and that they can possess those qualities only as they are given to them.

This now most obvious fact, so long hidden from the searchers after truth, opens to our race a new mine of truths and of happiness which time will fail to exhaust.

But to open this mine, and to work it to attain these glorious results, the sacrifice of many lives may be required, in resisting the ignorance, error, irrationality, insanity, and madness, of the system which has so long governed and afflicted the populations of all nations and of all peoples.

For so deep-rooted are the prejudices and habits in favour of the continuance of the ever-creating-evil system—so established are they by erroneous training, education, and surroundings, that the existing authorities under this system opposed to common sense for governing mankind, will endeavour to maintain it, with all its absurdities, even to the taking away the lives of those who attempt to introduce into practice the rational and true system for the universal government of mankind through all future ages.

Nevertheless the time is come for earnest foreseeing men and women, who desire to secure the permanent rationality and happiness of their race, to make this sacrifice, and now to unite for this purpose in such manner as by perseverence will be certain to effect their object.

This will be accomplished by the formation of a society which may be called " The Life and Death Society, for " changing the government of the population of the world, " from the absurdly false, ignorant, unjust, and cruel laws of

" men, to be under the government of the true, wise, just, and
" merciful laws of God and Nature."

The duties of the members constituting this society will be,

To attain a correct knowledge of the laws of God and nature
respecting humanity.

To commence a new mode of life based upon, and constructed
throughout in perfect consistency with, those divine laws, and
and to maintain this new life in all its purity, even, if necessary,
with the passive sacrifice of their lives, without attempting to
resist, or to inflict evil upon their falsely educated opponents
and oppressors.

This society will therefore be based on the knowledge—

" *That the Creating Power gives all the qualities possessed*
" *by the created, and that the created can possess no*
" *quality or power not thus given.*"

Consequently individual reward, praise, blame, or punishment, will be unknown in this society, composed of created
beings, whose qualities and powers are known to be all formed
for them.

And as the laws of God and nature respecting humanity
are,

That all *must* believe in obedience to the strongest impressions made on their minds ;—

And *must* like and love those things and persons made to
be agreeable or lovely to their individual organisation ;—

And *must* dislike and hate those things and persons made
to be disag reeab or hateful to their individual organisation ;—

Therefore, in this natural or rational state of existence,
effective arrangements will be devised to give to all from birth
true convictions only—that is, convictions derived from unchanging facts and self-evident truths, all consistent with
each other,—which they must be if true.

And arrangements also must be devised and combined with
the former, to give from birth to all, kind, good, and lovely
qualities only, in order that all may be loved according to
their degree of kindness, goodness, and loveliness, as these
are combined in their character.

By these arrangements no injury to individuals or to society
can ever arise from all freely expressing their compelled convictions and compelled feelings ; and more especially because
it will be the duty and interest of society to take especial care
that the received convictions shall be true to facts and to
nature, and that the feelings should be also naturally directed
for the happiness of the individual and of society.

These arrangements will render it imperative that all from
birth, as soon as the society shall be united for action, shall

be trained, educated, employed, placed, and governed, in accordance with these divine all-wise laws of God and nature.

But none can be rationally placed, trained, educated, employed, and governed, under the individualised selfish system of society, based on unnatural repulsive feelings and private property.

To be governed, therefore, by the laws of God and nature, entirely new arrangements and surroundings will be required, with a new classification of society according to age.

With these arrangements, consistently carried out and properly executed, universal peace and harmony may be made to reign perpetually over the earth, and mankind bound in chains of love and everlasting brotherhood.

But who are the parties willing to sacrifice their lives to break the existing bondage of sin against the laws of God and nature, and to establish the reign of the latter for ever over the population of the world?

Will the members of the *Society of Life or Death* first come from the superior and most conscientious of the Spiritualists, Shakers, Rappites, Zoarites, Full Socialists, or Fourrierite half Socialists?

Or will a yet more advanced band of martyrs arise out of all parties and nations—a select band of brothers and sisters, knowing the truth, and daring to act, and to persevere in acting, that truth, against the combined powers of this wretched old worn-out system of wars and conflicts, of error, ignorance, sin, and iniquity—a system based and constructed on the insane imagination, opposed to all facts, that the made and the created make their own qualities, and give to the made and created the powers which they possess?

Time will show whence will arise these self-sacrificing men and women, who will thus dare to confront and oppose with their lives the hosts of evil interests by which they will be assailed by an ill-taught, erroneously placed, and most injuriously surrounded population.

May the contest be short, and the sacrifice of lives few, although the change would be cheaply bought by the sacrifice of many.

ROBERT OWEN.

August 17th. 1857.

THE DIFFERENCE BETWEEN THE POPULATION OF
THE WORLD AS GOVERNED BY THE LAWS OF
MAN, AND WHAT IT WILL BE WHEN GOVERNED
BY THE LAWS OF GOD AND NATURE.

THE laws of men, as I have so often stated, are based on the
imaginary notions, opposed to all facts, that man, (the created
by God, nature, and society,) creates his own qualities, physical
and mental, and determines his belief and his feelings.

This false foundation on which all the laws of men have
been constructed. created evil, and is its sole origin.   It is the
source of all repulsive feelings between man and man and
nation and nation.   It is the source whence proceeds envy,
hatred, anger, jealousy, and revenge.   It is the cause of the
ignorance of the human race at this day, and of all the
poverty experienced through past ages.   It is the cause
of the general insanity and madness of the human race, and
of their more severe partial paroxysms of these maladies.   It
is the cause of the artificial divisions of society into opposing
classes, sects, and parties, and of the past and present Babel
contests and confusion in all nations and among all people.
And while these everlastingly changing laws of insanity shall
govern the human race, these evils must continue from generation to generation, creating evil, every kind of crime and
contest, and then irrationally and madly punishing what
society has thus blindly created.

Such has been and ever must be the condition of society
while governed by laws based upon an insane imaginary
notion.

See the latest results of these laws in the war of the Western
Powers against Russia; in the present war in India; in the
rivalries of nations; in the tyranny and slavery of the existing
classification of society; and in the universal mental degradation which these laws force upon all.

See also the unnecessary poverty; its especial crimes and
sufferings, continually experienced; or the fear of it by so
large a portion of the population of the world.

In addition to this, see the mass of error and evil; the loss
of knowledge, wealth, and of universal progress and happiness,
arising from the higher faculties of humanity lying dormant,
uncultivated, or most erroneously directed

These are beyond all human estimate, and will not be
imagined until the difference shall be experienced when men
shall be taught and governed by and under the laws of God
and nature, unobstructed by any laws of men

When men shall perceive the immense evil arising from

their laws made in direct opposition to facts and to the eternal unchanging laws of God and nature, and shall agree to abandon them, and to be governed solely by those laws given by the creating power to all humanity, they will all become conscious of the grevous wrongs and sufferings which man through all past ages to this day has inflicted upon man, to his own injury and to that of his race.

Under the laws of God and nature, based on the fact that the *Creator* gives all the qualities and powers to the created which it can possess, a new earth and a new heaven will be opened to the human race in perpetuity.

The broad path will be opened, freed from all obstructions, to give at once a superior character to all who shall be born under this change.

Arrangements will be made to give to the natural organs, faculties, propensities, and powers, their right direction from birth through life.

Attractive and lovely qualities will be given to all ; charity and kindness, by this instruction in nature's own laws, will be made to pervade the hearts and minds of each ; the knowledge to be derived from facts unmystified, will increase as all advance in years ; and this knowledge will be such, that each new fact will confirm the truth of all the preceding ; for truth is derived from facts, and truth is one throughout the universe.

Each will have an interest in the progress and happiness of all ; and all will aid the progress and endeavour to increase the happiness of each.

Human slavery and servitude will be unknown ; the sciences, wisely applied to practice, will be the faithful slaves and perfect servants of the human race.

These will be employed to cultivate the earth ; to make and manufacture superior things of evey description ; and to be effective to aid all nations gradually to form a terrestrial paradise within their dominions

There will be no necessity for armed men, police, officers for punishment, priests, lawyers, medical or commercial men, nor for any separate class or sect in society, opposed in interest and feeling to other classes and sects.

From one enlightened class, naturally trained and educated to be so from birth, when divided into classes according to age, and every division of age being on a just equality, and occupied according to age and natural capacity for the benefit of society, harmony to the highest practical degree will be attained.

Let the observing and reasoning faculties of all be now opened to calmly examine all nature, and they will discover that all that have life upon the earth, except man, act in obedience to the laws of their nature or of God, and are, when not obstructed in doing so, in the enjoyment of peculiar pleasure according to the organisation of each.

Man, while his faculties of observing and reasoning are slowly developing, is the only animal making laws to force his fellows, contrary to their natural feelings and wise instincts, to oppose the laws of God and nature; and in consequence he is the only animal that experiences so much physical and mental suffering, and the only animal so much or nearly so much afflicted with insanity and madness, or whose conduct through life is so inconsistent and irrational.

When, if rightly trained, educated, and placed, to act consistently in accordance with the laws and interests given to him by God and nature, man would become a superior being, actively engaged to the extent of his powers in promoting as far as practicable the happiness of all that has life upon the earth.

Let man then cease vainly to imagine that he can do good to, or alter the laws of the Power which creates him and all things created; and let him learn that the important lesson to be acquired is, to increase the happiness of earth's creations, and that the more he adds to this increase, the higher and more perfect and permanent will be his own enjoyment through life.

The only possible rational worship by man, of the creating intelligence of the universe, is for him actively, to the extent of the powers given to him, to endeavour to promote the happiness of all sentient beings created.

Ages of experience will prove that this is the whole duty of man.

And let it be held in everlasting remembrance, that the material means to give and secure this happiness for the human race in perpetuity, now abound, and are continually on the increase over the earth.

ROBERT OWEN.

Sevenoaks, August, 19th, 1857.

TO THE GOVERNMENTS, LAY AND ECCLE-SIASTIC, OF THE CIVILISED WORLD.

LISTEN now, and attend to the advice of a friend who has never deceived you, who has often told you most important truths;—one who has spent a long life in

the investigation of the causes which continually produce sin and misery to mankind, and of those causes
which in future will prevent their recurrence over
the earth.

The causes which have, of necessity, produced sin
and misery through all the past generations of men,
have been the undeveloped state and inexperience
of our early ancestors, in concluding, without thought,
that the created could and did create its own qualities ;—which upon reflection must appear an utter
impossibility, being opposed to the laws of nature.

On this false and insane foundation the characters
of men have been formed, human laws have been
made in direct opposition to nature's laws, and society
has been constructed in conformity with these fundamental errors.

In consequence, the characters of all have been
lamentably misformed, from birth through life ; and
society has been constructed in the most inconsistent and absurd manner, through all its ramifications in every department of life ;—making it literally
true that all are " doing that which they ought not
to do," for their own happiness, and " leaving undone all that they ought to do." And truly may all
say, " there is no health in us," — physically or
mentally.

In consequence, the world is filled with conflicting
and contending feelings and interests, making a perfect Babel of confusion, in language and conduct,—
exciting many to the madness of destroying life
and property to a fearful extent for no rational
object,—making light of human suffering and rivers
of innocent blood.

While, by forming character and constructing society on true fundamental principles, consistent with
common sense and all facts, attractive and kind
feelings would be universally created ; men would be
made to become good, wise, and happy ; society would
be constructed to produce perpetual prosperity ; and

truth and harmony would reign uninterruptedly over the earth.

By adopting the true principle respecting the created and Creator, and by your union in applying the principle consistently to practice, these results, with the enormous means now at the disposal of society, may be speedily attained, with the certainty of a law of nature ; and there would be found little or no difficulty in the execution. And this I now state in the most grave and solemn manner, on the faith of a true Christian, in spirit, principle, and practice, which teaches us to love our enemies, and to do good to those who hate and despitefully use us.

This, at my age, (upwards of eighty-six,) is probably the last communication I shall be enabled or impressed to make to you. May it be attended to, and thus prevent the impending conflict between the systems of good and evil; which conflict, if commenced, will probably be the most obstinate and bloody known in history.

May the Heavenly Powers of Goodness and Wisdom avert it!

ROBERT OWEN.

August 23rd, 1857.

THE EXPECTED-TO-BE LAST LEGACY OF ROBERT OWEN TO THE HUMAN RACE.

I HAVE previously published several legacies, supposing that each one would be my last ; but my life has been prolonged much beyond my anticipation—perhaps for some yet more useful purpose.

I now give to all my fellow men my experience and most matured thoughts, condensed into the fewest words.

The people, simply by their will and moral force, may now emancipate themselves from all the evils of life hitherto experienced through past ages and to the present time.

The *First* measure is to abandon the false foundation
on which from the beginning to this day society over
the world has been based,—that is, " the supposition
" that each one creates his own qualities, physical and
" mental;" and to establish society on its true foundation,—namely, " that the Great Creating Power of
" the Universe creates before birth all the divine phy-
" sical and mental qualities of each of the human
" race, and that society from birth gives these divine
" qualities a false or a true, an evil or a good direction,
" through the life of every individual of our race."

As soon as the people of the world can be taught
the first elements of common sense, they will adopt
this practical measure.

The *Second* step will be, for the people, by their will
and moral force, to induce their present governments to
form Federative Treaties with each other, until all governments and people shall be thus united to secure
permanent peace over the earth ; and this may now be
easily accomplished.

The first Federative Treaty, commencing with Great
Britain and the United States of North America, will
show to the remainder of the world the incalculable
permanent benefits to be derived from these justly
formed Federative Treaties.

The *Third* practical step will be, for the people to
induce their respective governments, by the same
united moral power, to reconstruct society, gradually,
with wise foresight, in order that there shall be no
confusion, disorder, or suffering, in any class in any
country, while the change shall be in progress.   As
was the case to some extent during the late changes
from the graveled roads to the new railways.

This reconstruction of society to be effected by a
gradual superseding of the existing false and evil surroundings, in which the human race are now placed, and
which have all emanated from the false fundamental
error of the imaginations of our ancestors, adopted in
ignorance, and on which error all society has been so

long based, and has therefore been made to become thoroughly irrational.

These evil surroundings to be superseded by a new class and combination of superior surroundings, which will necessarily arise from the new and true base of society.

These new combinations of good and superior surroundings will require the population of the world to be congregated into manageable masses, to enable each mass to conduct the whole business of life in the best manner, so that ultimately each one of our race shall be from birth through life better taken care of by society than any one has ever yet been, or than any can be under the existing irrational system for forming character, producing wealth, governing humanity, or devising and executing surroundings in accordance with the laws of our nature.

These new, rational, and superior combinations of surroundings will enable society, by a natural progressive process, to secure, by measures which will be made easy of execution, superior food, clothing, habitation, useful and pleasant occupation according to age, a good valuable character, physical and mental, for all, while all shall be better placed within these new and superior surroundings than any one is now, or ever has been, or ever can be under the existing false system and present irrational surroundings.

The new and true foundation on which to base society will open the path by which all anger, hatred, and jealousy between man and man will cease,—a new spirit of love and charity will be made to pervade the hearts and minds of all of our race,—the art of war, with all its cruelties and demoralising effects, will be known no more,—the earth will be made a fertile and beautiful paradise,—and the human race will be made to become rational, peaceable, wise, united, and happy, and at length, through a long, but perhaps necessary preparation, will be enabled to enjoy their natural existence under the All-Good and All-Wise Laws of God and Nature.

Hence is the plain broad road opened for the population of the world, to attain in peace the true, universal, permanent Millennial State of Existence on Earth.

It is but for the government and people to agree to abandon the fundamental false imagination on which society from the beginning has been based; to abrogate the laws of men which have all emanated from this false fundamental imagination, are opposed to the eternal laws of nature, and are therefore productive of all the vice, crime, and misery which now exist over the earth; to give from birth to each, a good, useful, and superior training and education, physically, intellectually, morally, spiritually, and practically; to enable each one so trained and educated to assist to produce, with pleasure to himself, his fair share of superior wealth to supply all abundantly with the necessaries, comforts, and highly beneficial luxuries of life; to create the new combinations of superior surroundings, scientifically calculated and arranged to effect all the preceeding results with the certainty of a law of nature.

That the period for this change may speedily arrive is the ardent desire of, your old friend,

ROBERT OWEN.

August 25th,, 1857.

THE CREATOR CREATES ALL THE QUALITIES AND POWERS OF THE CREATED.

It must be for some wise purpose, or from necessity in the order of creation, that man, a created being with certain intellectual faculties, should have been so long withheld from discovering a fact universal throughout nature, and on a knowledge of which depends the rationality, the well-being, and the happiness of his race.

That the created or made receives all its qualities and powers from its creator or maker, appears from observation and reflection now to be so obvious, that it appears like a miracle that it should have remained undiscovered for practical purposes in the affairs of men for all the generations which have passed. And more especially as the knowledge of this simple and now obvious fact leads direct to results of the highest and most lasting interest and importance to each of the human race through all time.

The knowledge of this fact opens the path to and developes the means by which the happiness of the human race may be attained and secured in perpetuity, and man may be made to become highly intelligent, consistent or rational, and through life superior in mind and conduct.

The knowledge that all the qualities and powers of thought and action are given to each individual of our race without his consent or consciousness, by a dual creation, will lead direct to universal happiness.

The *first* creation is directed by the Great Creating Power of the Universe, which gives to each at birth mysterious qualities and powers, to be afterwards cultivated and matured for thought and action.

Some, perhaps many, of these mysterious qualities and powers, which are made to differ in combinations in each individual, are yet unknown to man.

The *second* creation commences sometime prior to birth, and continues through life to death.

This is the creation of each from the birth-germ, by the combined surroundings of nature and those of human institutions for training, educating, employing, placing, and governing, all of our race.

It is important to know and always to recollect that no two of our race are created the same, either in the first creation, by God, or in the second creation, by nature and man ; nor does it appear to be possible for any two individuals to be created to be the same in qualities and powers during any period of their first or second creation ; and the first is the foundation for the second.

The knowledge of this dual creation in forming the character of our race, opens a new book of life to those who can observe accurately, compare correctly, and deduce just conclusions from those comparisons. The first page in this new book of life exhibits in strong colours the errors of our forefathers through all past generations, respecting a knowledge of themselves, or how their characters were formed for them individually,—much more respecting the means by which, with the certainty of a law of nature, all could be well formed by their immediate predecessors.

The second page of this new book shows the overwhelming influences of surroundings in the second creation of character by the union of nature and society, and that by the kind and quality of these surroundings any character, from the best to the worst, may be forced upon all that are born.

The third page will explain what are those surroundings made by man which will give the best character—physical, intellectual, moral, spiritual, and practical—to all of our race.

And the fourth page will show how those superior surroundings are to be attained, and to be applied to produce the best character for all.

This is the true foundation on which to construct social science.

The knowledge that the *Creator* gives all the qualities and powers possessed by the *created*, is the only true and solid foundation on which to construct social science, and to implant in man the pure spirit of universal charity and love for his race, and to make it easy and pleasant for him on all occasions to practice those truly divine qualities, without which no true social science can exist.

And it is this knowledge which can, and which alone can, unite the human race as one enlightened family, with one language, one interest, and one universal feeling, to promote at all times the permanent happiness of each other.

And this is the ultimate natural result of the true social science.

Some, even at this day, affecting to be wise men competent to lead the public mind, attempt to ignore the idea of the population of the world being made good, wise, and happy ; or that to attain a millennial state of existence upon earth is possible. To these men it may appear to be so ; but these are mere men of words, unknowing what is or is not practicable—men without a knowledge how character is formed, or on what base society is constructed.

They know not themselves, or the laws of nature which govern humanity. They know not that society has the means and the power to create a good and superior character for everyone, and that the common-sense surroundings required to create such character for all can be now easily devised and executed, and these surroundings and this formation of character might be made to be the means by which to attain and secure the millennial state of society, or the ultimate result of the true social science.

Little do these men of an old expiring system, too degrading and degraded to be much longer maintained or endured, imagine that it will soon be much easier to introduce the true, rational, social system, for the government of the world, than to continue to govern it by force, fear, fraud, and falsehood, which can only misform the character and misgovern society.

See, at this day, the confusion of all nations, and the contentions of all sects and parties in all countries over the globe,—all arising from the insane notion, opposed to all facts, that the *created*, and not the *Creator*, gives the qualities and powers to the created,

Never were any parties more mistaken than those now esteemed and believing themselves to be the clever practical men of the world, as writers for the periodical press, or carrying on any of the ordinary business of society in any of the branches

of business or commerce, when they imagine that they understand the true principles and practices of society.

From society having been based on a principle opposed to all
facts, all have been, to this day, trained, educated, employed,
placed, and governed, so irrationally, as not to know their own
nature, or the fixed laws of humanity, and are made to act continually in direct opposition to their own happiness and to that
of their race—to approve, in words, of universal charity and
love for our race,—and yet through their lives to forget or neglect
these divine principles, which by their practice can alone make
men to become consistent, rational, and happy.

So thoroughly blinded by a false education are what are
called the learned and the clever practical men of the world,
that they are taught and teach continually that the *Creator alone*
creates all things in the heavens and in the earth, and that
without this Universal Creating Power nothing is or can be made;
that man and all that have life are thus created, and to each is
given its own peculiar and distinctive qualities and powers : and
yet is man trained, educated, employed, placed, governed,
punished, and rewarded, individually, and society constructed
through all its departments, on the imaginary notion, and now
palpable falsehood, that he creates his own physical and mental
qualities and powers! In other words, that the *unconscious
created* gives *itself* its own *qualities* and *powers*, and *not* its *creator* !

While such errors shall be taught, believed, and acted upon,
by the population of the earth, and society shall continue to be
constructed throughout, in all its departments, on this most
erroneous foundation, this planet must as heretofore be inhabited
by a race trained to be opposed to their own happiness, and to
be irrational in mind and practice through life.

The approach towards a true and rational system of society,
(so strongly indicated by the government education through
material objects, as now commencing in South Kensington, and
by the forming of the Association, under the advanced minds of
the aristocracy of this country, for the promotion of social
science in all its departments and to their legitimate conclusions,) requires that the whole truth upon this subject should
be now faithfully stated to the public.

The foundation on which to construct the true social science,
in spirit, principle, and practice, was first published by me in
1813, in four essays, entitled " *A New View of Society*," or the
Formation of Character,—the teachings in which were at that
period too new and too much in advance of the public to be
then adopted in practice.

It may now be useful that the history of this publication
should be made generally known before this well-timed and
most important meeting of the Association for promoting social
science, in Birmingham, on the 12th of next month, takes place,
in order that it may be known what has been done in principle

and practice to prepare the world for the introduction of a true social science—for that science which can alone make man good, wise, and happy, to be cordially united to his fellows over the world, to abound in wealth, and to live in peace and without contests or competition ; and this must be the result of introducing a true social science to the public.

Knowing how little society was prepared in 1813 for a " New View of Society," or for the adoption in practice of the true social science, based on its only sure foundation—the formation of a superior natural and rational character, I adopted very singular and extraordinary measures to have the spirit, principles, and practices, advocated and put forth as the foundation of the only true social science in those Essays, scrutinized in a manner seldom or perhaps never practised in any other publication.

And in consequence of so trying an examination of that which was then so new to the world, I now refer to that publication, and to my " Address on opening the New Institution for the Formation of Character," on the 1st of January, 1816, in which I explained the objects to be attained by the Infant School which I had invented, and which I intended to exhibit and did exhibit in practice for upwards of twenty years in that institution.

And this Infant School was the first step in principle and practice of the social science explained in those Essays.

The history of its introduction to the public is as follows.

When the " New View of Society, or the formation of character," was written, I was a novice respecting the deep rooted influences which the old system of society had upon every class, sect, party, and colour, in all countries. I was then so inexperienced in the knowledge of the strength of early imbibed and long continued habits, and of what is called vested interests, that I imagined a plain statement of truths in accordance with all facts, and highly beneficial in their application in practice to all of our race, would be readily received, and would be applied to practice by those who had power and influence in society ; and that the publication of my Four Essays on the Formation of Character would be sufficient to induce all who felt an interest in the improvement, well-doing, and happiness of humanity, to accept the principles and adopt the practice which I advocated and explained in those Essays. And the extraordinary excitement generally created by their publication ; the interest taken in them by those then in authority in church and state ; the avidity with which five superior large editions were called for by the public, and the unlooked for attention paid to me by by those in the highest stations, tended for a time to strengthen my impression that a speedy change in the principle and practice of society would follow.

This impression was the more easily made and increased, because doubting my new knowledge when it appeared to be

opposed to the principles and practices of society past and
present, I felt the necessity of subjecting the principles to the
severe examination of the then most esteemed learned men of
different sects and parties and classes, being conscientiously
determined not to promulgate any new error, or to teach that
which was not important for the public to learn.

I therefore first sought for the most learned men in the universities, and in the cities of Edinburgh and Glasgow, among
the professed Church of Scotland and dissenters from it. Then
I enquired for the esteemed most learned among the Unita-
rians, and I was directed by Mrs. Fletcher of Edinburgh, to apply
to the Rev. Mr, now Professor Turner, of Newcastle,—to the
Rev. Mr. Wellbeloved, head of the Manchester College in
York, — to Mr. Belsham, Unitarian Minister, Essex Street
Chapel, London

I then enquired for the most learned theologian in the
Church of England, and was directed to Dr. Marsh, then
Margaret Professor at the University of Cambridge, and
afterwards Bishop of Peterborough; then to the Archbishop of
Canterbury, (Sutton,) to whom, after he had read the First and
Second Essays, I, at his particular request, read in his palace
at Lambeth, in manuscrpt, the Third and Fourth Essays; and to
his death he was ever after most friendly towards me.

And during this singular tour among the most popular in
religion and politics, and with the heads of the banking and
commercial classes, I was generally introduced also to the most
learned and esteemed friends of each, and with whom free discussion was courted, and generally much interest created.

Finding much and often strong and warm approval, and no
valid objection by these parties to the principles and practices
which I advocated, I then submitted them to our government,
(then under the administration of the Earl of Liverpool,) for its
consideration, and the MSS. were returned to me, saying " the
" government saw no objection to them, and wished to know
" my further intentions respecting them."

My reply was, that upon a subject so new I was most anxious
not to promulgate error, but was desirous to give important
universal truths for practice to the population of the world, and
therefore I wished to ascertain if the most learned men in the
governments or universities of Europe or America could discover
error in the principles or practices which had been submitted in
manuscript to them, and for this purpose, if government approved,
I would have two hundred copies of the four Essays printed, and
bound with alternate blank leaves, for our government to send
to all the governments with which they were in communication,
and to the most learned universities at home and abroad, and to
request these parties to have these Essays thoroughly examined
and scrutinised, and if errors or objections could be discovered,
that they should be written on the blank sheets, and returned

to our government—a promise being given that for every one so returned a corrected copy should be sent in exchange.

To this proposal the government readily assented, and they were highly pleased, they said, with the spirit and principle from which it originated.

The two hundred copies were sent, and in due time many were returned with remarks on the blank pages; but in no one case was a direct objection made to the principles or practices advocated.

This seemed very much to gratify Lord Liverpool and his cabinet, and I was asked what course I now intended to pursue with these Essays.

I said —" It appears to me necessary thet they should undergo " the criticism of all parties, and should pass the fiery ordeal " of the conservative principle of society ; and if the government " had no objection I would publish a large superior edition, and " would thus ascertain the influence which they would have on " all classes, sects, and parties."

The government agreed cordially to this proposal, for I afterwards discovered, from Lord Liverpool's then private secretary, subsequently Dean of Westminster, that his lordship and several of his cabinet were disciples and most friendly to " my New Views of Society," and were desirous that they should have a fair trial in practice.

But the church was at this period all-powerful in the state, and was opposed ; and being united on this measure with the Conservative Peers, headed by Lord Lauderdale, were too strong for Lord Liverpool's party in the house, and he was obliged to relinquish it as a government measure ; but the debates in both houses at that period when this subject was under discussion on my petitions, will show the opinion and temper of the government and popular members on both sides of each house.

I published this first edition in 1813, and four other editions were speedily called for by the public ; and it is worthy of remark that so popular were they, until I publicly denounced all the religions of the world as containing too much error in each for beneficial practice, that all the first London publishers of that day were desirous to have their names added to Longman and Co's., as publishers; and there they are now, in the copies which have been preserved of these several editions. While, subsequent to that denunciation, such is the all-powerful influence of the church over the book trade, not one of these parties dared to publish another edition or work of mine, nor any of what are called the respectable booksellers to offer a copy of my works for sale.

And the press caught the alarm, and was closed against my writings.

In fact, for forty years every means that could be devised have been resorted to by conservative power to keep my writings from what are called the respectable part of the public, and to prevent the principles and practices which I have so long advocated being known by the present generation ; and I could have them circulated only to a limited extent by a considerable private expenditure.

And even so late as this year, at the Educational Conference, many of the leading members of the church were alarmed lest I should explain my views on the subject for which the Conference was professedly called.

But in justice to the several administrations by which this country has been governed from that of Lord Liverpool to the present, I must state that they, knowing the truth and importance of the principles which I have now for so many years advocated without turning to the right or to the left, without private object, and against all the prejudices of an old worn-out system, have never at home or abroad attempted to interrupt my progress or to place obstacles in my way : but, on the contrary, they have often given me important facilities to aid my progress, when they could do so without compromising the government, as in the case of Lord Liverpool, the Duke of Wellington, and Lord Melbourne; the last, when prime minister, by presenting me to her Majesty, even at the hazard of his tenure of office.

Although for forty years I have been incessantly and strongly opposed both by honest and sincere and by interested opponents, I have never doubted the ultimate triumph of truths so important for the ultimate happiness of our race.

By the measures adopted, as previously stated, to ascertain the powers of the most advanced minds in the civilised world to discover error in the principles or practices advocated in these Essays to open to all a new view of society, founded on a new principle and practice of forming the character of the human race, I was well assured of their unassailable truths before I submitted them to the general public by printing the five editions in the manner explained.

I therefore at the termination of the Fourth Essay concluded " by stating—" Yet, as evil exists, and as man cannot be rational, " nor of course happy, until the cause of it shall be removed, the " writer, like a physician who feels the deepest interest in the " welfare of his patient, has hitherto administered of this un- " palatable restorative the smallest quantity which he deemed " sufficient for the purpose ; he now waits to see the effect which " that may produce. Should the application not prove of suffi- " cient strength to remove the mental disorder, he promises that " it shall be increased, until sound health to the public mind be " firmly and permanently established."

In conformity with this promise I have from that day to this been actively engaged in fulfilling it.

Knowing that the medicine of new ideas, in direct opposition to old deeply-imbibed conservative ideas, was most unpalatable

I have very gradually increased the dose, but to the full extent that the constitution of society could bear without altogether refusing to take it.

My medical practice with the national, or rather universal malady, has been, although slow, eminently successful ; for, nauseous as this new medicine has been to all classes, sects, and parties, in all countries, yet it has now prepared the body politic to receive the last dose, which will effect a perfect cure, and will change this planet, from being the abode of irritable irrational beings, to becoming the habitation of superior, enlightened, wise, and good, full-formed men and women, always thinking and acting rationally, and ever engaged in promoting each other's progress in excellence and happiness.

In continuance of this practice I have now my last disagreeable task to perform for my poor hitherto benighted fellow men, and have to declare to the esteemed learned, wise, and powerful of the earth, that the time has come for man's emancipation from ignorance, crime, and lunacy, and that the system based on a false principle, by which the world has hitherto been governed, by falsehood, force, and fraud, cannot be longer continued.

This system, so based and maintained, must now yield to a system based on truth, and supported by universal love and charity for our hitherto poor, blind, and deluded race.

And I tell the present rulers and teachers of mankind, from a practical experience with human nature and society, little imagined by the world, that it will be far more easy and practical to devise, form, execute, maintain, and govern society, when based on truth, and when *all* shall be well-trained, educated, employed, placed, and governed, and society thus made consistent in all its parts and as a whole, than it is now to hold this worn-out old system of false hood, ignorance, and crime, much longer together.

For there is a good time coming ; and it is near at hand, for the permanent benefit and happiness of every class, creed, country, and colour, over the world.

And this change will be the commencement of a New Era or Existence of Man upon the Earth.

ROBERT OWEN.

Sevenoaks Park, Sevenoaks,
    Sept. 20th, 1857.

PUBLISHED BY EFFINGHAM WILSON,
Price 5s., Cloth,

ROBERT OWEN'S MILLENNIAL GAZETTE of the 1st of August, 1857, explaining the greatest discovery yet made for the peaceable permanent Happiness of the Human Race, and the Means by which the Practice may be immediately commenced in all Countries.

Just Published, Price **10s.**

THE FIRST VOLUME

OF

THE LIFE OF ROBERT OWEN,

WITH SELECTIONS FROM HIS WRITINGS AND CORRESPONDENCE.

PUBLISHED BY EFFINGHAM WILSON, ROYAL EXCHANGE, LONDON.

THIS Life is written to disclose the ORIGIN OF EVIL among men, and to open the broad, direct, and certain road to the HAPPINESS OF OUR RACE THROUGH FUTURITY; to remove the CAUSE OF EVIL, and gradually to overcome the causes which now produce and continually reproduce the prejudices of creed, class, party, sex, country, and colour. And thus naturally and peacefully to prepare the ENTIRE POPULATION of the WORLD for a NEW EXISTENCE UPON EARTH, in which there shall be one language, one interest, and one universal desire to promote the highest, best, and permanent happiness of each other,—all living as one united, affectionate, and enlightened family, in the midst of superior surroundings, purposely calculated to attain and secure the permanent peace and harmony of all nations and peoples.

This apparently miraculous change in the condition and conduct of mankind will be effected by the most natural means, —simply by basing society on its true foundation, and making all the surroundings of man's producing, consistent with that foundation—surroundings, in and by which to new train, educate, employ, and place the population of the world, to make it natural, rational, wise, good, enlightened, and happy.

These new surroundings will emanate from the knowledge that the CREATING POWER of the UNIVERSE, called GOD, GIVES ALL THE QUALITIES AND POWERS WHICH ARE OR CAN BE POSSESSED BY THE CREATED.

The means and materials by which to produce these new surroundings abundantly exist over the earth.

Thus, in the due order of nature, by the gradual progress and development of the superior faculties, will order, unity, and harmony be established for ever.

And thus will terminate the first, or infant undeveloped state of man, while trained, educated, employed, placed, and governed, under the influences of ignorance, force, fear, fraud, and falsehood, and of the inferior surroundings which these necessarily produce.

This is the greatest discovery yet made by man for man.

ROBERT OWEN.

Sevenoaks Park, September 1857.

Registered for Foreign Transmission.

ROBERT OWEN'S
MILLENNIAL GAZETTE;

EXPLANATORY OF THE PRINCIPLES AND PRACTICES BY WHICH, IN PEACE, WITH TRUTH, HONESTY, AND SIMPLICITY, THE NEW EXISTENCE OF MAN UPON THE EARTH MAY BE EASILY AND SPEEDILY COMMENCED.

"The character of Man is formed *for* him, and *not by* him!"

No. 13.]   NOVEMBER 15th, 1857.   [PRICE 6d.

PAPERS SENT TO THE NATIONAL ASSOCIATION FOR THE PROMOTION OF SOCIAL SCIENCE AT ITS FIRST MEETING AT BIRMINGHAM, OCTOBER 12TH, 1857.

No. 1. *Social Science.*

SOCIAL SCIENCE, the most important of all sciences, and without which all other sciences are of much less value, is the latest to which the advanced minds of the world have turned their attention.

Its foundation has been ignored until this period. The principle for practice from which it emanates has been hidden from the human mind through all past ages. Yet are the facts from which the principle is derived the most universal throughout nature; and, when attention is called to them, they are perhaps the most obvious of all facts.

The National Association for promoting Social Science is well calculated, by the elevated station and known talents of its founder, now to draw attention to these facts, and to apply them for the permanent benefit of the human race.

Surely not one of the more advanced minds of the world will now deny that the Creating Power of the Universe gives to all things, animate and inanimate, throughout existence, all the qualities and powers which they possess; and that without this power nothing that has been made could have existed.

And these advanced minds will also admit that the Universal Creating Power is eternal, uncreated, and possessing powers competent to this universal creation,— or existence could not be, either in parts or as a whole.

Knowledge of these facts is the foundation of Social Science; and on a knowledge of this science, carried into practice, depend the unity, goodness, and permanent happiness of the human race.

The Great First Creating power of the Universe, or God, gives to the human race the faculties to enable them to discover the facts now stated, and, through the acquisition of this knowledge, to become agents or second creating powers to perfect the creation of the race, through the knowledge of the science of forming the human character and the science of society, which sciences combined constitute Social Science.

Having thus laid an immovable foundation for this science,— by keeping the foundation always in view a beautiful superstructure may be made to arise upon it—a superstructure in which all parts will harmonise and become perfect as a whole ; and the Social Science will become the science of sciences.

The superstructure will be raised in this manner.

The Great Creating Power of the Universe, or God, gives to man all the qualities and powers which he possesses. These are divine qualities and powers, coming direct from God ; and God, the Creator of them, is alone, and not man, responsible for them :—a fact, no doubt withheld so long from man for wise and beneficial future results, and now disclosed in the due order of creation.

A knowledge of this fact is directly calculated to elevate man to become, by comparison with the past, a superior being upon our planet.

It will withdraw all anger from man to man,—root out every evil or injurious passion,—prepare him to receive the pure spirit of universal charity and love for his race, to love his neighbours as himself ; not only to forgive, but to love his enemies ; and to do good to those who may now hate or despitefully use him,— knowing that the time approaches when there will be no enemies, or any who will desire to use him ill.

These will be the necessary results of the Social Science when generally understood and applied to practice.

Being based on its true foundation. it will not be difficult to raise the beautiful superstructure.

Previous to commencing this work, a new phase of knowledge is necessary.

This is a knowledge of the influences upon humanity of the surroundings made by man, and of those which man can make.

There are surroundings which produce influences which convey the extreme of evil and misery to man ; while surroundings may be made which shall convey to humanity the extreme of good and happiness.

And surroundings may be made to convey every shade of influences between these two extremes, and by these means to give any character, inferior or superior, bad or good, to any nation or people over the globe.

These surroundings consist of arrangements to lodge, feed, clothe, train, educate, employ, place, and govern the population. And experience will show that not one of these can be well done without having reference to all the others, as parts of a whole, in the right combination of which consists the Social Science, or the science of the happiness of the human race.

The surroundings to lodge, feed, clothe, train, educate, employ, place, and govern all, should be devised, executed, and combined, so as to produce the best influences through life upon every one within those surroundings.

And these new surroundings may be so devised, executed, and combined, as not to disturb the existing progress of society more than it was disturbed by the change from the old graveled roads to the new railways. By wise foresight the change from the existing random-made and most injurious surroundings to a new combination far superior in all respects to the present surroundings in any part of the world, may be commenced, and gradually continued until the whole change can be finally accomplished, without any real injury to one individual, and with unceasing advantages to all.

The means to commence this change, and to rapidly progress towards considerable perfection, abundantly exist over the earth, and it will be for the permanent interest and happiness of all that these means should be now so applied.

A question now arises in the mind of the writer, of the deepest interest to society. " Are the promoters of this association, and " the public, prepared to hear the whole on the subject of Social " Science, and, when developed, to follow it to its legitimate " results ?"

If they are,—then indeed is the good time coming, and it will be enjoyed to a considerable extent by some of the present gene-ration.

The writer will hope that the patrons of this new national association, and a sufficient number of the advanced minds of the world, are so prepared; and he will proceed under this hope and gratifying expectation.

He therefore states, without fear of rational contradiction, the following eternal truths respecting this science.

1st. Its base is, that the *Creator* gives to the *created* all the qualities and powers which are possessed by the created.

2nd. That some beings are created with faculties and qualities intended at maturity to become rational, and happy,—that is, to enable the being to perceive what is necessary to its happiness, and how to attain it,—to be consistent,—and to act consistently through life in such manner as to secure the object of its creation and existence.

3rd. That man is evidently a being so created, and intended at maturity to become rational in mind and practice, and to attain a high degree of happiness through life.

4th. For man to be rational, his ideas must be consistent with each other and in accordance with all facts. And, to be happy, his natural wants must be supplied in such manner that each and all shall give him gratification and pleasure in their use.

5th. That the means have been now attained by society, when it can be united to supply these wants of humanity abundantly for all in the manner required to insure their happiness.

6th. That Social Science, fully comprehended and consistently acted upon, will unite society in such manner that these ever-to-be-desired results shall be attained for all without contest or competition.

7th. And that they will be attained through a new combination of surroundings, so arranged that all shall at all times be lodged, fed, clothed, trained, educated, employed, governed, and placed, in such manner as to enable them to attain the highest state of physical and mental health and rational enjoyment.

But the science of surroundings, to comprehend their influences upon humanity, has been little studied by the population of the world, and is at this day but very partially known by the advanced minds in the most civilized countries.

The sovereigns of these countries are in general within the best material surroundings, but through their elevated position they are subjected to many imperfect mental surroundings. While the highest and more permanent pleasures are derived from the influences of superior mental surroundings.

The writer, early in life becoming conscious of the great importance of both physical and mental surroundings, made the science of their influences over humanity his chief study, and he has had peculiar opportunities to apply the science to practice through a long life, and by which he has attained knowledge applicable to the permanent improvement of society, which seldom falls to the lot of the learned or men of practical habits. From this experience he is now prepared to say, without fear of rational contradiction, that the means abundantly exist to enable society to form new combinations of superior surroundings, which shall permanently secure the happiness of the human race.

And that, to a combination of men familiar with the highest practice in the various departments of the business of life, he is prepared to explain what these surroundings are, and how they should be combined to produce the result stated.

This explanation of the writer's views of the Social Science, and of its importance to the public, may perhaps be as much as the association will yet require, or will desire in this division.

[The preceding paper was read for Mr. Owen by Sir Benjamin Brodie, Bart., F.R.S., President of the 5th department.]

No. 2. *Section First, Judiciary.*

" Any general character, from the best to the worst, from the most
" ignorant to the most enlightened, may be given to any community,
" even to the world at large, by the application of proper means ;
" which means are to a great extent at the command and under the
" control of those who have influence in the affairs of men."

In a rationally constituted society, based and consistently constructed on Social Science, human laws would be not only
unnecessary, but highly injurious. But while society is irrationally
constituted, and is based and constructed, as it has hitherto been,
in ignorance of and in opposition to Social Science, human laws
must be endured and supported, until a new character can be
formed for the population, based on and formed throughout in
accordance with Social Science.

Until that rational and happy period for the human race shall
arrive, it will be useful to consider what human laws, under the
existing condition of society, are necessary while the change from
a false to the true system of society is in progress, which evidently
it is now by the establishment of this society.

In a rationally constituted society, the laws of God, or, as
others prefer, the laws of nature, will be sufficient to govern it
in unity, peace, wisdom, goodness, and harmony ; but previously
all countries must continue to be governed by laws in conformity
with its religious and governmental institutions.

The laws of God or of nature respecting humanity being,
" that man is so created or constituted that he *must* believe in
" obedience to the strongest conviction made on his mind, and
" *must* feel pain and pleasure, love and hatred, in obedience to
" his peculiar and individual organisation ;" all human laws now
to be made should conform as near as practicable with these
unchanging laws of God or nature ; and those laws now existing,
made by human inexperience, which the most contravene those
natural laws, should be gradually repealed ; and the sooner they
can be repealed without too much immediate inconvenience, the
better will it be for all parties in the state.

The present condition of the British Empire is most favourable for the gradual repeal of the false and injurious laws made
by men, and for the gradual introduction of the all-wise, good,
and merciful laws of God, or of laws as nearly approaching to
these as the present imperfections of our existing political and
religious constitution will admit.

Consequently the best laws now to introduce into the government of the British Empire, are those which will the most favour
civil and religious liberty,— provide for a rational, natural, national
training and education of the people from birth,—and insure
constant beneficial occupation and employment according to age

for all the working classes, not only as an essential part of their
natural rational training and education, but as the best means to
make superior unadulterated wealth the most abundant, and to
terminate motives to crime from want or the fear of poverty.

In a rationally constituted society there will be no difficulty
in arranging for perpetual beneficial occupation or employment
for all who require them, and this will be one of the greatest
blessings that can be now bestowed on society for its safety, comfort, and happiness.

This may suffice to introduce useful discussion to this section
and to the general meetings of the association ; for, one part or
division of the social system cannot be consistently considered
without reference to some or all of the others.

No. 3.   Third Section Under the Presidency of the Right Rev. the Lord Bishop of London.

The Human Race governed without Punishment.

" Any general character, from the best to the worst, from the most
" ignorant to the most enlightened, may be given to any community,
" even to the world at large, by the application of proper means ;
" which means are to a great extent at the command and under the
" control of those who have influence in the affairs of men."

In a society based on its true foundation—" that the *Creator*
" gives all the qualities and powers to and possessed by the
" created," the punishment of man by man will be unnecessary
and unknown.

Look at the deeply interesting and most instructive engraving
from Mr. Wehnest's picture representing John Pound's natural
method of preventing the necessity for human punishment.
Can anyone, having an educated mind, and possessing feelings
of humanity, contemplate the details of that engraving without
becoming conscious of the overwhelming influences of surroundings for good or evil, for happiness or misery, of the human race ?

Is it not then time now to begin to acquire a knowledge of the
science of surroundings, so essential to unite with the knowledge
of social science, to make it complete ?—In fact the two sciences
are necessary to well-place and well-form the character of man.

It must highly gratify the best and foremost in church and
state, to learn that the discovery has been made by which the
human race may be far better governed without punishment, than
with any that man can devise.

By the aid of this discovery, the writer governed a population
originally very inferior, of between two and three thousand, for
upwards of a quarter of a century, without punishment ; and

they were by public consent allowed to be for that period the best and the happiest working population ever known to exist in any country. And all the children of this population were so trained, educated, and placed, from one year old, that vice, crime, or evil passions, or unkind conduct to each other, were unknown, and the strongest affection between them and their teachers were strikingly manifest at all times to all who witnessed their proceedings.

These previously extraordinary results were produced by measures which the church and state may gradually make universal throughout the British Empire, and by its example throughout the world.

These measures were,—

1st. To withdraw all punishment or *fear* of it from the children.

2nd. To instruct the younger children to six years of age by natural objects, or by the best representations of them that could be obtained,—these being fully explained to them by familiar conversation between the teachers and pupils as far as the latter could comprehend the formation, use, and other properties of the objects under inspection and examination; the pupils being freely allowed to ask their questions for additional explanation or information.

3rd. The surroundings in their schools and play-grounds for instruction were healthy, pleasant, and so furnished as to be attractive to the children, according to age, and as they advanced from one school to the next above in their New Institution for the formation of their characters.

4th. The teachers and taught were governed in *practice* by the true, simple, yet divine principles of pure undefiled Christianity, of universal love and charity—a love and charity emanating from the knowledge that the *Creator* gives all the qualities and powers to the *created* which it can possess, and that all the works of the Great Creating Power of the Universe are as perfect as the elements or materials for creation will admit.

And this Mysterious Power is the real God, under whatever name, of all nations and peoples.

It is therefore unwise, and indeed most irrational, for man, especially in his yet undeveloped state, to attempt to make laws to contravene the all-wise and all-merciful laws of God; for by so doing he mars and spoils to a great extent the perfect work of God.

No, my friends! the time shall surely come, when the population of the world shall be governed solely under the influences of universal love and charity; and, divine as these principles are, they are yet the principles of common sense for governing mankind and forming the character from birth to death.

Perhaps sufficient has now been said to open this division of the social science for useful discussion by the members of the association.

The writer concludes with the hope that the subject thus explained may be accepted by the Right Rev. Lord Bishop who presides over this section, and by the meeting, in the same spirit in which it has been written.

[This paper was read for Mr. Owen by M. D. Hill, Esq., Q.C., the Recorder of Birmingham, President of the third department in the absence of the Bishop of London.]

No. 4. *For the Educational Section.*

" Any general character, from the best to the worst, from the most " ignorant to the most enlightened, may be given to any community, " even to the world at large, by the application of proper means ; " which means are to a great extent at the command and under the " control of those who have influence in the affairs of men."

EDUCATION, or the formation of character, forms the most essential division of Social Science.   Education being understood as part of the Social Science, may now be made to effect, and with the certainty of a law of nature, the highest and most substantial services for the permanent prosperity and happiness of our country and of all countries.

If there is now sufficient moral courage in the public to look this subject fairly in the face, and to pursue it to its legitimate results, it will be found competent, united with the other branches of Social Science, to terminate, gradually and most beneficially for all, the present ignorance, poverty, disunion, evil passions, vice, crime, and misery, so prevalent at this day throughont society in all countries.

In fact, education, or the formation of character, when comprehended in its full extent, will be found to include within its legitimate range every other division of Social Science, as now divided by the association.   For it includes,

Instruction in a knowledge of the laws of God and of men, and of their influences upon humanity when applied to practice.

Instruction in the causes which have created humanly-devised punishments, and their influences upon society as now instituted ; and in those causes which when applied to practice will expose the error and great evil arising from man's ignorant and puerile attempts to punish man justly or with any permanent benefit to society.

Instruction in the never-ceasing beneficial influences, in a rationally constructed system for conducting wisely the affairs of life, arising from the punishments of nature, when punishment can be of use to the individual or to society.

Instruction in the Laws of Health, and their application to practice, as to food, dress, dwelling, air, exercise, occupations, sites for habitations, and how to warm, ventilate, and secure from fire.

Instruction in the principles how to create wealth in the most advantageous manner for the individual and for the aggregate of society.

Instruction in the formation of the best combinations for societies, and in a knowledge of the spirit, principle, and practice, by which these should be governed.

These and much more will be included in a *rational* system of *national* education, or in the *rational formation* of *character*, to train humanity into full formed men and women, or superior rational beings.

It will now be said, previously to sufficient knowledge and reflection upon the subject, that thus to educate the human race or any part of it is impracticable.

It *is* so on the old principles and practices of forcing false instruction upon humanity, and tormenting it to induce it to accept a most unnatural treatment to acquire superficial, useless, and often injurious knowledge.

The writer knows that by the principles on which half a century ago he established and continued the practice for upwards of a quarter of a century to new-form the character of humanity, by the most simple and natural method, in spirit, principle, and practice, and in strict accordance with the pure undefiled practice of Christianity, so far as the inventor's instructions could be carried out amidst many obstructions, he was eminently successful in demonstrating the truth of the principles and the advantages of the practice, until interfered with by old prejudices and quaker sectarianism.

Under the principle and practice of this then new mode of forming character by the eyes, by observing material objects, and by familiar conversation between pupil and teacher— the pupil was freely allowed to ask his own questions, and to receive rational answers. Under this principle and practice, fully understood, with proper arrangements, and conducted by the teacher without deviation in the true spirit of universal charity and love, more real, useful, well remembered knowledge of facts will be given and retained in one day, than is now received and retained through the old scholastic mode of giving instruction, in one month, and often in six months.

It is extremely gratifying to learn that our government has made a commencement in this direction in an establishment now in progress at South Kensington, which, as described to the writer, is much in advance of the general public, and is well imagined for the population of the metropolis, as society is now conducted. Its founders are in advance of the present instructors of the public. But until the different divisions of the science of society shall be united to act harmoniously as a whole, no one can have a correct conception of the superior character which may be formed for the human race.

c

One man thus full formed, physically, intellectually, morally, and practically, will be of more real value to society, than hundreds of the present misformed inhabitants of our earth.

The president of this section, if he pursues this subject through all its ramifications and extent, will open a new mine to the population of the world, of a value yet beyond human estimate, and will enter upon a cavern of more substantial wealth than the surface of the globe now contains.

That he may fearlessly enter this mine, and may succeed in working it with daily increasing satisfaction to himself, and lasting benefit to society, is the ardent wish of the writer.

The prize to be gained deserves the best efforts of the best men.

ROBERT OWEN.

Sevenoaks Park, Sevenoaks.
September, 1857.

No. 5, *For the Section of Health, under the Presidency of the Right Honourable Lord Stanley.*

" Unfavourable or inferior surroundings create disease and " misery; favourable or superior surroundings insure health " and happiness."

This is intended to be a paper to interest the population of the world through futurity; by exposing the origin of evil, and developing the means by which to establish the language of truth over the globe,—destroy all motive to falsehood, in look, word, or action,—and elevate man to the attainment of rationality, superior knowledge, and permanent happiness.

All who reflect will readily admit that sound health in body and mind of the population of the empire is of the first importance.

But society having been everywhere based on the false foundation that the *created* determines and forms its own qualities and powers, and being constructed in strict accordance with this fatal mistake, has given little attention to the laws of nature, or to the causes which alone can produce permanent health and happiness.

Hence old society has proceeded so far in error, in opposition to the laws of health, that not much can be done, even by large expenditures, to remove the causes of disease, as now experienced in London and other large cities and towns.

The laws of health, on which so much of our happiness depends, require that attention should be given in choosing sites for dwellings, to their plan and construction, the manner of warming, lighting, and ventilating them, &c., Also to the arrangements for training, educating, and employing their inhabitants, and to the aggregate combinations of these dwellings. And, in short, to the whole arrangements of the business of life ; and these are combined in one act or action.

These considerations, with innumerable others, show that it will be far the most economical and best course on all accounts to begin to re-arrange society from its base, on new sites, and to construct it throughout in accordance with the true principles of Social Science; which will be explained.

This change may be now easily effected, gradually, in the same manner as were the changes from the old roads, one by one, to the new railways, which required for adoption new sites, new principles and practices, and greatly superior surroundings for travelling.

Of course, innumerable ignorant and futile objections will be made to the proposed change from an old worn-out irrational system, only fertile in producing every kind of error, evil, and suffering, to another system, greatly superior in spirit, principle, and practice, and in its combinations for general permanent happiness, and which, by avoiding the errors, will *prevent* the evils and sufferings of the old system.

Superior as this new system will be in every respect when compared with the present, society will be strongly opposed to the change from the one to the other.

There is a recent strong warning to society respecting such changes.

Let the public call to recollection the varied absurd notions and fanciful objections made to a fundamental change from an inferior to a greatly superior mode of travelling, when first proposed by the untaught but nature-inspired George Stephenson, and how strongly he was opposed by the learned in the law, by the wealthy, and by many of the most powerful in the land, all combined in opposition to a simple untaught man of truth and integrity, but of native genius.

George Stephenson, strong in his internal convictions, persevered in what he felt and knew to be the truth and right ; and he thus overcame all the obstacles so unwisely brought to oppose his progress to the third great discovery of the age and the fifth of all ages for the benefit of universal man—a discovery which already, in a few short years, traverses the greater part of our globe, and promises soon to extend over the remainder.

And it will now soon appear to the astonished world, that for upwards of forty years the same false, futile, and frivolous objections have been continually opposed to the greatest discovery yet made by man, to enable him to attain and to secure the highest permanent happiness of his race—to a discovery which goes at once to the origin of evil and to the removal of its cause for ever ;—a discovery of the fundamental error on which society has been based and constructed, and in accordance with which the character of man has been misformed from the beginning to this day. And yet, like all the great truths of nature, it will be discovered to be simple, and will soon become obvious to the common mind of general society, and will be easily taught to children!

What, then, it will be now asked, is the origin of evil, and the great fundamental error which has been made by all of humanity?

It is the fatal, and, it may truly be said, on account of its consequences, horrible mistake, " that man, a created being, could " by any possible means determine upon or create one of the " qualities or powers which constitute his physical, intellectual, " moral, spiritual, and practical nature."

Yet, without deep reflection and much consideration, the truth cannot be made to enter the mind already filled with opposing ideas and associations of ideas; and so filled because, from the beginning, through all past ages to this day, all have been forced to receive the religions, laws, governments, and institutions, emanating from and based solely on the mere imaginary notion that the created determines upon and makes its own qualities and powers.

All, no doubt, will be anxious to learn what are the evils which have been and are produced and continually reproduced by this fatal, this horrible mistake of our early undeveloped ancestors, and transmitted through all succeeding ages to the present.

The catalogue would include all the evils experienced by man during this long dark night of mental insanity, moral degradation, and physical suffering.

To enumerate these in detail would exceed the limits here allowed, and indeed, would be endless. And to name a few of them now will suffice for present purpose.

This mistake of our poor ignorant inexperienced first parents has placed death obstructions to progress in real knowledge through every succeeding generation. It is therefore the cause of the gross ignorance which at this day pervades so large a portion of the population of the world.

Through this ignorance it has created innumerable obstructions to the production and preservation of real wealth; and it is therefore the cause of all the poverty and fear of it now suffered by the human race. For there exists no other necessity for poverty or the fear of it to be experienced by one human being.

It has created the repulsion so general between man and man and nations and nations, and has thus caused the religious and political wars, the sufferings, and the deaths, of the martyrs of all superstitions, and the present divided and opposing state of all creeds and political parties.

It is the cause of the atrocious cruelties of the Hindoos and Musselmen this day in India, and of our attempts to revenge them.

It represses the best and most attractive feelings, and creates the general falsehood and deception now in practice over the world.

It has created prostitution with its heart-rending unimaginable miseries and degradation,—the murder of children by their mothers,—murder of wives by husbands and of husbands by wives,—with all the hidden sufferings of forced cohabitation, directly opposed to the laws of God.

The mind of man cannot, but the mind of woman may perhaps imagine some of the dreadful sufferings created by this ignorance of an unchanging law of our common nature.

But few men or women can form any conception of the physical and mental diseases created by all the previously named causes of sufferings from ignorance, from poverty, from religious errors and repulsive feelings, from prostitution, from child murders, from bearing natural children, when not extended to the murder of offspring, from family feuds and quarrels arising from improperly forced legal cohabitation, and from the falsehood and deception existing between these parties.

These loathsome, degrading, and painful physical and mental diseases, are nature's punishments, continually increasing, for opposing her good, wise, and merciful laws; and they will increase until they shall compel men to perceive their errors and evil doings, and to abandon them altogether, by adopting the all-efficient laws of their Creator, and a new system based on everlasting truth.

Heartrending and numerous as the before-mentioned sufferings and diseases have been, and are, innumerable others remain to be noticed, but which notice the limit of these papers will not now admit here.

It is, however, not to be forgotten that this fatal error in founding society on so false a notion or mere undeveloped imaginary supposition, has caused men to make ignorant, absurd, inconsistent, and most presumptuous laws, in opposition to, and in defiance of, the laws of nature never known to change, and which, if attended to and consistently acted upon, would direct into the right path to wisdom, unity, peace, and happiness.

But what will the untaught mistaught among all classes, creeds, and parties, in all countries, say or do to the man who thus openly opposes these cherished errors in principle and practice, but which errors from their infancy they have been forced by a false instruction to believe to be truth and right?

They will agree in saying, that he cannot be in his right senses, that he is a dangerous man, and ought to be confined or put to death. I well know that these must be the feelings and desires of the unthinking and unreflecting, as well as of the erroneous thinkers and reflectors;—and this state of the human mind I have been conscious of, and calmly contemplated, from the commencement of my public proceedings. Witness what I said and did in the great public meeting held in the City of London Tavern, August, 21st, 1817.

Knowing the extent of the mental darkness in which so large a portion of my poor deluded fellow-men have been so long kept by the errors of our forefathers, and the horrible sufferings men have experienced from the same cause, I am conscious that strong, even that life and death measures, can alone arouse the human race from its present mental degradation and physical suffering, and that the most powerful medicine is now required to cure the bodily and mental diseases with which humanity has been so long afflicted.

This strong but nauseous medicine is now given under the heaviest responsibility, with full reliance in its efficacy to complete a perfect cure, and thus ultimately to create in the population sound minds in sound bodies.

ROBERT OWEN.

October 1st, 1857.

The following papers were not sent.

A TREATISE CALLED FOR BY THE PRESENT STATE OF THE POPULATION OF THE WORLD, EXPLANATORY OF THE ORIGIN OF EVIL AND OF GOOD TO THE HUMAN RACE, AND OF THE PLAIN PRACTICAL MEASURES TO SECURE THE HAPPINESS OF ALL THROUGH FUTURITY.

THE origin of evil is the impression made on the mind of all, through past time to the present, that the *created* creates its own qualities and powers, and should be made responsible for their actions.

The origin of the good which is to be experienced by the human race is the knowledge, derived from all facts, that the Creator determines upon and creates all the qualities and powers of the created, and is alone responsible for all the consequences of such creation.

What mortal man can trace and explain the errors, miseries, and sufferings of mankind, through past ages to the present, which have emanated from the fatal introduction of the origin of evil at the commencement of society ?

Or who can foresee and foretell the happiness which will be enjoyed by all through future ages, when the origin of evil, and its consequences, shall be peaceably superseded by the origin of good and its consequences?

An attempt, however, shall be made, to give a slight sketch of both, but these sketches will be slight indeed, compared with realities.

The belief that man, a new created existence, creates his own qualities and powers, deranged the rational and reasoning faculties of humanity, and made all of our race to see all things through a false medium, and to err in all their attempts to attain happiness—the ever-enduring object of human existence, and the ultimate destiny of all.

This derangement of the rational and reasoning faculties introduced the various superstitions, called religions, which have created the repulsive feelings between man and man and nation and nation, and which have filled the human race with erroneous ideas of truth and falsehood, and have generated the most savage feelings between those who differed on these matters ; all, at the same time, being most ignorant of the subjects about which they differed, and of the cause of their differences.

These superstitions, all dignified with the name of religion, soon created a favoured class to teach and maintain them; and this class became the priesthood in all these opposing superstitions.

These priesthoods gradually became masters of the human mind, and consequently the directors of all human affairs; and the population of the world during the darkest ages were completely under their control and government, possessing power to dethrone and degrade the highest secular potentates of the earth.

And for a long period they have ruled the population of the world with physical burnings and mental torments, to an extent unbearable to humanity, and which at length aroused some daring minds to question their claimed divine authority to assume the powers of God over their fellow men.

These daring minds, at the imminent hazard of their lives, met with some small success; just sufficient to induce others to follow their examples. Their attacks upon the superstitions of religious dogmas opened to view more and more the extent of tyranny which the priesthoods had for ages assumed over the intellects and affairs of men born with faculties equal to their own.

But the priesthoods, having acquired this power, gave to themselves high sounding titles, honours, and exclusive privileges, to enable them to keep the mass of the people in physical and mental slavery. Assuming to be made by some forms of their own contriving the equals and representatives of God, they claimed the direction in all things, from birth to death, of the entire population, but most especially the training of the young mind, that they might form it to perpetuate their influence and power over them when at maturity.

To this end they must name the child,—church the mother,—have the child taught and forced to receive their creed, however unintelligible to child and parent.

Then all their invented absurd ceremonies must be daily and weekly observed.

Then they assume to know better than their Creator when the sexes should be united, how long these unions should remain, and whether they were made and continued in accordance with or in opposition to the laws of God and of their nature; while, before and after these new-made, misery-producing, marriages, they must attend continually to their priestly instructors and teachers, in order that they should not acquire sufficient common sense to discover the fallacy and folly of their teachings, and the false foundation of all these superstitions conceived in opposition to all facts, to the first indications of common sense or sound judgment.

The whole of the proceedings of the priesthoods of the world through all ages, **having** emanated from the most gross and now palpable error " that the created makes its own qualities and " powers," nothing rational could proceed from that foundation.

In fact, the priesthoods of the present generation are, in consequence of their erroneous training, education, and placing, the unconscious obstructions to the elevation of man to the rank and state of a rational being.

With the ample appliances of materials, and of science to work them, all from birth, by being placed within such surroundings as society can now with ease and pleasure create to well-train and educate them, may be made, with the certainty of a law of nature, to become, not only consistent in mind and practice, but good, wise, healthy, united to their fellows, prosperous, and happy through life.

The priesthoods of the world, by their unconscious false teaching, and by the prejudices and injurious habits which they sanction, are the cause of the present wretchedly confused Babel condition of society, and of all the evil passions and immoralities of the human race.

Enormous and innumerable as are the evils and sufferings which the priesthoods of the world at this day inflict on themselves and on all of our race, yet the application of the Divine Principles of universal love and charity, teach all to avoid anger, or ill-will, or any injurious actions or proceedings against one of them in any part of the world, however erroneous, absurd, or foolish their teachings may be, and not even to deprive them of their living. And this for the strongest of all reasons :—because they have been so placed, trained, and educated by society, as to believe, and most likely the very great majority of them do believe most conscentiously, that they are right and good, and are doing the Great Moving Power or Spirit of the Universe,(blasphemous as is the idea) great service, by their creeds, forms, and ceremonies.

This is said from the knowledge of our nature, " that any one " from birth might have been so placed, trained, and educated, " as to be compelled by the force of surroundings to believe the " most contradictory to nature of these creeds to be divine " truths, and to be willing to sacrifice his life in many cases to " sustain and defend them as such."

O! My poor deluded fellow men! What have you not suffered?—What do you now suffer from the want of an unexclusive, sound, consistent, rational training and education from birth,—physical, intellectual, moral, spiritual, and practical. All that the population of the world now requires, to enable it to make a rapid progress in goodness and knowledge, to lead it to the full rational enjoyment of its existence, is the creation of common-sense surroundings, to well-form the character of each from birth ; for on the good or bad formation of character depends the good or bad, rational or irrational, miserable or happy state of the populations of all nations and peoples.

How easy, then, will it now be for the leading civilised governments to unite in peace to create these new, good, and superior surroundings, gradually so to train and educate their respective populations, that all shall become full-made well-formed superior rational men and women, knowing themselves, knowing society, and knowing how to act in such manner as to make each other permanently happy!

SECOND TREATISE ON THE ORIGIN OF EVIL AND OF GOOD TO THE HUMAN RACE.

THE leading liberal minds among the upper classes of society have now entered upon the right course to secure the progress and happiness of the human race, and it is hoped that, having commenced, they will now steadily pursue it, without stay or retrogression, or turning to the right or to the left, until full success shall crown their efforts.

The path now opened is probably new to many who have thus entered it, and it may appear to them to be full of thorns and briars and many perplexing obstructions.

The writer has employed many years, in fact a long life, in surveying every part of it, from its commencement to its termination, and he assures these young travellers on this most interesting road, that although formerly the obstructions to progress upon it were numerous, and indeed until lately insurmountable, yet have the most formidable now been removed or overcome, others are disappearing, and it is probable that the entire path will be soon cleared, and that the road may be with safety and great pleasure travelled through its whole course.

To cease metaphor;—until lately no one desirous to retain respectability, so called, in modern society, could venture to discuss the full subject of social science. All the educated prejudices of the public were so opposed, that it was tabooed, except among a party whose limited views and education precluded them from comprehending a science which provides for all the wants of humanity, and which, in fact, includes all other sciences and the whole business of life.

For it includes the development of the best means to place, train, educate, employ, feed, clothe, amuse, and govern the human race, in health, and so as to enable it to attain wisdom and happiness, increasing through futurity.

Until the origin of evil was discovered, no progress could be made in social science; for the origin of evil being opposed to the laws of God and nature, and the social sciences being founded and constructed on those laws only, the one has been throughout, in every department of life, opposed to the other; and it is utterly vain and useless to attempt in any manner to unite the ever-changing laws of ignorant men, with the unchanging divine laws of God and nature.

Let all now pause and reflect well on what is now going to be solemnly stated as an eternal truth. It is, that the population of the world must continue to be placed, trained, educated, employed, and governed, in accordance with the origin of evil, as it has been to this day,—or it must be placed, trained, educated, employed and governed, in accordance with the origin of good, the true and only foundation of social science.

The one, it is now evident, is now driving the human race to a state of Babel confusion which will lead to a pandemonium ; while the other will lead direct to knowledge, wisdom, goodness, unity, harmony, and ultimately to a terestrial paradise.

There can be no permanent happiness so long as society is based, constructed, and governed on the supposition " that the " created creates its own qualities and powers and should be " made responsible for their actions."

Nor will there be any permanent misery when society shall be based, constructed, and governed consistently on the knowledge of the universal fact " that the Creator gives all the qualities and " powers to the created, and is alone responsible for their " actions."

But, it will be said, this will overturn the whole principle and practice of existing society over the world.

The writer knows it ; and the sooner the old principles and practices of society are so overturned, the better it will be for every child of man, provided the change shall be effected in the spirit of universal charity and love for our race, with wise fore-sight, in order, in peace, gradually, and with harmony between the governors and governed.

The writer has now placed truth and falsehood, good and evil, discord and harmony, before the population of the world.

To do this was his mission from his birth. This mission is now fulfilled ; and he can do no more than trust to the Great Creating Power of the Universe, which has enabled him thus to feel, think, and act through life.

This power is the writer's God, from his infancy. What may be the God of others, he knows not, nor has he any business to pry into the interior thoughts and feelings of others : but as they are those which have been taught to them from their birth, he respects them as much as his own.

And let the republicans and democrats of all countries be assured, that these are the principles and practices by which alone true liberty, practical equality, universal unity, and a cordial fraternity, can ever be attained or maintained.

Let all now mark, learn, and inwardly digest what has been stated in this little publication. This is all that is asked.

EPITOME OF THE PRACTICAL MEASURES BY WHICH, IN PEACE, AND IN THE SHORTEST TIME, TO ATTAIN THIS ELEVATED, SUPERIOR, AND HAPPY STATE OF EXISTENCE FOR THE HUMAN RACE.

THE knowledge " that the Creator gives to the created all " the qualities and powers which they possess, and is alone " responsible for the action of those qualities and powers," is the broad and solid foundation for this new superstructure of society.

This knowledge at once becomes the base of the true universal religion for man, by creating within him that love and charity for our race, which can alone make him sincerely desirous to do to others as he would wish others to do to him, or, in other words, to love his neighbour as himself.

There is, then, but one road by which this practice may be made to obtain through the lives of all of our race.

The ruling powers of the civilised portions of the world must unite to abandon the false and fatal error on which society to this day has been based, and from which all its wars and wickednesses have of necessity emanated.

They must then make the required preparations well and wisely to re-base and re-construct society, on the divine truth,— " that God, and not man, gives all the qualities and powers of " thought and action possessed by everyone of our race ;" and to re-construct society in undeviating accordance with that glorious truth, and solid foundation by which forbearance, love, and charity will be made to pervade the hearts and minds of all, and the wants of all will be provided for by the most simple, rational, natural, and effective practical arrangements, which in execution will give health, security, satisfaction, and happiness to everyone through futurity.

The ruling powers of the civilised divisions of the earth will then have gradually to re-associate those whom they govern, into such masses as will be the most convenient to provide for their wants, and to enable those thus happily new-placed the most effectually to assist others to attain to this elevated and superior condition.

These arrangements will provide in the best manner for the training, education, employment, amusement, government, and surroundings of all—which surroundings will include all that superior made rational beings can or will desire to enjoy.

But to perfect these new combinations of arrangements, the permanent peace of nations is required ; and there never has been a period in the history of the world so auspicious for the inauguration of the universal and perpetual peace, first between the Christian nations, and by degrees to include all others.

There is now ordinary peace between Austria, France, Great Britain, Prussia, Persia, Russia, Sardinia, Turkey, and the United States.

The ordinary treaties of peace now subsisting between these parties, could easily be made into federative treaties, giving security and prosperity to each. These powers by such union could command the permanent peace of society, and induce all other powers gradually to join their great federation.

With a fair share of common sense and good intention among the present ruling powers of the world, that which has been stated would be found not difficult of practice.

And instead of the separated subjects proposed for discussion by the newly instituted "*National Association for the promotion of Social Science*," which can lead only to confusion and endless unsatisfactory discussions, let this association direct its attention in the manner now stated to the whole subject as one.

For upon reflection it will be obvious that social science includes every part of the business of life, in union; because each part has a direct reference to all the others, and cannot be considered separately.

I have thus explained the origin of evil and its necessary evil consequences, and the origin of good and its permanent happy consequences to the human race, by unfolding the true and superior surroundings necessarily emanating from the origin of good, and in which the human race should be placed for the perpetual advantage of every individual, whatever may be his present, country, creed, class, or political party.

THE ORIGIN OF GOOD AND EVIL, OF HAPPINESS AND MISERY, TO THE HUMAN RACE.

" Truth alone can set you free."

IGNORANT undeveloped, and inexperienced man, is a being of fear of unknown imaginary powers, and the very great majority of the human race are in that condition at this day.

As the mind gradually developes, this fear diminishes by a knowledge of facts superseding superstitious notions. Not, however, until this present period, had any minds acquired sufficient development and strength of mental powers to oppose facts to the oldest and strongest superstitions.

But now these facts are too obvious and palpable to be longer resisted, and superstitions must give way, strongly as they may be cherished, and at length " truth will prevail" over all opposing obstacles.

Mental liberty, so long repressed by ignorance and superstition, is now so far advanced, that the most developed minds of the present age will now venture to listen to truths heretofore tabooed by society; and listening, must reflect; and reflection will bring conviction.

The advanced public will now listen to the fact, which is an eternal truth, " that the maker makes the qualities of the made, " and is alone responsible for them ; " or " that the Creator creates " all the qualities and powers of the created, and is alone respon- " sible for their actions."

These facts are eternally true, and are all-important to be known to man, because they are the *origin* of *good,* and will guide all of our race through futurity to knowledge, wisdom, goodness, unity, health, and the permanent rational enjoyment of existence from birth to death—all-important to be known,— because the superstitious suppositions and imaginary notions,— " that the *made* makes its *own qualities,* that the *created* creates " its own nature and powers, and that the made and created " should be alone responsible for these qualities and powers," are the origin of all evil and misery to man ; and these fatal errors, emanating from our ignorant, undeveloped, and in- experienced early ancestors, and transmitted by them to us, have created all the superstitions, falsehood, deception, opposing interests, repulsive feelings, misguided education, erroneous social arrangements, defective governments, a false formation of character, and most injurious surrroundings within which the human race has been placed through past ages to this day.

The paths of good and evil are thus now opened to all. The path of good leads to truth, wisdom, goodness. unity, health, and rational enjoyment through life. The path of evil leads to falsehood, ignorance, poverty, opposing interests, disunion, con- flicts, wars, the injurious passions of anger, hatred, jealousy, malice, revenge,—to murders, prostitution, loathsome diseases, and all manner of crimes, arising from a false formation of cha- racter and a combination of irrational surroundings.

The path of evil has been the one universally followed, in opposition to facts, and to the direct and unchanging laws of God and nature.

The path of good will be universally pursued as soon as the advanced minds and ruling powers of society can be induced to attend to facts and to common sense.

It will be now seen which of these paths the men of influence in society will prefer. But the path leading to happiness being now made plain and easy to pursue, the public will not be long in finding out that the discovery of the path to good is the greatest discovery made by man for man ; because it will insure his everlasting peace and happiness.

The discoverer of the new path which leads direct to universal charity and love for our race,—to truth, goodness, knowledge and happiness,—will endeavour to make it plain to the public by an imaginary conversation between one of the most advanced minds of the age and himself.

And for this purpose, apologising to his lordship for the liberty he takes, he selects, as the representative of the active advanced minds of this country at this day, the Right Honourable Lord Brougham, Ex-Lord Chancellor of England, and now founder, patron, and president, of the "*National Association for the promotion of Social Science.*"

AN IMAGINANARY CONVERSATION BETWEEN THE RIGHT HONOURABLE LORD BROUGHAM AND VAUX, EX-LORD HIGH CHANCELLOR OF ENGLAND, AND FOUNDER, PATRON, AND PRESIDENT OF THE NATIONAL ASSOCIATION FOR THE PROMOTION OF SOCIAL SCIENCE, AND ROBERT OWEN, FORMERLY OF NEW LANARK IN SCOTLAND,—INVENTOR AND FOUNDER OF THE FIRST RATIONAL INFANT SCHOOL AND INSTITUTION FOR THE TRUE FORMATION OF CHARACTER, IN SPIRIT, PRINCIPLE, AND PRACTICE, AND THE INTRODUCER OF THE SAME SPIRIT, PRINCIPLE, AND PRACTICE, TO AN INFERIOR POPULATION, TO ELEVATE IT FROM IGNORANCE, POVERTY, RELIGIOUS DISSENTIONS, AND GREAT DEMORALIZATION, TO COMMON SENSE PROCEEDINGS, RELIGIOUS TOLERATION AND FRIENDSHIP, AND TO A GREATLY IMPROVED SOBRIETY AND GENERAL MORAL CONDUCT.

[L. B. will signify Lord Brougham, and R. O. the writer.]

L. B. You desire a conversation with me,—upon what subject?

R. O.—Upon the most important of all subjects,—Social Science; which appears to me to be the science of sciences, because on its true development depends the permanent happiness of our race.

L. B.—I agree with you as to the importance of the science; and for the general benefit of society I am willing to discuss the subject freely with you, although I know you entertain upon some matters what are deemed by many to be extreme opinions. But I apprehend no evil from any principles which can be demonstrated to be true or in accordance with facts.

R. O.—I am aware that I have long been deemed to hold extreme opinions; but all new truths are at first considered by the public to be extreme opinions, and not to be true.

L. B.—Admitted, as a general principle, to which there are exceptions. But now to the object of your visit. What are your views respecting the divisions of the science which the association is preparing to examine and discuss next week at Birmingham?

R. O.—I think the arrangements as stated in the printed papers so far issued to the public may prepare those who attend the meetings to begin to enquire in what the Social Science consists, and how it ought to be considered, to be understood for useful practical purposes.

L. B—.The association desires the subject to be so considered and discussed.   To what do you object ?

R. O.—To this science being attempted to be advantageously considered in sections ; when it is a science composed of such parts as cannot be understood separately.   Education, health, punishment, laws, all blend together and form one science, including the whole business of life.

L. B.—I do not yet see any reason why each of these subjects should not occupy the attention of the association as given in the prospectus.   Let me hear how you would have this science investigated and discussed.

R. O.—Social Science refers to the aggregation of men into societies, so constructed as to call forth the best qualities of each into daily action, by giving to each a good physical, intellectual, moral, spiritual, and practical character, in strict accordance with the laws of human nature, which are the laws of God :—into societies so constructed as to enable them to produce the greatest amount of the most valuable unadulterated wealth, in the shortest time, and in the best manner for the producers and consumers :—societies so constructed that the laws of health shall be systematically applied through all their details.   So constructed that all shall be well placed to perform all the duties of life in the best manner, and to enjoy the greatest amount of rational happiness during the performance of those duties.—So constructed as by the placing, training, and education, the punishment of man by man will never be required or useful, nor one human-made law, in opposition to nature's or God's laws, necessary for the good government of such societies.—So constructed that all the members shall be so placed, that each one shall be well cared for by the societies from birth to death.—So constructed that by this placing, training, and education, such attractive feelings shall be created between all the members of each society, that there will be no anger, ill-will, jealousy, or unkind feelings, at any time, between them, and they will have but one interest and one universally prevailing desire to promote the rational permanent happiness of each other.—So constructed that wealth shall always superabound in these societies, and be freely used by each member according to his or her wants.—So constructed that all the surroundings within and around each society shall be well considered with respect to their influences upon humanity, and shall be combined to create in all the members the best and most happy influences.

L. B—To effect these results will require superhuman powers, and they are beyond human nature to accomplish.

R. O.—Herein is the great error of the governing powers of the world, and the mistake of all statesmen.   Let society be at once placed on its true foundation, and all these results, with universal peace and harmony among men, will speedily follow.

L. B.—Why! What do you mean? Is not society now based on its true foundation?

R. O—No, my lord. It never has been based on its true foundation. But it ever has been, and is at this day, based on the origin of evil. And hence the sin and misery,— the repulsive feelings between men and nations,—the religious and civil wars,— the language of falsehood and conduct of deception,—the hatred of truth and opposition to open sincere minds,—the ignorance, poverty, superstitions, disunion, counteraction, cruelties, and Babel confusion and repulsive feelings now so prevalent over the globe.

L. B.—These are indeed strange doctrines; and well may they be called extreme opinions. Will you explain what you mean by a *false* foundation of society, the origin of evil; and by the *true* foundation of society?

R. O—With pleasure. For on a right understanding of these GREAT FUNDAMENTAL TRUTHS, depend the permanent peace and happiness of the human race. But to make the explanation more easy to be fully comprehended, perhaps your lordship will have the kindness, for the public good, to first reply to a few plain questions.

L. B.—I can have no objection to do so, provided they are relevant and are proper questions to answer.

R. O.—They shall be such in your lordship's estimation.

L. B.—Pray proceed—for my curiosity is now excited.

R. O.—When an inventor discovers and makes a curious, complicated, and most valuable machine, chooses his own materials, finishes it, and sets it to the action intended,—Is the inventor and maker, or is the machine itself, responsible for its working?

L. B.—The question answers itself. Who would ever blame the machine, however imperfect might be its actions?

R. O.—Good, my lord. But yet another question. When the Supreme Spirit and Great Creating Power of the Universe invents and creates the most complicated and wonderfully combined physical, intellectual, moral, spiritual, mechanical, and chemical, living machine, and places it within conditions, also of the Creator's creating—the living spiritual machine, thus wonderfully constructed and combined, not knowing how a particle of itself was created,—Should the existence thus produced,—the created, or should the Creator, be responsible for the action of the qualities and powers thus given to the created?

L. B.—This is a question which requires to be well considersd before a rational answer can be given.

R. O.—I know it, my lord, and while you have time to think of it I will proceed to reply to your lordships questions. *First*, the false foundation on which society has been based through all past ages, is the imagined notion that the made, made itself ; in other words, that the created creates its own qualities and powers, and ought to be responsible for their action.   This is opposed to all known facts, and is the true origin of evil to the human race.   *Second*, the true foundation on which to base society, is the fact that the Creator gives to the created whatever qualities and powers the created possesses. And that the Creator is therefore alone responsible for their action.

L. B.—Why this would be to upset the existing state of society over the world.

R. O.—I know it, and I have long foreseen that this is the great change, and the only reform that can ever benefit the human race.   On this true, solid, and unassailable foundation, it will be plain sailing to make the population of the world good, wise, united, ever prosperous, and happy.

L. B.—This, without much more elucidation, must be a mystery and enigma to every one.

R. O.—Only because every one has been taught to think, believe, and act on a false fundamental principle—on a principle opposed to nature and to all facts.

L. B.—Hitherto it has been universally received that man could be made to become good, only by being made responsible to man for his thoughts and actions.

R. O.—And this has been the direct road to make all men irrational in thought and action, as they are all over the world at this day.   And it has been the obstacle which has hitherto made it impossible that the pure spirit of universal love and charity for our race could ever enter the mind, or be reduced to practice.   While, on the knowledge of the fact, and therefore divine truth, that the Creator creates all the qualities and powers of the created, and is alone responsible for their action, every mind will be pervaded with this spirit of universal love and charity for our race, and it will be evident throughout the whole practice of their lives ; and evil thoughts and evil actions will be unknown among men.

L. B.—If this were not a merefanciful idea of yours, but were a reality, it would be indeed the greatest discovery ever made by man for man.

R. O.—Upon fair and full investigation, by your lordship and other advanced minds of the age, it will be ascertained to be the most important reality known among men.

L. B.—May it prove to be so, to terminate the sad sufferings of so large a portion of our fellow men.

R. O.—No efforts on my part shall be wanting to make this knowledge known to all, for the lasting benefit of all.

L. B.—But eternally true and highly important as you may imagine your discovery of the origin of evil may be, you will be strongly opposed by the conservative principle at every step of your progress, and the vested interests of the privileged classes will be insurmountable, supported, as they will be, by all the influential members of society.   What chance then have you of success ?

R. O.—From an early period in life, in fact, when I had made up my mind to bring the origin of evil before the public under the least offensive phrase I could devise, merely saying " that " the character of man is formed for him and not by him," I knew I should be opposed by every class, creed, and party, in every country, and I was prepared calmly to meet the result of that opposition, whatever form it might take, having full confidence in the ultimate success of the principle for the universal practice of the population of the world.

L. B.—Against the powers of such combined opposition, on what grounds was your confidence in success founded ?

R. O.—On the yet stronger powers which aided me.

L, B.—What are these ?

R. O.—First. An eternal truth, opposed by no one fact, and supported by all facts through all time.   *Second.* Universal humanity, or pure unprejudiced human nature.   And *Third.* The everlasting future happiness of all of our race.

L. B.—You are a strange man, so singular and extreme in all your ideas and combinations of ideas, I do not know what to make of you in your new system.   Good bye.

THE GREAT CREATING POWER OF THE UNIVERSE AND MAN.

IT is at this period of the first importance to the human race, that man should acquire consistent or rational ideas respecting the Great Creating Power of the Universe.

Without this knowledge, man may accumulate fact upon fact without limitation, and yet never progress in wisdom to apply those facts to attain goodness, unity, or united feelings, and happiness.

What, then, is this Eternal Power of unceasing action ? Where does it exist ?   How does it act?

In reply to these ever-recurring questions, the combined knowledge of the human race can only answer—" We know " not.   Our faculties are too limited and undeveloped to " comprehend the What, Where, or How."   We see the effects, and are conscious the cause of them exists, and must exist somewhere, and in some manner, eternally ; because nothing could never begin to create or produce something.

This power, in whatever form existing, is the All-Pervading Spirit of Eternal Action throughout the Universe ; and This is the God of the Human Race—by whatever name called, or in whatever manner worshipped.

This Power—the Eternal Godhead invented the mechanical, chemical, and spiritual parts of humanity, and wonderously combined them to form man and woman, the most mysterious of all living earthly existences—for they are yet mysteries to themselves; knowing but little of their own divine nature.

They are, however, conscious that they are created with a never-ceasing desire to attain and secure happiness.

This undying desire in man, to seek for happiness, is the germ which stimulates all his actions.

It is this germ which gradually developes the superior faculties combined within humanity. It is this stimulating germ which will enable him to progress until he attains the ultimate object for which he has been created—that is, the permanent happiness of his race.

But while man shall continue so undeveloped in his rational faculties as to degrade the Great Universal Spirit of Creation by attributing to it the present weakness and failings of humanity, very little progress can be made in a knowledge of our nature, or towards the permanent happiness of our race.

Men somewhat in advance of ordinary minds would deem themselves degraded were it imagined that they could consent to make machines, if they possessed the power, to worship, to praise, or to attempt to flatter them. To suppose that the Great Moving Spirit of the Universe should create beings for this purpose would be to give to God the attributes of inferior humanity.

The first rational step towards human wisdom, goodness, and happiness for our race, will be to abandon all ideas of worship, of praise or flattery of God, on the conviction that God can and will do, in the due order of creation, everything that, ultimately, is to make all humanity good, wise, united, and happy. And also that man, the created, cannot do a particle of good to the Power who or which created him.

Let men then cease contending about the attributes of an Eternal Existence of which they know nothing, and which cannot in any manner be effected by their puerile imaginations. Instead of which, let the advanced minds of the age pause, and ask themselves —" Do we understand the laws of nature " which are inherent in humanity, and which are evidently " the laws of the Great Creating Spirit of the Universe?"

The reply must convict them of ignorance of themselves, or of direct opposition to the laws of God.

For these laws of humanity declare that God has so created man that he *must* believe in accordance with the strongest conviction made on his mind, and that for this belief he can have no merit or demerit. And, again, that he *must* like and

dislike, love and hate, according to the organisation forced
upon him without his consent or knowledge, and that for thus
liking or disliking, loving or hating, man can have no merit.

Should the question be now asked—" Do the advanced and
" ruling minds of this age obey or disobey these laws of God?"
The reply must be " they disobey them."

They not only disobey them, but they make and enforce
laws in direct opposition to those unchanging laws of God,
and they thereby introduce innumerable unnecessary errors,
contentions, and sufferings, among the population of the
world, and make the language of truth impossible.

Instead of absurd ceremonies, intended for worship, useless
praise, and puerile flattery, all combined meaning nothing
rational,—let the laws of God be obeyed, and man will become
a superior happy being.

ROBERT OWEN.

THE FIRST MEETING OF THE NATIONAL ASSOCIA-
TION FOR THE PROMOTION OF SOCIAL SCIENCE.

THIS is the most advanced association which as yet been established, and it will prove of the highest importance to the future
permanent progress and happiness of the civilised world.

The first step for the first time has now been taken by the
governing and most influential class, commencing with the
British statesmen of the most advanced minds of the three
great contending political parties.   These noblemen and gentlemen have thus come forward to establish an open association
for all parties, for the free investigation of truth, when supported
by facts, to develope Social Science in principle and practice,
for the improvement and elevation of the working classes, and
thus to raise them from ignorance, poverty, and consequent
degradation and crime.

The men who have done this will have their names remembered through future ages as the best friends of humanity.

It is true the association has only taken the first step, but it
has taken that step well, in the right spirit, and in the right
direction.

And it appears that the three contending political parties have
chosen the men best calculated to conduct the association pru-
dently through its preliminary difficulties, and in such manner
as to satisfy all experienced intelligent parties who understood
the variety of opposing small views which they had to conciliate
and to unite for the general good.

As a proof of the fairness and fulness of the views of the council and committee who selected the papers which were to be read in the several sections,—two out of the five papers which I sent to the general Secretary of the Association were selected and read ;—No. 1, on *Social Science ;"* and No. 3, on *" The Human Race governed without punishment."*

The selection of these two Papers out of· the five, ιι once convinced me that the directing minds of the association were honest and sincere in their search for valuable and important truths, when consistent in themselves and in accordance with all facts.

The reading of these two papers must convince all who reflect on what they read, that the association is prepared to examine all statements, however startling they may at first appear, or from whatever source they may emanate.

It is but just in me to state, that the proceedings throughout the session of five days were so open, impartial, and liberal to all parties, that they greatly exceeded my most sanguine expectations on this occasion, and anything that I expected to witness during my life.

These proceedings are indeed the sure sign that the good time is coming, and that its commencement is near, and is not, as many suppose, afar off.

ROBERT OWEN.

London, Jermyn Street,
   October, 18th, 1857.

SPIRITUAL SOCIALISM IN TEXAS AND MEXICO—
A LETTER ADDRESSED TO ROBERT OWEN BY
R. B. HANNAY, OF CYPRUS TOP, HARRIS CO.,
TEXAS.

Cyprus Top, 28th *May*, 1857.

ROBERT OWEN, ESQ., LONDON.

MY DEAR SIR,

At our spiritual circles in Texas for some time past we have been directed by the spirits to investigate the principles of association, for the purpose of forming an association in Western Texas next Spring. The subject has taken hold of some advanced and vigorous minds, and a party of gentlemen will go west this Summer to explore the country, and there is every appearance from communications which we have received from socialists in the north, (where it appears they have had the same kind of spiritual communications,) that there will be a great many spiritualists and socialists at Galveston this winter, and that an important move will be made.

The spirits assure us that there are a sufficient number of advanced minds now in the world to make a successful beginning. Visions have been seen by mediums, from Maine to Texas, of the buildings of the association, and they are represented to be magnificent. Only those who are spiritualists and in interior harmony should be permitted to join ; and the object of my writing you is to open a communication with our English brethren on that subject, and to urge some who have the means, if any, to pay a visit to Galveston this winter,—where they will be welcomed.

I am a merchant and have to write in the distraction and interruption of a crowd in a country store. I am therefore unable to put my ideas into shape, and must write to you without any order. I have no time to do otherwise. I will therefore state that it is the spiritual communications at our circles which have stirred us up to think on this matter. I have seen a young man who will get up in the unconscious state, take a quire of blank paper, and read a most beautiful lecture, (professed to be from the spirit Swedenborg,) on association. Spirit wisdom would guide us, he said ;—spirit hands would aid us to build our buildings. We would hear music which mortal ear never heard ;—and by obeying the laws of harmony, would be filled with an interior delight which never had been felt.

They also impressed on us the idea that they could teach us laws of nature which would enable us to control the weather, —and that by organisation we could produce ten or twenty fold the wealth which we can now produce.

The occupation of the valley of the Rio Grande, the reception and spiritualisation of the poor and destitute of the world, and the establishment of a Great Spiritual Empire on the table lands of Mexico, which should in time revolutionise the world, seemed also to be the impression made on most of us. And it so happens, fortunately, that several of those most strongly interested are large land owners in that portion of the country—the door to the interior of Mexico, and that there are no physical obstacles in the way.

We see that society is in an inverted state ; that no man ever did or ever will gain any advantage over another which he will not have to repay, principle and interest, by the operation of the law of eternal justice or compensation ; and that we only have what we give, not what we reap ; that therefore in our present state of society we are toiling to heap up wrath against ourselves. As we become more *en rapport* with high spirits, and more sensitive to spiritual influences, the way we live becomes more and more unbearable. I find this to be the case with all those who have sat at circles for two or three years, and we must as a matter of necessity attempt a new system; for we cannot much longer live as we do now.

Our ideas as to the details of organisation are very crude and imperfect. We consider that practice and experiment alone can determine. But as to the general principles, the idea is, to cultivate all our faculties in harmony.

Every one will thus do his duty; and in that case every one able would supply himself with the necessaries of life in the field or the workshop, and would not deprive others of the time necessary for their moral, spiritual, and intellectual development. It requires labour to develop—to give stamina to body and mind.

In the first or material sphere there should be exact justice or reciprocation;—which principle contains all the higher and undeveloped; and this it appears can be be best carried out by—cost the limit of price.

You will see from this we want to throw overboard the lawyer, money-lender, banker, merchant, doctor, priest. The man must not lean on those expensive props. He must be thrown on his own resources, and stand alone.

We want those to join with us who have passed the Rubicon of selfishness—who have something of the heroic in them, and are willing to work for humanity, or, I should rather say, who are devoted to that work.

Although I have little respect for the fashionable drawing-room lady, yet I could fall down on my knees and worship the elegant and refined lady in a kitchen, working for humanity or a principle. Strong arms and true hearts would be there to help her.

I will also mention that most of us are successful men of business, and able to contend with the world; and it is not helplessness nor want which has directed our minds to this subject.

I am informed that several in the north have sold out their property by spirit direction, and are waiting with funds to make a beginning; but money is not of so much consequence to us, as the right kind of people.

I have expressed myself very imperfectly and have written so far, merely to give you an insight, however imperfect, into our views;—knowing well that you understand those matters better than I do.

Col. Ebenezer Allen of Galveston, an eminent lawyer there, is one of the principals in this move.

If yourself or others should answer me, he will correspond with you on the subject. In the mean time,

I remain, yours respectfully,

R. B. HANNAY.

P.S. Since writing the inclosed I may as well state that the country where we expect to locate is hardly settled. We are informed that land there can be purchased for from three to five hundred dollars per league of 4428 acres ; and on the other side of the Rio Grande for one hundred dollars per league.

Ebenezer Allen has a league over the Rio Grande, which will be devoted to that purpose if suitable.

One spiritualist owns 100,000 acres in the very part indicated by the spirits.

My friend Henry Allen is endeavouring to exchange 100,000 acres of Brazzos land, for land there; and others will do the same. At present it is an Indian country ; but a farmer here, who intends to join, and who is a medium, and a great hunter, and who is taken possession of by Indian spirits, says they tell him that the Indians there are spiritualists, and that they will be our best friends.

Some of us are slave owners ; but slavery will not be carried into the association. Although slavery is considered best for the Negro in our present organisation of society, yet it is not so in the new. As society is at present constituted, it is a protection to him ; but in the new, slavery would introduce discord—and we expect machinery to be our slaves.

A party of men headed by spiritualists went to Northern Texas hunting for gold three years ago, and they saw some beautiful valleys. In one, the valley of the Sacramento, (one hundred miles long and from two to four miles broad—a beautiful clear stream running through the whole length of it, one hundred feet wide, knee deep, and full of fish, and with a descent which would turn a mill every 40 yards,) they found strawberries, raspberries, peaches, cherries, and many other fruits, growing in vast quantities. There were high mountains on each side covered with timber,—the tops covered with snow around the valley, any quantity of minerals, lead ore, plaster of Paris, silver ore, marble, &c, &c., Deer, antelope, bears, in great number :—I cannot tell half of what they told me. Their health was so much improved I scarcely knew them. They left here yellow and dyspeptic ; and returned with the blood almost bursting out of their rosy complexions. Several have sold out and returned, but I have not heard of them since.

The spiritualists aim at occupying that as one of their homes or associations some day, with some other valleys, particularly as by law each family who settles there can have a pre-emption right to 160 acres of land. I would draw the attention of the English socialists to this ; and if one or two delegates will pay us a visit at Galveston next winter, every information will be given them. Those valleys are principally in New Mexico—the part ceded to the United States, and perhaps the greatest mineral country in the world, as well as the healthiest.

There were vegetables of enormous size, particularly onions; but when they planted the seed here, they grew no larger than any of our seeds.

They found a tribe of Apaches in the centre of the valley, who were very friendly.

Victor Considerant's association is succeeding. Although many have left, yet their places have been more than supplied by others from France; and he is now, I am told, contracting for 300,000 acres of land north of the city of Austin, for a large colony of French Socialists; and it appears to me that the foundation is laid in this State for a social revolution in time. And I cannot help being impressed with the idea, that it will be of importance to English Socialists and Spiritualists, to direct their attention to this country, and I do not see any other part of the world so well adapted to making a permanent beginning in effecting a social revolution in the world.

I will shortly write to S. P. Andrews of New York—author of "*The Science of Society*," to communicate with you on that subject. I have had a correspondence with him; and he amongst others will be at Galveston this winter.

We do not expect to make a beginning before the spring of the next year, and we want only men who are actuated by the loftiest and purest motives to associate with us at first—men whose highest ambition is to progress—to climb the steep heights of goodness and truth—greater heroes than those who can march to the cannon's mouth. We want experienced mechanics and men of science; men who can create wealth with a clear field before them.

Let it be clearly tested once, and successfully, and thousands are prepared to unite.

The Spirits say they are impressing men's minds to that effect.

I cannot say half of what I wish to say:—if you have an interest in this, you will write to me.

I remain, &c.,

R. B. HANNAY.

[The idea of individual sovereignty mentioned in the preceding letter, is opposed to nature, and is impracticable. Man is individualised and unsocial, while ignorant, inexperienced, and irrational. When the time arrives for him to be made rational, he will become eminently a superior social being. R. OWEN.]

CONCLUSION OF THIS PUBLICATION.

SINCE the previous articles were put into type, the printer informs me that a few pages more are required to complete the last sheet, and I desire to add that which will be of everlasting benefit to my poor deluded fellow men, who are so severely suffering from erroneous teaching and non-attention to the most obvious facts which have existed through all ages to the present day.

As soon as the population of this country can be taught how to overcome the strong prejudices of gross errors forced upon all from birth, not excluding any class or individuals of any rank or condition, and can be thus enabled to examine facts, past and present, to compare them accurately, and to deduce just conclusions from them, the most obvious of existing errors will be the total disregard of our ancestors, through the previous history of our race to this day, of the influences of circumstances, or of the effects of the surroundings in which all are placed from birth.

Attention to this subject would at any former period have stayed the evils which have been experienced by mankind, and would have put them in the path to become, without chance of failure, *rational, good, wise,* and *happy*. For the means have always existed, increasing through every succeeding generation, to effect these results, had the science of surroundings been known, and its application to practice understood.

Wealth for all would have been easily produced in abundance; union among the race easily effected; the spirit of universal love and charity would have been made to pervade all hearts and minds; and long since the earth would have been made a highly cultivated terrestrial paradise, inhabited by one brotherhood of full formed superior men and women, living in accordance with the laws of their nature, and all actively engaged in promoting each other's happiness, and knowing the true principles and action by which to attain it.

The British population is, in many respects, the most advanced practical nation, and it is perhaps in a better position at this day to make in peace and by wise foresight a yet greater advance than any other people.

I well know how difficult it is to move my countrymen out of their beaten track of error; but when this can be done, I know also how ardently they will pursue an improvement, when it can be made obvious to them that that which is proposed for their adoption is a real improvement.

In consequence, this population has at length, after years

of repeated reiteration of the influence of circumstances over human nature, been aroused by the no longer bearable bad circumstances in which so large a portion of it has been and is now placed, to make an infant commencement to try the effects upon the previously worst placed of this population, by removing it into somewhat better surroundings; and for this purpose it has become almost the fashion to patronise ragged schools and reformatory institutions—thus making the most puerile attempts to acquire some knowledge of the overwhelming power, for good, of the science of surroundings, when understood over the human race.

But these puerile attempts so slightly to improve the condition of the most ill-placed are already abundantly sufficient to prove the great truths,

1st. That as is the organisation of man, and as are his surroundings from birth, so must the individual become.

2nd. That through this knowledge, fully understood and applied to practice, the worst or the best character may be forced upon every one of our race.

3rd. That the surroundings are now known and could be easily applied by all people and governments, to force from birth a good and superior character upon every one.

4th. That it is now especially the interest of all of our race, that a good and superior character should be forced upon every child from birth.

5th. That this character might be easily given to all, by placing them from birth within surroundings which may now gradually be formed for the population of every country.

6th. That there is now a vast superfluity of dead and living capital to create these new surroundings, in comparatively a short time, in all nations and among all people; but more immediately in the British dominions and in those of the United States.

But in both these rich, powerful, and extensive empires, the metropolis of each (London and New York,) exhibits at this day a compound of the worst surroundings to promote health and goodness that could be well combined and hustled together, without foresight, knowledge of human nature, or common-sense observance of common facts.

These ragged schools, reformatory institutions, and every well-conducted experiment to improve humanity by placing it within improved surroundings, are sufficient to demonstrate that as are the surroundings—bad, indifferent, or good—so will be the children, men, and women, placed within them.

Now the conditions of London and New York are long since too far gone for any substantial improvement to be effected to make the surroundings in either sufficient to form, maintain, or retain, a rational population. All attempts to improve either will be time, talent, labour, and capital, wasted ; and the various expensive plans proposed to be adopted to diminish in a small part some of the worst evils now suffered in both capitals, will avail little to remedy them.

The same labour, capital, and talent, applied to create new surroundings on new sites, gradually to draw off the population of these already greatly over-crowded cities, would effect an hundred fold more benefit ; and if made with a knowledge of the science of the influences of surroundings, and how in the best manner to apply the science to practice, the permanent advantages of such change would be beyond estimate.

For not only are very large cities very evil surroundings, but all towns and villages, with streets, lanes, courts, and alleys, and all such arrangements of dwellings, are bad and inferior, on account of their injurious influences upon their inhabitants, when compared with the scientific surroundings which may now be made for human habitations all over the world.

By the change of system, from the false in principle and irrational in practice, the existing cities, towns, villages, and isolated dwellings, would gradually and peaceably disappear from the earth, and be universally superseded by convenient magnificent palaces, amidst gardens, orchards, and highly cultivated pleasure fields and groves, all made to have the best influences upon all of our race.

These palaces would be erected to accommodate in a very superior manner from two to three thousand souls, and with every requisite, by their well-directed exercise, physical and mental, to maintain themselves in the highest state of comfort and of superior existence, in perpetuity, and in cordial union with the human race.

And in this new rational existence, with these new surroundings, wars, conflicts, contests, or disunion of any description, would be unknown over the earth, and peace and harmony among men would be universal and everlasting.

These ever-to-be-desired results are to be accomplished to their full extent by the most simple means, based on truths which may now be made obvious even to children before they are twelve years old.

And it is the high permanent interest of governments and people, that these surroundings should be immediately commenced in all countries.

To effect this change in the condition of humanity, no sacrifice can be too great.

It would be cheaply purchased by the lives, not only of thousands, but of myriads.

And it might be accomplished with the sacrifice of few lives, and in a comparatively short period, by a few determined men and women, having sufficient wisdom and moral courage to live passively opposed, even to death, to all human being' and obstructions—to live a natural life of truth, love, and charity, and by their own well-directed physical and mental powers.

For man to attain this superior state of existence upon earth, he must be taught to comprehend, in spirit, principle, and practice.

1.—Pure, undefiled Christianity,—which is love and charity in practice for our race.

2.—Socialism in its full extent, without which Christianity cannot be introduced or maintained in practice, to enable as to love our neighbours as ourselves.

3. Spiritualism, rationally used to obtain from superior Spirits consistent knowledge how best to regenerate the present population of the world, and to unite all as one family, speaking only the language of truth, and living upon earth, as far as practicable, as they do in heaven.

Undeveloped men and women may continue to talk and to act at random, without compass or rudder to guide their thoughts or direct their actions to be consistent with each other or in accordance with facts; but by so doing they will never attain wisdom, unity, goodness, or happiness.

The road to good and to evil is now opened to all. Who will now prefer the evil and reject the good.

Having now said all that I have to say on the means by which to give permanent happiness to the human race,—my mission is ended; and this number will terminate the publication of the *Millennial Gazette;* and I trust that sooner or later it will accomplish the object for which it was commenced.

ROBERT OWEN.

Sevenoaks, September, 5th, 1857.

SECOND CONCLUSION.

I had, as I imagined, concluded the publication of my Millennial Gazette by the preceding article, when to my high gratification I was informed of the announcement that the " *National Association for the Promotion of Social Science*" would be inaugurated in Birmingham on the 12th of October—a glorious and auspicious day for the future permanent peace and happiness of the human race.

Until this ever-to-be-remembered announcement was made to the public by the leading British statesmen of all parties, little did I imagine that the seed which I had sown half a century ago and had daily cultivated and watered with the unceasing care of an anxious, cautious, and careful planter, had put forth such strong roots while in the earth and hidden from the cheering sun of public aid and encouragement; and still less did I suppose that it had made such vigorous shoots upwards as to defy the assault of the groveling and petty insects of the earth, the birds of the air, and the most savage beasts of prey.

But the proceedings during the conferences of this new-born wonder-working association in Birmingham have made these results certain, and the " Social Science" will henceforth be openly acknowledged to be, as it is, the *science* of *sciences*—the science which shall direct to the certain, easy, pleasant, practical, and peaceable means, by which through futurity to well-place, feed, clothe, lodge, train, educate, employ, unite, and govern, the human race.

Many will now ask—" Is it possible that this can be done?" I fearlessly answer that it may be done, and that with the open aid of the patrons and leaders of this new national association it may be commenced with the certainty of rapid progress to ultimate full success.

Do the Lords Brougham, John Russell, Stanley, and Lyttelton, the Bishop of London, Sir John Packington, Sir Benjamin Brodie, and the Recorder of Birmingham, desire to know how this great work can be legititimately commenced and successfully pursued? The path is clear.

I will petition both Houses of Parliament to appoint committees or commissions to examine the spirit, principle, and practice, which constitute Social Science in its outline and in all its details.

Or perhaps, yet better, to examine me on these matters at the bar of both Houses; because by this means all the members of the public will the more speedily learn the all-importance of this science for the practice of all people and nations.

The permanent progressive prosperity and happiness of the human race are now in the hands of the noblemen and gentlemen whom I have named, and of the British Parliament; and if there is sufficient wisdom and moral courage in these parties to pursue with persevering vigour the measures now proposed, they will soon terminate the present erroneous waste of the higher faculties of humanity, of the best feelings of our nature, of incalculable wealth, and means for its increase, of human blood, and of the certain means of universal happiness in perpetuity for our race.

———

I am just now informed that some parties interested in the success of these measures have decided to publish a weekly paper to instruct all parties in a knowledge of their own interests, by a full development of this science of sciences, now so little known, but so important to be known by all.

For the communication thus made to me, I beg leave in return to offer the following advice.

Let it be not connected with any party, class, or sect.

Let the spirit of universal love and charity, for all parties, classes, and sects, pervade the paper from its commencement through its entire progress; and without being turned aside from this course by the uninformed or deluded of any sect, class, or party.

Treat all your opponents with courtesy and consideration; knowing that, unfortunately for themselves, they have been from birth, not owing to their own fault, mis-placed, mis-trained, mis-educated, and mis-guided, as well as mis-governed. They will therefore really require your sympathy and pity, instead of anger or sharp rebuke.

And especially let all which you advance originate from the true first principle of society that " the character of man is formed *for* him;" and let every sentence be consistent with this divine truth; and then what you write and advocate will be of necessity in accordance with all facts, and you need fear no opponent,—for you have thus the sure criterion of truth to direct you always aright.

The all-important truth which I have so long endeavoured to teach the world—" that the character of man is formed *for* him," and without a knowledge of which, applied to every-day practice, Christianity must for ever remain a dead letter, may now be more fully explained as follows:—

" The *made* receives all its qualities and powers from its " Maker. The *created* receives all its qualities and powers from " its Creator."

Now that this first great and glorious step has been taken by the leading statesmen of the age, it will be seen how much longer the inhabitants of this planet will continue to prefer falsehood to truth,—ignorance to knowledge,—folly to wisdom, —poverty to wealth,—disunion to union,—wars to peace,—injurious and bad passions to beneficial and good feelings,—universal inconsistency to universal consistency,—universal action in opposition to facts, to universal action in accordance with facts,—universal counteraction to universal agreement,—and, consequently, irrationality to rationality and misery to happiness.

November 1st, 1857.   ROBERT OWEN.

THE ROYAL CONSORT'S SCHOOLS FOR ALL CLASSES.

AFTER this work was concluded, and while printing off, I visited the new establishment forming by the government, and aided by and under the patronage of the Royal Consort of the Crown of the British Empire.

Are the subjects of the British Empire at all conscious of what the Prince Consort and the government have already done for and are doing for them, have in fact done for all nations and all peoples?—No, they are not; their minds have not yet been trained and instructed to comprehend the truth, the value, and the magnificence of the ideas and combination of ideas, so beautifully, yet so quietly and unostentatiously given to the British people, and placed thus before the world for its inspection, admiration, example, and benefit.

When that which has been and which is now in progress of being done, shall be received into the minds of the public understandingly, they will know that a government for the first time in its records from its commencement has taken the first right step in practice in the right direction, and has thereby done more for the human race than all the heroes of war, who have murdered man, destroyed his property, and made his progeny beggars and miserable.

The Prince Consort and the government have fairly commenced to re-create the British mind by

E

so openly and liberally creating the most useful and
valuable influences to act upon it, under the best
conceived and most beautiful arrangements. All who
can appreciate the magnificence of the conceptions
now in progress in this new and greatest wonder of
world for the permanent benefit of mankind, will be
enabled to judge of the fortunate wisdom, of a mind
then so young, when her Majesty chose for her
Royal Consort Prince Albert.

And all classes in all nations will hereafter have
cause to bless the day when that union was ratified ;
but more especially the British population, from the
highest nobles to the lowest in mind and station,
whose ignorance and sufferings the results of this, apparently from the silence of the Press, unheeded
magical establishment will speedily put the public in
the way effectually to remove.

SUGGESTED BY READING TO-DAY OF THE MONEY PANIC.

IF the British public now possesses any practical common sense, it will take advantage of the present
financial confusion in the general affairs of life to
stay the absurdity of man being made the slave of
metals. And it will now, without loss of more time,
elevate the Bank of England to become the Bank of
the British Empire, based on the credit of the whole
wealth of that Empire, and then there will be no more
money panics or bankruptcies, but progressive prosperity to all. And let the New Bank at once issue

also one pound notes. Then could the British public and the government give and secure to all who required it, perpetual, highly remunerative, and most valuable employment.

Whatever any parties may now think, both these measures will be soon required for the safety and benefit of all.

Is real wealth created by man being idle or well-employed?

ROBERT OWEN.

London, Nov. 5th, 1857.

P.S.—In my haste to give an account in this publication of the Royal Consort's New Schools for all classes, I forgot to mention my satisfaction and pleasure while in the midst of my wonder at all I so unexpectedly saw around, to perceive a number of charity looking children passing me with gay and cheerful expressions of countenance. I asked one of the superintendents who was near me, how those children were there? "They are the children of schools for the " poor." But how admitted? I paid sixpence. "They " are admitted on these days free of expense."

And thus, with an intelligent leader for a teacher, may these poor children acquire far more useful knowledge in one day in these schools, than they could attain in any time in the present ordinary day schools.

ROBERT OWEN.

Registered for Foreign Transmission.

ROBERT OWEN'S
MILLENNIAL GAZETTE;

EXPLANATORY OF THE PRINCIPLES AND PRACTICES BY WHICH, IN PEACE, WITH TRUTH, HONESTY, AND SIMPLICITY, THE NEW EXISTENCE OF MAN UPON THE EARTH MAY BE EASILY AND SPEEDILY COMMENCED.

"The character of Man is formed *for* him, and *not by* him."

No. 14.]   FEBRUARY 10, 1858.   [PRICE 6D.

A LETTER

ADDRESSED TO THE POTENTATES OF THE EARTH, IN WHOM THE HAPPINESS AND MISERY OF THE HUMAN RACE ARE NOW INVESTED ; BUT ESPECIALLY TO AUSTRIA, FRANCE, GREAT BRITAIN, PRUSSIA. RUSSIA, SARDINIA, TURKEY, AND THE UNITED STATES OF NORTH AMERICA ; BECAUSE THESE POWERS ARE NOW AT PEACE WITH EACH OTHER, AND COULD, WITHOUT WAR, EASILY INDUCE ALL THE OTHER GOVERNMENTS AND PEOPLE TO UNITE WITH THEM IN PRACTICAL MEASURES FOR THE GENERAL GOOD OF ALL THROUGH FUTURITY.

POTENTATES, AND AT PRESENT ARBITERS OF THE HAPPINESS OR MISERY OF THE POPULATION OF THE WORLD ;—

You live in the period when, through the progress of physical and mental science, the past has prepared all the materials and means in superabundance to well-feed, clothe, lodge, train, educate, employ, amuse, and govern the human race in perpetual progressive prosperity,—without war, conflict, or competition, between nations or individuals.

All things are ready prepared to effect these results under your united control and direction.

All that the human race requires, to secure permanently its health and happiness, is to be peaceably well educated, and to be continually well-employed or occupied, alternately physically and mentally, but never over exercised in either respect.

Or, in other words, that all the faculties and powers of each shall through life be exercised up to, but never below or above, the point of temperance for each faculty, propensity, and power of humanity,—all of them being good, and all necessary to be so exercised.

But before this change can be accomplished, so much to be desired by all parties, you will be required to make scientific arrangements to well-place all, in such manner that all shall be well-trained, educated, and employed, physically and mentally, through life.

By your union for the purpose, these results may now, for the first time in the history of the world, be accomplished. And accomplished with far less difficulty and in less time than will be imagined, provided you adopt the only true course that can be pursued.

That course is—

Now to base society on its natural foundation, and to construct it in all its parts to be consistent with that foundation.

You will now naturally enquire—" what is this new founda-" tion, which can effect such magical results as you state ?"

It is a foundation in accordance with *all facts* from the beginning of time,—opposed by no *one fact* through the entire history of man,—ever in accordance with itself and with all nature,—and therefore true, beyond all rational contradiction. It is—

" That the maker of anything, gives to the made all its made " qualities and powers.

" That the Great Creating Power of the Universe gives to " all things created, the created qualities and powers which they " possess.

" That the maker and the creator, being the sole authors of " these qualities and powers, are alone responsible for them and " their actions during their existence."

You have been taught from your birth that the character of man could not be well-formed on this foundation, and that society could not be well-constructed or well-governed on this natural base, in accordance with all nature. But you might with more ease have been taught from your birth to believe the reverse to be true ; because it is much more easy to teach truth and to continue that instruction, than to teach falsehood and continue it ; and because truth is always consistent with itself, and falsehood, never.

It is for this reason that the present falsely based system of society for forming the characters of men and governing them is so grossly inconsistent in every department of life, and through every ramification in every department,—making society to be, as it is, one mass of contradictions, and a Babel of confusion, highly injurious to every one of our race. And especially is it injurious to all, by making a language of falsehood and conduct of deception a necessity upon all humanity.

Should your minds be now sufficiently opened and expanded to perceive the ALL IMPORTANCE of basing society on its natural and true foundation,—that is, " That the Creator not " only gives, but forces on the created all the qualities and powers " which it possesses or can acquire ;"—on this natural base the false language of men will be changed to the language of unde-viating truth, in look, word, and action ; their conduct of decep-tion, to that of undeviating honesty and open frank sincerity ; and their repulsive feelings to individuals and nations, to attrac-tive feelings to all humanity.

You will perhaps say " We do not comprehend these new ideas " and new combinations of ideas. They are to us as a new lan-" guage, untaught and therefore unknown to us."

This is quite natural as you have all been trained, educated, and placed, through your lives, amidst surroundings all produc-ing false and most injurious influences upon each of you.

And these evil results must continue until new surroundings shall be discovered and brought to act upon you, which shall pro-duce true and beneficial influences sufficiently powerful to over-come the false and injurious.

For years past I have been constantly engaged in preparing the means to admit of the introduction of such surroundings as should influence you to perceive the truth and its illimitable be-neficial results on yourselves, your families, and upon the human race in perpetuity.

To a certain extent I have so far succeeded ; and if you will now agree among yourselves to call a Congress of the leading governments of the world, inviting those of China, Japan, Burmah, &c., and to meet in London in May next, I will, should I live in my present health to that period, unfold to you at that Congress the natural means by which you may now, with ease and pleasure, gradually create those surroundings in peace and harmony, which shall have a perpetual good and superior in-fluence upon all of our race.

And the present most disordered and unsatisfactory system of society over the world shall gradually terminate, and cease for ever. And a new state of rational existence for men shall arise,. when truth, peace, harmony, perpetual prosperity, and happiness shall reign triumphant to the end of time upon the earth.

For no truth can be more true, or more important for man to fully comprehend, than this : —

" That the Great Creating Power of the Universe creates all " the organisations of men ; that as are these organisations, and " as are the surroundings in which the organisations are placed, " so, by the laws of their nature, must men become."

ROBERT OWEN.

Sevenoaks Park, 24th Nov. 1857.

LETTER

TO THE GOVERNED OF ALL CLASSES IN ALL NATIONS.

FRIENDS, CITIZENS, AND FELLOW SUBJECTS,—

You live in a period productive of more and higher events than have occurred in any former age, and yet these, great and important as they are, will ere long be known only as the necessary prelude to those of a character far greater, higher, and more important to the population of the world.

The industry of former ages, and the progress of science applied to practice in the present age, have prepared, in the most ample manner, all the means requisite to gradually attain and secure the future permanent happiness of our race

And as soon as you can acquire the necessary calmness, foresight, and practical knowledge to apply these means for this purpose, a commencement of this happy future may be made ; and a beneficial progress might be attained, by wise action on your parts, before the termination of the year 1858.

But to accomplish this result, the example must be made by the governed classes in the British dominions, as being the most favourably situated or surrounded to perform this task.

And I now more especially address myself to the sound thinking English, Irish, Scotch, and Welch, and of these Islands, being the centre and scene of government and of mental activity.

1st. You must openly abandon the absurd notion that the created can by possibility create one of its own qualities or powers, or be rationally made responsible for their actions.

This, when understood, will withdraw anger and all uncharitableness from man to man over the world, and will pervade all with the pure spirit of love and charity for all of our race, and will open the path to unite all by a universal principle and feeling of sympathy, which will make all to love their neighbours as themselves, and their enemies during the short space that there can be any enemies after this fundamental principle shall become general.

It is not by making men responsible for the actions of qualities and powers which they did not and could not create, that they can be made to become rational, good, wise, or happy.

This ever-to-be-desired result can be attained only by training and educating all to know that they are irresponsible for their feelings, thoughts, and motives to action ; and by society thus thinking and acting to all humanity, all could with ease be made from birth to have good and kind feelings, true and always consistent thoughts, and motives to perform the best actions only for the highest permanent happiness of our race, and to have the most merciful rational sympathy with all that has sensitive life.

2nd. You must no longer remain the blind, ignorant, and groveling slaves of metals; but, during the change from all that is false and wrong to all that is true and right, you must have a rational circulating medium, to represent the wealth which, when unrestricted by an insane gold and silver circulation, could be created with ease and pleasure to all, abundantly for all at all times, without the gross irrationality of money panics or any fear of them.

You must have the private banking company of the Bank of England to cease banking on their own account; all parties connected with it being fully compensated, and the present directors made to become, from their experience, the first directors of the National Bank of the British Empire, based on the credit of the fixed real and personal property of the empire, and in which all British subjects would be partners to the extent of their interest in the empire—the notes of this bank being made a legal tender by parliament throughout the British dominions. Branches to be everywhere established where they may be required; all private banking to cease for ever; the present private bankers to be made, as far as practicable, officers in the branch banks of the bank of the British Empire.

This bank and all its branches to purchase and keep as much gold and silver in each of these establishments as are ever likely to be wanted for real use when not attainable in the common marts of the world.

When other people and governments shall follow this example, as they soon will, these so-called precious metals will soon find their intrinsic values, which are below those of iron and steel. They will always be cheap and abundant, and man will be no longer the senseless slave of metals.

So long as the British Empire shall maintain its present rank among nations, the credit of this bank will remain undoubted.

Funds may be thus easily supplied to terminate the war in India rationally and beneficially for both parties and for the world. And all will admit that the present mode of governing India is the most irrational that could be devised to well-govern one hundred and fifty millions of human beings.

Arrangements could also be made with ease gradually to discharge annually an increasing amount of the national debt, and in such manner that none should remain at the termination of this century.

The profits of this national bank should go far towards paying the expenses of government.

This change in the currency and banking system of this empire would soon terminate poverty and all fear of it.

The next great evil to be overcome is—

3rd. The want of permanent beneficial employment for the working classes and for all who desire to be advantageously occupied.

Under the present system this can never be attained; while under the true and rational system which I am now proposing to you, everlasting good and most beneficial employment and occupation, physical and mental, may be easily provided for all who will desire them, and soon all will discover the many great advantages to themselves and to all others which they will experience by being so occupied. And in consequence of none of the working classes being forced to be idle, *real* wealth will be soon everywhere abundant.

The stupidity of forcing the working classes to be idle and to consume wealth, while more wealth is required which these forced to be-idle could, and if permitted would, easily produce, is equalled only by keeping persons idle, and distressing more or less all who are engaged in manufacturing and commercial pursuits, for want of the pernicious, called precious, metals.

It is the first duty now of all governments to find constant and beneficial employment for all the working classes; and this may easily be done by placing society on its true base, and making all things consistent with that solid foundation.

No government that is incompetent to find good perpetual employment for the working classes in such manner that in return for it they shall be well-placed, fed, clothed, lodged, trained, educated, amused, and governed, ought any longer to be allowed by the people to govern them.

4th. You require, as the second great duty of government, to have, united with the arrangements to insure perpetual beneficial employment for all the working classes, other arrangements to secure from birth a good, useful, and valuable physical and mental character for everyone; which may now be also easily effected with the certainty of the laws of nature.

To have this character formed for all, and to have this employment found and arranged for all, are now become, by the progress of mental and material knowledge, the birthright of every child given to man by the Great All-wise Creating Power of the Universe; and these, with their necessary consequences, are all that humanity will ever require while upon the earth.

But, from the public proceedings which I notice in the newspapers, I fear you do not know what your real wants are, or how to ask your government for them in the proper manner to obtain what you ask.

Your birth-right is as good a formation of character as your born organisation will admit, and perpetual temperate employment, to beneficially produce wealth abundantly for all, and, in return for your physical and mental powers so trained and employed, to be well-fed, clothed, lodged, amused, and governed, by being well-placed within the natural surroundings to produce, with the certainty of a law of nature, all these most desirable results.

Therefore, instead of wasting so much money, talent, and

valuable time in seeking to obtain that which will prove to be of very little value,—ask in a proper manner from the government your full birth-right; and you will be certain to obtain it.

The government has already shown its inclination to precede your asking, by giving so splendid, beautiful, and useful an example of what may be done nationally towards the commencement of forming a superior character for the people of this country. The Educational Establishment of the Prince Consort at South Kensington is indeed a magnificent and noble Institution for the formation of character, opened to the public on the most easy terms and under excellent arrangements.

Were you prepared to hear and to comprehend, I could now say much more that is deeply for your interests and happiness; but I refrain in order to see the result upon your minds, feelings, and conduct, of that which I have now stated, as a new year's gift for 1858.

But, working men! Remember, that you want real wealth, that is, good feeding, clothing, dwellings, training, and education; and that these can be obtained only by permanent beneficial employment and occupation, physical and mental; and that this necessary exercise of your invaluable faculties, when rightly trained and used, cannot be attained until you shall be well-placed within those surroundings which can alone produce the possibility of acquiring the necessaries and comforts of life, to enable you to become goood, wise, and happy.

The first practical step to give you immediate constant employment and good wages in return for it, is the establishment of the bank of the British Empire, based on the credit of all British capital and property, real and personal. Obtain this, and the others will speedily follow.

And if you do not obtain it you will remain blind slaves to base metals; for, intrinsically, gold and silver are base metals, compared with the most precious metals of steel and iron.

By this simple change the real wealth of the British Empire could be rapidly increased more than twenty fold.

                                        ROBERT OWEN.

December 1857.

In order to develope this subject more completely, I add a Memorial which I intend to present to the Lords of Her Majesty's Treasury, and a Petition to both Houses of Parliament, to be presented at the re-assembling of Parliament in February, 1858.

MEMORIAL

TO THE RIGHT HONOURABLE THE LORDS OF HER MAJESTY'S TREASURY.

THE MEMORIAL OF ROBERT OWEN, LATE OF NEW LANARK, BUT NOW OF SEVENOAKS PARK, SEVENOAKS, KENT; JAN., 1858.

SHOWETH ;—

That your Memorialist has devoted a long life to the study from facts of the laws of human nature and the construction of society as it has existed under its various forms, at different periods, in the same and in other countries, opposed in religion, language, and government.

That he has discovered the origin of the errors on which the human-made part of the character of man has been based and society constructed at all times and among all people.

That this error has been fatal to the rationality and happiness of man over the earth, and to the true construction of society to produce permanent prosperity to all of our race.

That this fatal fundamental error has from birth destroyed the germ of the rational faculties and powers of humanity, and has given a false direction to all man's invaluable instincts, which are the laws of his nature and are amply sufficient to secure the well-being, well-doing, and permanent high happiness of all nations and peoples.

That your Memorialist, in looking back through the past history of humanity to the present hour under all its ever-changing forms, has seen that it has always denied the wisdom of nature's most beneficent laws, and endeavoured to counteract them by the puerile and futile conceptions of men calling themselves legislators—of men in every age totally ignorant of the most common (it might be supposed the most obvious) laws given to man by the Great Creating Power of the Universe, to give goodness, wisdom, and happiness in perpetuity to all of our race.

That, by men legislating in direct opposition to God's and nature's legislation, they have made all of our race through all time, arrant, ignorant, presumptuous fools, living in the midst of innumerable tribes of animals living in accordance with the laws and instincts given to them by their Creator and therefore much wiser and happier in reference to their respective natures than are any divisions of the human race in any part of the earth.

That your Memorialist has long known and deeply lamented this insanity of our race, and sought in all directions for a peaceable remedy that should not irritate and increase this malady, made now hereditary through so many thousand generations.

That your Memorialist has discovered the only remedy which can go to the root of this venomous evil, so deeply imbedded in the minds, manners, customs, and habits of all from birth through life.

That this sovereign remedy for the cure of error and of evil is " truth, without mystery, mixture of error, or fear of man" given openly, freely, and frankly to the population of the world, in the pure spirit of love and charity for our race, regardless of class, sect, party, country, colour, or any natural or acquired differences.

That the great truths which will break down and destroy the insanity of humanity may be advantageously stated in the following order.

1st.—That the Creator creates all the qualities and powers of the created, and is alone responsible for its actions, thoughts, and feelings, through life.

2nd. That to this period humanity has been passing through the infant or preliminary state of its existence upon earth, necessary, in the order of creation and progress, to enable man to acquire the experience, through error, suffering, and mental development, to know good and evil, that he might in due time enjoy supreme uninterrupted happiness.

3rd. That this period of infant ignorance, error, suffering, evil, and deficient experience, could not cease until humanity attained so much knowledge, by its gradual mental development, as to discover that it could not make one of its own qualities and powers, and that hitherto it has not known what is good or evil in man, and that during this necessary preliminary night of mental darkness all things have been in an effervescence of apparent confusion, when all things were called by wrong names, and men were blindly acting a forced part, the object and end of which they knew not and had not mental powers to divine.

4th. That the discovery of this great truth opens a new life to man, of goodness, wisdom, and happiness, which will speedily be uninterrupted in its progress.

5th. That this truth, which in its consequences is the greatest discovery ever made by man, will create the spirit and induce the practice of love and charity of man to man over the earth,. terminate the inferior and bad passions created only by error, and gradually make the human race in harmony with itself and all nature, when all from birth shall be placed, trained, educated, and governed, in accordance with the laws of our nature, and no longer as heretofore in opposition to those unchanging laws of God and nature, or of God in nature.

6th. That as a necessary consequence of this great discovery, all anger and ill-will from man to man will gradually cease over the earth, being obviously too irrational to be retained in this new mental state of existence; peace and good-will among men will become universal ; and harmony will be perpetual among all nations, tribes, and people.

That your Memorialist, an old experienced practical man in the affairs of this worn-out system of buying and selling for a monied profit, has deeply reflected upon the measures which may best be immediately adopted to commence this glorious change for all humanity, in the spirit, principle, and practice of conducting all the future affairs of humanity,—the change commencing in this country, when it will be speedily followed by all others.

That, first, to effect this change, a great increase of funds will be required by government, to terminate the present war in India, created solely by the ignorance of the old worn-out system by which it and the world have been so long attempted to be governed on wrong principles.

That these funds are to be naturally obtained by making the British Empire its own banker and the legitimate authorizer, and maker, and issuer, of a medium to circulate the real wealth which the British people, so aided, could so easily create in abundance sufficient for all their natural wants and desires.

That the change from the Chartered private Bank of England to the National British Bank should be effected in the following manner :—

The present share-holders of the Bank of England to be paid the full value of their shares by the National Bank of the British Empire.

The present machinery for conducting the Bank of England to be purchased by the new National Bank, and used for the latter.

The present directors and officers of the Bank of England to be continued and made directors and officers of the Bank of the British Empire, with adequate liberal salaries for the governor, deputy governor, and directors.

The bank notes of the British Empire to be made by law a legal tender throughout the British dominions, and they will soon become accepted as such by all commercial nations and peoples.

Every British subject to be a share-holder to the full extent of his property and personal interest, the National Bank being based on the national wealth and credit of the empire.

The new National Bank to always keep as much gold in its possession as will be found by experience to be required for any foreign purposes, which it is presumed will be seldom if ever required.

The present governor, deputy governor, and directors of the Bank of England to be the governor, deputy governor, and directors of the Bank of the British Empire for three years certain, to give time for the change from the one to the other to be calmly and well conducted by approved men of experience.

At the end of three years the House of Commons to elect the governor, deputy governor, and directors of the Bank of the British Empire, the present being eligible for re-election.

The House of Commons also to elect three auditors to make full quarterly reports to the nation, of the business and state of the bank.

Arrangements to be made by which the Bank of the British Empire shall gradually purchase and pay off the national debt,— which it will not be difficult in this manner to accomplish.

That your Memorialist, knowing that the British nation will make any sacrifice before it will abandon its power over the tribes of India, so long so unwisely governed for the interests of humanity, of India, and of this country, recommends the most grave attention of the present administration to this subject.

And seeing that the establishment of the National Bank of the British Empire, based on the credit of the British Empire, will immediately, in the most legitimate manner, supply funds sufficient to bring the present unnatural contest to the most speedy termination, it is necessary that the population of India and the populations of all civilised nations should know, when India shall be reconquered, how it is in future to be governed; and your Memorialist recommends the adoption of the following outline for this purpose.

1st. That India be made an empire or kingdom, under one of our young princes, with an upper and lower house of assembly, the members of both to be elected after the model of the United States.

2nd. That this empire or kingdom be hereditary, and the king or governor be assisted by a cabinet council not exceeding twelve, appointed by the crown, but made strictly responsible to the two houses of legislation for their proceedings.

3rd. That until the young sovereign shall attain the age of twenty-one, India shall be governed by the British Government, on the principles afterwards stated, and that when the sovereign shall have attained his majority, British rule shall cease, and a treaty of federation on equal terms be made between Great Britain and this new Indian government.

4th. That from the majority of the sovereign of India, its government shall be independent and self-supported, except being federatively united with Great Britain in peace and war and commerce.

5th. That, for a period to be fixed, the bank notes of the Bank of the British Empire shall be legal tenders in all payments; but as soon as the new Indian government shall be sufficiently established, it shall establish a Bank of the Indian Empire, based on the credit of India.

6th. That British subjects in India shall have all the rights of Indian subjects, while all Indian subjects shall have the full rights of British subjects throughout the British Empire.

7th. That the officers and soldiers employed to regain and to retain India until the Indian government can support itself, shall be entitled according to rank and service to certain portions of land in India—their proportions to be decided by the British Parliament.

8th. That the government of India shall be by British born subjects, until the sovereign shall be of age ; after which period the natives of India to have the full right of subjects, except to the high offices of government and to the two houses of assembly,—and to these also in ten years from the time when they give in their adhesion to the new government.

9th. That the directors of the East India Company and its shareholders be amply compensated for their present interests in the company ; but all their right to rule India to cease for ever.

10th. That during the period while the sovereign shall be attaining his twenty-first year, the British government shall take into its most grave consideration the best practical means, as the opportunity is so peculiarly favourable for the purpose, to arrange new surroundings in which to place the native subjects of the new Indian Empire while under British rule. These surroundings to be scientifically combined through a knowledge of the social science, in such manner as shall secure to all, by their own well-directed industry within those surroundings, the means by which they shall all, at all times, be well-fed, clothed, lodged, trained, educated, occupied, amused, and locally well governed by themselves ; all of which, with the knowledge now acquired of social science and of the origin of evil, may be by due foresight and wisdom easily accomplished, if set about in the true spirit of determination to succed in new measures.

That by thus adjusting the pecuniary affairs of this country, and by adopting the measures recommended for the adjustment of Indian affairs, the present government will have ample time to attend to the claims of British subjects to have these Islands now well governed, in accordance with the true principles of social science, and your Memorialist recommends the following measures to be immediately adopted.

As the mercantile, manufacturing, and trading interests will be at once relieved by the establishment of the Bank of the British Empire, they will be satisfied, and will be enabled to employ the now unemployed for want of work, and thus the floodgates to the creation of real wealth will be opened independent of any metal circulation.

Public attention has been long directed to a reform in Parliament as a panacea for all political evils, in which the expectants will be sadly disappointed, for it can effect no good or evil. A

Parliament elected by manhood suffrage, things remaining as they are, would make little or no change for the better to the working classes, but would create perhaps more useless debates on subjects little understood by the new debaters. It would, however, be wisdom in the government to bring in and pass a bill for reform on the most liberal conditions—however liberal it will be harmless, and it will prevent more waste of invaluable time.

As members elected to the House of Commons have been prejudiced from birth by their erroneous training, education, and surroundings, they can see and comprehend private interests only; they are unprepared to legislate for the general public good; and such would continue to be the case with the elected members under the full manhood suffrage. This result is demonstrated by the manhood elected members of the Congress of the United States, where an entire reform in the character and condition of the mass of the people is quite as much required as in the British dominions.

But as manhood suffrage is at present a popular bauble, that will do neither good nor harm in its practical results, it will satisfy the most energetic but least experienced of the population of these islands to have it made a law of the constitution of this country, and it may now be safely granted to them.

When these preliminary measures shall be arranged, and with men of real habits of business, and understanding what they have to do, they may be fully explained to Parliament and the country, and passed into laws, in six or eight weeks at the latest, the government will thus be supplied legitimately according to law with the necessary funds to bring the war on just and humane principles to a speedy termination, and to satisfy the legitimate wants of the trading, manufacturing, and commercial interests, to enable them immediately to employ every forced-to-be-idle subject in these Islands, and will have satisfied also the well-meaning but sadly inexperienced parliamentary reformers, who themselves require to be reformed under a rational system for conducting the affairs of this country and of the world.

That Parliament and the public mind, being relieved from these necessary preliminary measures to give immediate relief and present prosperity to this old worn-out dying system, fit only for the undeveloped infancy of humanity, both will be at liberty to calmly and gravely consider what are the surroundings which can in the best manner form the most useful and valuable character for all British subjects, and enable them also to produce the greatest amount of the most valuable wealth in the shortest time, most advantageously for producers and consumers.

That it has been long obvious to the far-seeing practical men of the world, that that which its population has required through all past ages was, to have their characters well formed from birth, and to be so placed and surrounded that they could with ease produce annually a superabundance of wealth for all;—both of which, if present knowledge had been acquired, could have been, as they may now be, speedily and easily accomplished.

That your Memorialist prays your Lordships to take the measures now proposed into your most grave consideration, and to use your utmost energies and powers to carry them into immediate practice.

And your Memorialist will ever pray, &c.,

ROBERT OWEN.

Jan., 1st. 1858.

PETITION

TO BOTH HOUSES OF PARLIAMENT.

The Petition of Robert Owen, late of New Lanark,

Sheweth,

That your Petitioner has been enabled and permitted, under divine providence, to make the greatest discovery for the permanent happiness of the human race that man has yet made for man.

1st. He has discovered the means by which, with the certainty of a law of nature, a good and superior character may be given to all from birth, and yet that there shall be an advantageous difference in each.

2nd. He has discovered how to new-place all whose characters shall be so formed, that through their own physical and mental powers wisely applied, and united with their fellows, they shall always abound in superior wealth.

3rd. That those thus formed, placed, and employed, will be through every succeeding generation well-fed, clothed, lodged, trained, educated, occupied, amused, and locally governed by themselves, so as to constitute a new and very advanced state of existence—so far superior to any society known in any part of the world, that no comparison can be made between them.

4th. That to form and govern this superior state of society will be far more simple and easy of practice than to attempt longer to maintain the Babel confusion called society which now universally prevails among all nations and peoples.

5th. That your Petitioner has been enabled to attain these all-important results by patiently tracing each evil experienced by society to its original source, and thus discovering that all had one and the same source, and that this was the origin of ignorance, falsehood, the injurious passions, poverty, disunion, crime, evil thoughts, and inferior selfish motives of action, in all governments and people; thus destroying and preventing the otherwise easy attainment of the universal harmony of humanity over the earth.

6th. That this origin of evil to the human race, as experienced to the present day, is the insane supposition that the made or created could by any possibility create any one of its own powers or qualities, and be rationally made responsible for the actions of the former or the thing made, or for the feelings, thoughts, motives, and actions, of the created.

7th. That this fatal fundamental error has so deranged the mental faculties of humanity, that they are unconscious of the most glaring universal facts, and instead of understanding and following, as all other living beings do, the good and wise natural instincts given to them for their guidance and happiness, they have been made through this error to deem it right to exert all their power to oppose them, and have always insanely legislated to endeavour to destroy these instincts or laws of nature, which calmly, regardless of these puerile attempts, retain their full strength and power over man, as at the beginning of his legislating folly and mad attempts to oppose his own beautifully and wonderfully created nature.

8th. That your Petitioner, by discovering the origin of evil and of all falsehood, became conscious of the origin of good and of all truth ; and that when the origin of good shall be made to become the foundation of society, truth will become of necessity the only language known to man. And it will be vain to look for goodness and happiness until truth shall be the only language of society.

9th. That the change of system, from the origin of evil and of falsehood to the system of goodness and truth, which may appear to those inexperienced in extensive practical combinations to be difficult or impracticable, is known by your Petitioner to be most easy of practice, when it shall be commenced in a proper spirit and with a knowledge of what will be required, and when the proceedings shall be directed by wise foresight.

Your Petitioner therefore prays that he may have a fair and full opportunity to make these truths known to your Right Honourable (or Honourable) House, by a committee or commission appointed by your Right Honourable (or Honourable) House ; or that he may be heard at the bar of your Right Honourable (or Honourable) House, or in any manner your House may deem better.

And your Petitioner will ever pray, &c.,

ROBERT OWEN.

January 1, 1858.

NOT knowing the day or the hour when I may be called hence, I make the following memorandums, with the request that, if not published in my life-time by myself, they shall be given to the public for the benefit of all governments, nations, and peoples.

Little do the children of the present generation suspect the all-important truth for them to know, that the preceding generation has trained, educated, placed, employed, and governed them under the system so false and injurious to all, that when stripped of its tinsel covering, and when the true names are given to all things, it will be discovered that this system is based on the origin of evil, and is directly calculated to force men to become liars, fools, knaves, and most ignorantly selfish, and women to become fools and prostitutes; and that all are not of these characters is only owing to the strong natural good and superior qualities of humanity, as given to every one at birth by the all-wise and good Creator of all things.

But man, by that wise and good Creator, and no doubt for the best of all ultimate results, has been destined to pass through all the evils of this system, the better to fit him for a much higher and superior sphere of existence, in which he will enjoy without retrogression, but always progressing, a state of excellence and happiness unknown under the existing first or infant life of humanity.

All things over the earth indicate that this infant system of falsehood and ignorance is undergoing rapid changes to come to its termination, when the true, good, wise, and happy system for the government of the population of the world through futurity will commence.

The tragedies now acting in India may probably be the last act of this fearful but highly instructive infant drama.

Man can know only that which he is taught by external means, or by interior inspiration, coming to him he knows not whence or how.

The present generation having been taught and practised only in this false and ignorantly selfish system of individualism and of all repulsive feelings, has now, under a system of truth and wisdom, to be taught a new spirit, a new principle, and a new practice.

The spirit of that universal love and charity which feareth no evil, the principle which creates the desire to do good to all of our race, and the practice of union, are to be obtained only under the true unmixed social system, which until now could not be introduced.

This new teaching, so loudly called for by the signs of the times, exhibiting the extraordinary events daily occurring—events which create so much now-seen-to-be unnecessary misery to our race, should be now commenced, and continued without retrogression through all future ages.

This new teaching will instruct all that man, being created with qualities and powers in a manner mysterious to him, and yet more mysteriously combined to constitute him a living physical, intellectual, and spiritual existence, has been forced to be what he has been through all past ages, as he is now forced to be what he is.

That to apply responsibility or blame to a being so created and enforced to feel, think, and act, is most irrational—not to say insane.

Under the new and true system, instead of wasting time in vain attempts to oppose and counteract the beautiful and wonderful organs, faculties, qualities, propensities, and powers of humanity, superior scientific surroundings will be devised and executed to develope them in their natural order of time and of action, as nature or God has by their creation intended; and the present jarring conflicts of insanity over the earth will gradually cease, and be superseded by universal concord of action and harmony of feeling.

To all appearance this great and glorious change will commence in Great Britain, and thence spread gradually over the earth.

The change can be more easily effected through the British government, parliament, and people, than by any other government and people.

They could more easily establish a national bank, and give the necessary confidence and credit to its notes, than any other government or people; and this is the first practical step required to free industry from gold slavery, and to open the floodgates of universal prosperity to the population of the world.

The new superior surroundings, in accordance with the true social science, are immediately required in India, where they could be now easily introduced; and they would at once satisfy and harmonise the natives to British rule, as long as it would be necessary to maintain that rule, or until an Indian Empire could be established, federatively united to the British Empire.

The extraordinary beneficial effects which this system would produce in practice in India would soon induce all nations to adopt it; and the true social system would in a few years become universal over the earth, and distinctions of opposition between men would everywhere terminate.

Men would cease to make their puerile and foolish laws to endeavour to counteract nature's unchanging, wise, and most beneficent laws for the government of all humanity.

All punishment of man by man would cease, and anger and all evil passions would be unknown—the path to wisdom and happiness would be opened to all, and would be so delightful to follow, that all would readily enter and pursue it, not turning to the right or to the left to the end of their journey of life.

But to make the best use of invaluable time for the population of the world, seeing how all now suffer, the practical measures which ought to be immediately adopted by the British government and people shall be now stated.

· They should openly declare through parliament their determination to abandon the origin of evil as the foundation of society ; and gradually to supersede all the practices so fatal to harmony and happiness which have of necessity emanated from it.

This would be to commence at the right point, by going at once to the root of all evil. And by thus at the outset taking the bull by the horns, every succeeding measure in advance would become more and more easy, and every advance would prove the superiority of the true and good system over the false and evil one.

The next step is the establishment of the Bank of the British Empire, to supersede the present nominal Bank of England and all private banking, as I have previously explained. This will soon supply the necessary funds to relieve the public, and give the required assistance to the immediate wants of government, regardless of all immediate supplies of gold—that senseless root of so much unnecessary evil to man over the world.

The government should then declare its intention to govern India on the true principles of man's nature,—that is, of the highest humanity, and that it would as speedily as possible abandon the government of the old system of error, by force, fear, fraud, and falsehood ; and instead thereof commence in all parts of India to form the new superior surroundings to enable the natives by their own well-directed industry to be well-fed, clothed, lodged, trained, educated, and surrounded by those influences which would substantially contribute to their progress and permanent happiness. And thus could the greatest possible surplus revenue be obtained from them without reluctance, for the necessary aids to well govern them, and without any interference with their present religious insanities, which, under this new system, will gradually die their natural death.

The next measure which should engage the attention of both Houses of Parliament is that which should at the earliest period have been its chief business :—that is, to discover the most natural and rational means to give from birth a good, useful, valuable character, physical and mental, to every British born subject, and to supply permanent beneficial employment through life for every one of them ; which may now be done most advantageously for all. These will be easily attained by the creation of new and superior surroundings in which to place all from birth.

And as easy practical steps to pass from this old, evil, and thoroughly worn-out sytem, to the new, now so anxiously looked for, parliament should by one act repeal all the laws opposed to good laws which it had previously made and enforced, every one of which opposing laws has produced only evil; and should then make laws, when any shall be required, in accordance with the laws of God, called laws of nature.

These suggestions being adopted, it will be found that the necessity for human laws will be difficult to discover; ample laws, when understood, having been given for man's guidance and government by his Creator.

As one of the measures of preparation to new form the character of all British subjects, the priesthood of every denomination, in return for their support, should be required to teach in all churches, chapels, meeting-houses, synagogues, and all other places now of worship, the necessity for all to acquire a knowledge of the pure and undefiled spirit of universal love and charity, and to apply it constantly in practice in every day life, and that the priests of each sect should especially exhibit this practice in all their doings, and should cease to torment humanity by their much-worse-than-useless dogmas which no one understands.

The priesthood of this generation will thus become really useful, in assisting to effect the change from the evil to the good system. And in the coming generations none will be trained to be priests of any sect; as in the true and rational system not one will be required, or could be made as such to be of any use.

For in making the new and superior surroundings to well place, feed, clothe, lodge, train, educate, employ, amuse, and govern the entire population, they will be useless as priests; for hereafter there will be no possible requirement for priests, but a new and very superior class of instructors will be formed of the entire population.

In the next generation, under the rational system of society, Lawyers also will be useless, and none will be trained for an obsolete profession.

And under the true and natural system of society it is yet doubtful whether it will be necessary to have any especially trained for the Medical profession.

The division of powers will be obtained by mechanism and chemistry; and the union of powers will be trained in all men and women.

Instruction to the young will be given from facts, all at first demonstrable to the senses, and explained to the taught by familiar conversation, as nature dictates. And by the arrangements and surroundings which the rational and natural system of society will require, all will be so well instructed, that they will become the best formers of the characters of the young from their birth.

They will be early taught an accurate knowledge of themselves and of human nature generally, to the extent that facts have yet disclosed this knowledge. And the most advanced knowledge given to any, will, under this natural system for forming the character of and governing man, be given to all, as far as their born capacities will admit.

Those trained under the old, false, and artificial system, and knowing only this system, can form no conception of the extent of the correct, useful, and valuable knowledge which can, with ease and pleasure to teachers and taught, be given to every man and woman before they attain man and woman-hood. And this great advance in accurate knowledge, useful for every-day practice, will arise from the difference between false and artificial, and true and natural teaching—the one under injurious, and the other under superior surroundings—the former made at random, without knowledge or foresight ; the other scientifically devised, by wise and experienced foresight, to produce, with the certainty of a law of nature, the superior effects desired.

Under this change of system it will be soon discovered that to govern the population of the world well and wisely, a good, useful, and valuable character from birth should be formed by one generation for the succeeding, and that the time is come, in the due order of creation, for this to be now accomplished.

And until a good natural character shall be formed for our race, governments will have failed to perform their first, most essential, and highest duty.

So erroneously have the ruling influences of society hitherto thought and acted, that they have so far exerted all their powers to keep the mass of the people grossly ignorant, and to give them a false and most injurious character—injurious to themselves and to society : Witness the existing state of the population of the world, speaking, to all who can observe and reflect, in a voice louder than thunder, extending to and over all nations and peoples.

My last word in this publication, and perhaps the last which I may be permitted, by the infirmities of age to publish, shall be addressed in an especial manner to the existing ruling influences over the world.

And these words should be written in letters of gold, and placed conspicuously in every palace, and be held in everlasting remembrance by all of our race.

These words are,—

First.—That to insure your own happiness and the safety and well-being of your families and of all society, you should immediately adopt decisive measures to have taught to all the great truth—" THAT THE CREATOR CREATES ALL THE " QUALITIES AND POWERS OF THE CREATED, AND " IS ALONE RESPONSIBLE FOR THE ACTIONS OF " THE CREATED THROUGH ITS EXISTENCE.

This never-to-be-forgotten truth, derived from all past and present facts, can alone create that pure spirit of universal love and charity, which will be with perpetually increasing pleasure applied to practice in every thought and action of our lives.

And this great truth will thus harmonise all humanity through every future age.

Second.—That you adopt immediate measures to have created new combinations of surroundings, all based on and consistent with that great fundamental truth, to well educate and well employ all within your influences.

This will insure a good, useful, and valuable character, and a superfluity of unadulterated superior wealth for all, through futurity ; and will destroy for ever the existing individual ignorant selfishness of our race.

In further explanation of the subjects here treated of, the following observations are added :—

ON THE ABSOLUTE NECESSITY, IN THE NATURE OF THINGS, FOR THE ATTAINMENT OF HAPPINESS, THAT THE SYSTEM OF FALSEHOOD AND EVIL SHOULD PRECEDE THE SYSTEM OF TRUTH AND GOOD.

THE rulers of nations and peoples need not longer to halt in deciding which of these systems should now prevail for forming the character of and governing man.

The existing system of fraud, delusion, and wickedness, is everywhere disjointed, opposed to itself, and, by the unnecessary sufferings, physical and mental, which it creates to all, must soon fall of itself, and at this period intended by nature be left without defenders.

It is evil in spirit, false in principle, and most injurious to humanity in all its practices.   It has taught man to know evil, and to experience all its varied miseries ; and without this knowledge man could never enjoy the high permanent happiness intended by his Creator to be his future inheritance and superior state of existence.

Had not a system of falsehood and delusion existed through the past, with its necessary innumerable evils, the value of a system of truth, in every look, word, and action, could never be estimated or highly enjoyed.

Had the pains and the sufferings, physical and mental, experienced by humanity during the centuries which have passed, been unknown, the pleasures to be derived from their total absence must ever have remained unknown.

Had the vices, crimes, diseases, murders, and destruction of property, so universal through unknown time, not taken place, no one could estimate the extent of safety and satisfaction that will be experienced in a state of society in which these evils will be unknown except from the history of the miseries which they inflicted on humanity during its infancy of error and mental weakness.

Had the demoralisation, desolation, cruelties, and slaughters of wars been unknown, the happiness to be derived from universal peace, undisturbed by the fear of war, could not be felt or understood.

Had the effects of a false and most unnatural formation of character not existed, to exhibit all its evil and injurious results, the exquisite pleasure to be derived from a true formation of character, consistent with nature in spirit, principle, and practice, must for ever have remained unexperienced and unenjoyed.

Had the evils arising from forced idleness, and its sufferings for want of occupation and from poverty, not been experienced, the constant means of rational, healthy, and pleasant occupation, physical and mental, and of freedom from poverty and the fear of it, could never be appreciated.

Had not the evils arising from discordance, contests, disunion, and repulsive feelings, been experienced through the past, the high happiness to be derived from accordance, union, and attractive feelings, could never be experienced, understood, or enjoyed.

Had not the extent of the evil of the ignorant selfish individual system of buying and selling for a money profit been experienced, with its poverty and injurious luxury and all their demoralising results, the happiness of having the best unadulterated wealth of all kinds and at all times for all without money and without price, could never be fully appreciated or enjoyed.

Had not the innumerable evils arising from the populations of the world being governed by the repulsive and ignorant system of individualism been experienced, the happiness to be derived from the full social system in practice could never be felt or known.

Had not the ignorance, poverty, fear of it, general demoralisation, murders, and wars, with endless individual contentions, arising from the various attempts to circulate an illimitable increase of wealth by a metal circulation, greatly limited in amount compared with the overwhelming means discovered by which to increase real wealth, been experienced,—the advantages of a circulating medium co-extensive and co-equal with the most rapid increase of real wealth could not be known or appreciated, and could be very imperfectly enjoyed while the change from the false and evil to the true and good system shall be in progress; for when the change shall be completed no circulating medium will ever be required or in anyway necessary.

Had not the varied punishments inflicted by man on man been known and suffered, the happiness to be experienced when man shall no longer ignorantly punish or in any manner deceive or injure his fellow man, could not be known or enjoyed.

Had not all the varieties of ignorant, cruel, and bad governments, been experienced, the advantages and pleasure to be derived when man shall be rationally and well-governed could not be known.

Had not the ever-to-be-remembered evils arising from the ignorances, incongruities, irrationalities, insanities, and madness, arising from the various superstitions with which the populations of the world have been physically and mentally tormented through all the ages which have passed been experienced, the happiness to be enjoyed when entirely freed from these hydras of misery and suffering to all of our race could never be felt or comprehended.

It is for a similarly good ultimate result that man has had to experience the unspeakable and often unbearable miseries which arise from the artificial marriages and forced co-habitation of the sexes against nature, invented by these superstitions, and by which they have forced the creation of prostitution, a crime unknown to nature—for prostitution, with its gross injustice, and often unbearable mental cruelties to a large proportion of the best especially of the two sexes, is an unnatural crime created solely by the ignorant and insane contrivances of the priesthood for the artificial compulsory union of the sexes.

By inventing the varied, imaginary, insane, artificial marriages against nature, (for if they were not against nature they would be useless and most unnecessary,) the priests of the world, in order to give themselves power over their fellows, have created and forced upon society all the loathsome sexual diseases and gross evils of prostitution; and by thus most ignorantly opposing one of the strongest and most beautiful laws of God and Nature, they have opened Pandora's box upon poor undeveloped, ignorant, and inexperienced humanity—ignorant and inexperienced in a knowledge of the most simple yet important laws of its nature.

When the superstitions of the world had first the temerity and unblushing audacity to presume to propose to society their unnatural laws of artificial marriages, in direct opposition to the ever unerring, most wise, merciful, good, and efficient laws of God—of that Power which gave man all his qualities and means to continue his species and his own life—if any individual had, at that period, possessed the first indication of a knowledge of himself, he would have simply asked the presuming priests— " Have we the power by our will to love and hate? I find I am " forced to like and love certain things and persons, and to dis- " like and hate certain things and persons. How then dare you

" to attempt to make your laws, based on ignorance of the laws
" of humanity, in opposition to the God-made laws of humanity,
" forced at birth on both sexes ?"—What answer could any of
the innumerable contending priesthoods of the world have then
made, or when the question is now put to them what answer can
they now make to these obvious and straightforward enquiries ?

They could only honestly reply to the present population of
the world, — " experience has now proved that we erred in
" ignorance, and that your ancestors were fools for attending to
" us, and you will be, with the experience now acquired, much
" greater idiots if you continue to do so."

To conclude,—had evil not existed through the past, to produce the present state of knowledge and feeling of the past, the
happy future, now immediately before humanity, could never have
been attained, or enjoyed as it will be, with the pleasure arising
from the knowledge of the past merciful sufferings of humanity ;
—the past being a speck in time of pain and misery, to produce
a future eternity of superior pleasure and happiness.

Thus naturally are the ways of God justified to man, and the
origin of evil shown also to be the necessary origin of much
greater good than otherwise could have been attained, known, or
enjoyed.

Had the irrational not preceeded the rational, the latter would
not have been appreciated.

Let man, therefore, henceforth cease to blame or punish man
for the exercise of qualities and powers which he did not and
could not create.

These truths being now known, a great change over the earth
is about to commence. The longer necessity for the reign of
evil to prepare future perpetual good to man is drawing to its
termination, and men and women will now speak openly that
which they have been compelled to feel and to know, but which
they have not had the moral courage openly to express from fear
of the governments of evil.

Let the nations of the earth therefore now attend, and hereafter never forget the *Great Fundamental Fact* " that the Creator
" creates all the qualities and powers of the created throughout
" the universe, and forsees and directs all the consequences of
" these creations through every period of eternity,"—and man
must and will now learn and begin to obey this Great Truth, on
the knowledge of which his happiness will commence and for
ever progress.

Man is a necessity in creation, created to acquire knowledge by
experience, and happiness by obeying the laws of his nature.

ROBERT OWEN.

January, 1st., 1858.

SECOND LETTER

TO THE RULING POWERS OF THE WORLD.

SOCIAL SCIENCE.

EXPERIENCE, the appointed teacher of man, through gradually developing his organisation and giving strength and power of action to all his faculties, qualities, and propensities, from their incipient to their matured state, has now, in the due order of nature or of progressive creation, brought to light the most advanced of all human discoveries,—namely, that man could be perfected for the high enjoyment of a life of permanent rational happiness only by passing through an unknown preliminary period of evil, in which the consequences of error through all its ramifications should produce all its varied innumerable miseries and sufferings, and during which period, force, fear, fraud, and falsehood should reign supreme, and in which repulsive individualism should create contests, conflicts, and wars, with all their demoralising, cruel, and destructive results; and that these evils should extend to their extremes of afflicting humanity in every form and manner.   In which period, in addition, the most ignorant, wild, incongruous imaginations were conceived, and were formed into deadly opposing superstitions, all called the " true religion," devised with consummate wisdom and foresight to create the highest bearable degree of varied mental torments, so that the race should know by experience the utmost extent of physical and mental sufferings that humanity could sustain before yielding up its earthly short life.

All this was necessary to enable man to know good and evil. For it is now evident that without this preliminary life of evil and falsehood, an eternal life of truth and good could never be enjoyed.

For the individual it is a short life of necessary physical and mental suffering, to enable him to enjoy a future eternity of supreme felicity.   And without this short life of pains, the future eternal life of high and superior pleasures could never be appreciated, felt, or understood.

Modern Spiritualism confirms this most important truth.

The change from this reign of evil, falsehood, sin, and misery, to the reign of universal truth, goodness, and happiness, is to be effected by the governments of the world adopting direct and efficient practical measures to teach all, in the shortest time and best manner, the new born SOCIAL SCIENCE, in spirit, principle, and practice.

This Science will be soon found to be the science of sciences, through a knowledge of which the population of the world will be permanently well-fed, clothed, lodged, trained, educated, employed, recreated, and governed, by being placed within circumstances or surroundings scientifically devised and executed to produce with the certainty of a law of nature all these results.

It is true that, for the ultimate high permanent happiness of our race, the organisations of all humanity, although possessing the same general qualities, differ in their combinations in every individual. Through this all-wise and all-good law of nature, God has devised the most simple and certain means by which, under the new reign about to commence, of truth, union, and happiness, each one of our race will, to the extent of his educated enlarged capacity, enjoy the benefits to be derived from this incalculable variety of invaluable superior qualities; for each will be for all, and all will be for each.

Under this new reign no one will withhold any good thing from another ; and thus will these trained-to-be superior qualities of all be blended to create perfection in each, so far as humanity can upon earth attain perfection.

The preliminary and temporary reign of falsehood and all evil could have been effected only by man's imagination being so far perverted as to suppose that he, a created being, unconscious how the nail of his little finger could be brought into existence, created all his own qualities, faculties, propensities, powers, and entire organisation, and should be made responsible to his fellow men for their ideas respecting the manner in which these wonderful combinations, physical and mental, spiritual, chemical, and mechanical, should feel, think, and act ; while his fellow men, as well as himself, were profoundly ignorant of the secret springs by which this yet great mystery to man, lives, feels, thinks, and acts.

But it is only now, after the lapse of unknown ages, that experience has taught man to know that he ever has been and is incompetent to create his own qualities and powers, or to know how they were created, and that ignorance of and inattention to the unchanging laws of humanity could alone have given rise to his insane notions, " that the created could be rationally made " responsible for the actions of qualities and powers which he " did not and could not create."

But the period for the commencement of the termination of this insanity begins, when the knowledge is acquired " that the " created cannot be made rationally responsible for the actions of " qualities and powers which it could not create."

With the acquirement of the knowledge that it is blasphemy

against the Great Creating Power of all things created throughout the universe, to imagine that he has not foreseen all the results from the beginning of this creation, and that he is not alone responsible for those results, will commence the new reign of truth, knowledge, wisdom, union, peace, and happiness, which will rapidly spread over the earth.

The new Spiritual Manifestations are now powerfully influencing the ruling earthly powers to stand still in their irrational and evil career, to look around them to know what they should do to avert a storm such as men have not yet encountered, and fearful to contemplate.

But good and superior Spirits are actively engaged in their new spheres of existence to turn the threatening evil to good. They are now employed in measures to reconcile these powers, and to convince them that their safety and the means to accomplish the most good in the shortest time will be, first, in a cordial union among themselves, and second, in promoting that union between all over whom they rule.

This will be easily effected by now superseding the fundamental principle of evil and repulsion—" that the created creates its " own qualities," by the fundamental principle of good and attraction—" that God alone creates all the qualities of humanity, " and ever guides and governs their actions."

Hence will immediately arise universal charity and love between all of every shade of difference in body or mind. And there is no other principle under heaven which can create among men universal charity and love for every-day practice. And without this universal charity and love, in spirit, principle, and practice, man must remain an ignorant, inconsistent, contending animal, ever fighting against his own best interests and highest happiness.

But the Superior Spirits give assurance that soon the ruling earthly powers will discover it to be for their interests to cordially unite, and as cordially to unite those over whom they rule.

Then the Spirits suggest that their first united great measure will be to change their expensive, idle, useless, demoralising standing armies, into easily managed masses of from two to three thousand, in due proportions of men, women and children, each mass forming a new superior military and civil colony, in which both the civil and military duties may in each be carried to a high point of perfection in the most simple manner, by each colony being made of scientific surroundings especially calculated to enable each in every colony, by their united, well-directed, healthy and pleasant, regular industry, itself a source of perpetual enjoyment, to be, without stay or retrogression, well fed, clothed, lodged, trained, educated, recreated, and locally self-governed; and humanity, when this rational change shall, as it now easily may, be peaceably extended over the earth, can ask no more.

By this being done with foresight and wisdom, each country will become impregnable for home defence, and foreign wars must cease.

And by this simple change each country may speedily be made to become a beautiful highly cultivated earthly paradise, governed through existing governments solely by the laws of God, yet called by many the laws of nature ; but names change not things, and men will soon learn no longer to differ about words meaning nothing substantial.

The Spirits are more especially occupied in preparing the British, Russian, and French governments for this change. The British to commence now in India ; the Russians and Indians being well prepared for this new mode of domestic colonising. And the French population has for some time had a strong liking for some such change. Her Britanic Majesty and Royal Consort, with their Imperial Majesties of Russia and France, are at this time much under the influence and inspiration of superior Spirits, to induce them to unite and lead in this great change, and then to induce all other governments to follow their example.

Mechanism and chemistry may be made with ease to become the most efficient slaves and servants of the population of the world in these domestic colonies, and thus gradually to prepare for permanent progress, peace, good will, and harmony, over the earth.

For these rationally formed united military and civil domestic colonies will combine, under scientific arrangements, the most effective means to make a rapid progress in agriculture, manufactures, trades, exchanges, in the arts and sciences, and especially in social science, on the perfecting of which the happiness of the population of the world depends.

For in these colonies, when rightly constituted, all gross ideas and conduct will be unknown.

Refinement of mind and manners will attain their highest perfection, combined with undeviating truth and sincerity.

The sexes will be equal in rights, perfect in their associations, and their unions always those of mutual sympathy and affection. The ignorance of man's interference, with his gross ideas of artificial bondage and mental slavery, will be unknown ; true chastity will be understood and will be thus purified and made perfect. Sexual diseases, crimes, disappointments, and jealousies, will be unknown ; and humanity will begin to know and understand itself, feeling its natural and beneficial wants, and knowing how rationally best to supply them.

To attain some knowledge of the extent of the gross ignorance of humanity and of society under the system of falsehood and evil by which the population of the world has been and is now governed,—contemplate the present condition of the United States of North America. Here is a most splendid empire, possessing within itself all climes, soils, and minerals, sufficient to maintain in the highest comfort the present population of the world, and to give them a superior character and happy existence, with less than four hours daily, upon the average, of healthy pleasant exercise. It now contains less than thirty millions, including Indians. Then consider its present state of slavery, its late panic, its civil dissentions, the demoralisation which these create, and the small share of truth, knowledge, wisdom, charity, and love, which it at this day exhibits as an example to the world.

And yet, being the latest constituted nation, without obstruction to apply in its construction the entire experience of the past, it might be expected to have become a shining light to all nations. But it was based on the system of falsehood and evil; and hence the deplorable condition of this easily-to-be-made most magnificent and happy empire.

May you, the present rulers of the earth, mark, learn, and inwardly digest these sayings, and act wisely in accordance with them, and let the change from evil to good commence this year.

ROBERT OWEN.

1st January, 1858.

THE SCIENCE OF POLITICS AND SOCIAL SCIENCE.

THE science of Politics, so called, has hitherto governed all nations and peoples under all its various forms of governing.

It has been tested through the past history of man, and see its effects at this day in all nations and among all people! In no corner of the earth, even at this day, is there to be found anything approaching to national truth, wisdom, and happiness.

The reason is now obvious to those who can trace effects to their ultimate causes upon earth. The science of politics is based on the origin of evil, which is the foundation of all physical and mental suffering and spiritual ignorance.

Politics, then, is the science of mental and spiritual ignorance, now carried to its ultimate attainable folly and absurdity, as seen in the forms, ceremonies, and pageantries in the courts of laws, legislative assemblies, human punishments, and grave superstitions of every sect over the world.

This science, which should be called the science of ignorance, has long since become so glaringly inconsistent in its theories and injurious in its practical results to the mass of mankind, that it could not have been so long maintained had it not been upheld by a long established system combined of force, fear, fraud, and falsehood, exercised through the armies and the superstitions of the world—the one to have power to govern by physical force and fear, the other to aid by fraud and falsehood to train the mental and spiritual faculties and powers to become its abject slaves.

This spell over all humanity has been thus apparently long continued for, no doubt, an ulterior great good to man ; this good being to some extent already made obvious to advanced minds,— and advanced minds always lead the way and open the path to newly discovered truths.

There are no new truths. All truths are as eternal as the universe, which is one great truth, ever consistent with itself.

But this spell is broken, and the origin of evil has been disclosed to man. Ignorance will disappear ; force, fear, fraud, and falsehood will lose their power ; and the superstitions of the earth will vanish as wild imaginations having no material or spiritual base, but all emanating from the origin of evil.

The spell is broken ! Advanced modern statesmen have at length ventured openly to announce to the world the *Social Science* as something new, and as if just dug out of the ruins and wreck of all past ages, and now first approaching the light.

The birth of this newly-found science, made first known to the political world by statesmen in 1857, will be an event to be remembered with joy and gladness by all future generations.

For the social science is destined to secure the permanent happiness of humanity, by making known the means by which, under the most natural and beautiful combinations of new arranged surroundings, the human race may be, and will be, fed, clothed, lodged, trained, educated, employed, recreated, and locally and generally governed and placed in a manner greatly superior to any ever known, and yet these shall be for ever improving through every succeeding generation.

Through a knowledge of this science, in its spirit, principle, and practice, the world will gradually cease to be tormented by the ignorances of wild superstitions, by force, fear, fraud, and falsehood. Humanity, in each one from birth, will be made gradually to become full formed, physically, intellectually, morally, spiritually, and practically ; injurious passions by these means will cease to be cultivated, and soon will not exist ; truth will be the sole language of all ; every mind will be pervaded with the pure spirit of universal love and charity ; and all will be actively engaged in promoting the highest happiness of each other ; wars will cease ; and the art, expense, demoralisation, and destructive powers of life and wealth will be unknown. The necessity for any money circulation will terminate, for wealth will everywhere abound and be used freely without price, and its creation will be a pleasure and pastime to all. Peace will be universal and perpetual, and harmony will reign for ever through all the generations of men. These blessings will be the natural and necessary results of the change from the population of the world being governed by *politics*, as through all past time, to the government which will arise from the introduction of the *Social Science*, when understood and rationally and consistently applied to practice.

But who now comprehends the newly announced Social Science, in spirit and principle, and how to apply it consistently in practice to produce the results previously stated ?

Is this knowledge to be found among the most learned in any of the superstitions of the world ?

Or among the first statesmen in the most liberal and advanced governments ?

Or among the *élite* in the most learned and scientific societies ?— Or among the monied millionaires ?—Or among the most experienced practical men ?—Or among the profound philosophers of the day, who have had the advantage of acquiring the knowledge of all recorded facts and the wisdom of the wise collected from the entire history of man ?

Enquire of each of these separately, and the true Social Science, of divine origin, in spirit, principle, and practice, is yet to be taught to and acquired by all ; for it is now destined to form a new and very superior character for man, to govern the world wisely, in peace and perpetual prosperity always increasing. And instead of governing by force, fear, fraud, and falsehood, as heretofore, to govern without human punishment, and solely through the spirit and practice of universal love and charity, which will be found sufficient to supersede all the puerile, futile, and everchanging laws of men, made until now in ignorance of their own nature and while their mental faculties were undeveloped for rational action. Hence the variety of superstitions, governments, laws, and customs, forming so many experiments of society to obtain happiness, their utter failure, and the Babel confusion of the population of the world at this day as to the best mode to pursue to attain a state of truth, goodness, and wisdom, or of true physical and mental liberty for the individual, without which there can be no permanent happiness for the human race.

Some of the advanced minds of the world now say—" We admit that that which you have stated is in accordance with facts, " consistent with itself, with the laws of humanity, and therefore " true ; but how is such an overthrow of all existing prejudices " in favour of things as they are, to be effected ?"

It is to be effected, as I have often stated, in the manner in which the old roads of the world are now being superseded by the new railways,—and as the old comparatively slow modes of communication between distant places are now being superseded by the electric telegraphs.

The same parties then ask—" Who will take the initiative and " introduce the change ?"

My reply hitherto has been that the leading governments of the civilised world will introduce the change, because they are well-placed to effect it, and have so deep an interest in heading and directing so momentous a change in the spirit, principle, and practice of society.

Again they say—" But what if governments will not intro-" duce it ?"

Then, as it is the business of all society, all society must interest itself to have the change effected in the shortest peaceable practicable time. I say " peaceable"—because nothing can be permanently well done by violence.

But to accomplish this change by society, however highly advantageous it may be for all of our race, society has yet much new knowledge to acquire.

It has to learn Social Science, in principle, spirit, and practice, that it may attain to the knowledge of the science of society, of which, from anything yet published or said in public, all appear to be profoundly ignorant. Yet Social Science and the science of society must be acquired before any parties can know how to take one step rationally in practice in either of them.

They must learn the principle, spirit, and practice, by which to work the mine of humanity—a mine intrinsically of more value than all the material mines of the world.

Hitherto the entrance to this mine of incalculable value has been deeply covered, and thus hidden from human discovery, by the rubbish produced from the origin of evil, creating the religious superstitions, the political governments, the absurd classifications, and all the other fooleries of the past and present state of society over the world.

The entrance to this mine being found and opened, its first fruits are—

1. The discovery of the origin of good in perpetuity to the human race.

2. The discovery of the true principle of forming character for the human race, and by which any character, from the worst to the best, according to the natural organisation of each, may be given from birth with the certainty of a law of nature.

3. The discovery of the natural means of creating at all times a superfluity of superior unadulterated wealth, with health, comfort, and pleasure to its producers, and to be at all times freely partaken of by all.

4. The discovery of the universal principle of attraction between man and man, and by which the human race will be ultimately united as one enlightened family, superior in all its attainments, and bringing its aggregate knowledge to bear upon everything, and to influence every mind in spirit, principle, and practice.

5. The discovery of the means by which to supersede gradually and peaceably all the existing surroundings made by the human race—surroundings all of which have emanated from the origin of evil, by new arrangements of surroundings, so combined as to form over the world comparatively perfect scientific societies. It is said " comparatively perfect"—because these societies, although at first greatly superior to any yet known, will be improved by experience and the progress of mental and material knowledge through every succeeding generation, and to make that progress will be the pleasure and delight of all through all time.

But if the first fruits of working this mine single-handed produce the results stated, what may be expected from it when it shall be regularly worked by the human race, after man has been properly trained, educated, and placed for the task ?

No mind has been yet sufficiently developed to comprehend the extent of the extraordinary results which will be attained and enjoyed by man upon earth when the whole of humanity from birth shall be naturally and rationally trained, educated, employed, placed, and governed ; future generations, yet unborn, under a higher development of all our faculties, physical, intellectual, moral, spiritual, and practical, will be required, to encompass a knowledge so new and so far beyond the teachings of individualism, based on the origin of evil.

It is of the first interest to the leading governments of the civilised world that they should systematically work this mine on the now known principles of mental and social science. They possess the machinery, habits, and means of governing, and for founding society anew on its true base, the origin of truth and good, forming the character of all on these principles, and constructing society on the newly acquired knowledge to be derived from the social science.

Should there not be sufficient foresight and wisdom in existing governments to unite to attain these results, now so necessary for the happiness of the human race, I will unfold the means by which the people may peaceably form themselves into the scientific social societies mentioned in a previous part of this article.

But it is much better that the governments should lead in this new mental, moral, and practical revolution of the human race.

It may be here remarked that until the human mind had been developed to the point of freedom only just attained in the most advanced nations by the most advanced individuals, neither governments nor people could accomplish this task, owing to the educated ignorance of both.

But this is destined to be a century ever-to-be remembered in the future history of man—the century in which he first gained the victory over ignorance, to openly speak the truth respecting the natural feelings and convictions which by the laws of his nature he is compelled to have, and upon which freedom the union, rationality, permanent peace, and happiness of the race depend.

I will now wait to see if the medicine now given to my poor deeply suffering fellow men is sufficiently strong to cure them of the fatal disease of ignorant prejudices which has so long rendered them unable to see the plain open path to truth, union, wisdom, goodness, and happiness.

ROBERT OWEN.

Sevenoaks Park,
Sevenoaks, Jan. 25th, 1858.

THE SPIRIT, PRINCIPLE, AND PRACTICE, BY WHICH THE OLD SYSTEM OF FALSEHOOD, IGNORANCE, AND EVIL IS TO BE SUPERSEDED BY THE NEW SYSTEM OF TRUTH, WISDOM, AND GOODNESS.

FALSEHOOD, ignorance, and evil, emanate from the extraordinary delusion which has pervaded the human mind through all past ages,—" that the created could " and " did create its own qualities and powers, whether material, or mental, or spiritual."

Truth, Wisdom, and goodness, can alone emanate from the knowledge of the fact that the created cannot by any possibility possess one quality or power not given to it by its Creator.

The consequence of the universal delusion on this all-important subject has been *all the evil* of man's past existence to the present hour.

The consequence of the truth of this subject will be universal perpetual progress and happiness.

For this great fundamental truth is the only true and solid foundation for universal love and charity;

and until these two great principles of action can be made to pervade the human race, it will be vain to look for rationality among mankind. But as soon as arrangements shall be made to give this character from birth to all for every day practice, then will man become rational in mind and practice, and the population of the world will enjoy perpetual peace and harmony.

The great fact and eternal truth, " that the Creator " alone creates all the qualities of the created, and " that the created cannot possess any power which " has not been previously given to it by its Creator," is the keystone to the ultimate union, peace, harmony, and happiness of the human race. It is that great truth which can alone create the feeling of attraction between all of our race, and terminate the destructive and most injurious feelings of repulsion between man and man on account of educated differences of mere imaginary notions—notions which for so long a period have kept men estranged from each other, and made enemies of those whose highest interest it was to be as cordially united as friends.

To simplify this subject in such manner that all may comprehend the great change now contemplated, it may be thus stated :—

Firstly. The Great Creating Power of the Universe, called God, creates all the qualities and powers of the created, and is alone the cause or author of all its actions through its whole existence, and the same whether it is mineral, vegetable, animal, or spiritual, or any combination of these.

Secondly. This principle applied to the creation of man, when fully comprehended, will of necessity create in the race the spirit of universal love and charity, knowing no exceptions of colour, country, creed, class, sex, or party.

Thirdly. This principle, of necessity producing this spirit, will of like necessity cause all born and educated differences, having been forced on the individual, to be treated with respect, and never abused either by word or action.

Fourthly. The criterion of truth being now known, (namely, " that truth is always consistent with itself " and with all facts,") *that* only which is in accordance with this test will be taught to the rising generation, and then all their ideas and associations of ideas will be in accordance with each other and in harmony with all nature.

Fifthly. Man will then for the first time in the history of humanity be relieved from the many-folded bandages of ignorance by which our forefathers have been so long blinded, and he will be enabled plainly to perceive the causes of the prejudices which have thus kept him in mental darkness and Babel confusion in the affairs of life at this day.

The spirit of love and charity thus based on their only true foundation, will not only destroy all angry and repulsive feelings between all of our race, but will induce all to have kind feelings of forbearance of abuse for any born or educated differences, whatever may be their character; it being at the same time ever remembered that education from birth may be made to give any direction for good or evil to the natural born qualities of humanity.

From this knowledge of the formation of character, the educated prejudices of all will be respected by all, and, as previously mentioned, will never be abused by word or action.

But truths consistent with themselves and in accordance with all facts known or that can be known being alone taught to the rising generation, all prejudices, whether religious, civil, or military, will gradually and quietly die a natural death, and will then no more disturb the harmony of the human race, and thus, in accordance with the laws of nature, by extending the mental powers of man, will error cease, and truth and wisdom will become triumphant, universal, and perpetual.

Let all therefore now begin in earnest to learn the laws of their nature, and to obey them and them only, and then will knowledge and happiness become the birthright of all, and perpetually progress towards higher and higher perfection.

This conduct will be for the permanent interest of all.

ROBERT OWEN.

Sevenoaks Park,
    January 15th, 1858.

THE GREAT CHANGE IN ALL HUMAN AFFAIRS, ARISING FROM THE DISCOVERY OF THE ORIGIN OF EVIL AND OF THE ORIGIN OF GOOD TO THE VARIOUS RACES OF MEN OVER THE WORLD.

THE happiness of the human race in perpetuity is now attainable, but attainable only through truth, goodness, wisdom, and unity.

Truth, goodness, wisdom, and union, have now to

be given to man, from whom they have been hitherto hidden by reason of the origin of evil having been taught to all past generations as the origin of good, and the origin of good as the origin of evil.

Before this great discovery could be made it was necessary that the true criterion of truth should be discovered—a criterion which should be competent to prove in every case what is true and what is false.

This criterion being ascertained to be " that truth " is ever consistent with itself and with all facts," it has opened a new volume in the book of human life, and will sweep away all the rubbish produced through past ages while under the government of the origin of evil.

While thus governed all the rational faculties of humanity have lain dormant and undeveloped, and all men from their birth have been trained and educated to acquire a language of falsehood to support a false principle, which has created the false and evil spirit and false and evil practice which have hitherto pervaded all men, nations, and peoples, over the globe.

The criterion of truth proves that with the irrational first principle of society as hitherto existing, " that " man forms his own qualities and powers, and directs " them for good and evil throughout his life," there is nothing consistent in the mind and practice of the human race.

This false language, principle, spirit, and practice, with all their endless miserable results, are at this day taught, maintained, and encouraged most blindly by all the superstitions, called religions, and by all the governments on the earth.

Hence the cause of all the ignorance, poverty, false-

hood, disunion, crime, or sin and misery of past ages
and as these similar evils exist so prominently at
this day.

Any additional discussion on these subjects would
be now useless and a waste of the most valuable time
of the human race, suffering so severely day by day as
it is now doing from these causes.

That which is required is a knowledge and the
adoption of the *practice* which will in the shortest time
peaceably relieve the population of the world from the
degradation of this physical and mental bondage, which
has so long held in chains the natural feelings and
thoughts of our race, forcing all as far as possible to
falsify both, and thus keeping man ignorant of himself
—a knowledge the most valuable for him to acquire.

Under this reign of evil all nations are compelled
to talk nonsense, to act absurdities, and to be the dupes
of physical and mental oppression supported by force,
fear, fraud, and falsehood.

A true course of action founded on the origin of
good must commence somewhere and at sometime.
And why not at this time in the metropolis of the
British Empire and of the world?

To commence, (for everything on earth must have a
beginning,) I propose, then, now to commence a new
practical society, based on the origin of good, and that
the society shall be consistent with this foundation in
principle, spirit, language, and practice, and that
nothing inconsistent with its origin shall be admitted
to form any part of it.

The members who will form this new society will be
required to sacrifice everything for that which, by the
criterion stated, shall be proved to be true, and they

will form a band of brothers and sisters, which will gradually re-people the earth with full-formed men and women, wholly different in character from any who have yet lived upon it.

Their language will be that of truth, without deviation in look, word, or action; the genuine feelings and thoughts of all will, when required, be freely given to every one who shall ask for them; and thus will men and women begin to learn to know themselves and each other.

Entirely new surroundings will be made, in which to place all, to enable them without fear of giving offence to speak on all occasions the simple language of truth, and to act continually in consistent accordance with the origin of good.

In these surroundings there will be no private property, no private interests; and property, being public, will be freely used when required without money and without price by all, it being the joint production of all according to capacity.

The children of the members of the society will receive from birth the best formation of character that their created faculties and powers will admit, and they will be placed through life within the best surroundings that can be devised with existing means, to enable all to be at all times well fed, clothed, and lodged,—to be trained and educated naturally in the best manner,— to be employed and recreated most beneficially for the individual and for society,—and to be governed locally according to the laws of God and nature.

By these means the present generation, as soon as placed within these rational surroundings, will be very greatly im roved in their general character; and all the children born, trained, educated, and living within them will be made to become good, wise, united with their fellows, and happy in the natural enjoyment of all their faculties, physical and mental, highly cultivated and refined.

By these simple rational natural means the rubbish which has been created so abundantly in every department of this false and most artificial state of society, based on the origin of evil, will be removed and burnt up through the common sense of all, by this new society founded on and emanating from the origin of good.

Large portions of this rubbish will be found to consist of the various contending superstitions called religions, laws, governments, institutions, and classifications of society, as these now exist over the earth, all directly emanating from the origin of falsehood and evil, and which if it was to be much longer suffered to continue would gradually lead the human race down to a Pandemonium existence, of utter Babel confusion, of public wars, and of private assassinations.

But these natural, rational, and superior surroundings cannot be commenced until the society shall be sufficiently numerous and wealthy to create them in the most scientific and complete manner to attain the objects stated.

But when so created and carried into full practical effect, it will be found to be greatly more economical than the existing random mode of conducting society.

Under the new system every one will be secured in an existence so far superior to any yet known, that no comparison can be made between the future and the past, and at an expenditure of labour, let it be said, of one-fourth now required to maintain the same number in the middle class of life. I say "one-fourth" on the same principle that the highly-gifted late George Stevenson said his projected new railways would enable us to travel at the speed of fifteen miles an hour, when he knew the speed attained could easily be made to exceed thirty miles an hour. And I well know that much less than one-tenth the labour now required to support this wretched retificial false and evil state of existence would make our earth a paradise, and would insure high permanent happiness to all.

The change from the population of the world being governed by the erroneous principles and injurious surroundings necessarily proceeding from the origin of evil, to the same population being governed by the uniformly true principles and the beautiful surroundings which will as necessarily emanate from the origin of truth and good, will at first appear to all to be the greatest miracle that the nations of the earth have yet witnessed.

To give a full detail of all the differences which will arise in spirit, principle, and practice, when the origin of truth and good shall be made to supersede the origin of falsehood and evil, would require a large volume.

That which has been written to introduce this all-absorbing subject to the public may suffice until more shall be required.

But let it be remembered by every one of every class over the world, that their character from birth has been based on a falsehood which pervades their whole mind and conduct, and that every arrangement of society known to the human race has had this foundation, and that it is therefore at this day that the mass of the population in all countries are in gross ignorance, in abject poverty or the fear of it, disunited, continually opposed to or estranged from each other, and that so much sin and misery are experienced by all, from the greatest to the least; while the most ample means exist, if they were properly applied, based on the origin of truth and good, to gradually remove all these evils, and to prevent their recurrence through all future time.

It is now for the British government and people to consider and decide whether in future they shall have the character of their children formed and themselves governed under the origin of falsehood and evil, or under a scientific system based on the origin of truth and good?

For myself, so long as I shall have mental health and physical strength I shall continue to advocate the introduction of the pure, uncontaminated, consistent system of truth and good, for forming the character of and governing the human race.

                    ROBERT OWEN.

Sevenoaks Park, 4th Feb., 1858.

The following Circular was sent by R. Owen to the leading members of both houses of Parliament between the 2nd and 4th of February, 1858—previous to the re-assembling of Parliament:—

" Mr. Owen presents his compliments to and requests to be informed if (his **Royal Highness,** his Grace, his Lordship, or he, as the case required,) can give his support to the prayer of the inclosed petition to change the present system of falsehood and evil for governing society—a system which through all past time has been most injurious to all; for the system of truth and good, which through all future time will be highly beneficial to all of our race."

N.B.—The Petition referred to is that which is printed in No. 14 of the *Millennial Gazette*, published February 10th, 1858.

Lately Published, Price 10*s.*

The first Volume of the Life of Robert Owen, written by himself, with selections from his writings and correspondence. Effingham Wilson, Royal Exchange, London.

Will be Published shortly. A Supplement to the First Volume of the Life of Robert Owen. Containing a collection of Mr. Owen's early Publications, &c. Price 10s.

Robert Owen's Millennial Gazette.

No. 13. Containing the Papers read at the first meeting of the National Association for the promotion of Social Science, at Birmingham, in October 1857, and other articles.

Report of the Meetings of the Congress of the advanced minds of the world, convened by Robert Owen, held in St. Martin's Hall, Long Acre, and in the Literary and Scientific Institution, John Street, Fitzroy Square, from the 12th to the 25th of May, 1857, to consider the best peaceable methods and means for changing the present most ignorant, false, unjust, cruel, and evil system of human Society, and for introducing the enlightened, true, just, merciful, and good system of Society, for forming men's character, producing wealth, and governing the human race.

As the object of the Author is to attain unchanging everlasting truths, to secure the permanent happiness of all through futurity, irrespective of every natural or acquired difference, he will be obliged to the intelligent reader to state his or her matured objections to the spirit, principles, or practices, recommended in this pamphlet, after a due study of the entire new system of society which it advocates, and which the Author now submits to the unprejudiced consideration of all nations and peoples.

THIS WORK

IS WRITTEN AND PUBLISHED TO PREPARE, ASSIST, AND ENABLE THE POPULATION OF THE WORLD TO OVERCOME AND ABANDON THE SYSTEM OF FALSEHOOD, EVIL, AND MISERY, BY WHICH IT HAS BEEN SO LONG GOVERNED, AND TO COMMENCE AND MAINTAIN THE SYSTEM OF TRUTH, GOODNESS, AND HAPPINESS, FOR THEIR FUTURE GOVERNMENT. THE OLD SYSTEM LEADING TO A TERRESTRIAL PANDEMONIUM, AND THE NEW TO A TERRESTRIAL PARADISE.

Registered for Foreign Transmission.

ROBERT OWEN'S
MILLENNIAL GAZETTE.

DEDICATED

TO THE

FAITHFUL UNTO DEATH

IN

OPENLY DECLARING AND MAINTAINING THE ALL-IMPOR-
TANT TRUTHS ON WHICH THE PERMANENT
HAPPINESS OF OUR RACE DEPENDS;

TRUTHS

PROVED TO BE SUCH BY THEIR EVER CONSISTENCY
WITH THEMSELVES AND ALL FACTS;

THE ONLY SURE CRITERION OF TRUTH
EVER YET GIVEN TO MAN.

No. 15.
MAY 1, 1858.

SECOND EDITION.

LONDON:
PUBLISHED BY EFFINGHAM WILSON,
ROYAL EXCHANGE

Price 8d.

THESE WRITINGS

ARE INTENDED TO EFFECT AN ENTIRE REVOLUTION
IN THE SPIRIT, MIND, MANNERS, HABITS, AND CON-
DUCT, OF THE HUMAN RACE ;—A RATIONAL, PRAC-
TICAL REVOLUTION, TO BE INTRODUCED GRADUALLY,
IN PEACE, WITH WISE FORESIGHT, AND TO BE
HIGHLY BENEFICIAL FOR ALL THROUGH FUTU-
RITY ;—A REVOLUTION TO SUPERSEDE A SYSTEM
OF INDIVIDUAL IGNORANT SELFISHNESS, BASED
ON THE ORIGIN OF FALSEHOOD AND EVIL; AND
WHICH CAN BE SUPPORTED ONLY BY FORCE, FEAR,
FRAUD, AND FALSEHOOD, SUPERSEDED BY A
SYSTEM BASED ON THE ORIGIN OF TRUTH AND
GOOD, WHICH CAN ALONE PRODUCE THE SPIRIT,
KNOWLEDGE, AND WISDOM, BY WHICH TO GOVERN
SOCIETY PERPETUALLY ON SOCIAL PRINCIPLES,
SOLELY BY LOVE AND CHARITY ;—A REVOLUTION
WHICH WILL DESTROY EVERY IGNORANT SELFISH
FEELING, WILL UNITE MAN TO MAN, AND WILL
THEN HARMONISE ALL TO NATURE AND TO GOD,
MAKING OUR GLOBE INTO AN EVER-IMPROVING
EARTHLY PARADISE, WHICH IS NOW EVIDENTLY
THE INTENTION OF OUR CREATOR. THIS UNIVERSAL
REVOLUTION WILL BE EFFECTED BY THE MOST
NATURAL MEANS ;—SIMPLY BY BASING SOCIETY ON
ITS ONLY TRUE FOUNDATION, IN ACCORDANCE WITH
ALL FACTS, AND MAKING THE SURROUNDINGS IN
WHICH TO PLACE THE HUMAN RACE SUPERIOR,
AND ALWAYS CONSISTENT WITH THAT BASE AND
THOSE FACTS. THE MEANS TO ACCOMPLISH THIS
TASK ABUNDANTLY EXIST, AND BY THE UNION OF
GOVERNMENTS IT MAY EASILY BE EFFECTED.

ROBERT OWEN.

March 30. 1858.

MANIFESTO

OF

ROBERT OWEN

ON THE PRESENT FALSE CONDITION OF SOCIETY, AND WHAT IS NOW REQUIRED TO BE DONE TO OVERCOME ITS EVILS AND SUFFERINGS.

THE population of the world through all past time has been trained, educated, and placed, on principles opposed to facts and to the unchanging laws of humanity. It has therefore never attained to goodness, wisdom, union, peace, or happiness, or been enabled to use the language of truth on the most important subjects respecting the nature of man and the laws of his being.

In consequence of this long mysterious universal ignorance of and inattention to the plain and obvious laws of human nature, man from his birth has been forced by the injurious surroundings in which he has ever been placed to this day, to become a mere superstitious fighting animal, not sufficiently developed mentally to acquire the first degree of common sense in common things.

And therefore, with the most ample means at the immediate control of society to create a vast superfluity of superior, real, and substantial wealth for all in perpetuity, and to form a good, rational, and superior character for all from birth, man is compelled by the ignorance of society to grow up in utter ignorance of the laws of his nature, to speak the language of falsehood, to acquire the arts of deception, to be opposed to his fellows in feelings and interest, to act continually in opposition to his nature, and to become an artificial fool, in the midst of an animal creation all acting wisely according to the laws of their respective natures, and therefore enjoying much happiness in accordance with their natural qualities and conditions.

But man is now approaching the first step towards becoming a rational being, and to know something of the laws of his

nature. As a localised animal he has now power to look around
him and to perceive that in other localities the human animal has
been forced to acquire languages, superstitions, habits, manners,
customs, and ideas, opposed to his own, which he has been forced
to receive and believe to be *the true* and *right*, in opposition to
the innumerable varieties around him, extending in all directions.

But he has yet only just sufficient mental power developed
within him to enable him to discover that all those varieties
which are opposed to those which he has been forced to believe
true and right are the very essence of ignorance and insane superstitions, and he wonders that any one could be made to be
sincere in that which to him appears so glaringly absurd :—never
in the least suspecting that these parties as glaringly perceive *his*
ignorance and superstitions, which are equally irrational ; and
still less does he suspect the truth, that *he* could from his birth
have been easily made to become a sincere believer in the truth
and superiority of any one of those varieties which he now deems
to be insane and absurd both in mind and practice.

All these errors necessarily emanate from the origin of falsehood and evil, which, happily for mankind, has been now discovered, and will soon be made familiar to the population of the
world, and will be superseded by the knowledge of the all-
important fact, that " the Creator, and not man, creates every
" quality and power, physical and mental, of humanity, and
" also continues them with more or less differences in each in-
" dividual, so that no two have been the same through the
" existence of man upon the earth, or ever will be the same as
" long as the race shall inhabit this globe, and that, therefore,
" God, the Creator of all within the universe, can be alone re-
" sponsible for the feelings, thoughts, and actions of beings so
" created, and more especially of beings so varied in their created
" qualities and powers."

Undeveloped man, before he understood facts or how to ascertain them, imagined that, to make his offspring good, he must
make them responsible for the feelings, thoughts, and actions,
which emanate from qualities and powers which were forced
upon them without their consent or knowledge. By this fatal
error he necessarily trained his descendants to become through
all past time false, deceitful, repulsive, fighting animals, presuming that they were good and wise and competent to know
themselves, while to this day they exhibit in all public affairs
over the world the most gross irrationality, insanity, or madness,
and a total ignorance of themselves and of the most important
laws of human nature.

Seeing that this melancholy condition is at this day the actual
state of affairs in all nations and among all peoples,—how are
the rays of heavenly truth to be made to penetrate all hearts and
minds, so as to enable them to comprehend and appreciate these

divine truths, on which the permanent goodness, progress, wisdom, rationality, and happiness of our race depend?

These divine truths must be taught to the existing governments of the world in the spirit of kindness, charity, and love; they must be carried calmly into execution under their direction, in peace, in order, and with wise foresight. And the entire change from the false and evil system, to the true and good, over the world, may be made a plain straight-forward matter of business, far more simple than to establish railways, steam navigation, and electric telegraphs over the earth, as now in progress.

And under their direction also, the press in every country should immediately promulgate these divine truths, that they may speedily become universally known, in order that real knowledge may " cover the earth as the waters cover the seas."

And thus, in the fulness of time, and in the due order of nature, shall falsehood, evil, ignorance, and misery, be changed to truth, goodness, wisdom, and happiness.

ROBERT OWEN.

Written in Sevenoaks Park,
   Sevenoaks, February 16th, 1858.

SOCIETY OF SOCIAL SCIENCE CHARTISTS.

PREAMBLE.

THE members of all governments can know only that which they have been taught in their respective localities; and this instruction, however apparently different, being only varieties of the same system of falsehood, repulsion, and evil, which through all past time has been taught to and forced upon all the preceding generations of men, governments cannot know the true and good attractive system for governing wisely, or for forming a rational, useful, truthful, and superior natural character for any portion of those over whom they govern.

This knowledge in principle and practice, valuable beyond all estimate which can be made in the present state of human faculties, is yet known only to a few of the most advanced minds over the world, and to these only in the general outline, and they will not know more until the discoverer of the origin of falsehood, repulsive feelings, and evil shall disclose to them and to the population of the world the full system of truth, goodness, and of universal attractive feelings between all of the human race through futurity.

And the most rapidly to promulgate this knowledge, which to

our race is beyond price, I propose to found the "*Society of Social Science Chartists,*" to effect in peace, in order, and with wise foresight, the change of the false, evil, and repulsive system of society for governing mankind, for the true, good, and universally attractive system for forming a superior character in man and for the government of our race in accordance with the unchanging laws of God and nature.

In addition to this all-absorbing change of system, from falsehood to truth, from evil to good, and from repulsive to attractive feelings, this society will be established to give immediate relief to all the suffering working classes,—suffering solely from the general ignorance of society, and from the want of a true natural formation of character from birth, to give them the spirit of universal charity and love for their fellows, and also from their want of the natural, perpetual, beneficial, reproductive occupations and employments which may now be so easily given to all.

For the means everywhere amply exist to insure this character and employment for all, and this character and employment may be given to all through their own well directed industry.

This industry could be now applied to insure the creation of new combinations of surroundings, in which all, without contest or competition, could be permanently well-fed, clothed, lodged, trained, educated, occupied, recreated, and locally governed. And now to have these secured to all is the birthright of man over the world; and they are to be secured simply by man being well placed from his birth.

Let there be, therefore, no more wasting of most valuable time, wealth, and talents, in agitating for a reform in parliament, which, if obtained to the extent of the six points of what is called "The People's Charter," would not for twenty years or more benefit the working classes, or put one penny into their pockets, nor indeed until they can have an unexclusive, national, natural formation of character from birth, and permanent beneficial occupation.

These two united can alone permanently and substantially benefit the working classes; and for the attainment of these they should continually agitate society until they shall be secured to them in perpetuity.

This change, now so loudly called for by the unnatural and most unnecessary suffering of the producing classes, would essentially and speedily improve the condition of all classes above them; and these classes in various ways also call loudly for improvement.

The six points of the Charter which the people are now taught to ask for are of the least possible value, except when united with the superior natural formed character, and with permanent beneficial occupation. With these first obtained, their real value will become known; but the formation of this character must be immediately commenced, and the occupations provided, both of which may be made to be in active progress this year.

These are the reasons for now commencing the " *Society of* " *Social Science Chartists, for improving the social condition of* " *the industrious producing, peaceable, working classes.*"

Conditions of Membership.

1st.—As in the present false and artificial state of society no important permenent benefit can be obtained for the poor and working classes without sufficient funds and practical knowledge how to apply those funds, each member must pay an entrauce fee of twenty shillings, or £1. sterling, and subscribe regularly one shilling per week.

2nd.—Every member must possess a knowledge of some useful occupation, in which, as employer or employed, he is daily engaged.

3rd.—The members must abandon all party politics, and give all their spare time, from business and necessary recreation for health, to promote the objects of the Society of the Social Science Chartists, these objects being paramount to all others except employment for existence and a respectable living.

4th.—All sectarian dogmas and superstitious notions and ceremonies to be given up and entirely abandoned, and these to be superseded by the spirit, principle, and practice of universal charity and love for all of our race, exercised on all occasions without deviation, based on the knowledge " that the natural " faculties and qualities of every one are forced upon them, and " that the wise or foolish direction from birth is alone the work " of the society by which they are surrounded ; and that a good " or bad, a truthful or a false, a useful or a useless character may " now be forced upon all of the human race."

5th.—That each member, thus knowing how every character is formed, shall treat all kindly, and consider them as brothers and sisters of one family, and who, if in error, physically or mentally, or both, deserve our aid and sympathy, and never our anger or abusive language. And this conduct to be uniform to all, whether members of the society or not. For the members must be known by their love and charity, not only for each other, but for all of their race, knowing no exception of colour, country, class, creed, or any natural born differences, physical or mental.

6th.—That all attend the Sunday meetings of the society, which shall be always held, in every locality where a branch society shall be established, at least once on each Sabbath day, for rational enjoyment, and to assist constant progress in all useful knowledge. None to be absent except from unavoidable necessity.

7th.—The non-payment of the weekly subscription, or absence from the weekly meeting, except from unavoidable necessity, will preclude the continuance of membership—members who are indifferent to the objects and proceedings of the society being worse than useless.

8th.—At the social meeting on Sunday, some one of the members should deliver a useful lecture on the views and objects of the society, or read some paper, valuable for its information, explanatory of the difference which will arise when society shall be governed by the all-wise laws of God and nature, instead of the absurd and evil-creating laws of undeveloped men. The members of the society should govern themselves and be governed, as far as practicable in the present false and artificial state of the laws and customs of all countries, by the known unchanging, merciful, and all-wise laws of humanity, as given to man by his Creator.

The society to be inaugurated the 14th May next. ·

ROBERT OWEN.

February 18, 1858.

FURTHER PARTICULARS.

THE greatest change ever made in the condition of humanity, or perhaps the greatest that ever can be made while man inhabits the earth, may be thus briefly stated.

1st.—All to be taught to know and to abandon the Origin of Falsehood and Evil, which, be it ever remembered, is the insane notion " that man creates by his will his own physical and " mental qualities and powers, and should be made responsible to " his fellow men for the thoughts and actions which they directly " or indirectly create."

2nd.—All should be taught to know and to abandon the insane combinations of surroundings for governing society, under all its apparent varieties over the world, and which have necessarily emanated from the Origin of Falsehood and Evil.

3rd.—All must be taught to know and to adopt the Origin of Truth and Good, which is the knowledge " that man cannot make " one of his physical or mental qualities or powers, or rationally " be made responsible for their actions."

4th.—All must be taught to know and to adopt universally the new combinations of surroundings which will necessarily emanate from the Origin of Truth and Good

Men of all ranks and conditions !—from the highest to the lowest—from the supposed best to the supposed worst ! learn the preceding short lesson! The study of it will open your minds to perceive the truth in all things, and the practical measures by which the present and future of our race may be made to become *good* and *wise*, and may be secured in an *everlasting joyous happiness*.

To commence this change in the present year, and to make it to progress steadily onwards, the following is proposed and recommended to every shade of reformers who sincerely desire to permanently speedily improve the condition of their poor unnecessarily suffering fellow men, who, millions upon millions, are at this moment grievously afflicted, physically, mentally, and spiritually, without knowing the cause, or that it may now be removed with the certainty of a law of nature.

Then behold! a short, direct, and certain road to the speedy relief of all, from falsehood and evil, and their innumerable direful effects in practice,—among which are ignorance, *poverty*, *crime*, tyranny, and slavery.

This change must commence by improving the condition of those now made the degraded poor and the working classes; for until these are elevated to become rational and superior in mind, manners, and habits, no permanent good can be effected for society.

This can only be done by giving to these classes a new natural national training and education, and by arranging practical measures to give them a constant supply of beneficial employment.

As there are no other means under heaven by which they can be permanently raised from their present degraded state of slavery and suffering, no time should now be lost in commencing those measures in practice.

To accomplish these results in peace, in order, and with wise foresight, two new societies are necessary, to new train and educate both the working and the upper classes, and to give them the necessary knowledge to comprehend the spirit, principle, and practice, by which alone these superior results can be obtained for all.

The first of these societies may be called " *The Society of* " *Social Science Chartists, to improve the social condition of* " *the poor and working classes, and ultimately to prepare them* " *to become, in mind, manner, and habits, equal to any class.*"

This Society to be composed of the Working Classes who desire their social condition to be improved by a national, unexclusive, natural training and education from birth, and by a national, natural, reproductive, beneficial employment according to age, provided for them through life, and thus *prevent* the continuance of *ignorance*, *poverty*, *crime*, or the necessity for punishment of man by man.

This society to be inaugurated on the 14th of May next, in St. Martin's Hall, Long Acre, at seven o'clock in the evening, when the details of the practical working of the society will be explained.

These proceedings are intended to prepare a solid and lasting base on which to construct a superior society, new in spirit, principle, and practice, for the human race, and to give permanent peace, harmony, and happiness to the population of the world.

To perfect this work a second society will be required.

This second society to be formed from what are now called the upper classes, of well-intentioned, thoughtful, and reflecting men and women, superior in mind, manner, and habits.

These classes now have accomplished the work for which they were destined, and are now worse than useless in their present positions ; while under the new combinations of surroundings in which society will place them, they will become highly useful, greatly superior, and much happier than they are or can be in the existing system.

This society will be called " *The Social Science Society of the superior Middle and Upper Classes who sincerely desire to improve the general condition of humanity.*"

These will show to the world what may be now attained by man for man with the means which an all-wise and all-good Providence has provided in the due order and progress of nature's creations, to enable man, through his present advanced development and wisely directed industry, to attain permanently the happiness of his race through all succeeding generations.

The period for the inauguration of the second society will be announced at the inauguration of the " *Society of Social Science Chartists*" on the 14th of May next.

Let it now be distinctly impressed on the minds of all, that without a real substantial and permanent equality in training, education, and condition, according to age and physical and mental capacity, there can be no public truth, justice, or moral and honest proceedings in society :—that under the present *classifications* over the world there can be no real liberty, equality, or fraternity ; for all existing classifications necessarily create tyrants and slaves, under various denominations :—consequently, that while society shall continue to be governed under the system of falsehood and evil, it will be useless for the democracies to expect to attain their long cherished desire for " liberty, equality, and fraternity." For so long as those who are now made poor, ignorant, and degraded, shall continue to be by society so wickedly and insanely trained, educated, placed, as they have been and are, there can be no practical equality for them with those made by society to become the upper classes, by being differently trained, educated, and surrounded with ideas, habits, and manners so opposed to those by which the minds, habits, and manners of those who are now called the lower orders are formed. Nor will it be possible for this desire of all enlightened humanity to be attained until all from birth shall be nationally equally trained, educated, placed, and surrounded.

Let it now be had in everlasting remembrance, that abundant means have been provided, even far more than sufficient to train, educate, and place all over the earth within much superior surroundings to those now possessed, and to any that can be attained by the *greatest* and most *powerful Potentate* upon *earth*, under the satanic working of society while governed by the origin of evil.

With this knowledge now disclosed, can men continue so blind as to persevere in maintaining this system, now no longer necessary or useful, of satanic superstitions and governments, ever supported by fire and sword, by force and fear, or by fraud and falsehood, and which can be supported only by these scourges of humanity—a system which has perfected its destiny, of creating limited evils, that far greater illimitable good may be known by its contrasts, and enjoyed for ever by all through knowing these contrasts by their authentic details as past history; a system which nature, in her own quiet and effectual way, is now actively preparing to destroy all over the world, and to supersede it by the system of truth and good, and then to govern mankind solely on the divine principles of love and charity for all humanity ; when, in consequence, evil and suffering, physical, mental, and spiritual, will be unknown, and the inhabitants of the earth will enjoy perfect harmony, and be in possession of real liberty, equality, and fraternity.

But to effect this glorious change for humanity,—a change yet difficult for the most advanced in knowledge to comprehend or appreciate, nature's course must be pursued, and no impossibility in practice attempted.

As stated, a second society will be required, composed of men and women superior and refined in mind, manner, and habits, in order to become an example to teach all others to acquire the same attainments, to be united with a knowledge of practice in all the business of life.

This knowledge will be acquired by those placed within the new combinations of superior surroundings—superior for training, educating, and employing all, according to age, in the best manner for the individual and for the whole of society.

By this change, which will be found simple and beautiful in practice, all necessity for standing *Armies* will soon cease, and their enormous waste of labour, property, and life, with all their demoralizing effects and inexpressible sufferings to the millions, will become so glaring to all, that all will cry " shame ! shame !" on them, and the people will acquire too much knowledge and power, and too much love and charity for each other, to allow the practice to continue.

The knowledge of the origin of truth and good will open the

eyes of all to the enormity of this great, standing, satanic evil—this hydra, with its millions of heads continually pouring forth the most scientific discoveries of tremendous power to destroy the life, liberty, property, and morality of the peaceable inhabitants of the earth.

These armies now waste and destroy more labour and materials, ten times told, than if they were wisely applied and directed would create superior surroundings for the population of the world, in which through all future generations they would all become *good, wise, united, ever prosperous,* and *happy.*

With the ceasing of standing armies—the greatest scourge of humanity—must cease also their great and main support, the insane ever-contending *Superstitions* of all nations and peoples—superstitions which ever have been, now are, and, while continued, ever will be the hydra of obstacles to prevent the possibility of the human race being taught to acquire, in heart, mind, and practice, the divine spirit of universal love and charity, to be applied in every day practice by each to all of our race ; and this is the only True Religion that can be taught to man while living upon the earth.

The gradual ceasing of these two monsters of iniquity and hydras of evil will make room for a new and just and good classification of mankind—a classification according to age, formed into armies of civilization, to create, with the most beautiful order, wealth and goodness and happiness for every portion of the human race, leaving no child of ignorance, poverty, and misery to be found in all the earth.

Human made *Laws,* all being based on the origin of falsehood and evil, and all in direct opposition to the laws of God and nature, as written unchangeably in the constitution of all humanity and in the feelings of every one born of man, will be entirely abandoned, with all their demoralizing and misery-producing results, by all of the human race ; and man will thereafter be for ever governed by the known laws of God and nature.

Wealth will be naturally produced and naturally used, and in consequence will be always superabundant for the population of the world. It has hitherto been artificially produced and artificially used ; and this error has alone created poverty through all past ages, and alone continues to create it at this day.

These combined hydras of evil one and all emanate from the origin of evil.

CHALLENGE TO BOTH HOUSES OF PARLIAMENT.

It is time to bring the worldly contending contradictions of an insane system, based on the origin of falsehood and evil, for governing the human race, to a speedy termination, that the po-

pulation of the world may be trained and educated to become
sane, good, wise, united, and happy, and be for ever hereafter
governed in the spirit and practice of universal love and charity,
emanating direct from the origin of truth and good, on which
foundation alone man can ever be taught to know his own nature and the laws which govern it, or be so trained, educated, and
placed, as to become a sane being, consistent in mind and practice, or to become, or to know what is, good or wise, or to be
competent to understand or to enjoy rational happiness.

Having year after year, with exceptions only when I was pursuing the same great objects in foreign lands, exhausted without
success all the usual legitimate means according to the usages of
what is deemed respectable society to bring these now become all
absorbing subjects before Parliament for fair and full examination and open discussion, I must now for this purpose resort to
the only means l ft to me by which I can speedily and permanently benefit my poor suffering insane fellow men. It is the
last resource which I possess to give that divine knowledge in
spirit, principle, and practice, by which alone man while inhabiting the earth can be made to become sane, good, wise, united, or
happy.

I now come forward to this great and good work, not in my
own strength or powers—for I have none. Those which I possess
have been given to me by that Power which gives their qualities
to all things and beings created, and which excites them to every
movement of action.

Say not, then, that this proceeding emanates from the presumption of Robert Owen, to whom one particle of merit never did
and never can be rationally attributed. That which Robert Owen
is about to do, he, as a passive agent, is forced into action to do,
by that Power which, although yet unknown to men in essence
and mode of action, does all things well and wisely for ultimate
good and happiness—evil itself, as previously shown, being an
essential means to this end.

Having stated in all sincerity, in good feeling, and in good
faith, the preceding preliminaries, I now challenge the British
Parliament, in its aggregate of members of both Houses, to discuss with me, in any manner it may prefer, the following all-important subjects, involving the permanent happiness or misery of
the human race :—

I will maintain :—

First.—That society over the world is based on the origin of
falsehood and evil, and that all existing surroundings have
emanated from the origin of evil, and are everywhere producing
avoidable misery to mankind.

Second.—That the existing contending *Superstitions* have all
emanated from the same source, and are at this day producing

incalculable disease, crime, and misery, in all countries, and which may now be easily prevented.

Third.—That all *Governments* emanate from the same source, and, in consequence, are of necessity governments supported only by force, fear, fraud, and falsehood, and are in their varied forms of action, highly injurious to and destructive of the rationality and happiness of governors and governed.

Fourth.—That all human *Laws* have proceeded from the fountain of evil, and that to this day there has not been one human-made law which has not been productive, directly or indirectly, of crime and misery, and opposed to the laws of God and nature, as permanently existing in humanity. And that it will be for the perpetual good and happiness of mankind these laws of men should gradually cease, and that man should be governed alone by the well ascertained fixed laws of God and Nature respecting humanity.

Fifth.—That the existing *Classifications of society* over the world have emanated from the origin of falsehood and evil; that they are directly calculated to make the human race insane, divided in interests and feeling, and to degrade physically and mentally all classes. And that a far more simple and much superior and more beneficial classification may be now easily adopted.

Sixth—That the present *Financial Arrangements of society* are absurd, insane, and highly injurious to every class over the world; destructive of good feelings between men, the cause of great suffering from poverty and of more from the fear of it, and most uselessly occupy and waste nine-tenths or more of the faculties and time of humanity, both of which, rightly applied, are of inestimable value, and capable of producing knowledge, wealth, unity, and happiness, utterly unknown to or unimagined to be capable of being attained by one member in either House of Parliament. I say this, because I have been made conscious that all are yet without knowledge of the mine of superior goodness and faculties now kept dormant within each individual in consequence of being coerced by the whole system of falsehood and evil.

Seventh.—In short, I engage to prove that the *Entire of the present system* of the world is satanic evil, having its origin in error; and that it is false and injurious in spirit, principle, and practice; and that it is incapable of any change for the happiness of our race, except by an entire change of system, in its spirit, principle, and practice, and by a new combination of surroundings, based upon and emanating from the system of truth and good, and which would insure the permanent happiness of all through futurity.

Eighth.—That it will be for the highest interest of every

British subject, and of the population of the world, that these subjects should be openly discussed and decided upon by the British parliament, before it proceeds to discuss and debate uselessly upon the petty temporary matters of no real interest to one human being—for with such only has the parliament of Great Britian been engaged through its whole existence. It has been occupied in making laws to endeavour to oppose the laws of God and nature—the most vain of all attempts in which men could occupy their time.

It is true that, at this day, the British parliament is the most advanced and free of all public assemblies now existing, or which perhaps ever existed, or can exist under a system of falsehood and evil. Nevertheless it is now useless, except to effect the change in peace and with order and wise foresight from this miserable state of existence, to the system of truth and good, which will of necessity produce universal goodness, wisdom, and happiness.

I could proceed in the same manner to all the details of the old, false, evil, and now thoroughly worn-out system for the future government of the human race; but I deem it unnecessary, and hope that sufficient has been said to induce parliament to enter with fairness and fulness upon the investigation of these subjects, involving the happiness or misery of the human race.

ROBERT OWEN.

March 1, 1858.

THE FALSE, EVIL, AND REPULSIVE SYSTEM, BY WHICH THE WORLD HAS BEEN HITHERTO GOVERNED, AND THE TRUE, GOOD, AND ATTRACTIVE SYSTEM, BY WHICH IN FUTURE THE WORLD WILL BE GOVERNED, AS SOON AS THE FIRST GLIMMERINGS OF COMMON SENSE CAN BE IMPRESSED ON THE MINDS OF GOVERNORS AND GOVERNED, MASTERS AND SERVANTS, TYRANTS AND SLAVES.

This change, the greatest ever made in the condition of humanity, and the greatest which can be made while man retains his present physical condition upon the earth, may be thus briefly expressed.

It will be a change from ignorance, violent and injurious passions, disunion, repulsive and uncharitable feelings, competition, conflicts, wars, poverty, crime, human punishments, and deceit of every shade and character, all of which have emanated directly from the origin of falsehood and evil; to an entirely new state of existence, emanating from the origin of truth and good, which will form a new character for the human race—a character which will combine wisdom or real knowledge rightly directed, attractive feelings for the confidence and sympathies of all humanity; a character which will create in all the true spirit of universal charity and love for our race, knowing no exceptions of colour, country, creed, sex, class, party, or born differences, but viewing each as a brother or sister of one united and enlightened family, forming by the union the aggregate of humanity, or the combined full-formed man and woman.

As soon as this character shall be well and wisely formed from birth, and all shall be rightly placed to be well occupied through life, the universal harmony of a useful active life for each will commence, will be perpetually progressive, and will be highly enjoyed, freed from all contending ignorant and most repulsive superstitions, and leaving this earthly state of existence for the future amidst superior eternal joys.

Such has been the past—such will be the future.

Let the watchword of all future agitation be " The society of " Friends of Social Science, established to give peace, prosperity, " unity, and harmony to man while upon earth, and to prepare " him for more joys when leaving this state of existence for the " future."

All classes, but more especially the producing classes, are now deluded and made antagonistic to other classes, necessarily creating a most miserable and irrational condition. This change will be effected by the creation of new combinations of surroundings, to give a national, rational, natural, good character, and perpetual national or local employment, to all within those surroundings.

These surroundings to be purposely devised to enable those within them, by their own well-directed industry, to be well fed, clothed, lodged. trained, educated, employed, recreated, and well locally governed by themselves, in gradations of office, according to age, without election or selection, after the death of the present generation, all born within these surroundings being from birth so well trained and educated as to be more than superior to the business of the office to be filled.

Such has been the error of the system under which the human-made part of the character of the population of the world has been formed, and all nations and people governed, that all classes in all countries appear to be overwhelmed with the ignorance and prejudices of localities which this system has inflicted upon all through the past ages of human existence, and all now are incapable of perceiving the most obvious and important truths.

Through the errors forced into their minds from birth, they cannot see the plain straightforward road to the attainment of those never-ceasing desires implanted by nature in every child of humanity—the desire to be good and the desire to be happy—the one unattainable without the other.

This ignorance we must conclude has been retained over all

humanity for some ultimate wise and good purpose, or the universe is not governed by infinite wisdom and goodness. But all the works of God will be gradually justified to man; for now, in its right time and due order of nature, this ignorance is removed by the discovery being made of the plain, simple, practical means by which, with the certainty of a law of nature, all of our race through futurity may be made to become good and happy, and gradually to increase in knowledge and in the power to use it wisely for the benefit of our race.

This discovery, by far the greatest ever made for the happiness of man, consists in the knowledge of the means by which a *national, natural, and superior training and education* may be economically given to all; by which *national, natural, beneficial reproductive employment* may be for ever insured to all; and by which training, education, and employment, all, by being rightly placed, may be for ever well fed, clothed, lodged, and have leisure for healthy and pleasant recreations, and to acquire high attainments in arts and sciences; while their habits and manners will be refined to the highest useful degree attainable by humanity.

This discovery includes a knowledge of the science of surroundings, which may truly be called "The *Divine Science* to insure the permanent happiness of the human race;" for on the good or evil, wise or foolish surroundings, depend the destiny of man.

Surroundings may now be formed to give to the entire family of man the qualities which men have attributed to angels, and to place them within an earthly paradise. Or to give to all the character attributed to demons, and to place them within a pandemonium.

It is for the new administration now to look immediately to this subject; for it will no longer be allowed to sleep. Man cannot remain as he now is made to be; he must be made to become much superior, or he will be made a slave in mind and station.

The Earl of Derby and his friends will have to decide this matter with the British public and with foreign powers; for the change will affect all nations and peoples. And it will also now have to be decided whether this change shall be effected calmly, in peace, with wise foresight; or through opposition or Babel confusion.

The change by the one or the other will soon become inevitable; for the present system, or rather disorder, of society, physically and mentally, cannot long continue without producing a sanguinary revolution over the world.

ROBERT OWEN.

March 3rd, 1858.

A NEW GOVERNMENT.

AN experienced, faithful, and talented Prime Minister of this country, seeing now the cause of its past ignorance, poverty, and fear of it ; of its disunion, its language of falsehood and conduct of deception ; of its erroneous superstitions, fatal classifications, and injurious institutions ; its neglect or ignorance of the true principles and by which to give a substantial good character from birth to all ; of its laws, based on falsehood, professing to prevent crime, while in reality they *create* and *encourage* it ; of its foreign public wars, with their wasteful expenditure, and destruction of valuable life and property, moral degradation, and endless miseries ; of its civil dissentions, conflicts, competitions, and endless opposing interests, with the miseries and sufferings which this cause has inflicted upon the human race through all past ages, and which at this day it inflicts upon all of our race, from the highest to the lowest, from the youngest to the oldest, of every rank and of every class—a faithful and talented Prime Minister, knowing these truths, as he ought to know them, would, at once, openly declare his determination to abandon this system of falsehood, evil, and misery, and to adopt the spirit, principle, and practice emanating direct from the origin of truth, goodness, and happiness ; but that he would effect the change so gradually that none should be injured by it, and all should be in their respective stations and conditions essentially benefited by every step made in this progress from the false and evil to the true and good state of our earthly existence.

All this a faithful, experienced, and talented Prime Minister could now effect, without any real difficulty or successful opposition to his measures.

A sufficient number of details for carrying this change into successful practice have been given in the preceeding pages of this publication, and the results may be thus briefly stated.

1st.—A good understanding for perpetual peace, and an offer of a federative honest treaty, with all foreign nations. Without this peace the nations of the earth can never become good, rational, wise, or happy.

2nd.—The establishment of the Bank of the British Empire, for the sole benefit of the nation ; to supersede the private Bank of England and all other private banks, making full compensation to all parties suffering by the change.

3rd.—A liberal, good, practical reform of Parliament, which shall give a vote to all competent to make a rational use of it.

4th.—Practical arrangements of new combinations of surroundings, which shall enable the government, by the wisely directed talents and industry of those within them, to well-feed, clothe, lodge, train, educate, employ, re-create, and amuse, and locally govern in perpetuity.

5th.—While this change shall be in gradual progress, a natural national system of training and education by object teaching and through familiar explanations and friendly conversations between teachers and taught,—the only rational mode of giving real knowledge and forming a consistent or sound mind in a sound body.

6th.—Perpetual national employment in forming these new combinations of surroundings for those who cannot better employ themselves or obtain superior occupation.

7th.—The establishment in India of a just and rational government for the natives and for the Europeans who may live and settle among them. This government to proceed from and be under the direction of the British government, until it shall be so organised and experienced in governing as, with a federative treaty with this country, to be competent to govern by its own knowledge and power.

8th.—A national property tax, graduated to increase according to the amount of increased wealth, and the abolition of all other taxes.

9th—Liberty to express, in speech or writing, on all proper occasions, the convictions and feelings which we are compelled, by the laws of our nature, to feel.

10th.—To abandon, as speedily as practicable, the unwise and most injurious laws of men, all directly or indirectly creating crime and misery, for the all-sufficient and all-wise laws of God and nature.

By these simple practical changes, ignorance, poverty, or fear of it, disunion, crime, and human punishments, would speedily become unknown within the British Empire at home and abroad.

ROBERT OWEN.

March 8th, 1858.

THE CONCLUSION OF MY MISSION TO THE HUMAN RACE.

THE experience derived from all facts through the past history of man demonstrates, that from the beginning the true nature of his formation and of the laws by which he should be governed have never been understood, and hence the Babel confusion and unnatural sufferings with which every generation to the present has been afflicted.

Let the nations and people of this globe now, for their permanent progress and happiness, attend to the following.

Man is created, unknown to himself, by the Great Mysterious

ever-Creating Power of the Universe, or God; and every organ, faculty, propensity, quality, and power, is directly calculated, when comprehended and naturally used, to promote the continued pleasure and happiness of the individual and of society, and ultimately, by the natural action of these combined qualities and powers, to make every one good, wise, united to his race, consistent in mind and practice, and, therefore, happy.

Evidently, now, God has created man to be happy in all his thoughts and actions, as soon as his reasoning faculties and judgment are sufficiently developed and matured; and facts prove that some individuals must make the advanced progress in these respects in order that the multitude may see and follow.

God has not created man to flatter his Creator by useless words or ceremonies; but to obey the laws of that nature which God has given man solely for the happiness of the individual and of humanity; this being the only possible means, if possible, to add to the happiness and satisfaction of the Great Creating Mysterious Power of the Universe.

To imagine that man could originate any of his natural qualities and powers, or unite them in the wonderful manner in which they are combined and entwined in each of our race for such a complication of action during the life of each, is opposed to all facts and is blasphemy against God; nor is this the natural way by which it is possible to make man a good, wise, consistent, and happy being, or enable him to become charitable and kind to all, or to acquire the spirit to give him the motives and power to love his neighbour as himself, and to forgive and love his enemies, as being made to be such because they had been mis-educated and mis-placed by the ignorance of their ancestors.

On the contrary, to suppose man competent to create his own will, or any one of his own qualities or powers, and to make him responsible to his ignorant and undeveloped fellow man, as now so generally practised over the world, is to compel him to become unnatural and to be false and deceitful and full of miserable and most injurious errors in mind and conduct, as he is at this day.

Man of himself cannot think a thought or do an action, but as he is empowered by his Creator.

" Man of himself can do nothing;" for by the laws of his nature he is *compelled* to *believe* and is *compelled* to *feel*; and it is a proof of general insanity for man to make man responsible to him for either his beliefs or his feelings; for this is the sure method to make him deceitful and a weak coward, and to cause him to lose the character of humanity and never to attain to being a full-formed man or woman through life.

Ascertaining these fixed and unchanging laws of humanity, I was led to the discovery of the Origin of Falsehood, Evil, and Misery, and of the Origin of Truth, Goodness, and Happiness;

hence to the knowledge of the Science of Surroundings, or of the Social Science; and hence to all the practice necessary to ensure the new Millennial Existence of Man upon the earth through futurity.

The Science of Surroundings or the Social Science developes the means by which, with the most useful and beautiful surroundings, the human race through futurity may from birth be well fed, clothed, lodged, trained, educated, employed, amused, or healthily recreated, and locally self-governed; and these results to arise from all being well or naturally placed.

Thus shall " old things pass away and all become new;" and yet the change may be made so quietly, peaceably, and so beneficially for all, that it will come " like a thief in the night," and disturb no one interest throughout the whole of society, nor injure one individual during the whole change.

If the Earl of Derby and his political friends desire to establish their administration on a permanent foundation, they must govern through the knowledge of the Social Science or the Science of Surroundings; for as these surroundings are wise or foolish, so will mankind be.

The present surroundings over the world are an absurd compound of folly. These may now be made by the governing authorities in churches and states gradually and quietly to pass away, and be superseded by new combinations wisely imagined and wisely executed.

Let the population of the world mark, learn, and inwardly digest what has been now said and written for durability.

ROBERT OWEN.

March 9th, 1858.

ADDRESS

TO THE SOCIAL CHARTISTS OF THE BRITISH EMPIRE.

This address is intended not to flatter, but to express to you truth, without mystery, mixture of error, or fear of man, that will for ever essentially benefit you and your children's children.

Hitherto you have been taught to be politicians—tell me now, what good have politics ever done for you, or can ever do for you? They have kept you, and now keep you, ignorant talkative slaves, about that of which you appear to have no knowledge —that is, of your interests,—your duties to yourselves, to your families, and to society,—and your natural rights. And they have thus kept you ignorant slaves, for the imagined benefit of others, who have thought that they had an interest in giving your minds a wrong direction.

Your rights are—the best natural practical training and education from birth that society possesses the knowledge and means to give you, and without this you must continue ignorant slaves to the idle, whom you alone support.

Your duties are—to learn your rights, and how to obtain them by rational proceedings.

You are now born and bred, grow up, and live, within *slave surroundings;* and so long as you are continued within them you must remain *ignorant oppressed slaves* to task-masters a little less ignorant than yourselves.

While you are continued within these surroundings, neither you nor your children can ever receive a natural, practical, rational, useful, and good training and education.

The surroundings in which alone you can receive this training and education require to be such as will, by their natural combinations and progress, of necessity enable you, without contest, to be permanently well employed, and by that employment to be always well-fed, clothed, lodged, healthily recreated, rationally amused, and locally well governed by yourselves; and all this in consequence of being well placed within surroundings all devised to be in accordance with the natural constitution or general organization of humanity, and in perpetual harmony with the laws by which it ever has been governed.

Your duties, therefore, are to learn the theory and practice of these surroundings, and the social science from which they emanate, and also the natural or best mode to make the change from the present false, artificial, and most injurious surroundings, to the true, the natural, and the good surroundings.

Your interests are to unite cordially and heartily as one man, and quietly, peaceably, but in the most firm and determined manner, to petition or rather memorialize government and parliament now to give you your rights, in such manner as shall not prematurely disturb the existing order (if order it can be called when all is disorder,) of society, and to effect this change by the usual organs and agents of government, without your inexperienced interference.

And, above all things, eschew all attempts at violence, and avoid abusive language; for both exhibit total ignorance of human nature and of common sense.

If you firmly unite among yourselves in asking for your rights, no government that can retain its position will refuse that which you require of them. It is their interest and safety to willingly and pleasantly grant you your rightful request.

It is true that, as members of an artificial representative government, you have a just right to *all* the points of the so-called people's charter,—but, my friends, in your present ignorant and dependent slavish state, mentally and physically, and in the ignorant state in which those are who would solicit your votes, of what possible use would the full charter be to you for many years to come? The whole Charter, if granted to-morrow, would not put one penny, except bribes for votes, into your pockets, for half a century to come.

Your wants are immediate, and, to a considerable extent, may be relieved this year.

Your friend,

The discoverer of the true social science

And system for practice.

ROBERT OWEN.

Sevenoaks, March 10th, 1858.

ADDRESS

TO THE MIDDLE CLASSES INCLUDING THE PROFESSIONS WITHIN THE BRITISH EMPIRE.

FRIENDS,—You now possess the most ample means to secure to yourselves, your children, and society, in perpetuity, a superior character, increasing prosperity, and wisdom to attain a high degree of happiness, constantly progressing as your knowledge of facts shall extend.

But for want of that which now appears to be the rudiments of the most useful and valuable practical knowledge, you are retained slaves and pack horses to the upper classes, to your and their permanent loss and grievous injury; for the upper classes appear to have nothing to do but to devise laws to keep you in bondage, physically and mentally, to make you task masters over the working classes to provide wealth, not only for luxurious living, but for them to squander in the most insane manner in fomenting wars highly injurious to the entire family of man over the earth, and in the support of the most irrational superstitions, which serve no good purpose whatever, but which, on the contrary, derange the rational faculties of humanity, by promulgating and teaching the most gross falsehoods as divine truths which no one must doubt or call in question,—being, as they say, too sacred to be discussed. And they say this, knowing them to be so false as easily to be proved so in the first common sense discussion to which they shall be submitted without the fear of man. For the heads of all the superstitions in the world say—" Be-

" lieve what I tell you to believe ; disbelieve what I tell you to
" disbelieve ; reverence me ; and pay me well ; and you will be
" God's good children, and when you die you will go to heaven."

Such, and such only, is the true meaning of every superstition
invented by man from man's creation upon earth ; for there
never was, there is not, there never will be, a particle of merit in
any man or woman for any belief whatever, any more than they
can have merit or demerit for the colour of their hair or the
complexion of their skin.   All are compelled by the laws of their
nature to have their hair and skin of the colour given to them
by their Creator, and all are compelled to have their belief in
accordance with the strongest convictions made on their minds
by the circumstances in which they are placed.   And facts, from
the beginning of man's history to this day, in all the nations of
the world, prove that *any* belief may be *forced* into the mind of
any child, commencing in its infancy.

Who can tell of the severe mental and physical torments which
have been and are experienced by man through this taught error
of all the superstitions known to the human race, of which those
which history narrates are comparatively few compared with
those endless untold sufferings which no history narrates or can
narrate ?

Again ; who, possessing the first grains of common sense, does
not know, that by the laws of his nature, fixed more firmly than
the stars of heaven, he must like and love, dislike and hate,
according to the feelings of his organisation ; and that by his
will he cannot create those feelings, or prevent circumstances
changing them at any moment.

What right, then, in the name of common sense, have any of
these insane superstitions to interpose their absurdities to direct
these feelings according to their whims and fancies, in opposition
to the direct laws of God and of human nature, never known to
change ?

Do they know the crimes and diseases which they by these
errors have *created* and *inflicted* upon *man* and *woman* through
past ages ?

Do they know the crimes, the diseases, and the hellish torments
of prostitution in Europe and America ?

Do they know that, erroneous as Smith's Mormonism is, in
many ways, it is not so demoralising as prostitution is at this
day in all Christian countries, nor the cause of a tythe of the
crimes, including child murders, husband and wife murders,
loathsome disease, and mental and physical sufferings, occasioned by the marriage laws without divorce ?

This last error, by creating prostitution, is by very many degrees worse than Mormonism. Mormonism is also one of the
innumerable superstitions emanating direct from the origin of
falsehood, evil, and misery, and it has as much right to be tole-

rated by society as any of the other insane isms which now cover
the earth and torment the human race.

These isms have all originated from the source of all falsehood,
evil, and misery, and are all based on the two insane errors of all
past and present superstitions :—" that man has merit or demerit
" for his belief, and for his feelings of liking and loving, disliking
" and hating persons and things;" and all human laws have
the same insane base, although that base is opposed by all known
facts. Now you, the middle class, including the professions, are
in a position the most effectually to aid the other classes to make
the change from ignorance to knowledge, from folly to wisdom,
from poverty to wealth, from an inferior and irrational character
in all, to a superior and rational character for all, from crime and
punishment to the absence of both, in short, from this insane
Babel confusion of society through all its ramifications, to a new
state of social existence upon earth, nor yet imagined by statesmen or even poets.

But none of you know how to begin to make such a change.
Your training, education, habits, and prejudices, have so blind-
folded you, as to prevent you seeing your highest permanent interest, or deriving wisdom from the most common facts daily
existing around us.

You perceive not the overwhelming influence of the science of
surroundings over all humanity ; you are deaf and blind to its
hourly practical teaching around you in all directions, and to its
teachings through all past ages in every district over the earth.

And yet, how simple are these teachings ! They continually say
to the unprejudiced observers,—" make rational, good, and supe-
" rior surroundings, and you will make the human race rational,
" good, superior, and consequently peaceable, wise, and happy."

Your position and your interests call upon you to know the
principle and practice by which in the best manner to create,
use, and distribute wealth ; yet are you profoundly ignorant of
both the principle and practice.

Your position and your interests direct you to form the best
character, physical, intellectual, moral, spiritual, and practical, for
your children and for all society. You take this task especially
upon yourselves. You attempt by your teachings to form the
character of the upper, your own, and the lower class ; and a
pretty mess of confusion have you made by these attempts
through all the ages which have passed, and by your supposed
increase of knowledge on this subject even at this day ! You
have made, and continue to make, of the human race, blind, prejudiced fools, unable to see one of their true permanent interests,
and who prefer an inferior, disunited, repulsive, and miserable
state of existence upon earth, to a superior, united, attractive,
and happy existence.

It is especially your province to show good examples of local self-government; but you are without knowledge of the science or practice of good government, and spend your time, wealth, and talents, in vain talking, and in attempts to govern on erroneous principles, and by practices directly opposed to the unchanging laws of humanity.

You take upon yourselves, when members of the House of Commons, to make laws for the nation; while you are too uninformed in a knowledge of yourselves to make one law to benefit one of our race permanently, or which is not indirectly or directly opposed to the eternal, all-wise, and all-efficient laws of God and nature.

Learn the origin of falsehood, evil, and misery,—the origin of truth, good, and happiness, and the science and practice of surroundings; and then you will possess some useful practical knowledge now unknown to your class.

ROBERT OWEN.

March 12th 1858.

ADDRESS

TO THE UPPER CLASSES IN THE BRITISH EMPIRE.

I address you as members of a class which has directly or indirectly influenced for a long period the destinies of the human race, savage, barbarian, and civilized.

With your power and influence, had you possessed the practical knowledge now familiar to a few of the most advanced and experienced of our race, and had you known how to apply it wisely, you might centuries ago have taught the population of the world to live in peace, to attain high prosperity, without knowing crimes or experiencing any of their direful consequences, but, on the contrary, to be now enjoying permanently increasing happiness without chance of stay or retrogression.

Yet you, like all of our race, have been and are the natural and necessary results, physically and mentally, of your surroundings. You could not have been any other, and you were therefore without the knowledge of the power which your position gave you, to make yourselves and the population of this globe, good, wise, united, and happy.

Much of the power, influence, and respect, possessed by your ancestors, even in the last century, have been lost, and what remains is daily diminishing, Many causes, too obvious to be detailed, now contribute to this result, and if not arrested, these causes will ere long greatly lessen that which remains.

You have thought, and those below you in rank and station have thought, that you had reached the highest attainments that humanity could enjoy ; and the anxious concern of your class is to maintain its order and present position.

Fortunately, however, for your class, this is now impracticable.

Progress in the sciences, material, mental, and spiritual, has outstripped all your esteemed noble acquirements, and you must, as a class, yield to them ; but not to your injury, but for your highest permanent advantage.

Those privileges and honours which you now so much prize, and which are so much envied by all in inferior stations, have been derived solely from the origin of falsehood, evil, and misery, and can now be supported only by the force, fear, fraud, and falsehood, emanating directly from that source.

To maintain this position is no longer possible. The powers which have so long supported you were the powers of the dark-ness—superstitions, which, for wise pruposes, have so far been made to govern the infant progress of humanity.

These superstitions have performed their mission, and will now be deprived of all their power and influence, and man will now be made to become a rational being, instead of an irrational animal, which he has been made to be through this infant period of his past existence.

It has been said that, " fortunately for you and society," your present position cannot be much longer maintained. It is a position desirable only in a false and artificial state of society, emanating from the origin of evil.

This origin must now give way to, and be superseded by, the origin of truth, good, and happiness, which will create a new state of existence for man upon the earth, the lowest condition of which will be greatly to be envied by the highest condition at-tainable under the systems of society emanating from the origin of falsehood, evil, and misery.

You have stretched the human faculties to the utmost to place yourselves within the best surroundings that wealth and power could devise under a system of such base origin   And what do these surroundings effect for you, although obtained at an extra-vagant expense and waste of valuable materials ?

They give you a grossly false and irrational training and edu-cation ; they give you a most injurious estimate of yourselves ; they surround you with flattery and deception ; they induce you to be miserably idle, or to be actively occupied in various public and private affairs to the injury of society, while pretending to benefit it ; often indeed, intending to do so, but without having the ground-work in principle, or having the practical knowledge to ascertain any mode of effecting any real benefit for society.

Your order and class are essentially at all times highly inju-rious to every other class, and you keep all other classes in bondage, while you are yourselves subject to the most grievous bondage of an artificial system, based on falsehood, evil, and misery; a bondage which is so opposed to the rational happiness of all humanity, that it can be supported only by the extremes of force, fear, fraud, and falsehood; and these will soon fail you through the rapid progress making in physical and mental knowledge.

Your lives now are far from being rational or happy. They are too artificial to satisfy any one who can comprehend a well and highly cultivated natural existence, enjoyed with others equally well and highly cultivated.

But you are especially favourably placed to escape now from the evils which you suffer, and from those greater dangers to which you will be exposed from unguided, ungoverned, and uncultivated human passions.

You may so direct the wheels of state, as to turn them into a new direction, so as to give you safety, and more valuable power and permanent substantial happiness than in your present uninformed and artificial condition you can form any adequate conception of.

This path can be easily opened for you, and you may pursue it daily through your lives, in accordance with all the laws of God, with increasing pleasure, until you attain the happiness to be enjoyed by the highest cultivation, physical, intellectual, moral, spiritual, and practical, that the human faculties can receive.

These joys are in store for you.

                                   ROBERT OWEN.

March 14th, 1858.

A PROGRAMME

FOR

THE EARL OF DERBY

BY WHICH

HE MAY MAKE HIS ADMINISTRATION PERMANENT.

ROBERT OWEN'S REPLY,

Upwards of twenty years since, to the Question

"WHAT WOULD YOU DO IF YOU WERE PRIME MINISTER OF ENGLAND."

AN intelligent friend, who has long studied with deep interest the system which I recommend for general investigation, and who approves of it to the extent to which it has been explained, lately suggested the great utility that would arise to the public from my supposing myself invested with full power to administer the affairs of this country, and stating the measures which in that case I would adopt to obtain and secure the permanent prosperity and happiness of the people.

And as many of my disciples in this and in other countries have at various times expressed a similar wish, and as the continuance of life, especially at my age, is uncertain, I now feel it a duty incumbent upon me to comply with the request.

But to perform this task as it ought to be executed, it is requisite that I should take into consideration the existing prejudices, customs, and practices of the lower, the middle, and the higher orders; the present state of parties, religious, political, and commercial; the new position in which late events have placed the two Houses of Parliament with respect to each other and to the country; the condition of Ireland, as it bears upon the general interests of England and of the empire; and our present foreign relations.

Under the supposition, then, that I was appointed by the Crown, with the consent of the People, to effect for them the greatest amount of advantages, in the shortest time, and with the fewest evils to individuals, the question is, What course would I adopt, and what are the practical measures which I would recommend?

My answer to these questions is, that I would change all the existing low, inferior, and vicious circumstances, for others of a very superior character. I would, therefore, commence my administration by informing all foreign states that the British Government was about to change its national proceedings, both domestic and foreign ; that it was going to effect this change in consequence of having detected the source of the errors on which all governments have been hitherto founded and governed, and from which, in fact, all laws and institutions have emanated ; and because it had discovered the principles on which society ought now to be based, and upon which all laws and institutions ought now to be established, for the general benefit of all nations ;— that the whole extent of the change should be fully explained to them, and their aid and cordial co-operation solicited to carry it into effect, without injury to individuals or nations ; that the old mode of conducting the diplomacy between nations, should, on the part of Great Britain, be abandoned : and, instead thereof, the plain, simple language of truth should be used, and no attempt should be made to deceive any party, or to take advantage of their ignorance or weakness ; but, on the contrary, that Great Britain would exert all her power and energies to promote the improvement and happiness of all nations

I would also inform them, that, while this change from wrong to right principles and practices was in progress, Great Britain would adopt, and maintain, an attitude of national power that would render all attacks upon her from without so hopeless of success, that none would be attempted. While, on the other hand, all nations would become conscious that the new principles which she had adopted would prevent, on her part, any aggression or injustice of any kind.

Great Britain would by these means acquire the confidence and friendship of all nations and people, and soon terminate the necessity for the continuance of the present extravagant and injurious system of diplomacy, with all its absurd and unmeaning phraseology.

I would next make arrangements to give, after proper preparation for the purpose, political freedom to all our dependencies in the four quarters of the world, and to enable them to govern themselves ; but I would, as at present, protect them from foreign attack or subjugation. These colonies should also, as long as it was necessary, receive every aid from the mother country to improve their character and condition, and increase their wealth.

I would also institute measures to induce all nations to adopt a common language, in addition to their own, to facilitate the communication between the most distant parts of the world, and, by degrees, to make all men of one nation, with one language and one interest.

Simultaneously with these proceedings relative to foreign nations and our colonies, I would announce to the population of the British empire the change of the fundamental principles which was about to commence, for the benefit of all persons of every rank, and of their posterity through endless ages. And, to calm the minds of those who now hold private property and possess exclusive privileges, it should be declared, and so arranged, that none should be deprived of the one or the other, or disturbed in their present position, until their increased intelligence should induce them to desire the change.

I would then inform the population that the existing laws, customs, and institutions should remain in force until new arrangements could be made to supersede them, without any violent or sudden change; but that the evils arising from the present order of things should be prevented, by removing, as rapidly as the national means would admit, the causes which produce them : and the causes being the mal-arrangements of society, formed under the most mistaken notions of human nature, and a total ignorance of the mode of adjusting the affairs of life, new and very superior arrangements should be adopted for educating, employing, and governing the whole population.

All who can observe and reason now know " *That man is* " *the creature of circumstances in which he is placed :*" therefore the vicious and inferior circumstances which the want of better knowledge and more experience in our ancestors has allowed to grow up to their present complication of error, should be made gradually to yield to new and improved arrangements, in which the superior natural qualities of man might be called into full action, and in which he should obtain all the advantages of a wise association of his powers with those of his fellow-men, for their highest mutual advantage.

And this is, really, all that is now required, to change the present most cruel and irrational condition of the human race, into a state of terrestrial paradise. Ignorance has produced the one ; while wisdom, which includes knowledge and goodness, will produce the other.

I would then have explained to all parties the following great and everlasting truths, on which alone universal charity and affection can be established and applied in practice to the daily and hourly transactions of every individual : viz.—

" That man is not a being formed by nature to deserve indi-
" vidual reward or punishment ; but a being so totally different,
" that he may be educated from his birth, by the arrangements
" of others, to become good in all his relations in life ; highly
" useful to himself, and beneficial to his fellows ; rational and
" wise in all his conduct, so as to insure happiness to himself
" and others. Or, with the same certainty, he may be educated to
" have his faculties so neglected, or erroneously cultivated, that
" he shall be made to acquire the worst qualities that can be
" given to human nature, and to become, to himself and others,
" through his life, the cause of much misery."

As all who consider themselves in a comparatively better
situation than the great mass of the people are unwilling to risk
any great change, and would therefore oppose everything that
indicated the introduction of an entirely new system,—I would
calm their fears by showing them the change of character and
condition which I would make, first on those who now the most
require to have them changed; that is, upon the ignorant, the
vicious, and the miserable. And I would convince all of the practi-
bility of this change, by creating new circumstances for these
individuals, which should gradually turn their ignorance into
intelligence, their viciousness into real goodness, and their misery
into happiness.

From this alteration in the minds, manners, and conduct of
these *now* poor, unfortunate, because neglected, beings, all should
be satisfied of the overwhelming power of the influence of external
circumstances. Of the full extent of this power all parties are
yet without knowledge: it is unlimitable, and competent to make
man, angel or devil.

By these preliminary proceedings all would be convinced, by
ocular demonstration, that a due cultivation and wise exercise
of all our natural powers, physical, intellectual, and moral, are
absolutely necessary to give a high degree of happiness to each
individual ; and that the over-employed and under-employed, the
uncultivated and ill cultivated are necessarily imperfect and
unhappy beings.

These preliminary proceedings would also prove to the world,
that the necessity for poverty or the fear of it has ceased,
through the discoveries in various sciences ; for these discoveries
should be so applied under our new arrangements, that with
their aid every portion of the population should be enabled,
with light labour, or rather with necessary and pleasant exercise,
to produce more of all the necessaries, comforts, and beneficial
luxuries, than the same population would desire to use or consume ; and thus real wealth would be continually upon the increase in every part of the British dominions, and, soon, in every
other part of the world.

I would effect this change without adding any new burdens to
the people. The funds which are now wasted in what is called
supporting the poor and bringing criminals to justice, as the
poor and criminals would rapidly be diminished, would be ample
to defray the expense of the great change proposed ; and by the
creation of these new arrangements, the annual wealth produced
would be very speedily doubled, then trebled, and quadrupled.
It is a great want of a knowledge of facts which prevents parties
from discovering how easily wealth may be produced by every
population, greatly beyond the most extravagant wants of that
population.

I would raise the funds requisite for the objects to be attained, by making the poor national, and collecting an equitable rate from all parishes; which rate would be speedily diminished below the average parish rate now collected, and then it would be gradually reduced to nothing. As long as there shall be one shilling raised for poor-rate in Great Britain; that is, as long as a system shall be allowed to continue which permits one British subject to be in poverty or in idleness, or in the most distant fear of poverty, Great Britain will be ignorantly governed. And so long as there shall be one person in the British dominions allowed to grow up in ignorance, vice, and bad habits of any kind, Great Britain will be ignorantly and viciously governed; for both of these evils may now, by good government be easily avoided.

To prevent these enormous national evils I would make immediate arrangements to employ every person willing to be, and capable of being, employed in creating the new circumstances, in which the present unemployed and ignorant should find useful work and instruction, at all times, suitable to the age and capacity of the individual; and within these arrangements, young, middle-aged, and old, should immediately be instructed in the most useful knowledge.

To attain these objects I would make arrangements to purchase, at a fair price, all such estates, proper for the purpose, as were offered for sale in England, Ireland, and Scotland. On these estates the new superior circumstances should be created, that should gradually render the continuance of the present inferior and vicious circumstances unnecessary and impossible.

These new superior circumstances would consist in a different disposition and internal arrangement of the domestic dwellings and public buildings for instruction and recreation; in a different disposition and better arrangement of manufactures and trades, and for distributing the various productions among the population upon these estates, and for exchanging them with more distant populations, in other countries.

By these changes it might be expected that, before the expiration of four or five years at the most, two millions per day of additional substantial valuable wealth would be produced in Great Britain and Ireland, and that there would be, what to the ignorant would appear a miraculous change in the character, condition, and happiness, of the population of these Islands.

There is now no one obstacle to this change being immediately commenced, and to a great progress being made in it annually, except the want of knowledge on the part of those individuals who influence the measures of our government.

And the change may be effected by the most plain, simple, straight-forward, practical measures; such as farmers, gardeners, manufacturers, tradesmen, teachers of youth, sea-faring persons, and practical statesmen, could readily comprehend, and, by di-

D

rection, put into practice. And these changes would naturally arise from acting consistently upon a few fundamental principles, now admitted by all well-educated, reflecting persons, and upon facts well known to all scientific and intelligent practical men.

I would thus, as director of the administration of this country—

First.—Obtain for Great Britain the confidence and friendship of all foreign nations and people, by so decidedly deserving both that they could not be withheld.

Second.—The same confidence and friendship should be, on the same principles, secured from all our present dependencies.

Third.—Arrangements would be thus made to remove the cause of poverty, or the fear of it, in one year, from the British dominions, and to make it evident to the least experienced in the production of wealth, that we possess, in our mineral productions, in our surface soil, in our climate, in our peculiar native physical and mental energies, in the already acquired skill and habits of industry of the people, in the national and private capital, in the domestic and foreign political or national power of the population, in the knowledge of the principles by which these may now be united to effect the most gigantic and mighty purposes, a mine of inexhaustible materials, affording the most ample means that can be desired to create wealth so rapidly, abundantly, and permanently, that, as soon as all the private property shall be purchased by the nation or government from individuals, at a full price, which it soon may be, all will perceive the gross folly or madness in the inhabitants of this or of any country hereafter misdirecting their invaluable faculties in degrading, demoralizing, useless contests for individual possessions or private wealth of any kind; those faculties which might be employed for the attainment of excellence in all knowledge, and for the enjoyment of high happiness in the due cultivation and temperate exercise of each of those faculties. Were it not for the overwhelming influence of early impressions, continually repeated, from external circumstances, the folly and madness of all people and governments, relative to the creation, distribution, and enjoyment of wealth, would appear so glaringly absurd, that children, rationally trained and educated, would, at a very early age, be astounded at the gross inconsistencies of the present nations of the earth,—but more especially of the people and government of this country, who have unlimited means of increasing their powers to produce wealth beyond the possible wants or use of rational creatures.

Fourth.—Arrangements would also be thus made to arrest, at once, the flood of ignorance which is daily overspreading the land, flowing from those appointed to instruct the people in kindness, justice, and charity; which knowledge they have been trained to mistake, and, instead thereof, to be employed most actively in teaching the principles and practices of superstition, oppression, and uncharitableness. These unwise (may we not say, insane?) proceedings, would be superseded by decisive practical measures to prevent one British or Irish child being allowed to remain in ignorance, or permitted to acquire any superstitious or unjust notions, or any uncharitable feeling towards one human being. But, on the contrary, every British and Irish child should have all the faculties of his nature cultivated in their due proportions, and called forth into regular healthy exercise, in such a manner that the individual and society should be the most permanently benefited by them.

Fifth.—Arrangements would be thus made to supersede as speedily as possible all the present inferior, vicious, and insane circumstances within which so large a portion of the British and Irish people are now involved. These evil circumstances would be superseded by a new creation of good circumstances, through the irresistible influences of which, these same individuals would have their persons, minds, and morals so changed and improved that they would not, in a comparatively short period, be deemed, by those who had not witnessed the progress of the change, and who were uninformed respecting the means applied to effect it, to belong to the same species: the one would be thought to be the irrational, while the other would be deemed the rational beings, of the same genus.

These are the changes, or the new circumstances, which, as Prime Minister, or Adviser of the Crown and People, I would immediately begin to form; and in less than twelve months the population of this country could be made to think, feel, and act so differently, that their characters should be the reverse of what they now are, or have ever yet been: anxiety would be unknown amongst them, and confidence, arising from the perpetual practice of truth and sincerity, would pervade all, from the oldest to the youngest.

Were these measures adopted with decision throughout the British dominions, they would also soon change the condition of other nations; for those who have been trained in erroneous principles only, and have never seen any other practices than those which have emanated from erroneous principles, can form no adequate conception of the rapidity with which the human character, in the mass, may be changed, and improvements of every kind made to advance, as soon as public opinion and the public institutions shall be based upon true fundamental principles, and when public measures shall proceed in strict accordance with them.

It is upon this part of the subject that the world is in complete darkness. It has hitherto known error only in principle and practice; it has found itself involved, by these errors, in continual difficulties, and has met with never-ceasing obstacles to its progress towards excellence and happiness; and it has imagined that evils, and their innumerable obstructions, were to keep man in the bondage of ignorance and of the inferior passions, which ignorance alone engenders, for ever. The world could have no belief in the statements which affirmed that the cause of these errors and miseries was known and could be removed ; and that the earth, with less human labour than is now required, and without anxiety, could be made a paradise.

The immediate conversion of men and women from an irreligious to a religious state of mind and feelings, has been often known. But truth, without mystery or mixture of error, being publicly taught from authority, and enforced with the powers of eloquence, which would then be eager to enlist under its banners, could be made by the existing governments to banish all error, and falsehood, and deception, in a period so short, that the regeneration of the public mind would, at first, be considered as the most extraordinary of all the miracles of past times. And it would be so considered until it should be made manifest by the fact, that the laws of nature, when understood, are capable of effecting more extensive and wonderful changes than any of the petty local proceedings, even supposing them to have been true, that have been recorded as miracles in any of the religious or other writings of the ancients.

Let the British government now adopt these principles, and act decisively upon them, and all the governments of Europe and America would be induced, or irresistibly impelled, for their own safety, interest, and happiness, to follow her example ; and thus would the more civilized portion of the earth be relieved from the oppressions and bondage of ignorance, and of all the inferior and vile passions which it cultivates in man ; and human society would become the abode of high intelligence, under the perpetual influence of the kindest and finest sympathies of our nature ; and thus would knowledge, charity, and love fill the minds and hearts of men, and pervade all the transactions of the human race.

What a glorious position is now held by the present administration of the British government, if it had knowledge and firmness to make the best use of it !

The most intelligent and best disposed of the Tories, Whigs, and Radicals, and the most enlightened of all parties in church and state, are conscious that a revolution, such as history has not recorded, is now taking place in the human mind ; and they must desire that it should proceed and be completed without violence, and, if possible, without evil of any kind.

Let the present administration, then, communicate frankly and freely with these individuals ; explain to them the necessity for union among them to direct this great change in the destiny of mankind, and the incalculable benefits which one and all may be made immediately to derive from it.

Let them, at the same time, invite the people to turn their attention from their present petty, useless political and religious squabbles about folly and insanity, (for they produce only a total absence of justice, charity, and kindness,) and encourage them to give their whole powers to understand the new order of things which this revolution in public opinion will effect; and then truly may it be said, that the great change from evil to good will come " like r thief in the night," and be produced by a Power, of which no man knows " whence it cometh, or whither it goeth."

Thus, by the most simple and natural means, might the present administration speedily remove ignorance and poverty, or the fear of it, and all uncharitableness and unkindness, from the British dominions, and speedily from all other nations, for ever; and thus might they effect, at once, that great reform, to which, if they had had foresight, they might have been sure the reform of the Commons' House of Parliament would ultimately lead. The deed is done, and it cannot be undone! The decree has gone forth that " the mind (of man) shall be born again, the " world shall be regenerated, a new heaven and a new earth shall " arise, and sin and misery shall be known no more!"

ROBERT OWEN.

Extract from Robert Owen's Address to the Electors of Great Britain and Ireland.

It is for you, by the members whom you elect, to convince the world that you have advanced beyond the narrow and most injurious views of mere party and personal considerations;— that you desire, as speedily as possible, to terminate class legislation and obtain the rights of humanity for yourselves and your children, that you may no longer remain the slaves of an ignorant system which is most injurious to all classes.

To secure these rights, and gradually to prepare society to abandon class legislation, or the oppression of wealth over poverty, the following measures are necessary;—

1. *A graduated Property Tax, equal to the necessary National Expenditure.*
2. *The abolition of all other taxes.*
3. *Free Trade with all the World*
4. *National Education for all who desire it.*
5. *National Employment for all who require it.*
6. *Liberty of speaking and writing on all subjects, civil, religious, and political.*
7. *Full and complete Freedom of Religion for Christians, Jews, Mahomedans, Hindoos, and every other form, under every name by which men may call themselves.*

HOW THE BRITISH EMPIRE UNDER EXISTING CIRCUMSTANCES SHOULD BE GOVERNED.

A prime minister who desires to govern the British Empire faithfully and well for the government and people, would adopt the following measures to raise the population to the level of society changed by the great progress made in science, arts, and general knowledge, physical and mental—a progress attained within the last hundred years, but more especially within the last half and quarter century.—

1st.—He would commence his administration by assuring all foreign governments that the British government sincerely desired permanent peace with them, and that, as far as their position permitted, his government would afford them every assistance which it could give them consistently with good government at home and in its colonies.

And in proof of the sincerity of his statements, his government would be willing to enter into federative treaties with all or any of them upon equal terms of reciprocity, by which each nation would be an immense gainer, and would experience no loss or disadvantage in return.

He would openly declare to these nations, as well as to the British Empire, that as the Origin of Falsehood, Evil, and Misery had been fortunately discovered in his day, and also the Origin of Truth, Good, and Happiness, he would *gradually* adopt the latter, and in peace, in order, and with due foresight, as *gradually* relinquish the former.

Men of mind will now perceive that the Origin of Falsehood, Evil, and Misery, leads direct to the individual, ignorantly selfish, repulsive, and fighting system, now in practice for forming character, governing man, and degrading humanity to every kind of injurious demoralization—in many cases to a far worse condition than animal life among the superior tribes of animals.

Men of mind also perceive that the Origin of Truth, Good, and Happiness, will lead direct to a knowledge of the true social science, which abandons all ignorantly selfish feelings, and opens a beautiful path, by persuing which, truth alone will become the universal language of mankind, without a motive arising to express a falsehood in look, or word, or action. And until this state of society shall be attained, it will be vain to look for goodness, honesty, or happiness, among men.

This beautiful path will also lead direct to the practical knowledge by which, with ease and pleasure, the human race, without contests and in everlasting perpetuity, may be well born, fed, clothed, lodged, trained, educated, employed, and governed, by being well-placed within the proper surroundings, now not difficult to devise and execute, and by which these blessings, now the birthright of all, may be attained with the certainty of a law of nature.

The discovery being made public of the Origin of Falsehood, Evil, and Misery, the faithful and good prime minister would, at once, openly declare his determination to abandon it and all its baneful practices as speedily as circumstances would admit, and to begin to prepare to enter the beautiful path, now so broadly opened, by the discovery of the Origin of Truth, Good, and Happinesss; and, as soon as entered upon, to pursue it, neither turning to the right nor to the left from the direct line of perpetual peace, progress, and true prosperity.

But preliminary measures would be immediately required to make the present system of Falsehood, Evil, and Misery, more bearable by the now living generation, while the preparations for the great change of system were in progress.

His first preparatory step would be to make liberal arrangements with the private Bank of England, to change it as speedily as practicable to the Public Bank of the British Empire; by which change the requisite means would be found to give legitimate relief to the existing commercial order of society, to give full beneficial employment to all the working classes, and to supply an honest government with all the funds it could require for national purposes, without requiring additional taxes.

These purposes would rapidly diminish the national expenditure in its most useless and wasteful direction, while these savings would be most advantageously applied in another direction,— that is, to do what all governments will soon be required to do, and what would have been done many centuries ago had it not been for the destructive, repulsive, selfish, demoralising, impoverishing, and degrading individual system, maintained solely by the insane superstitions of past and present times, in opposition to common sense and to the social practice so wisely adopted by the early Christians, and recommended by every truly great, good, and honest man through all past ages; although until this generation none knew how to combine the spirit, principle, and practice, in new combinations of surroundings, to make the social system of union permanently practicable.

But this difficulty has now been overcome.

That which the population of the world has always required has been the knowledge how to make the surroundings to give to all from birth a good rational natural character, and to give to all permanent natural reproductive occupation, beneficial to the individual and to society.

These two things the British population and the population of the world require to-day; and they are the only two things, properly executed, that the population of the world will ever require; for these two will include every desire of man.

But while the preparations are in progress to well train, educate, and employ all,—as the British government calls itself a representative government, it should become really so, and a good and faithful prime minister would in this session of parliament give the nation a liberal instalment of the six points of what is now called "*the People's Charter*," and at once, to appease a popular bubble, pass a Reform Bill that would satisfy the reasonable portion of the public.

It is true the nation has a full right, being under a representative government, to all the points of this Charter; but in the present state of ignorance, poverty, and degradation of the lower orders, including a large portion of the working classes, the six points, if given to them before they are better trained, educated, and employed, would be a great evil to them and to all classes.

And were a Reform Bill to be passed this session, to include the Six Points of the Charter, it would not for twenty or thirty years put one penny into the pockets of the working classes, and the business of good governing would be greatly retarded.

How, would the multitude discover men to elect who possessed good governing administrative knowledge?

Does not experience prove that no such men have been yet trained and educated for the task? And that the present system of Falsehood, Evil, and Misery, cannot train and educate men to attain such knowledge.

No men in either house of parliament have given any indication that such knowledge has yet been given to one of them, or the present Babel confusion of society could not long continue.

Universal peace,—universal natural training and education,—universal natural reproductive permanent beneficial employment,—all based on the Origin of Truth, Good, and Happiness, or, which is the same in other words, on the Principle and Practice of universal Love and Charity, are alone what all nations and all peoples require.

The means abundantly exist to accomplish all these results.

A good and superior faithful prime minister would, in addition to the preceding, bestir himself to prepare a permanent government for India—one that would gradually improve the character and condition of the natives, and which would ultimately become independent of the mother country, and be substantially beneficial to the Europeans and natives who would form the empire, and be federatively united in peace and war with Great Britain, and thus continue to be as one nation.

If we do not govern India for the ultimate permanent benefit of its natives, we have no claim but that of brute force to go and govern that empire, which may now be made the most splendid and happy of all empires.

A prime minister equal to this task is now urgently required for the British Empire.

ROBERT OWEN.

Sevenoaks, March 6th, 1858.

ON MAN.

Man is a dual creation.

The first is the germ of humanity created by God.

The second, under the full control and direction of society, is the growth of the germ to maturity and death ; but society, through the agency of man, is indirectly, also, the creation of God,—as are all things created in the universe.

The early made and wholly undeveloped state of the human faculties, when solely under the guidance of an inexperienced imagination, created Original Sin, by attributing the qualities and powers of the made and created to the made and created, and not to the maker and creator.

This error is the Original Sin of mankind, and the cause of all the irrationality, insanity, and madness of the human race through all past generations to this day.

It is the cause of man over the earth being now opposed to his own well-being, well-doing, and happiness; and of the repulsive feelings which so universally prevail among mankind.

The religions of the world are all imaginary superstitions, based on this Origin of Falsehood and Evil, and on total ignorance of the unchanging laws of humanity, as given to man from his first creation, and continuing to this day.

These laws demonstrate that there is but one true, useful, good, and practical religion for all men—a religion not derived from any human name, but direct from the source of all truth and of the unchanging nature of man. This one true universal religion for all humanity is the practice of unceasing love and charity of each for all and all for each, to the end of time.

This religion of man is derived direct from the Origin of all Truth and Good, namely, "That the creator creates all the qualities " and powers which the created can possess, and that the creator " alone is the cause, immediate or remote, of all results emanating " from these creations, which are in every instance forced by the " creating power on the created, whether material or spiritual, " so called in the language of men while ignorant of both, or of " spirit and matter combined."

On this foundation the well-being, well-doing, progress, and happiness of all humanity will be placed on the rock of truth, eternal as man's existence.

And now all that will be required to give permanent increasing knowledge and happiness to all humanity, will be to place it in new combinations of surroundings, emanating from and always consistent with the origin of truth and good.

The materials have been abundantly acquired, and the scientific knowledge now to work and to apply those materials to form those surroundings, and to make them superior to any which now exist, or which have ever been on the earth, and thus to elevate the human race through future ages to a much higher and happier state of existence than the present erroneously trained, educated, employed, placed, and governed generation can comprehend or appreciate.

This great and glorious change is the good time coming, and when the long promised and anticipated happiness of man should be attained and secured.

ROBERT OWEN.

March 21st, 1858.

Registered for Foreign Transmission.

———

ROBERT OWEN'S
MILLENNIAL GAZETTE.

" The character of Man is formed *for* him, and *not by* him."

No. 16.]　　　JULY 1, 1858.　　　[PRICE 1*s.* 6*d.*

PRESENTED

BY

THE AUTHOR,

WITH HIS EARNEST REQUEST THAT THE RECEIVERS
AND READERS OF

THIS PAMPHLET

WILL PLACE THE FOLLOWING ALL-IMPORTANT
TRUTHS DEEP IN THE TABLET OF THEIR
MEMORY, TO ENABLE THEM IN ALL THE
AFFAIRS OF LIFE TO APPLY THEM
CONSISTENTLY TO PRACTICE.

———

THE infancy of humanity, and while its natural
faculties were slowly developing, has been, by the
necessary laws of nature, a period of inexperience,
of errors, and of sufferings, evidently made to be so
in order to prepare it, through gradual experience and
the natural growth and development of the reasoning
and rational faculties, to overcome error, and by so

doing to terminate all evil, and the sufferings which error creates.

This infant, inexperienced, and suffering state of humanity, is, by all the signs of the times, about to be gradually superseded by a matured, experienced, and developed state of the rational faculties; a state in which the evils and sufferings arising from the progress of infancy towards maturity will cease and die their natural deaths.

In the infant, inexperienced, and undeveloped state of hmanity, man has been made to prefer falsehood to truth, folly to wisdom, ignorance to knowledge, repulsive to attractive feelings for his race, disunion to union, hate to love, uncharitableness to charity, war to peace, the means to obstruct the productions of wealth and to waste and destroy it, to the means by which to create, preserve, and protect it. To prefer human-made, ever-changing, and most injurious laws, to the unchanging, all-wise, and all-efficient laws of God; the former always producing evil—the latter always producing good. To prefer an inferior general character for the human race, to a superior general character,—irrational, inferior, and often degrading surroundings, to rational, superior, and elevating surroundings,—to prefer the cause which produces prostitution and all its horrid crimes, diseases, demoralisation, and sufferings, especially to the female sex, to the only cause which can create pure chastity and conjugal affection and happiness.

These combined errors necessarily produced the individual selfish and most demoralising system of society, by which the population of the world has been so far governed.

The matured, experienced, and developed state of the reasoning and rational faculties, now attained by some of our race, having discovered the evils produced by the errors of the past or infant state, now prefers truth to falsehood, wisdom to folly, knowledge to ignorance, attractive to repulsive feelings for our race, union to disunion, love to hate, charity to the want of it, peace to war, the means by which to produce, save, and protect wealth from destruction, to the means to obstruct its production, to waste, and to destroy it;– to prefer God-made laws to man's,—a superior to an inferior general character for the human race,—rational, superior, and elevating surroundings in which to place the whole of the human race, to the irrational, inferior, and degrading surroundings in which they are now placed,—the cause which will create and maintain pure chastity and conjugal affection, to the cause which creates prostitution and destroys conjugal affection. In short to prefer all the causes which will produce happiness, to those which produce misery.

In consequence of these new preferences, a strong desire is arising to change the ignorant selfish individual system for the government of the human race, for the full social system, based on the knowledge of the origin of truth and good and of the laws of social science, and made consistent throughout its entire combinations and ramifications, by the creation of new and superior surroundings, in which to place all of our race, and thus to insure their permanent happiness.

Thus, in brief, are the true and the false, the good and the evil systems for governing mankind placed before the human race.

Is the time come for the false and evil to be abandoned, and the true and good to commence ?

ROBERT OWEN.

THE

REPORTER'S REPORT

OF

ROBERT OWEN'S

MAY MEETINGS IN LONDON FOR 1858.

PREFACE.

How blind to their true position are the most advanced in the most civilised nations at this day!

The means to attain universal superiority of character, truth, prosperity, and happiness, are at their feet. They know them not,—they cannot yet perceive them, but insanely spurn them away, not only as worthless, but as things positively injurious to humanity. Instead of which, until the foundation shall be laid to form a universal good and superior character for man, to establish truth as the only language of our race, and to create useable wealth annually to exceed the wants of all, it will be vain to expect that man can be made to attain and enjoy happiness.

A

Every government may now with ease and pleasure form a good, useful, and superior character for all its subjects,—enable them annually to create a superfluity of useable and the most desirable wealth to satisfy all without contest or competition,—and make truth the only language known to and spoken by all. This will be soon their sole duty; and is their only road to safety and happiness for the members of all governments and their posterity.

Henceforth it will be much worse than a farce, for it must become a tragedy, for them to continue to talk of their desire to make their subjects good, prosperous, and happy; for they have hitherto, perhaps in most cases blindly, adopted the most direct and effectual measures to force them to become untruthful, inferior or bad in character, and to lead a life of mental weakness or hypocrisy, and of misery.

The means to attain truth, goodness, wisdom, and happiness can be no longer spurned by governments. They must be now brought into every day practice for the use and benefit of all, or universal revolutions of violence and every kind of mis-rule will speedily arise.

All governments are now in the midst of vicious, inferior, or very imperfect physical and mental surroundings. They have only to re-place themselves in the midst of good, superior, and more perfect surroundings, which, with present knowledge of the sciences, physical and mental, may be easily accomplished in all countries—one country aiding another.

Surely the human race, with the late extraordinary discoveries made in the material sciences to facilitate rapid communications between them, may be taught to observe the most numerous and ordinary facts daily existing around them and on the knowledge of which their permanent happiness depends, and to deduce from these facts their natural self-evident conclusions!

Place the germs of all individual things in the three kingdoms of nature, mineral, vegetable, and animal, within, for them, inferior and bad surroundings, and they will grow up with inferior and bad qualities. Place the same quality of germ within, for them, good and superior surroundings, and they will become good and superior. For, according to a universal law of nature, as are the qualities of surroundings, so must the thing surrounded become.

What a glorious lesson is this to our race, from the great book of nature! It teaches the direct road to universal happiness and to misery, and makes it evident that man has hitherto pursued the latter until the seven fold bandage of ignorance and prejudice has fallen from his eyes. Behold the great fact which explains this hitherto hidden mystery of nature! Do you want a Catholic to be made a Protestant? Place the infant Catholic in a Protestant family. Do you wish a Jew to become a Christian? Place the infant Jew in a Christian family. Do you desire a Quaker to become a Jew? Place the infant Quaker in a Jew family. Or a Mahometan, Hindoo, or Chinese, to become an English Christian? Place the infants of each in an English family in England. And so on throughout the world.

It is the Christian, Jew, Hindoo, Mahometan, Chinese, &c., surroundings, which make the Chinese, Mahometan, Hindoo, Jew, and Christian character, full of prejudices in opposition to each other, and all egregiously in the dark respecting the formation of their own absurd notions and unnatural repulsive feelings to each other.

How much longer will nations and peoples and their governments remain ignorant of the greatest and most important of all facts for universal practice, —namely, that, of necessity, inferior and bad surroundings make inferior and bad men and women, and that, of like necessity, superior and good surroundings will make superior and good men and women? And that it is now especially the highest interest of the human race that every one of its offspring from birth should be made superior and good.

Have governments and people yet any consistent ideas of the spirit, principle, and practice, by which, with ease, pleasure, and delight, they could rapidly and most beneficially for all supersede the present insane surroundings in which all of our race are now placed, by the most rational and superior, which would insure the permanent happiness of all? To acquire them let the following pages be well studied, and the practices which they recommend be immediately commenced.

ROBERT OWEN.

TO HER MAJESTY VICTORIA, QUEEN OF THE BRITISH EMPIRE.

HIGHLY RESPECTED AND BELOVED SOVEREIGN,—

You have been destined to reign during a crisis in the history of humanity which will be fondly cherished and retained in everlasting remembrance by all of our race.

It is the crisis of man's destiny from his undeveloped state of falsehood, contention, conflicts, and evil, to truth, peace, harmony, and good to all.

The ruling power of the universe has enabled man, through the experience of the past, now to prepare all things upon the earth to commence at this period, during your Majesty's reign of moral example to the rulers of other states, the change from evil to good throughout the world.

The materials to insure the universal permanent happiness of our race now abundantly exist in great superfluity, and require only to be rightly applied; and this is the work which all nations have now to do.

They have to reconstruct society, by forming new social surroundings over the world, each of which surroundings to be calculated to promote the progress and happiness of all. For unless all are known to be happy, none can be perfectly so,—not even God himself until He effects this change throughout His creation.

To ensure the happiness of all, the wants of our nature, when it shall be highly and rationally cultivated from birth, must be supplied in a superior manner, and with the regularity of the seasons, without anxiety or injustice on the part of the producer.

By these measures all will be naturally well-trained, educated, and employed, so as to have a good, useful, valuable, and superior character formed for each, and a plentiful supply of all things necessary to ensure the happiness of all provided.

It is now evident, by these means being so amply provided and the knowledge being now given how rightly to apply them, that the ultimate object of nature and intention of our Creator are to effect the permanent progressive happiness of our race.

By all the materials for universal happiness being thus so amply provided, it is evident also that this is the period, in the order of nature, when the great change from the preliminary necessary evil and suffering to the good and happy state of humanity should commence and progress without stay or retrogression, until happiness shall be permanently secured for all.

This is now to be the great business of life for all society.

All nations and peoples will now have to be occupied to build up and arrange the new combinations of superior surroundings to insure the permanent progress and happiness of all.

This is a glorious work for the governments of the world now to enter upon, and it will afford all their members a source of happiness in continued perpetuity, of which at present they have no means to form an adequate conception. It will exceed in reality the utmost imaginations of any of the undeveloped mis-taught race now upon the earth; for truth, in thought, word, and action, will universally prevail.

It is now for the other members of your Majesty's government to be aroused to feel the dignity of the position in which they are placed by being the government of the wide-extended British empire in this auspicious crisis in the existence of humanity.

It is for them at once now to learn, mark, and inwardly digest the signs of the times and the all-important new knowledge pressing upon them from so many sources.

It is for them to follow in the wake of the Prince Consort, who, by the wise foresight of his well conceived and well founded establishment at South Kensington, has laid the corner stone of a fabric whose adamantine strength will increase with the increase of ages. It is the commencement of the easy, pleasant, and certain means of forming a superior character for all of our race; and this being accomplished, the utmost wishes and desires of highly cultivated and refined humanity will be speedily attained.

It is true all the powers of the ignorance of dark-ness and of mind-destroying superstitions will be aroused to their utmost violence and strongest exer-tions of opposition against a government beginning to attempt to govern rationally. But let the government heed them not; they are now, except in wordy warfare, powerless as an infant; their power has been in this century effectually undermined, and now there is not a foot of even apparent rational ground for them to take their stand upon.

They have sown broadcast, with high cultivation, ignorance, disunion, and every kind of evil; and they are now reaping a most fruitful harvest of them. But universal love and charity, guided by knowledge and wisdom, come to the aid of even these, the destroyers of the past happiness of our race. These divine powers say " the children of darkness have " themselves been the victims of dark surroundings. " By these were they taught and their characters " formed; and their teachings have been as they were " themselves taught. They are therefore to be pitied, " and call for the sympathy of enlightened humanity. " They must, then, be amply and justly provided for,

" and a new character must be formed for them, and
" they must be clothed in bright and brilliant, instead
" of dark and dismal garments—garments fit for the
" marriage feast of the union and happiness of our
" race."

And thus will terminate all insane disputes about
words having no practical meaning.

That this great and glorious change may be commenced and made rapidly yet wisely to progress
during your Majesty's reign, is the ardent wish of
your Majesty's faithful subject and friend,

May 25, 1858. ROBERT OWEN.

ADVERTISEMENT.

*Important Public Meeting to advocate an entire change
in forming the Character of Man and governing
Society.*

NOTICE TO ALL.

GLAD TIDINGS TO THE HUMAN RACE, AND NO MISTAKE
THIS TIME.

A PUBLIC meeting will be held in St. Martin's Hall on
the 14th of May, at eight P. M., to consider the
best means immediately to commence practical measures to NEW-FORM MAN and NEW-FORM
SOCIETY, by new-placing all within new and very
superior surroundings, in order that, in future, each

one of the human race may be well-born, well-fed, well-clothed, well-lodged, well-employed, well-re-created, and amused, well-governed, locally and generally, and well-placed, under such new combinations of physical and mental conditions, as will induce and enable all to act in their every day practice in accordance with the only true and Divine Religion of Universal Love and Charity, irrespective of colour, country, creed, and class, and thus to secure the permanent well-doing and happiness of all.

And these results are to be attained, with the certainty of a law of nature, through all coming ages, with the regularity of the seasons without contest or competition.

The PRINCIPLES, SPIRIT, and PRACTICE by which these glorious attainments are to be accomplished will be more explained at this meeting, in a manner easily to be comprehended by all accustomed to think and reason for themselves.

But it may be useful in this Advertisement briefly to state, that the intention of the writer is to revolutionise the population of the world, by peaceable, well-digested measures of foresight, derived from a calm, long-continued study of the natural laws of humanity, extended experience in applying those laws to practice and a strong conviction that there is no earthly power competent to disprove the truth of the principles, the

purity of the spirit, or the undeviating consistency
with these principles and spirit of the practice to be
recommended for universal adoption. " Universal"
is written with full knowledge of its importance
where placed,— because there can be but one true
fundamental principle on which to base a rational
system for the government of mankind,— one undefiled spirit of universal love and charity, uncontaminated by individual or private selfish feelings,
— and one practice in accordance with that fundamental principle and divine spirit.

Soon it will be discovered that truth is one throughout the whole affairs and details of human life, as
well as throughout the great illimitable universe.
There is therefore one, and but one, true mode of
governing the human race,—one and but one true
practice by which to form all of our race to become
united, wise, and permanently happy,—one and only
one true practice by which to produce the greatest
amount of the most valuable wealth in the shortest
time, in the best manner, and with the most pleasure
and advantage to the producers and consumers of it,
— one and only one principle, spirit, and practice, by
which our race can be cordially and permanently
united as one family, with one language, one interest,
and one universal desire to promote the best, highest,
and most permanent happiness of each other, without

wars, individual contests, or competition,—one and only one rational proceeding by which the earth can be laid out and made to become a terrestrial paradise and all its inhabitants made to become good, wise, united, and happy.

The means are now prepared, through the experience and discoveries of past ages and the progress of science and of mental knowledge in the present century, to commence this universal revolution in the principle, spirit, and practice of governing the population of the world,—in creating a new superior character for man,—in producing a superabundance of wealth for all,—in uniting all as one family by gradual practical changes,—in making the human race rational and consistent in mind and practice,—and in securing universal peace, prosperity, and happiness, to all future generations living upon our planet.

But the undeveloped, the neglected uneducated, the falsely educated, and the practically inexperienced, will say, not knowing better, that to produce such changes is not only impracticable but impossible.

To them, with their limited knowledge and experience of what is impracticable and impossible and what is practicable and possible, the results stated must appear as the tales of steam power and navigation, of railway travelling speed, and of electric telegraph messages, appear to savages who never saw or before heard of these wonders of the present age. But let any one possessing the same study of human history, of human discoveries and inventions, of human nature and its laws ; the same experience in applying those laws to practice in organising and governing most successfully on new principles and by a new practice a considerable population for upwards of a quarter of a century, and who has had the same free and confidential communications with the most advanced statesmen and philosophers living in the past three quarters of a century in the civilised world, come forward and state his objections to the possibility or practicability of any one of the results stated, and the writer will undertake satisfactorily to remove all such objections from his mind.

The writer states this with confidence, because he knows the practice by which, with the certainty of a law of nature, a useful, good, and truly valuable character may be given to all from and before birth,--by which a superfluity for all of the most useful and valuable wealth may be annually created with pleasure to all,—by which all can be united in one interest, feeling, and language, and gradually be made to think, feel, and act, as one family, on a perfect system of equality according to age and capacity,—by which, with pleasure to all, the earth may be made rapidly to become a terrestrial paradise, and all its inhabitants placed within surroundings greatly superior to any now enjoyed by any of the human race, and thus the writer knows how, by rational progressive practical measures, this great revolution of all humanity may be naturally, peaceably, and most pleasantly accomplished.

What more can any individual of any rank or class over the world desire ? This is much more than the philosopher's stone, or the perpetual motion, can be ; and it is emphatically asked—Why is the population of this planet to be longer prevented the rational enjoyment of these natural blessings ?

ROBERT OWEN.

Sevenoaks Park, April 20th, 1858.

REPORT.

AMONG the May meetings in London, this year, three were held of a most extraordinary character. They were commenced in St. Martin's Hall on the 14th of May, and terminated on Tuesday the 18th instant.

At these meetings, composed of all parties and creeds, there was an unanimity of feeling in favour of the extraordinary measures proposed for adoption, seldom, if ever, witnessed in public meetings free and open to all without restriction. The first meeting was called together by the preceding advertisement, published in the newspapers and also widely circulated privately among the governing classes, both lay and ecclesiastical. It commenced at eight, P.M., with a full audience. Robert Owen, the well known of New Lanark celebrity and as the perpetual opponent of the existing system of society, and proposer of another, new in spirit, principle, and practice, was unanimously called to the chair. But the old veteran said, as he could not hear the distant speakers, he should request the aid of his friend and disciple also, until he, the newly appointed chairman, had openly declared his knowledge of the truth of the new spiritual manifestations, to assist him in the arduous task which he was about to commence; and to this proposal Mr. Cooper willingly consented, and he became to some extent, eyes, ears, and voice to the chairman.

The business then proceeded by Mr. Cooper reading the following opening address, which the chairman had previously prepared; but frequently Mr. Owen stopped the reading that he might more fully explain parts of the subject which he thought might be usefully enlarged upon. These explanations were given with great clearness and force, and, as well as the whole of the opening address, were received with extraordinary fervour by the entire meeting.

SOCIAL SCIENCE

IN ITS FULL SPIRIT AND PRINCIPLE, AND IN ITS FIRST, SECOND, AND THIRD STAGES FOR THE PERMANENT PRACTICE OF IT BY THE HUMAN RACE, TO SECURE THE FUTURE HAPPINESS OF ALL.

By the first annual report published by the National Association for the Promotion of Social Science, it is evident that this science is yet unknown to the public.

Social Science is based on the origin of truth and good, on the knowledge of ourselves, on the permanent laws of humanity and of society.

True Social Science is thus based to secure to all, in perpetuity, the means by which they shall be for ever well-born, well-fed, well-clothed, well-lodged, well-trained, well-educated, well-employed, well-recreated, well-governed, and well-placed, in order that from birth to death they shall be well-surrounded. For as these surroundings are over the world, inferior, mixed, or superior, so are the human race, and so will they ever become, with the certainty of a law of nature.

B

Almost every paper in the report of the association previously mentioned confirms the last stated fact.

But, to attain these results, certain definite surroundings must be created, and, fortunately for the population of the world, these surroundings are attainable in practice for the human race.

But this is the earliest period in the history of man, by reason of his inexperienced and undeveloped state, when these surroundings could be devised and executed for universal practice.

1st.—To be well-born, the immediate parents must be in the proper condition, physically and mentally, to produce a full-formed superior infant, and the mother, during the whole period of internally sustaining this invaluable germ, should be unruffled by passion, calm, kindly treated by all, and surrounded only by superior objects and persons; her mind freed from anxieties, and, as far as practicable, beautiful forms only should be within her sight.

2nd.—To be fed well and rationally, the qualities, quantities, and kind of food best suited to the individual constitution during every period of life should be studied, known, produced, and applied to practice.

3rd.—To be well-clothed, the best texture and form of garments for the different periods of life, and the most convenient and graceful, when occupied in the various departments required from each by society, and also when dressed for the leisure hours of social enjoyment, should be well studied and made appropriate for health, utility, and appearance.

4th.—To be well lodged, dwellings must be erected to receive and accommodate each of both sexes, separately, from the age of puberty, with apartments suitable for men and women trained and so far educated from birth to become superior full-formed rational beings, and members of the best society which can be formed upon the earth. Such apartments, to accommodate each one in the best manner, may be now easily constructed, having reference to heat, cold, ventilation, and the permanent health and convenience of the individual, whose highest progress in knowledge, wisdom, and happiness will be the guiding star to direct all these arrangements ; for unless the *individual* can be made superior and happy, it will be vain to expect that *society* can ever become so.

5th.—To be well trained from birth, the feelings, temper, habits, and manners of each must be carefully attended to, by previously well-trained experienced persons, naturally fond of children. This extreme care in infancy is necessary that in these respects all shall by degrees be made to become superior ; and this, by due attention, will be practicable.

6th.—To be well educated. This, connected with the previously stated training from birth, and which is, in fact, important preliminary education, will be found to be the all-in-all by which to secure the un-changing well-being, well-doing, and permanent happiness of mankind. On the formation of character for the human race depends the formation of a pande-monium or a paradise for man through all future ages. To well educate, each one must have his character well-formed; and to well-form the character of each, every organ, faculty, propensity, quality, and power of our nature must be well cultivated and directed as they appear and advance with our growth;—that is, the organization of each, whether physical, intellectual, moral, spiritual, or practical, must be not only well-cultivated, but all these must be regularly exercised to the point of temperance for each power and pro-pensity in each individual; for this point will vary in every organ and propensity of each man and woman. Yet will this apparent perfection of humanity be attainable when society shall be truthfully based and rationally constructed. Then all may be made to acquire the best character, physical and mental, that their born organization will admit.

7th.—To be well employed is to be properly occu-pied, physically and mentally, in their natural pro-portions of time for each, through life, according to age, sex, capacity, and inclination. To be thus occupied, day by day, will be the zest of human exist-ence. With men and women trained and educated as previously stated, idleness will be unknown, rest will arise from change of occupation, physical to mental, but neither must be continued too long at any time for the health of the individual. These occupations will always be desired, pleasant to perform, and useful to the individual and to society. All that will be too unhealthy, too laborious, or too unpleasant for superior men or women or their offspring to perform, will be readily done by innumerable obedient servants or slaves, always ready and willing at command to execute whatever may be required that will be necessary— hundreds, thousands, and millions upon millions of mechanical and chemical slaves may be always placed at the service of the human race, to assist, by direction, to supply, and, if there could be use in it, to far over-supply all the wants of humanity, so as to secure the permanent happiness of our race through futurity. To supply the ever-existing wants of humanity will afford ever-existing joyous occupation to all in directing the sciences to perform the work required. The sciences have been given by our Creator that they should relieve man, in producing wealth, from slavery, servitude, and all anxiety. These material slaves and servants, illimitable in number and power, will assist the human race rapidly to make this globe into an earthly paradise, to be enjoyed as such by all of human kind.

8th—To be well recreated. The sciences and arts already known may now be easily applied and directed to give full leisure to humanity to have abundance of time for physical and mental recreation, to be rationally enjoyed by societies composed of superior full-formed men and women, trained and educated to well choose their means of, and objects for, recreation—if indeed they did not in two or three generations make their whole existence a life of high intelligent recreation and perpetual rational enjoyment.

9th—To be well governed is to be well trained, educated, employed, and placed. Social societies thus created will require little or no governing. As all will be enabled to well-govern themselves, and will be trained and educated to desire at all times the best interests and highest happiness of every one of our race, a few simple regulations for each society and their relations to other societies will be sufficient for the government of the world fraternally, without elections or selections, but according to the natural divisions of age in the life of humanity,—each division of age being made much more than equal to the task which society will require from them. Under the full scientific social system, the characters of all will be made so superior from birth, and society will be so simplified, that both sexes, at the age of puberty, will be taught to comprehend the spirit, principle, and practice of society, as carried on over the world, and to be competent, at once, to take some useful active part on entering as visitor or new member into any one of these new social societies in any division of our globe. Every such society being, when vacancies arise, open for the admission of any of our race, and each society possessing a knowledge of, and being governed by, the spirit of true religion, that is, of universal love and charity perpetually practised, and therefore knowing no exceptions of natural or acquired differences will readily admit any new comer.

But this high and comparatively perfect state of social science is not to be attained at once. This is utterly impossible. It can be attained only by passing through several preliminary stages; but each stage will be a great advance over the best state of the present disorganized, contending, repulsive, and most ignorant and unjust system, or rather no system, of society.

Social Science may now be explained to the public in this manner.

Suppose an individual from birth to have all his organs, faculties, propensities, qualities, and powers, trained, educated, and cultivated, naturally, in the best manner, by being placed within the surroundings by which alone such a result could be attained. Such an individual would be of greatly more value to society than any one now living or who has yet lived upon the earth.

Then suppose every one born to have all their natural powers so trained, educated, cultivated, and placed—What would be the increased value, by this process, of the entire population of the world? Who can make the estimate of this calculation? Not one of the present generation; nor will there be one until some can be made fully conscious of the spirit, principle, and practices of the Social Science in its purity, undefiled by the ignorance and gross prejudices of the existing system of falsehood and evil.

But now for the gradual measures by which this new paradise is to be gained, and these superior full-formed men and women are to be educated to possess the character fit for such an advanced state of earthly existence. In this advanced state, and without which there can be no justice in society and happiness for man, there must be real " liberty, equality, and fraternity" throughout the population of the world.

Yet at this day real liberty, equality, and fraternity, are unknown over the earth. They cannot be understood, and are thoroughly impracticable under a system based, as the entire system of the world now is, on falsehood and evil. It is this system which the preliminary stages of new practical measures have been devised to supersede in such manner that none shall be injured, but all essentially benefited by the change, even while in progress.

Liberty cannot be given to the robber or murderer.

Equality cannot take place between St. James's and St. Giles's.

Fraternity can never arise between filth, grossly bad habits, self-degradation,—and cleanliness, superior habits and manners, and rational self-respect.

Yet full liberty, real equality, according to age, in education and position, and a cordial fraternity among all of our race, must be attained, before man, enlightened man, can be made to become good, wise, and happy.

The unceasing desire of humanity is to attain happiness.

Social Science, fully understood, and applied wisely to practice, will accomplish this result.

But from the latest publications in the new and the old world, it is now evident that this science has yet to be developed so as to enable the public to comprehend it in principle, spirit, and practice.

The principle is, " That the physical, intellectual, ' moral, spiritual, and practical qualities and powers of " each of the human race are formed for them without " their consent or knowledge. In other words, That the " character of man over the world has ever been, is now,

" and ever will be formed for him, and now may be
" scientifically well or ill formed for him by society."

The spirit, naturally arising from this knowledge,
is the spirit of universal love and charity for our race.

The knowledge of this principle, governed and
guided by this spirit, will enable society, with the
ample means which it has acquired for the purpose, to
insure from birth a superior physical, intellectual,
moral, spiritual, and practical character for every one ;
and by the formation of that superior character to
attain and secure in perpetuity the happiness of our
race.

It being now known that the origin of truth and
good among men is the knowledge that the Great
Creator creates, governs, and guides all things within the
universe, and that He gives to man his every power of
feeling, thought, and action,—the broad path to love,
charity, unity, wisdom, and happiness, is opened to
our race.

All the natural faculties and qualities of men are
therefore divine, and are calculated for perpetual
progress and happiness through every stage of his
existence ; and all now required to effect these results
is to place all of human kind within superior surroundings, scientifically devised and well executed to
insure this perpetual progress and happiness for all.

This will be a work to be commenced in the spirit

of love and charity, of persevering labour without stay or retrogression, and the result will be a continual increase of pleasure and happiness to all engaged in the task.

It has been said that many stages of progress must be passed through before the full advantages of the science in practice can be attained.

The first step in this progress will be to give to the ignorant, the poor, the idle, the filthy, the depraved, the degraded, the robber, and the murderer, a new character, and to give them knowledge, industry, cleanliness, self-respect, and a standing to be desired by the mass of the present working classes, whose means of maintaining a comfortable support of themselves and families are now precarious.

This change will be effected by the new combinations of surroundings, ultimately most economical, devised and executed in accordance with the science of society, called now " Social Science," by the British National Association for the promotion of it.

Those who comprehend and are familiar with the practical formation of character, know that it is a most lamentable error in society to allow one of its members to grow up in ignorance, poverty, idleness, crime, dirt, depravity, and degradation; deeply lamentable, because society has long possessed the most ample means to give to every one of its members from birth a character the most opposite in every one of these particulars.

But society to this day has been kept thoroughly blind to its best and highest interests, being enveloped in the dense mists of the most fatal prejudices. To overcome this state of human depression and misery, superior good Spirits in the spirit life, deeply feeling the physical and mental degradation of man over the earth and the utter confusion of all in mind and practice, have united their newly acquired superior powers to regenerate and redeem the human race from the sin and misery which ignorance of the unchanging laws of humanity, given to it by its Creator, have inflicted upon all past generations even to this day, continually increasing until they can be no longer suffered with impunity by the degraded millions in every nation over the globe.

These Spirits are now actively engaged, through the new and all-important spiritual manifestations, to open and expand the minds of many men in different nations and in various ways, to prepare mankind for this great revolution from evil to good, from ignorance to knowledge, with wisdom to apply it to unite and harmonise humanity, irrespective of natural and all present acquired differences.

They teach that truth, ever consistent with itself and

in accordance with all facts, taught without mystery, mixture of error, or fear of man, can alone effect this ever-to-be-desired glorious change.

Their teachings, to their present full extent, I mean to adopt, and in the spirit of true religion, that is, of love and charity, which they never fail to inculcate in the daily practice of every one to all of human kind.

In conformity with these teachings and this spirit of universal love and charity, I have now to announce that the religious and secular governments of the world have so far been taught to govern the governed only by keeping the great mass of mankind in physical and mental bondage, ignorant, poor, disunited, continually tempted to commit crimes, created solely by the governments, and then punishing these poor degraded working slaves, who, without knowledge of themselves, their rights and powers, are often most severely punished for these artificially made crimes. And all this error and evil continues so glaringly conspicuous at this day, that the advanced minds of the world are beginning to have the faculties of their minds opened to perceive the absurdity and gross injustice and cruelty of this wretched state of humanity over the earth.

A little reflection now will enable those who can reflect, to perceive that the state of ignorance, disunion, poverty, crime, punishment, incessant toil, and suffering, all now perfectly unnecessary, could not be maintained in opposition to the knowledge of facts, daily accumulating, and the rapid progress making in material and mental sciences, except by the union of religious and secular governments of Force, Fear, Fraud, and Falsehood. And by these only is the population of the world now governed.

The governments of the world have been taught this mode of governing, and know no other. For this mis-instruction and ignorance they are now very much to be pitied; for some, and I think many of them, are alive to the gross errors of this highly artificial, false, and most injurious system of governing, and are earnestly looking around in all directions for knowledge to enable them to govern on true principles and in accordance with the wise, all-efficient, and eternal laws of God, as given by the Creator of man to all of human kind, to direct their whole conduct through life, as soon as their mental and spiritual faculties shall be sufficiently developed to enable them to commence this superior and happy state of governing for themselves and the governed. Governments, lay and ecclesiastical, have no conception or belief that through their want of knowledge they keep the great mass of mankind in gross ignorance and superstition, in poverty or constant fear of it, in degrading toil and labour, disunited, committing crimes of which their governments continually encourage the creation, and then punish their poor deluded victims, and force upon all a false, wicked, and most injurious character; when, at less than a tithe of the present expence of time, labour, and capital, a good, useful, and superior character may, with the certainty of a law of nature, be given from birth to all of human kind, and the present diabolical mode of governing all of our race be gradually and peacefully superseded by the divine spirit, principles, and practices of Love and Charity directed by wisdom from above.

When have love and charity, directed by judgment, upon any scale yet tried, failed to produce the most beneficial and happy results, even when exercised in and counteracted by the present Babel confusion of falsehood, injustice, crime, and a system which encourages all manner of oppressions and evils?

Of the causes which of necessity create this diabolical state of human existence, the governments, civil and religious, daily evince the most profound ignorance. Were it not so, and if they knew the causes which day by day produce and encourage the rapid growth of these curses to humanity, and also knew how easily they, with their present powers, could remove them for ever, and supersede them by introducing causes which would produce universal love, charity, and wisdom, and establish ever progressing knowledge and happiness—I repeat, in the most emphatic manner that words can express, the thought, that if they were not without practical knowledge on this subject, and declined to unite to at once commence to change these evils for good, no language could describe the extent of horrid errors which they commit by attempting now, in opposition to the most glaring facts, to maintain this most injurious and irrational mode of mis-forming the character of, and mis-governing the human race.

But they do not know the practice by which the population of the world *can* be governed by the spirit of love and charity, directed by experienced judgment or true wisdom.

It is intended, by the publication of this pamphlet, to give this knowledge.

The Creator of all things created, has now, by gradually developing the faculties of man, enabled the human race, by extraordinary inventions and by the yet more extraordinary discoveries of many laws of nature, to acquire a knowledge of the means by which, when rationally used and applied, to provide in the most ample and sufficient manner to satisfy all the wants and desires of humanity, when the characters of all shall be naturally well-formed from birth, in a manner far better calculated to insure permanent happiness, than by the modes now in practice by the most favoured individuals living in any part of the world.

And these means, when applied as stated, will for ever abundantly suffice to meet the wants and desires of every succeeding generation. And all wants will be thereafter delightfully supplied—except the never dying desire to improve in every divine quality to which humanity can attain.

The everlasting wants of the human race are, and will be, to be well born, fed, clothed, lodged, trained, educated, employed, amused, governed, and so placed that all the surroundings, material, mental, and spiritual, shall be good and superior.

The means, rightly applied, to attain all these results, already amply exist, and they are daily increasing in a continually increasing ratio, and to their increase there is no assignable limitation.

In the British Empire more especially the means abound to over supply these wants of all through futurity.

Why, then, it may be now asked, are arrangements not made to allow of these wants being supplied,—seeing that all would be permanently benefited by their desires being satisfied?

The reasons are—

1st.—That the government is unconscious of the natural and acquired powers of the empire.

2nd.—That if it knew these powers, the members of it, not being scientifically trained practical men, would not know how to apply these powers to satisfy the wants and desires of all.

3rd.—The members of government are trained, educated, and placed, to acquire ignorant prejudices, strongly opposed to the well-being, progress, and happiness of the entire population, including themselves and families.

4th.—The people have been so educated and placed by the government, lay and ecclesiastic, as to be filled with strong prejudices against the only principles and practices which could give and secure to them their rights—the rights of all humanity, by which alone happiness can be attained and secured for them.

5th— That this is the very earliest period when the population would allow their rights to be taught to them, and how they are rationally to apply them to practice.

6th.—No one having a knowledge of the principles and practices of the science of society, or of the true Social Science, has ever yet possessed the requisite wealth to form a working model of the new combinations of surroundings to constitute the model arrangements which the advanced state of scientific knowledge now demands to complete the first practical society in accordance with Social Science, or the science by which to produce universal permanent happiness. The writer, some years ago, being strongly urged by the public to form one of these societies of new surroundings, and many offering their subscriptions, allowed the attempt to proceed to ascertain if sufficient funds could be so obtained to effect the object proposed. The writer knew that success could not be attained with less than *seven hundred thousand pounds*, or perhaps *one million* sterling. He asked the former sum, well knowing at the time it could not be raised unless the government would lend its countenance and aid. Lord Liverpool the then prime minister, and a large majority of his cabinet, were favourable to the trial of the full experiment; but it was too much in advance of the ecclesiastical power of the state, and of many of the old conservative aristocracy, and also of the sectarian superstitions of all classes, at that period, to pass successfully through either house of parliament, although, as will be seen very imperfectly reported in Hansard, the motion for its introduction into both houses met with much favour from high secular quarters. And it may be here noted that the then Archbishop of Canterbury (the liberal Archbishop Sutton,) was most friendly to my *"New Views of Society."* But also the great majority of the public of all parties were at that period too deeply imbued with the most ignorant and injurious superstitious prejudices, for truth and right reason, however beneficial these would prove for all, to be listened to in opposition to the strongholds of the conscientious prejudices of the sectarians, although these latter were opposed otherwise to the religion of the state. The writer broke the ice by openly advocating his " New Views of Society" in opposition to the entire old system by which the world had been so long, and yet is, so wrongly and injuriously governed, making it impossible under such a system of error in principle and practice that happiness or even common sense in forming the character of man or national surroundings in which to place him, or for the good government of the world, in principle, spirit or practice, could be attained.

But now a great change has come over the world The progress made by tracing facts to their principles, and thus acquiring real knowledge, has given sufficient strength to the public, aided by science and art, to put the axe to the root of all the superstitions which have so long stood in the way of all substantial progress in mental knowledge, and has opened the passage by which a flood of new and invaluable knowledge will be freely allowed to flow into the minds of the population of the world ;—new knowledge, by which all, with the certainty of a law of nature, will be made from their birth to become truly good, wise, united, ever consistent in mind and practice, continually increasing in real knowledge and progressing in happiness.

Under this change the existing evils of the world will rapidly die their natural death, and will be known no more except through history, to heighten the pleasures by contrast between the reign of evil and of good—of falsehood and truth in the language and conduct of all nations and peoples.

This is the great change in the public mind and feelings which was required to be made before a knowledge of the science of society could be suffered to be taught even in its baby-hood as introduced into legitimate society last year, when it was inaugurated at Birmingham by some of the leading statesmen of the day. This inauguration and the report of its proceedings will be long remembered with interest as proceedings by which the door has been opened, never again to be closed, to allow all to enter and to eat of the tree of knowledge, to learn to know good from evil, truth from falsehood, to adopt the good and true, and to abandon for ever the false and evil.

But how is this change to be introduced?

This is the great problem of the age to be now solved, and it is to be solved only by one mode of proceeding, which is the following.

1st.—The governments and people, lay and ecclesiastic, must, in the spirit of charity and love, be made conscious of the origin of good and evil to man, and of the necessary consequences of each to all humanity.

2nd.—This knowledge will give to all a correct idea of the principle on which the character of man should be based and formed for him. and on which society should be founded and constructed, and both made throughout to be consistent with that first principle.

3rd.—This knowledge will soon pervade all humanity with universal LOVE and CHARITY, PURE in PRINCIPLE, SPIRIT, and PRACTICE, and so perfect that the latter, even in every day intercourse of life, shall never deviate in principle or spirit, but be ever consistent in motive, feeling, mind, and conduct.

4th —Man will be, therefore, understandingly united to man, to nature, and to the Creator of all things within the illimitable universe, and in consequence, peace, harmony, and happiness will reign triumphant over the earth through all future ages, until as a planatory orb this earth shall cease to exist.

Such will be the future of humanity, to arise from man being taught to know the origin of evil and of good to all of his race.

Upon finishing this address, which many in the meeting declared was the best they had ever heard, even in his younger days, from the venerable chairman, he then said he had also prepared some resolutions which Mr. Cooper would read to the meeting, and if approved by any parties who would move and second them, they could be submitted to be approved or rejected by the audience thus met, consisting of every shade of party and creed. They were so moved and seconded. Explanations of some of them were called for and given. These were satisfactory to the questioners. The Resolutions were then put and unanimously adopted amidst much cheering.

An Address to Her Majesty, a Memorial to Her Majesty's Lords of the Treasury, and Petitions to both Houses of Parliament were then proposed, seconded, put to the meeting, and unanimously agreed to.

The following are the Resolutions, Memorial, and Address.

RESOLUTIONS.

RESOLVED :—

1st.—That at length the cause of evil and of good to man has been discovered, and that the evil may be now overcome and superseded by good.

2nd.—That the cause of evil is the undeveloped imagination of all past ages to the present, that man, contrary to every known fact, forms his own qualities, powers, and propensities, physical, intellectual, moral, spiritual, and practical; and that this error is the cause of all falsehood and deception.

3rd.—That the cause of all good to man is the knowledge that God creates in the germ all the qualities, powers, propensities, and faculties of humanity, and that matured society cultivates these qualities, powers, propensities, and faculties, from the germ in each individual for evil or for good.

4th.—That when the germ is placed before and after its birth within inferior, injurious, or evil surroundings, so must the individual become, with very few exceptions; and that when placed within superior and good surroundings, the individual will become good and superior.

5th.—That in consequence of the training and education of all past generations on the cause which has necessitated falsehood and evil, the surroundings in which the human race have been and are now placed are inferior and most fatal to the happiness of all.

6th.—That the British government now possess the most ample means to gradually supersede these inferior and injurious surroundings by good and superior, in which to place all the subjects of the empire at home and abroad, including our Indian possessions.

7th.—That in consequence of these discoveries it now becomes the first and highest duty of the government to investigate these subjects to their foundation and through all their ramifications, that it may learn to know how to begin the great work of superseding the present evil surroundings in which all are placed, by good and superior.

8th.—That as such immense permanent interests, affecting all classes, are involved in these matters, this meeting do address Her Majesty, memorialize the lords of the treasury, and petition both houses of parliament, to take these subjects into immediate consideration.

That the following be the address to Her Majesty.

ADDRESS OF A PUBLIC MEETING, HELD ON THE 14th OF MAY, 1858, IN ST. MARTIN'S HALL, LONG ACRE, LONDON; ROBERT OWEN, ESQ., IN THE CHAIR; TO HER MAJESTY, VICTORIA, QUEEN OF THE BRITISH EMPIRE.

WE, Your Majesty's faithful subjects, have now ascertained that the discovery has been made of the Cause of the Origin of Falsehood and Evil among the human race, and also the natural means by which that Cause can be removed, and Falsehood and Evil made to terminate for ever.

That the Cause of the Origin of Truth and Good

has been discovered, and at the same time the natural means by which Truth and Good may be made universally to supersede Falsehood and Evil.

That the means to effect this change throughout the British dominions, in peace and order, and with wise foresight, are at the command of Your Majesty's government.

We therefore pray Your Majesty to use your powerful influence with the chief officers of the government to begin to apply the means with the least delay to practice, that Your Majesty's subjects may be relieved from the many severe sufferings which they now most unnecessarily experience.

And, wishing Your Majesty a long, prosperous, and happy reign, we will for ever pray, &c.

TO THE LORDS OF HER MAJESTY'S TREASURY.

THE MEMORIAL

Adopted at a Public Meeting held in St. Martin's Hall, on 14th of May, 1858, to take into consideration the best practical means to new form man from birth, and to new construct society, &c.

YOUR MEMORIALISTS, having ascertained the Origin of Evil and Good, and of Falsehood and Truth throughout the past of human existence, and also the natural easy means by which the Falsehood and Evil may be gradually overcome and superseded by Truth and Good, and in which results there can be no mistake, pray your Lordships to use your influence with the Government and Parliament, to take these now all-important subjects into their most grave and immediate consideration, with the view to speedily terminate in peace and with order the present physical and mental sufferings of the millions, and the existing artificial and Babel confused and involved state of society.

And your memorialists will for ever pray.

PROPOSED PETITIONS TO BOTH HOUSES OF PARLIAMENT.

SHEWETH,

That your petitioners have after much study, observation, and reflection, ascertained the Origin of Evil and of Good, of Falsehood and of Truth, and also the natural and now easy practical means by which Evil and Falsehood may be overcome and gradually superseded by the Good and the True to the exclusion of all Falsehood and Evil.

Your Petitioners therefore pray, that your Right

Honourable (or Honourable) house will appoint a committee or commission, or examine a deputation of your petitioners at the Bar of your Right Honourable (or Honourable) house, to investigate this now all-important subject, with the view to speedily terminate in peace and with order the present physical and mental sufferings of the millions, and the existing artificial and Babel confusion and involved state of society.

And your petitioners will for ever pray.

———————

Thanks to the chairman and also to Mr. Cooper were likewise passed, and the meeting was adjourned to the 16th inst.

═══════════

THE SECOND MEETING ON THE EVENING OF THE 16TH OF MAY.

THIS Meeting was composed of an audience from 900 to 1000, who appeared to be deeply interested in the subject to be propounded and discussed.

The early portion of the evening was occupied with a Soiree, given by the Committee of the Literary and Scientific Institution, John Street, in commemoration of Mr. Owen's 88th birthday. During this period Robert Cooper, Esq., St. John's Terrace, Clarendon Road, Notting Hill, presiding, proposed the toast of the occasion in the following useful and well imagined speech, explanatory of the gross error of practice by all parties in every class throughout society. It was seconded by Mr. John Scott, civil engineer, who had come purposely from Belfast to attend this meeting. This compliment to Mr. Owen was received by the meeting in such manner as to prove that their hearts and souls were intensely interested in the success of the changes of society which he had so long advocated.

Mr. Cooper said—

Ladies and gentlemen,—I deem it no less a pleasure than a distinction to preside on this occasion—the last anniversary meeting that will be held in this Institution. This is the eighty-eighth birthday of Mr. Owen—an extraordinary age in itself, but singularly remarkable in one who has led so active, so industrious, and so eventful a career.

His presence amongst us once more, still youthful in his hopes and buoyant in his sympathies, still calling for an inquiry into the great social problems which have engaged his attention for upwards of fifty years,—is indeed, a lesson to us all: it teaches us patience, perseverance, consistency—the highest attributes of a true reformer.

And is it not time these questions were inquired into? Better, indeed, would it be for England, better would it be for Europe and the world, were the

British Parliament to investigate these subjects with the earnestness and dignity their vital importance demand, instead of expending their time and talents in party contests and diplomatic intrigues. While they are squabbling, the people are starving, mentally and physically. I hold it to be the duty of a state not merely to secure the liberties of the nation, but to promote its general well-being. And how can this noble work be accomplished while the intellectual, social, and moral development of the community are so grossly neglected. Disease, crime, and destitution are increasing around us, while the means to *prevent* these evils are also increasing. Whence these anomolies? Why is it that though Great Britain is the richest empire in Europe, it is one of the most immoral? Though we have more churches, we have more crime—though we have more manufactories, we have as large a number of artizans reduced to compulsory idleness. Gentlemen, is it not time such discrepancies in the state were inquired into?

Mr. Cooper proceeded at some length to remark upon the moral and social aspect of England during the last century. Dr. Wade tells us in his History of the Middle and Working Classes, that in 1805 our committals for crime in England and Wales did not exceed 4,500. In 1832 they had increased to upwards of 20,000 committals. From that time to the present they have averaged probably 25,000. The social condition of the nation during a large portion of that period is exemplified by the fact that the poors' rates in 1750 were under £700,000, while in 1832, they had increased to £7,000,000! and since that time they had averaged that amount at least. Now, our population had little more than doubled during this interval—that is, while our population had increased cent. per cent., crime had increased 500 per cent., and pauperism 700 per cent. !

Should not these appalling anomolies be investigated? Should not Mr. Owen, who has studied these subjects more than any man living, be fairly and fully heard by the British Government, not merely at the bar of the house, but *in* it.

Mr. Gaskell informs us in his book on the manufacturing population that in some departments of production one person can produce as much in one *day* as he could have produced less than a century ago in a whole *year.* Eighty years ago, one person, by hand, could attend only to one spindle, while in Manchester at this moment there are men who attend to two spinning frames which carry 2,000 spindles ! And these spindles, worked by steam power, go at *three* times the speed they did by hand last century. So that in the spinning department one man produces as much in the same time as 6,000 men could have done at that period !

Mr. McCulloch himself, so long ago as 1834, stated there were 9,000,000 spindles in use in this country. This multiplied by three would equal 27,000,000 spindles worked by hand—that is, about 5,000 spinners by steam power can now do the work which it would have required 27,000,000 spinners to do by hand seventy or eighty years since.

And yet, though our powers of production have increased so enormously, pauperism and crime have increased also.

Mr. Colquhoun in 1812 estimated the wealth annually produced in this country at £450,000,000. Mr. McQueen in 1840 estimated it at £820,000,000! Still we have more moral and social degradation. Is it not time, I again ask, these discrepancies were inquired into? Were Mr. Owen's views upon these subjects carried out into practice, these anomolies would be impossible.

It is probable their full importance may not be appreciated or even understood at this moment, perhaps not in this generation, but it is not the less our duty to recognise the services of those who, like Mr. Owen, have devoted a life to their exposition. Our venerable friend has pursued these grave problems with an earnestness, a devotion, a singleness, and benevolence of purpose unparalleled in our times, and though his contemporaries may not appreciate them, an enlightened posterity will revere his name

as one of the highest and purest in the history of
this century.

Mr. Owen then requested of the meeting that all
personalities might cease, and that it would resolve
itself into the adjourned public meeting, as advertised,
from St. Martin's Hall, of the 14th instant.   This
was immediately assented to, and Mr. Owen was
unanimously voted to the chair, when he opened the
meeting by stating its objects.   He then requested
Mr. Cooper to read the address which he, (Mr.
Owen), had prepared in continuation of the previous
meeting on the 14th instant.

THE ORIGIN OF EVIL.

THE origin of evil, as written frequently in my late
publications, but hitherto so little understood or believed, is the erroneous, undeveloped, crude imagination of our first ancestors, " that the created could
" and did create its own qualities and powers;" and
especially " That man created his own physical,
" intellectual, moral, spiritual, and practical, qualities
" and powers, and that therefore he should be made
" responsible to his fellow men," while ignorant of
the motives, thoughts, and feelings, whence his actions
emanated—actions which these divine qualities and
powers of necessity produced in all.

D

The consequence of this crude notion and totally unsupported wild and absurd imagination, is insane anger, ill-will, pride, vanity, self-conceit, egotism, self-aggrandisement, tyranny, robbery, and murders for property, competition, contests, individual conflicts, and national wars, envy, malice, jealousy, revenge, and murders from hatred—human laws in direct defiance of nature's instincts and the Creator's unchanging, all-efficient, and all-merciful laws. These laws of poor deluded man, created superstitions, poverty, prostitution, and every other crime known to human nature, and these cruel and most unjust laws have alone for so long a period maintained the origin of evil, and encouraged its continuance, and retarded the progress of knowledge and the attainment of permanent general happiness to all of our race.

The origin of evil is at this day creating and encouraging the growth of all these sins and miseries to their full state of ripeness, even to rank corruption in the body politic, physical and mental. While, through this origin of all that is evil to man, true religion, or the *spirit* and *practice* of universal love and charity, can no longer be found on the earth, having been driven by force, fear, fraud, and falsehood, from every hole and corner of it.

It is indeed full time in the order of nature for the origin of good to destroy the origin of evil, to commence its reign, and give health of body and mind, rationality, and happiness, to poor long-suffering and long-deluded humanity—to our common humanity, which has thus suffered from the most gross ignorance of its nature and divine qualities, fitting it for the attainment of every kind of excellence, and for the enjoyment of the highest degrees of rational happiness.

And a knowledge of the *Origin of Good will produce these ever to-be-desired results.* For the Origin of Good will destroy in man all motive to anger, ill-will, pride, vanity, self-conceit, egotism, desire of self-aggrandisement, to steal, rob, or murder for property, to engage in individual conflicts, contests, competition, or national wars, to become envious, malicious, revengeful, or to desire to murder from hatreds. It will also destroy all motive to make laws in defiance of nature's instincts and the unchanging divine laws of the Creator, and consequently will destroy all motive to prostitution, unchaste desires, and indelicacy of practice, with all their horrid diseases and hydras of evil.

The discovery of the Origin of Good and Evil will be first received, comprehended, and accepted, by the more advanced minds in churches and states and among the people ; and these, seeing the natural and necessary consequences emanating from both, will be eager and anxious to spread the knowledge of them far and wide, even into the most distant lands and among the present least civilized of our race.

Thus will a natural revolution in the motives, thoughts, feelings, mind, and language or general phraseology of the world, be effected.

And this mental revolution is a necessary preparation before the material revolution can be commenced, to execute the superior new surroundings which necessarily emanate from the Origin of Good, to gradually and peacefully supersede the inferior, unjust, and cruel surroundings which from like necessity have emanated from the Origin of Evil.

But the intelligent public will not now be satisfied without some immediate practical preparatory measures; and these practical measures it will be for the interest of all that government should undertake and superintend to their completion.

The best energies and highest talents of the empire, not refusing willing aid from the acquirements of other nations, should be called to this all-glorious task of creating new combinations of surroundings to make it unavoidable that man shall become good, wise, healthy, and society united, wealthy, consistent, and happy, in making a continual progress towards every kind of excellence.

These preparatory practical governmental measures should consist of three preliminary model societies.

One, in which to new-train properly chosen persons of both sexes from the working class; one from the middle class; and the third from the higher class:— the establishments having reference in their construction and general arrangements to the previous surroundings of each class. And in due time, to complete these preliminary arrangements, a fourth establishment or society will be required, in which to receive and train certain selected infants and children and young persons from the first named three societies.

These four to be nursing societies for the different classes under the government of the Origin of Truth and Good, and to be brought as near to perfection in principle, spirit, and practice, as old prejudices, customs, and habits will admit, under new surroundings, to improve the inmates to the greatest extent practicable in one generation in the three first societies, and in the second generation in the fourth.

It is expected that decisive improvements will be made in the mind, manner, and conduct of the inmates placed within the three first preparatory societies, but that in the fourth, additional substantial acquirements of a high order will be attained—such as, by the example, will induce the population of the world to be eager and to desire to imitate and to adopt them with the least delay.

The essential difference between old society, based

on the Origin of Falsehood and Evil, and the proposed
new society, based on the Origin of Truth and Good,
is, that in the old the individual is made responsible
for his thoughts and feelings, and for the actions
thence ensuing; while under the proposed new dispensation for the government of the human race,
matured society will be made responsible for the
thoughts, feelings, and conduct of every individual
trained, educated, and placed by society, directly or
indirectly.

The reason, when the bandages of ignorance, error,
and prejudices shall be withdrawn from the so blinded
mental vision of all nations and peoples, will be obvious
to every one so relieved.

For when these bandages shall be withdrawn, it will
become vivid to the mental faculties of all, that individuals are passive recipients of the physical, mental,
moral, spiritual, and practical powers of their organization before birth, and equally so in receiving their
locale, language, religion, habits, manners, position,
ideas of right or wrong, truth and falsehood; for these
differ more or less according to localities among all
nations and peoples.

For the organization of the germ *before* birth, the
Great Creating Power of the Universe or God is alone
responsible; for the acquisitions given to the individual
from the germ *after* birth, of his language, religion, habits,

manners, position, ideas of wrong and right, of truth and falsehood, matured society is alone responsible.

Hence the now loud call upon society to abandon the origin of falsehood and evil in principle, spirit, and practice, and all the tremendous evils which it is hourly creating and inflicting upon poor ignorantly passive humanity.

And hence the now overwhelming necessity for the population of the world to adopt the origin of truth and good, in principle, spirit, and practice, and to make the new surroundings in undeviating accordance with this divine origin, and ever consistent with its principles, spirit, and practice ; and then will the earth be speedily made into a terrestrial paradise, occupied by human beings possessing the qualities hitherto given to angels, and yet only preparing for a much higher and more glorious future existence in a new and superior life.

To comprehend this change, let the mind imagine our globe to be a training school, to form the character of its inhabitants to fit them for a future higher life, while they enjoy the pleasures to be derived from a well arranged and well conducted seminary of instruction in the art of acquiring the most useful and valuable knowledge in the manner most accordant with the beautiful laws of nature.

By so attaining these new acquisitions, guided by

the principles, spirit, and practice emanating from the origin of truth and good, a source of happiness will be opened to all, daily increasing without limitation, such as the old world has never yet imagined.

The population of the world will thus be congregated in societies, scientifically arranged and combined to perform all the business of this life in a very superior manner, with pleasure to all engaged in it; while at the same time these societies will be in fact the best schools for the formation of a good, wise, and happy character for all within them, ever yet, perhaps, conceived by humanity; for all societies, large or small, are now schools for the formation of character of those living within them, and most wretched combinations are they for this all-important purpose.

In these schools for business and the formation of character, all will have their natural liberty to speak, write, and publish the thoughts and feelings which nature and society have forced them to receive, and with these, all knowing their source, none will ever be offended.

But the only *public* religion taught within these Seminaries of industry, union, knowledge, and affection, will be the unceasing practice in spirit and conduct of universal love and charity. This being the highest and only acceptable worship of an infinitely wise and good being, who created all things, knowing what He makes, and that evidently all are made for the harmony and happiness of all life.   All practising this universal public religion, each one will of necessity have his or her own impressions of the Universe, its Cause and its Government, and the variety of opinions upon these and other subjects will always be a source of new knowledge and a pleasurable mental exercise to all.

These scientifically constructed, arranged, combined, and united societies, will offer the most easy and ready means by which to teach the population of the earth to acquire one language, one religion, one interest, and one general feeling of desire to promote to the utmost the happiness of all, and by degrees to acquire a real practical equality of condition according to age.

To govern the population of the world will then be simply to well-form the character of all from birth, and to accomplish this merely by placing all within new surroundings, which will enable all to live and enjoy life according to their highest cultivated nature.

Before concluding it may be stated that the proposed preliminary model society No. 1, will have the appearance of a well-constructed, arranged, and conducted village, with about *one thousand* inhabitants, surrounded by gardens and a well-cultivated, well-laid-out farm of about *one thousand* or *fifteen hundred* acres.

That the second proposed preliminary model will have the appearance of a small well-constructed, well-arranged, and well-conducted town, surrounded by gardens, and by farms containing from *two to three thousand* acres, well laid out and well cultivated; the number of inhabitants *about two thousand.*

The third proposed preliminary model of society will have the appearance of a superior moderate sized town, in the form of a large square of superior buildings, sufficient to contain *two thousand five hundred* or *three thousand* inhabitants, surrounded by beautiful gardens, pleasure grounds, and highly cultivated farms, together containing from *three thousand five hundred* to *five thousand* acres, more or less according to soils and other local considerations.

It should now be had in everlasting remembrance, that by the discoveries of the past century the human race may from birth be so surrounded by the creations of society, as to force each one, unknown to himself or herself, to become a human demon or a human angel.

And that it is the highest possible permanent interest of all, from the highest to the lowest, that arrangements should be made with the least delay over the world, to give this superior character to all of our race. And thus may the will of God be done on earth, as it is now in the superior heavens of the spirit life.

It may be useful to add, that the principles, spirit, and practice, now advocated, are universally applicable to all of our race; and that from these will arise one beautiful system, by which the population of the world will be governed with ease, pleasure, and entire satisfaction to all.

The first measure towards the attainment of this most desirable object will be for all nations to agree to form and to be cordially united by federative treaties, based on equal justice to all; none by their physical force or position to attempt to take advantage of the weakness of others in these respects; and the more civilized taking the necessary means, in the pure religious spirit of charity and love, with patience and kind perseverance, to enlighten the less civilized, even down to the most ignorant and barbarous savages; for by these means a good and valuable character may be now easily given to all possessing the organization of humanity.

The next measure to attain the beauty, simplicity, and innumerable advantages of the universal government, will be to establish the central executive government of each nation as near to the centre of the dominions to be governed as a proper site for it can be found. This site will require an area of from 4000 to 6000 acres, well chosen to maintain for ever by good culture from 2000 to 3000 inhabitants;—for, to obtain the full advantages of society in its highest perfection, the population of the world should be gradually withdrawn from all cities, towns, villages, and isolated dwellings, and be newly congregated within new scientific surroundings to contain not more when complete than from 2000 to 3000 men, women, and children, in their usual proportions.

The advantages of this arrangement are too numerous and important to be particularized, but the reasons for it I have detailed in my official report to the County of Lanark, made in the year 1820, and now re-published in the supplementary appendix to the first volume of my Life; and that document I now most earnestly recommend to the study of every statesman, philanthropist, and philosopher, and especially to all engaged in the practical improvement and progress of humanity, irrespective of colour, country, creed, or class. They will find that in that document the foundations of a scientific practical society, and especially of the science of society in its social perfection, were then for the first time in the history of mankind given, and given in the most plain and simple manner, to the world. But the popular mind, although greatly admiring it, was then too undeveloped to admit the practice. This, indeed, is the very earliest period when public prejudices and popular ignorance could be made to receive the full instruction before the practice of this divine system for the government of humanity could be commenced with the least chance of success.

Time will now permit me only to state in addition, that this central government will be surrounded in circles by the federatively associated families, from 2000 to 3000 each, with their natural proportion of domain around them; and thus circle after circle will extend like the waves in a lake when a stone is thrown into it, from the centre to the circumference.

Within these family societies, in all these circles from the centre to the circumference of the territories governed, the arrangements will be such that each one born within each, after they shall be established and regularly organized, will be well-born, well-fed, well-clothed, well-lodged, well-trained from birth, well-educated, well-employed, well-recreated, well-locally governed, and well-placed for the highest enjoyments of a superior life.

So trained, educated, and placed, all will be made to become, good, enlightened, rational, or consistent in mind and practice; consequently each one will be competent to govern himself and herself, without troubling the government, the chief business of which will be to receive from, and impart to, each of the associated families in these federated circles useful information, within the national domains. And also to communicate in like manner by telegraph with the central governments of all nations, giving and receiving useful and curious information daily, when necessary, to the uttermost inhabited parts of our globe. In fact, making, by means of the telegraph when carried to its full practical extent, one family of all the governments and people of the population of the earth. And no more private property among them than there is now in a private family before its property is divided among the children.

Why, then, should these universal blessings, now so easily attainable, be longer withheld from all humanity?

ROBERT OWEN.

During the reading of this address Mr. Owen frequently requested Mr. Cooper to stop while he, Mr Owen, made additional explanations of some of the more important statements. These were generally well timed, and were well received by the audience, as was the whole address when concluded.

It was then proposed, seconded, and unanimously carried, that this division of the meeting should also address Her Majesty, Memorialise the Lords of the Treasury, and Petition both Houses of Parliament; and the following Address, Memorial, and Petition, were moved for adoption and were unanimously agreed to.

ADDRESS
TO HER MAJESTY THE QUEEN OF THE BRITISH EMPIRE.

MAY IT PLEASE YOUR MAJESTY,

WE, the subscribers, have held a numerous meeting, called by public advertisement, Robert Owen, Esq., in the chair, at which it was unanimously resolved to address your Majesty to disclose the important discovery which we have made for the benefit of all your Majesty's subjects at home and abroad, and ultimately for the population of the world.

It is—that we have ascertained the certain means to attain universal goodness, prosperity, and happiness, and the manner in which the practical measures by which the change from the existing system of ignorance, disunion, poverty, crime, and misery, may be gradually, peaceably, and most advantageously for all, carried speedily into execution.

We therefore pray your Majesty to use your royal influence with your Majesty's Government to have this now all-important subject fully investigated.

And your petitioners will for ever pray, &c.

PETITION TO BOTH HOUSES OF PARLIAMENT.

SHOWETH,—

That your petitioners have discovered the fatal errors of all past legislation for the good government of mankind.

That to govern humanity rightly and in accordance with its nature is now ascertained to be simple, easy, and straightforward.

That it is but to well-form the character from birth for all, by a natural training in accordrnce with our created character before birth, and by a continued education by the natural means to form good and superior men and women. And then to supply all the wants of our nature at all times in a superior manner by the only just mode through which this all-important result can be attained, that is, by healthy, pleasant, superior, and delightful employment and occupation for all, according to age, capacity, and inclination.

We therefore pray your Right Honourable (or Honourable) house now, with the earnestness and gravity required, to investigate to its foundation, and through all its ramifications, this now most vital of all subjects.

And your petitioners will for ever pray, &c.

TO THE RIGHT HONOURABLE THE LORDS OF HER MAJESTY'S TREASURY.

A Memorial passed unanimously at a most numerous and crowded public meeting, Robert Owen, Esq., in the chair,—

SHOWETH,—

That your Memorialists have made the great discovery so long sought for by the human race, but hitherto without the slightest prospect of success.

That this great discovery is the certain knowledge of the means by which to insure the goodness, wisdom, prosperity, and happiness of all in perpetuity.

Your memorialists therefore pray your lordships to use their influence with the other members of the Government to bring this now all-important subject under the immediate consideration of Parliament.

And your memorialists will for ever pray, &c.

The chairman then suggested that the meeting might desire to pass their opinion upon the Resolutions, Address, Memorial, and Petitions, which were so unanimously agreed to at the previous meeting in St. Martin's Hall. These were then proposed, seconded, and enthusiastically approved and confirmed, and the meeting was adjourned to Tuesday the 18th, at eight o'clock.

THE ADJOURNED THIRD MEETING, HELD THE 18TH MAY. COMMENCED AT 8 P.M.

THIS will be perhaps considered by the public to be the most important of the three meetings, although not so numerously attended as the second. Mr. Owen was again voted to the chair, and was, as in the previous meeting, assisted in reading for him by Mr. Robert Cooper.

E

The proceedings were commenced by a short explanation by the chairman, stating the importance of the objects to be brought that evening under the consideration of the meeting, which he said were never exceeded by the proceedings of any other public meeting. They would have to express an opinion after hearing the statements which would be presented and explained to them, whether they would prefer the continuance of the present false and evil system for forming character and governing society, or the true and good system by which a natural, superior, and good character could be formed from birth for all, a superabundance of the most valuable wealth produced for all, and society could be, with ease and pleasure to all, well-governed.

Mr. Cooper was then requested by the chairman to read the following paper :—

TO COMMENCE PRACTICAL MEASURES.

BEFORE there can be Truth, Justice, Goodness, and happiness among men, there must be a new formation of their character from birth ; this character to be formed through the influences of a new combination of surroundings, in which to new place all and to reconstruct society, in such manner as to make it competent to supply, with ease, pleasure, and regularity, all the ever recurring wants of humanity when it shall be most highly cultivated in each individual ;

and to satisfy these wants in the best manner is the direct and only road to insure the highest permanent happiness of our race. But to accomplish these results, measures entirely new in spirit, principle, and practice will be required.

To discover how to commence these practical measures on a sure foundation, and in a right direction, has required long and deep study of the past, present, and future; and the following has been the result :—

That an association will require to be formed of men and women competent in mind and manner to become students to acquire a comprehensive and accurate knowledge of the past and present system of society based on the origin of Falsehood and Evil, and of the errors and miseries which have necessarily arisen from a foundation so fatal to goodness and happiness, and even to common sense.

And to become students also of the future system of truth and goodness, by which the population of the world will be hereafter governed and their characters formed; and thus to acquire the capacity to form a correct judgment between the Evil and the Good system for the government of all nations and peoples, and of the consequences which must emanate from each—the one to inflict misery on, and the other to insure happiness to, all of our race.

The association may be called " The Association

of Student Co-operators, to change Evil into Good."
And to effect the change peaceably, gradually, and
rationally, by measures easily to be understood in
spirit, principle, and practice, when commenced on
its true foundation and with a full knowledge of that
which is intended to be accomplished. But every
measure must now be viewed practically, and every
difficulty fairly and fully met.

It is the duty of the British government now to
adopt, guide, and direct, the change proposed, from
the system of falsehood, repulsion, and evil, to the
system of truth, attraction, and all good; and the
first difficulty which the people have to learn is to
acquire the knowledge how to act peaceably and
effectually on the government, to enable it to make
the change in opposition to all the discordant factions
which may not yet discover the universal advantage
that will be derived when the repulsive and evil
system shall be abandoned and the attractive and
good system adopted.

But the time limited for a public meeting will only
admit of general statements without entering too
much into detail. Yet it will be useful here to observe, that the attempts of the people to obtain a
Reform in Parliament are a waste of most valuable
time and means; for if all the points of what they
call their charter were to be obtained to-morrow, they,

the people, would derive no benefit from it to relieve them from their present difficulty. The whole population now require very different practical measures to give them immediate permanent relief.

That which they require may be thus put in the form of

A NATIONAL CHARTER.

1st.—To change the origin of falsehood and evil for the origin of truth and good for the foundation of society.

Until this shall be done all attempts at reform will be a mere mockery to give permanent relief.

2nd.—A national natural education, to form a good, useful, and valuable character for all, and thus to insure a superior state of society.

3rd.—National natural employment and occupation for all who require them, in order that the wants of all may be always regularly supplied. And they may with ease be now thus supplied without contests or competition.

4th.—The construction of national improved combinations of new surroundings, in which to place the hitherto most neglected of the population of these islands and thus to remove them out of those most irrational surroundings which while suffered to continue will be a disgrace to British legislation, and must of necessity

perpetually encourage, enforce, and maintain ignorance, depravity, filth, poverty, prostitution, crime, and
wretchedness, on all trained and living within them—
a public scandal to the British name and nation.

5th.—That to assist to make the change from the
system of evil to good, and to make it gradually and
peaceably,—national new combinations of rational
surroundings must be constructed, in which to place the
working classes, to enable them to be well educated
and employed beneficially for themselves and society.

6th.—That the Bank of the British Empire be
established with branches throughout the British
dominions for the benefit of the nation. The security
to be Her Majesty's subjects. And by thus providing a
sure, sound, and most convenient circulating medium
our immense wealth would daily rapidly increase
under the change, and panics could never occur.

7th.—That government and people should cordially
unite in aiding each other in peaceably and gradually
effecting the change from the practice of all that is
evil and now so injurious to every class and rank in
the state. And that

8th.—To facilitate this change and simplify the
present involved system of conducting society, all
taxes should be repealed, and an honest property tax,
equal to the real wants of the nation, should be alone
the tax of the nation.

When the government and people can attain the good common sense to unite cordially to terminate the reign of falsehood and evil, and to desire the reign of truth and goodness, the mysteries of govern‑ing will cease, and to the surprise and delight of both parties it will be discovered that good governing con‑sists in devising and well executing new rational combinations of surroundings to well form the cha‑racter of all from birth and to well employ all through life.   So simple will it be thus to govern the popu‑lation of the world in peace, universal prosperity, and happiness, without conflicts, or wars, or contests of any kind.

National education and national employment, well conceived, combined, and executed, will be found to be all that the world will hereafter require.

And the watchword of the British nation hence‑forth should be, " national unexclusive education, and national, useful, natural employment and occupation."

The more effectually to forward these great national measures, the resolutions adopted by the previous meetings were then agreed to, with the addition of the following :—

" That a deputation of the friends of national un‑exclusive education, and of national natural employ‑ment for all the unemployed poor and working classes, wait upon the Prime Minister and the Secretary for the Home Department, to impress them with the urgent necessity which exists for the poor and working classes to be immediately nationally well-educated and usefully and beneficially employed for themselves and for society."

These statements were considered and approved by the meeting.

Next followed

THE FIRST LESSON OF TRUTH, EMANATING FROM THE NEW SYSTEM FOR THE GOVERNMENT OF THE WORLD, FOUNDED ON THE ORIGIN OF TRUTH AND GOOD. ADDRESSED TO THE BRITISH GOVERNMENT AND PARLIAMENT.

ARISING from a combination of circumstances of unnumbered ages in progress, your present position has become the most important of any governing power upon the earth, and especially at this crisis, when a revolution is in its progress which must influence the population of the world for good or evil through all succeeding generations, and when you have one of the most extensive empires in the world to re-establish and to re-model.

At this day you hold in your hands the government of the British Empire, extending into every quarter of the globe, and a fearful responsibility depends on your wise or unwise direction of this charge.

To become men equal to this high position, and to give an example to the world, such as the world ought

now to adopt, you must drop party politics, **class**
interests, and all ignorant individual selfish considerations.   You must look to eternal principles, and
endeavour to attain a knowledge of great and permanent interests of humanity; and when you fully
comprehend them in all their wide extended connexions
then fearlessly apply them consistently to practice,
throughout the British Empire.

What, then, you ask, are these eternal principles?
They are

1st.—That humanity has ever been created with
Natural Wants, and that the right satisfying of these
wants will give high happiness, universal harmony, and
the enjoyment of a superior earthly existence, to all
of our race.

You will now say that these wants never have been,
and never can be satisfied.

You thus speak as you have been taught; not as
men trained to observe facts, to draw the most natural
conclusions from them, and to acquire valuable practical experience for the direction of human affairs and
the government of a great empire.   The course to
pursue to attain these objects is, to ascertain what these
natural wants of humanity are,—whether the British
Empire possesses the means to satisfy those wants,—
and, if the means are found to be superabundant for
this purpose, then the important question will arise

How can these means be applied in the best manner to practice?

2nd.—What are these eternal wants of humanity?

Answer.—To be well-born,—well-fed—well-clothed, —well-lodged,—well-trained,—well-educated, so as to have the character well formed, physically, mentally, morally, spiritually, practically, and affectionately, (that is, to have love and charity for all, irrespective of every natural and acquired difference),—to be well-employed,—well-recreated,—well-governed,—and well-placed.

3rd.—Do the means exist in the British Empire to satisfy all the wants permanently of its subjects?

Answer.—Yes. The most abundant means exist at this day, and have long existed, most fully to satisfy all these wants, and to secure happiness to every one at home and abroad.

4th.—What, then, has prevented this happy state of existence from being introduced, and enjoyed by the whole population of the British Empire?

Answer.—Your trained ignorance in favour of human-made laws, and their endless evil consequences;—laws made in direct opposition to the eternal, wise, and all-efficient laws of God, as daily exhibited through all nature: and the equally ignorant prejudices thence arising, which by your ever criminal-making laws, you have forced into the minds of the people. And thus

most unnecessarily, except for your want of knowledge, do the mass of the people now wallow in dirt,
disgrace, crime, ignorance, want, prostitution, and its
never-ending miseries.

5th.—You ask, like helpless infants, what can we
do to prevent the continuance of these evils, and especially prostitution, the greatest of them all?—What
can all the men and women upon the earth do with
them under the existing system, or with prostitution,
the man-made social evil?

Answer.—Nothing, but to make them worse. And
while this cancer of prostitution shall be allowed to
remain in the body politic, and shall continue to be
created and encouraged, as it now is, and as it has
been through so many past generations, by the
blinded and most ignorant superstitions and governments among all nations and all peoples, who, with
experience and a grain of common sense, will ever
expect to introduce health, peace, truth, and virtue,
among the human race?

It is for you, the British Government and Parliament, to look at this and all other subjects on which
the permanent happiness of man depends, fairly and
fully, and to stand forth like men to investigate every
social evil to its source and true cause; and then,
with minds fully master of the subject, like men determined to do their duty to their race, at once to

eradicate the evil at its root, to supersede it by the ever wise, merciful, and efficient eternal laws of God, given to humanity to conduct it the direct road to real knowledge, to unity, and to happiness.

Every crime upon the earth has been created by man-made inhuman laws—laws made ignorantly, presumptuously, in opposition to daily occurring millions of facts, against, and as it were in open disregard and defiance of these unchanging laws of God.

At present you are governing and legislating like school children, continually afraid of the birch of truth; for through all past periods of your governing and legislating you have been more afraid of the truth being promulgated to the world, than of all the armies and navies ever opposed to you. And yet it is these divine truths which can alone set the nations free, and give to each of you the strength of mind which you now ought to acquire, and the permanent high happiness which you and all men might now be made to possess.

But to reach these high attainments, in order that all future generations may be well-born, well-fed, well-clothed, well-lodged, well-trained, well-educated, well-employed, well-recreated, well-governed, and well-placed,—present society must pass through certain stages of refining surroundings.

The lower and inferior class must be placed within

these divine refining surroundings, yet not too refined for their present habits and state of mind; but sufficiently refined to give them new ideas, habits, and conduct, equal to the best of the present middle class; while all that is really useful among the working class must be retained.

Then there must be superior surroundings in which to place the middle class, to elevate them to attain all that is truly valuable in the present refinement of the upper classes, but carrying with them and retaining all that is useful in the present middle class.

To these must be added new combinations of yet superior surroundings in which to place the present higher classes; for all require to be practically re-educated. In these advanced surroundings the upper class, retaining their desirable refinements, will acquire the most useful knowledge of the lower and middle classes; for there are qualities in each, necessary to be combined in each individual, to train them to become full-formed, rational, and superior men and women, prepared to live in harmony and to enjoy the happiness which all such may now derive from the earth.

But there is yet a fourth and higher stage to be attained. The children of these three surroundings, who shall be born, trained, educated, and employed within them, will acquire a new spirit of love and charity, and be prepared with new tempers, habits, manners, ideas, and useful practical knowledge of themselves, of man, and of society. They will thus constitute a full nucleus society, composed of full formed men and women of what may be termed a new and superior race, to commence, without crime, human punishment, evil passions, or misery of any kind, a new existence of man upon the earth, far surpassing in wisdom, goodness, and happiness, the imaginations of any of the misformed, not to say mentally malformed men and women of the present generation. Although it is this generation which must be new taught and trained, to prepare the *new surroundings* by which this apparent miracle is to be introduced and finally accomplished; not, indeed, by a miracle, but by the most simple and natural practical measures, gradually carried into execution in a manner essentially beneficial to all.

It may be effected with the order and regularity of the seasons, nor need there be any disturbing cause introduced through the whole progress of the change.

And truly a new book of life will be opened to man, by which he will be enabled to put off his present worn-out garments of filthy rags of ignorance and corruption, in order that " old things may pass away, and become new."

Briefly now to recapitulate :

1st.—The human race can never enjoy the happiness to which its natural qualities are capable of attaining, while it shall be based on a system of falsehood and evil ; because under such a system all the natural wants of humanity can never be supplied, or the repulsive feelings be withdrawn from society.

2nd.—Under a system based on the origin of truth and good, all these wants may with pleasure and delight to every one be abundantly supplied through futurity, and the repulsive feeling withdrawn and superseded by the universal feeling of attraction.

3rd.—Society being so based, no obstacle will arise to prevent the present generation from commencing the all-pleasing task of making the first, second, third, and fourth preliminary stages of the new surroundings, which, when completed, are to effect this glorious change in man and society ; because by the kind and quality of these surroundings man may be made to acquire the character now given to angels or devils.

4th—The science of surroundings, hitherto hidden from and unsuspected by all generations to the present, and its right application to practice over the world, may now be taught, in a well devised training school, with ease and pleasure to teachers and taught ; and this is that knowledge which will lead direct to universal peace, harmony, and happiness.

5th.—Through the knowledge of this science and of its right application to practice, the great problem of the age will be solved,—that is, How to give the greatest individual liberty practicable, with the best and highest social arrangements of society, and how to form the best and highest social arrangements of society, compatible with the full liberty of thought, speech, writing, and action of the individual, in order that the full advantages of the individual and social state of existence may be united and permanently enjoyed by all through every succeeding age.

How simple, plain, and beautiful, may these principles and practices be soon made to appear to the human race! It is but to teach them the origin of truth and good, and the science and application to practice of the surroundings which will of necessity emanate from that divine foundation.

But it will be now, of necessity, under the existing state of things emanating from the origin of falsehood and evil, thought and said by every colour, creed, and class, in all countries, that to commence such a change in human affairs is impracticable and impossible by you, unless you had a large and powerful party to back and sustain the attempt, and yet that you are now without any party, creed, or class, to second your proceedings.

All this I well know, and see as vividly as you see the sun when it shines at noon day.

But I am not alone. I am aided and assisted by Truth, unerringly consistent with itself and in accor-

dance with all facts.   I have all natural humanity, and
the high permament interest of every individual living
or who may live hereafter, and I have the eternal, unchanging, all-wise, merciful, and all-efficient laws of
God and nature.

With these weapons, thus shielded, I now stand
forth, confront, and defy all the powers of darkness,
come from whence they may.   Will they now venture
to come openly to the attack?   They will not—they
dare not.   The sun of truth is now unclouded,—is
too high in the heavens to feel the puny attempts of
creed, class, or party.   Against its mid-day brilliancy
they will become powerless and fail in all their attempts
longer to deceive or mystify.   TRUTH IS NOW GREAT,
AND WILL PREVAIL ; and the human race must be
placed within new surroundings from birth, to make
all, with the certainty of a law of nature, good, wise,
united, and happy.

ROBERT OWEN.

The reading of this document created an intense
interest in the audience, and when finished it was proposed for their approval or rejection, and was
enthusiastically and unanimously adopted.

It was then moved and seconded that this meeting
should also petition both houses of parliament.

It was then proposed, seconded, and unanimously
adopted—

That the following Petition be presented to both Houses of Parliament—

PETITION TO BOTH HOUSES OF PARLIAMENT.

THAT your Petitioners have now ascertained that their condition and the condition of the population of the empire can be alone substantially and permanently benefited by a national, unexclusive, useful, natural system of education, and by its union with a national well-arranged system of useful permanent employment for the unemployed, and that these, combined, may be now introduced into practice most advantageously for the interests of the nation and for every class within it.

We therefore pray that your Honourable (or Right Honourable) house will now abandon petty, personal, and party politics, and give your attention to the national governing of this, by nature, highly favoured empire, by well-educating and employing all the people—measures which may now be easily and speedily carried into practice, and which will give permanent high prosperity to the British empire.

And your petitioners will for ever pray, &c.

It was then resolved that Lord Brougham be requested to present the petition to the House of Peers, and that Mr. T. S. Duncombe be requested to present the petition to the House of Commons.

Mr. Scott, of Belfast, then desired to read some papers which he had prepared, but they were found not to be in the order of the meeting, but an excellent essay for a lecture for a mechanic's institution or other literary or political society. They were therefore withdrawn.

Mr. McBean, of Belfast, then read the following address—

Address of the Social Reformers attending the public meetings held in St. Martin's Hall, Long Acre, and in the John Street Institution, Fitzroy Square, London, from the 14th to the 18th May, 1858, (to advocate an entire change in forming the character of man and in governing society,) to Mr. Robert Owen, the great philanthropist,

Venerable and beloved Sire,—Though we are composed of persons very variously educated, differently formed and trained, and consequently differing in our opinions and views in many respects, yet we are unanimous in expressing to you our deep satisfaction at having had the opportunity and privilege of assembling again this year under your venerable auspices; at having listened to the profound principles, and comprehensive plans of social regeneration, contained and explained in your several sublime addresses on the present never-to-be-forgotten occasion. We are unanimous in expressing to you our sincere congratulations, that at the advanced age of eighty seven years you still enjoy so large a measure of bodily health and mental vigour; that with mental powers and faculties unimpaired you are still able clearly to unfold truths the most important to all mankind; still able successfully to propound the grand fundamental principles and plans which have been the undivided study and practice of your long and valuable life; still able to teach your fellowmen the true science of human nature and of society—a science which is yet known to a few advanced minds only; still able to point out the grand principles and practices which shall secure the permanent union, welfare, and perpetual happiness of all mankind. And we are unanimous in admiring the great philosophic power, the dignified patience, the all-pervading perseverance, and the beautiful consistency, which have characterised all your addresses, explanations, and proceedings on this momentous occasion. We are now (happily for ourselves, and for all those of our fellow-beings with whom we may come into contact for the future,) unanimously convinced, that true social science consists in the real knowledge of what human nature is, of what is best for man physically, intellectually, and morally; that social science is, indeed, but another name for the accurate practical knowledge by which the adult men and women of every community, in every country on earth, at every period of time, shall be enabled successfully to organise, regulate, and direct all the arrangements and operations which will secure to all in perpetuity, with the certainty of a law of nature, the grand advantages of being well-generated previous to birth, of being well-born, of being well-fed well-clothed, well-lodged, well-educated, well-trained, well placed, well-exercised, well-employed, well-governed, well-associated, and well-surrounded with harmonious, beautiful, and virtuous objects and influences from birth, during life on earth, and to the period of the physical dissolution of each individual. For as men are generated before birth, are exercised, employed, directed, governed, and constantly surrounded, so will men be, and become, with the certainty of the laws of nature. When we take a survey of your long and eminently useful life, and consider your valuable services in the cause of humanity, labouring in all seasons, among all classes, in many different countries, to diffuse correct practical views of fundamental principles by which the permanent welfare and the perpetual happiness of mankind shall be certainly secured, we cannot but admire the power, the patience, the perseverance, and the consistency, which you have displayed throughout your long and valuable life; nor can we fail to observe and appreciate the evident success which has attended your unparalelled exertions, and the steady progress of your practical views—as seen in the partial adoption of your plans in many new public establishments and arrangements throughout every civilized country—as manifest in the improved tone of society, in the improved and improving condition of portions of the people of this and other countries.

Venerable and beloved Sire.—We recognise and appreciate the potent and beneficial influence which your long active career and widely circulated enlightened views have exercised and are producing on public opinion in this and other countries—in opening the way for uninterrupted progress, for laying wide and deep the foundation of the great social edifice of the future—in preparing the general mind for the great improvements in the character of men, and the great changes in the construction of human society, which all who are capable of accurate thinking now comprehend as certain and inevitable, as alike possible, beneficial, and desirable for all classes of human beings.

To your profound and instructive views, to that active and intelligent philanthropy which has led you to sacrifice personal ease and a large fortune to devote the whole of your time and talents to discover and diffuse the knowledge of the causes which have led to the production of all existing evils and human division, discord, and sufferings, and by which all human miseries can be effectually removed and prevented : to that genuine heroism and moral courage which enabled you to brave obloquy and every form of prejudice, to fearlessly and boldly proclaim your fundamental principles opposed to established system and institutions ; to that consistency of character, indomitable energy, patience, perseverance, and continuity of purpose which have contributed so largely to the success of your exertions, and without which, success in any such great undertakings cannot be reasonably expected ; to that universal and all-embracing benevolence which you have always preached and uniformly practised,—we owe the vigorous liberality of the present— the free unfettered inquiry going on around us, and the bright hopes of future advancement which constantly sustain us in all our varied efforts in the cause of humanity.

Your benign principles have been misrepresented ; your benevolent character and virtuous purposes have been falsely slandered, maligned, and cunningly calumniated by bitter bigots, by erroneously educated preachers and politicians ; but calmly, mildly, and dignifiedly you have pursued your onward course, earnestly reiterating your grand charitable principles, trusting to produce conviction by the power of facts, by the force of truth, always consistent with itself, and feeling pity and the kindest sympathy for all those who had sought to injure you and your cause, because you knew well that they did not know what they did.

Let those who have been accustomed in their ignorance to sneer at your name, or who may have heard your views described as " visionary and impracticable," learn without delay to make themselves fully acquainted with the facts of your long and industrious life—with the comprehensive measures which you have always advocated, and the results which you have achieved—with the large amount of practical good already effected by your unwearied exertions— and they will soon become better men and more useful reformers. Let them learn to know that you were the founder of the first and most efficient institution ever established in this country for the purpose of infant training, for the proper formation; of human character in harmony with the laws of nature, that you were the first who publicly advocated and prepared a Bill for limiting the hours of labour for children in the Mills and Factories of this country; that you were the author of the plans of SELF-SUPPORTING HOME COLONIES, which, if established throughout the country, would soon lead to the extinction of pauperism and poor-rates; your practical views of education and employment, of equal rights and perfect liberty of conscience, the complete development of all man's powers and faculties, and the proper supply of all man's real wants,—and they will learn to comprehend, admire, and imitate the unceasing exertions which have been so successfully consecrated to these all-glorious objects.

Among the multifarious and inestimable blessings of Divine benevolence, practical brotherly love, we must regard as not the least the new force with which this principle now induces some advanced men to look upon their fellow beings; the new interest which it awakens in the unprejudiced, the unsectarian towards universal humanity; the new importance which it gives to the poorest and humblest human being; the new energies which it enables the truly sincere and active to put forth, for the improvement of human society. It is long since brotherly love began a mighty new revolution, which has been spreading itself throughout society, and which will not stop until new ties shall have taken the place of those which have hitherto connected the human family. Brotherly love has, as yet, but began its work of human reformation: under its influence a new era of society is fast advancing, surely, though slowly; and this grand change it is to accomplish by revealing to men the knowledge of their own nature, of their natural rights, of their supreme importance, individually and collectively considered. We cordially and fully concur with the valuable principles, explanations, and remarks, contained in your splendid address to us in St. Martin's Hall, on Friday evening, May 14th; and in your address to us in the John Street Institution on the occasion of the celebration of your eighty-eighth birthday, on the evening of May 16th; and we especially commend them to the most serious attention of the entire population of the world.

Venerable and beloved Sire, in conclusion, we would earnestly express the hope that the present proceedings shall not be suffered to drop and die away without producing their proper results ; and that they may be followed up by the most active systematic organisation of the social reformers and advanced minds of this and of all other countries, that the knowledge of the most important discovery ever made by, or known to man—viz , ' *That any general character, from the best to the worst, from the most ignorant to the most enlightened, may be given to any community even to the world at large, by the application of proper means, which means are, to a great extent, at the command and under the control of those who have influence in regulating and directing the affairs of men in society,*' may be circulated to the utmost extent among every class and section of mankind.

We are, venerable Sire, in our own names, and on behalf of this meeting, your affectionate and devoted admirers, and shall continue to be the faithful promoters of the knowledge of your comprehensive principles and benevolent views

G. N. B. McBean.
John Scott.
Joseph Franklin.

London, May 18*th*, 1858.

The above address being most cordially concurred in and highly approved of was proposed to the meeting by Mr. McBean, and seconded by Mr. Scott, and the meeting unanimously agreed that it should form part of the proceedings. Mr. Owen then rose and took an affectionate farewell of his followers and friends, wishing them all a long, peaceful, prosperous, happy life. Thanks were then voted to the chairman, and to Mr. Robert Cooper for his assistance, and the meeting separated.

We shall never forget the deeply-impressive eloquence of the glorious aged philanthropist as he stood up disclaiming all personal merit for what he had done for his fellow men through life, and said that there was no man living, whatever might be his wealth or position, with whom he would exchange places—his face brightening up to express the faithfulness of his modesty and the fervour of his benevolence—his eyes glistening with young hope and fresh energy, while descanting upon his favourite theme—with the burning zeal and inspiring ardour of youthful enthusiasm—with his faith as firm, his hope as high, his love of human nature as strong and unbounded as ever. As we gazed upon the good old man and attempted to recall our first impressions and remembrance of him twenty-five years ago, how small and insignificant compared with him appeared the artificially titled men of the age !

Mr. Owen has no doubt of the ultimate success of his grand views; he is never assailed by any misgivings as to their future triumph. So long, however, as the people and government of this or any other country shall suffer the true and the false, the upright and the perverse, the practicable and the chimerical, the salutary and the pestilent, to be constantly mingled and confounded in their opinions, institutions, and in the management of their affairs, chaos and confusion will reign, and their liberty, security, dignity, prosperity, and all real material and moral benefits will be deferred But these great fundamental truths, proclaimed by Mr. Owen and his followers, can neither be any longer hidden in obscurity nor cowardly passed over in silence. These great truths are now penetrating everywhere; their action is constant and tending to universality. They now form a torch which is never extinguished—a voice which is never wearied or hushed. Our recognised duty is to give these great truths publicity universally.

CONCLUDING STATEMENT.

I now conclude my public mission with the following statement, explanatory of that which is necessary to be done with the least delay by the union of governments and people.

And this statement should be written in letters of gold, and placed conspicuously in every public building and private dwelling over the world, until it shall be understood and become familiar for practice to every one of our race; because the knowledge which this document contains will insure to all, for ever, peace, prosperity, harmony, and happiness.

THE STATEMENT.

Evil and good,—truth and falsehood,— misery and happiness, are now brought prominently before all nations and all peoples.

It is the everlasting interest of all, that good, truth, and happiness, should now supersede the evil, falsehood, and misery which at this day so universally prevail over the earth.

The change is desired by all; but the practical knowledge by which to accomplish this task is not to be found throughout existing society. And yet the past experience of humanity should now be sufficient to attain this all-important result, and to attain it with ease and pleasure and in a comparatively short period.

Nature, in millions of lessons in her daily teachings to man, says—" Observe, throughout my three king-
" doms, that when I am placed within inferior
" surroundings, my children, in each of my kingdoms,
" of necessity become inferior,—but when placed
" within superior surroundings, they with the same
" certainty become superior.

" This is a law enforced upon me from the
" beginning of all formations, and when thoroughly
" investigated it will be found to be universal without
" an exception.

" Attend to this law, and place your offspring
" within superior, good, true, and happy surroundings;
" and as these surroundings are, so must your offspring
" become; and by such a simple process may all my
" children of the human race be made, with the

" certainty of the strongest of my laws, good, truthful
" and happy.

" All which you have now to do, is to learn how to
" apply this lesson to universal practice; and you will for
" ever destroy evil, falsehood, and every cause of misery.

" All existing surroundings, over the world, have
" emanated from a false fundamental principle ; and
" they are therefore bad, inferior, or injuriously
" mixed, even in the apparently splendid and imagined
" most perfect.

" To understand and make good surroundings,
" society must first be based on its true fundamental
" principle, and then every surrounding must be
" devised and combined to be consistent with that
" principle.

" The materials to create these new surroundings
" for all of your race now abundantly xist, and wait
" only your right application of them to practice to
" permanently supply all the wants and desires of
" every succeeding generation, in a manner greatly
" superior to any arrangements for this purpose
" enjoyed now by any earthly potentate, however
" powerful and wealthy."

To this statement of self-evident truths, or self-
evident deductions from them, it is unnecessary to
attempt any reply.

ROBERT OWEN.

Sevenoaks Park, Sevenoaks.   June, 1858.

THE

WORLD'S RACE.

TO BE RUN ON THE WORLD'S COURSE.

PRIZE

" THE PERMANENT HAPPPINESS OF MAN."

THIS race takes place at the end of June, and in consequence of Owen's challenge in favour of his young horse " New Social System for the Government of Mankind," against all the most experienced and long-tried old horses which have been hitherto unsuccessfully contending for this prize.

The horses previously entered to contest for this great prize are—Confucius, Brama, Moses, Christian, Mahomet, Philosopher, Sceptic, Infidel, with many hobbies only calculated to crowd the field during the first heat, in which they are all expected to be distanced.

Conditions.

The race, to try the soundness of the constitution of each horse, is to be five heats,—each heat five miles.

A well-cleared course, and no favour.

Present state of the Betting.

Twenty to one against Confucius, considered ori-

ginally of a good stock, but degenerated, yet many
excellent qualities remain in the present horse, having
the most numerous backers, but now expected to have
too old a rider to be equal to some of the other most
knowing jockies.

Seventy to one against Brama, supposed to be too
aged to contend with any chance of success against
the younger horses. Yet numerous backers

Sixty to one against Moses. A good old horse for
former times; some useful points in the present
horse, but with very small chance of success.
Backers not numerous, but some of them yet hopeful.

Ten to one against Christian, original stock very
pure, and by many deemed perfect, but the present
now most lamentably degenerated through mixtures
with inferior breeds, and especially latterly. The present horse is one of great show and high pretensions,
with much promise for success in his bearing; but the
knowing ones have discovered that these are sham
appearances, for he has hitherto always, when put to
the test, disappointed the expectations of those taken
at first by his assumed pretensions. He is however
expected to make play until the last heat, when it is
calculated he will be broken-winded through his over-
strained exertions to win; and that before the last
time round in the fifth heat he will be compelled to
give in, having no power remaining for further con-

test. Although he has many backers of great pretensions, the knowing ones have no faith in his strength for this race.

Eighty to one against Mahomet. The original stock high mettled, and often successful against powerful opponents; but latterly degenerated; and the present horse said to be too sick and weakened to have much chance in a severely-contested race.

Thirty to one against Philosopher, of ancient breed, but through all their paces too slow for any chance to win in such a race.

Fifty to one against Sceptic, who has little faith in himself, yet appears to despise all his opponents. His backers are however on the increase.

Seventy to one against Infidel. The original stock sturdy, obstinate animals, confident in their own powers, but in any course uncertain what direction to pursue, and from this uncertainty, failing to have any chance of ultimate success. Many silent friends, but few open backers.

New System, long kept in the background, has lately risen to be the favorite. Many already back him against the field, and the most knowing of these, having investigated the manner of his training, the great care taken to exercise him regularly in all his points for a hard and severe contest, and having quietly tested his powers on many trying occasions, have great confidence that the soundness of his well-tried constitution will give him the victory in this greatest of all contests, and more especially as he will be ridden by Spiritualist, a first rate rider from the higher country, who has come purposely for this race, and who knows the powers of his horse and the strong and weak points of all the rival horses, and feels secure of winning the great prize against all competitors.   They therefore offer *fifty to one* that he will win the race in a hand canter in the last round of the fifth heat, if the victory has not been previously accorded to him.

Who will venture to accept this last offer?

The knowing ones of all nations to be the judges, to decide and declare the winner.

TRUTH,

Clerk of the Course.

FOR THE GRAVE CONSIDERATION OF GOVERNMENTS.

SHOULD the race previously announced be won by " Social System," of which there can scarcely be a doubt, as he has all the good and true points for winning in his favor, he cannot fail to become a great favorite with all well-disposed imperial, royal, and republican governments, all of which, to drop meta-

phor, must become desirous to see made in the shortest
time the most perfect model that existing circumstances
will permit to be executed of those superior surroundings which will be required to secure the great prize of
man's permanent happiness, and to form a complete society, wisely devised and constructed in its various
combined parts to create new full-formed men and
women, who, through their own well-directed newly
acquired physical and mental powers, will be enabled unitedly to be always well-fed, clothed, lodged,
trained, educated, employed, recreated, governed, and,
in the second or third generation, to be always well-
born.   And these results will arise from their being
well-placed within superior surroundings, purposely
devised and executed to secure all these objects with
the certainty of a law of nature, and also to unite
them cordially as one family, with one interest and
one general feeling to promote the highest permanent
happiness of each, and of society outside of these
apparently, as they will appear, magic surroundings.

The world now requires one of these models to
form a full scientifically arranged and complete
society, to contain about 3000 of the most advanced
in spirit, principle, and practice, from the various
departments of the active business of life, to properly
exhibit the working of such new surroundings.

Such model should be made as perfect as minds

can conceive and hands execute, and would require an expenditure of about *one million sterling ;* but to the present governments, lay and ecclesiastic, such a model would be worth countless millions,—and the million may be raised without any expense to the nation.

So far as my experience extends among books and men, no one living in past time has possessed the knowledge, in spirit, principle, and practice, to conceive and get executed such models; nor do I know of any one living who is so far advanced as to be competent to direct the execution of this task as myself.

I am now past my 87th year, and not physically strong; the contingencies of my life therefore are very uncertain ; my mental faculties yet good, but declining.

I could yet instruct a well-appointed national or international committee, of men of the first practical talents in the most useful departments of the true business of life, to construct the new combinations of superior surroundings as they now exist in my mind, and this committee could afterwards instruct nation after nation to follow the example. But it may be centuries before such a succession of singular and extraordinary events as have occurred to give me this knowledge in principle and practice may happen to another.   It would be true wisdom, therefore, in the governments of the civilized world, to make use of this most precious knowledge and experience while it is to be obtained without trouble or expense.   It is now most evident that no one except myself has ever acquired a knowledge of the *science* of the influence of surroundings, nor is there one living who dare openly to advocate the laws of God and to abrogate all the laws of man.   And until the necessity for the laws of God for the government of the world can be understood, applied to practice, and made to supersede all the laws of men, there can be no rationality or wisdom in human affairs.   At present all is Babel confusion over the earth; while as soon as God's laws shall govern man, peace, order, and harmony will universally prevail, and the heterogeneous mass of involvement and disorder now perplexing every one, through the contending, contradictory, and unnatural laws of men, will cease, and their puny attempts at legislating against God will be abandoned for ever.

And let it never be forgotten that the now three greatest taught prejudices of the human race, and strongest imbibed from infancy by all, are the three greatest causes of ignorance, crime, and misery, and now the real obstacle to all progress to general happinesss, and that these are, *the Superstitions of the*

world, called by the disciples of each " the true religion,"—*the unnatural Marriages of the Priesthoods of
the world,* the real cause of all past and present prostitution, the curse of humanity,— and the practice,
most selfish and demoralising, of *Private Property.*
With these there can be no good surroundings, nor
truth, goodness, wisdom, unity, or happiness, in any
society formed by men.   Also, that the two systems
never can be united, in spirit, principle, or practice.

ROBERT OWEN.

June, 1858.